Christopher Taylor

IN DEFENCE (

CU00921725

Other books by Brian Vickers

As author:

Francis Bacon and Renaissance Prose (Cambridge, 1968)
The Artistry of Shakespeare's Prose (London, 1968, 1976)
Classical Rhetoric in English Poetry (London, 1970)
Towards Greek Tragedy (London, 1973)
Shakespeare: *Coriolanus* (London, 1976, 1981)

As editor and contributor:

The World of Jonathan Swift (Oxford, 1968)
Rhetoric Revalued (Binghamton, NY, 1982)
Occult and Scientific Mentalities in the Renaissance (Cambridge, 1984)
Arbeit, Musse, Meditation: Betrachtungen zur *Vita activa* und *Vita contemplativa* (Zurich, 1985)

As editor:

Henry Mackenzie, *The Man of Feeling* (Oxford, 1967, 1987)
Shakespeare: The Critical Heritage, 1623–1801, 6 vols. (London and Boston, 1974–81)
Public and Private Life in the Seventeenth Century:
     The Mackenzie–Evelyn Debate (Delmar, NY, 1986)
English Science, Bacon to Newton (Cambridge, 1987)

IN DEFENCE OF RHETORIC

Brian Vickers

CLARENDON PRESS · OXFORD

Oxford University Press, Walton Street, Oxford OX2 6DP

Oxford New York Toronto
Delhi Bombay Calcutta Madras Karachi
Petaling Jaya Singapore Hong Kong Tokyo
Nairobi Dar es Salaam Cape Town
Melbourne Auckland
and associated companies in
Berlin Ibadan

Oxford is a trade mark of Oxford University Press

Published in the United States
by Oxford University Press, New York

First published 1988
First issued as a paperback with corrections and additions 1989

British Library Cataloguing in Publication Data

Vickers, Brian, 1937–
In defence of rhetoric.
1. Rhetoric
I. Title
808   PN187

ISBN 0–19–811791–4

Library of Congress Cataloging in Publication Data

Vickers, Brian,
In defence of rhetoric/Brian Vickers
p.   cm.
Bibliography: p.   Includes index
1. Rhetoric
I. Title
PN175.V53 1987   808—dc19   87–26222

ISBN 0–19–811791–4

Printed and bound in
Great Britain by Biddles Ltd,
Guildford and King's Lynn

Amicis defensoribus rhetoricae

MARGARETA FREDBORG
GEORGE KENNEDY
JOHN MONFASANI
ILSE NEW-FANNENBÖCK
DONALD RUSSELL
JOHN WARD
MICHAEL WINTERBOTTOM

PREFACE

THE goal of this book is to remove the misapprehensions and prejudices that still affect our appreciation of rhetoric. For many years scholars have been telling us about the great importance of rhetoric as a key to understanding the past, its history, literature, art, architecture, music—such distinguished writers as E. R. Curtius, Henri Marrou, Erwin Panofsky, Sir Ernst Gombrich, C. S. Lewis. Their encouragements to study rhetoric as a communicational system used for over two thousand years to shape literary and artistic creation, and the critical processes by which the arts were judged, have been matched by the work of other more specialized students of rhetoric, amply represented in the bibliography and notes to this book. Yet neither group has managed to overcome the prejudices, or lack of response affecting people who otherwise take a wide and keen interest in history, literature, and the arts. Some people are aware of the importance of rhetoric, but have never bothered to find out how it works, and are content to let someone else do it for them. In the memorable words of Wilhelm Busch describing the common response to a strongly-smelling cheese, 'Bedenk: Man liebt den Käse wohl, indessen / Man deckt ihn zu' ['Consider: We like cheese well enough, but we still cover it up'].

Rhetoric is not merely put at a discreet distance, however, it is actively distrusted, and attacked. By an ever-present irony, the first written accounts of Greek rhetoric to survive come from rhetoric's most influential enemy, Plato, attacks which anyone truly concerned to rehabilitate rhetoric cannot simply pass by. I have long felt that the account of rhetoric, and politics, in the *Gorgias* was a violent travesty of both disciplines, but not until I sat down to write the studies that form Chapters 2 and 3 (in part) of this book did I realize just how systematically Plato distorted both evidence and argument to build up his case. Most of those who study Plato do so because he is a great philosopher, and either ignore rhetoric altogether (as the indexes or contents pages to most modern studies will show), or endorse his view of it. To show how much misrepresentation,

animus, and covert manipulation of argument Plato carries out I
have used two outstanding modern editions of the *Gorgias*, by
E. R. Dodds and Terence Irwin. The resulting analysis is
lengthy, but I make no apologies for it on that account. As the
later part of Chapter 3 shows, Plato's travesty of rhetoric
influenced Kant, Croce, and continues to influence a majority of
classicists and philosophers today. I hope that they won't ignore
this discussion. I also attempt to validate the Sophists, whose
reputation has never recovered from the drubbing Plato gave it,
drawing on Eric Havelock's sympathetic account of Protagoras,
and making my own evaluation of Isocrates. It seems to me that
their school, with its conception of rhetoric as public debate in a
society guaranteeing free speech, a debate in which both sides
of the case are heard and those qualified to vote come to a
decision binding on all parties, has much more to offer us
(although such a society continues to seem Utopian) than Plato's
equation of it with cosmetics, cookery, and other more
disreputable arts designed, according to him, to satisfy base
pleasures rather than promote knowledge.

One part of this book, then, lives up to its title as a defence of
rhetoric by actively engaging with its attackers. Yet, as a reading
of Chapter 3 will show, I regard such controversies between
rhetoric and philosophy as pointless, ultimately damaging to
both sides. It is only because rhetoric has been given negative
connotations of insincerity, mere display, artifice, or ornament
without substance, that I think the argument worth engaging in.
More important is to understand what rhetoric really can do in
the right hands, at the right time. Aristotle defended rhetoric
against Plato on several heads, but on this one he made the
general point, which I imagine most people who study it would
agree with, that rhetoric is a tool which, like all other human
resources, can be abused. (He excluded virtue from this
category—but he did not know *Othello*.) Contemporary history
will confirm the truth that all forms of knowledge, even science,
can be misused for evil purposes. Studies of totalitarian rhetoric,
then, are valuable, if depressing, analyses of the power of the
word and other forms of communication in the wrong hands.
(Plato claimed that all rhetoric belonged to tyranny, except his
own.) By 'the right hands' I mean those of public speakers and

writers in a state where free speech is still possible; by 'the right time' I mean one in which rhetoric is still flourishing.

Rhetoric has existed for two and a half millennia, but its fortunes have always depended on external factors, whether political—in Rome free speech was drastically curtailed once emperors ruled; or educational—it figured strongly in the school curriculum between 200 BC and AD 400, and again between 1450 and 1850; aesthetic—its dominance over music and the visual arts being only challenged by the rise of non language-based aesthetic systems. In the first part of this book I have treated rhetoric as a general cultural phenomenon, in historical and analytical terms. In Chapter 1 I begin, as rhetoric itself began, with real life, showing how eloquence was seen as a natural phenomenon, practised by all human beings, merely written down and systematized in rhetoric-books. Then I give a brief history of rhetoric in the time of its first, and lasting formulation, together with an introduction to the major texts in classical rhetoric, from Aristotle to Tacitus. I also outline the main teachings of rhetoric on the processes of composition, the attitude of the orator or writer towards his audience, and the concept of style. It is a rather summary treatment of these topics, but I wanted to make this book relatively complete within itself, given the obvious limitations on size.

Chapters 4 and 5 carry on the historical survey into the Middle Ages and the Renaissance, respectively. These chapters started off as my own attempt to understand why the medieval treatises on poetry were so different from those in the Renaissance. What I ended up writing was a study, first, of what happens when a body of knowledge gets broken up in the process of transmission, the fate of the classical rhetoric texts during the Middle Ages, and what becomes of a culture when its basic assumptions and institutions cannot be reconstituted. The converse process, the rediscovery of texts, learning how to fit them into a newly-recovered sense of place and time, gave Renaissance rhetoric a remarkable boost, resulting in thousands of books and hundreds and thousands of readers between the time of Petrarch and Wordsworth. Rhetoric developed new literary genres, notably the letter and the oration, and helped writers of all kinds—including scientists such as Kepler and

Galileo—to structure their work clearly and make their arguments more effective.

From these essays in historical analysis I turn back to the nature of rhetoric, and the link between style and persuasion. One important theme of Chapter 5 is the way in which Renaissance rhetoric laid increasing stress on its power to move the reader's or listener's feelings, the concept of *movere*, with a parallel emphasis on developing *elocutio,* understood not just as style but as expressivity. In Chapter 6 I show that the crucial link in this process was the doctrine of the figures and tropes, which were seen as recording powerful emotions in normal speech, re-creating those emotions in a speaker, and so arousing them in the audience. Contrary to what even historians of rhetoric have thought, both classical and Renaissance rhetoricians had an explicit rationale for these individual forms of style to which they, and everyone who had an education in Europe over a 400-year period, devoted so much time and energy.

The attraction of rhetoric as an instrument of persuasion and instruction was recognized by its sister arts, music and painting. In Chapter 7 I follow the ways in which theorists of both arts took over from the rhetorical treatises such concepts as the duties of the orator (to move, to delight, to instruct), the importance of the fable (*historia*) as an imitation of life—the main principle in both music and painting—and even the tropes and figures. Some of these essentially verbal devices can be transposed to an art not based on language, but only up to a certain point. Both composers and painters found the general teachings of rhetoric more useful than its details.

The last chapter traces the survival of rhetoric in the modern novel. In it I show how the figures and tropes that we find in Aeschylus, Shakespeare, or Racine, are used again, and to very individual purposes, in novels by Joyce, Orwell, Randall Jarrell, and other more recent writers. The same point could be made about modern poetry in English, a topic well worth pursuing.

Finally, in the Epilogue, I survey the current state of rhetoric studies and try to judge which directions are likely to prove fruitful, and which not. In the linguistic theories of Roman Jakobson, and in the deconstructionist criticism of Paul de Man, I find, rhetoric is once again fragmented, as it was in the Middle

Ages, but now reduced to two or three tropes only, or else forced into a critical theory of opposition and self-destruction. This unfortunate degeneration of rhetoric in some ahistorical (or even anti-historical) schools of literary criticism is set against the range and fertility of rhetoric studies which accept the relevance of history.

Another writer wanting to defend rhetoric might have opted for a briefer treatment, with more emphasis on the polemical element. It seemed to me important to include an exposition of the content and emphases of rhetoric as a coherent system, rather than only describe perversions of it—especially since I could not assume any shared knowledge among people likely to use this book. The result is rather lengthy but, I hope, at least clearly structured and argued. I have wanted to convey an accurate overall view while also giving enough detail to re-create the reality of the text, and show how rhetoric actually works. All I can hope for now is to find open-minded readers, who are interested to see what case can be made for rhetoric and against its enemies, and who have not already prejudged the issues. I invoke the 'candid reader', in the older senses of that word, from 'innocent of evil' to 'generous', well-disposed. May you read this and be persuaded by it!

In Chapters 1 and 6 I have used some material that appeared first in my *Classical Rhetoric in English Poetry* (1970), long out of print, while Chapter 3 draws on an essay published in *Rhetoric Revalued* (1982). In all cases this material has been rethought and rewritten.

I am grateful to all the scholars, poets, and dramatists from whom I have learned about rhetoric, and especially to the friends to whom the book is dedicated. They are not responsible, of course, for my errors or opinions. I should like to thank Kim Scott Walwyn of Oxford University Press for her patient encouragement of my work, and Alice Park for her efficient copy-editing. Andrea Eckert and Sabine Köllmann of the Wissenschaftskolleg zu Berlin have kindly helped with the last stages of typing. I am as ever much indebted to my Zurich assistant Dr Margrit Soland for her care with my manuscript through its many metamorphoses, not least its final appearance on a video screen.

Cambridge—Zurich—Berlin   B.V.

CONTENTS

LIST OF ILLUSTRATIONS

I am grateful to the institutions listed above for permission to reproduce their copyright material.

REFERENCES

Books and articles referred to more than once in the footnotes are cited in an abbreviated form, full titles being given in the Bibliography. Thus George Kennedy, *The Art of Persuasion in Greece* (London, 1963) appears as Kennedy 1963. Primary texts are cited usually by the author's name or by an abbreviated title, with book, chapter, and paragraph references; but where differing translations are cited, then by the translator's name, such as the two versions of Matthew of Vendôme cited here: cf. Gallo 1974 and Galyon 1980. Aristotle's *Rhetoric* is abbreviated as '*Rhet.*' and quoted in the translation of W. R. Roberts in *The Works of Aristotle*, ed. W. D. Ross, vol. xi (Oxford, 1924). The major texts in Latin rhetoric are cited from the Loeb Classical Library translations: Cicero, *De Oratore* (*De Or.*), tr. E. W. Sutton and H. Rackham, 2 vols. (London, 1942; 1948), including *Partitiones Oratoriae* (*Part. Or.*), tr. H. Rackham; *Brutus* (*Brut.*), tr. G. L. Hendrickson, printed with *Orator* (*Or.*), tr. H. M. Hubbell (London, 1939; rev. 1962); *De Inventione* (*De Inv.*), with *De Optimo Genere Oratorum* (*De Opt. Gen.*) and *Topica*, tr. H. M. Hubbell (London, 1949; 1960). The anonymous *Rhetorica ad Herennium* (*Ad Her.*), tr. H. Caplan (London, 1954). Quintilian, *Institutio Oratoria* (*Inst. Or.*, or 'Quintilian'), tr. H. E. Butler, 4 vols. (London, 1920–2; 1963). An important anthology of primary texts, in outstanding translations, is *Ancient Literary Criticism. The Principal Texts in New Translations*, ed. D. A. Russell and M. Winterbottom (Oxford, 1972).

AN OUTLINE OF CLASSICAL RHETORIC

i RHETORIC AND LIFE

ALFRED DOOLITTLE. I'll tell you, Governor, if youll only let me get a word in. I'm willing to tell you. I'm wanting to tell you. I'm waiting to tell you.
PROFESSOR HIGGINS. Pickering: this chap has a certain natural gift of rhetoric. Observe the rhythm of his native woodnotes wild. 'I'm willing to tell you: I'm wanting to tell you: I'm waiting to tell you'. Sentimental rhetoric! thats the Welsh strain in him. It also accounts for his mendacity and dishonesty.

Shaw, *Pygmalion*, Act II

Rhetoric, the art of persuasive communication, has long been recognized as the systematization of natural eloquence. According to this tradition, the first writers of rhetoric-books observed situations in real life where eloquence succeeded, analysed the resources used by such speakers, and developed a teaching method which could impart those skills. As one of the speakers in Cicero's dialogue *De Oratore*,[1] having summarized the main doctrines in rhetoric, puts it:

the virtue in all these rules is, not that orators by following them have won a reputation for eloquence, but that certain persons have noted and collected the doings of men who were naturally eloquent: thus eloquence is not the offspring of the art, but the art of eloquence. (1. 32. 146)

Quintilian, author of the most comprehensive classical treatise 'On the Teaching of Oratory', the *Institutio Oratoria*, noted that 'everything which art has brought to perfection originated in nature' (2. 17. 6), be it medicine, architecture, music, or oratory:

It was, then, nature that created speech, and observation that originated the art of speaking. Just as men discovered the art of medicine by observing that some things were healthy and some the

[1] For the conventions governing quotations and references see above, p. xvii.

reverse, so they observed that some things were useful and some useless in speaking, and noted them for imitation or avoidance, while they added certain other precepts according as their nature suggested. These observations were confirmed by experience and each man proceeded to teach what he knew. (3. 2. 3)

The same process, the art of rhetoric codifying natural ability, also determined the invention of topics: 'the discovery of arguments was not the result of the publication of textbooks, but every kind of argument was put forward before any rules were laid down' (5. 10. 120).

While writers of rhetoric-books collected, analysed, and classified methods of discovering and organizing arguments, eloquence itself continued to flourish in a natural state. Defending rhetoric from Plato's charge in the *Gorgias* and *Phaedrus* that it was a mere 'knack' or 'routine', not worthy of being declared a *technē* or *ars*, Aristotle, in the opening paragraph of his *Rhetoric*, pronounced rhetoric to be the analogue or counterpart of dialectic (whose status as a serious discipline was indisputable), since

Both alike are concerned with such things as come, more or less, within the general ken of all men and belong to no definite science. Accordingly all men make use . . . of both; for to a certain extent all men attempt to discuss statements and to maintain them, to defend themselves and to attack others. Ordinary people do this either at random or through practice and from acquired habit.(1354^{a}1–7)

The parallel existence of natural and acquired eloquence means that the latter must always resemble the former. 'For as art started from nature', one of Cicero's speakers in *De Oratore* warns, 'it would certainly be deemed to have failed if it had not a natural power of affecting us and giving us pleasure' (3. 51. 197). Hence 'the very cardinal sin' of oratory 'is to depart from the language of everyday life, and the usage approved by the sense of the community' (1. 3. 12). For Cicero, the orator is—as Wordsworth said of the poet—'a man speaking to men', and the proverbial injunction of the rhetorical tradition, *ars est celare artem*, reminded the orator that however elevated his style and feelings became he should not lose touch with what an ordinary person could think and feel. As Quintilian advised him, 'fix your eyes on nature and follow her. All eloquence is concerned with the activities of life, . . . and the mind is always readiest to accept what it recognizes to be true to nature' (8. 3. 71). To develop ability in speaking, Quintilian wrote, is as natural as to develop the body by exercise, 'consequently the more effective a man's speaking the more in accordance with the nature of eloquence will it be' (12. 10. 43–4). The successful speaker 'stimulates us by the animation of his delivery, and kindles the imagination, not by presenting us with an elaborate picture, but by bringing us into actual contact with the things themselves' (10. 1. 16).

The theoretical insistence on the naturalness of eloquence also had a historical grounding, for rhetoricians could evoke, as the best proof of the existence of eloquence before the codification of rhetoric, the poems of Homer. Aristotle, living in what was still to a great extent an oral culture, refers to and quotes from Homer some forty times in his *Rhetoric*, drawing on him for examples of speech and behaviour which are given the same evidential status as references to contemporary life or history. So he distinguishes two types of witnesses, 'recent' and 'ancient', the latter comprising 'the poets and all other notable persons whose judgements are known to all. Thus the Athenians appealed to Homer as a witness about Salamis' (1375[b]25 ff.). Aristotle even believes that the 'most trustworthy of all are the "ancient" witnesses, since they cannot be corrupted' (1376[a]16), which to a modern reader seems to carry reverence too far. Homer or Hesiod may state general principles, but they are surely not on the same level as people who have observed something connected with a crime!

The reverence for Homer shared by Greeks and Romans, for whom he was already the classic literary text, meant that the poems were closely scrutinized for evidence of rhetorical activity. Crassus, Cicero's mouthpiece in *De Oratore*, deploring the separation between rhetoric and philosophy created by Socrates, observes that in the old days

the same system of instruction seems to have imparted education both in right conduct and in good speech; nor were professors in two separate groups, but the same masters gave instruction both in ethics and in rhetoric, for instance the great Phoenix in Homer, who says that he was assigned to the young Achilles by his father Peleus to accompany him to the wars in order to make him 'a speaker of words and a doer of deeds'. (3. 15. 57; *Iliad*, 9. 443)

Quintilian picks up the same point, and adds that not only does Homer mention 'a number of orators' but 'the various styles are represented by the speeches of three of the chiefs, and the young men are set to contend among themselves in contests of eloquence [*Iliad*, 15. 283 f.]; moreover, lawsuits and pleaders are represented in the engravings on the shield of Achilles [*Iliad*, 18. 497 ff.]' (2. 17. 8). In his influential survey of classical literature in Book 10, which discusses the authors whom the budding orator should read, Quintilian follows the principle of Aratus— ' "With Jove let us begin" '—in starting with Homer, who is as multiple as 'his own conception of Ocean', the source and 'inspiration for every department' of eloquent speech.

For, to say nothing of his eloquence, which he shows in praise, exhortation and consolation, do not the ninth book containing the embassy to Achilles, the first describing the quarrel between the chiefs, or the speeches delivered by the counsellors in the second, display all the rules of art to be followed in forensic or deliberative oratory? (10. 1. 46–7)

Homer was 'master of all the emotions, tender and vehement alike', and instinctively observed such rhetorical devices as *exordium, narratio*, proof and refutation, peroration, and all the ornaments of speech. 'They are so numerous that the majority of writers on the principles of rhetoric have gone to his works for examples of all these things' (48–51).

The significance of eloquence in Homer is double. Writers on rhetoric continued to cite his work, classifying the speeches into various categories. Menelaus represents the plain style, Nestor the middle, the 'resourceful Odysseus' incarnates the grand style.[2] He may seem unimpressive before he speaks,

But when he let the great voice go from his chest, and the words came
drifting down like the winter snows, then no other mortal
man beside could stand up against Odysseus.[3]

---

[2] Kennedy 1963, pp. 35–9. Kennedy 1980, pp. 9–15, gives an excellent analysis of Homeric speeches.

[3] *Iliad*, tr. Richmond Lattimore (Chicago, 1951), 3. 216–23.

As late as Alexander Pope's translation of the *Iliad* (1720), the speeches were indexed under the rhetorical categories, 'the Exhortatory or Deliberative, the Vituperative, the Narrative, the Pathetic, and the Sarcastic'. But in addition to his exemplary value to rhetoricians, Homer has an added significance in the history of eloquence in that his orators are all presented speaking according to the needs of an immediate situation, political, military, or personal. Rhetoric has always existed in a symbiotic relationship with society, expanding or contracting itself according to the demands that a social group makes on it. Since 'almost half of the *Iliad* and more than two-thirds of the *Odyssey* are devoted to speeches by the characters'[4]—at meetings of the army-leaders in council, of the soldiers' assembly, of embassies, of citizens—we find there all the basic forms of communication that exist in oral cultures (and not only there): face-to-face political conflict, threats of force, dissimulation, appeals for mercy. Speakers do not always get what they want, since the word is subject to the will, and in Homer, as in real life, persuasion does not always succeed (a propagandist for rhetoric might have constructed things differently).[5] But in these poems men invest their whole beings in their eloquence and the success they hope it will bring, none more poignantly than Priam, begging Achilles to return the body of his son Hector for burial (*Iliad*, 24. 476 ff.). The status and power of eloquence in later Greek life is already visible in the *Odyssey*, where Odysseus explains to Euryalus that

> the gods do not bestow graces in all ways
> on men, neither in stature nor yet in brains or eloquence;
> for there is a certain kind of man, less noted for beauty,
> but the god puts comeliness on his words, and they who
>   look toward him

---

[4] Curtius 1953, p. 64.
[5] Kennedy 1980, p. 15, describes the ninth book of the *Iliad*, in which Odysseus, Phoenix, and Ajax come as ambassadors to persuade Achilles to return to the battle, but fail, as 'a picture of the failure of formal rhetoric in dealing with a highly personal situation. . . . In the first work of European literature we are brought face to face with some of the limitations of rhetoric.' Yet Homer is surely facing the fact in life that human desires will inevitably conflict, and that language has only a limited ability to resolve disputes or change people's goals. If it were otherwise, one exposure to good—or evil—speech would fix us for ever.

are filled with joy at the sight, and he speaks to them
without faltering in winning modesty, and shines among
those who are gathered,
and people look on him as on a god when he walks in the city.[6]

Greek society needed orators, and valued rhetoricians.

The first teachers of rhetoric that we know of emerged precisely
in answer to a new social need. A systematic rhetoric was first
developed in the Greek towns of Sicily after the expulsions,
between 471 and 463 BC, of tyrants who, among other illegal
acts, had seized property. To re-establish its ownership
widespread litigation was necessary, and one Corax and his
pupil Tysias set up in Syracuse the first rule-based methods for
handling judicial disputes. Little is known of the detail of their
teaching, but it included a rudimentary account of the structure
of a speech, while to Tysias (among others) is ascribed the
definition of rhetoric as the *demiurgos*, or artificer, of
persuasion.[7] Much more is known about Gorgias, another
product of the Greek province in Sicily, who came to Athens
from Leontini in 427 BC to request Athenian help, and made a
great impression with his eloquence.[8] Gorgias was a Sophist,
one of that school of philosophers who devoted themselves to
the practicalities of civic life, and whose advocacy of rhetoric
was based, as Plato recorded, on its ability to make men its
slaves by persuasion, not force (*Philebus*, 58 a–b.). His arrival
was timely, for changes in both Athenian politics and law in the
second half of the fifth century put a much greater premium on
the citizen's direct involvement with community decisions. The
system of single magistrates or the select group of judges on
the Areopagus gave way to one involving large popular juries,
the *dikastēria*, consisting of from 201 to 501 citizens, with
complete jurisdiction over trial proceedings. There being no
public prosecutor, criminal cases were brought by citizens who
appeared in person to argue their case in a single set speech for
either side. It is no accident that the early handbooks of rhetoric,
including Aristotle's, pay so much attention to the techniques of
successful litigation. An ability to speak effectively was a

[6] *Odyssey*, tr. Richmond Lattimore (New York, 1968), 8. 166–73.
[7] Marrou 1964, p. 53; Kennedy 1963, pp. 26, 58–61.
[8] Kennedy 1963, pp. 26–7, 47, 61–8, 168–73; Kennedy 1980, pp. 29–31.

necessity for the liberty and prosperity of any proper Athenian. The need to address a large jury coherently on a single appearance encouraged the composition of speeches that were carefully reasoned, clearly arranged, and also appealed to the emotions, much to the dislike of Aristotle and other more conservative thinkers.[9] In politics, too, democracy was broadening the base of participation in public life, so that the citizen who wanted to speak successfully in the Assembly or Council might take lessons from the Sophists, who specialized in political oratory. In the dialogue named after him, Plato makes Gorgias set out the practical advantages of eloquence. Rhetoric

is in very truth the greatest boon, for it brings freedom to mankind in general and to each man dominion over others in his own country . . . . I mean the power to convince by your words the judges in court, the senators in Council, the people in the Assembly, or in any other gathering of a citizen body.[10]

To Plato, of course, it was deplorable that the rhetorician, not the philosopher, should have such power, but to the majority of students of rhetoric down to the Renaissance its great attraction was just this promise of success in civic life, and its upholding of liberty.

It is a historical fact, more familiar in this century than in any other, that tyrants and totalitarian states destroy freedom of speech. Under the Thirty Tyrants in Athens at one point the teachers of rhetoric were forbidden to work, and when Latin teachers of rhetoric appeared in Rome at the beginning of the first century BC, 'the senatorial party, regarding them as a sign of democratic progress, tried to silence them'.[11] An involvement in politics was ranked highly in ancient society, since it implied that the individual was escaping from self-centredness and devoting his abilities to the *vita activa*, for the common good. This attitude is particularly strong in the Sophists, as we shall see, from Protagoras to Isocrates. For Aristotle political oratory 'is a nobler business' than forensic (judicial) oratory, 'and fitter for a citizen than that which concerns the relations of private

---

[9] Kennedy 1980, pp. 26–9, 42.
[10] *Gorgias*, 452 d–e; tr. W. D. Woodhead in Plato 1963.
[11] Kennedy 1963, p. 29, citing Xenophon, *Memorabilia*, 1. 2. 31 and Suetonius, *De Rhetoribus*, 1; Marrou 1964, pp. 338–9.

individuals' (1354^{b}23). To him, indeed, politics was 'a more instructive art and a more real branch of knowledge' than rhetoric (1359^{b}5), but for Isocrates, the leading representative of the Sophists (the rival tradition to Plato and Aristotle), rhetoric was the primary tool in education, and education was directed towards political activity and practicality.[12] For Roman rhetoricians, above all Cicero, the link between rhetoric and the *vita activa* was fundamental. In the early *De Inventione* (c. 87 BC) rhetoric is held to have taught men, when society was still unformed, 'that they must work for the common good' (1. 2. 3). When rhetoric became corrupted men opted out of the active life (1. 3. 4), but Roman orators and politicians reclaimed the art in order to protect the state (1. 4. 5). Rhetoric is now defined as a department of 'the scientific system of politics', while oratorical ability is subsumed under politics as essential to the state (1. 5. 6).

The mature *De Oratore* (55 BC) includes numerous passages praising rhetoric in glowing terms for giving those who master it the power 'to get hold on assemblies of men':

In every free nation, and most of all in communities which have attained the enjoyment of peace and tranquillity, this one art has always flourished over the rest and ever reigned supreme. . . . What function is so kingly, so worthy of the free, so generous, as to bring help to the suppliant, to raise up those who are cast down, to bestow security, to set free from peril, to maintain men in their civil rights? . . . The wise control of the complete orator is that which chiefly upholds not only his own dignity, but the safety of countless individuals and of the entire State. (1. 8. 30–4)

The connection between rhetoric and political life, reiterated so frequently by Cicero,[13] and so influentially for the Renaissance, is also found in Quintilian's *Institutio Oratoria* (AD 92–4), but inevitably with less emphasis.[14] Cicero had achieved fame in a long career (81–43 BC) as an orator on political and legal affairs,

---

[12] Kennedy 1963, p. 17.

[13] See *De Oratore*, 1. 46. 202, 1. 48. 211 and 214, 2. 8. 33, 2. 9. 35, 2. 16. 67–8, 2. 82. 337–8, 3. 1. 1–3. 2. 5, 3. 2. 8–3. 9. 12, 3. 4. 13, 3. 15. 57, 3. 16. 1, 3. 16. 59, 3. 17. 63, 3. 19. 72, 3. 20. 74, 3. 28. 109, 3. 32. 131, 3. 33. 133, 3. 34. 139; *Brutus*, 2. 6–7, 6. 22, 12. 45, 14. 54, 76. 265, 94. 324, 96. 328–31; *Orator*, 41. 141–2, 43. 148.

[14] See Quintilian, 1. Pr. 10, 2. 16. 1 and 8, 11. 1. 35, 12. 2. 6 and 20, 12. 7. 1, 12. 11. 1.

and his two greatest campaigns, the defeat of Catiline and the attack on Mark Antony, displayed both oratorical power and admirable integrity. Yet the collapse of the Republic and the establishment of the Empire in 31 BC meant that rhetoric and free speech no longer flourished in public affairs, the orator being 'driven from the helm of State', as Crassus had put it in *De Oratore*, 'thrust down and locked up exclusively in law-courts and petty little assemblies, as if in a pounding-mill' (1. 11. 45). Quintilian was confined to an even smaller space, the school-room, first as a state professor of rhetoric and then as tutor to the Emperor Domitian's nephews. From that position he naturally disagreed with those who 'identify rhetoric with politics' (2. 15. 33), arguing that political questions provide only part of its material (2. 21. 2). Yet his comprehensive enquiry into the career of the orator, from boyhood to retirement, typified an important process in which rhetoric became essential to public life in another sphere, education.

The pioneer who took the logical step of developing a school to train the Greeks for political and legal speaking, with a fixed school (as distinct from the Sophists, who travelled from place to place), was Isocrates (436–338 BC).[15] In about 393, several years before Plato founded the Academy, Isocrates opened a small school whose graduates included some of the outstanding men of their generation, among them the general Timotheus, the historians Theopompus and Ephorus, and Nicocles, the king of Cyprus. As Cicero recorded, at this time 'there arose Isocrates, the Master of all rhetoricians, from whose school, as from the Horse of Troy, none but leaders emerged', some of whom 'sought glory in ceremonial, others in action' (*De Or.* 2. 22. 94). Isocrates' system, partly described in the fragmentary speech *Against the Sophists*, emphasized three fundamental elements

[15] On Isocrates see Kennedy 1963, pp. 174–203 (a somewhat harsh account); Kennedy 1980, pp. 31–6; Marrou 1964, pp. 119–35; Werner Jaeger, *Paideia: the Ideals of Greek Culture*, tr. G. Highet, 3 vols. (Oxford, 1939–45), iii. 46–155; H. M. Hubbell, *The Influence of Isocrates on Cicero, Dionysius and Aristides* (New Haven, 1913); August Burk, *Die Pädagogik des Isokrates als Grundlegung des humanistischen Bildungsideals* (Würzburg, 1923); L. Gualdo Rosa, *La fede nella Paideia: Aspetti della fortuna europea di Isocrate nei secoli XV e XVI* (Rome, 1984); Christoph Eucken, *Isokrates. Seine Positionen in der Auseinandersetzung mit den zeitgenössischen Philosophen* (Berlin, 1983); and O. A. Baumhauer, *Die sophistische Rhetorik* (Stuttgart, 1986).

in rhetorical education—nature, training, and practice. The teacher must not only explain principles but provide examples of oratory as models, and guide his students to the acquisition of practical wisdom. Isocrates' importance as the founder of a rhetoric-school is marked by the many similar institutions that sprang up in the ancient world, and his influence on education extended to Renaissance Europe. But his significance far exceeds his actual teaching practice. In his extant speeches, which were written for reading rather than public delivery, Isocrates saw language as the defining mark of humanity and civilization:

> In most of our abilities we differ not at all from the animals; we are in fact behind many in swiftness and strength and other resources. But because there is born in us the power to persuade each other and to show ourselves whatever we wish, we not only have escaped from living as brutes, but also by coming together have founded cities and set up laws and invented arts, and speech has helped us attain practically all of the things we have devised. For it is speech that has made laws about justice and injustice and honour and disgrace, without which provisions we should not be able to live together. By speech we refute the wicked and praise the good. By speech we educate the ignorant and inform the wise.

Since 'nothing done with intelligence is done without speech', then 'speech is the marshal of all actions and of thoughts, and those most use it who have the greatest wisdom'.[16]

Isocrates' praise of language was taken over unacknowledged by many other writers, and achieved its widest diffusion through Cicero, in passages that, right up to the eighteenth century, played a major role in forming the image of the orator as a culture-hero. The early *De Inventione* elaborates on the Isocratean model by positing a time 'when men wandered at large in the field like animals and lived on wild fare', lacking reason, religion, society, and law, until one 'great and wise' man 'transformed them from wild savages into a kind and gentle folk' by use of 'reason and eloquence', *ratio* and *oratio* (1. 2. 2). Once social order was established, according to this mythical history, persuasion was still the crucial factor in leading men to submit themselves to authority and justice

---

[16] Nicocles, 5 ff. (= *Antidosis*, 253 ff.); tr. Kennedy 1963, pp. 8–9.

(1. 2. 3). Rhetoric continues to play a crucial cultural and political role, for it preserves the community, 'renders life safe, honourable', and protects friends, so that just as men excel animals 'most by having the power of speech', that man has 'won a splendid possession who excels men themselves in that ability by which men excel beasts' (1. 4. 5). Although Cicero disowned *De Inventione* thirty years later as 'the unfinished and crude essays which slipped out of the notebooks of . . . my youth' (*De Or.* 1. 2. 5), it was the only one of his rhetorical works to have an unbroken tradition, with hundreds of manuscripts and commentaries surviving from the Middle Ages and Renaissance. Nor was Cicero deterred from repeating this *laus eloquentiae* almost verbatim in the mature work (1. 8. 32–3). The picture given there of the orator leading 'scattered humanity . . . out of its brutish existence in the wilderness up to our present condition of civilization as men and as citizens', helping to create 'social communities, . . . laws, tribunals, and civic rights', was taken over bodily by many Renaissance writers on rhetoric.[17] Quintilian similarly described oratory as 'the highest gift of providence to man' (1. 10. 7), and echoed Isocrates and Cicero in crediting eloquence with a civilizing function (2. 16. 9), *ratio* and *oratio* being a divine gift to elevate us over the beasts (2. 16. 12–15, 2. 20. 9, 3. 2. 1, 3). Hence the orator, in excelling other men in these capacities, becomes the highest realization of humanity (2. 16. 17).

The effect (and perhaps intention) of these programmatic celebrations of rhetoric was to confirm the validity of a rhetorical education and to attract both teachers and pupils. By the middle of the fourth century BC rhetoric had become the central discipline in Greek education, affecting 'all public utterances' and indeed all intellectual activity,[18] and it became yet more widespread in the Hellenistic period (338 BC onwards). Greek rhetoricians began teaching in Rome in the second century BC, with great success. Cicero recorded that when the Romans had 'heard the Greek orators, gained acquaintance with their literature and called in Greek teachers, our people were fired with a really incredible enthusiasm for eloquence' (*De Or.*

[17] Vickers 1983a, pp. 412–16.
[18] Kennedy 1963, pp. 7, 237, 268–72; Clarke 1953; Marrou 1964, pp. 267–81, 338–9, 381–5.

1. 4. 14). The rhetor was the best paid and most respected of teachers: Vespasian paid them salaries of up to 100,000 sesterces, and in AD 74 he even excused grammarians and rhetoricians from local obligations, such as taxes and billetting.[19] A boy's education began with grammar and rhetoric, and the study of rhetoric could last from four to eight years, indeed 'higher education was reduced to rhetoric in the strictest sense of the word', which dominated teaching in Rome by the first century BC.[20] The Romans made rhetoric even more systematic, unlikely though that seems, but added little of their own to the Greek corpus. Yet although rhetoric affected many areas of Roman life and literature, it never became the organic link between school and adult activity in politics and law that it had been in Greece. For whereas all Greek citizens could exercise the right to speak on their own behalf, 'oratory in Rome, in the lawcourts, the senate, and assemblies, was practised chiefly by a relatively small number of professional orators, highly conscious of techniques and of their own roles'.[21] Paradoxically, then, the number of people studying rhetoric increased vastly while the number practising it was reduced. Furthermore, 'freedom of expression in Rome was a relative matter. It was not something to which every citizen was entitled', and although he might acquire it by birth, wealth, or service, this freedom was always limited by hierarchy.[22] But the widespread knowledge of rhetoric through the school system undoubtedly accounts for its dissemination through the whole of Latin literature,[23] and writers could be sure that their readers were able to appreciate their art. From Rome rhetoric, in education, in public activity, and in all forms of writing, spread through the world, its influence waning only in the nineteenth century.

ii THE MAJOR TEXTS

Rhetoric was a central element in education—setting aside the losses suffered by literary culture in general—from before Plato

[19] J. Bowen, *A History of Western Education*. Vol. 1. *The Ancient World* (London, 1972), pp. 197–8, 205.
[20] Marrou 1964, pp. 284, 204, 285; Bonner 1977.
[21] Kennedy 1980, p. 23.
[22] Kennedy 1972, p. 302.
[23] Curtius 1953; Clarke 1953; D'Alton 1931; Bonner 1977.

to after the Romantics. During most of this period rhetoric was passed on either by direct teaching, where the master expounded principles from his own knowledge, the students making notes and performing exercises under his guidance, or else by textbooks that circulated in schools, universities, or in society at large. Any one wishing to learn the range and capability of rhetoric must still have recourse to such a textbook, if he can find one adapted to his needs.

It is essential to know the major texts, but also to realize that they are very diverse compositions. Some of them begin, as the opening lectures in medieval and Renaissance universities began, as this book begins, with praises of eloquence as a humanizing discipline in which man realizes to the full his God-given faculty, whose cultivation will benefit both society and himself. Other general topics may include a history of rhetoric, or of one particular branch, oratory, style, epistolary theory. Such passages can build up to the importance of and need for this particular treatment, and include disparaging remarks about rival texts. Aristotle does this, as does Quintilian on many occasions, and it continues as a topos down to the Renaissance, some writers even claiming that all previous treatments are defective, theirs alone perfect. (Naïve though this may seem to all but the most gullible readers, such disparaging comments on other rhetoric-books may have had a cumulatively damaging effect on rhetoric itself.) When the texts get down to detail they can fulfil a prescriptive function, giving speakers or writers instruction in methods of composition, invention, expression. They can also be descriptive, analysing notable examples of oratory: Cicero takes Demosthenes, Quintilian both Demosthenes and Cicero for instances of logical development, emotional appeal. Other writers analyse style, either in terms of specific qualities—clarity, ornateness, appropriateness—or larger schools of style, such as Asianism and Atticism. Rhetoric books can devote themselves to a single type of oratory, forensic (judicial) being the most popular in Roman eloquence, or a single genre, such as the sermon or letter in medieval and Renaissance times.

The reader must take this diversity of material as it comes, accepting the fact that it is not all of equal interest. The perfect rhetoric text has never been written, nor one that could meet the needs of users of every level, although the Renaissance saw several attempts at the comprehensive rhetoric-book, vast and unwieldy tomes of over a thousand folio pages, or rhetorical lexicons containing five thousand entries. The modern reader, like his predecessors no doubt, will have to make a synthesis of various texts at various stages in the development of his interests and knowledge. But one preliminary point should be kept in mind, that while studying such texts is of immense value for the recovery of the verbal culture of the past, and its manifestation in poetry, drama, fiction, history, politics, painting, and music, in so doing we are not using them for the purposes for which they were designed. That is, although the descriptive and historical parts can be read as they were read then, the prescriptive texts were never meant to be read as works of literature or history. They were 'how-to-do-it' manuals, and reading them without the intention of putting their teachings into practice would be as perverse as studying a book on tennis, or bridge, if we never intended to play those games. It is perhaps not yet time for a complete revival of rhetoric as a systematic discipline of speaking and writing, and in this interim period our study of the prescriptive texts, the handbooks of tropes and figures, ought to be undertaken with a view to evaluating the literature of the past which was created in accordance with this system, as I attempt to do in a later chapter of this book. But no one should complain that the textbooks are boring or 'sterile', as so many modern historians of rhetoric do, without really taking the practicalities seriously.

Not all authors of rhetoric-books have accepted the prescriptive role as legitimate. Plato, the earliest surviving writer on rhetoric, had largely negative feelings about a discipline that represented the main challenge to Socratic dialectic. In his *Phaedrus*[24] (266 d ff.) he makes Socrates reel off, in a slightly contemptuous manner, the contents of the early *technai* or arts of rhetoric. The 'niceties of the art', he records, include the teaching that 'a speech must begin with a preamble', then move on to

[24] Quotations are from the translation by R. Hackforth, reprinted in Plato 1963. One can still use with profit W. H. Thompson's edition of the *Phaedrus* (London, 1868), which reveals far more clearly than many recent commentators the extent of Plato's animus against rhetoric.

exposition, direct and indirect evidence, probabilities, proof and supplementary proof, and 'refutation both for prosecution and defence'. Socrates even includes a potted history, but given Plato's general hostility to rhetoric and rhetoricians one detects a note of irony in his references to 'the admirable Evenus of Paros . . . the inventor of covert allusion and indirect compliment and . . . the indirect censure', all memorized with the help of a mnemonic system.—'A real master, that', says Socrates ironically, leaving us to wonder about that strange combination of deviousness and prepared devices. Tysias and Gorgias are also called to mind, 'who realized that probability deserves more respect than truth'—so much the worse for rhetoric, then!—and had what Plato alleged to be the Sophists' dangerous ability to transform their subject-matter by their handling of it, making 'trifles seem important and important points trifles by the force of their language' (267 a–b). Plato's hostility to rhetoric is so great, and his misrepresentation of it so extreme, that it is impossible to take his accounts as reliable history or exposition.

Yet, as any reader will observe, his own dialogues included both theoretical discussions of eloquence and practical examples, just like self-confessed rhetoric-books, even though he would have disowned the label. George Kennedy has argued that the two parts of the *Phaedrus* reflect the two main types of rhetorical teaching in ancient Greece, the first part comprising three speeches (although here they are hardly 'specimens' for imitation, as they would be in a normal treatise), the second discussing the nature of rhetoric and its formal properties.[25] The *Phaedrus* might be called an anti-rhetoric, then, or an 'alternative' rhetoric, and in a certain sense it is true that Plato thought 'he could do a better job teaching rhetoric than the rhetoricians'.[26] The first part begins with a written-out speech, read aloud by Phaedrus, and supposedly composed by Lysias, which describes 'how a handsome boy was tempted, but not by a lover—that's the clever part of it. He maintains that surrender should be to one who is not in love rather than to one who is' (227 c). This is meant to be a pastiche and a parody of Sophistic rhetoric, a destruction by creation (230 e–234 c). In reply to what

[25] Kennedy 1963, p. 74.
[26] Monfasani 1976, p. 243.

the naïve youth Phaedrus describes as an 'extraordinarily fine' speech Socrates seems to extemporize a reply which has both a clearer rhetorical structure and better logical development than Lysias' attempt. I say 'seems to', to draw attention to the fictions within Plato's carefully composed dialogues, and to point up the fact that since Plato had also written Lysias' speech he was able to make it inept in order to outshine it. Socrates now sets out the answering case, the disadvantages of accepting such a lover (238 a–241 d), and there in the hands of a lesser writer the debate might have ended. But Plato makes Socrates feel that his *daimon* is rebuking him for having done something wrong, insulting love, who is after all a god, and he then delivers a much longer and more personal speech, which makes the one preceding seem like a rhetorical exercise. Now he argues in favour of the lover, in his famous account of the nature of the soul and the forms of love through the myth of the charioteer (244 a–257 b). This is the first, and still one of the most brilliant examples of the rhetorical practice of arguing *in utramque partem*, on both sides of an issue.

Plato's critique of existing rhetoric in the *Phaedrus* has a reforming, as well as a destructive intent. Although he sets Socratic dialectic and the spoken word above all other forms of communication, he is still concerned with improving the art, urging the rhetorician to learn from dialectic how to make definitions, distinguish genus from species and subspecies (the process of *diairesis* or division being accorded an almost mythical power to divine the truth), and produce an organic whole. In what has been called 'probably the most influential critical statement in Plato',[27] Socrates points to the deficiency of Lysias' speech in failing to unify its component parts: 'any discourse ought to be constructed like a living creature, with its own body, as it were; it must not lack either head or feet; it must have a middle and extremities so composed as to suit each other and the whole work' (264 c). That concept of organic unity will reappear in Cicero, in Horace's *Ars Poetica*, and in countless later treatises. Moving from formal properties to the goal of rhetoric, which has earlier been defined as 'a kind of influencing the mind by means of words, not only in courts of law and other public gatherings' (261 a) but also in Socrates' preferred face-

[27] Kennedy 1980, p. 56.

to-face dialectical encounter, Plato outlines a new approach to rhetoric. Socrates develops the implications of the fact that the 'object on which our discourse is brought to bear' is the soul. Anyone 'who seriously proffers a scientific rhetoric, will, in the first place, describe the soul very precisely' (270 e–271 a), considering 'what natural capacity it has to act upon what', and how itself is acted upon. Then, relating this psychological knowledge to the verbal artefact, the maker of a scientific rhetoric 'will classify the types of discourse and the types of soul, and the various ways in which souls are affected . . .' (271 a–b).

The orator's purpose in making such an inventory is to achieve a higher degree of persuasion:

Since the function of oratory is in fact to influence men's souls, the intending orator must know what types of soul there are. Now these are of a determinate number, and their variety results in a variety of individuals. To the types of soul thus discriminated there corresponds a determinate number of types of discourse. Hence a certain type of hearer will be easy to persuade by a certain type of speech to take such and such action for such and such reason, while another type will be hard to persuade.

The orator must study this reaction, watching it 'actually occurring, exemplified in men's conduct', for the 'keenness of perception' that he develops will give him the ability to know just 'what type of man is susceptible to what kind of discourse' (271 d–e). Knowing the character, he must also know the right occasions for speaking and for keeping quiet, the 'right and wrong time for the brachylogy, the pathetic passage, the exacerbation, and all the rest of his accomplishments' (272 a). This is the first sketch of a concept of rhetorical decorum, adjusting style to audience-response.

Plato does not tell us how to classify either souls or types of discourse, but we can accept his general argument that successful persuasion of human beings depends primarily on a knowledge of psychology, to which verbal devices are subordinate. We can also accept Socrates' dismissing 'the present-day authors of manuals of rhetoric' for never having concerned themselves with the soul (271 c). Most important, yet tantalizingly so, this passage places Plato's attacks on rhetoric in a new light. He evidently felt himself able to establish the art on a fresh scientific basis, had it been important enough for him to do so. One wishes that he had, being left as we are with a *pars destruens* (to be considered in the next chapter) that far exceeds in length and energy the *pars construens*. This sudden concern to work out the connection between rhetoric and psychology seems to lead nowhere in Plato's system, unless it lies behind the application of persuasion for state propaganda that emerges, as we shall see, in the late dialogues. Otherwise we are left with the three paradoxes of Plato as 'the rhetorician who distrusts rhetoric, the poet who abolishes poetry from his state, and the admirer of oral dialectic who publishes dialogues worked out with extraordinary care'.[28] Plato is simultaneously eloquent and deeply distrustful of his own powers of expression, rather like Thomas Hobbes, who writes at the end of *Leviathan* (1651) that 'there is nothing I distrust more than my elocution'.[29]

.To posterity Plato has more often seemed the out-and-out enemy of rhetoric, greeted or scorned accordingly. Yet his immediate impact within the Academy was constructive. His pupil Aristotle began lecturing on rhetoric before Plato's death, evidently with his master's approval, and in lectures extending over a period of years both expanded Plato's positive suggestions and refuted some of his attacks (as will be seen in Chapter 3 below). Awareness of the extended genesis of Aristotle's *Rhetoric*[30] is essential for the understanding of a text that otherwise seems in places self-contradictory. As Friedrich Solmsen was the first to show,[31] Aristotle probably started this lecture-course (given in the afternoons, when less intellectually demanding topics were treated) when he returned to Athens

[28] Kennedy 1980, p. 59.
[29] 'A Review, and Conclusion', *Leviathan*, ed. M. Oakeshott (Oxford, 1946), p. 466.
[30] English readers of this text have had to rely for many years on E. M. Cope, *An Introduction to Aristotle's Rhetoric: with Analyses, Notes and Appendices* (London, 1867) and E. M. Cope and J. E. Sandys, *The Rhetoric of Aristotle* (Cambridge, 1877), a 3-vol. commentary. Now W. M. A. Grimaldi, SJ, who published *Studies in the Philosophy of Aristotle's Rhetoric* (Wiesbaden, 1972), has begun to produce a *Commentary*, so far on Book I (Bronx, NY, 1980). For a compact bibliography of classical rhetoric see Fuhrmann 1984, pp. 153–60.
[31] Solmsen, *Die Entwicklung der aristotelischen Logik und Rhetorik* (Berlin, 1929); Kennedy 1963, pp. 82–7; and various essays collected in Keith V. Erickson (ed.), *Aristotle: The Classical Heritage of Rhetoric* (Metuchen, NJ, 1974).

and opened his own school in about 335 BC, although it may contain material from his earlier period at the Academy (367–347), and even from his period in Macedon (347–335), while the 'final version' may have been edited by pupils after his death. The resulting text does indeed read as if three or more sets of lecture-notes have been joined together by someone concerned to preserve everything the master had said, not daring to edit out discrepancies between them. As every reader will find, the opening section attacks the extant rhetoric-books on two grounds, for discussing the arousal of the emotions instead of the true topic, persuasion; and for enumerating such things as the parts of an oration. But Aristotle devotes much of Book Two to the first topic, and part of Book Three to the second. Again, in some places Aristotle makes great advocacy of the enthymeme and logical proof, linking rhetoric closely to his dialectic (although with many gaps in the execution), while in other places he describes purely rhetorical devices. The composite nature of the text makes it impossible to form a clear view of Aristotle's final thoughts on the subject, but at least the *Rhetoric* survives. Other rhetorical works he is known to have written are lost, including an early dialogue in the Platonic mode, *Gryllus* (around 360 BC); a *Synagoge Technon*, summarizing the handbooks of earlier rhetoricians; and a *Compendium of the Art of Theodectes*, rhetorician and dramatist.

Aristotle's preoccupation with rhetoric, we can see, was lifelong, which is hardly surprising in view of its importance in Greek life and education, and the threat to Plato's school posed by the Sophists. Aristotle shared Plato's disapproval of Isocrates, but he shows himself his own man by challenging Plato's own prejudices head-on, as we shall see. He announces that he will describe 'the systematic principles of Rhetoric itself', and defines it as 'the faculty of observing in any given case the available means of persuasion', a goal that sets it apart from all other arts (1355^{b}22–35). This is to differ both from Plato, by seeing persuasion as the goal that may not always be attained, and from other rhetoricians who would link it immediately with ethics. He then distinguishes three kinds or modes of persuasion: the first 'depends on the personal character of the speaker' (*ethos*); 'the second on putting the audience into a fit state of mind' (*pathos*); 'the third on the proof, or apparent proof, provided by the words of the speech itself' (1356ª1–3). *Ethos* involves the speaker in appearing to be good and hence worthy of trust, for 'we believe good men more fully and more readily than others', and a speaker's 'character may almost be called the most effective means of persuasion he possesses' (3–13). *Pathos* works when the speech stirs the reader's emotions, for 'our judgments when we are pleased and friendly are not the same as when we are pained and hostile'. Aristotle postpones detailed discussion of the emotions to what is now known as Book Two, chapters 2–11. (I retain these traditional divisions for ease of reference, but they are not Aristotle's, nor do they mark any clear division of subject-matter.) He then turns to persuasion by proof, outlining the logical resources of rhetoric, the example and enthymeme, that correspond to the induction and syllogism in dialectic. The length of this last section (1356ᵇ1– 1358ª33) and the easy familiarity of the detail show where Aristotle's greater sympathies lie, inspiring later rhetoricians to attempt a closer union between rhetoric and logic.

These three modes of persuasion are taken up in varying detail later. *Ethos* is given the least space (Book Two, first half of chapter 1), followed by *Pathos* (second half of that chapter, and the next ten, with a further six chapters appended on the various types of human character). Forms of argument are discussed for the remainder of Book Two (chs. 19–26), but recur in Book Three, which is notionally devoted to Style (chs. 1–12), when Aristotle comes to arrangement, listing forms of argument in general (ch. 17), and specific arguments to excite or allay prejudice (chs. 14–15). This triple division is the main organizing thread of the *Rhetoric*, and was to prove very influential, but the heterogeneity of the work allows Aristotle to discuss several other topics. Equally influential, and apparently original, was his classification of rhetoric into

three divisions, determined by the three classes of listeners to speeches. For of the three elements in speech-making—speaker, subject, and person addressed—it is the last one, the hearer, that determines the speech's end and object. (1358ª36–8)

That is a classic statement of what I would call a functional or holistic view of rhetoric, the three elements of speaker, subject, and audience being seen as an interdependent triad. It is a typical Aristotelian ploy, of course, to seek out the determining factor on which others depend, and in this case it results in the important classification of the hearer as 'either a judge, with a decision to make about things past or future, or an observer'. The 'judge', as member of a jury in a lawcourt, decides about things that have already happened, which gives the category of forensic (legal or judicial) oratory; as member of a political assembly he decides on what must be done, in political (or deliberative) oratory; and as 'observer' or onlooker he merely listens to a set speech of display on ceremonial occasions, epideictic oratory, on which no formal judgement is expected (1358ᵇ1–13).

The division is elaborated further in a pregnant formulation which describes the action and purpose relevant to each:

Political speaking urges us either to do or not to do something: one of these two courses is always taken by private counsellors, as well as by men who address public assemblies. Forensic speaking either attacks or defends somebody: one or other of these two things must always be done by the parties in a case. The ceremonial oratory of display either praises or censures somebody. (8–13)

The three kinds also involve three different phases of time, past, future, and present, and, more importantly, they have 'distinct ends in view':

The political orator aims at establishing the expediency or the harmfulness of a proposed course of action; if he urges its acceptance, he does so on the ground that it will do good; if he urges its rejection, he does so on the ground that it will do harm; and all other points, such as whether the proposal is just or unjust, honourable or dishonourable, he brings in as subsidiary and relative to this main consideration. Parties in a law-case aim at establishing the justice or injustice of some action, and they too bring in all other points as subsidiary and relative to this one. Those who praise or attack a man aim at proving him worthy of honour or the reverse, and they too treat all other considerations with reference to this one. (1358ᵇ21–8)

While admitting the justice of that classification, one's first response is of surprise at the clarity with which Aristotle shows the realm of politics to be unethical, essentially concerned with the good of a state, its survival or prosperity, and ready to set justice or honour on one side. Not many rhetoric-books continually stimulate their readers to consider fundamental issues, and no other sustains analysis so cogently.

This ability to get at essentials, to discover the determining factors or actual modes of operation in human life, makes Aristotle's *Rhetoric* compelling reading, and of far greater significance than the usual *technē*. Pursuing his classification of the three kinds of rhetoric he notes that what they have in common is that speakers in each kind 'attempt not only to prove the points mentioned but also to show that the good or the harm, the honour or disgrace, the justice or injustice, is great or small, either absolutely or relatively' (1359^a17–21). That is, the speaker in each kind of oratory must know the effects on human beings of certain modes of action, whether acting or suffering. The political speaker, as well as knowing about national defence, war and peace, ways and means, law and legislation (Book One, ch. 4), must, since he urges his hearers to take or avoid a course of action, show that he is concerned with their happiness. This fundamental point leads Aristotle to 'ascertain what is in general the nature of happiness' (Book One, ch. 5). He, gives four definitions of happiness, and lists fourteen constituent parts, divided into external values—good birth, friends, money, honour—and internal values—goods of the soul and body (1360^b7–27). The definitions and discussions are not as rigorous as in Aristotle's ethical and political works, but they are ample enough to justify his claim that 'rhetoric is an offshoot of dialectic and also of ethical studies', which may also be called political (1356^a25–6). Although the political orator was originally seen as concerned solely with a country's welfare, in order to appeal to the interest of his hearers he must know what things are 'good', so Aristotle adds a discussion of 'the main facts about Goodness and Utility in general', absolute and relative (1362^a20–1365^b20). By allowing topics to branch out organically from the main trunk of discourse, he leads us into ever-widening areas of life.

Turning to the epideictic speaker, who praises virtue and censures vice, Aristotle surveys these topics, defining virtue as 'a faculty of providing and preserving good things; or a faculty of conferring many great benefits . . .' (1366^a36–8). He defines the forms of virtue, 'justice, courage, temperance, magnificence, magnanimity, liberality, gentleness, prudence, wisdom', and immediately ranks them: 'if virtue is a faculty of beneficence, the highest kinds of it must be those which are most useful to others, and for this reason men honour most the just and courageous, since courage is useful to others in war, justice both in war and peace' (1366ᵇ1–6). This 'other-centred' concept is one of the key principles of the *vita activa*, and Aristotle invokes here some of the basic principles of his ethics, albeit in simplified form. The forensic speaker is also sent back to first principles. Since his subject is in effect wrongdoing, he must first ascertain 'the nature and number of the incentives to wrongdoing; second, the state of mind of wrongdoers; third, the kind of persons who are wronged, and their condition' (1368ᵇ2–5). Wrongdoing is defined as 'injury voluntarily inflicted contrary to law', law being then defined as either 'special', that is the 'written law which regulates the life of a particular community', or general, 'all those unwritten principles which are supposed to be acknowledged everywhere' (6–11). There follows a brief but penetrating essay into the psychology of the criminal (who acts either for vicious motives or lacking self-control); his goals and avoidances, which leads to a classification of human action into seven causes: three involuntary—chance, nature, compulsion— and four voluntary—habit, reasoning, anger, and appetite (1368ᵇ10–1369ᵃ6). Voluntary actions are undertaken because they promise either what is advantageous or good (a topic already discussed), or what is pleasant, which leads to a definition and discussion of pleasure (1369ᵇ30–1372ᵃ3). Having considered 'the motives that make men do wrong to others' Aristotle next reviews 'the states of mind in which they do it, and the persons to whom they do it', which leads him on to a more detailed discussion of justice, natural law, unwritten law, equity, and the comparative badness of criminal actions (1372ᵃ4– 1375ᵃ20).

In this way Aristotle's classification of the three kinds of rhetoric and their goals has led him into discussing politics, ethics, criminology, jurisprudence, and the causes of human drives and desires. This remarkably open-minded spirit of enquiry into everything that depends on language gives Aristotle's *Rhetoric* its unique quality. It also reinforces the point from which I began, that, as originally conceived, rhetoric is intimately concerned with every aspect of human life. This reciprocal relationship becomes still clearer in Book Two, where he reverts to his original categories of persuasion, *ethos, pathos,* and proof. *Ethos* receives the smallest space again, simply listing 'the three things which inspire confidence in the orator's own character' (1378^{a}6–18). Passing on to *pathos,* Aristotle begins by defining the emotions as 'those feelings that so change men as to affect their judgments, and that are also attended by pain or pleasure' (1378^{a}20). He devotes the next ten sections to pithy discussions of anger and calmness, friendship and enmity, fear and confidence, shame and shamelessness, kindness and unkindness, pity, indignation, envy, and emulation. The over-riding analytic approach is shown in the opening account of the emotion of anger: 'here we must discover (1) what the state of mind of angry people is, (2) who the people are with whom they usually get angry, and (3) on what grounds they get angry with them.' Partial knowledge is not enough, for without mastering all three points 'we shall be unable to arouse anger in anyone' (1378^{a}23–6). Here the orator is clearly seen in his prime role of persuading his hearers by arousing their feelings, the rhetorical doctine of *movere.* But elsewhere Aristotle's eye seems to be on the nature of the emotions in general, and he produces what are in effect moral-psychological essays, which provoked imitation both in classical times (Cicero, Seneca, Lactantius) and in the Renaissance (Montaigne, Bacon). Setting aside specifically Greek social and religious attitudes, these discussions show great penetration into psychology and motive, and any reader will derive knowledge and stimulus from them. They have the value that Dr Johnson ascribed to Bacon's *Essays,* being 'the observations of a strong mind operating upon life'.[32]

The same judgement applies to his account of 'the various types of human character', considered 'in relation to the

---

[32] *Johnsonian Miscellanies,* ed. G. B. Hill (Oxford, 1897), ii. 229. Roland Barthes praised Aristotle's discussion of the *pathē* for avoiding the reductive tendencies of modern psychology in dealing with such feelings as anger, hatred: 'toutes ces passions sont prises volontairement *dans leur banalité*: la colère, c'est ce que tout le monde pense de la colère. . . . La psychologie rhétorique est donc tout le contraire d'une psychologie réductrice, qui essayerait de voir ce qu'il y a *derrière* ce que les gens disent et qui prétendrait réduire la colère, par exemple, à *autre chose,* de plus caché.' Rejecting 'aucune idée herméneutique (de décryptage)'. Aristotle sees the passions as 'des morceaux de langage tout faits', and applies a more advanced 'psychologie classificatrice, qui distingue des "langages" [des passions]' (Barthes 1970, p. 212).

emotions and moral qualities, showing how they correspond to our various ages and fortunes' (1388ᵇ32 ff.), an enquiry that anticipates developmental psychology yet adds the dimension of ethics. The discussion of ages produces a brilliant juxta-position of youth and age, one that any essayist could be proud of. 'Young men have strong passions, and tend to gratify them indiscriminately'; their desires are violent but quickly over. 'They trust others readily, because they have not yet often been cheated. . . . Their lives are mainly spent not in memory but in expectation. . . . They have exalted notions, because they have not yet been humbled by life or learnt its necessary limitations. . . . They would always rather do noble deeds than useful ones; their lives are regulated more by moral feeling than by reasoning.' Old men, by contrast, 'have often been taken in, and often made mistakes. . . . The result is that they are sure about nothing and *under-do* everything. They "think", but they never know. . . . They tend to put the worse construction on everything', life having made them distrustful. 'They live by memory rather than by hope. . . . They guide their lives by reasoning more than by moral feeling', considering utility rather than goodness, and not caring what people say about them. If they feel pity it is for a different reason: 'young men feel it out of kindness; old men out of weakness, imagining that anything that befalls anyone else might easily happen to them . . .' (1389ᵃ1–1390ᵃ25). But, a modern reader might object, what has all this to do with rhetoric? Everything! a fourth-century Greek might answer, since the rhetorician needs above all to know about life. He must be aware, too, of the effects on human character of the gifts of fortune such as good birth, wealth, and power, especially their corruption, as when 'wealth becomes a standard of value for everything else' (1390ᵇ15–1391ᵇ8). As Aristotle remarks later, 'Educated men lay down broad general principles' (1396ᵇ30), and the breadth of his discussion shows how widely rhetoric can be conceived.

The final book is devoted to style, and is the part which, along with the intricacies of logical proof (which I shall not broach here), the modern reader is likely to find least rewarding. One problem is that many of his remarks refer specifically to Greek prose composition, such as the need to use 'pure, correct Greek' (1407ᵃ19), or to avoid using compound words or fancy epithets that belong to verse, not prose (1405^b35–1406^a15). The whole discussion of prose-rhythm and sentence-structure (1408^b21–1410^b5) only really makes sense for Greek. Further, the concluding enumeration of the parts of a speech, for including which he had censured other rhetoric-books, seems sketchy and unrelated. If the extant sequence of the *Rhetoric* leaves the reader with a sense of anticlimax, the work as a whole remains the most penetrating analysis of speech in its full individual and social dimension.

To Aristotle, writing in the Athenian *polis*, just as politics was superior to rhetoric as a discipline, so 'political oratory is a more difficult task than forensic' (1418^a21). To the authors of the first two Latin rhetorics, both published in the first century BC, Cicero's *De Inventione* (*c*.87 BC) and the anonymous *Rhetorica ad Caius Herennium* (*c*.84 BC), that position was reversed. 'There are three kinds of causes', the author of the latter writes, 'Epideictic, Deliberative, and Judicial. By far the most difficult is the judicial', therefore he devotes two of his four books to it (2. 1. 1). We note that the subject is now a 'cause', or 'issue' (the nearest English terms for the Greek *stasis, systasis,* and the Latin *status, constitutio*), for the focus of attention is now courtroom oratory. 'Of the five tasks of the speaker Invention is the most important and the most difficult', he continues, and he is referring to the discovery of legal arguments. In *De Inventione* (which was to have treated all five parts of rhetoric, but only completed the first), Cicero agrees that invention 'is the most important of all the divisions, and above all is used in every kind of pleading' (1. 7. 9: *omni causarum genere*). Both Cicero and his anonymous compatriot imported into Roman rhetoric the doctrine of *constitutio causae*, or determination of the nature of the issue under dispute, from a Greek rhetorician of the second century BC, Hermagoras of Temnos, whose own work has perished but who elaborated a systematic classification of the kinds of legal dispute that was to prove influential.[33] As the *Ad Herennium* explains,

The Issue is determined by the joining of the primary plea of the defence with the charge of the plaintiff. The Types of Issue are . . .

---

[33] On Hermagoras see Dieter Matthes, 'Hermagoras von Temnos, 1904–1955', *Lustrum*, 3 (1958), 58–214, and Kennedy 1972, p. 61.

three: Conjectural, Legal, and Juridical. The Issue is Conjectural when the controversy concerns a question of fact . . .; Legal, when some controversy turns upon the letter of a text or arises from an implication therein . . .; Juridical, when there is agreement on the act, but the right or wrong of the act is in question. (1. 11. 18–19, 1. 14. 24)

The status system addresses such topics as whether the act was committed or not; who committed it; which part of the law applies; whether it covers this case; and, if the act is admitted, the extenuating circumstances, if any. Cicero distinguishes four causes, the conjectural, the definitional, the general, and the translative (1. 8. 10–1. 12. 17).

In effect these first two Latin rhetoric-books turn out to be legal treatises, drawing on the general system of rhetoric (which they summarize with commendable brevity), but adapting it to specific legal problems, and illustrating their doctrine with examples from courtroom situations. The problem facing the modern reader with a general interest in rhetoric is that the greater part of these texts is only comprehensible to specialists in Roman law, or social history. The outline of the basic issues given above seems simple, but we will be bemused by the amount of detail that accumulates and the number of categories that are distinguished. The *Ad Herennium* divides the legal issue into six types (including 'Letter and Spirit', 'Ambiguity', 'Reasoning from Analogy'), the Juridical into Absolute (the act was correct) and Assumptive, which has four main headings (acknowledging the charge, shifting the responsibility to some other person or circumstance, shifting the question of guilt, and comparison with an alternative act); while the Conjectural is divided into six main headings (probability of defendant's guilt; comparison—no one else likely to be guilty; signs pointing to guilt; presumptive proof; subsequent behaviour; confirmatory proof), and more than a dozen subheadings. Rhetoric had a tendency towards elaborating classification to the maximum possible degree, whether in these Hellenistic legal rhetorics, medieval epistolary manuals, or Renaissance compilations on style, gesture, and memory. Since all these treatises are how-to-do-it manuals an attempt at complete coverage of the subject is laudable, but even the dedicated rhetoric-student reaches the point of asking whether the subdivisions are justified, or whether they represent an impulse to classify 'in excess of the facts' (as T. S. Eliot said of Hamlet's preoccupation with his mother's sex-life). In this instance, the answer seems to be, as Harry Caplan (whose *Ad Herennium* in the Loeb Library is one of the best editions of any rhetoric-book) reports, that 'modern students of Roman Law for the most part think that from the juristic point of view, as against the rhetorical, the *status* system was over-intricate and impractical', and had no real influence on judicial decisions: 'the rhetorician's method of interpretation is rationalistic and schematic, the jurist's is casuistic.'[34] The two methods could not really cohere.

Yet, the *De Inventione* and the *Ad Herennium* were the two most popular rhetoric-books of antiquity, and perhaps the two most disseminated works of any kind. More manuscripts of them survive than of any other classical texts, and the total of copies and commentaries originally circulating was probably in the thousands.[35] Since neither medieval nor Renaissance legal systems resembled Roman law-court practices, we are forced to conceive of generations of users 'reading past' the law, as it were, ignoring this doctrine while searching for other matters. What they found in both texts were brief and coherent definitions of the main rhetorical doctrine, the three kinds of oratory, the five stages of composition (*inventio, dispositio, elocutio, memoria, pronuntiatio*), and the six parts of a speech. Book 3 of *Ad Herennium* itemizes the topics of deliberative and epideictic oratory, discusses memory and gesture, while Book 4 deals with qualities of style and lists over a hundred figures of speech—for centuries the most-used section. It is in general an admirable textbook, rationally organized, clearly expounded, and with excellent illustrations. But one must add that it contains not a single memorable sentence on rhetoric, or on anything else, over and above its self-appointed tasks. *De Inventione*, although not as comprehensive, has many of the same virtues and vices, while opening up a slightly wider horizon in the procemium, with its Isocrates-inspired praise of language and eloquence. But both are essentially *technai*, works used by the ancients in order to learn rhetorical skills, and

---

[34] Caplan (ed.), *Ad Herennium*, pp. 32–3, 90–1; W. Trimpi, 'The Quality of Fiction: The Rhetorical Transmission of Literary Theory', *Traditio*, 30 (1974), 1–118, pp. 26 n., 36 n.

[35] Ward 1978.

whose popularity proves how well they satisfied those needs. They are books we turn to for information, but not for stimulus, and after Aristotle's *Rhetoric* they cannot but seem narrow, lacking interest in wider human issues.

In his major rhetoric-book, the *De Oratore*, which is also his longest work, Cicero attempted a wider scope, indeed the widest, bringing into the rhetorician's field of competence everything under the sun. It is a work over which he laboured long, and all who appreciate Cicero's enormous importance for Western culture from classical times to the early nineteenth century will want to study it.[36] Yet two difficulties confront us at the outset. One concerns content, the other form. The widest scope is claimed for rhetoric, but it is claimed only, not demonstrated. Whereas Aristotle was able to give, in relatively brief compass, numerous practical demonstrations of the relevance of rhetoric to politics, law, ethics, psychology, criminology, and other subjects, Cicero and his speakers continually urge the need for the orator to master the whole of knowledge, but they never outline a practical method of doing so, nor do they give any examples. One can always resort to Cicero's moral works, of course, such as *De Officiis* ('Of duties') and *De Finibus* ('Of the ends or goals of human action'), but a rhetoric-book that sets out to be as comprehensive as this one surely ought to be complete in itself. As for its form, it is one of the few classical rhetorics to be written as a dialogue, less in the Platonic dialectical than in the Aristotelian expository mode, as Cicero himself recorded[37] (having access to dialogues of Aristotle subsequently lost). By making the participants in his dialogue famous Roman orators of the past Cicero expressed his constant desire to set his own work and career within the pantheon of Latin eloquence, and the historical dimension so created is valuable. But Cicero was no Plato, much though he wanted to emulate him, and neither in setting nor in characterization does he rival the *Phaedrus* or *Gorgias*. A more serious fault is that we

---

[36] A major commentary is in progress (in German): *De Oratore Libri III*, ed. Anton Leeman and Harm Pinkster, Vols. 1 (Heidelberg, 1981) and 2 (Heidelberg, 1985) having reached Book 2, para. 98. See also Alain Michel, *Rhétorique et philosophie chez Cicéron* (Paris, 1960).

[37] Cicero, *Letters to Atticus*, tr. D. R. Shackleton Bailey (Harmondsworth, 1978), xiii. 19—'my recent compositions follow the Aristotelian pattern, in which the other roles in the dialogue are subordinate to the author's own' (p. 533).

sometimes feel that the dialogue form is being used for what is essentially a task of exposition, with the risk that the personae will either give us great slabs of information or, at the other extreme, dismiss a topic perfunctorily. Cicero was evidently aware of both dangers, and is more successful with the first, breaking up expository passages by interventions from the other participants. For the second failing he is perhaps himself responsible.

The great problem in the dialogue form is to relate the speakers to clearly differentiated attitudes. Where Plato uses the dialogue to downgrade rhetoric by a direct confrontation between its proponents and their implacable enemy Socrates, Cicero makes his a dispute among friends, that is between people who basically agree about the nature and value of rhetoric, but who disagree on the way it should be acquired. Cicero could not just repeat Plato's structure, obviously enough, and certainly no part of him could have formulated the ruthless critique made by Socrates, but the consequence is that the issues which divide his speakers seem by comparison relatively unimportant. The main speaker, and for much of the time Cicero's mouthpiece, is L. Licinius Crassus, born 140 BC and aged 49 when the discussion is supposed to have taken place, 91 BC (he died shortly afterwards). A leading politician, he was the most illustrious Roman orator before Cicero, whom he taught as a boy. His notional opponent in the dialogue is M. Antonius (143–87 BC), grandfather of the triumvir, an outstanding public servant. The other speakers who take part in the whole dialogue are P. Sulpicius Rufus and C. Aurelius Cotta, both members of the party of conservative reform. Q. Mucius Scaevola the Augur, a lawyer and Stoic, appears in Book I only, in order to deliver a token attack on the proposal to educate the orator in literature and philosophy. Two speakers who figure in Books II and III are Q. Lutatius Catulus, a successful consul, and C. Julius Caesar Strabo, lawyer and aedile. All of Cicero's characters, then, are practising politicians and lawyers, all committed to public speaking as a way of life, and all marked as representatives of the *vita activa*, servants of the state.

Apart from Scaevola, whose objections (1. 9. 35–1. 10. 44, 1. 17. 74–79) are given only to motivate their refutation by Crassus, what opposition there is comes from Antonius. In Book I he attacks as unpracticable Crassus' claim that the orator should master all knowledge (1. 18. 80), a point that he later develops at greater length (1. 48. 209–1. 61. 262). Crassus suggests that Antonius, who had earlier described the practice of the Athenian Academy in taking the opposite side on every issue (1. 18. 84), is merely 'gratifying [his] singular liking for contradiction' (1. 62. 263), and invites him to state his own views. Antonius does so on the following day, first admitting that he had calculatedly disagreed with Crassus before: 'it was my design, if I should have succeeded in refuting your arguments, to steal these pupils from you' (2. 10. 40). But now, instead of fighting, he outlines his own ideas, of which the most contentious is that oratory 'owes little to art', which is concerned with the things that are known, while 'the orator has to do with opinion, no knowledge' (2. 27. 30)—Plato's contention in the *Gorgias*. Antonius denies the need for special rules in composing official dispatches, history-writing, or philosophical topics (2. 12. 49–2. 15. 64), thus representing Nature, while Crassus stands for Art. This opposition had been prefigured in the introduction, addressed by Cicero to his brother Quintus, who holds that rhetoric 'must be separated from the refinements of learning and made to depend on a sort of natural talent and on practice', while Cicero, on the other hand, believes that 'eloquence is dependent upon the trained skill of highly educated men' (1. 2. 5). But in practice the opposition between Antonius and Crassus constantly breaks down.

Antonius believes in natural eloquence (1. 21. 94), but Crassus similarly holds that 'natural talent is the chief contributor to the virtue of oratory' (1. 25. 113), and later comes even closer to Antonius' position, stating that the orator doesn't learn his skill from 'artificial devices', but uses them to confirm 'the soundness, or reveal to us the weakness, of whatever resources we attain by native talent, study, or practice' (2. 57. 231). Antonius attacks the need for rules, but when he comes to discuss specific topics he inevitably descends to precepts and detailed advice. He recommends the orator to 'have in readiness certain commonplaces [*locos*] which will instantly present themselves for setting forth the case' (2. 30. 130). Discussing the importance of moving the audience's feelings, he follows Aristotle by enumerating the most common emotions likely to affect the jury's mind: 'love, hate, wrath, jealousy, compassion, hope, joy, fear, vexation', going on to give advice on how to arouse each of these (2. 51. 206–2. 52. 211), and adding the injunction not to make emotional appeals at the beginning of the speech (2. 53. 213 f.). In this mode of exposition Antonius is not noticeably shamed by Crassus, who turns out to show an equal dislike for formalities. If Antonius deals with the five rhetorical processes and the six parts of speech with great brevity, scorning technicalities (2. 19. 79 f.), that is exactly the spirit in which Crassus had dealt with them (1. 31. 142). When Crassus has to deal with the figures of speech he rattles off a great list of them equally perfunctorily (3. 53. 200–3. 54. 208).

Viewing *De Oratore* from the perspective of the author, we can say that at this stage of his career Cicero scorned the idea of writing a rhetorical handbook. One can reconstitute the main topics of such a text from his book, but they are overlaid by such a vast freewheeling discussion that it seems perverse to do so, especially when clear and straightforward guides are available, the *Ad Herennium* and *De Inventione*. Cicero evidently wished to write a comprehensive treatise, and therefore put such matter in (writing to Atticus that he had included the *technologia* or technicalities of rhetoric),[38] but he then reduced its value by the brevity of treatment and the dismissive tone. Authorial attitudes come to dominate those of the characters, and the notional separation of viewpoints necessary to sustain *decorum personae* vanishes as we realize that Antonius and Crassus are actually united in their scorn for the usual kind of rhetoric teaching and textbook. Antonius describes the masters in the rhetoric-schools as 'dull and inelegant', uninventive (2. 31. 133), 'untiring people who hammer day and night on the same anvil at their one and only task', chewing up rhetoric to make babies' pap (2. 39. 162). Crassus explicitly approves of Antonius for having attacked the 'narrow pettifogging argumentation' of the usual handbook (3. 30. 121), and on his own account mocks the 'exceedingly foolish persons' who write about elementary rules (3. 20. 75), whether Latin or Greek (3. 24. 93–4). Antonius and Crassus agree on so many topics, in fact: that rhetoric is the highest human cultural achievement (C: 1. 8. 30–4, 1. 46. 202; A: 2. 8. 33–2. 9. 35); that the orator needs to have a vast knowledge,

[38] Cicero, *Letters to Atticus*, iv. 16 (p. 174); Fuhrmann 1984, p. 53.

theoretical and practical (*C*: 1. 13. 59, 1. 28. 128, 1. 36. 165 ff.,
etc.; *A*: 1. 18. 80, 2. 9. 38, 2. 16. 67–8, 2. 20. 85)—a point
endorsed by Cicero himself *in propria persona*, so collapsing any
character separation (2. 1. 5, 2. 2. 5); that rhetoric gains its effects
by moving the passions (*A*: 2. 16. 70, 2. 27. 114–15, 2. 28. 121, 2.
42. 178, etc.; *C*: 3. 6. 23, 3. 14. 55, 3. 27. 105, etc.); that rhetoric
must adapt its presentation according to its audience (*C*: 1. 23.
108; *A*: 2. 38. 159); that rhetoricians must learn by imitating good
models (*C*: 1. 34. 154, 3. 31. 125; *A*: 2. 22. 90, 2. 23. 96); and that
students must be able to move from the shelter of their schools
into 'political hurly-burly', 'the dust and uproar . . . of public
debate'—a prefiguration of the British House of Commons!
(*A*: 1. 18. 81, 2. 20. 84; *C*: 1. 32. 147, 1. 34. 157).

Antonius and Crassus are not fully-formed independent
characters, then, but complementary, both expressing many of
Cicero's own convictions about rhetoric. Much of *De Oratore*
only seems like a debate, it is in fact an exposition split up
between two personae. The division of labour, basically, setting
aside numerous digressions and interventions, is that Antonius
deals with *inventio* (2. 27. 114–2. 54. 216—at which point a
disquisition on wit is provided by one of the other characters;
2. 71. 290–2. 75. 306), *dispositio* (2. 76. 307–2. 85. 350), and then
adds 'something on the subject of memory, in order to lighten
the task of Crassus and to leave him nothing else to discuss
except the method of elaborating these subjects' (2. 85. 350, 2.
86. 351–2. 88. 360). This comment makes the characters' role of
sharing the exposition transparent. Cicero indeed draws
attention to the fact (as an attempt to excuse it?) by making
Crassus express his delight 'to see you at last known as a master
of the theory, finally unmasked and stripped of the veil of your
pretended ignorance' (2. 86. 350). But this remark wholly
destroys the characters' notional differentiation, as does
Crassus' praise of Antonius' wisdom as being the product not
only of practical experience but of 'the most diligent study'
(2. 89. 362). So where is 'nature without art' now? The agreed
division between the two orators was that Antonius should
'expound the speaker's stock-in-trade' while Crassus should
deal with its 'elaboration and embellishment' (2. 28. 121–4, 2. 90.
366, 3. 5. 19), the ubiquitous distinction in Roman rhetoric
between *res* and *verba*. But every schoolboy knew that that pair

should never be split up, indeed Cicero gives Crassus an explicit statement of this principle (3. 5. 19–24), together with an eloquent passage on the disastrous consequences of Socrates having divided *cor* and *lingua* (3. 16. 60–1). Crassus duly treats *elocutio* (3. 5. 19–3. 55. 212) and *pronuntiatio* (3. 56. 213–3. 61. 228), but often unwillingly, and with unforced digressions in Cicero's own style on the present lamentably reduced scope of rhetoric, heroes of the past, outstanding Greek orators, the ideal orator, and so on (3. 14. 52–3. 35. 143), to the point where Cicero has to make one of the other speakers comment on a digression in order to justify it (3. 36. 144–5). But *qui s'excuse, s'accuse*. Crassus, and Cicero, complete the allotted task ungraciously.

A critical evaluation of the dialogue form of *De Oratore* reveals it to be cumbersome, inefficient in exposition, and frequently breaking its own supposed distinction between the personae.[39] As for the content, almost every issue in contemporary rhetoric is touched on at some point. Although Crassus affects to despise forensic oratory for 'making the orator abandon a vast, immeasurable plain and confine himself to quite a narrow circle', and summarizes its topics in a throw-away paragraph (3. 19. 70), Cicero continues the emphasis on judicial rhetoric already established in Rome. Antonius echoes the two earlier Latin rhetoric-books by saying that 'the battles of the law-courts involve really great difficulty and, I rather think, by far the most arduous of human enterprises' (2. 17. 72). Book II accordingly contains much lore about court-room practice (2. 24. 99 ff.), the right way to conduct prosecutions (2. 48. 199 ff.), and to protect one's own case (2. 72. 292 ff.). As a complement to Antonius' concern with the law Crassus is given many passages exhorting the importance of rhetoric in politics and civic life. Developing the connection between rhetoric and liberty made in his opening

---

[39] I am not persuaded by George Kennedy's estimate of it as standing 'beside or only slightly behind Aristotle's *Rhetoric* and Quintilian's *De institutione oratoria* as a rhetorical classic' (Kennedy 1972, p. 199). He himself comments on 'the lack of precision in the treatise' (p. 212), its inconsistencies (pp. 219–20), the way the dialogue form 'covers up some imprecision' and does not allow Cicero to work out his ideas 'in an entirely satisfactory way' (p. 226), and the fact that although the account of invention in Book II draws on Aristotle, 'the real keystone of logical proof in the *Rhetoric*, the theory of enthymeme and example, is totally lacking' (p. 222). These are serious deficiencies in a 'classic': although I agree that *De Oratore* is a major work, Cicero's choice of the dialogue form seems to me unfortunate.

laus eloquentiae, Crassus describes how the outstanding orator
'can either inspire a lukewarm and erring nation to a sense of
the fitting, or lead them away from their blundering, or kindle
their wrath against the wicked, or soothe them when they are
excited against good men . . .' (1. 46. 202)—an account repeated
in almost identical language by Antonius (2. 9. 35, 2. 82. 337).
Crassus' words gain more authority, of course, from our
knowledge of the historical Crassus' commitment to civic
liberty, and at the opening of Book III Cicero—*in propria persona*
—recalls his last brave and triumphant speech to the Senate
shortly before his death (3. 1. 1–8). At least, Cicero adds, he was
spared the sight of 'Italy ablaze with war, the Senate inflamed
with passion', and all the savagery and corruption that followed
in the civil war (3. 2. 8–3. 3. 12). Mention of this unhappy
sequence in Roman history makes Cicero recall 'the reverses'
suffered by his own 'incredible and unparalleled patriotism',
enough to make anyone wish to opt out of civic duties (3. 4. 13).
Here, I feel, Cicero inserts himself legitimately in the great
tradition of Roman orators who defended the state and its
liberties. Cicero's significance in the history of rhetoric may
finally be not as a theorist but as a practitioner, author of the
fifty-eight extant speeches which were pillaged by Quintilian for
examples of virtually every rhetorical procedure, and which had
an immense popularity in the Renaissance.

The *De Oratore* treats many topics in rhetoric, but invents few.
According to George Kennedy, Cicero's 'one major contribution
to technical rhetoric [was] the concept of the *officia oratoris*, or
duties of an orator'.[40] As Antonius is made to say,

for purposes of persuasion the art of speaking relies wholly upon three
things: the proof of our allegations, the winning of our hearers' favour,
and the rousing of their feelings to whatever impulse our case may
require. (2. 27. 115)

But Cicero's triad evidently draws on Aristotle's three modes of
proof: *ethos, pathos,* and logical argument, so that there is not
much originality here. Yet this formulation, or its variant in
Orator (69), was handed down for centuries while Aristotle's
Rhetoric was unknown, and Cicero must be given credit for

---

[40] Kennedy 1980, p. 100; Kennedy 1972, p. 207 describes the affective triad
(*movere—docere—delectare*) as 'the central concept of Cicero's rhetorical theory'.

being the channel by which posterity gained much of its knowledge about classical rhetoric.

In *De Oratore*, we may feel, content is obscured by form, as if somewhere inside the dialogue a rhetorical handbook was trying to get out. Cicero's three other works on rhetoric use simpler structures. *Partitiones Oratoriae* (*c.* 52 BC), written for his son Marcus Tullius, is a dialogue in the 'magistral' style, involving simple questions and answers rather like a catechism. It briefly reviews the processes of composition, the parts of a speech, the *quaestio* or matter at issue, and other topics related to judicial rhetoric. *Brutus* (44 BC) is another dialogue, like *De Oratore* in the Aristotelian mode of longer speeches, in which the interlocutors are Cicero himself, Cicero's friend Atticus (109– 32 BC), and Marcus Junius Brutus (85–42 BC), at this point one of Julius Caesar's chief lieutenants, later one of his assassins. The subject-matter is a history of Roman oratory, anchored to Cicero's own situation in two ways. The recent death of Hortensius, friend and patriot, alluded to at the beginning and end (1. 1–2. 6, 88. 301–97. 333) gives Cicero occasion once more to lament the effects of Caesar's dictatorship on free speech, 'the Roman forum . . . robbed and bereft' of eloquence, the courts of criminal and private justice all hampered, and Cicero himself forced into ignoble retirement:

> For me too it is a source of deep pain that the state feels no need of those weapons of counsel, of insight, and of authority, which I had learned to handle and to rely upon,—weapons which are the peculiar and proper resources of a leader in the commonwealth and of a civilized and law-abiding state. Indeed if there ever was a time in the history of the state when the authority and eloquence of a good citizen might have wrested arms from the hands of angry partisans, it was exactly when through blindness or fear the door was abruptly closed upon the cause of peace. (2. 7–8)

Cicero's connection of rhetoric with liberty and democracy, and his justifiable reminder of his own political career, were inspirations to proponents of the *vita activa* when this work was disseminated after its rediscovery in 1421.

Brutus is a work of self-justification on another plane, that of style. At this period in Rome a controversy raged over the proper style of oratory, between the Atticists, who wished to recall Greek to its original purity in grammar and vocabulary, reclaiming it from the copiousness of 'Asiatic' rhetoric (so called from the Greek colonies in Asia, where a more effusive form of oratory prevailed). Cicero attacks Calvus, one of the younger school of Attic orators, for a style which he characterizes as meagre, pinched and dry, quite lacking in the emotional force needed by the speaker who hopes to succeed in real-life public disputes. To mark the difference between their style and his own (for Cicero is defending himself by attacking them), Cicero gives an idealized but marvellously vivid picture of the successful public speaker:

This is what I wish for my orator: when it is reported that he is going to speak let every place on the benches be taken, the judge's tribunal full, the clerks busy and obliging in assigning or giving up places, a listening crowd thronging about, the presiding judge erect and attentive. When the speaker rises the whole throng will give a sign for silence, then expressions of assent, frequent applause; laughter when he wills it, or if he wills, tears; so that a mere passer-by observing from a distance, though quite ignorant of the case in question, will recognize that he is succeeding and that a Roscius is on the stage. (84. 290)

Questions of style also dominate *Orator* (44 BC), a treatise on the perfect orator cast in the form of a letter to Brutus, who had replied to the dialogue named after himself. Devoting three-quarters of his text to *elocutio*, Cicero again defends his own oratorical practice against the Atticists, purists and dry logicians, competent in *docere* or instruction, wholly lacking in *movere*, the orator's power over the audience's feelings. As in *Brutus*, Cicero holds up as the great model for orators Demosthenes (7. 23, 8.26–7, 31. 110–11, etc.), although here even Demosthenes is found wanting in the highest qualities, and Cicero celebrates his own work as having attempted every kind 'of oratorical merit' (29. 102–4, 30. 106–8). The *Orator* is less carefully written than *De Oratore*, but the modern reader may prefer its directness and spontaneity. If one relatively brief work had to be chosen to give an impression of the role rhetoric played in Roman life, this would be it.

Viewed as a whole Cicero's seven rhetorical treatises[41] suffer from a deal of repetition and overlapping. They were not

[41] I have not discussed *De Optimo Genere Oratorum, c.* 44 BC, which was designed as an introduction to Latin translations of two famous speeches by Aeschines and Demosthenes.

planned as a unity, although he did once claim that five of them constituted a corpus, and they range from elementary treatises designed for himself aged 19, or his son at the same age, to considered statements of his deepest beliefs, and a series of occasional polemical and self-justifying works. The reader working through them in the space of a few weeks inevitably finds that the author, writing across a period of over forty years, repeated the same ideas many times, yet also failed to treat some important topics, notably the tropes and figures, in anything like the detail they deserve. In this sense Quintilian (c. 40–96 AD) had the advantage over Cicero, for his *Institutio Oratoria* was written in two years (92–4), and was designed as a unified and comprehensive treatise. Its length, at about 200,000 words, as long as many Victorian novels, may be discouraging at first, but it is clearly constructed, and a little judicious browsing will soon locate the sections of greatest interest to the individual reader. It comprises twelve books, which the author describes as follows:

My first book will be concerned with the education preliminary to the duties of the teacher of rhetoric. My second will deal with the rudiments of the schools of rhetoric and with problems concerned with the essence of rhetoric itself. The next five will be concerned with Invention, in which I include Arrangement. The four following will be assigned to Eloquence, under which head I include Memory and Delivery. Finally there will be one book in which our complete orator will be delineated. (1. Pr. 21–2)

That disposition, Books 3 to 7 on *inventio*, 8 to 11 on *elocutio*, with the other processes subordinated, reflects a basic distinction between *res*, or subject-matter, and *verba*. The *res*, once again, is judicial oratory, with the other genres, deliberative and epideictic, receiving a brief mention (3. 4, 3. 7–8). Dismissing those writers who limited the duty of the orator to instruction and denied him appeals to the emotions, Quintilian agrees that such arts form a legitimate part of oratory, but holds that 'its special and peculiar task is to make good the case which it maintains and refute that of its opponent' (5. Pr. 1). Quintilian goes into more detail about specific courtroom techniques than any other classical rhetorician, and his work is an invaluable guide to Roman legal practices.

Yet the *Institutio*, although covering the whole rhetorical tradition systematically, devotes only just over half its space to rhetoric. Quintilian gives lengthy accounts of two topics that endeared him especially to readers between the fifteenth and nineteenth centuries: literary criticism and education. Indeed, to him the two were closely related, for

Unless the foundations of oratory are well and truly laid by the teaching of literature, the superstructure will collapse. The study of literature is a necessity for boys and the delight of old age, the sweet companion of our privacy and the sole branch of study which has more solid substance than display. (1. 4. 5)

Quintilian's belief that 'the love of letters and the value of reading are not confined to one's schooldays, but end only with life' (1. 8. 12) is so great that in one place it leads him to a distinctly un-Roman recommendation of abandoning the *vita activa*:

Perhaps the highest of all pleasures is that which we derive from private study, and the only circumstances under which the delights of literature are unalloyed are when it withdraws from action, that is to say from toil, and can enjoy the pleasure of self-contemplation. (2. 18. 4)

This concern with the student orator reading the best authors partly for self-improvement and partly for sheer pleasure (a refreshing exception to the usual utilitarian justification for literature), results in the famous survey of Greek and Roman literature from this standpoint (10. 1), one of the first and most influential histories of literature.

The formation of the orator is Quintilian's whole concern, leading the reader 'from the very cradle of speech through all the stages of education which can be of any service to our budding orator till we have reached the very summit of the art' (1. Pr. 6). Where other writers began with the rhetoric-schools, which boys visited from the age of 14 or 15, Quintilian starts from the time when the future orator is still *infans*, unable to speak, and it was this account of primary education, at once practical and humane, that won him so many admirers in posterity.⁴² Children, he writes, are by nature 'quick to reason

---

⁴² On Quintilian's reputation and influence see F. H. Colson (ed.), *M. Fabii Quintiliani Institutionis Oratoriae Liber I* (Cambridge, 1924), pp. lxiv–lxxxix; the

and ready to learn. Reasoning comes as naturally to man as
flying to birds, speed to horses, and ferocity to beasts of prey'
(1. 1. 1). The human mind is endowed with activity and
sagacity, but deserves the best possible teacher, who should
make education a process to be enjoyed, not hated. The child's
'studies must be made an amusement: he must be questioned
and praised and taught to rejoice when he has done well' (1. 1.
20). The teacher must encourage minds with praise and refresh
them with relaxation, for 'study depends on the good will of the
student, a quality that cannot be secured by compulsion' (1. 3.
7–8). Quintilian despises all forms of coercion, rejecting flogging
as degrading, fit only for slaves (1. 3. 13–14). The teacher must
be sensitive to a child's development, and not object to 'a little
exuberance in the young learner', for such daring and
inventiveness can be controlled: 'Exuberance is easily remedied,
but barrenness is incurable, be your efforts what they may' (2. 4.
5–7). The teacher's job is to guide his students through the
learning process until they can 'find out things for themselves'
and no longer need him. 'For what else is our object in teaching,
save that our pupils should not always require to be taught?'
(2. 5. 13)

The humanity and adaptability seen in Quintilian's approach
to general education is found in his specific teaching on rhetoric.
While affirming that 'the art of speaking can only be attained by
hard work and assiduity of study, by a variety of exercises and
repeated trial, the highest prudence and unfailing quickness of
judgment' (2. 13. 15), and insisting that since rhetoric *is* an art,
the more training an orator receives the better he becomes—'If
this were not so, there would not be so many rhetorical rules,
nor would so many great men have come forward to teach them'
(2. 17. 42)—Quintilian is the great enemy of pedantry,
unnecessary technicalities, and mindless rote-learning. He
attacks the 'affectation of subtlety in the invention of technical
terms' as a 'laborious ostentation' that is educationally harmful.
An 'instructor proceeding on less technical lines' should not
'destroy the coherence of his teaching by attention to such

French edition of Book I by Charles Fierville (Paris, 1890); Marianne Wychgram,
Quintilian in der deutschen und französischen Literatur des Barocks und der Aufklärung
(Langensalza, 1921; *Pädagogisches Magazin*, Heft 803), with useful bibliography
at pp. 139–47; Muntéano 1967, pp. 177–85, 297 ff., and *passim*; Kennedy 1969,
pp. 139–40.

minute detail' (3. 11. 21). Those authors of textbooks who fall into the trap that rhetoric was always prone to, of inventing a verbal equivalent for every situation, are bound to fail, for there are 'such a variety of causes' in real life 'as to render classification by species impossible' (4. 1. 43). These attempts at all-inclusiveness are not only self-defeating, as we are frequently reminded,[43] they also destroy the prime rule in rhetoric, that it should draw from life and be lifelike. 'The majority of students, finding themselves lost in an inextricable maze, have abandoned all individual effort . . . and keeping their eyes fixed upon their master have ceased to follow the guidance of nature' (5. 10. 101). The practising orator, on his feet in a lawcourt, needs above all a clear grasp of the immediate situation, and lacking this, knowledge of the most elaborate rules is 'a dumb science' (5. 10. 119). The message is repeated frequently: the ability that matters most is to be able to address the actual situation, with a readiness to abandon fixed ideas and prepared scripts according to the needs of the moment.[44] This ability can be acquired both by practice in writing, 'the best producer and teacher of eloquence'—a topic discussed with many helpful practical tips that a modern reader can still learn from (10. 3. 1.–10. 5. 7)—and, above all, by daily speaking before an audience whose judgement we value. 'Theory once mastered is not forgotten', but 'promptness and readiness for action can be maintained by practice only' (10. 7. 24). Quintilian's emphasis on daily practice reminds us that oratory is, properly speaking, a performing art, like violin playing or ballet dancing.

It could be argued that Quintilian's greatest service to rhetoric lay in his humane and practical approach to the related tasks of learning and performing. No topic is too small or unimportant if he has something useful to say. The range of his work is so all-embracing that we find here almost everything we need to know. It is necessarily eclectic, absorbing the tradition, as so many rhetoric-books do, python-like. The major source and inspiration, acknowledged time and again in the most fulsome

---

[43] See 1. Pr. 24, 3. 8. 67, 3. 11. 21, 4. 1. 43, 4. 1. 70, 5. 10. 100, 5. 11. 30, 7. 1. 37, 8. Pr. 4, 8. 4. 15, 9. 3. 99.
[44] See 2. 13. 2 and 6, 5. 10. 109 and 119, 5. 13. 60, 5. 14. 31, 6. 1. 5, 6. 5. 2, 7. 1. 2, 10. 6. 5, 10. 7. 24, 12. 9. 17–18.

terms,[45] is Cicero, 'who shed the greatest light not only on the practice but on the theory of oratory; for he stands alone among Romans as combining the gift of actual eloquence with that of teaching the art' (3. 1. 20). Cicero's influence is clearly seen in the broad lines of Quintilian's argument. Just as he had deplored the separation between philosophy and rhetoric, so does Quintilian, who urges even more aggressively that the rhetoricians should invade the philosophers' territory and reclaim their own. Cicero, the model of the orator actively engaged in civic affairs, had stressed the mutual importance of rhetoric and the *vita activa*; Quintilian, once a lawyer and now a schoolmaster, dutifully follows him, even though he seems to have been almost wholly apolitical.[46] His complete orator is 'the man who can really play his part as a citizen and is capable of meeting the demands both of public and private business, the man who can guide the state by his counsels, give it a firm base by his legislations and purge its vices by his decisions as a judge' (1. Pr. 10). The orator has 'often revived the courage of a panic-stricken army' (2. 16. 8), can assist 'the public at large . . . in the most serious emergencies' (10. 7. 1), and in his dedication to the community the orator is to be set far above the philosophers, who have withdrawn themselves, refusing to take part 'in the government of the state, which forms the most frequent theme of their instruction' (12. 2. 6–7; also 11. 1. 35, 12. 2. 21, 12. 3. 1, 12. 7. 1, etc.).

Yet although Quintilian follows Cicero, the passage of time and differences of temperament account for varying emphases. Cicero had undoubtedly conceived of the orator as a man of virtue (*De Or.* 2. 2. 85–6), but Quintilian developed this notion of the *vir bonus* to a far greater, indeed extreme and unrealistic degree (12. 1. 1.–44). On the links between rhetoric and philosophy Cicero, who was much closer to Greek culture, having studied in Athens with several distinguished teachers, emphasized the need for the orator to master a wide philosophical syllabus, particularly dialectic.[47] Quintilian pays

[45] For Quintilian's admiration of Cicero see, e.g., 5. 11. 17, 6. 3. 3, 8. 3. 3–4, 8. 3. 64, 9. 2. 53, 10. 1. 105–9, 11. 1. 85, 11. 3. 47 and 108, 12. 1. 19–20, 12. 6. 4, 12. 10. 12.
[46] Kennedy 1969, p. 23.
[47] *De Or.* 1. 3. 9, 1. 28. 128; *Brutus*, 6. 23, 41. 153, 89. 306, 90. 309, 93. 322; *Part. Or.* 40. 139; *Orator*, 3. 12, 4. 14, 4. 16, etc.

lip-worship to the principle of wide education (1. 10. 34 ff., 12. 2. 20), but in practice for him philosophy is reduced to ethics. The orator must master 'the better part of philosophy', with its 'task of forming character and establishing rules of life' (1. Pr. 14), the 'discourse of what is good, expedient, or just' (2. 21. 12; also 1. Pr. 10, 10. 1. 35, 12. 2. 5–9, etc.). Rhetoric may use some logical processes, but dare not be fettered by them (5. 19. 29–31), for dialectic is ultimately too limited and cerebral for oratory. If it claims to control 'the struggles of the forum' it will just be an obstacle to rhetoric, and 'by its very subtlety will exhaust the strength that has been pared down to suit its limitations' (12. 2. 11–14).

This increased emphasis on practicality, and distrust of theory, marks a last major difference between these two great rhetoricians on the teaching of the art of language itself. Both agree that while philosophy can offer the *res*, or subject-matter of communication, only rhetoric can supply the *verba* that turn it into effective and persuasive discourse. This is a position affirmed in the *De Oratore*, significantly enough, by both Crassus (1. 11. 49–50) and Antonius (1. 21. 94, 2. 9. 38), in terms repeated elsewhere (*Or.* 14–44). But where Cicero, the supreme master of rhetoric, is reluctant to descend to the detail needed to show how *elocutio* can be mastered, Quintilian the schoolmaster follows out the consequences and gives a full account of style as the crowning point of the whole rhetorical edifice. We are justified in expending 'the greatest care' on 'the rules for the cultivation of eloquence', he writes,

For the verb *eloqui* means the production and communication to the audience of all that the speaker has conceived in his mind, and without this power all the preliminary accomplishments of oratory are as useless as a sword that is kept permanently concealed within its sheath. Therefore it is on this that teachers of rhetoric concentrate their attention, since it cannot possibly be acquired without the assistance of the rules of art: it is this which is the chief object of our study, the goal of all our exercises and all our efforts at imitation, and it is to this that we devote the energies of a lifetime. (8. Pr. 15–16)

Of course, he goes on, this does not mean that we should study words at the expense of subject-matter, but rather unite the two in an oratory that will be 'natural and unaffected', which will 'give the impression of simplicity and reality', appeal to 'the common feeling of mankind' while preserving 'the natural current of our speech' (18–28). Quintilian is outstanding as a teacher for his humanity and practicality, but his lasting importance is as the writer who, more than any other, fully realized the claim of rhetoric to be a coherent system.

No other rhetoric text in classical antiquity offered a complete account of the art. Of the lesser works extant some touch on the problematic status of rhetoric in society. Tacitus' dialogue *De Oratoribus*[48] (probably A D 97) juxtaposes several contemporary attitudes not easily reconciled. In the prefatory epistle Tacitus writes that his dialogue addresses the problem why Rome previously had so many outstanding orators, while 'our own times' are 'barren, bereft of distinction in eloquence—scarcely, indeed, even retaining the name "orator"' (1). The persona chosen to defend modern oratory is Marcus Aper, a distinguished lawyer, who revives the Isocratean-Ciceronian celebration of the utility of rhetoric to society, upholding justice and virtue for the common good, also the pleasure and celebrity that his art brings to the orator (5–10). Aper vaunts the legal profession further by attacking poetry, while Maternus, a poet present, comments on Aper's use of the stock rhetorical trick of passing from eulogy to disparagement, before himself defending poetry for its antiquity, peace, and the fame that it, too, can bring (11–13). The dispute is also one between the contemplative and active lives, and Maternus does not fail to make the expected denunciation of the perils and uncertainties of the public life, attacking 'the profiteering and bloodstained eloquence of today . . . a new thing, born of evil habits' (12). A new character enters, Messalla, an admirer of the ancients, who provokes Aper to a defence of modern oratory (14–23), in which he claims that 'eloquence has no single face' (18), and that 'as times change and audiences vary, the style and appearance of oratory must change too' (19). These days judges won't put up with long philosophical disquisitions and clumsily developed

---

[48] See the Loeb edition of Tacitus, Vol. 1 for the *Dialogus* tr. W. Peterson, rev. M. Winterbottom (London, 1970), and Winterbottom's more fluent translation in Russell and Winterbottom 1972, pp. 432–59, from which my quotations are taken (references are to the paragraphs). For the dating, I have been persuaded by C. E. Murgin's arguments, 'The Date of Tacitus' *Dialogus*', *Harvard Studies in Classical Philology*, 84 (1980), 99–125.

speeches, but demand 'fluent arguments, brilliant reflections, refined and colourful description', so that contemporary orators have had to 'become more pretty and more ornate in style' (20).

This apology amounts to a denunciation, of course, and Messalla comments on the effect of this sort of 'refinement', which has made modern oratory theatrical in a bad sense, 'language obscene, thoughts frivolous, rhythm licentious' (26). Challenged to name the causes of the decline, Messalla replies:

Everybody knows that eloquence, and the other arts too, have declined from their old heights not for any lack óf exponents, but because the young are lazy, their parents neglectful, their teachers ignorant—and because the old ways are forgotten. (28)

The lost ideals are those of Cicero's *Brutus*, with its autobiographical account of the orator's education as including philosophy, law, music, mathematics, dialectic, ethics, since 'wonderful eloquence is the lavish overflow from great learning, wide skills, and universal knowledge'. Messalla restates the old (and, one would have thought, increasingly impracticable) image of the orator, able to 'speak on any question brilliantly and splendidly and persuasively' (30), going into the forum 'armed with all the arts like a fully-equipped soldier striding into battle'. Modern orators are ignorant of law, philosophy, and all other arts, can merely 'squeeze eloquence into a handful of bright ideas and a narrow range of epigrams—dethroning it' (32). The cause of the decline is that whereas orators previously had a broad general education, and were apprenticed to an orator active in politics and law, so that they 'learned to fight, you might say, in the battle-line' (34), today they go to 'the schools of the so-called rhetors', and learn to declaim 'in imaginary debates that have no sort of relation to reality', instead of discussing 'Good and Evil, Right and Wrong, Just and Unjust' (31).

The last speaker in the dialogue—traditionally the one whose words carry most weight—is the poet Maternus, who turns the discussion to the more general question of the nature of rhetoric itself, which he sees as stimulated more by a disturbed society than a settled one: 'Great eloquence is like a flame; it needs fuel to feed it' (36). In the unsettled earlier days of Rome orators saw 'that they could reap advantages from the confusion and licence then prevailing', and achieved great rewards by exploiting dissension, eloquence being the one accomplishment needed for success in the *vita activa* (36–7). Maternus claims that rhetoric 'flourishes more easily in stormy and troubled times' (37), and he appears to be attacking the ancient orators for making their reputations out of discord. Yet an unmistakable note of admiration comes through as he describes 'the importance of the cases' in politics and law that were treated then, which provided 'immense scope for eloquence': 'A talent swells with the size of the events it has to deal with; no one can produce a famous and notable oration unless he finds a case equal to his powers.' The celebrity of Demosthenes and Cicero derives not from petty legal disputes but from their defence of the state against its enemies. Just as 'wars produce more good fighters than peace',

So it is with oratory. The more often it stands in the firing-line, the more knocks it gives and receives, the greater adversaries and the more bitter battles it takes on, the higher and more sublime it reigns, ennobled by those crises. (37)

The old lawcourts gave the orator more time, space, freedom to develop his ideas, a large audience, 'noise and applause': today cases are conducted in 'public record offices' before one or two people, under strict time-limits, subject to the constant interference of the judge, so that eloquence has been emasculated (38–9).

Of course, Maternus concludes, with transparent irony— Tacitus was writing under the emperor Domitian, we recall, although the dialogue is set in about A D 74, under Vespasian— 'the great and famous eloquence I have in mind is the nurseling of licence—which fools call liberty—and the companion of sedition'. In 'well-organized states it does not arise', for where states have 'the severest constitutions and the severest laws', where the rulers are powerful and the citizens dutiful, there is no need for eloquence (40). With perfectly balanced irony Maternus concludes by praising present-day Rome for having made rhetoric unnecessary:

What need of long speeches in the senate? Our great men swiftly reach agreement. What need of constant harangues to the people? The deliberations of the state are not left to the ignorant many—they are the duty of one man, the wisest. What need of prosecutions? Crime is rare and trivial. What need of long and unpopular defences? The clemency of the judge meets the defendants half way. (41)

Truly, rhetoric would have no role in such a society—but neither would justice or liberty.

Tacitus' *Dialogue* is an anatomy of the decline of eloquence which in one respect echoed many complaints. Messalla denounces the rhetors' schools for their two practice exercises in declamation, the *suasoriae* and *controversiae*. The *suasoriae* or 'persuasions', given to the younger boys, were speeches offering advice to a historical personage, such as Hannibal deliberating 'whether to remain in Italy, or to return home, or invade Egypt' (*Ad Her*. 3. 2. 2). The older boys practised *controversiae* (cases in dispute), speeches for the prosecution or defence based on imaginary cases in law—as Messalla says,

—God, how do I describe those? They are fantastically put together; and moreover these deliberately unreal subjects are treated with declamatory bombast. So it comes about that the most grandiose language is lavished on rewards for tyrannicides or choices by the raped or remedies for plague or adultery by matrons, or any of the other topics that come up daily in school, in the forum rarely or never. (35)

In order to give the best scope for debate and ingenuity the *controversiae* represented some absolute dilemma, often one based on made-up laws in fantastic circumstances:

The law ordains that in the case of rape the woman may demand either the death of her seducer or marriage without dowry. A certain man raped two women in one night; one demanded his death, the other marriage. Which one should have your decision?[49]

Two collections of declamations are extant, one by Seneca the Elder, the other ascribed to Quintilian,[50] and their bizarre themes were constantly criticized for their remoteness from the realities of life, notably by Quintilian and Petronius.[51] Yet the

[49] Clarke 1953, p. 90. See also Marrou 1964, p. 202.
[50] Michael Winterbottom has edited *The Minor Declamations Ascribed to Quintilian* (Berlin, 1984) with a valuable commentary, and has translated the Elder Seneca's *Declamations*, 2 vols., Loeb Classical Library (London, 1974), Vol. 1, *Controversiae*, Books 1–6; Vol. 2, *Controversiae*, Books 7–10 and *Suasoriae*.
[51] See Quintilian, e.g. 2. 20. 3, 4. 2. 28 f., 5. 12. 17 ff., 5. 13. 36–43, 6. 1. 41–3, 6. 2. 36, 8. 3. 23, 10. 2. 12, 10. 5. 14–18, 12. 2. 7 f., 12. 6. 4, 12. 11. 15; Juvenal,

declamation schools left their mark on those who had attended them—including Ovid, Juvenal, Lucan—while the printed collections had an amazing influence. Curtius noted that Seneca's *Controversiae* were 'a principal source of the *Gesta Romanorum*', so popular in the Middle Ages, and that one of Seneca's most celebrated creations (a young man secures his freedom from pirates by marrying the pirate-chief's daughter: thus unable to marry the heiress selected by his father, he is disinherited) provides the plot of a romance by Mlle de Scudéry, *Ibrahim ou l'illustre Bassa*, as late as 1641.[52] E. M. Waith has shown that the Senecan *controversiae* were a source for several of the Beaumont and Fletcher plays. The plot of *The Queen of Corinth* (1617) is based entirely on 'The Man Who Raped Two Women' (Book 1, no. 5), and even the twist that in fact he 'rapes' the same woman twice (*sic!*) is derived from Seneca.[53]

The survival of the declamations in such places and forms is a freak, no doubt, but it shows the tremendous persistence of texts used in education. Just as influential were the *progymnasmata* or preliminary exercises in composition taught in the grammar schools. The earliest extant treatise is by the Greek Aelius Theon, dating from about A D 100 followed by Hermogenes a century later (whose work was widely disseminated in Priscian's Latin translation). The most popular text (because it included worked-out examples of each exercise) was produced by Aphthonius in the fourth century; it had a great vogue in the Renaissance, with commentaries by Rudolph Agricola and Reinhard Lorich.[54] These collections of

Satires, 7. 150–4, 168–70; and Petronius, *Satyricon*, 1–4 (included, with other relevant material tr. Winterbottom, in Russell and Winterbottom 1972, pp. 344–71). For modern studies see D. A. Russell, *Greek Declamation* (Cambridge, 1983); S. F. Bonner, *Roman Declamation* (Liverpool, 1947); Bonner 1977, pp. 250–87, 309–27; M. Winterbottom (ed.), *Roman Declamation* (Bristol, 1980); and Winterbottom, 'Schoolroom and Courtroom' in Vickers 1982a, pp. 59–70; J. Fairweather, *Seneca the Elder* (Cambridge, 1981). On the decline of oratory see also K. Heldmann, *Antike Theorien über Entwicklung und Verfall der Redekunst* (Munich, 1982).

[52] Curtius 1953, p. 155.
[53] Waith, *The Pattern of Tragicomedy in Beaumont and Fletcher* (New Haven, Conn., 1952), pp. 86–98, 203–7 on additional influences.
[54] See Bonner 1977, pp. 250–76. Baldwin 1928, pp. 23–38, summarizes the treatise of Hermogenes, while Ray Nadeau gives 'The *Progymnasmata* of Aphthonius in Translation' in *Speech Monographs*, 19 (1952), 264–85; good treatment in Kennedy 1983, pp. 54–73. For the later diffusion of these exercises

composition-models started with simple forms, such as the fable (*apologus, fabula*), maxim (*sententia*), instructive saying (*chreia*), and mythological narrative (*narratio*), giving a set of rules for each. Boys would gradually move on to more demanding exercises, commonplace, encomium and denunciation, speech in character or impersonation (*ethopoeia* or *prosopopoeia*), and description (*ekphrasis*). By this time pupils were producing quite elaborate essays, and learning how to vary and above all to amplify material ('elaboration', *ergasia, expolitio*). With such topics as praise and blame, thesis (arguing both sides of a question), *narratio*, and the discussion of a law, students could make the transition to a rhetorical training proper. The justification for such exercises is that they provided a framework within which a student could develop his own individuality. As one of the best students of classical education, Henri Marrou, has written, rhetoric had its own conventions,

but once these had been recognized and assimilated, the artist had complete freedom within the system, and when he had mastered the various processes he could use them to express his own feelings and ideas without any loss of sincerity. Far from hindering originality or talent, the restrictions enabled very subtle, polished effects to be produced.[55]

The treatises mentioned so far have all been prescriptive, giving instructions on how to use rhetorical processes in composition. One last example of this tradition worth including is Horace's 'Epistle to the Pisos', which Quintilian nicknamed the *Ars Poetica* (*c.* 16 BC).[56] Horace was drawing both on an immediate Greek source, one Neoptolemus of Parium, and on a tradition going back to Aristotle's *Poetics* and *Rhetoric*. His work, although eclectic and bewilderingly structured, owes a great deal to rhetoric, especially Cicero, taking over for poetry and drama many of the traditional precepts of the orators.[57] The

see Curtius 1953, p. 442 and Baldwin 1944, with, however, an unconvincing claim for their influence on Shakespeare (2. 231–49). See also Quintilian 1. 9, 2. 1–2. 4.

[55] Marrou 1964, p. 204.
[56] See the Loeb edition, *Satires, Epistles, and Ars Poetica*. tr. H. R. Fairclough (London, 1929) and the excellent translation by Donald Russell in Russell and Winterbottom 1972, pp. 279–91, used here (references by line-number).
[57] The erudite edition and commentary by C. O. Brink, *Horace on Poetry*, 3 vols. (Cambridge, 1963–82), is very thorough on the post-Aristotelian rhetorical

prescriptive part of the poem is arranged according to the rhetorical triad of *ordo*, arrangement (42–4), *facundia*, style (45–118), and *res*, subject-matter (119–294). But within this division we find comments on the rhetorical processes of *inventio*, *dispositio*, and *elocutio* (38–58), and especially the need for decorum between style, genre, and subject (1–21, 85–92, 108–23, 155–78—a juxtaposition of youth and age obviously inspired by Aristotle's *Rhetoric*: see p. 25 above—, 225–32, 309–19). Horace's debt to the rhetorical tradition is unmistakable when he describes the affective intention of the poet towards his audience, the *officia oratoris* as formulated by Cicero (p. 35 above):

It is not enough for poetry to be beautiful; it must also be pleasing and lead the hearer's mind wherever it will. The human face smiles in sympathy with smilers and comes to the help of those that weep. If you want me to cry, mourn first yourself; *then* your misfortunes will hurt me, Telephus and Peleus. If your words are given you ineptly, I shall fall asleep or laugh. (99–107: cf. Cicero and Quintilian, pp. 77 ff. below)

After *movere* come *docere* and *delectare*. For the first, the poet, like the orator, is advised to study philosophy, acquire wisdom from the 'Socratic books', learning 'his duty to his country and friends, the proper kind of love with which parent, brother, and guest should be cherished' (309 ff.)—common themes in ethics, especially in Cicero's *De Officiis*. For the second, *delectare* must always accompany *docere*:

Poetry aims either to do good or to give pleasure—or, thirdly, to say things which are both pleasing and serviceable for life. . . . The man who combines pleasure with usefulness wins every suffrage, delighting the reader and also giving him advice; this is the book that . . . gives your celebrated writer a long lease of fame. (333 ff.)

Many of those ideas, taken from the rhetorical tradition and formulated here with unequalled pithiness—*si vis me flere, dolendum est/Primum ipsi tibi; aut prodesse volunt aut delectare poetae,/aut simul et iucunda et idonea dicere vitae; omne tulit punctum qui miscuit utile dulci*—were taken back by the rhetorical

tradition, but insists on a too sharp distinction between poetics and rhetoric, and undervalues Horace's debt to the rhetorical tradition. This gap is partly filled by the older studies of G. C. Fiske and M. A. Grant, *Cicero's 'De Oratore' and Horace's 'Ars Poetica'* (Madison, Wis., 1929), and 'Cicero's *Orator* and the *Ars Poetica'*, *Harvard Studies in Classical Philology*, 35 (1924), 1–75.

tradition, and echoed a thousand times. Horace's fame as a poet helped to make this work accepted as a fusion of rhetoric and poetics, with an incalculable influence in the Renaissance and after.[58]

The preceptive tradition in rhetoric continued in the handbooks of figures and tropes, and in composition manuals addressed to specific genres. But some apparently prescriptive rhetorics also included much descriptive material, analysing the styles of individual writers or specific stylistic qualities, marking a transition from rhetoric to literary criticism. The work *On Style* attributed to one Demetrius, and dating from the second or first century BC,[59] defines four styles and analyses each, together with its anti-type (grand: frigid; elegant: affected; plain: arid; forceful: unpleasant). Within each the writer analyses further the role played by diction, word-arrangement, and subject-matter, discussing grammatical, syntactical, and rhetorical aspects, with apt quotations from a range of Greek writers. A later Greek critic, Dionysius of Halicarnassus (in Rome by 30 BC), used a less elaborate theory of style (preferring the Attic style as exemplified by Demosthenes), writing treatises on individual Greek writers—Lysias, Isocrates, Plato, Demosthenes—and a work on prose style, where four main elements producing pleasure and beauty are distinguished: melody, rhythm, variety, and appropriateness.[60] One stylistic feature was singled out by a critic called 'Longinus' in a treatise *On Sublimity*, written in the late first century AD,[61] which is arguably the most

[58] See Weinberg 1961, i. 71–200, and M. T. Herrick, *The Fusion of Horatian and Aristotelian Literary Criticism, 1531–1555* (Urbana, Ill. 1946).

[59] See Demetrius 1961; useful translation by Doreen Innes in Russell and Winterbottom 1972, pp. 171–215, with unfortunate omissions of sections on the rhetorical figures.

[60] See Dionysius of Halicarnassus, *The Critical Essays*, tr. S. Usher, 2 vols., Loeb Classical Library (London, 1974, 1985), and substantial excerpts tr. D. A. Russell in Russell and Winterbottom 1972, pp. 305–43. S. F. Bonner, *The Literary Treatises of Dionysius of Halicarnassus* (Cambridge, 1939; Amsterdam, 1969) somewhat overvalues its author, I feel, and takes a too negative view of rhetoric (e.g. pp. 41, 82, 99). There is much intelligent analysis of Dionysius and other writers reviewed here in D. A. Russell, *Criticism in Antiquity* (London, 1981), while the earlier period is well covered by A. D. Leeman, *Orationis Ratio. The Stylistic Theories and Practice of the Roman Orators, Historians, and Philosophers*, 2 vols. (Amsterdam, 1963).

[61] See Longinus 1964; the complete text is admirably translated by Russell in Russell and Winterbottom 1972, pp. 460–503.

sensitive application of rhetoric to literary criticism made in antiquity, or since (further discussion in Chapter 6 below). Finally, another Greek rhetorician, Hermogenes of Tarsus (born c. AD 160), took the move towards ever more detailed classification of style as far as it could go, in a series of works which schematized stylistic qualities on to a grid, almost reducing writing to a mechanical process. On the horizontal plane, as it were, he distinguishes seven characteristics of style: clarity, grandeur, beauty, speed, ethos, verity, and gravity. (As in all the works of this school, the attempt to sum up qualities of style with one epithet seems a hopeless task.) Vertically, each head is given such subcategories as diction, syntax, rhythm, sound, length of sentences, word-order, and a selection of rhetorical figures. All that the writer has to do, supposing that he wants to reproduce one of these styles, is to run his finger down the list and find which vowels or consonants to use, which to avoid, whether to use the nominative or ablative cases, whether to use nouns or (!) verbs, and all his problems are solved.[62] Hermogenes' works, which include treatises *On Ideas* or *On Types of Style (Peri Idēon)* and *On Staseis* (with three other works ascribed on doubtful evidence) had a great, and in some ways surprising diffusion in the Renaissance.[63] The appetite for rhetoric texts at that time was inexhaustible, and these stylistic treatises were regarded as extending the main prescriptive tradition from the *De Inventione* to Quintilian rather than replacing it. But their vogue shows that the demand for detailed help in composition did not decline in the period that historians now describe as 'early modern'.

iii THE MAIN PROCESSES OF RHETORIC

Inspired by Quintilian's example, and wishing to make this book contain in itself, as far as possible, all the material necessary for its understanding, I shall now outline the major

[62] Excerpts from *Peri Idēon*, tr. Russell (with abridgements) in Russell and Winterbottom 1972, pp. 561–79. See now Wootten 1987.

[63] Annabel Patterson, *Hermogenes and the Renaissance. Seven Ideas of Style* (Princeton, NJ, 1970) is unsatisfactory in several respects (see my review in *TLS*, 28 May 1971, p. 626); more reliable treatment in Kennedy 1972, pp. 619–33 and Kennedy 1983, pp. 76–103; Monfasani 1976, pp. 18, 248–54, 322–7, and Monfasani 1983, pp. 176, 183–6.

doctrines of rhetoric briefly, and with very selective annotation.[64] This will be more than just a summary, since I wish to develop two of the themes of this book, the rhetorical tradition's emphasis on persuasion by moving the feelings, and the revival of classical rhetoric in the Renaissance.

The Three Genres

The three main genres of oratory, as Aristotle classified them, were the judicial, the deliberative, and the epideictic. The first two were covered most fully by the major classical rhetoric texts, but with a certain discrepancy between theory and practice, especially in the case of deliberative or political oratory. Despite the rhetorician's celebrations of the power of speech in open political gatherings, the fact is that oratory was never the sole source of political influence, and what power it had was always at the mercy of changes in the state. As George Kennedy describes it, the Roman senate was 'a highly oligarchic body whose decisions, though influenced by speeches, were also very much the result of ties of family or personal friendship and the prior decision of an inner group of senators'. In theory it was 'an advisory, not a law-making body'.[65] Kennedy's history of rhetoric at Rome conveniently traces the stages by which the influence of political rhetoric diminished. Already in the Roman revolution 'the role of oratory . . . steadily declined as the military might of individual generals rose' (pp. 74–5). In the Augustan period 'judicial oratory flourished under only slightly altered conditions; political oratory, however, lost ground while new forms of persuasion, a new rhetoric in the verbal and visual arts, arose to influence public opinion' (p. 302). By the first century AD deliberative oratory was much changed, 'the factionalism and bitter debates of the late republic were gone

---

[64] The most comprehensive summary is still Richard Volkmann, *Die Rhetorik der Griechen und Römer in systematischer Uebersicht*, 2nd edn. (Leipzig, 1885; Hildesheim, 1963). German scholars have also provided the most complete modern surveys, such as Josef Martin, *Antike Rhetorik, Technik und Methode* (Munich, 1974), and Heinrich Lausberg, *Handbuch der literarischen Rhetorik*, 2 vols. (Munich, 1960)—with some eccentricities. On the other hand, nothing in any language matches George Kennedy's ongoing history of rhetoric: Kennedy 1963, 1972, 1980, 1983.

[65] Kennedy 1972, pp. 20–1; the quotations following are also from this source.

from the assembly and the senate. Indeed the assembly now existed only in name' (p. 430). Lawcourts were still important, and the early empire saw an expansion both in the number of legal cases and the courts trying them, as well as a striking spread of bureaucracy, which made use of rhetorical forms of communication (p. 434). But two new elements in the lawcourts of the first century A D 'served further to undermine the freedom of speech'. These were the treason-trials, and the rise of informers, the *delatores*, 'clever, unscrupulous men [who] won position, wealth, and notoriety by feeding on the suspicions of the emperor and his officials' (pp. 440–2). Tacitus' *Dialogue on Orators* and other texts of the late first and early second centuries show the continuing decline of eloquence, as the links between rhetoric and politics weakened further (p. 446). This is the historical reality against which we must measure the rhetoricians' claims for their pet topics or achievements. The fact is that Cicero's major treatises 'were produced at a time when Roman rhetoric in its traditional forms was being checked' (p. 239). An air of fantasy or wish-fulfilment hangs over the *De Oratore* in particular.

This progressive decline of both deliberative and judicial oratory helps account for what might otherwise seem the surprising success of the Cinderella of the three. Epideictic rhetoric turned out to be the most generally applicable in later periods, especially following the collapse of Graeco-Roman political and legal systems. It was, indeed, the only form still usable as a whole (although parts and processes from the other two survived, sometimes adapted to strange contexts). It is for this reason that, in the Middle Ages and Renaissance, all literature became subsumed under epideictic, and all writing was perceived as occupying the related spheres of praise and blame.[66]

Yet in classical theory epideictic oscillated between a functional and a purely ornamental concept. Both Plato and Aristotle relate epideictic to ethics, considering praise to be the correct response to virtue, blame to vice. Plato banished the

---

[66] On epideictic see Burgess 1902, Baldwin 1928, Buchheit 1960, Hardison 1962, Kennedy 1963, Vickers 1982b, and Helen North, *From Myth to Icon. Reflections of Greek Ethical Doctrine in Literature and Art* (Ithaca, NY, 1979), pp. 135–76, an excellent discussion of *ethos*, epideictic, and persuasion.

poets from his state but allowed the poetry of praise to remain, 'hymns to the gods and encomia to good men' (*Republic*, 10. 607), in which the poet was expected to show that 'the just are happy and the unjust unhappy' (3. 392). In the *Protagoras* (325–6) Plato saw encomium as being useful in exciting the young to virtue, while in the *Laws* (659–61, 801 ff.) he approved of communal celebrations in which songs of praise to the gods and to 'citizens who have departed and have done good and energetic deeds' will benefit morals and virtue. Isocrates, too, in his *Evagoras*, eulogized the virtues of his hero consciously, in order to stimulate emulation for virtue among the young.[67]

Plato and Isocrates give epideictic a social function, reinforcing the norms of public morality. Aristotle's account is less concerned with its role in the state, but always conceives of it ethically. As he says in the *Rhetoric*, those 'who praise or attack a man aim at proving him worthy of honour or the reverse' (1358ᵇ28). One ground for praise is heroic activity, where a man 'has neglected his own interest to do what was honourable. Thus, they praise Achilles because he championed his fallen friend Patroclus, though he knew that this meant death', and 'to die thus was the nobler thing for him to do, the expedient was to live on' (1359ᵃ1 ff.). The 'objects of praise and blame', he writes later, are 'Virtue and Vice, the Noble and the Base', the highest form of virtue consisting in being useful to other people (1366ᵃ23–1366ᵇ5). It follows that praise can only be given to noble acts made intentionally, as the result of a man's moral choice, where his actions are the product of his good qualities (1367ᵇ20 ff.). Aristotle at least joins Plato and Isocrates in ascribing a pragmatic or persuasive function to epideictic, which can rouse the listeners to emulation:

> To praise a man is in one respect akin to urging a course of action. The suggestions made in the latter case become encomiums when differently expressed. . . . Consequently, whenever you want to praise any one, think what you would urge people to do. (1367ᵇ35 ff.)

Here Aristotle qualifies his original distinction, where deliberative (political) oratory was said to address a judge and to refer to future acts and decisions, while epideictic was merely directed towards an onlooker, and had no concern with the

---

⁶⁷ Cit. Hardison 1962, p. 30.

future ($1358^{b}1$ ff., $1377^{b}21$). Subsequently he breaks down his categories still further, stating that 'the use of persuasive speech is to lead to decisions', even if we address only a single person, 'as when we scold a man for his conduct or try to change his views'. The 'judge', then, is not just the formally constituted arbitrator of a trial, or a political assembly, for 'anyone is your judge whom you have to persuade' ($1391^{b}8$ ff.). This deduction at last allows Aristotle to see epideictic, too, as involving decisions: 'our principle holds good of epideictic speeches also; the "onlookers" for whom such a speech is put together are treated as the judges of it' ($1391^{b}15$).

Aristotle's enlarging of the rhetoric of praise and blame to the affecting of internal decisions—opinions and attitudes—is important for the later history of rhetoric, when epideictic became the sole genre to survive intact. Medieval and Renaissance writers seldom regard their subject-matter neutrally, but usually express a clearly positive or negative evaluation which attempts to change the reader's views. Aristotle would have been an excellent model for them, but Roman rhetoric presented a more ambivalent attitude toward epideictic. In the three centuries between Aristotle's *Rhetoric* and the first Latin handbooks, epideictic had been developed in the panegyrical orations to emperors and rulers, and had come to be associated with the praise of a specific outstanding person, rather than a virtue, developing in the process connotations of flattery and insincerity. The *Rhetorica ad Herennium* gives only a sketchy treatment of epideictic (3. 6. 10 ff.), listing the topics for invention under 'External Circumstances', deriving from Fortune (descent, education, wealth, kinds of power), 'Physical Attributes', coming from Nature (agility, beauty, health, strength), and 'Qualities of Character', stemming from Virtue (wisdom, justice, courage, temperance). This listing of the primary virtues goes back to Plato (*Rep.* 4. 428 ff.) and Aristotle (*Rhet.* $1366^{b}1$ ff.), but the author fails to develop its importance, and in one place seems to identify epideictic with the 'speech of entertainment' (4. 23. 32). He also discusses the 'praiseworthy' under deliberative or political rhetoric (3. 4. 7), revealing a certain blurring of categories. Cicero's *De Inventione* is more coherent, accepting the by now standard division into three classes of subject and linking epideictic with *honestum* (1. 5. 7,

2. 4. 12). Yet, like this anonymous colleague—both writers evidently drawing on a common source—Cicero invokes *honestas* as 'the greatest necessity' but places it under deliberative oratory, being future-oriented towards 'things to be sought and . . . avoided' (2. 52. 157 ff.). In this way epideictic linked politics and ethics.

In Cicero's mature rhetorical works epideictic is given two conflicting evaluations. In *De Oratore* the orator is seen as excelling all others in his power to encourage men to virtue or reclaim them from vice through *vituperare* and *laudare* (2. 9. 35). But while accepting the ethical nature of epideictic here, some speakers in the dialogue dismiss panegyrics as 'serviceable' but not 'essential', not needing the exposition of rules, since the panegyrist is concerned with the unpredictable favours of fortune (2. 11. 44 ff.). Antonius even makes an opposition between epideictic and other genres, saying that the Greeks practise it 'more for reading and for entertainment, or for giving a laudatory account of some person, than for the practical purposes of public life' (2. 84. 340). Epideictic is thus identified with *delectare*, rather than with *movere* or *docere*, and denied a serious political or social function. This judgement is repeated in the *Orator*, which describes epideictic speeches as 'show-pieces', designed to give pleasure and entertainment, 'unconnected with the battles of public life' (11. 37, 12. 38, 12. 42, 61. 207–8). Yet in *De Oratore* Cicero also gives his protagonists a defence of epideictic for showing how virtue manages the gifts of nature and fortune (2. 84. 342–8), and as a fertile field for the exercise of amplification (2. 85. 346, 3. 27. 105; also *Brutus*, 12. 47). This view is developed in *Partitiones Oratoriae*, where Cicero concedes epideictic both an ethical and a social function, praising

the form that we adopt for panegyrics on distinguished men and for censuring the wicked. For there is no class of oratory capable of producing more copious rhetoric or of doing more service to the state, nor any in which the speaker is more occupied in recognizing the virtues and vices. (20. 69)

Like Isocrates, Cicero believes that the practice of celebrating virtue and detesting vice will benefit the orator's own life: 'the principles awarding praise and blame . . . have a value not only for good oratory but also for right conduct' (21.70). This judgement leads on to a long discussion, in the Platonic–Aristotelian mode, of the virtues and their place in life (22. 75–23. 81), an issue referred to more briefly in the *Topica* (23. 89–91).

At various times in Cicero, then, epideictic is both display, for entertainment only, and of great importance to inculcating ethics in the individual as in the state. In Quintilian the same dichotomy exists. On the one hand epideictic is said to provide *delectatio*, only (3. 4. 6.): it 'aims solely at delighting the audience, and . . . seeks not to steal its way into the mind nor to wrest the victory from its opponent, but aims solely at honour and glory' (8. 3. 11, 3. 4. 13, 3. 7. 1). It can be compared with poetry, since both aim solely at giving pleasure (10. 1. 28), and epideictic therefore can allow itself 'much more elegance and ornament' than deliberative or forensic oratory (11. 1. 48). Yet Quintilian also opposes this view, noting that 'panegyrics are advisory in form and frequently discuss the interests of Greece' (3. 4. 14), and even rejecting Aristotle's triadic definition as 'easy and neat rather than true: for all three kinds rely on the mutual assistance of the other. For we deal with justice and expediency in panegyric, and with honour in deliberations' (3. 4. 16). Roman oratory, he claims, unlike Greek, has given epideictic

a place in the practical tasks of life. For funeral orations are often imposed as a duty on persons holding public office, or entrusted to magistrates by decree of the senate. Again, the award of praise or blame to a witness may carry weight in the courts, while it is also a recognised practice to produce persons to praise the character of the accused. (3. 7. 2)

Aristotle himself had broken his initial categorization, and Quintilian follows him in stressing the identity between those actions or qualities praised in epideictic and advised in deliberative oratory (3. 7. 28), so that epideictic can take over the goals of that genre, too, being concerned with both *honestas* and *utilitas* (8. Pr. 8).

The amount of space that Quintilian devotes to epideictic shows its importance to Roman oratory. We praise both gods and men, celebrating the gods' majesty, power, exploits, and the discoveries by which they benefited mankind (3. 7. 68).

For men, we can begin with factors preceding birth, such as the native land, parents, ancestors, and can continue by reviewing character, physical endowments, and external circumstances such as fortune. But, Quintilian adds,

the praise awarded to external and accidental advantages is given, not to their possession, but to their honourable employment. For wealth and power and influence, since they are the sources of strength, are the surest test of character for good or evil: they make us better or they make us worse. (3. 7. 10–14)

This caveat was to become extremely important in the Renaissance debate over the relative merits of 'virtue' and 'nobility'. In formal terms, Quintilian advises, an encomium can be constructed by taking a man's life, deeds, and words 'in due chronological order'. At other times we do better to 'divide our praises, dealing separately with the various virtues, fortitude, justice, self-control and the rest of them and to assign to each virtue the deeds performed under its influence' (3. 7. 15). This kind of approach was to become influential in Renaissance epic and epic-theory, where characters were often seen as embodying separate virtues and vices. Cities can also be 'praised after the same fashion as men', for 'the virtues and vices revealed by their deeds are the same as private individuals' (3. 7. 26). And in all these cases, as Aristotle (*Rhet.* 1368ª35) and the *Ad Herennium* (3. 6. 10) had shown, the same methods can be 'applied to denunciations as well, but with a view to opposite effects' (3. 7. 20), by merely inverting the judgements.

Later rhetoric-books consolidated the position of epideictic. In his treatise *On Ideas* Hermogenes defined encomium as 'the setting forth of the good qualities' of mankind in general or in particular, differing from the other forms by having no other end than 'the witness to virtue'.[68] In his 'treatment of all poetry as a subdivision of epideictic' George Kennedy sees the final 'victory of rhetoric over poetics';[69] but the two arts had been closing on each other for a century or more. Aristotle's *Rhetoric* had taken many of its examples from the poets, and had discussed the similarities and differences between prose

[68] Cit. Baldwin 1928, pp. 30–1.
[69] Kennedy 1972, p. 632.

and poetry. Literary language legitimately uses 'foreign' or unfamiliar expressions, but these are more common in verse than prose, where 'the subject-matter is less exalted' (1404^{b}8 ff.). Prose oratory, however, should certainly use metaphor, since it is used in everyday conversation (1404^{b}31 ff.), and prose-writers are urged to 'pay specially careful attention to metaphor, because their other resources are scantier' than the poets' (1405^{a}5 ff.). Prose should avoid compound epithets and other poeticisms, however (1406^{a}5– 14). In an often quoted passage from *De Oratore* Cicero had laid down that

> the poet is a very near kinsman of the orator, rather more heavily fettered as regards rhythm, but with ampler freedom in his choice of words, while in the use of many sorts of ornament he is his ally and almost his counterpart. (1. 16. 70; also 3. 7. 27)

Although we still have no adequate study of rhetoric in Latin poetry and drama, poets were educated by the *rhetores*, acquired a considerable knowledge of rhetoric, and saw their art as complementary to the prose of oratory. Writing to Salamus (a rhetor who had taught Germanicus Caesar) Ovid proclaimed the poets' use of rhetoric: 'Our work differs, but it derives from the same sources; we are both worshippers of that liberal art. . . . as my numbers receive vigour from your eloquence, so I lend brilliance to your words' (*Ex Ponto*, 2. 5. 65 f.). Quintilian advised the orator to read the poets in order to find examples of the figures (10. 1. 27 ff.), and in his own work takes his examples from poet and orator alike, a practice followed by almost all subsequent rhetoric-books. Perhaps, then, rather than speaking of a 'victory' we should think of an alliance between poetics and rhetoric.

To return to epideictic, the techniques of panegyric set out by the *Ad Herennium* and Quintilian were simplified for use in schools by the *progymnasmata*, as we would expect, but also formed the basis of separate treatises. The most elaborate of these was the *Peri Epideiktikon*, dating from the late third or early fourth century AD, and ascribed to Menander the Sophist,[70] which contains two treatises, both incomplete, and not necessarily by the same author. The first discusses hymns to

[70] See the admirable edition and translation of *Menander Rhetor* by D. A. Russell and N. Wilson (Oxford, 1981).

the gods (subdivided into eight different types), celebrations of countries, cities (including harbours, citadels; the city's origins, accomplishments, virtues). The second treatise explains how to write an 'imperial oration', or encomium of the emperor; a speech of arrival at a city; a 'talk' or more casual form of encomium, less bound by rules; a 'propemptic talk', or speech 'which speeds its subject on his journey with commendation'; an epithalamium or wedding speech, with its more specialized appendage, the bedroom speech; birthday, consolatory, and funeral speeches, speeches of invitation, leavetaking, lament, and many more. If this profusion of genres seems another example of the rhetorician's 'taxonomania',[71] his desire to take account of every possible eventuality, in language or life, we might note the impressive range of authors drawn on for examples (Homer, Isocrates, Plato, Thucydides, Xenophon), which justify the isolation of this literary genre. Historically, Menander enjoyed a wide dissemination in the Renaissance. First published in the Aldus collection of *Rhetores Graeci* (Venice, 1508–9), his system was taken over and elaborated further by J. C. Scaliger in his *Poetices Libri Septem* (Lyons, 1561), and left its mark on George Puttenham's *Arte of English Poesie* (London, 1589).[72] Later poets whose works exemplify Menander's categories, whether or not due to direct knowledge, include Spenser, Shakespeare, and Milton.

As for epideictic in general, as E. R. Curtius noted, 'the epideictic oration had by far the strongest influence upon medieval poetry', since 'stylistic elements belonging to panegyric can find application in all genres and to all kinds of subjects'.[73] Edmond Faral and Douglas Kelly have shown that the tendency to divide all utterances into praise or blame affected much medieval literature, resulting in the virtual absence of neutral descriptions and an enlargement of the writer's affective intent, addressing the emotions of his audience.[74] In the Renaissance many influences converged to give epideictic the leading status, among them the allegorical

[71] The coinage is D. Shackleton Bailey's: *TLS*, 20 June 1986, p. 672, commenting on the passion for classification in the late Roman republic (Varro distinguished 'at least 99 classes of soil').
[72] An ambitious but over-stated attempt to apply Menander's categories is F. Cairns, *Generic Composition in Greek and Roman Poetry* (Edinburgh, 1972).
[73] Curtius 1953, pp. 69–71, 154–82.
[74] Faral 1924, p. 76; Kelly 1978, pp. 232, 242.

interpretations of the *Aeneid* as a work exemplifying virtue; the Latin translation of Averroës' paraphrase of Aristotle's *Poetics*, which begins 'Every poem and all poetic discourse is blame or praise . . . [of] the honourable or the base'; and the techniques of debate in schools and universities, where opposed arguments fell naturally into the moulds of *laus* and *vituperatio*.[75] As a result of these and other influences epideictic was indissolubly linked with ethical themes, and deeply affected all literary genres. Epic was the form most obviously influenced, with its tendency to divide characters into the polar extremes of virtuous and vicious, but the injunction to make moral discriminations by praise and blame was applied even to lyric. As Ben Jonson said of the the poet,

We do not require in him mere elocution; or an excellent faculty in verse; but the exact knowledge of all virtues, and their contraries; with ability to render the one loved, the other hated, by his proper embattling them.[76]

The Stages of Composition

Classical rhetoric distinguished five stages in the composition of speech: *inventio, dispositio, elocutio, memoria,* and *pronuntiatio* or *actio*. As Cicero defined them in his youthful handbook,

Invention is the discovery of valid or seemingly valid arguments to render one's cause plausible. Arrangement is the distribution of arguments thus discovered in the proper order. Expression is the fitting of the proper language to the invented matter. Memory is the firm mental grasp of matter and words. Delivery is the control of voice and body in a manner suitable to the dignity of the subject matter and the style. (1. 7. 9; very similarly, *Ad Herennium*, 1. 2. 3)

Both Cicero and his anonymous contemporary reveal their concern with forensic rhetoric, describing *inventio* as 'the most important of all the divisions', to be 'used in every kind of pleading' (1. 7. 9; *Ad Her.* 3. 8. 15). In *De Oratore* Cicero's main protagonists, Antonius and Crassus, echo each other by making

---

[75] Hardison 1962, Vickers 1982b, and '*King Lear* and Renaissance Paradoxes', *Modern Language Review*, 63 (1968), 305–14.

[76] Jonson, *Timber: or Discoveries*, 1038–45, in Jonson, *Works*, ed. C. H. Herford, P. and E. Simpson, 11 vols. (Oxford, 1925–52), viii. 595. Jonson's model is of course Quintilian, 1. Pr. 9–14.

the briefest references to the compositional processes (1. 31. 142, 2. 19. 79 ff.), but in *Partitiones Oratoriae* Cicero presents a more helpful account in the form of a dialogue between himself and his son:

> c. jun. Inasmuch then as the first aim of the speaker's functions is to invent, what will be his aim?
>
> c. sen. To discover how to convince the persons whom he wishes to persuade and how to arouse their emotions.
>
> c. jun. What things serve to produce conviction?
>
> c. sen. Arguments, which are derived from topics that are either contained in the facts of the case itself or are obtained from outside.
>
> c. jun. What do you mean by topics?
>
> c. sen. Pigeonholes in which arguments are stored.
>
> (1. 2. 5)

This doctrine of the topoi derives from Aristotelian rhetoric, but is developed very differently by Cicero in his *Topica*. It derives some of its categories from dialectic, a curious hybrid. (Some modern accounts have overemphasized the link between *inventio* and logic.) Readers will have noticed that Cicero immediately connects invention with the main goal of rhetoric, 'how to convince the persons whom he wishes to persuade and how to arouse their emotions'.

The construction of an argument ('a plausible device to obtain belief', as Cicero defines it) involves the orator in analysing the case at hand against an array of possibly relevant categories. These ' "places" of argument', as Quintilian sums them up, can be drawn

> from persons, causes, place and time (which latter we have divided into preceding, contemporary and subsequent), from resources (under which we include instruments), from manner (that is, how a thing has been done), from definition, genus, species, difference, property, elimination, division, beginnings, increase, consummation, likes, unlikes, contradictions, consequents, efficients, effects, results, and comparison, which is subdivided into several species. (5. 10. 94)

It would seldom occur to a modern lawyer to make up a list of all the categories of argument, especially not such a heterogeneous one as this, but doing so would encourage him to be systematic, and undoubtedly bring out every aspect of the case in hand. After *inventio* comes *dispositio*, and for Quintilian it is 'not without good reason' that arrangement is 'treated as the second of the five departments of oratory, since without it the first is useless'. A sculptor can have cast all the limbs of a statue accurately but unless he can assemble them in the right position the result will be a monster (7. Pr. 1–2). *Dispositio* concerns the best arrangement of arguments and also the structure of a whole speech.

From the discovering and arranging of arguments we pass to their verbal expression, *elocutio* being the specific domain of the orator, the 'supreme power of speaking [being] granted to him alone', as Cicero puts it (*Orator*, 19. 61, 14.44; also *De Or.* 1. 13. 56–1. 14. 67; Quintilian, 1. Pr. 12; 17; etc.). The orator needs above all *copia verborum ac rerum* (10. 1. 5), a phrase of Quintilian's that provided the inspiration for one of Erasmus' most popular works,[77] fullness of matter and language, *eloqui* as opposed to *loqui* (natural or dialectical speech). Quintilian, quoting some of these passages from Cicero, and enlarging on this etymology, justifies his illustrious predecessor's emphasis from the nature of eloquence itself.

The rhetoric-book's teaching on *elocutio* can be divided into two unequal categories, the doctrine of tropes and figures, often seen in a functional context as the main agents of persuasion (see Chapter 6 below), and the less important topic of the 'qualities of style'. This concept, developed by the pupils of Aristotle, notably Theophrastus and Demetrius, held that the style of the finished oration should possess a number of positive qualities, including correctness (pure Greek, or pure Latinity), clarity, ornateness, and appropriateness. Taken over by Cicero (*De Or.* 3. 3. 7), it reappears in Quintilian and is much enlarged in the Greek stylistic treatises[78] mentioned above (although the inherent vagueness of many of the definitions of style prevented it ever becoming generally usable). Development of this doctrine in the Hellenistic period marks a shift from rhetoric as a persuasive process, involving artist, artefact, and audience, to a concern with the artefact alone, detached from the speaker–hearer relationship. It comes close to what we understand today as poetics, yet of course, once elaborated, it could always be reinserted in the full rhetorical context.

---

[77] Erasmus, *De Utraque Verborum ac Rerum Copia* (1512; 3rd, rev. edn., 1534) had at least 150 printings by 1600 and about 200 all told. See Erasmus 1978.
[78] See Kennedy 1963, pp. 273–90; Kennedy 1972, pp. 225, 349, 628–9.

The two remaining processes only make proper sense when rhetoric is a performance-art. *Memoria* involves the orator memorizing his speech for delivery, and discussion of this stage usually included encomia to the faculty of memory itself, 'the treasure-house of the ideas supplied by Invention' (*Ad Her.* 3. 16. 28). Quintilian, quoting that description, says that memory is a natural gift that must be improved by training, for 'all the labour of which I have so far spoken will be in vain unless all the other departments be co-ordinated by the animating principle of memory. For our whole education depends' on it (11. 2. 1). The rhetorical doctrine of *memoria* was based on the association of specific sounds, words, ideas, or arguments with a physical space—a wall, or part of a building—divided into a matching number of compartments. The classic anecdote illustrating the power of a trained memory was that of Simonides of Ceos, who left a banquet he had attended just before the roof collapsed, destroying the remaining guests. Thanks to his use of the rhetorical *loci* Simonides could recall who had sat where, allowing the relatives to identify the deceased for burial (*De Or.* 2. 86. 351 ff.; *Ad Her.* 3. 16. 28–24. 40). Like every department of rhetoric, *memoria* was elaborated into a vast number of categories, taken even further by some Renaissance texts, carried indeed beyond the stage of usefulness or practicality.[79]

The final stage in the composing and delivering of a speech is the orator's use of voice (*pronuntiatio*) and gesture (*actio*). Quintilian says that this dual skill 'has an extraordinarily powerful effect in oratory. For the nature of the speech we have composed within our minds is not so important as the manner in which we produce it, since the emotion of each member of our audience will depend on the impression made upon his hearing' (11. 3. 2). As classical rhetoric was a performance-art,

---

[79] On *memoria* see Herwig Blum, *Die antike Mnemotechnik* (Hildesheim, 1969). Frances Yates, *The Art of Memory* (London, 1966), has attracted a great deal of interest to the topic, which is all to the good, but it is an unreliable study on several heads. David Newton-de-Molina, reviewing Blum's book in *Essays in Criticism*, 20 (1970), 353–9, says that it 'serves to refute nearly all the conjectures made in the opening chapters of *The Art of Memory*, conjectures upon which the rest of Dr. Yates's argument is based', and provides 'an implicit correction of Yates's hectic theorising' (p. 354). See further Newton-de-Molina's Cambridge Ph.D. dissertation (1972), 'A critical select history of the classical arts of memory and their interpretation, with special reference to English arts of memory, 1509–1620'.

its teachers went to extraordinary lengths to inculcate effectiveness in this single appearance before the judge and jury. Aristotle found the subject neglected (1403ᵇ20), and realizing that delivery 'affects the success of a speech greatly' he made this acute analysis of its constituent parts:

It is, essentially, a matter of the right management of the voice to express the various emotions—of speaking loudly, softly, or between the two; of high, low, or intermediate pitch; of the various rhythms that suit various subjects. These are the three things—volume of sound, modulation of pitch, and rhythm—that a speaker bears in mind. It is those who *do* bear them in mind who usually win prizes in the dramatic contests; and just as in drama the actors now count for more than the poets, so it is in the contests of public life, owing to the defects of our political institutions. (1403ᵇ28–35)

Aristotle would no doubt have been appalled at the importance ascribed to vocal delivery and gesture in Roman rhetoric. In *De Oratore* Crassus actually asserts that delivery 'is the dominant factor in oratory; without delivery the best speaker cannot be of any account at all, and a moderate speaker with a trained delivery can often outdo the best of them' (3. 56. 213). Cicero justifies this emphasis on the grounds that since 'reality beats imitation in everything' the art of rhetorical gesture should not just imitate life but improve on it, bringing out more clearly those signs of emotion that exist in real life, but sometimes indistinctly: 'For nature has assigned to every emotion a particular look and tone of voice and bearing of its own; and the whole of a person's frame and every look on his face and utterance of his voice are like the strings of a harp, and sound according as they are struck by each successive emotion. For the tones of the voice are keyed up like the strings of an instrument' to answer every touch, and all can be 'regulated by the control of art; they are the colours available for the actor, as for the painter, to secure variety' (3. 56. 214–15: a passage extremely interesting to Renaissance art-theorists, notably Leonardo da Vinci). In *Brutus* Cicero says of *actio* that 'nothing else so penetrates the mind, shapes, moulds, turns it' (28. 142). In the *Orator* delivery is described as 'a sort of language of the body' (17. 55), and Cicero quotes again the famous anecdote of Demosthenes who, being asked three times what the most important faculty of the orator was, replied each time 'action'. The *Ad Herennium* does not find it the most important accomplishment, but concedes its 'exceptionally great usefulness' and gives it pithy but detailed treatment (3. 11. 19–3. 15. 27). Quintilian agrees that delivery 'has an extraordinarily powerful effect in oratory. For the nature of the speech that we have composed within our minds is not so important as the manner in which we produce it, since the emotion of each member of our audience will depend on the impression made upon his hearing' (11. 2. 2). His account is appropriately full, discussing a remarkable repertoire of gestures, involving the head, eye (most expressive), arms, hands, fingers, and even the placing and movement of the toga, which, like every other resource, is under the orator's alert control (11. 3. 1–184). Classical rhetoric tried to allow for any eventuality in life, but the best writers made it into a system in which all the parts cohere. Its teachings on gesture had a remarkable afterlife, as we are just finding out, in baroque opera-performance and eighteenth-century acting.[80]

The Parts of a Speech

'A speech has two parts', wrote Aristotle, moving from *lexis* to *taxis*, 'You must state your case, and you must prove it' (1414ª30). Impatient with over-elaborate divisions, he dismissed those rhetoricians who, unconcerned with what had actually been done in the case at issue, instead laid down rules about 'what must be the content of the "introduction" or "narration", or any of the other divisions of a speech'. Such theorists were 'theorizing about non-essentials as if they belonged to the art' (1354ᵇ16 ff.). Yet, since the *Rhetoric* conflates material from two or more lecture courses, we subsequently find Aristotle himself adopting the prescriptive role, giving details of 'heightening the effect' (1368ª1–22), of effective ways of arguing (1375ª7, 27 ff.; 1376ª18 ff.), or of 'investing speeches with moral character' (1391ᵇ20). So he, too, comes to discuss the parts of a speech, starting with the procemium, which he compares to the

---

[80] See Angelica Goodden, *'Actio' and Persuasion. Dramatic Performance in Eighteenth-Century France* (Oxford, 1986), a somewhat disappointing study, and Dene Barnett, *The Art of Gesture: the Practices and Principles of 18th Century Acting* (Heidelberg, 1987), which promises to be comprehensive.

prologue in poetry and the prelude in flute-music (1414ᵇ20). The essential function of the introduction is

to show what the aim of the speech is; and therefore no introduction ought to be employed where the subject is not long or intricate. The other kinds of introduction are remedial in purpose, and may be used in any type of speech. They are concerned with the speaker, the hearer, the subject, or the speaker's opponent. (1415ᵃ22 ff.)

The type that was to receive most attention in classical rhetoric, needless to say, was the one appealing to the hearer. As Aristotle said, this 'aims at securing his goodwill, or at arousing his resentment, or sometimes at gaining his serious attention to the case, or even at distracting it', by making the judge or jury laugh, or telling them that the case 'does not affect them, or is trivial or disagreeable' (1415ᵃ34–1415ᵇ5). The rhetorician is told to lose no time in trying to establish an emotional hold over the judges, especially those with 'the weak-minded tendency . . . to listen to what is beside the point' (1415ᵇ7)—the sarcasm reveals Aristotle's contempt for the democratic jury-system, composed of amateurs, not professional philosophers. In the narration, too, Aristotle advises, 'you must make use of the emotions. Relate the familiar manifestations of them, and those that distinguish yourself and your opponent' (1416ᵃ36). In the epilogue you must continue as you have begun, exciting 'the required state of emotion in your hearers', including 'pity, indignation, anger, hatred, envy, emulation, pugnacity' (1419ᵇ12, 25).

From Aristotle and other now-lost texts in the Greek tradition students of rhetoric could learn that a speech has certain formal divisions, and that each carried with it a specific persuasive function. While various systems emerged, a popular division was into six parts: *exordium, narratio, partitio, confirmatio, refutatio* (or *reprehensio*), and *conclusio*. As the *Rhetorica ad Herennium* defined them,

The Introduction is the beginning of the discourse, and by it the hearer's mind is prepared for attention. The Narration or Statement of Facts sets forth the events that have occurred or might had occurred. By means of the Division we make clear what matters are agreed upon and what contested, and announce what points we intend to take up. Proof is the presentation of our arguments, together with their corroboration.

Refutation is the destruction of our adversaries' arguments. The Conclusion is the end of the discourse, framed in accordance with the principles of the art. (1. 3. 4)

The author discusses each part in some detail (1. 3. 4–2. 31. 50), in terms similar to Cicero's in *De Inventione* (1. 4. 19–1. 56. 109), but at greater length and with more attention to the types 'of issue', that is, legal status-theory. Both writers see the structure of an oration as providing a variety of ways of bringing pressure to bear on the judge, direct and indirect, and of affecting his judgement of the opponent. There are two kinds of *exordium*, the direct (*principium*), which uses plain language to make the auditor 'well-disposed, receptive, and attentive', and the subtle or indirect (*insinuatio*), 'which by dissimulation and indirection unobtrusively steals into the mind of the auditor' (*De Inv.* 1. 15. 20; *Ad Her.* 1. 4. 6). The speaker will use the latter if he knows that his cause is shaky, or downright discreditable. The *captatio benevolentiae*, winning the audience's goodwill, involves the orator setting out his good qualities (*ethos*), lamenting his or his client's misfortune (*pathos*), and working up hatred of his opponent (*Ad Her.* 1. 4. 6.–1. 7. 11; *De Inv.* 1. 15. 20–1. 18. 26). Strategies of gaining advantage are already being prepared at the outset of the speech.

The *narratio* is by no means a neutral statement of facts, for if used skilfully the orator can 'turn every detail to our advantage so as to win the victory', both by 'winning belief' and 'incriminating our adversary' (*Ad Her.* 1. 8. 12). There are three types of narrative, he goes on, 'legendary, historical, and realistic' (1. 8. 13; *De Inv.* 1. 19. 27; Quintilian, 2. 4. 2). Whichever form we use, the *narratio* ought to be 'brief, clear, and plausible' (*De Inv.* 1. 10. 28; *Ad Her.* 1. 9. 14); plausibility being achieved if the story told has characteristics that 'appear in real life', such as action appropriate to character (*decorum personae*), coherent motives, opportune time and space for 'the events about to be narrated', all of which will bring verisimilitude (*De Inv.* 1. 21. 24). We should remember that Cicero is visualizing the advocate for either prosecution or defence reconstructing the events that gave rise to the legal dispute as he wants them to have occurred. We are in the realm of the argument from probability, or plausibility, which in

Graeco-Roman law—strange though it may seem to modern ears—was deemed more credible than the 'truth' of witnesses or evidence. Since the opposed parties are bound to disagree, the *partitio* divides up the points at issue, showing 'in what we agree with our opponents and what is left in dispute; as a result of this some definite problem is set for the auditor on which he ought to have his attention fixed' (*De Inv.* 1. 22. 31; *Ad Her.* 1. 10. 17). Here brevity, completeness, and conciseness are essential, above all the orator should refer to each of the heads of his division, no fewer, no more.

The *partitio* effected, we pass on to the crucial stages of *confirmatio* and *confutatio* (or *refutatio*):

The entire hope of victory and the entire method of persuasion rest on proof and refutation, for when we have submitted our arguments and destroyed those of the opposition, we have, of course, completely fulfilled the speaker's function. (*Ad Her.* 1. 10. 18)

The essentially pragmatic, adversarial nature of Roman judicial rhetoric emerges very clearly in that comment. Cicero shows his own philosophical approach by inserting a long excerpt from his studies of Greek dialectic, concerning propositions, attributes of persons or of actions, and the two main forms of argument, inductive and deductive, or syllogistic (1. 24. 34–1. 41. 77). But he shares the Roman legal profession's concern with learning how 'to impair, disprove, or weaken the confirmation or proof in our opponent's speech' (1. 42. 78), and in his practical performance more than fulfilled these goals. In the judgement of a modern historian, Cicero's eminence as 'the greatest Roman orator can hardly be questioned. . . . He was almost equally adept at argument, at presentation and destruction of character, and at emotional appeal.'[81]

The emotional or affective intent of the orator dominates all accounts of the peroration, which was said to have three parts, 'the summing-up; the *indignatio* or exciting of indignation or ill-will against the opponent; and the *conquestio* or the arousing of pity and sympathy' (*De Inv.* 1. 52. 98). Of the second Cicero writes that, if properly done, the *indignatio* 'results in arousing great hatred against some person, or violent offence at some action', and, like his anonymous compatriot, he lists a number of topics effective in working up the hearers' anger (1. 53. 100–1. 54. 105: *Ad Her.* 1. 30. 47–9). Cicero advises his fellow orators to accompany the narrative 'with reproaches and violent denunciations of each act, and by our language bring the action as vividly as possible before the eyes of the judge' (1. 54. 104). Classical law-trials were evidently emotionally uninhibited to a degree that will surprise the modern reader getting to know these texts. Roman lawcourts must have resembled theatres, indeed 'cases were divided into sections known as *actiones*, and the prosecutor was known as an *actor*', while both Cicero and Quintilian compare the orator's art with the actor's.[82] The *conquestio* or lament reverses these tactics, seeking to 'make the auditor's spirit gentle and merciful that he may be more easily moved', using such *loci communes* as 'the power of fortune over all men and the weakness of the human race'. Like so many rhetoricians, Cicero guarantees the efficient functioning of the device: 'When such a passage is delivered gravely and sententiously, the spirit of man is greatly abased and prepared for pity, for in viewing the misfortune of another he will contemplate his own weakness' (*De Inv.* 1. 55. 106). Both authors list ways of producing this effect, and both end by warning us not to go on too long with the famous saying of the rhetorician Apollonius, 'nothing dries more quickly than a tear' (*Ad Her.* 2. 31. 50; *De Inv.* 1. 56. 109).

These two unpretentious textbooks give the most helpful account of the parts of an oration. It is obviously beneath the mature Cicero's dignity in *De Oratore* to make more than the briefest reference to such elementary matters (1. 31. 142, 2. 19. 79 ff., 2. 76. 307 ff.), but Antonius does at least give some account of *exordium* (2. 79. 30 ff.), and *narratio* (2. 80. 326 ff.). Quintilian discusses the whole sequence, as one might expect, fully, with much mature and sensible advice. The *exordium* is not always needed in deliberative oratory, 'since he who asks an orator for his opinion is naturally well-disposed to him' (3. 8. 6),

[82] Kennedy 1972, p. 18; Cicero, *De Or.* 3. 56. 214–20; Quintilian 11. 3. 61–3, 158; Aristotle, *Rhet.* 1417[b]3.

but in forensic oratory its main use is to render the audience attentive (4. 1. 1–79). Quintilian's most concise advice on composing an *exordium* is that

he who has a speech to make should consider what he has to say; before whom, in whose defence, against whom, at what time and place, under what circumstances he has to speak; what is the popular opinion on the subject, and what the prepossessions of the judge are likely to be; and finally of what we should express our deprecation or desire. (4. 1. 52)

The *narratio* is equally directed at the hearer, its purpose being 'not merely to instruct, but rather to persuade the judge' (4. 2. 21). It is difficult to achieve simplicity and clarity here, indeed most speakers 'will never find anything more difficult in the whole range of oratory' (4. 2. 38). The *partitio* can also clarify the issue, if properly used, for 'it follows nature as a guide', helps the speaker's memory (4. 5. 3.), and not only makes our argument clearer by isolating the points 'and placing them before the eyes of the judge, but relieves his attention by assigning a definite limit to certain parts of our speech, just as our fatigue upon a journey is relieved by reading the distances on the milestones which we pass' (4. 5. 22). Quintilian describes the peroration as 'the most important part of forensic pleading' (6. 2. 1), in which 'we may give full rein to our emotions' (4. 1. 28), for it offers great 'opportunities for exciting the passions of jealousy, hatred or anger' (6. 1. 14), opportunities that he analyses in impressive detail (6. 1. 1–55).

The Orator's Three Duties

Readers of Aristotle's *Rhetoric* will discover two conflicting accounts, once again, of the orator's duty towards his audience. In one Aristotle takes the severely philosophic line that 'the modes of persuasion are the only true constituents of the art' of rhetoric, and that 'enthymemes . . . are the substance of rhetorical persuasion', for they alone deal with 'the essential facts', everything else being merely accessory (1354^{a}12). The enthymeme in rhetoric is the counterpart of the syllogism in logic, both being structures of argument governed by rules, albeit less strict in rhetoric. From this first, austere position Aristotle rejects 'the arousing of prejudice, pity, anger, and similar emotions' as being beside the point, 'merely a personal appeal to the man who is judging the case' (18). In 'well-governed states'—such as Athens used to be when murder-cases on the Areopagus were tried before a small group of experienced magistrates—appeal to the emotions would be irrelevant, and the litigant had only to show 'that the alleged fact is so or not so, that it has or has not happened' (24). Yet, as things are now, Aristotle concedes, with orators addressing massive juries (of 201 to 501 citizens), and having to appeal to their emotions (1354ᵇ8), one had better master this art. And so he switches to the other attitude, which was to be much more influential in classical and Renaissance rhetoric, that 'since rhetoric exists to affect the giving of decisions' the orator must 'put his hearers, who are to decide, into the right frame of mind', this being particularly important in lawsuits (1377ᵇ21 ff.), where 'to conciliate the audience is what pays' (1354ᵇ22).

Accepting the realities of the rhetorical situation Aristotle defines three modes of persuasion, as we have seen, *ethos*, *pathos*, and logical proof. He bases his argument on the underlying link between feelings and thoughts, arguing that reason is seldom unattended by emotion: 'When people are feeling friendly or placable, they think one sort of thing; when they are feeling angry or hostile', they think differently (1377ᵇ21 ff.). The lawyer must show his opponents in an unfavourable light, then work up the judges' feelings against them, carefully unleashing emotion so as to effect persuasion. In the *Phaedrus* Socrates had defined rhetoric as 'a kind of influencing of the mind by means of words' (261 a), but Aristotle sees that words alone are not enough: 'those who heighten the effect of their words with suitable gestures, tones, dress, and dramatic action generally, are especially successful in arousing pity' (1386ᵃ30 f.). In his own body and dress the orator has a whole arsenal of expressive devices at his disposal.

The triad of *ethos*, *pathos*, and logical proof eventually reached Roman rhetoric, but not in time for the *De Inventione* and the *Rhetorica ad Herennium*. Whatever the common Hellenistic source of those works, they lack the Aristotelian triad, and this presumably reflects the fact that Aristotle's *Rhetoric* was lost for a certain period, being rediscovered only in 82 B C.[83] But in the *De*

---

[83] Kennedy 1972, pp. 114–15.

Oratore (55 BC) Cicero clearly draws on Aristotle when he makes Crassus say that 'the speaker will not be able to achieve what he wants by his words, unless he has gained profound insight into the characters of men', knowing 'all the mental emotions', all their 'natural characters and . . . habits of conduct' (1. 12. 53; 1. 5. 17; 1. 14. 60). The other main protagonist, Antonius, refers specifically to Aristotle, stating that since the essential point is how 'to sway the feelings of the tribunal', then 'for purposes of persuasion the art of speaking relies wholly upon three things: the proof of our allegations, the winning of our hearers' favour, and the rousing of their feelings to whatever impulse our case may require' (2. 27. 114). Antonius recurs later to 'those three things which alone can carry conviction; I mean the winning over, the instructing and the stirring of men's minds', the basic topics to consider in *inventio* (2. 28. 121, 2. 29. 128). In his other rhetorical works Cicero repeats the triad of *movere* (or *flectere*), *docere*, and *delectare* in a more pithy form (*Brutus*, 49. 185, 80. 276), but with the emphasis gradually shifting: 'the orator is in duty bound to instruct; giving pleasure will win him the audience's favour; to move them is indispensable' (*De Opt. Gen.* 1. 3). Or, as the *Orator* puts it, 'to prove is the first necessity, to please is charm, to sway is victory; for it is the one thing of all that avails most in winning verdicts' (21. 69). *Movere* becomes the most important power.

Yet, while this doctrine derives from Aristotle it has suffered a sea-change. We find occasional traces of the original Aristotelian distinction between *ethos* and *pathos*, as in the *Orator*, where *ethikon* is said to refer to the orator's self, *pathetikon* to the emotions he arouses. But even here we can see the strange Roman adaptation by which *ethos* becomes merely a more gentle form of the emotions aroused by *pathos*. 'The former is courteous and agreeable, adapted to win goodwill; the latter is violent, hot and impassioned, and by this cases are wrested from our opponents; when it rushes along in full career it is irresistible' (36. 128). The process involved in working up the feelings is known as *amplificatio*, which is a 'forcible method of arguing, argument being aimed at effecting proof, amplification at exercising influence', when it becomes 'a sort of weightier affirmation, designed to win credence in the course of speaking by arousing emotion' (*Part. Or.* 8. 27, 15. 53). Cicero tended to see *amplificatio* on a scale extending to infinity, declaring that 'there is no limit to the power of an oration to exalt a subject or render it contemptible' (36. 126–7), success in *amplificatio* being 'the one distinction that most specially marks the orator' (*De Or.* 3. 27. 105: so often in classical rhetoric we find this or that skill singled out as 'the one essential' faculty). The orator who is fully able to master his audience's feelings can move them in any direction, arouse any emotion, achieve any goal he wishes. Of all the topics in the *laus eloquentiae* this was the one that most fascinated Cicero, and most affected the Renaissance, the promise of absolute power over the audience's mind and feelings.

This theme runs through the *De Oratore*, emerging in each speaker and in every discussion. Crassus begins it:

there is to my mind no more excellent thing than the power, by means of oratory, to get a hold on assemblies of men, win their good will, direct their attentions wherever the speaker wishes, or divert them from wherever he wishes. (1. 8. 30)

The great attraction of rhetoric is that the orator who has mastered it can, at will, arouse 'men's hearts to anger, hatred, or indignation', or calm them down 'to mildness and mercy' (1. 12. 53, 1. 36. 165, 1. 46. 202, 2. 44. 185 and 189, 2. 81. 332, 3. 6. 23, 3. 30. 118, 3. 51. 197). He has *carte blanche*, the power to arouse 'whatever passion the circumstances and occasion may demand' (1.46. 202, 2. 27. 114), to lead his audience 'whithersoever he pleases' (2. 41. 176, 3. 14. 55). Cicero follows Aristotle in subjecting reason to emotion, the most important achievement for the orator being, Antonius states, to have his hearer

so affected as to be swayed by something resembling a mental impulse or emotion, rather than by judgement or deliberation. For men decide far more problems by hate, or love, or lust, or rage, or sorrow, or joy, or hope, or fear, or illusion, or some other inward emotion, than by reality, or authority, or any legal standard, or judicial precedent, or statute. (2. 42. 178)

The orator can only do this if he is himself moved by the emotions he seeks to arouse, indeed if the 'speaker is not himself aglow with passion' the minds of the listeners will not be ready to absorb his influence (2. 44. 189–90). Antonius declares that 'I never tried, by means of a speech, to arouse either indignation or compassion, either ill-will or hatred, in the minds of a tribunal, without being really stirred myself', and gives a vivid account of how the 'vast indignation' he had shown aroused deep feeling in a court, working up its hatred against a tyrant (2. 47. 195–2. 49. 200).

If the *De Oratore* has one unifying thread it is this celebration of the power of 'Eloquence, rightly styled, by an excellent poet [Pacuvius], "soulbending sovereign of all things", that she can not only support the sinking and bend the upstanding, but, like a good and brave commander, can even make prisoner a resisting antagonist' (2. 44. 187). Cicero's other rhetorical works reiterate the idea, if with less intensity of emphasis. The power of *movere* is constantly granted the highest place among the orator's resources (*Brutus*, 23. 89, 52. 193, 54. 198–9, 80. 276 and 279; *Part. Or.* 4. 13; *Orator*, 28. 97, 36. 126–7). The speaker who can 'inflame the minds of his hearers' can 'turn them in whatever direction the case demands' (*Brutus*, 80. 279, 84. 290, 93. 322; *Part. Or.* 3. 9, 19. 67, 27. 96; *Orator*, 5. 20, 25. 122, 36. 131–2). In the *Brutus* Cicero gives a vivid picture of how, when 'a real orator' speaks,

the listening throng is delighted, is carried along by his words, is in a sense bathed deep in delight. . . . They feel now joy, now sorrow, are moved now to laughter, now to tears; . . . are stirred to anger, wonder, hope, fear; and all these come to pass just as the hearer's minds are played upon by word and thought and action. (49. 187; compare 84. 290)

And in the *Orator* he gives an account of his own achievements that shows how he regarded himself as having fulfilled all the requirements of the ideal speaker (36. 129–32). As George Kennedy aptly reminds us, 'the lack of modesty which we sometimes think of as a peculiar weakness of Cicero was a permanent feature of Roman oratory, especially in the case of a new man like Cicero or Cato'.[84] They knew that self-advertisement sometimes does work.

Quintilian accepted Cicero's estimate of his rhetorical

---

[84] Kennedy 1972, p. 101.

performance, indeed never ceased to hold him up as the paragon or orators. In his fifth Verrine oration, describing the scourging of a Roman citizen, he judges that Cicero's *narratio* 'excites the warmest indignation' and 'moves us even to tears' (4. 2. 113). Elsewhere Quintilian celebrates 'the sheer force of his eloquence' (9. 2. 53), the skill of that 'supreme artist in playing on the minds of men' (11. 1. 85). On the place of emotional appeal in rhetoric Quintilian follows Cicero closely, but where Cicero is usually content just to praise the ability to arouse the emotions, Quintilian works out the practical details. He accepts the Aristotelian–Ciceronian triad, ranking both *docere* (4. 5. 6) and *delectare* (5. 8. 3) far below *movere*, where eloquence shows its true power. Quintilian adapts this topic, too, to the teaching situation, advising the teacher to read great speeches with his class and show 'how the orator establishes his sway over the emotions of his audience, forces his way into their very hearts' (2. 5. 8). Where Aristotle had given logical proof joint status with *ethos* and *pathos* Quintilian plays down logical processes as too intellectual, the real aim of oratory being to drag the audience by the force of our discourse 'and occasionally throw them off balance by an appeal to their emotions' (5. 19. 29–31). This is both 'the most powerful means of obtaining what we desire' and the hardest of tasks (6. 2. 1), yet 'it is this emotional power that dominates the court' (6. 2. 4), 'it is in its power over the emotions that the life and soul of oratory is to be found' (6. 2. 7). Like Cicero, Quintilian sees the emotions as existing on a scale, *pathos* including 'the more violent emotions', which command and disturb, while *ethos* refers to the 'calm and gentle' ones which 'persuade and induce a feeling of goodwill' (6. 2. 9). When *pathos* is properly aroused and the judge is overcome by feeling, he is unable to consider reason or truth, and his emotions give the verdict despite himself (6. 2. 6–7)—another claim for rhetoric's automatic success. *Pathos* is largely concerned 'with anger, dislike, fear, hatred and pity', there being various kinds of each (6. 2. 20–1). The orator should draw on all of these, since

the force of eloquence is such that it not merely compels the judge to the conclusion toward which the nature of the facts leads him, but awakens emotions which either do not naturally arise from the case or are stronger than the case would suggest. This is known as *deinosis* ['making terrible'], that is to say, language giving additional force to things unjust, cruel, or hateful. (6. 2. 24)

Demosthenes was outstanding in this respect.

Quintilian thinks that appeal to the emotions is necessary in all three kinds of oratory (3. 4. 15), including deliberative, for the audience must be worked on in political no less than in legal debates (3. 8. 12). Emotional appeal should be used in every part of the speech, in the *exordium* (4. 1. 5), in digressions (4. 2. 104), in the *narratio*—for in that part of the speech the judge is most attentive and can be aroused more easily (4. 2. 113–15, 119, 128) —and above all in the *peroratio*, where 'we have to consider what the feelings of the judge will be when he retires to consider his verdict' (6. 1. 10). Quintilian's long analysis of the arousal of emotion in the peroration (6. 1. 1–55) is an admirably practical account—whatever we may feel of the ethical issue—of how the Roman advocate went to work. The prosecution counsel 'has to rouse the judge, while the defender has to soften him' (6. 1. 9), so that each will be trying to 'win the judge's goodwill and to divert it from their opponent' (6. 1. 11). The prosecution must excite the passions of jealousy, hatred, or anger in the judge (14), make the accused seem as atrocious or deplorable as possible (15), using *amplificatio* to enhance effects (6. 1. 16, 51). The defence counsel must arouse pity by describing the 'previous or present sufferings' of the accused, and contrasting his present fortune with what will happen if he fails (23–4). He can also use *prosopopoeia*, an impersonation speech put into the mouth of his client (25), while—developing one of Aristotle's points—

Actions as well as words may be employed to move the court to tears. Hence the custom of bringing accused persons into court wearing squalid and unkempt attire, and of introducing their children and parents, and it is with this in view that we see blood-stained swords, fragments of bone taken from the wound, and garments spotted with blood, displayed by the accusers, wounds . . . , scourged bodies bared to the view. The impression produced by such exhibitions is generally enormous, since they seem to bring the spectators face to face with the cruel facts. (6. 1. 30–1)

Readers of Shakespeare will recall the tremendous effect made by Antony showing Caesar's blood-stained toga (which Quintilian refers to here); or the political success that the patrician class hopes to gain by having Coriolanus display the wounds he has received fighting for his country (a real Roman custom); or Volumnia's stage-managed *conquestio* which deflects her son's revenge on Rome (*Coriolanus*, 5. 3. 21 ff.).

Effective though these external devices may be, to Quintilian 'the prime essential for stirring the emotions of others is . . . first to feel those emotions oneself' (6. 2. 26). To 'counterfeit grief, anger and indignation' without adapting our own feelings to them is ridiculous. We must 'assimilate ourselves to the emotions of those who are genuinely so affected', for then our eloquence will really derive from the feeling we want to produce in the mind of the judge:

Will he be angry, if the orator who seeks to kindle his anger shows no sign of labouring under the emotion which he demands from his audience? Will he shed tears if the pleader's eyes are dry? It is utterly impossible. (6. 2. 27)

As to how the orator induces such emotions in himself, to Cicero this depended on the language he uses, 'for the very quality of the diction, employed to stir the feelings of others, stirs the speaker himself even more deeply than any of his hearers' (*De Or.* 2. 46. 191). Quintilian's account is more subtle, appealing to the visual sense, for his orator should 'generate' the emotions he wishes 'to prevail with the judge' by using 'visions' (the Greek term is *phantasiai*),

whereby things absent are presented to our imagination with such extreme vividness that they seem actually to be before our very eyes. It is the man who is really sensitive to such impressions who will have the greatest power over the emotions. (6. 2. 29–30)

This 'power of vivid imagination, whereby things, words and actions are presented in the most realistic manner', is known as *enargeia* (also *illustratio* and *evidentia*: 32), and depends on our being able to 'identify ourselves with the persons' we represent, 'and for a brief space feel their suffering as though it were our own' (34). Actors are sometimes overcome by emotion after completing their part ('What's Hecuba to him, or he to Hecuba?'),

But if the mere delivery of words written by another has the power to set our souls on fire with fictitious emotions, what will the orator do whose duty it is to picture to himself the facts and who has it in his power to feel the same emotion as his client whose interests are at stake? (35)

Quintilian testifies that he himself has often been so much moved while speaking 'that I have not merely been wrought upon to tears, but have turned pale and shown all the symptoms of genuine grief'. In rhetoric art not only imitates, it re-creates nature.

The Three Styles

All of these emotional states must, of course, be represented in the appropriate language. Aristotle had laid down the first principles of linguistic decorum, stating that in rhetoric language 'will be appropriate if it expresses emotion and character, and if it corresponds to its subject' (1408ª10). So he instructs his pupils that 'to express emotion, you will employ the language of anger in speaking of outrage; the language of disgust and discreet reluctance to utter a word when speaking of impiety or foulness; the language of exultation for a tale of glory', and humiliation for pity (1408ª15 ff.). This 'aptness of language is one thing that makes people believe in the truth of your story' (20), and reinforces the impression of your *ethos* (25). Aristotle discusses prose style more fully in Book Three, without however reverting to this functional, persuasive view of language, being more concerned there with the artefact than with the speaker–hearer relationship (see e.g. 1404ª8 ff., 1404ᵇ1, 1405ª7, 1407ᵇ25, etc.). The early Roman rhetorics share this concern with the artefact rather than with the persuasive process. The *Rhetorica ad Herennium* makes the first extant division of the kinds of style into three, but as regards their stylistic components:

The Grand type consists of a smooth and ornate arrangement of impressive words. The Middle type consists of words of a lower, yet not of the lowest and most colloquial, class of words. The Simple type is brought down even to the most current idiom of standard speech. (4. 8. 11)

Although the author does link the grand style with 'Amplification and Appeal to Pity', it is in terms of 'ornate words' and 'impressive thoughts', *gravitas* or grandeur, and his concern, too, is with the language of the artefact rather than its varying degrees of emotional impact.

That connection seems to have been made first by Cicero, who took the very influential step of correlating the three styles with the three *officia oratoris*. In *De Oratore* Antonius repeats his aims as an orator, 'the winning of men's favour, secondly their enlightenment, thirdly their excitement', and then links them in general terms with the appropriate language: 'the first calls for gentleness of style, the second for acuteness, the third for energy' (2. 29. 128–9). Later he goes into more detail on the 'passionate style', which 'searches out an arbitrator's emotional side [*perturbatio*] rather than his understanding [*cognitio*]' (2. 53. 214). The correlation of goal and style was properly systematized in the *Orator*, where Cicero earmarked 'the plain style for proof, the middle style for pleasure, the vigorous style for persuasion; and in this last is summed up the entire virtue of the orator' (21. 69). Of them all, the orator using the grand style

undoubtedly has the greatest power. This is the man whose brilliance and fluency have caused admiring nations to let eloquence attain the highest power in the state; I mean the kind of eloquence which rushes along with the roar of a mighty stream. . . . This eloquence has power to sway men's minds and move them in every possible way. Now it storms the feelings, now it creeps in; it implants new ideas and uproots the old. (28. 99)

Orators of the grandiloquent style 'were forceful, versatile, copious and grave, trained and equipped to arouse and sway the emotions' (5. 20), none more so than Demosthenes (8. 26). Cicero goes into for him an unusual amount of detail defining the plain (24. 81), middle (26. 91 ff.), and grand styles (28. 97 ff.), emphasizing that the perfect orator must be able to manage all three: 'He in fact is eloquent who can discuss commonplace matters simply, lofty subjects impressively, and topics ranging between in a tempered style' (29. 100).

Quintilian's account of the role of language in rhetoric extends through Books 8, 9, 10, and part of 12, covering an enormous range of linguistic effects which resist brief summary. On the detailed resources of *elocutio* he writes that 'there is no more effective method of exciting the emotions than an apt use of figures' (9. 1. 21), and a later chapter will evaluate his contribution to this topic. As for this issue of the three styles and the three *officia oratoris*, it is only towards the end of his book that he takes up his earlier promise (12. 10. 1 f.) to discuss the 'kind of style' the orator should adopt. He is obviously unhappy with Cicero's tidy designation of three styles, because of the great varieties of style that exist in oratory, as in painting (12. 10. 2 ff., 10). But subsequently he does discuss them, and makes the Ciceronian correlation, though rather grudgingly (12. 10. 58). The orator should use the plain style to instruct, the grand style to move, the intermediate style to charm: 'for instruction the quality most needed is acumen, for conciliation gentleness, and for stirring the emotions force' (59). Once again the *genus grande* gets the lion's share. The other styles have their merits,

but he whose eloquence is like to some great torrent that rolls down rocks and 'disdains a bridge' and carves out its own banks for itself, will sweep the judge from his feet, struggle as he may, and force him to go whither he bears him. This is the orator that will call the dead to life . . . it is in his pages that his native land itself will cry aloud. (12. 10. 61)

These praises of eloquence are themselves demonstrations of their own art, and in them we note how the rhetorician seeks to align his power with the great forces of nature, rivers in flood, thunder and lightning, or snow-storms (as with Homer's Ulysses). The 'streams' of eloquence must flow 'as mighty rivers flow, filling whole valleys' (5. 14. 31); 'It is this force and impetuosity that . . . Aristophanes compares to the thunderbolt' (12. 10. 65). What impressionable person, reading these words in a time when rhetoric was still alive, would not also want to acquire 'the power of true eloquence'?

2

PLATO'S ATTACK ON RHETORIC

Finally, in forming our judgements on Plato's procedure, we must not forget that Plato likes to argue against rhetoric and sophistry; and indeed that he is the man who by his attacks on the 'Sophists' created the bad associations connected with that word. I believe that we therefore have every reason to censor him when he himself makes use of rhetoric and sophistry in place of argument.

Sir Karl Popper[1]

The very success of rhetoric was sometimes its own undoing. Rival disciplines challenged its eminence, attacked its principles and methods. The most prominent attacks on rhetoric, from the ancient Greeks to the late nineteenth century, came from philosophy, which felt itself threatened by rhetoric's status in education and cultural life generally. As H. M. Hubbell wrote of the attacks by philosophy against rhetoric in the first century BC, the dispute over whether rhetoric was a *technē* or only a *tribē* (knack) may seem futile to us:

But the question was evidently felt to be of vital importance, and we may not be far from wrong in assuming that the bread and butter of many a philosopher and rhetorician was at stake. So long as the rhetorician was a mere declaimer, there was little danger that he would attract any considerable portion of the student class. But the rejuvenated rhetoric of the last days of the Roman republic claimed to be a complete education in itself, supplanting philosophy, or at least reducing philosophy to the position of a handmaid of rhetoric. To combat the new rival philosophy put forth its utmost strength.[2]

Once attacked, rhetoric defended itself or counter-attacked, so that in this and other periods we find bitter disputes over the territory that each discipline occupied, with fundamental criticisms of the other's subject-matter and method.

[1] Popper 1966, p. 263 n. 52.
[2] Hubbell 1920, p. 368.

The first and most sustained attacks from Plato, at the very beginning of the Western rhetorical tradition. Alarmed by the role of oratory in what he saw as the decline of values in Athenian society, and partly stung by the success of the Sophists, those rival teachers of philosophy, politics, and eloquence, Plato devoted large sections of two dialogues, *Gorgias* and *Phaedrus*, and a number of passages elsewhere, to attacking rhetoric. To the reader who does not know them it must be said at once that these are not balanced and dispassionate evaluations of rhetoric's validity or contribution to society, but frank polemics against it. Since they have enjoyed great prestige, no honest student of rhetoric can avoid confronting them for himself. I shall try to isolate the grounds of Plato's hostility towards rhetoric, and also the methods he used to express it.

I

The *Gorgias* is a long and complex dialogue, densely argued, whose subject shifts unpredictability, concerning politics, ethics, and rhetoric in its relation to both politics and ethics. It is difficult to keep a balance between all three subjects when discussing it, yet essential to do so if we are to understand the associations that Plato gives to rhetoric. One modern editor sees it as a treatise on 'the foundation and justification of ethics',[3] as indeed it is, but for its attitude to rhetoric the discussion of politics is more important. This is because Plato does not treat rhetoric as an educational subject, nor as an aesthetic system, nor—least of all—as a branch of philosophy. In the *Gorgias* rhetoric is treated as subservient to politics, being indeed the main tool of politics in Athenian democracy. E. R. Dodds's view that 'the dialogue is primarily concerned with the moral basis of politics'[4] seems more accurate.

To understand the *Gorgias* we must briefly recall both the political situation in fourth-century Athens and the philo-

---

[3] Terence Irwin, Plato, *Gorgias, Translated with Notes* (Oxford, 1979), p. v. Future references to this edition will be incorporated in the text with the abbreviation 'I' prefixed, e.g. 'I 27'.

[4] E. R. Dodds, Plato, *Gorgias. A Revised Text with Introduction and Commentary* (Oxford, 1959), p. 1. Future references to this edition will be incorporated in the text with the abbreviation 'D' prefixed, e.g. 'D 27'. The translation of the *Gorgias* used here, except otherwise stated, is by W. D. Woodhead in Plato 1963.

sophical careers of Socrates and Plato, his disciple. Socrates was put to death by the Athenian people in 399 BC, on the charges of refusing to recognize the gods recognized by the state, and corrupting the youth. Plato's hostility to the democracy of Athens, to its social structure, legal system, and to the medium which sustained that system—the oratory of the *rhetores* or public speakers in the Council, the Assembly, and the lawcourts—found intense expression in this dialogue. As E. R. Dodds writes in his great edition, answering the question, 'Why is the *Gorgias* so bitter?': it 'stands out among the early dialogues by the tragic tone of its later pages and by the direct and bitter criticism which it levels against Athenian politics and politicians' (D 19). Plato was born in 427 BC, at a time when 'the Periclean society still seemed intact', but he 'witnessed as a boy its gradual disintegration under the stress of war; as a young man in his early twenties he had experienced its death-agonies' (D 32). After the twin disasters of the Spartan victory in the Peloponnesian War, and the siege and capitulation of Athens in 404–403, Athenian democracy rebuilt itself in economic and military terms, but 'Plato viewed with disfavour these attempts at recreating vanished glories' (D 361–2). The Athenians may have pursued building and defensive programmes, but they wholly failed, according to Plato, to evolve that system of values needed to create the good society. Realizing 'the growing demoralization of Athenian society in the nineties', Plato described in his Seventh Letter (if it be authentic) his disillusionment with politics and the social order:

At last I decided that all existing forms of society are wrong: their institutions are pretty well past remedy, unless some quite unexpected force should intervene at a lucky moment. I was thus constrained to give my devotion to a true philosophy, and say that only from the standpoint of such a philosophy could one get a comprehensive view of what was right, for the social order as for individuals; so that mankind would never be rid of its miseries until philosophers, in the genuine sense of the term, gained political power, or else, by some miracle, the governing classes took to genuine philosophy. (326 a; D 25)

At about this time (389–387); Plato went to Sicily; the *Gorgias* was written either just before this visit or just after, and is roughly contemporary with the *Menexenus* and *Meno* (D 18–30).

The responsibility for the decline of Athenian society is placed, in the *Gorgias*, not with the contemporary leaders but with their famous predecessors, the 'Four Men', Pericles, Cimon, Militiades, and Themistocles (515 d). They failed, according to Socrates, in the task of the statesman—and philosopher—the 'tending of the city and its citizens with the aim of making the citizens themselves as good as possible' (513 e). Pericles evidently failed to teach the Athenians justice and gratitude, for 'at the end of his life, he was convicted of theft by them and narrowly escaped a death sentence, obviously because they held him an evil man' (515 e). Cimon was ostracized for ten years; Themistocles was ostracized and banished; while 'Militiades, the victor of Marathon, they voted to throw into the pit, and he would have suffered this fate but for the president of the Council' (516 d). These leaders failed, as their successors have failed, in the task that Socrates sees as 'the only true office of a good citizen', that of educating the citizens. We must note from the outset that Plato presents his ideas on education in the form of a strict dichotomy. The true statesman must take the base 'desires' of the populace, which are assumed to be in constant war against their reason (if they have any), and give 'those desires a different direction instead of allowing them free scope, by *persuading and compelling* citizens to adopt courses that would improve them' (517 b–c; my italics). As his editors have pointed out, this notion of the statesman applying the doctor's mandate to a sick society ruthlessly, to restore it to health, is the first sign of the 'authoritarian strain in Plato's thinking' which comes out so strongly in the *Republic* and in the *Laws*, with its recommended 'conditioning' of the masses (D 328). Socrates' 'authoritarian views' appear in his belief that the politician's task is 'to "force change" . . . in people's desires, with or without their consent' (I 236). Instead of doing this, Socrates claims, Athenian politicians have 'catered to the desires' of the people (518 c), like purveyors of consumer goods (517 d–e), and have been celebrated by the Athenian populace for just this 'flattery' of their wishes:

You praise those who have banqueted our citizens with all the dainties they desire. And men say it is these who have made our city great, never realizing that it is swollen and festering through these statesmen of old. For they have paid no heed to discipline and justice, but have filled our city with harbours and dockyards and walls and revenues and similar rubbish, and so, when the crisis of her infirmity comes, they will hold their present advisers responsible and will sing the praises of Themistocles and Cimon and Pericles, who caused their misfortunes. (518 e–519 a)

The present corruption of values is the outcome of an earlier failure of rule.

The choice, as Socrates presents it through a whole range of analogies from medicine, gymnastics, and political philosophy, is expressed in the strict dichotomy, whether or not he and any other responsible citizen should 'do battle with the Athenians, like a doctor, to make them as good as possible', or else just 'serve and minister to their pleasures' (521 a). This absolute, uncompromising dichotomy between either indulging their appetites or correcting them is extended and correlated with the dichotomy between the politician and the doctor-like philosopher. Socrates alleges that although the citizens, victims of their rulers, are suffering from being fed on dainties that titillate the appetite but cause the body to waste away, they 'will not blame for their maladies . . . those who feasted them', that is, the politicians. However, 'any who may . . . give them advice when the surfeit of the past has some time later brought sickness upon them, because it disregarded the rules of health— these they will blame and abuse and injure' (518 d). Here is the role the historic Socrates set himself, to point out to his fellow-citizens their corruption of values, to set philosophy against politics and against rhetoric, its tool and medium. Plato makes Socrates the persona in his dialogue foreshadow the fate that actually befell the historic Socrates, saying that in the uncertain climate of Athens, where 'anything whatever may happen to anybody', he is quite likely to be brought into court, prosecuted by some evil man, 'and it would not be surprising if I were put to death' (521 d). Plato's image of Socrates' total isolation, of being the only man in Athens who knows the true values needed for society, is expressed in a form that reiterates the operative dichotomy and also prefigures the events at his actual trial:

I think that I am one of the very few Athenians, not to say the only one, engaged in the true political art, and that of the men today I alone practise statesmanship. Since therefore when I speak on any occasion it is *not with a view to winning favour*, but I *aim at what is best, not what is most pleasant*, and since I am unwilling to engage in those 'dainty devices' that you recommend, I shall have nothing to say for myself when in court. (521 d–e; my italics)

And in effect Socrates offered no defence, although Plato, Xenophon (each in an *Apology*), and at least seven other ancient writers composed one for him.[5]

It is important to register the intensity of Plato's hatred of Athenian democracy, and especially its use of oratory as the main visible means of influencing opinion at public gatherings. To reconstruct this alienation from the norms of a society in which, as commentators have noted, Plato himself felt as isolated as the historical Socrates (D 16, 31–2, 243), is to realize the extent to which the *Gorgias* is the product of a specific time and place, and the work of a very individual writer. It is not, as some critics suggest, a universally valid critique of rhetoric. To reach the closing position of Socrates, that since all modes of address to the public are tainted by flattery and corruption, it is better to lose your life than to pollute your soul by speaking in your own defence, is to have reached such an extreme position regarding the possibility of honest communication to a large group—'the masses' seems to be the appropriately pejorative word—that any fair or balanced discussion of rhetoric is impossible. Socrates practises dialectic but wholly rejects rhetoric: 'I know how to produce one witness to the truth of what I say, the man with whom I am debating, but the others I ignore. I know how to secure one man's vote, but with the many I will not even enter into discussion' (474 a). Dialectic involved individuals, rhetoric approached the masses, and was therefore corrupt.

Modern commentators, usually more interested in Plato's use of dialectic, tend to pass over this passage without comment. But it is essential to grasp that the image Plato gives of Athenian politics is biased to an extreme, and that rhetoric suffers in the same way. Much of Plato's criticism of his society, as Dodds says, 'looks unfair today. He mentions the dockyards (517 c, 519 a) but not the Parthenon; he condemns the dramatists along

---

[5] Kennedy 1963, p. 149 and note.

with the politicians for flattering the prejudices of the mob (502 b), but forgets the *Trojan Women* and the *Knights*; he ignores the economic condition which made the Periclean' introduction of payment for service on juries and other bodies (515 e) 'a necessity if democracy was to be more than a façade' (D 33, 356–7). The treatment of the 'Four Men' is unfair in several ways. Plato has an absolute concept of successful education being a once-and-for-all conversion of its recipients to virtue, and so the fact that the Athenian citizens disagreed with its leaders proves to him that they had not been educated properly, and hence that the leaders were at fault. But, as Dodds says, this argument is weak: 'If the masses turn against their leader, this is no proof that they have deteriorated morally; it may be the leader who has deteriorated . . . or it may prove merely an ingrained fickleness which no statesmanship can cure' (D 355). Socrates believes that a virtuous man can make others virtuous, and according to the Socratic Paradox whoever knows what virtue is will embrace it. But, as Terence Irwin puts it, 'why might not some cognitive deficiency make someone fail to grasp the argument showing this?' (I 233–4).

Plato's charge that Pericles' introduction of maintenance allowance to citizens empanelled on juries damaged the state reflects, in fact, the attitudes of other conservative critics, who 'probably objected to political pay because it made democracy work' effectively (I 234). Yet there is no evidence for his further claim that its introduction made Athenians 'cowardly' (D 356). As for the trial of Pericles on the charge of embezzlement, 'Socrates does not mention that the Athenians soon restored Pericles to office' (I 234). Similarly, for Plato to cite Themistocles' 'condemnation simply as proof of Athenian ingratitude clearly begs the question of his guilt' (D 359). The condemnation probably expressed their disapproval at the failure of his policy on a specific issue, as was the case with Miltiades, where 'it is not obvious that the Athenians were unfair to him' (I 235).

If Plato has not acually distorted the facts here, he has 'selected his details in such a way as to put the conduct of the Athenians in the worst possible light' (D 359). The walls that Socrates refers to so dismissively are 'the defensively vital "Long Walls" connecting Athens and its harbour at Peiraeus', while the dockyards at Peiraeus 'were important in Athenian defence and sea power', both being 'examples of shrewd and far-sighted strategic projects undertaken on the advice of popular leaders by a democratic assembly' (I 119). (It is due to them both, one might add, that Athens enjoyed the stability that made Plato's career at all possible!) Socrates later subsumes Themistocles' ship-building proposal under the charge of gratifying the people's desires, but he 'omits to mention' that it had to compete against a 'proposal to distribute the necessary money among the people', so that 'it is a gross over-simplification—typical of Socrates' political comments—to suggest' that Themistocles was 'just humouring political whims', and not showing statesmanly foresight in persuading the people to accept a long-term asset for national defence (I 237). As Irwin judges, 'Socrates' version of these incidents conceals the serious questions of policy sometimes at stake and the solid grounds for measures taken against these politicians. His story is a perversion of the historical conditions, as far as we know them' (I 235). Popper's comment that 'Plato's description of democracy is a vivid but intensely hostile and unjust parody of the political life of Athens'[6] does not, perhaps, seem so far out.

   I have cited informed opinion on Plato's political attitudes in the *Gorgias* to bring out its polemical intent, which in turn affects his account of rhetoric. Politicians addressing the people—*rhetores* as they are called here, the normal word for those who spoke in public (466 c; cf. D 194)—it is claimed, can *either* educate them to virtue and justice *or* join in their corruption by gratifying their desires. Rhetoric, also, is hacked into two by this powerful dichotomy, for Plato reduces the whole of human communication to these two poles, education *or* corruption. If public speaking fails in the one area, this must be because it belongs to the other. The first point to register is the reductivism implied in these binary oppositions, as a very wide range of possibilities of discourse is boiled down to two, and two only. Secondly, the binarism is only a stage on the process towards monism, in which only one of the poles is accepted, the other being cancelled out. Politics is 'flattery'; rhetoric is 'flattery': both can be abandoned in favour of Socratic philosophy, which alone has access to the truth. Socrates is the only true rhetor in Athens, and he refuses to speak in public.

[6] Popper 1966, p. 42.

This is the position reached in the last of the three conversations recorded in the *Gorgias*, between Socrates and Callicles, where, as Dodds notes, we come to the real heart of the dialogue (D 260). To see the full extent of Plato's attack on rhetoric we must go back to the beginning, bearing in mind that the earlier discussion is intended to establish the logical grounds for some of the later polemic. Thus the dichotomy between 'indulging' the populace's desires or 'educating' them—which means restraining them—develops out of a long argument that pleasure, seen as the satisfaction of bodily desires, is evil, and that virtue depends on temperance. Plato, unfairly enough, makes the proponents of rhetoric claim that the advantage of acquiring it is to be able to indulge their own pleasures at other people's expense. They are also made to claim that rhetoric concerns justice and virtue. This second assertion is countered by Socrates, who argues that rhetoricians do not know what justice is, and that their teaching is in any case ineffective. The method used to establish these positions is sometimes the *elenchos*, the method of 'cross-examination' or 'refutation' which is applied to the interlocutors' argument, exposing its inadequacies until the other speaker concedes the point. But when it suits Plato, Socrates is allowed long speeches, although his interlocutors are criticized when they do the same.

The dialogue falls into three sections, as Socrates engages in dispute successively with three proponents of rhetoric: Gorgias, the distinguished elder Sophist; Polus, a younger and inexperienced teacher of rhetoric; and Callicles, an anti-democratic advocate of political power as achieved through the spoken word. In each section Socrates outwits his opponent, bringing the discussion to a stalemate. At the end, in fact, he is left holding forth in a monologue, Callicles having been reduced to asking him to carry on the discussion 'alone, either speaking on your own or answering your own questions' (505 d). It is a victory for the more persistent speaker, yet one achieved by some rather dubious manœuvres.

In the first encounter Socrates gets Gorgias to agree to the question-and-answer method of dialectic, instead of long discourses (448 d, 449 b), and asks him to define rhetoric. Gorgias makes five attempts at definition, but Socrates rejects each of them. To the statements that rhetoric is concerned with

'words', or with 'discourse' as its instrument, Socrates objects
that each of the arts is concerned with words that have to do
with its own subject-matter (449 d–450 b). What then is the
subject-matter of rhetoric? Gorgias answers, 'the greatest and
noblest of human affairs'; but Socrates replies that the best
things in life are health, beauty, and wealth obtained without
dishonesty (451 d). Gorgias then states that rhetoric is 'the
greatest good', for it is 'responsible for freedom for a man
himself, and at the same time for rule over others in his own
city' (452 d; tr. Irwin). As noted above (p. 25), Plato now makes
Gorgias deliver the traditional praise of rhetoric in society, which
persisted from Isocrates to the eighteenth century, associating it
with liberty and power in a democracy. Socrates will return to
some of these issues (especially power) later, but for now he
picks up the assertion that 'rhetoric is a creator of persuasion' or
'conviction' (453 a), and argues that other arts—arithmetic, for
instance—also teach us their lore 'and consequently persuade
us' (453 d–e). Gorgias fatally agrees to this proposition—he
ought to have argued that persuasion implies moving the will by
speech, not just communicating knowledge[7]—and falls into a
worse trap in his fifth definition, responding to Socrates'
question, 'what kind of persuasion?': 'The kind of persuasion
exercised on juries and other mobs . . . about good and evil'
(454 b; tr. Dodds). Athenian juries were very large, usually of
several hundred men, but the word 'mob' expresses Plato's
personal contempt for the mass involved (D 205). The final
phrase, 'good and evil', or 'the things which are just and unjust'
(tr. Irwin) will turn out to be important, but Socrates sometimes
lets his targets rest for a while.

Still unsatisfied with Gorgias' account of the kind of
conviction that rhetoric induces, Socrates now defines two
forms of 'conviction' (*pistis*), one resulting from learning
(*mathesis*) and systematic teaching, the other from persuasion
alone (454 e; I 118). The distinction may seem unexceptionable,

[7] Having written these words I was glad to discover H. M. Hubbell's analysis
of Greek reactions to Plato: 'The definition of rhetoric as the power of persuasion
which Plato ascribed to Gorgias contained an ambiguity which gave an
opportunity for reply. Other things, the opponents said, persuade,—wealth,
beauty, reputation.' Philodemus, Sextus Empiricus, and Quintilian (2. 15. 6–9)
'give the natural and normal answer that it is not persuasion but persuasion by
speech which is the end of rhetoric' (Hubbell 1920, pp. 380–1).

but experienced readers of Plato will be wary of what he can do with the cutting edge of a dichotomy. Plato duly makes Gorgias fall into a trap that any tyro in logic could have avoided, so demonstrating, as E. R. Dodds says of a later passage, 'the rhetorician's ineptitude at the philosopher's game of dialectic' (D 223).

SOCRATES. Then do you want us to lay down two forms of persuasion, one yielding conviction without knowing, the other yielding knowledge?

GORGIAS. Quite.

SOCRATES. Then which persuasion does rhetoric produce in jury-courts and the other mobs, about just and unjust things? The persuasion from which conviction comes without knowing, or that from which knowing comes?

GORGIAS. Presumably it's clear, Socrates, that it's the kind from which conviction comes

—'without knowing', that is.—'O foolish Gorgias!', a Renaissance reader might have noted in the margin here.

SOCRATES. Then it seems rhetoric is the craftsman of persuasion which yields conviction but does not teach about the just and the unjust.

GORGIAS. Yes.

SOCRATES. Then neither does the rhetor teach juries and the other mobs about just and unjust things, but only produces conviction. For presumably he couldn't teach such great matters to such a large mob in a short time.

GORGIAS. No indeed.

(454 e–455 a; tr. Irwin)

A more intelligent or experienced interlocutor—would that Plato's desire to discredit rhetoric were not so strong that he gives it such incompetent defenders!—might have replied that rhetoric *is* concerned with persuasion producing knowledge, precisely depends on its audience knowing what the points at issue are (see, e.g., Quintilian 4. 1. 6–7) and that Socrates is using the term 'instruct' in too absolute a manner. The rhetorician may not indeed be able to 'instruct' a court 'in a short time' about right and wrong; but he does not need to, for his task is not to give the court a complete education in ethics, or justice, from scratch. Its members are educated adults, Greek citizens at that, and although Plato expresses nothing but contempt for

the citizens of Athens he cannot convince everyone either that
the court is essentially ignorant of such matters or that the
rhetorician can get away with mere 'opinion'.

One of Plato's most effective ploys is that he never allows
Socrates' opponents to go back over his arguments critically, but
forces them to accept Socrates' terms and Socrates' tempo—as
Socrates puts it, 'in order that the argument may be carried
forward consecutively' (454 c). So Gorgias is now asked to
define the subjects on which a rhetorician is able to advise the
city, lacking as he does technical knowledge in building, or
medicine, or soldiery (455 b–d). Gorgias answers that none the
less the orator can give decisive advice on such issues (455 e–
456 a)—as Themistocles had done—and is emboldened by that
argument to make the greater claim that 'rhetoric includes
practically all other faculties under her control', for 'there is no
subject on which a rhetorician would not speak more
persuasively than any other craftsman, before a crowd'
(456 a–c). For instance, a rhetorician could persuade a patient to
undergo surgery, although a doctor might fail to.

The weakness of Gorgias' first argument is that he has
conceived of rhetoric as a 'competitive art', with the rhetor
holding forth 'among a mass of people' like a boxer or athlete
(456 c). This is to confuse setting with purpose, accident with
essence. He claims, further, that the rhetor is competent 'to
speak *against anybody* on *any subject*, and to prove himself more
convincing before a crowd on practically every topic he wishes'
(457 a–b; my italics). After a subtle digression, disarming
Gorgias' suspicions and getting him to allow the 'cross-
examination' to continue—a true *captatio benevolentiae*—Socrates
picks up the words 'before a crowd', and applies another of his
inclusive/exclusive dichotomies. If Gorgias agrees that the
rhetorician 'would be convincing about any subject before a
crowd, not through instruction but by persuasion'—*Gorgias*:
'Certainly'—and if 'before a crowd means among the ignorant',
then, Socrates concludes, 'when the rhetorician is more
convincing than the doctor, the ignorant is more convincing
among the ignorant than the expert' (458 e–459 b).

Someone allowed more sense than Plato has granted Gorgias
might have said at this point that the rhetorician took over the
relevant medical knowledge from the doctor on one special

occasion, and could put that knowledge into words more forcefully and persuasively, but that of course he never implied that the rhetorician was an expert on medicine.—Nor, of course, can people be divided into such absolute categories as 'those who know' and 'the ignorant', for many people have some knowledge of matters that concern them, or else how could they tell a good doctor from a bad one? (A rather important point in the fourth century, as it happens.)—But Plato pushes on to grant Socrates his first major conclusion against rhetoric, that 'it has no need to know the truth about things but merely to discover a technique of persuasion, so as to appear among the ignorant to have more knowledge than the expert'. At this point anyone still capable of thought would object to this *reductio ad absurdum* created by manipulating antithetical categories that privilege one side ('truth', 'expert') and downgrade the other ('persuasion', 'ignorant'). But Gorgias, dialectician's dummy that he is, having accepted the argument placidly so far, actually plays into Plato's hands: 'But is not this a great comfort, Socrates, to be able without learning any other arts but this one to prove in no way inferior to the specialists?' (459 b–c). This is to brand oneself an impostor and a simpleton to boot!

Some sense, perhaps, that he might reveal the fragility of his persona makes Plato refrain from having Socrates expose the absurdity of that position—it exposes itself—so he makes him revert to the question of good and evil. Gorgias had earlier stated the obvious, that 'competitive arts' such as boxing, or weapon-combat, or rhetoric should not be used indiscriminately against other people, especially not friends or relatives, and are in any case to be used for self-defence, not aggression. However, should someone misuse their skills, he states, 'the teachers are not guilty, and the craft is not for this reason evil or to blame, but rather, in my opinion, those who make improper use of it' (456 c–457 b). Now Socrates, who had not commented on this remark at the time, quietly shifts the discourse from medicine to ethics, and suggests that the same dichotomy between the expert and the amateur applies to Gorgias' earlier claim—also left unexploded until Socrates was ready—that rhetoric produces conviction 'about the just and unjust' (454 b). Socrates now alleges that the rhetorician 'does not know what is right and wrong, noble or base, just or unjust, but has contrived a technique of persuasion in these matters, so that, though ignorant, he appears among the ignorant to know better than the expert' (459 d). Presumably, too, as a teacher of rhetoric he will train a pupil to 'appear before the crowd to have such knowledge, when he has it not, and appear to be a good man, when he is not' (459 d–e).

Gorgias fails to see the effects of accepting this devastating dichotomy between seeming and being, and replies that if a pupil 'does not possess this knowledge, he can learn these things also from me' (460 a). Terence Irwin notes the unreality of this reply: 'Why should Gorgias obligingly give the answer that causes him trouble? Would he not have been better off insisting that the rhetor needs no special competence in justice and injustice?' (I 125). Socrates, having received this free gift, states his belief that 'the man who has learned anything becomes in each case such as his knowledge makes him'—the assumption that education is instantly and totally effective—so that 'he who has learned justice is just' (460 b). If so, then the teacher *must* be responsible for the ethical behaviour of his pupils. Gorgias had denied this earlier, as Socrates reminds him—in such a case 'we should not censure or banish his instructor but rather the guilty man who wrongly employs rhetoric' (460 d)—but he had also agreed that the rhetorician 'must wish to do just actions' (460 c), and had affirmed that rhetoric is concerned with right and wrong (454 b, 460 e). At that point, Socrates now tells us, hearing Gorgias, he had

considered that rhetoric could never be a thing of evil, since its discourse is always concerned with justice. But when a little later you said that the rhetorician might actually make an evil use of rhetoric, I was surprised, . . . considering that what was said was inconsistent . . . [for] it is admitted that the rhetorician is incapable of making a wrong use of rhetoric and unwilling to do wrong. Now, by the dog, Gorgias, it will need no short discussion to settle satisfactorily where the truth lies. (460 a–461 b)

This clever collapsing of several arguments into a state of confusion can be defended on logical grounds (D 220), but we should note that Socrates plays on the ambiguity between what 'the rhetorician' as a genus ought to be, and what the student of rhetoric whom Gorgias referred to hypothetically would be who 'makes a wrongful use of this faculty'. The genus cannot be equated with one of its species.

At this point, with Gorgias reduced to silence, the young Polus takes up the case for rhetoric, and Socrates instantly changes tack. Where he had seemingly humoured the distinguished public figure and allowed him to blunder into traps of his own making, now he allows himself to be cross-questioned by Polus, which might suggest that his opponent has seized the initiative. Yet Polus is shown to be so inept in dialectic (Socrates even has to put questions into his mouth) that Socrates can exploit his opponent's ineptitude to deliver his most scathing attack on rhetoric. He 'presents a definition of rhetoric', as Irwin says, 'embedded in a fairly elaborate taxonomy of genus and differentiae, and showing none of his usual hesitation' (I 7): the hunt is up. It is obviously a carefully prepared speech, which makes nonsense of Plato's claim elsewhere as to the superiority of spoken over written argument, for this arraignment has not just emerged spontaneously from Socrates' pate. Whether written down or not, it is prepared, not spontaneous. Rhetoric is said to be not a *technē* or 'art', as Polus had claimed in his treatise on rhetoric, but 'a kind of routine. . . . One that produces gratification and pleasure' (462 c). The hidden link between this passage and the earlier discussion is Gorgias' insistence that the rhetorician will always succeed 'in front of a crowd', a point to which Socrates will revert. Here Socrates introduces cookery as an analogous 'routine', with the same goals, both being 'part of a not very reputable activity', demanding a mind that is good at guessing what people want, namely *kolakeia*, a word usually translated as 'flattery' (462 c–463 a). But, as Dodds writes, 'the Greek term applies to a wider range of actions and also carries a more emphatic implication of moral baseness', the kind of 'time-serving opportunism which panders to public taste instead of trying to educate it' (D 225). Furthermore, rhetoric is said to be merely an *empeiria*, an 'empirical knack', having no rational principle or *logos*, and hence no scientific status as a *technē*. (As we will see later, these dichotomies do not correlate very successfully.) Socrates now offers a long, carefully thought-out, and wholly destructive division of the human arts (464 b–465 e), employing another inclusive/exclusive dichotomy. Regarding

the mind and body there are four genuine arts, and four
spurious ones, namely:

	Genuine Arts	Spurious Arts
Body:	Gymnastics	Cosmetics
	Medicine	Cookery
Mind:	Legislation	Sophistic
	Justice	Rhetoric

The four spurious arts are controlled by *kolakeia* (now
personified as the agent of temptation), who, 'having no
thought for what is best, . . . regularly uses pleasure as a bait to
catch folly and deceives it into believing that she is of supreme
worth' (464 d). Plato has thus opened up another yawning
dichotomy, reiterated in Socrates' statement that each of these
impersonations of a genuine art 'aims at what is *pleasant*,
ignoring *the good*' (465 a; my italics). This dichotomy is further
reinforced by Socrates' claim that if the false and the genuine,
'cookery and medicine', for instance, 'were not investigated and
distinguished by the soul, but the body instead gave the verdict,
weighing them by the bodily pleasures they offered', then 'all
things would be mingled in indiscriminate confusion' (465 d).

Polus is not allowed to take up any part of this harangue, but
every reader may, indeed must do so if the case for rhetoric is
not to go by default. Plato denies rhetoric any involvement with
virtue or 'the good', that is, 'what humanity really desires'
(D 228). One can simply deny this premiss, and argue the
opposite. The orator, just as much as the philosopher, we could
say, will and must support causes that may be unpopular with a
section of the community, or indeed with all of it, since he
knows or believes it to be in their better interest. He has a case
to argue, and may possess just as much of 'the forthright
integrity of word and act practised by Socrates' which, as Dodds
puts it, forms the positive pole opposing *kolakeia* (D 225). The
reinforcing claim, that if the mind (of the philosopher,
evidently) did not investigate and distinguish as Plato's has
done, we will be plunged back into the time described by
Anaxagoras when 'chaos existed before the intervention of *nous*'
(D 231), is merely an attempt to pressurize the reader into
agreement, and may be rejected too, as a *non sequitur*.
Rhetoric, we must counter, has a legitimate claim to a position in

society and within education—a subject strikingly omitted by Plato—and does not automatically endorse corruption or injustice.

Polus, having been bullied and chivvied along by Socrates (466 a–b) and denied any comment on this indictment, is then made by Plato to revert to Gorgias' earlier claim that rhetoric gives its user 'the power to convince people by your words' (452 d–e). Are not public speakers, what we would call politicians (*rhetores*: D 194), Polus insensitively asks, 'most powerful in the cities? . . . Do they not, like tyrants, put to death any man they will, and deprive of their fortunes and banish whomsoever it seems best?' (466 c–d). Once again Plato has sabotaged the defence of rhetoric by giving its proponent an outrageous claim. Gorgias was merely inept, but Polus is amoral, putting orators and politicians in the role of being able to do wrong at their pleasure. We note the cunning with which Plato makes all three of his rhetors invoke the power of rhetoric (Gorgias: 452 d; Polus: 466 bc; Callicles: 483 cd, 488 cd, 492 b), and take that power to imply a good for the rhetor, namely the maximizing of their own desires (see Irwin on 491 e–492 a, 500 ab). But of course he has crudified the argument, for the power traditionally ascribed to rhetoric was not the un-scrupulous power of the tyrant, autocrat and voluptuary at once, but the power to influence decisions in open meetings. What is actually a mark of democracy—which Plato abhorred—is turned by him into an attribute of tyranny.

Having incriminated rhetoric good and proper, Plato now sends Socrates off at an apparent tangent, denying that in fact such speakers do what they want, but only what seems good to them, an 'apparently senseless distinction', as Dodds puts it (D 232), which baffles and enrages Polus. With this tactic Socrates can take the initiative and develop his own beliefs that power is 'something good for its possessor' (466 b), and that only 'good' actions are willed (468 c). The working-out of Socrates' paradox is complex, turning as it does on a shift in the meaning of 'good', and modern editors are indispensable guides to this long digression (D 235–54; I 141–62). The core of Socrates' argument is the claim that 'to do wrong'—by now inescapably associated with the power of the *rhetores*—'is the greatest of evils', greater than to suffer wrong (469 b). Polus replies that 'many men who do wrong are happy', citing—unfortunately, once again, for rhetoric—the example of Archelaus the Macedonian tyrant, who enjoys great prosperity despite his terrible crimes (470 d–471 d). To Socrates, however, 'education and justice' are the only criteria to judge a person's happiness, for 'the man and woman who are noble and good I call happy, but the evil and base I call wretched' (470 e).

The discussion only makes full sense when set in the wider context of Plato's philosophy, and the reader concerned with the discussion of rhetoric may wonder where the conversation is leading, that is, towards what hidden goal Socrates is working. The turning-point comes when 'Polus admits that doing wrong is "uglier" or less admirable (*aischron*) than suffering it (474 c 8), while still maintaining that to suffer wrong is "worse" (*kakion*)' (D 248). As Dodds says, this position proves fatal to Polus' case, for 'it amounts to divorcing the "right" from the "good", morality from the true interest of the individual' (D 249). As a wider study of Greek ethical concepts has shown, Polus represents 'the confusion of values existing in Athens at this period'.[8] Yet, although Polus is muddleheaded, Socrates' refutation 'seems to turn', as Dodds puts it, 'merely on the ambiguity of the word *ophelimon*', beneficial, taken by Polus in the sense of '*beneficial for the community*', but applied by Socrates to mean '*beneficial for the agent*' (D 249). Socrates uses the equivocation for his own victory here, as he later exploits the ambiguity of *kakon* as referring to either the community or the agent (D 252). Such verbal tricks may be a way of using the Sophists' tools against them (D 249), but they seem to reduce the contest to a farce.[9] The real point of the excursus finally emerges

[8] A. W. H. Adkins, *Merit and Responsibility. A Study in Greek Values* (Oxford, 1960), pp. 266–9.

[9] Adkins notes that 'Polus goes down almost without a fight', his mistake lying 'in the agreed definition' of *kala*, good things, as being so termed 'either because they are pleasant, *hēdu*, or because they are beneficial, *ophelimon*'. It is interesting that Adkins feels so moved by the lacunae in the argument exploited by Socrates that he writes the reply which Polus should have been allowed to give: 'Polus *may* agree that there is a reason why *kala* are so termed; but to Socrates' suggestion as to the nature of that reason he should have replied: "No, Socrates. I maintain that the reason that *kala* and *aischra* [shameful things] are so termed is that people in general conspire to do so. Admittedly in the past *aischron* has generally been used to decry military, social, and other failures, and *these* situations do exceed their converses in the amount of pain or harm caused to the person who experiences them; but there has recently been a considerable

when Polus is forced to agree that the 'most unhappy man' is
the one 'who is afflicted with evil and does not get rid of it'.
Now Socrates can turn the tables on his second opponent:

SOCRATES. And is not this just the man who does the greatest wrong
and indulges in the greatest injustice and yet contrives to escape
admonition, correction, or punishment—the very condition you
describe as achieved by Archelaus and other tyrants, orators, and
potentates?

POLUS. It seems so.

(478 e–479 a)

In his earlier assertion of the power of the *rhetores* Polus had
unwisely linked orators and tyrants (466 d). The pairing comes
back to him like a boomerang, but now 'the Athenian politicians
(*rhetores*) are invidiously sandwiched between tyrants and
dunastai' (D 256). *Dunastaia*, as Dodds shows, represents 'group-
tyranny, and as such is opposed to the rule of law': the rule of
the Thirty Tyrants is described as a *dunastaia* (D 295). All such
men of power, according to Socrates, avoid punishment or cure
by 'providing themselves with money and friends'—of course!
—and 'the highest attainable powers of persuasive rhetoric'
(479 c). And so, to finally polish off Polus, and Gorgias, Socrates
asks 'what great use is there in rhetoric?' and answers his own
question (this is the rhetorical figure *anthypophora): Rhetoric 'is of
no use whatever . . . for the purpose of defending *one's own guilt*
or that of his parents or friends or children, or his country *when
guilty* . . .' (480 a–b). I have italicized the qualification that
Socrates has smuggled in, one that Polus is too dazed to notice.
Yet, although Socrates did not deign to use it, we must retort
that rhetoric can also defend an innocent person, or one
unjustly accused, and 'to be wronged is undesirable even to
Socrates (469 c)': (D 259). But such commonsensical objections
seem flat and irrelevant when put side by side with the state of
righteous indignation into which Socrates now works himself,
saying that rhetoric is truly only useful to expose one's own
misdeeds, and visualizing an inescapable series of consequences

extension of usage, and I see no reason why the criterion of 'pain or harm'
should be held to apply to all cases. That, Socrates, is what you have to prove: it
would be folly if I were to admit it without a struggle." ' (ibid., p. 267.) But Plato
will not grant him that much intelligence.

following such a self-denunciation: 'evil . . . guilty deeds . . . worthy of flogging . . . the lash . . . imprisonment . . . bonds . . . fine . . . exile . . . death' (480 c–d). This is indeed to use rhetoric against rhetoric, to wish it to perform its own destruction, and doing so even down to the verbal detail of putting that self-laceration into the form of the rhetorical figure *auxesis* (moving from a lesser term to a greater), with emotion-inducing repetition. By a kind of grotesque, parodic extrapolation, Socrates urges that 'Rhetoric is of service for such purposes' as conniving with someone to escape punishment for robbery or murder, 'in defiance of God and man', and helping him to 'live forever in his wickedness', but that it is of no use 'for a man who does not intend to do wrong' (480 e–481 b)—that is, by the association established, one who (like Socrates) does not wish to take part in Athenian politics. One can only admire the ingenuity and vehemence with which Plato derives this grotesque account from Polus' failure to counter Socrates' inimitable dialectical tricks and fallacies. The spectator concerned with Dame Rhetorique, as a medieval poet might put it, will be wondering, is there no one in Athens who can defend her?

At this point Callicles, the third and last interlocutor, enters the fray. As Dodds has shown, Callicles represents an anti-democratic attitude with which Plato fundamentally sympathized (D 13 f., 267, 350). Callicles scorns the people—'a rabble of slaves and nondescripts' as he calls them—'who are of no earthly use except for their bodily strength' (489 c), yet he is committed to the Athenian political system. Socrates' case against him is that Callicles is 'in love with two objects . . . the Athenian demos and Demos, son of Pyrilampes' (a fortuitous parallel between names allows Plato to pun rhetorically from one to the other). And the object of his love determines the lover's whole behaviour, Socrates alleges:

Now I notice on every occasion that, clever though you be, whatever your favourite says and however he describes things to be, you cannot contradict him, but constantly shift to and fro. In the Assembly, if any statement of yours is contradicted by the Athenian demos, you change about and say what it wishes, and you behave much the same towards the handsome young son of Pyrilampes. For you are incapable of resisting the words and designs of your favourite . . . (481 d–e)

His infatuation with Demos, the son of Pyrilampes, is obviously a special case, but to Socrates Callicles is otherwise a typical representative of the politician in a democracy.

Callicles' answer, in a long speech (482 c–486 c), in which he is allowed to set out his personal beliefs in a form that will ultimately damn him, is to defend his brand of politics and to attack philosophy. He introduces the distinction between *physis* and *nomos*, 'nature and convention', which he sees as 'antagonistic to each other' (482 e), in order to argue that convention imposes restrictive moral laws formed by people who are too weak to realize their own desires. But Callicles soon illicitly equates 'nature' with 'desires', and hence with power. In order to defend their weaker state against 'the stronger, who are able to overreach them', he claims, the law-abiding weaklings frame social attitudes condemning such 'seeking the advantage' as wrong, shameful, and unjust. Callicles, putative representative of the *rhetores*, knows that 'nature herself makes it plain that it is right for the better to have the advantage over the worse, the more able over the less', and envisages a man 'endowed with a nature sufficiently strong' to burst these fetters of convention and law (483 a–e). (We are not surprised to learn that Nietzsche was attracted by this section: D 387–91.) As for philosophy, he says, it is a suitable occupation in one's youth but unfit for a grown man or a gentleman (484 c–d, 485 a–486 a), and shameful in the way it opts out of public life. The philosopher 'is doomed to prove less than a man, shunning the city centre and market place, in which the poet has said that men win distinction, and living the rest of his life sunk in a corner and whispering with three or four boys' (485 d). Self-excluded from society, philosophers won't know 'the language they should use in their business associations both public and private with other men' (484 d), and will be at a disadvantage in practical affairs, unable to 'contribute a useful word in the councils of justice, either to help another or themselves if unjustly accused' (486 a–c).

Although Callicles' invocation of the language needed for survival in public life will ultimately lead us back to rhetoric, Plato has now brought the dialogue to its real subject, the rival claims of politics and philosophy to represent the good life. The switch to this topic has been signalled by quotations from the famous debate in Euripides' lost play *Antiope* between Zethus the herdsman and his brother Amphion, a musician, representing the public and the retired life, respectively. Socrates has already affirmed his rejection of politics as practised in Athens (473 e–474 a), and at the end of their encounter Plato will allow Socrates to resolve the debate, in favour of philosophy (526 c). What is at stake, he reminds Callicles, is 'the noblest . . . of all inquiries'—so rejecting Polus' claim that rhetoric is 'the noblest of arts' (448 c)—namely, 'what a man should be, and what he should practise and to what extent, both when older and when young' (487 e–488 a). The goal is to discover

what kind of life one should live, the life to which you invite me, that of a 'real man', speaking in the Assembly and practising rhetoric and playing the politician according to your present fashion, or the life spent in philosophy. (500 c–d; 492 d)

Given that 'there are two such lives distinct', their task, Socrates proposes, is 'to distinguish between them, . . . to consider in what way they differ from one another and *which one should be lived*' (500 d; my italics): from dichotomy to monism again. We should regard the closing part of the dialogue, then, as an exercise in epideictic rhetoric, a *laus philosophiae* accompanying a *vituperatio politicae et rhetoricae*.

Socrates premised his discussion with the statement that, unlike politics, philosophy is not 'unstable', nor at the whim of its favourites (482 a), and he briefly outlines his own beliefs (508). Otherwise his energies are devoted more to the destructive part of the contract, denigrating Callicles' way of life by exposing its values as corrupt. We may agree that his values are debased, but not that they are innate to rhetoric. Socrates first attacks Callicles' immoralist equation of the good with the powerful, showing that both nature and convention agree 'that justice means equal shares, not excess' given by right to the stronger (489 a–b). Then he refutes Callicles' belief that 'anyone who is to live aright should suffer his appetites to grow to the greatest extent and not check them', using 'courage and intelligence . . . to satisfy every appetite' (491 e–492 a). Whereas Callicles believes that 'luxury and intemperance' are true 'virtue and happiness' (492 a) Socrates soon makes him see the shocking consequences of such a belief (494 c–e), and agree that temperance and self-control are true virtues. Having downgraded hedonism as a way of life, Socrates now reminds Callicles of his previous conversations with Gorgias and Polus, in which rhetoric was said to be one of those spurious routines designed to give pleasure, those purely empirical and 'unscientific' knacks that are 'preoccupied entirely with the pleasure' of body and soul 'and how it may be achieved—but as to which pleasures are better or worse, this they have never considered, their sole concern being to gratify these pleasures' in the practice of *kolakeia* (500 e--501 c). Only philosophy can distinguish between the 'better' and 'worse' pleasures (500 a, 503 d, 510 a). The devaluation of pleasure, we see, has had several goals.

Now, finally, we return to rhetoric, as the tool of politics. But before getting there, Plato builds up his case by indicting other analogous activities that indulge in gratification, namely music and drama. Callicles is made to agree that 'flute playing . . . conforms to this type, pursuing our pleasure only, with no thought for anything else', likewise playing the lyre (501 e). As for the dithyrambic poet, Socrates asks, is he 'in the slightest concerned with saying anything likely to *improve* his hearers, or merely what will *gratify* the mob of spectators?'—the rhetorical question requires no answer. And 'tragic drama', too, she is out 'merely to *gratify* the spectators', rather than 'if there be anything pleasant and charming, but evil, to struggle against uttering it, but [instead] to declaim and sing anything that is *unwelcome but beneficial*, whether they like it or not' (502 b; my italics). As Irwin notes, 'here the tragedian is said to ignore what *benefits* his audience; previously artists were said to ignore what *improves* the audience. As usual, Socrates seems to identify the two criticisms' (I 212). Either way, tragedy, too, can be dismissed as a *kolakeia* or gratification of the consumer. Poetry, finally, being 'a kind of public address', is by definition 'rhetorical', and represents 'a form of rhetoric addressed to a people composed alike of children and women and men, slaves and free'—experienced readers of Plato will recognize the disapproval contained in that itemization of the indiscriminate nature of its audience[10]—and thus constitutes 'a form which we cannot admire, for we describe it as a kind of flattery' (502 c–d).

Callicles, who has long since ceased to be an independent judge of the proceedings, says 'Evidently' and 'Certainly' at the appropriate moments, which is all that the defeated interlocutor in the Platonic dialogue needs to do. We are more surprised that E. R. Dodds, besides explaining what Plato means, has attempted to defend him on this score. Plato's attitude, he writes, represents a 'widely held opinion'; there are bits in Euripides where we suspect him of playing to the gallery (as usual, this great dramatist becomes a butt); tragedy 'shares with rhetoric its subservience to the whims of the *dēmos* and its incapacity to distinguish between "good" and "bad" pleasures'; Socrates' complaint about the tragic dramatists is 'that like the politicians they pander to the prejudices of an ignorant audience', namely the Athenian theatre festival, 'with its unselected mass audience and its competitive system', where judges were 'exposed to mass suggestion, even at times to intimidation' (D 320–2). That so great a scholar, and such an acute critic of drama as Dodds[11] could have gone along with Plato here shows, perhaps, the continuing prestige of philosophy over literature in classical circles. Yet the corpus of Greek tragedy surely gives the lie to all these accusations. There could be no better tribute to the critical intelligence of the Athenian audience than the plays that Aeschylus, Sophocles, and Euripides wrote for it. The Greek tragedies may not distinguish between 'good' and 'bad' pleasures in the same way that Plato's philosopher would, but few works have ever equalled their discrimination of evil and destructiveness in human behaviour, and few have responded with such

[10] Irwin notes: 'Tragedy, unlike other forms of rhetoric, is not addressed to the parts of the free adult male population who are present in the Assembly or the courts, but to all citizens and non-citizens in Athens' (I 212). In another context Sir Karl Popper quotes the passage from the *Republic* (562 a–563 b) in which one sign of the 'democratic city athirst for liberty' and developing the 'anarchic temper' out of which tyranny can arise, the 'height of all this abundance of freedom', is 'when slaves, male as well as female, who have been bought on the market, are every whit as free as those whose property they are' (Popper 1966, pp. 42–3). Imagine going to a poetry performance and having to sit next to a slave!

[11] See his excellent edition of Euripides' *Bacchae* (rev. edn., Oxford, 1960), and *The Greeks and the Irrational* (Berkeley and Los Angeles, 1951).

compassion to suffering, or affirmed human dignity in the face of power and oppression. [12] The student of rhetoric may feel very glad that Plato wrote this 'digression', as Dodds calls it, in which he 'has simply taken the opportunity to point out in passing that his condemnation of rhetoric applies equally to certain other types of public performance' (D 320). If there are to be two opposed sides, and two only, then we are happy to be aligned with tragedy, poetry, and music.

At this point Socrates switches back to 'the rhetoric addressed to the Athenian people and other free peoples in various cities', insinuating that these orators also do not try to 'improve' the citizens but merely to 'gratify' them, both 'neglecting the common good for their personal interest' and 'treating the people like children, attempting only to please them' (502 d). Then he goes on to attack the Four Men and, as we have seen, the whole structure and conduct of Athenian politics. Now we can see how Socrates has arrived at his utterly jaundiced view of rhetoric, politics, and 'other types of public performance'. This whole diatribe derives, or so I think, from Plato's mis-interpretation of the true nature of communication between an individual and an audience. If, like Aristotle, we distinguish three elements, speaker, speech, and audience (which we could divide into public and private), Plato imagines that the goal of public communication is solely to please the audience, whereas dialectic, as practised by Socrates, actually improves the interlocutor by making him reconsider his life and values. (I would not dispute this last possibility: what an uncomfortable— if beneficial!—experience it might be to be cross-questioned by Socrates.) The nature of the audience, then, is used to determine the whole nature of the communication, and to downgrade public address. Such a speaker, Plato suggests, will have no programme of his own other than what the audience wants to hear; he will have no integrity, readily adapting his ideas to the whim of the audience—as Socrates accuses Callicles of doing before the Assembly (481 d–e). Of the three goals later given to rhetoric, to move, to instruct, and to please, Plato grants it only the last; and since his philosophy takes such a wholly negative view of pleasure then rhetoric, too, is degraded to the level of gratifying the baser appetites.

[12] See Vickers 1973, especially pp. 70–96, 438–89.

In the Athenian democracy, as Plato sees it, the politician who wishes to succeed is reduced to the level of adapting himself to the prevailing power, that is, the *dēmos*. Socrates now develops a tendentious argument by imagining the case of a 'savage and illiterate tyrant' who has gained power in a city. Anyone who wishes to succeed there must imitate the tyrant's likes and dislikes, even though he may become 'depraved of soul and ruined through his imitation of his master, and through his power'. At this point Callicles protests that, given the realities of power, whoever refuses to identify with such a tyrant is likely to be killed or have his property confiscated (510 b–511 a). Socrates then embarks on a disparaging and apparently unrelated analogy between rhetoric and 'the skill of a ship's pilot'—which also saves lives, and is, moreover, an 'unpretentious and orderly' art, and inexpensive—but unexpectedly draws the discussion back to the subject. As Dodds says, 'the "tyrant" with whom Callicles must identify himself is suddenly revealed as none other than the Sovereign People whom Callicles despises as much as Socrates' (D 350). If a man chooses to live his life 'by assimilating himself to the type of government under which he lives', then, Socrates tells Callicles, 'you must become as like as possible to the Athenian people, if you are to be dear to them and wield great power in the city' (512 e–513 a). The *technē* which 'will win you great power in the city' is not one of words but of deeds, namely self-transformation, or in this case self-degradation. Power will only come if 'you resemble its government', indeed 'You must not be a mere imitator, but must bear a natural resemblance, if you are to effect a genuine friendship with the Athenian demos' (513 a–b). Hence, 'whoever makes you most resemble these'—the author of some new rhetorical *technē*, perhaps, such as the one parodied by Swift, 'The Art of Lying in Politics'—'will make of you the kind of statesman and rhetorician you desire to be' (513 b).

Politics is thus another form of *kolakeia*, the politician pandering to the people being their *kolax* or lickspittle, their 'servant' in the ignominious sense that Plato attaches to the word here (517 b). Politics is seen as one of the 'servile and menial and illiberal' arts, its practitioners being 'servants who cater to our desires', rather like a *kapelos*, a retailer or petty trader. Plato's 'contempt for the Athenian politicians is bitingly expressed in the comparison with the *kapelos*: in return for power they serve the public with the goods it wants, and the customer is always right'. In this way Callicles' accusations (485 b–c) are flung back at him, for 'it is not the philosopher whose occupation is "servile" and "unfit for a gentleman", but the politician, who must cringe like a servant or shopkeeper' (D 361). Socrates has vindicated his own form of life, and, he thinks, demolished that of Gorgias, Polus, and Callicles. In the mythical 'Vision of Judgement' that closes the dialogue, where souls are examined after death and sent either to Tartarus (hell) or to the Isles of the Blessed, the judge consigns all those guilty of luxury and incontinence to 'the prison house' (525 a). Not having lived the life of Plato's philosopher, a grisly fate awaits them, which our author contemplates with some satisfaction.[13] Occasionally, however,

> the judge sees another soul, that has lived in piety and truth, that of a private citizen or any other—but in especial, I maintain, Callicles, the soul of a philosopher who has applied himself to his own business and not played the busybody in his life—and he is filled with admiration and sends him forthwith to the Isles of the Blessed. (526 c)

Socrates does not explicitly state what becomes of the politicians and rhetoricians who have 'meddled' in politics, but his silence on this head gives greater force to his concluding exhortation 'that we should avoid every form of flattery', and that rhetoric 'should ever be so employed to attain justice' (527 b–c). When dichotomies have been used as remorselessly as Plato's have, it is only necessary to mention one pole, and rely on the other resonating in the reader's mind.

The separation between philosophy and rhetoric in the *Gorgias* is almost total. The single exception seems to be the passage where Socrates describes how, 'with his eye on' lawfulness, justice, and temperance, 'our orator, the good and true artist, will bring to bear upon our souls the words he utters and all his actions too' (504 d). This might seem to open the possibility of a truly ethical function for rhetoric, but I agree with Dodds that its real implication is to affirm that the only true

---

[13] Terence Irwin comments: 'Plato takes a rather unattractively malicious pleasure in depicting the incompetence of the unjust and unphilosophical man (often identified) facing the life after death; cf. *Tht.* 174 a–176 a' (I 248).

rhetor in Athens is Socrates himself (D 330). Or, as Irwin puts it, 'someone becomes a "true rhetor" only in so far as he abandons rhetorical techniques, and simply prescribes what is needed whether or not it is palatable' (I 215)—that is, gives up rhetoric as a verbal art for philosophy, viewed as 'medicine for the state'. The two ways of life are not just 'distinct', as Socrates says on several occasions, they are 'distinguished' or 'divided' into two antithetically opposed and mutually exclusive options. Like the Pythagorean upsilon, the Y that symbolized the choice of life, such as that faced by the young Heracles, to take one path means to exclude yourself from the other.[14] This use of binary categories to privilege one pole and exclude the other is Plato's favourite weapon throughout the *Gorgias*, and reference to Dodds's notes will show the extent to which Plato either invented new antitheses or pushed them farther than any Greek had done before. The distinction between knowledge and opinion is 'formally drawn for the first time in Plato' at 454 e (D 206). In Socrates' distinction between genuine arts ministering to the body or mind and their spurious imitations (463 e–466 a), Dodds describes 'the most important element' as being 'the distinction of principle which Plato draws between "scientific" and "unscientific" procedures. . . . It is one form of that distinction between being and seeming, inner reality and outward appearance, which runs through the whole of the dialogue from this point' (D 227). The distinction is between a *technē* (based on a rational principle) and an *empeiria* (discovered by trial and error), which seems to have been coined for this occasion. 'The sharp antithesis between the two terms appears nowhere in the Hippocratic corpus; it is typically Platonic, and is probably due to Plato himself' (D 229). The other binary opposition underlying the whole dialogue is between mind and body, and again Plato innovated: 'the sharp Platonic antithesis between mind as the dominant and body the subject part of man appears here perhaps for the first time' (D 231). The distinction —and the superior valuation of the mind—recurs many times, indeed 'Plato never tires of restating' it (D 252).

[14] See Robert Joly, *Le Thème philosophique des genres de vie dans l'antiquité classique* (Brussels, 1955); Erwin Panofsky, *Hercules am Scheidewege und andere antike Bildstoffe in der neueren Kunst* (Leipzig and Berlin, 1930); and Vickers 1985, Introduction, pp. 1–6.

The real function of these antitheses, I suggest, is less neutral classification than polemical discrimination. The terms are not just differentiated but ranked as superior and inferior, good and bad. As mind is to body, so is virtue to pleasure. Those who follow *hēdonē* will end up in Tartarus; lovers of *aretē*, as Plato defines it, will go to the Isles of the Blessed. Callicles, exponent of *hēdonē*, initially believes that the proper use of courage and intelligence is not to repress the passions but to gratify them (491 e–492 a). Socrates shows him that virtue consists in 'not indulging in pleasure but battling against it' (513 d). It follows that all the arts that seek to 'gratify' the audience rather than 'improve' them (501 e–502 d)—music, poetry, tragedy, rhetoric —are to be battled against. Callicles also sets nature or *physis* above *nomos*, convention or even law (482 e–484 a), 'a fresh weapon of formidable destructive power', as Dodds puts it, which Callicles uses for consequences that 'go beyond anything known' in Greek thought before that point (D 263). Yet this is Callicles' antithesis, not Plato's—or at least not used for this end— and Socrates subsequently refutes it (D 337), just as he mocks Callicles' use of the word 'manly' to upgrade politics and downgrade philosophy (484 c–485 e; 500 c). Callicles thinks in sharp antithetical categories, like Plato, only unfortunately they happen to be ones that would favour his brand of politics.

Terence Irwin has also noted the frequent use of antithesis in the *Gorgias*, and reference to his commentary will show that the dichotomies all have in common the privileging of philosophy and the rejection of rhetoric.[15] Irwin also brings out the violence

[15] See Irwin's edition, pp. 120 (Socrates claims that dialectic 'benefits' man, while rhetoric merely brings 'pleasure'), 130 (*empeiria*/*technē*: 'the two are not always opposed' elsewhere in Greek), 132 (rhetor out for his own interest, not the people's), 132–3 (spurious/genuine), 133 (body/soul), 134 (impersonated/ real), 135 (arts with a *logos*/without), 140 (craft/knack), 150 (Socrates says that 'Polus is well educated in rhetoric, but not in what matters', namely dialectic), 169 ('Plato implies that Socrates' values allow him the kind of integrity and self-respect in his attitude to others which Callicles can never achieve'), 183 ('the insistence on sincerity is no doubt meant to distinguish dialectic' from rhetoric and eristic), 190 (self-indulgence/self-control), 232 (soul/body, and their respective benefits), 233 (science/pseudo-science), 237 ('ruling' and 'serving' crafts), 240 ('the real political craft'), 241 ('really practising politics'), and 244 ('Socrates claims that the conditions which Callicles praised as virtues . . . are treated as vices, and "dishonoured" in the afterlife'). Plato tried to privilege dialectic, setting it above rhetoric and eristic (the practice of disputation on specious grounds, or 'fighting with words'), but, as Richard Robinson commented, 'the reason why Plato constantly pillories eristic and distinguishes

to logic or consistency often made in Plato's attempt to force such distinctions, as when 'the various techniques of flattery are said to "impersonate" crafts, or "dress themselves up" as crafts': 'But surely Socrates is wrong to say that cookery pretends to offer healthy food. Children or foolish people may not know the difference between tasty or enjoyable food and healthy food, but surely adults know the difference . . . ?' (I 134). Again, Socrates mentions two objections to rhetoric: '(1) It is shameful because it aims at the pleasant without the best. (2) It is not a craft because it offers no "rational account", *logos*, and cannot give the "cause" or "explanation" of its treatment.' Irwin objects:

But Socrates has not shown why there cannot be an 'Art of Rhetoric' explaining why each rhetorical device is the right one to use to persuade different audiences in different conditions. He apparently thinks that the concern of rhetoric with pleasure disqualifies it from being a craft. But why is that? (I 135)

Objection sustained, we reply, noting how the forks of two binary categories have become muddled here. Sir Karl Popper comments on another binary opposition central to the *Republic*, where 'Plato divides his ruling caste into two classes, the guardians and the auxiliaries, without elaborating similar subdivisions within the working class . . . [because] he is interested only in the rulers'. Additional 'pressure can be secured by emphasizing and widening the gulf between the rulers and the ruled. The stronger the feeling that the ruled are a different and altogether inferior race, the stronger will be the sense of unity among the rulers'.[16] Weakening one pole strengthens the other.

it from dialectic is that in truth his own dialectic very closely resembled eristic': *Plato's Earlier Dialectic* (Oxford, 1953), p. 85. H. I. Marrou has synthesized other scholarly work to show that *technē* and *epistēmē* were interchangeable terms in fifth-century Greece and beyond: 'Les arts libéraux dans l'antiquité classique', in *Arts libéraux et philosophie au moyen âge* (Montreal and Paris, 1969), pp. 5–27, at 6–7. It follows that Aristotle's rehabilitation of rhetoric as a *technē* gives it the status of *epistēmē*, which Plato denied it.

[16] Popper 1966, pp. 46–7. For further analyses that bring out binary oppositions see ibid., pp. 74–5, 78, 80, 82, and 84–5 on the 'fundamental metaphysical dualism in Plato's thought'. Popper lists the main dichotomies in Plato's logic, mathematics, epistemology, ontology, cosmology, ethics, and politics. They are not neutral distinctions, it seems to me, but value judgements posing as neutral distinctions.

Binary oppositions were extremely common in Greek thought, of course,[17] but their function in Plato's hands is to relegate rhetoric to the inferior, the lowest possible category. It is spurious; a mere routine. It ministers to the base end of pleasure; connotes degrading flattery of the audience; perverts justice and integrity; will not be rewarded in the afterlife. It must be clear by now that Plato is not using these binary oppositions in a heuristic, exploratory way. They may masquerade as logical or value-free categories, but they merely reflect, and enforce, a prejudice. The real target is Athenian politics, but rhetoric is put in the same boat, and sunk without trace.

II

My analysis of the polemical and prejudiced attitudes in the *Gorgias*, which inevitably reduce its claims to be taken seriously as a work of philosophy, may be dismissed as a partisan reply from the camp of rhetoric. But the most recent commentator on the *Gorgias*, Terence Irwin, author of a full-length study of Plato's thought,[18] has given the text perhaps the most rigorous sustained scrutiny it has ever received, and if we extract from the dense mass of commentary some of his recurring criticisms of Plato's methods of argument the results are devastating. In his Preface Irwin states that the *Gorgias* 'is amply stocked with apparently fallacious arguments', and says that in his notes he has 'tried to say what is wrong with them' (I v). In the Introduction he draws attention to some implications of the *elenchos* form, Socrates' 'method of "cross-examination" or "refutation" ', where the interlocutor offers an account of a topic and Socrates 'presents counter-examples . . . or attacks it in some other way, until the interlocutor agrees that it is wrong' (I 1). As Irwin notes, the successful working of this method 'depends on the interlocutor's co-operation in answering sincerely and facing the consequences of his own admission' (ibid). Dialectic 'can never certify that the conclusion is beyond challenge', for the method 'rests on the agreement of the interlocutor' (I 129)—which in effect means his being outwitted

---

[17] See Geoffrey Lloyd, *Polarity and Analogy. Two Types of Argumentation in Early Greek Thought* (Cambridge, 1966).
[18] Irwin, *Plato's Moral Theory: The Early and Middle Dialogues* (Oxford, 1977).

by Socrates. Yet, as Irwin candidly notes, 'it is sometimes hard to decide whether the interlocutor's defeat shows a genuine flaw in his position, or only a mistake in his defence of it, or failure to detect an illegitimate Socratic move' (I 152). In a discussion organized on such severe conventions much will depend on the mental abilities of the interlocutors, and on Plato's handling of his personae and their arguments. 'We must decide then', Irwin writes, 'whether Plato argues soundly against each interlocutor, but also whether he is right about the logical relations between their positions, and whether he presents them in the fairest way' (I 9).

As concerns the personae, Plato may be showing historical characters, 'with their actual inconsistencies', or he may be 'trying to develop the strongest anti-Socratic case for Socrates to refute'. There is some evidence for the first of these possibilities, the information we have on Gorgias revealing several areas where his views coincide with those attributed to him by Plato. But the second aim is the crucial one for 'assessing the philosophical merits of the dialogue' if it is to 'provide a convincing defence of Socrates', since 'it does not help much if he can defend himself against foolish but historical opponents, or against straw men'. So, Irwin concludes, 'we need to ask whether [Plato] has done the best he could for each opponent', and he directs the reader to some fourteen longer notes where this issue is brought to the surface (I 10). An attentive reading of the commentary will show surprisingly many places where Irwin feels that Plato has not done his best for both sides of the dispute. Sometimes Socrates' opponents are given perfectly reasonable arguments. Thus, Irwin argues, 'we might say that Polus' distinction between the fine and the beneficial is quite legitimate, and indeed even a central feature of morality, since he sees, or at least does not deny, that we may have reason to act morally even against our own interests' (I 155). In the later dispute Callicles 'appeals plausibly' to one principle, 'plausibly denies' another (I 192), gives a 'reasonable' reply (I 194), and 'justifiably disputes' one of Socrates' assumptions (I 196).

Yet, more often, Irwin notes that Socrates' opponents have not been given the pertinent reply—Plato has deliberately withheld from them an argument that would have strengthened their case and weakened his own. In his definition of rhetoric

'Gorgias could avoid some of these difficulties by saying more exactly how rhetoric is a craftsman of persuasion. He might distinguish the formal and material elements of a convincing speech. . . . Now Gorgias might say . . .', and so the note goes on for a long paragraph as Irwin finds himself, like other readers of Plato, adducing further or better arguments for the characters (I 117). 'Gorgias might defend himself here by pointing to an ambiguity' in Socrates' 'claim that the rhetor is more persuasive than the doctor "about the healthy" ' (I 124). 'A rhetor might claim' a different argument (I 124); Polus 'could withdraw his agreement to [Socrates' assumptions] without any further inconsistency in his position' (I 146); Polus is not allowed to 'challenge the Socratic Paradox, which has so far been accepted with neither challenge nor defence' (I 159); Irwin notes 'several ways for Polus to avoid Socrates' conclusion' (I 168). As these comments accumulate we realize that Plato never allows the defenders of rhetoric to engage Socrates on equal terms. Even if Gorgias or Polus had made the concession to conventional scruples of which Callicles accuses them at 482 cd, Irwin writes, 'he could still have blocked the rest of [Socrates'] argument' (I 179). The fact that Callicles 'does not exploit' a line of argument open to him (I 177) makes us wonder whether it might have damaged Plato's case. At times interlocutors agree with Socrates for no apparent reason (I 125, 185), or fail to see a possible reply (I 197, 206). The puppets are kept well under control.

This withholding of intelligence or keenness from Socrates' interlocutors is something that any critical reader of Plato will have noticed. What is more surprising is the number of times Irwin has to indict the Socrates of this dialogue for inadequacies of argument. The faults itemized include lack of clarity, ambiguity (often deliberate), inadequate reasoning, illegitimate inference, and unjustified or unacknowledged assumptions. At least a dozen times Irwin finds the basic sense or implication of an argument to be 'unclear' or 'vague', or both:[19] 'like many others who talk vaguely of the effects of moral degeneracy, Socrates does not make his diagnosis very clear, or support it with the evidence it needs' (I 239). More damagingly for the

---

[19] See Irwin's edition, pp. 130, 150 (twice), 178 (twice), 221, 226, 249 (twice), and no doubt elsewhere.

thrust of Plato's argument in the later stages, 'Socrates is never clear about how this ideal of a moral and political craft is to be realized; for he offers no clear account of happiness showing how it requires justice; and without such a clear account of its goal, in "undisputed" terms (cf. 451 d), the political craft cannot begin' (I 240–1). One form of unclarity, even more frequent in the *Gorgias*, is ambiguity. Sometimes, as Dodds noted, Plato uses ambiguity for his own purposes, playing off the second sense (the rhetorical figure *syllepsis*). Gorgias says that rhetoric is about *logoi* in the general sense of 'what is spoken or thought', but in his reply 'Socrates plays on the suggestion that *logos* must be *rational* discourse, and later rejects the claim of rhetoric to be about *logoi* in this sense, saying that it is "irrational", *alogon*, 465 a' (I 114). More common are cases where the ambiguity is not intentional but a sign of confusion or inconsistency in argument,[20] often at crucial stages. Irwin breaks down Socrates' argument that doing injustice is more evil than suffering it (475 c) into seven stages, and notes that three of them are ambiguous, bearing two or more meanings, and a fourth becomes ambivalent in consequence. This may seem accidental but Irwin detects design, for the 'failure to disambiguate' three of the stages 'can easily make the premises seem plausible and the argument seem valid; and Socrates may well be sliding between the two readings of the ambiguous steps' (I 157–8). A certain manipulation of the evidence is not beneath Plato in his campaign against rhetoric.

Judged by the canons of consistency or coherence the argument of the *Gorgias* is found lacking, amazingly enough, in some fifty places. Irwin shows that one position in Socrates' argument 'does not follow' from what preceded it (I 143, 185, 213); some arguments are 'not valid' (I 135, 235), or 'misleading' (I 145); others involve an 'illegitimate' inference (I 127, 146, 170, 203) or an 'illicit substitution' (I 135). Socrates is 'wrong to infer' a certain point (I 141), is 'inconsistent' in his reasoning (I 145, 191, 228), 'has no right to' a conclusion (I 146, 245), gives a 'poor' explanation (I 128), fails to make the necessary logical connection (I 248). He simply 'has not shown' that his

---

[20] For instances of intentional ambiguity see ibid., pp. 165, 198, 223, 235; for involuntary ambiguity see pp. 134, 139 (both at crucial stages in the argument), 140, 144 (leading to further inconsistencies), 158, 184, 216, 230, etc.

arguments hold up (I 158, 236, 249, etc.), has failed to find the proper criterion (I 163, 165), has defined premises inadequately (I 166), has 'wrongly conflated' arguments (I 178, 216), has identified positions that are different (I 221), has 'grossly over-simplified' the issue (I 246), has 'confused' different virtues (I 218), and is in general 'careless' (I 222). He claims that a previous opponent has agreed with him, when this is demonstrably not so (I 208, 229), and he several times 'does not mention difficult cases; he sticks to those cases where his principle looks plausible' (I 159, 163–4, 225). Sometimes a reply 'is stated in deliberately paradoxical terms—and, we will find, over-stated' (I 137): a degree of over-kill can be detected. In one place 'Socrates' actual conclusion is unjustifiably strong, [for] a weaker conclusion is all he needs for his main point—as we often find in the dialogue' (I 146).

The crime that Plato commits even more frequently is to allow Socrates to make unjustified assumptions: Irwin notes this on some eighty occasions.[21] This would be a serious enough failing in any discourse that purports to be closely argued, but the frequency here is so great that it testifies once again to the intensity of Plato's desire to put rhetoric down, once and for all. The positions taken for granted by Socrates are often key ones, concession of which effectively hamstrings rhetoric's defence. Gorgias argued that the rhetor will be more persuasive on certain issues among the non-expert than an expert would be, thanks to his gifts of persuasion. So at 459 c

Socrates now suggests that the rhetor makes himself appear to know more than the expert, which Gorgias has not so far conceded. Socrates must assume that the rhetor can persuade his audience only by appearing to know more than the expert. But this assumption is dubious. Why could a rhetor not appear to know the *relevant* facts, even though in general the expert knows more about the subject? Or why could the rhetor not be more persuasive because he appeals vividly and powerfully to people's feelings? Socrates ignores this possible reply, as though the only successful persuasive device could be the appearance of knowledge; see 465a. He makes the rhetor appear a suspicious

---

[21] See, e.g., pp. 111 (2 instances), 113, 115, 119 (2), 124 (2), 126, 127(2), 128, 129, 142 (4), 143, 144 (4), 145, 146 (2), 160 (2), 161 (2), 162 (3), 164, 166, 167, 168 (2), 170, 188 (4), 196, 199, 200, 209 (3), 213 (2), 216 (2), 217 (3), 218 (2), 219, 220 (4), 224, 225 (4), 229 (2), 233, 236, 239, 245, 248, 250; no doubt I have missed some occurrences.

character with a false pretence to knowledge; but why is any such false
pretence needed? (I 123–4)

—Because it is in Plato's interest to paint rhetoric as black as
possible, we reply.

The forms taken by these unjustified assumptions highlight
another tactical feature of Plato's control of his personae.
Socrates is frequently allowed to assume fundamental
principles, or conditions of method and procedure, without
bringing them into the open for discussion and agreement. In
other words, he makes up the rules as he goes along. So he
relies on conditions which are not explicitly stated (I 135); he
takes a term in a wider sense than his interlocutor had meant
(I 115, 188); or he proposes restrictions in the ordinary meaning
of the words like 'want' or 'good', restrictions that he nowhere
justifies (I 141, 142, 144–5), in which tactic he sometimes presses
'ordinary language too far' (I 162). He conceals his own
assumptions (I, 144, 222), ignores his own distinctions (I 202),
does not explain what he means by such key terms as
'education', 'justice', or 'injustice' (I 148, 228, 238), or the
relation between 'being just and doing unjust actions' (I 167),
and he offers 'no argument for some of the most disputable
assumptions used in reaching [a] conclusion' (I 146). Polus 'has
not challenged these assumptions', indeed time and again the
modern commentator finds Socrates' interlocutors meekly
accepting positions which have never been argued, even the
highly controversial Socratic Paradox that knowledge is
sufficient for virtue (I 159). Polus 'concedes more than he needs
in saying that injustice' is 'bad for me': 'Polus has been driven to
agree that somehow it *is* bad for me, but Socrates has not
explained how' (I 160, 161, 162). Callicles 'remarks neither on
the tacit acceptance of Socratic assumptions in the argument nor
on the danger of fallacious inference' (I 170). Although 'the
initial claim against Gorgias is supposed to be proved', there are
'many unanswered questions' (I 226–7).

Plato, we can only conclude, manipulates the interlocutors,
denying them the right to challenge Socrates when he begs the
question or uses words and ideas in some private sense not
disclosed to them. What he might gain as a philosopher, or at
any rate as someone 'arguing for victory', he loses as an artist,

for we cease to respect a writer who has to reduce Socrates'
opponents to straw men. Something must be wrong with a case,
we feel, that needs to be protected so solicitously. Indeed, closer
examination of some sequences will show that Plato has loaded
the scales heavily in his own favour. In the first encounter
Socrates argues that 'the rhetor produces conviction resulting
from persuasion, not the reasoned conviction that a teacher
would produce, and hence is not a teacher'. As Irwin rightly
asks, 'Is this necessarily discreditable to the rhetor?' (I 118–19).
As we know from other Platonic dialogues dealing with the
Sophists, Gorgias disclaimed any power to teach virtue, other
than the 'virtue' or power of speaking (Meno, 95 c, 71 e, 73 a–c).
As Irwin says, 'Gorgias does not promise to "teach virtue" in the
sense of making people virtuous', merely to 'tell his pupils
the sorts of things that are just and unjust. Learning this and
acting justly or being just are, for Gorgias and for most people,
two very different things; it is Socrates who holds the beliefs
which imply their identity.' That is, Socrates assumes that 'virtue
is a craft, a systematic, rationally teachable body of knowledge',
which will not fail to be effective, and Gorgias is never allowed
to challenge that assumption. So that when Socrates accuses
Gorgias of 'disharmony' in his views on the relations between
rhetoric and justice, he is simply relying on

Socratic assumptions. The 'disharmony' is between Gorgias' views and
Socrates' views, not internal to Gorgias' views. Socrates might say that
Gorgias' views are disharmonious, given the Socratic assumptions he
has left unchallenged. But this reply shows only that the Socratic
assumptions still need defence. (I 126–8)

This judgement also applies to the later part of the dialogue,
where Socrates indicts the rhetors of Athens for having failed to
make the people virtuous. Since they never claimed to be able
to make the citizens just, they 'need not be surprised at their
injustice; only Socrates' ideal rhetors and politicians will claim to
make people just' (I 239).
Readers of Plato become used to commentators and editors
pointing to parallel passages in other works which help to clarify
a specific point, or show how the system hangs together. This is
perfectly correct practice, but in treating the corpus as a system

it overlooks the fact that the interlocutors in the actual dialogues do not have access to this material. They are out there, under a plane-tree or in a private house, subjected to Socrates' cross-questioning, a disconcerting process at the best of times, but made harder by this practice of concealing assumptions or taking other parts of the system for granted. Some crucial issues, although clear to us with our annotated editions, remain opaque to them, and they are easily discomfited. So at one point 'Polus misidentifies Socrates' false move' (I 128), giving Socrates the chance to score some points off him, while Socrates later misrepresents Polus' arguments (I 152). Callicles is not allowed to 'provide an amended account' of what he has said so as to answer Socrates' objections (I 174), for the dialectical method must sweep forward. 'While Socrates successfully ridicules Callicles' at 490 c, 'he does not show that he has himself adequately considered the questions of distributive justice' (I 189), although he assumes the rightness of his own position. The largest assumption of all is the Socratic Paradox, that knowledge is sufficient for virtue, which is taken as read from its first appearance at 468 ab, and provides an occasion for further assumptions (I 143, 167, 188, etc.). But, as Irwin shows, Socrates fatally compromises his own argument by recognizing non-rational or 'good-independent desires'—that is, bodily appetites that are intemperate or insatiable—and therefore advocating self-control (I 191, 195, 208), thus making temperance the primary virtue (I 220–1). The relevance of this strand of argument to his campaign against rhetoric is that throughout the *Gorgias* Plato identifies rhetoric with the desires to gain power and benefit the self by the unrestrained indulgence of desire. Yet, as Irwin points out,

Socrates' previous argument against the value of rhetoric assumed the truth of the Socratic Paradox. The defence of temperance and continence assumes the falsity of the Paradox. The conclusions of these two main lines of argument in the dialogue are never satisfactorily reconciled. (I 218)

In a careful reading, then, Plato's case against rhetoric in the *Gorgias* is based on a calculated perversion of his own principles of dialectic. We can no longer be taken in by Socrates' claim that he is pursuing the truth.

III

The *Gorgias* is one of several attacks on the Sophists, and the reader coming to this subject for the first time might now be wondering what they had done to arouse Plato's ire, and what their real views on language and philosophy were. If we turn to the *Protagoras*, and to Eric Havelock's placing of it within the 'liberal tradition' in Greek politics,[22] we can discover something of their attitude to rhetoric and public debate. In this dialogue Socrates is presented cross-examining Protagoras, Prodicus, and other Sophists, in order to elicit a definition of their activity. As Havelock summarizes the crucial passage (318 e–319 a),

I have indeed an intellectual discipline (*mathema*), says Protagoras, which consists in the 'formation' of correct decision (*euboulia*) covering the most effective management of the household, and the most capable administration of civic business and expression (in discourse). You mean, says Socrates, the political (civic) technique? Precisely, replies Protagoras. This is my professional competence. (p. 164)

'Household', there, refers to the Greeks' conception of the *oikos* as including the house, estate, family, ancestors, servants, cattle, and all the processes of rearing, guiding, and taking part in social relations that flowed from this nucleus.[23] The Sophists were concerned with the life of democracy at all levels, but especially with the democratic processes of debate and decision. Although the Athenians rightly believe that advice on technical matters should come from the experts, Protagoras says, in

[22] Havelock 1957, especially chs. 4, 7–9 (on Plato). I quote Havelock's own translations, which aim to be literal, rather than elegant. It is generally agreed, as E. R. Dodds puts it, that 'Protagoras' discourse (320 c–328 d) can be taken as a broadly faithful reproduction of views which Protagoras actually held, though certainly not as an excerpt or précis from one of his works' (*The Greeks and the Irrational* (Berkeley and Los Angeles, 1951), p. 198 n. 31). Here, at least, Plato allowed a Sophist to present the gist of his philosophy undistorted. The rhetorical practices of the historical Gorgias have been well expounded by George Kennedy (Kennedy 1963, pp. 61–8). Geoffrey Lloyd, in *Magic, Reason and Experience* (Cambridge, 1979), pp. 79–102, usefully discusses the contribution of rhetoric to the development of Greek science, noting in passing that in his *Helen* Gorgias recognizes "the negative or destructive possibilities of persuasion", whereas Plato makes him "claim the superiority of rhetoric to all other arts precisely because it is unconcerned with the truth and confines itself to . . . persuasion" (p. 84 n.).

[23] The best introduction to the Greek concept of *oikos* remains Moses Finley, *The World of Odysseus* (New York, 1954; rev. edn. Harmondsworth, 1967).

politics there are no 'experts', for everyone takes part (322 d–323 c). When the Athenian, or any other democracy, reaches

> the stage of forming joint decisions in the field of civic excellence—a process which wholly involves righteousness and temperance—with good reason they tolerate any man's voice, it being axiomatic that every man properly partakes in this excellence as a condition of cities existing. (p. 169)

As Havelock says, 'these are memorable words', forming 'a reasoned defence of democratic process as it obtained in the mother of all democracies', and is one of only three such utterances in classical literature (p. 170).

Protagoras goes on to expound the Sophists' attitude to social morality (323 c–324 a), which the citizen learns by growing up in a family and community, where *mores* condemning immorality and impiety as anti-social are passed on from one generation to the next by custom, or *pragmata*—that is, 'things that happen or that you do' (p. 228). Rather than endorsing Plato's a priori theories of how society ought to be, the Sophists study it as it is. They believe that virtue must be shared by all citizens if the state is to exist (324 e–327 b), and that 'the right and the lawful' are not topics reserved to an élite class of philosophers, but are open to all: 'everyone is so zealous in the cause of the right and the lawful, ready to speak and give instruction to everyone else about them' (p. 185). Nor does Sophistic education elevate the teacher, putting the pupil 'at an intellectual disadvantage', for 'either side can ask questions and expect answers' (p. 212). In discussion the Sophist exercised a similar equality, being ready, as Socrates puts it, sympathetically for once (329 b), to 'pose a question and then wait while the answer is given and taken in' (p. 210). The same spirit of balanced exchange marks their theory of parliamentary debate, where conflicting ideas are put before an assembly which makes a collective decision accepted by all parties as binding. As Plato allows Prodicus (another Sophist taking part in the dialogue) to say (337 a–b), those listening to a discussion must divide their attention between two speakers impartially, but then vote for the wiser course, in a spirit of good will: 'Debate on the one hand is characteristic of amicable relationships involving good will; contention on the

other is of mutually irreconcilable relations between enemies'
(p. 217).

To the Sophists rhetoric was less an arsenal of verbal devices
than a process of interaction in which the norms of justice and
social order were worked out by those taking part. For them, as
Havelock puts it,

discourse is social or it is nothing; its topics and problems are by
definition common ones, group notions; the words of men act on other
men and vice versa. There is an exchange of opinion, alteration of
opinion, discovery of common opinion, consensus and decision. It is
not a discourse carried on in the private soul. (p. 193)

The word 'opinion' emphasized there refers to *doxa*, the term so
irrevocably downgraded by Plato's evaluation of *epistēmē*. The
Sophists' whole political theory is based on the premiss that the
opinion of the people constituting a democracy is to be treated
with respect, granted seriousness and dignity. The audience will
vote, having listened to both sides and made up their mind,
because they have the ability—utterly denied them by Plato—to
take part in a learning process, forming a commitment involving
'an intellectual conscience', answerable for its decisions (pp.
219–20). So *doxa* becomes a collective view which absorbs the
opposed arguments and transcends them in a judgement
accepted by all parties. In Havelock's words, 'when the debate is
conducted properly neither side wins an exclusive victory'—
unlike Socratic dialectic! Belief in the open-ended nature of
democratic discussion meant that

Sophistic distinguished between power which used sheer force as its
instrument, and that power exercised in free assemblies, which has to
rely on the effects of communication, and therefore on consent. . . .
Persuasion, in short, is the art of leadership in a free assembly [where]
the act of persuasion, to be effective, must engage at some level with
the minds of those being persuaded, for they do the voting and
make the decisions. (p. 248)

The dialectic between persuasion and force recurs in Plato, as
we shall see, but in a much more repressive form.

    At almost every point in that brief exposition of the Sophists'
views on politics and rhetoric—which will be extended by the

discussion of Isocrates in the next chapter—Plato's views were diametrically opposed to theirs. Their virtues of flexibility, pragmatism in a good sense—working with things as they are— and realism about the existence of conflict in any group, with the need to find a system that will allow it expression yet contain it by an agreed political procedure—these seemed to him a dereliction of the philosopher's duty to improve society by reference to a metaphysics of Forms, eternal verities lying beyond time and space. Yet Plato does not simply accept this fundamental difference as given, as a more tolerant thinker might have done, nor record the Sophists' ideas in their own social and cultural context. As Havelock shows so effectively— and here the parallels with the *Gorgias* become clear—Plato not only judges their philosophy in terms of his own but presents it in those terms. In his politics the formation of political decision relies on the expert, who can discipline his soul and bring it 'into contact with formal laws, cosmic and moral', eternal verities apprehended in a form of self-dialogue—a total remove from the democratic negotiation of consensus. From the outset the two systems are alien, and Plato exploits this incompatibility to his own advantage. For

the problems set by Plato in his dialogues for the Sophists to solve, or to fail at solving, are Platonic questions to which sophistic was not equipped to give an answer; and quite properly so, because it did not ask them. If therefore sophistic is, so to speak, put in the witness box and allowed only a yes or no to the questions selected by the prosecuting counsel, it is likely to stutter and mumble. It is not being allowed the privilege of speaking its own language, nor of addressing itself to those specific questions which sophistic considered important, though Plato did not. (pp. 167–8)

In just the same way, in the *Gorgias*, rhetoric was allowed to make a token statement of its goals before Socrates treated it with such withering contempt.

    In playing off his system against its rival Plato exploits, in both dialogues, the technique of engineered discord between argument and setting. Where Protagoras has defined his 'discipline' as the study of the 'formation of correct decision' in the family as in the state, that is, 'political technique', Plato immediately transfers these principles 'into a non-political context'. Socrates' question, 'is virtue teachable?', in effect 'foists an alien context—the educational—upon an original system of ideas which was sociological' (p. 168). Socrates' question implies a more intellectual conception of virtue.

The question meant: Is there an independent scientific procedure for formulating and communicating this (Platonic) excellence of man? To this kind of problem Protagoras never addresses himself. For him, human excellence is not a conscious science but a conditioning. The Platonic problem would be meaningless to him. That is why his answers are made to seem so ineffective. (p. 178)

Just as Irwin noted Plato in the *Gorgias* setting up a calculated 'disharmony' between Gorgias' views and Socrates' views, so here the Sophist is made to seem incompetent in terms of Platonic assumptions and Platonic method. Plato gives us an account of his opponents' philosophy which is sufficiently detailed and close enough to its actual content as to make it seem reliable, yet he does so in such a way as to rob the original of its validity. The reader moves through the pages of the *Protagoras* 'carefully conducted within the framework of ideas and problems postulated not by sophistic but by Socratic logic' (p. 195). The result, as every reader can report, is disastrous for Protagoras, who is led by Socratic 'guided thinking', denied the chance to formulate his own position in his own terms, and made a target for ridicule. 'Sophistic is allowed to present itself only as it fails to meet Socratic requirements', so that Protagoras' desire 'to preserve ambiguity and flexibility and the like is made to appear as a failure of mental precision' (ibid.). His 'qualifications look pretty lame and muddled when they are made to strike their heads against the unyielding structure of Socratic logic' (p. 200). In just the same way Gorgias, Polus, and Callicles were disposed of. We might apply to their account of rhetoric Havelock's comment on Protagoras' system, that it was not 'confused until made to appear so by the use of formal logic' (p. 201). Context determines meaning.

In the Socratic *elenchos*, as we have seen, argument continues until the interlocutor concedes the issue. The privileging of this mode of discourse, and the discrediting of longer speeches, is carried out with even more force here than in the *Gorgias*. Having written a long speech for Protagoras, Plato then (328 d–

329 a) undermines it by making Socrates mock him and other 'public men', such as Pericles, who have 'adequate powers of expression' to make long discourses, but when asked a question on a specific point merely 'echo back like a brass gong that goes on booming till you stop it' (p. 190). Socrates makes many speeches just as long when he wants to, of course, or longer, but the law of these dialogues is that anyone else who does so can be mercilessly mocked. (Much of the *Protagoras* is narrated by Socrates himself, who interlards his report with passages describing his opponents' discomfiture. As soon as one starts to ask if the 'report' is fair, the fiction of the Platonic dialogue collapses.) A few pages later he plays this trick even more blatantly, protesting that he cannot remember long speeches (334 c), so cancelling any effect that the paragraph describing the Sophists' economics might have had by representing it as 'a lapse into rhetoric'—rhetoric and fee-taking being 'the two characteristics of sophistic which Plato continually exploits as though they were the essentials' (p. 206). Plato uses another tactic to pursue 'the antithesis between Platonism and sophistic, at the expense of the latter', seeming to dramatize 'something which sophistic has to say' but in fact presenting the views of Platonism. Thus 'the former is reported through the medium of the latter and suffers refraction in the process' (p. 207). The *Gorgias* applied a similar technique to rhetoric.

Socrates' continued insistence that Protagoras should take part in the 'proper' dialectical method (334 c, 335 b, 336 a, 336 c) appears to invite an open-ended conversation, with a real exchange of opinion. But in fact, as Havelock shows, this involves a form of discourse having quite different rules:

(1) the requirements laid down are restricted to the conduct of an interrogation, not that of a dialogue;
(2) the rules prescribed are restricted in purpose, being designed to control the respondent, not the questioner;
(3) replies must be confined strictly to the point raised by the previous question;
(4) they must be as brief as humanly possible;
(5) the purpose of numbers 3 and 4 being to maintain the strict continuity of the questions asked. (p. 209)

That seems to me the definitive exposure of the hidden rules of

Socratic dialectic, and explains the sense one has of it as a constrictive system. As Havelock rightly says, the questioner thus gains complete control of the discourse, which is neither 'a conversational method, nor a genuine exchange of ideas', which was in any case never intended. Throughout the whole of Plato's dialogues 'a genuine conversational handling of serious ideas between equal minds is not to be found' (p. 209). The only kind of thinking they allow is 'dogmatic thinking', knowledge being passed on from the learned to the ignorant or deluded. A further trick is that the respondent's ideas 'can be reduced to apparent self-contradiction by the device of getting each of them reworded in terms of the questioner's own principles' (ibid.)— as was done in the *Gorgias*, with the added element of those principles being silently assumed. The confusion is not inherent in the system Plato is attacking, but is created by Plato's way of presenting it.

The much-vaunted Platonic dialectic begins to look like an opportunistic debating method. On the questioner's side, the advantage of restricting the answers to brief replies

is to allow the Platonic system of ideas to be broken up and developed step by step in logical series. That is to say, the questions could just as well be statements, so far as content is concerned, but by requiring answers the questioner provokes a series of interruptions to indicate the rungs in the ladder which he is climbing. (p. 210)

The respondent is in effect a necessary foil who is made to look a fool. He guarantees the 'correctness' of each step, but always at his own expense, for every stage tells against him. Thus Protagoras is made to speak of the practice of 'holding dialogue' (335 a) in terms of competition (as did Gorgias), *agon* being a perfectly acceptable word in ancient Greece for any form of competition, including oratory. Socrates then makes this seem a superficial attempt to evade the Socratic terms for holding a dialogue, but 'the real reason is that Protagoras requires the condition of a genuine discussion conducted on a fifty-fifty basis' (p. 215).

Every aspect of Socratic dialectic is alien to the Sophists' conception of *logos* as open-ended verbal exchange, in small groups or public assemblies, where the outcome depends on the judgement of the hearers. Havelock judges that Plato's dramatization of the Sophists' theories of language is 'partly confused and partly disguised in order to cast over all of them a colour of irresponsibility, shallowness and irrelevance to Socratic aims and principles' (p. 216). In addition, Plato parodies parliamentary procedure (which the Sophists did much to regularize), mocks debates (pp. 216–17), giving one of his fictionalized Sophists a 'laboured artificiality of style' (p. 217), another a ridiculous habit of mixing metaphors (pp. 225 f.). He 'satirizes the institution of chairmanship which had been devised to assist assembly procedure' (p. 226), and ridicules the Sophists' appeal for Pan-Hellenic unity based on an idea of 'man's common nature and brotherhood and world citizenship', a dismissal which Havelock finds hard to forgive (pp. 224–9). Plato also creates the very influential myth of Sophistic rhetoric as 'concentrating on the speakers at the expense of the audience' (p. 221), and reduces 'speaking on either side of the question' to a sign of irresponsibility and demagoguery (p. 240). The distortion that occurs when 'positions occupied by one school of thought are reported in terms of the premisses of another' (p. 244) has probably fixed the Sophists' unfavourable image for ever. Yet, as Havelock rightly says, rhetoric was to them merely 'ancillary to a bigger thing, a larger view of life and man altogether', involving a sense of 'social and political responsibility'. They were not interested in 'the authoritarian leader', even less in 'the practice of unscrupulous persuasion upon the blind emotions of masses of men'. What really exercised them were 'those complex processes and subtle currents of judgement which go to the making of the collective mind and the group decision' (p. 230). The gap that Plato opened up between their system and his own is undeniably there, but it does not render them worthless, and the virulence with which he denigrated their aims and methods goes far beyond the justification of philosophy, into some obsessive need to eliminate rivals.

IV

Plato's hostility towards rhetoric and the Sophists, most fully expressed in the *Gorgias* and *Protagoras*, never died out, although towards the end of his life it took some strange forms.

In *Theaetetus*[24] the *bios* or way of life of the philosopher is opposed to that of the rhetorician as lawyer. Whereas the philosopher has been trained as a free man, Socrates claims, and 'always has time at his disposal to converse in peace at his leisure' (172 c–d),

The orator is always talking against time, hurried on by the clock; there is no space to enlarge on any subject he chooses, but the adversary stands over him ready to recite a schedule of the points to which he must confine himself. He is a slave disputing about a fellow slave before a master sitting in judgment with some definite plea in his hand, and the issue is never indifferent, but his personal concerns are always at stake, sometimes even his life. (172 e)

This is an amusing, if exaggerated account of the constraints of time, place, and argument within which a lawyer operates, having to keep one eye on the *klepsydra,* the water-clock. But the disparaging description of everyone involved in law as a 'slave' heralds the ethical criticism, Socrates' account of the effect this way of life has on the lawyer's character:

Hence he acquires a tense and bitter shrewdness; he knows how to flatter his master and earn his good graces, but his mind is narrow and crooked. An apprenticeship in slavery has dwarfed and twisted his growth and robbed him of his free spirit, driving him into devious ways, threatening him with fears and dangers which the tenderness of youth could not face with truth and honesty; so, turning from the first to lies and the requital of wrong with wrong, warped and stunted, he passes from youth to manhood with no soundness in him and turns out, in the end, a man of formidable intellect—as he imagines.

So much for the orator.   (173 ab)

With such a devastating account of the opposed discipline there seems little point in enquiring about its justice, and none in complaining of prejudice. One can always enjoy the comparison as a superb piece of epideictic rhetoric, setting praise against blame, *laus* against *vituperatio*.

The philosophers' life is free, of course, from any taint of business. They 'have never known the way to market place or law court or Council Chamber or any other place of public assembly; they never hear a decree read out or look at the text of

[24] The translation is by F. M. Cornford, repr. in Plato 1963.

a law' (173 cd). As in the *Gorgias* (526 c) Plato describes with proud approval the philosopher's state of 'not interfering' (*apragmosunē*), contrasted with political activism, or 'doing many things' (*polupragmosunē*).[25] Unconcerned with business or politics, the philosopher holds aloof because

> it is really only his body that sojourns in his city, while his thought, disdaining all such things as worthless, takes wings, as Pindar says, 'beyond the sky, beneath the earth', searching the heavens and measuring the plains, everywhere seeking the true nature of everything, as a whole, never sinking to what lies close at hand. (173 e)

His lack of concern with the social or mundane means that the philosopher may look ridiculous when he appears as a speaker in a court of law (172 c), where his clumsiness arouses laughter. But of course his weakness there is really a sign of strength: 'he cannot engage in an exchange of abuse for, never having made a study of anyone's peculiar weaknesses, he has no personal scandals to bring up' (174 c). His real superiority appears when such questions as 'justice and injustice' arise, or 'the meaning of kingship and the whole question of human happiness and misery' (175 c). In all this field, 'when that small shrewd legal mind has to render an account, then the situation is reversed'. The lawyer is 'lost, dismayed and stammering', and 'will be laughed at by everyone whose breeding has been the antithesis of a slave's' (175 d). What began as a metaphor for the lawyer as a 'slave' of business has been turned into a fact of slavery, or at least invested with all of an aristocrat's contempt. And so Socrates sums up his antithesis:

> Such are the two characters, Theodorus. The one is nursed in freedom and leisure, the philosopher, as you call him. He may be excused if he looks foolish or useless when faced with some menial task, if he cannot tie up bedclothes into a neat bundle or flavour a dish with spices and a speech with flattery. The other is smart in the dispatch of all such services, but has not learned to wear his cloak like a gentleman, or caught the accent of discourse that will rightly celebrate the true life of happiness for gods and men. (175 d–176 a)

[25] See Irwin's edition, p. 247, and V. Ehrenberg, '*Polupragmosunē*', *Journal of Hellenic Studies*, 67 (1947), 46–67; A. W. H. Adkins, '*Polupragmosunē* and Minding One's Own Business', *Classical Philology*, 71 (1976), 301–27; and L. B. Carter, *The Quiet Athenian* (Oxford, 1986).

So much for the lawyers, those menial flatterers, incapable of abstract thought, corrupted by their practice of vilification and abuse! Although Plato's animus against rhetoric is brilliantly formulated, to the non-prejudiced reader a defence of philosophy which elevates itself by such a denigration is itself suspect.

From dismissive mockery Plato now turns to warnings. As in the *Gorgias*, Socrates contrasts this world with the next, urging us to 'make all speed to take flight from this world to the other, . . . becoming like the divine so far as we can', uniting righteousness with wisdom. This course is set against the world of appearances, where it is enough to seem good, but where all 'forms of seeming power and intelligence in the rulers of society are as mean and vulgar as the mechanic's skill in handicraft'. With a flurry of antitheses setting the 'divine . . . perfection of righteousness' against 'godless misery' (176 a–177 a), Socrates warns politicians, rhetoricians, and anyone else involved in public life in this world of 'the penalty of injustice' that they cannot escape. If such men do not 'rid themselves of their superior cunning, that other region which is free of all evil will not receive them after death, but here on earth they will dwell for all time in some form of life resembling their own and in the society of things as evil as themselves . . .' (177 a). For Plato there can be no worse fate than to spend eternity in the company of men devoted to the public life of the *polis*! But not all need suffer this dreadful fate, Socrates adds charitably; some might be lucky enough to be disabused by his *elenchos*. For

when you get them alone and make them explain their objections to philosophy, then, if they are men enough to face a long examination without running away, it is odd how they end by finding their own arguments unsatisfying. Somehow their flow of eloquence runs dry, and they become as speechless as an infant. (177 b)

That is the ultimate triumph of Platonic philosophy: it will deprive rhetoric of utterance, reducing it to silence. Later in the dialogue Socrates returns to the attack, mocking a 'whole profession' that exists 'to prove that true belief is not knowledge', namely that practised by

those paragons of intellect known as orators and lawyers. There you have men who use their skill to produce conviction, not by instruction, but by making people believe whatever they want them to believe. You can hardly imagine teachers so clever as to be able, in the short time allowed by the clock, to instruct their hearers thoroughly in the true facts of a case of robbery or other violence which those hearers had not witnessed. (201 a–b)

Within the familiar dichotomy of *pistis* (conviction) and *epistēmē* (knowledge), Plato reverts to the charge made in the *Gorgias*, of the impossibility of truly instructing the jury in the short time available. But is this the task of the rhetor?

In *Theaetetus* the use of binary oppositions to dismiss rhetoric has been largely concentrated into one passage, 'a digression', as Socrates calls it (177 b–c), which in effect constitutes a piece of epideictic rhetoric resembling a *synkrisis* or formal comparison. In *Phaedrus*[26] the binary method is all-pervasive. The first part of this dialogue, as we have seen, presents three formal speeches, starting with Lysias' sophistic argument that a young man wooed by two men should surrender to the admirer 'who is not in love with him rather than to one who is' (227 c). Socrates, in his first speech replying to Lysias, attacks any form of love dominated by desire and a longing for pleasure as leading to obsessive behaviour, jealousy, domination, exploitation, distrust, and faithlessness. Socrates' starting-point is the by now familiar distinction between pleasure, in Plato's eyes an irrational desire which drags us unavoidably towards wantonness, lust, gluttony, and other sins, and temperance, the 'acquired judgment that aims at what is best' (237 c–238 a). Socrates delivers this address forcefully enough, but is suddenly rebuked by his *daimon* for having offended the god of love (242 b–e). Even Socrates can pervert language and argument, we notice to our surprise. But, unlike his interlocutors, he is given the chance to put things right, now delivering the third speech 'in awe of love' as a purification of his offence. Yet his persuasion to love shares with the dissuasion the same organizing antithesis between virtue and pleasure, expressed in the famous myth comparing the soul to a chariot where the charioteer has to control two steeds, one 'noble and good', the other its opposite, the eternal conflict between reason and appetite (244 a–257 b).

There is 'nothing shameful in the mere writing of speeches',

---

[26] The translation is by R. Hackforth, repr. in Plato 1963.

says Socrates defensively, having completed his task, only 'in speaking and writing shamefully and badly' (258 d). The second half of the dialogue reviews rhetoric, starting with shameful speaking, as in the cynical opinion reported by Phaedrus, 'that the intending orator' does not need to know 'what is truly just, but only what is likely to be thought just by the body of men who are to give judgment; nor need he know what is truly good or noble, but what will be thought so, since it is on the latter, not the former, that persuasion depends' (260 a). That opposition between knowing and thinking, between truth and plausibility, is the basis of much of the following discussion. If the orator does not know the difference between good and evil, Socrates says, then he is liable to persuade 'a community as ignorant as himself . . . by extolling evil as being really good' (a perversion of the true role of epideictic), with disastrous results (260 c–d). The case against rhetoric here partly echoes its indictment in the *Gorgias*: it is 'no art, but a knack' (260 e), and whoever has this knack 'can make the same thing appear to the same people now just, now unjust, at will', good or evil, like or unlike (261 c–e). But, Socrates adds, the orator cannot misuse appearances in this way without deceiving himself, and therefore needs to know the truth, not appearances, else his will be 'a comical sort of art' (262 a–c).

This is a back-handed way of saying that although rhetoric as now practised is corrupt (the orator is one 'who intends to mislead another, without being misled himself'), it at least needs to know what it is talking about. Socrates then recommends the orator to learn how to define concepts which 'fluctuate in meaning' (263 a–e), to use proper methods of order, especially division (264 b–266 b), and to know the nature of the human soul, his main focus of interest (270 b–272 a). This is Plato's longest exposition of a reformed, philosophical rhetoric, which, as we have seen, inspired Aristotle to emulation. But it is still a project directed against extant rhetoric, so that, following his favourite A–B–A structure, Plato brings Socrates back to the view reported by Phaedrus 'at the beginning of this discussion', that as things now stand no 'budding orator' need bother with

the truth about what is just or good conduct, nor indeed about who are just and good men whether by nature or education. In the law courts

134 PLATO'S ATTACK ON RHETORIC

nobody cares a rap for the truth of these matters, but only about what is plausible. And that is the same as what is probable. . . . Even actual facts ought sometimes not to be stated, if they don't tally with probability.

If you wish to succeed in a legal career, Socrates advises, just pursue 'probability' and 'say good-bye to the truth forever' (272 d–e).

That antithesis is as sharply inclusive—exclusive as any Plato has used. Rhetoric may teach the plausible, but only his philosophy has access to the truth. Yet, at the end of the *Phaedrus*, Plato adds an even sharper dichotomy, setting verbal far above written communication. This is the fable of Theuth's invention of writing, attacked by Ammon (and Socrates) as an art that will inevitably destroy the memory, deny spontaneous progressive thought, fix the same ideas for ever (274 c–275 d). Here Plato means to privilege dialectic (276 e–277 a) against rhetoric or any art written down, a deconstructing manœuvre which, if carried through, would imply the destruction of all written words, including his own. However, its real point is to elevate the philosopher, who delivers 'lessons on justice and honour and goodness that are expounded and set forth for the sake of instruction, and are veritably written in the soul of the listener' (278 a)—positive pole!—over any practitioner of 'written discourse', especially one 'which aims at mere persuasion' (277 e). The man who has devoted himself to the study of truth, and is ready to acknowledge 'the inferiority of his writings', may be called a 'lover of wisdom' to designate 'his serious pursuit' (278 b–d). Then follows the matching, and negative pole:

On the other hand, one who has nothing to show of more value than the literary works on whose phrases he spends hours, twisting them this way and that, pasting them together and pulling them apart, will rightly, I suggest, be called a poet or speech writer or law writer. (278 d–e)

Terms not perhaps of abuse, but of definite and assured inferiority.

Plato's use of binary oppositions to elevate philosophy and cast down its rivals mostly involves the subject-matter and ethical nature of the disciplines involved. But the conclusion of the *Phaedrus* links up with other moments where the differentiation is made in terms of form—always, predictably enough, to the benefit of philosophy as practised by Plato. One distinction is between the question-and-answer method of dialectic, Plato's ideal instrument, and the longer, continued speeches of rhetoric, which are seen as both cumbersome and blocking access to the truth—presumably since the speaker can develop his own argument from his own premisses without having to submit to the terms of the Socratic *elenchos*. But the distinction is capable of a more aggressive formulation, as in the *Sophist*,[27] where the Eleatic Stranger defines two types of mimic, sincere and insincere, dividing up the latter category into two kinds, one who 'uses short arguments in private and forces others to contradict themselves in conversation'—here the Sophist, aping the true dialectician; the other 'who can keep up his dissimulation publicly in long speeches to a large assembly', namely—the demagogue! (268 a–b).[28] In Plato writers of speeches never appear in a good light. At the end of the *Protagoras*,[29] we recall, Socrates attacks the 'popular orators' of Athens, who deliver written-down, memorized speeches mechanically, like a gong being beaten, having nothing of their own to add (328 d–329 b). In the *Euthydemus*[30] Socrates asks Clinias, 'if we should learn the art of speechmaking', will it make men happy? He receives the expected response: no. Clinias then describes 'certain speechmakers who do not know how to use the speeches which they make themselves, like harp makers with their harps; but here also there are others able to use the speeches which the others have made, some who are themselves unable to make the speeches. It is clear then that, in speeches also, making is one art and using another.' Either way, Socrates concludes, 'the art of the speechmakers' will not bring anyone happiness, let alone make them a better human being (289 c–d).

[27] The translation is by F. M. Cornford, repr. in Plato 1963.
[28] So in the *Republic* Adimantus, as the devil's advocate speciously defending the evil man's preference for false appearances over the truth, 'seeming' over 'being', states that one way of concealing wrongdoing is given by the 'teachers of cajolery', who 'impart the arts of the popular assembly and the courtroom, so that, partly by persuasion, partly by force, we shall contrive to overreach with impunity' (365 b–d).
[29] The translation is by W. K. C. Guthrie, repr. in Plato 1963.
[30] The translation is by W. H. D. Rouse, repr. in Plato 1963.

Socrates, of course, is never guilty of the calculated manipulation of language and ethics that Plato associates with any written-out discourse. At the outset of the *Apology*[31] he makes Socrates deny being, as his accusers have claimed, 'a skilful speaker', since he tells the truth rather than speaking well (the poles are mutually exclusive), and will therefore give a 'straight-forward speech in the first words that occur to me' (17 a–c). Plato will not conceive that anyone who writes out a speech in advance can still be sincere, or trustworthy. Phaedrus, naïve in his admiration for Lysias' rhetorical skills at the beginning of that dialogue, praises the pains that the Sophist put into writing his speech—'it took him weeks to compose at his leisure' (228 c): in Plato's eyes that is precisely what disqualifies it. In the *Menexenus*[32] Socrates mocks the epideictic funeral oration for being 'an elaborate speech' made over the corpse 'by a wise man who has long ago prepared what he has to say' (234 c). An objection follows:

MENEXENUS. You are always making fun of the rhetoricians, Socrates. This time, however, I am inclined to think that the speaker who is chosen will not have much to say, for he has been called upon to speak at a moment's notice, and he will be compelled almost to improvise.

SOCRATES. But why, my friend, should he not have plenty to say? Every rhetorician has speeches ready-made, nor is there any difficulty in improvising that sort of stuff. Had the orator to praise Athenians among Peloponnesians, or Peloponnesians among Athenians, he must be a good rhetorician who could succeed and gain credit. But there is no difficulty in a man's winning applause when he is contending for fame among the persons whom he is praising. (235 c–d)

That is an acute, and amusing, comment on the nature of such occasions, where the speaker was indeed expected to expatiate on the virtues of the deceased, his ancestors, family and friends, many of whom would be present. But Plato's most telling riposte is that he now makes Socrates, claiming to be inspired by memories of his teacher of rhetoric, Aspasia, who 'made so many good speakers, and one who was the best among all the Hellenes, Pericles' (235 e), deliver an impromptu funeral oration

[31] The translation is by H. Tredennick, repr. in Plato 1963.
[32] The translation is by B. Jowett, repr. in Plato 1963.

of his own, using all the appropriate topics (236 d–249 d).
Socrates and Menexenus pay tribute to Aspasia's skill (249 d–e),
but readers are left with the interesting dilemma whether the
oration is a parody (as of Pericles' funeral oration), or meant to
be taken seriously.[33] It seems to me that the speech works
equally well either way, and really serves to show that Socrates,
like Plato, thought that he could beat the rhetoricians at their
game, any time he chose.

What Socrates does in the *Menexenus* is to copy other
rhetoricians, who 'steal away our souls with their embellished
words' (235 a). Plato usually concedes the power of rhetorical
persuasio, but sometimes reluctantly, by making it comic or
sinister. In the *Phaedrus* Socrates defines rhetoric as 'a kind of
influencing of the mind by means of words' (261 a), but says no
more on this head apart from a mocking reference to 'the mighty
man of Chalcedon' (a parodistic reference to the Sophist
Thrasymachus, cast into choryambic rhythm). Thrasymachus, he
reports sarcastically, in addition to being skilful in applying
'pathetic language to the poor and aged . . . was also expert at
rousing a crowd to anger and then soothing them down again
with his spells, to quote his own saying' (267 c–d). The 'spells'
of rhetoric also figure in the *Euthydemus*, where Socrates
ironically describes the makers of speeches as 'superwise', and
ascribes to their art

something divine and lofty. However, that is nothing to wonder at, for
it is a portion of the art of enchanters, but falls short just a little. For the
enchanter's art is the charming of adders and tarantulas and scorpions
and other vermin and pests, but this is really the charming and
persuasion of juries and parliaments and any sort of crowds. (289 e)

While that passage has provoked serious discussion of the
relationship between Greek rhetoric and magic,[34] in the context
of Plato's sustained quarrel with the art of eloquence it seems

[33] Kennedy 1963, pp. 158–64, takes it as a serious composition; most other
commentators see it as a parody. See ibid., p. 159 n., and Popper 1966, pp. 96,
197 ('that sneering reply to Pericles' funeral oration') and pp. 255–6 (n. 19), 278
(n. 48). For a recent study of the Athenian funeral oration see Nicole Loraux, *The
Invention of Athens* (Cambridge, Mass., 1986).
[34] See Jacqueline de Romilly, *Magic and Rhetoric in Ancient Greece* (Cambridge,
Mass., 1975).

another indirect insult, equating popular assemblies with 'vermin and pests', and rhetoric with snake-charming.

Yet rhetoric does work, it does have 'a very substantial power, at all events in large assemblies', as Phaedrus puts it. Socrates' response there is to invite his young friend to 'have a look at it, . . . and see whether you discern some holes in the fabric, as I do' (268 a). In the hierarchical, strictly regulated communities outlined in the *Republic* and the *Laws*, every possible hole has been blocked, for Plato gives very little space to writers of any kind, and none to critics of the established order. 'Free speech' might call the system in question, and since the poets have done just that with their fables of the gods' immorality they are to be excluded or silenced, apart from when allowed to sing hymns to the gods or use panegyric to celebrate the deeds of good men (*Rep.* 607 a). In the *Laws* encomia of topics approved by the ruling powers are permitted, all other utterances being censured (2. 662 b–664 d; 7. 801 b–803 a; 11. 937 d–943 a). As E. L. Hunt has said, Plato's 'later utopia' allowed 'no freedom of utterance', so denying rhetoric any chance to develop. 'With the dogmatism of age upon him, he laid down laws which were to be permanent. The games of children, the restrictions upon foreign travel, the denial of freedom of speech, and the enforcement of ethical and political dogmas, were all designed to protect the city against changes of any sort.'[35]

In the later dialogues Plato's whole system has become rigidly authoritarian. The rulers of his city are given total control over the citizen, including the power to use lies and propaganda. In Book Three of the *Republic*[36], after the attack on the poets for giving false accounts of the gods' weaknesses, 'neither true nor edifying to men who are destined to be warriors' (386 a), and which might make them too "sensitive and soft" (387 c), the Socrates of this dialogue recurs to an earlier part of his discussion in which he distinguished falsehood in the soul, 'the veritable lie', from 'falsehood in words'. There he had stated that verbal falsehood, although deplorable, can be 'serviceable . . . against enemies', or against friends who have gone mad, or are trying to commit a crime, when it helps 'to avert the evil—as

[35] Hunt 1961, p. 34.
[36] The translation is by Paul Shorey, repr. in Plato 1963, apart from some passages where I prefer Popper's rendering.

a medicine' (382 a–c). Gods do not need it, but since to men falsehood is 'useful as a remedy or form of medicine', then such a craft must be 'assigned to physicians' (sc. rulers) and denied to laymen (sc. citizens). With no sense of shame, Socrates declares that

> It is the business of the rulers of the city, if it is anybody's, to tell lies, deceiving both its enemies and its own citizens for the benefit of the city; and no one else must touch this privilege. . . . If the ruler catches *anyone else* in a lie . . . then he will punish him for introducing a practice which injures and endangers the city. (389 b–c)[37]

Sir Karl Popper comments that this pronouncement contradicts Socrates' definition of the philosopher as one who loves truth, and that Plato has now discovered a higher value: 'the appeal to the principle of collective utility is the ultimate ethical consideration. Totalitarian morality overrides everything, even the definition, the Idea, of the philosopher.'[38] Where Max Weber would define the state as that body which claims the monopoly over using violence,[39] Plato would add the monopoly over using lies.

The rulers of the state are its doctors, and must be prepared to prescribe strong medicine when needed, even 'to administer a great many lies and deceptions' for the benefit of their subjects (459 c). The occasion when lies are most blatantly needed is for Plato's eugenic projects, in which the breeding of future warriors will be strictly controlled to yield perfect physical specimens (414 b–415 d). Here Socrates introduces two myths, one of the warriors of the city being autochthonous, 'born of the earth of their country', the other correlating the various social classes with the metals, (gold, silver, iron, brass), in order to discourage interbreeding between classes. Socrates introduces his account of these myths by asking

> could we perhaps fabricate one of those very handy lies which indeed we mentioned just recently? With the help of one single lordly lie we

---

[37] Tr. Popper 1966, p. 138; his italics.
[38] Ibid.
[39] Weber, 'Politics as a Vocation' (1919), in *From Max Weber: Essays in Sociology*, tr. H. H. Gerth and C. W. Mills (London, 1948; 1970), p. 78: 'a state is a human community that (successfully) claims the *monopoly* of the legitimate use of physical force within a given territory. . . . The state is considered the sole source of the "right" to use violence.'

may, if we are lucky, persuade even the rulers themselves—but at any rate the rest of the city. (414 b–c)[40]

What he proposes is that

the best men must cohabit with the best women in as many cases as possible and the worst with the worst in the fewest, and that the offspring of the one must be reared and that of the other not, if the flock is to be as perfect as possible. And the way in which all this is brought to pass must be unknown to any but the rulers, if, again, the herd of guardians is to be as free as possible from dissension. (459 d–e)

In order to achieve these ends with the minimum of embarrassment Plato is not above fiddling the outcome of a lottery, as Socrates recapitulates in the *Timaeus*.[41] To get the right people together the chief magistrates 'should contrive secretly, by the use of certain lots, so as to arrange the nuptial meeting that the bad of either sex and the good of either sex might pair with their like'. Rigging the draw will eliminate quarrels, for the 'inferior man' who has been landed (or rather, bedded) with an inferior woman will 'imagine that the union was a mere accident and was to be attributed to the lot', while outstanding warriors can have 'more frequent intercourse with the women' of comparable biological excellence (*Tim.* 18 e; *Rep.* 459 e).

While finding this method of strengthening and perpetuating a ruling élite repellent, Popper is surely wrong to describe Plato's project as a 'racialism' planning '*the breeding of the master race*', thus making him a precursor of the Nazis. Plato is against mixing social classes, not races. But I agree with Popper on the connotations of the term 'persuade' here: 'To persuade somebody to believe a lie means, more precisely, to mislead or to hoax him',[42] now with the additional hope that even the ruling

[40] Tr. Popper 1966, p. 140. I agree with Popper's rendering of *gennaios* as '*lordly* lie' (Shorey has 'noble lie'). See Popper's account pp. 270–1 (n. 1), 330–1, 336–8.

[41] The translation is by B. Jowett, repr. in Plato 1963.

[42] Popper 1966, p. 140. For other passages in Plato with this association of persuasion with deception see *Republic*, 364 e, where Adimantus says that the poets ' "persuade", i.e. mislead into believing, "not only individuals, but whole cities"', that the gods will be placated by prayers and thank-offerings into 'granting remissions of sins and purifications for deeds of injustice' (tr. Popper, p. 271 n. 10, and Shorey). Popper notes the use of 'persuasion' in the sense of 'bribery' at *Republic*, 390 e–f, and to connote 'delusive opinion' (as opposed to rational knowledge) at *Rep.* 511 d, 533 e, and *Tim.* 51 d–e.

class will take this 'fiction' to be the truth. Where propaganda is normally directed against the citizens, here the state must somehow believe its own propaganda, a dangerous, indeed fatal step, one might think, from some twentieth-century instances.

Persuasion in the political context of the later dialogues is also connected, as Popper was the first to show, with force. In the *Gorgias*, we may recall, Socrates laid down that the true statesman must take the base desires of the populace and 'give those desires a different direction instead of allowing them free scope, by *persuading and compelling* citizens to adopt courses that would improve them' (517 b–c; my italics). Here, one might feel, the presence of compulsion renders persuasion redundant. Elsewhere Plato associates persuasion with deception and propaganda, keeping force in reserve should other means fail. So, in Book Two of the *Republic*, Adimantus, espousing injustice so that Socrates can define justice, apes the arguments of men who deliberately follow the path of injustice, and make sure that their wrongdoings lie hid by founding social institutions and learning rhetoric (a gross slander, one need hardly add):

For with a view to lying hid we will organize societies and political clubs, and there are teachers of cajolery who impart the arts of the popular assembly and the courtroom, so that, *partly by persuasion, partly by force*, we shall contrive to overreach with impunity. But against the gods, it may be said, neither *secrecy* nor *force* can avail. [Or, in Popper's version, 'one cannot cheat, or force the gods'.] (365 d; my italics)

Here Plato is denouncing corrupt and successful politicians for being ready to use both persuasion and force: yet in his own republic he advocates exactly the same combination. His 'law' is concerned to produce happiness 'in the city as a whole, harmonizing and adapting the citizens to one another by *persuasion and compulsion*' (519 e). We might say, then, that Plato first degraded rhetoric and then made use of it for degrading others.

In the *Statesman*[43] the Eleatic Stranger considers the case of a 'scientific legislator' who, like a doctor, knows 'what benefits society, and what hurts it' (295 e). If such a man 'discovers

[43] The translation is by J. B. Skemp, repr. in Plato 1963.

better laws than those already enacted' he is entitled to get them brought into effect, without having 'first persuaded his own city to accept them', just as a doctor who 'fails to persuade the patient' of the value of a remedy legitimately 'forces a particular treatment' on him for his own good. As with the individual body so with the state, both may be *subjected to compulsion . . . with or without persuasion'*, if the appointed authority 'does what is really beneficial' (296 a–e; my italics). Socrates (here presented as a youth) agrees to all this, and to the later sequence of division and subdivision which defines 'the precious elements which are akin to' statesmanship (303 c–e). As the Eleatic Stranger expounds them, they are three in number, 'the art of generalship, the art of administering justice, and that department of the art of public speaking which is closely allied to the kingly art. This last persuades men to do what is right and therefore takes its share in controlling what goes on in a true community' (303 e–304 a). Having elicited the agreement of Socrates that 'the art which decides whether we learn a skill or not ought to have control of the art which actually teaches us that skill', the Eleatic Stranger asks: 'Which is the art to which we must assign the task of persuading the general mass of the population by telling them suitable stories rather than by giving them formal instruction?' (304 c–d). (Presumably Plato feels that 'the general mass' cannot or should not be educated 'formally' other than by having improving myths told them, or hymns to the gods and good men, 'state epideictic', as we may call it.) Young Socrates gives the expected answer, that 'this is the province to be assigned to rhetoric', only to be questioned further:

STRANGER. But to which art must we assign the function of deciding whether in any particular situation we must proceed *by persuasion, or by coercive measures* against a group of men, or whether it is right to take no action at all?

YOUNG SOCRATES. The art which can teach us how to decide that will be the art which controls rhetoric and the art of public speaking.

STRANGER. This activity can be none other than the work of the statesman. (304 d–e; my italics)

Oratory, then, 'distinct from statesmanship, and yet its auxiliary', is openly given the task of state propaganda, while the government may decide whether or not to use force as well.

In the *Laws*,[44] that final and most authoritarian statement of Plato's views, the poets, so often rudely treated, are recalled— for propaganda duties. The Athenian, advising Clinias on how to institute his ideal city, holds that 'justice and virtue' are the greatest of goods: 'this is my teaching, and I conceive you will *persuade, or constrain,* your national poets to teach it too, and likewise to produce correspondent rhythms and scales for the education of your young people' (661 c; my italics). The 'lawgiver' knows that

the youthful mind will be persuaded by anything, if one will take the trouble to persuade it. [What a contempt for innocence this shows!] Thus he need only tax his invention to discover what conviction would be most beneficial to a city, and then contrive all manner of devices to ensure that the whole of such a community shall treat the topic in one single and selfsame tone, alike in song, in story, and in discourse. (663 e–664 c)

So 'all our choirs . . . must enchant the souls of our children, while they are still young and tender, by reciting' the 'noble doctrines' that Plato would inculcate (664 b). Yet the poets are not needed all the time. For adult society 'the actual recital of the laws will, with heaven's consent, ensure our society bliss and well-being, *in part by persuasion,* and *in part by enforced and legal correction* of characters not amenable to persuasion' (718 b; my italics).

As the Athenian pursues the goal of making the citizens 'a ready audience to persuasions to virtue' (setting aside 'utterly brutal souls') he recommends that the lawgiver, once 'he has finished the rest of his discourse to the best of his power'— presumably Plato has swallowed his objections to written discourse, unless prodigies of memorization are expected of his legislators—should then 'propound a sample' before he 'enters on his actual enactments' (718 c–d). The appointed lawmaker must not just 'tell us curtly what we are to do or not to do, add the threat of a penalty, and then turn to the next enactment, without one word of exhortation or advice to the recipients'; rather, he must add a 'prefatory statement in front of his code' (719 e–720 a). So, ironically enough, he now needs rhetoric again! To begin with 'the first stage in the creation of any

[44] The translation is by A. E. Taylor, repr. in Plato 1963.

society' marriage, and the marriage law, the law itself is uncompromisingly rigorous: a man must marry between the ages of thirty and thirty-five, or else be 'yearly mulcted in such and such a sum', and deprived of all public honours. To that bare injunction with penalty-clause Plato now adds a specimen 'persuasion to virtue'. A good citizen will do this, the state rhetorician will tell him,

> bethinking him that there is a sense in which mankind naturally partakes of immortality, a prize our nature makes desirable to all of us in its every form, for to win renown and not lie in our graves without a name is a desire [for] this. Thus the race of man is time's equal twin and companion, bound up with him in a union never to be broken, and the manner of their immortality is in this wise. By succession of generations the race abides one and the same, so partaking in immortality through procreation. Whence piety flatly forbids a man to deprive himself of the boon of his own act, as he wilfully deprives himself who takes no thought of children and wife. So him who will obey the law we will hold scatheless. (721 a–e)

Under this system, laws, 'thus *joining persuasion to menace*' might be longer than usual, but would be more effective. As it is now, the Athenian complains, the legislators in Athens have never noticed that 'they rely wholly on one instrument in their work, whereas there are two available, so far as the mass's lack of education will permit, *persuasion and compulsion*. Authority is never tempered in their lawmaking with *persuasion*; they work by *compulsion* unalloyed' (722 b–c; my italics). Plato could easily provide the persuasive element, as he has just shown by this specimen address, so identifying himself with the poets and rhetoricians who now stand ready to do the state's bidding.

Indeed, one more resource is available to the lawgiver from the rhetorician's shop administered by Plato, namely the 'preamble', which will soften up the populace. Just as 'discourse and vocal utterances of every kind have their preludes, their preliminaries, . . . which furnish a useful methodical introduction to the coming performance', so the laws should have their preambles attached, as the Athenian has just demonstrated. The marriage law was enunciated as 'unqualified law', a 'dictatorial prescription in tones' comparable to those in which a physician treats slaves, or an 'empirical injunction' delivered 'in the brusque fashion of a dictator' (720 c), not bothering to use persuasion. The Athenian's specimen invocation of the benefits of immortality, by contrast, was 'persuasive' since it had

the rhetorical character of a preamble. For I find I framed the whole of this discourse, uttered by its speaker in the tones of persuasion, to prepare the auditor of the legislator's enactments to receive his prescription, that is to say his law, in a spirit of friendliness and consequent docility. (722 e-723 a)

Here Plato reduces rhetoric to perhaps its lowest point, helping to produce a citizenry that will follow docilely the directions of its leaders.

The state not only uses rhetoric, but insists on a monopoly over it, as over violence and law. Free speech, open discussion, especially criticism of the state, are forbidden, as we might expect; but so is any attempt to interpret the laws, or speak on behalf of the accused. Towards the end of Book 11 the Athenian discusses the activity of legal orators, starting with this crushing judgement: 'Life abounds in good things, but most of those good things are infested by polluting and defiling parasites'— such as lawyers. Justice is a blessing to mankind, and advocacy ought also to be a boon. But

both blessings are brought into ill repute by a vice which cloaks itself under the specious name of an art. It begins by professing that there is a device for managing one's own [and other's] legal business . . . and that this device will ensure victory equally whether the conduct at issue in the case, whatever it is, has been rightful or not. And it then adds that this art itself and the eloquence it teaches are to be had as a gift by anyone who will make a gift in money in return. Now this device—be it which it may, art or mere artless empirical knack—must not, if we can help it, strike root in our society. The legislator will call for obedient silence in the presence of right, and departure to some other territory.

Whoever fails to obey this law, and is suspected of 'attempting to pervert the influence of justice upon the mind of a judge', or 'wrongfully multiplying suits of law', may be prosecuted 'by all who choose', and will face penalties ranging from deportation to death (937 d–938 c). Surely no Sophist, opening a school that will charge fees (as did Plato's Academy too, incidentally),[45] and

[45] As Eric Havelock notes, 'we know from Middle Comedy that Plato's Academy charged fees and high ones at that': Havelock 1957, p. 162. It seems as

penning optimistic claims for the success of his art, can have imagined the consequences when they fell under the baleful eye of the elder Plato!

Elsewhere in the *Laws* Plato conceives of 'persuasion and coercion' as being combined (711 c), or as alternatives ('either with their free consent or by a modest measure of compulsion': 753 a). But there is no doubt that he would prefer to eschew violence where possible, and rather apply persuasion to all the other ways of producing a docile and unquestioning citizen body. In the frightening passage that Popper took as an epigraph to his account of 'The Spell of Plato', the 'greatest principle of all is that nobody should be without a leader. Nor should the mind of anybody be habituated to letting him do anything at all on his own initiative', not even getting up, washing, or taking his meals unless 'told to do so. In a word, he should teach his soul, by long habit, never to dream of acting independently, and to become utterly incapable of it' (*Laws*, 942 a–c).[46]

That is one of a number of passages in Plato, as discussed by Popper, that makes one wonder about the relationship between *The Open Society* (1945) and *Nineteen Eighty-Four* (1949). Orwell's fable reads at times like the logical extension of everything that a closed society would consist of. In these late dialogues persuasion and coercion are two sides of the same weapon with which the state ensures its dominance over its citizens. Readers of Cicero will recall the two dominant modes of seizing power that he regarded as evil—force or fraud—and which Machiavelli was to recommend to would-be princes with his studied avoidance of the ethical issue.[47] It is sad to think that Plato saw

---

if Plato had one standard for the Sophists and one for himself. Havelock later comments that Plato 'revolutionized' educational methodology by 'founding an institution in which pupils were enrolled to hear lectures' for which they paid fees to the institution' (p. 214). But Isocrates had already made the transition from the itinerant life of the Sophist by founding a permanent school in Athens, one more cause of offence in the eyes of Plato and Aristotle.

[46] Popper 1966, pp. 1, 102–5, 258–9 (nn. 32–4), and 338–42 (a reply to his critics).

[47] Cicero, *De Officiis*, 1. 13. 41: 'While wrong may be done, then, in either of two ways, that is, by force or by fraud, both are bestial: fraud seems to belong to the cunning fox, force to the lion; both are wholly unworthy of man, but fraud is the more contemptible.' Machiavelli, *Il Principe*, ch. 7, holding up the deeds of the ruthless Cesare Borgia as 'a model' for 'any new prince who deems it

both as legitimate tools of the state. Here, at any rate, the Sophists were ethically superior to him, for as *Philebus*,[48] another of the later dialogues, tells us, the historical Gorgias 'regularly said that the art of persuasion was greatly superior to all others, for it subjugated all things not by violence but by willing submission' (58 a–b). Later Sophists held the same belief, as the next chapter will show.

The ultimate attraction of rhetoric to Plato, as to so many, was its power to win conviction in political life. For the Plato of the *Gorgias* rhetoric was the tool of Athenian democracy, and therefore as corrupt as its users. Now, however, in his descriptions of society as he wants it to be, it becomes a valued weapon, with which one can control 'the general mass of the population' by telling them what they ought to think, and what they should love or hate. Rhetoric is only a tool, of course, and can be abused by Plato as by anyone else. To modern readers his move from an anti-democratic to a totalitarian position can only underline, whatever the defects of its users and teachers, the value of free speech.

necessary to safeguard himself against his enemies; to win allies over to his side; to conquer either by force or by fraud . . .' (*The Prince*, tr. J. B. Atkinson (Indianapolis, 1976), p. 173).

[48] The translation is by R. Hackforth, repr. in Plato 1963.

3

TERRITORIAL DISPUTES:
PHILOSOPHY VERSUS RHETORIC

> Good philosophy will always have a place in the
> investigation of any matter of deep human importance,
> because of its commitment to clarity, to carefully drawn
> distinctions, to calm argument rather than to prejudice and
> dogmatic assertion.
>
> Martha Nussbaum[1]

While Plato's hostility towards rhetoric, expressed over a thirty-year period, was idiosyncratic and extreme, the rivalry between the two disciplines persisted just as long as rhetoric was a living force. It flared up in the second century BC; again in the first century AD, in the movement known as the 'second Sophistic'; in the Middle Ages it formed part of the recurring 'Battles of the Liberal Arts'; in the Renaissance it was largely found in the humanists' attack on scholastic philosophy; while in later periods it has been the work of individuals rather than coherent groups.[2] Rather than attempt to summarize the continuous history of this dispute (which would be a challenging subject for a book), I shall pick out three episodes that represent classical, Renaissance, and modern phases of the quarrel. One *point de repère*, inevitably enough, was Plato's attack, with which I begin.

---

[1] *The New York Review of Books*, 18 Dec. 1986, p. 52.
[2] For the dispute between rhetoric and philosophy in the classical period see Havelock 1957; Mario Untersteiner, *The Sophists*, tr. K. Freeman (Oxford, 1953); Hans von Arnim, *Leben und Werke des Dio von Prusa, mit einer Einleitung: Sophistik, Rhetorik, Philosophie in ihrem Kampf um die Jugendbildung* (Berlin, 1898), pp. 4–114; Kennedy 1963, pp. 13–23, 78–9, 83–4, 321–30; Kennedy 1972, pp. 220, 351, 502, 513, 557–8, 582–5; Kennedy 1980, pp. 16–17, 37–40, 103. For the medieval period see Abelson 1906; Paetow 1910; L. J. Paetow (ed.), *Two Medieval Satires on the University of Paris: La Bataille des vii arts of Henri d'Andeli and the Morale Scolarium of John of Garland* (Berkeley, Ca., 1927). For the Renaissance and after see E. Garin (ed.), *La disputà delle arti nel '400* (Florence, 1947); Seigel 1968; IJsseling 1976.

i RESPONSES TO PLATO

One of the targets of Plato's criticism was the Sophist Isocrates, who replied to Plato in several works, but indirectly, never mentioning him by name.[3] The works of Isocrates most relevant to the debate between rhetoric and philosophy are *Against the Sophists*, an early (*c.* 390 BC) and fragmentary account of the curriculum of his school, of which only the introduction, attacking rival teachers for their unscrupulous promises, survives (ii. 162–77); *On the Peace* (355 BC), a plea for an end to the exhausting Social War which Athens was fighting against her former allies, the Chians, Coans, Rhodians, and Byzantines (ii. 6–97); and the *Antidosis*, or 'On the Exchange' (354–53 BC). The last refers to an incident in Isocrates' life, and to the Athenian custom of 'liturgies', by which wealthier citizens bore the expense of public services. As George Norlin explains, 'anyone allotted to such a duty might challenge another to accept the alternative of either undertaking this burden in his stead or of exchanging property with him' (ii. 181). Isocrates had undergone such a trial and had been ordered to fit out a ship of war. Feeling that he had been misrepresented, Isocrates decided to publish a self-defence which would also be an *apologia pro vita sua*, an account of his life and works cast in the form of a speech for the defence which deliberately echoes Plato's *Apology* some twenty times (ii. 184–365). In many ways Isocrates modelled himself on Socrates,[4] which perhaps increased Plato's irritation, who may have felt that he himself owned all the rights in that property.

The term 'Sophist' at this time meant no more than a 'teacher' of various subjects in the new learning—oratory, literature, ethics, science. Some of his fellow-teachers, Isocrates felt, were 'making greater promises than they can possibly fulfil', so bringing the profession into 'bad repute with the lay-public'

---

[3] All quotations are from Isocrates, *Works*, tr. G. Norlin (vols. i and ii) and La Rue Van Hook (vol. iii), Loeb Classical Library (London, 1928, 1929), with title and paragraph number following the quotation in the text, and titles abbreviated as follows: *Against the Sophists: S; On the Peace: P; Antidosis: A* (all the texts I quote are in vol. ii). Other references will be to volume and page number, as ii. 290. See also the introduction to *Helen* (1–13) on the social functions of language and philosophy.

[4] See Norlin's edition i, pp. xvi ff.; ii. 28, 203 ff. (*passim*); and Kennedy 1963, pp. 179–85.

(S 1). Although Isocrates regards himself as one of the Sophists (A 220), he prefers to call his activity *philosophia* (A 270). As Norlin says, 'the word has at this time no definite association with speculative or abstract thought, signifying only a lover of wisdom or a seeker after the cultivated life, and is in fact more general and modest than the honourable title of Sophist' (i, p. xxvii)—'wise man', or 'sage'. Modesty is one of Isocrates' most appealing qualities as a teacher, for he consistently disclaims any dogmatic intent, affirming that

since it is not in the nature of man to attain a science by the possession of which we can know positively what we should do or what we should say, in the next resort I hold that man to be wise who is able by his powers of conjecture to arrive generally at the best course. (A 271)

Mankind must work with *doxa*, 'opinion' or theory, 'for no system of knowledge can possibly cover all occasions' (A 184). Thus *doxa* is redeemed from the wholly negative implications given it by Plato, and seen, in Norlin's words, as 'a working theory based on practical experience—judgement or insight in dealing with the uncertain contingencies of any human situation which presents itself' (ii. 290–1).

Isocrates underlines his lack of dogmatism in the field of ethics—as if to avoid the punishment that Plato handed out to Protagoras—asserting several times that he makes no claims to be able to make men virtuous who do not want to be so. While other teachers lack all scruples and make 'vain pretensions' to inculcate virtue (S 21; A 84), he says, 'let no one suppose that I claim that just living can be taught; for I hold that there does not exist an art of the kind which can implant sobriety and justice in depraved natures' (S 21; A 274). 'I could wish', he writes elsewhere, 'that even as to praise virtue is a facile theme, so it were easy to persuade hearers to practise it' (P 36). This is neither cynicism nor amorality, but honesty, a scrupulousness about being able to carry out what one promises. From this realistic basis Plato's criticism of 'the Four Men' for not having totally and irrevocably educated the Athenians to virtue seems groundless, and it is perhaps no accident that Isocrates several times singles out three of them for praise. In *On the Peace* he compares Aristides, Themistocles, and Militiades to their degenerate successors Hyperbolus, Cleophon, 'and those who today harangue the people' (Aristophon and Eubulus). The 'people who then governed the state were not given over to slackness and poverty and empty hopes', but were distinguished in generalship and valour, and were trusted by most of the Greek states (*P* 75–6). A year or two later he extols the 'greatness of the deeds wrought by' these past leaders, all men 'pre-eminent, not only in birth and reputation, but in wisdom and eloquence': Cleisthenes, who 'expelled the tyrants . . . and established our democratic state'; Militiades, who 'conquered the barbarians in the battle at Marathon and won for the city' much glory; Themistocles, who 'liberated the Hellenes, . . . led our forefathers . . . to leadership and power, and whó . . . girded the city with walls in despite of the Lacedaemonians'; and Pericles, who 'made the homes of the Athenians to overflow with prosperity and wealth' (*A* 306–8). Three of these figures are accused by Plato of sycophancy and greed.

Isocrates differed from other Sophists in being a staunch believer in democracy, writing in 359 that 'the honours of a free state seemed to him sweeter than those of a monarchy' (i, p. xxxviii). In celebrating the leaders of Athens' great days, then, he was also celebrating freedom of speech, and eloquence used neither for personal advantage nor flattery, as Plato alleged, but for responsible public service. In the *Antidosis*, defending civic eloquence, he writes that 'among the ancients it was the greatest and the most illustrious orators who brought to the city most of her blessings' (*A* 231). Solon and Cleisthenes, the founders of Athenian democracy, gave the people laws, constituted a government, and used oratory for the public good:

> Cleisthenes, after he had been driven from Athens by the tyrants, succeeded by his eloquence in persuading the Amphictyons to lend him money from the treasury of Apollo, and thus restored the people to power, expelled the tyrants, and established that democracy to which the world of Hellas owes its greatest blessings. (*A* 232)

Themistocles, with his 'surpassing eloquence' in the service of a shrewd tactical sense, during the Persian War 'counselled our ancestors to abandon the city' for a short time, a tactic which resulted in them becoming 'masters of the Hellenes'. Pericles, 'both a good leader of the people and an excellent orator', made

Athens so richly adorned with temples and monuments that visitors still 'think her worthy of ruling not only the Hellenes, but all the world' (A 273-4). And of all of these leaders, Isocrates writes,

> not one neglected the art of discourse; nay, so much more did they apply their minds to eloquence than to other things, that Solon was named one of the seven Sophists ['Sages', or 'wise men'] and was given the title which is now dishonoured and on trial here; and Pericles studied under two of the Sophists. . . . Could one, then, show more clearly than by these examples that the powers of eloquence do not turn men into evil-doers? (A 235-6)

Plato's identification of rhetoric with flattery and corruption is refuted by examples taken from recent history, and with none of Plato's bias; indeed historians have commented on Isocrates' reliable 'version of the facts' (ii. 259 n.).

As to the causes of Athens' subsequent decline, Isocrates locates these partly in politics, partly in the kind of rhetoric those politics produced. In political life he denounces Athenian greed, aggression, and imperial ambitions. The Athenians 'crave great possessions contrary to justice', are 'insatiate in seizing, . . . always grasping after more and so risking the loss of what they have' (P 6–7). Building a great fleet and forcing other states to pay tribute money has only produced 'hatreds and wars' (P 29). 'Mad and bereft of our senses . . . we seek to enslave' the cities of Hellas (P 41–2), and 'setting our hearts on the empire of the sea' the Athenians lust after 'imperial power' (P 64–5), trying to acquire an empire that they could not retain (P 69). Their desire for *archē*, empire, however, is really 'a misfortune', and 'depraves all who have to do with it' (P 94). The Athenians wish 'not to rule but to dominate', but 'those who attempt a despot's course must encounter the disasters which befall despotic power' (P 91). The tyrant with unlimited power lives a life of fear, trusting none, trusted by none (P 111–13)—an analysis which agrees with Plato's (*Rep.* 579 ff.). All that Athens has gained from her 'arrogance and insolence' (P 119) has been a series of disasters, battles in which they lost 200 ships and their crews off Egypt, 150 ships off Cyprus, in the Decelean War 10,000 troops, in Sicily 40,000 men and 240 ships, and finally, at the battle of Aegospotami in 405 BC, another 200 ships. The disasters were so frequent that it became 'a matter of regular routine to hold public funerals', and the civic burial-grounds were full (*P* 86–8). The whole course of the Peloponnesian War, including the oligarchy of the Four Hundred in 411 BC, and the rule of the Thirty Tyrants in 404 BC, has been disastrous to the Athenians:

We have . . . seen many of our fellow-countrymen suffer, some of them dying in battle, some made prisoners of war, and others reduced to the last extremities of want; we have seen the democracy twice overthrown, the walls which defended our country torn down; and, worst of all, we have seen the whole city in peril of being enslaved, and our enemy encamped on the Acropolis. (*A* 319)

This whole analysis gives great force to Isocrates' repeated appeals for Athens to 'make peace, not only' with her immediate enemies, 'but with all mankind' (*P* 16).

As a social critic Isocrates resembles Socrates both in the targets he attacks and in the forthright way he does so. I have summarized his long and detailed account very briefly, partly to show that Plato was not the only critic of Athens, but also because Isocrates derives his analysis of the corruptions of rhetoric from these forces of greed and ambition in society. Where Plato crudely lumped all politicians and rhetors together as flatterers and corrupters of the people, Isocrates draws a broader and more differentiated picture, particularly emphasizing the role of the sycophants, 'false accusers, slanderers, professional blackmailers', as Norlin defines them, 'a class of persons which sprang up like weeds in Athens after the age of Pericles. Their favourite device was to extort money by threatening or instituting law-suits' (ii. 84–5 n.). Isocrates applies the word 'sycophant' to the demagogic leaders of the war party, but he is also, I think, refuting the accusations of the *Gorgias*, for he twice applies to the sycophants the unusual word *kolakeia* (*P* 4; *A* 315), and describes their rise in terms of Plato's dichotomy between 'gratifying' the hearers and 'doing them good'. So he takes the Athenians

to task because, while you know well that many great families and estates have been ruined by flatterers and while in your private affairs you abhor those who practise this art, in your public affairs . . . you place greater confidence in them than in the rest of your fellow-citizens.

Indeed, you have caused the orators to practise and study, not what will be advantageous to the state, but how they may discourse in a manner pleasing to you. (*P* 4–5)

We note that the responsibility for this corruption is placed with the people, greedy for war as a means to gain land and riches, not with the orators, and not with rhetoric itself. Isocrates is using Plato's categories, but emptying them of their animus. The whole city is responsible, not just the rhetors.

The Athenians are only willing to listen to those 'who speak for your pleasure'. Yet, Isocrates tells them, borrowing Plato's dichotomy, 'if you really desired to find out what is advantageous to the state, you ought to give your attention more to those who oppose your views than to those who seek to gratify you', even though 'those who say what you desire are able to delude you easily', while the others cannot cloud your judgement in this way (*P* 10). Isocrates agrees with Plato that such a form of flattering rhetoric exists, but draws a clear line separating the corrupt rhetors from those concerned with the state's true health. He also takes over Plato's analogy between politics and medicine, urging the Athenians 'to choose, not those discourses which are agreeable to you, but those which are profitable', since while physicians have discovered many treatments 'for the ills of our bodies, there exists no remedy for souls which are ignorant of the truth and filled with base desires, other than the kind of discourse which boldly rebukes the sins which they commit' (*P* 39–40). Athens has enough honest orators, in fact, but the people 'distrust and dislike men of that character and cultivate, instead, the most depraved of the orators who come before you on this platform' (*P* 13)—men who have indeed gone down in history for their vice and corruption (ii. 14–15 nn.). Echoing Socrates (*Apology*, 31 e), Isocrates complains that 'it is hazardous to oppose' the views of the majority in Athens, for 'although this is a free government there exists no freedom of speech except that which is enjoyed in this Assembly by the most reckless orators, who care nothing for your welfare, and in the theatre by the comic poets' (*P* 14). Such depraved orators were actually bribed to speak, 'paid for what they say' by those who wished Athens to go to war (*P* 36, 50), telling her people that 'they ought to rule over the rest of the world' (P 125). They 'gratify' the Athenians 'for the moment, while caring nothing for the future', professing to love the people while really holding them in contempt (P 36, 121). Within the city the impeachments and indictments they continually foment bring many unnecessary but profitable lawsuits (P 129–32; A 314–16). Yet far from being punished, society grants them status and power.

Against the corruptions of the demagogues and sycophants Isocrates sets true and responsible rhetoric, as taught by himself and practised in his own writings. Despising the rhetoric of the lawcourts as petty and ignoble (i, pp. xxii f., xxx f.; A 36–7, 42, 46–9, 228–9), Isocrates devoted himself to civic or political rhetoric, trying to 'persuade the whole state to pursue a policy from which the Athenians will become prosperous themselves' and 'deliver the rest of the Hellenes from their present ills' (A 85). 'We who are occupied with political discourse' (A 260), he states, believe in tolerance and fairness, knowing that men cannot 'wisely pass judgment on the past or take counsel for the future unless they examine and compare the arguments of opposing speakers, themselves giving an unbiased hearing to both sides' (P 12). Isocrates shares Protagoras' concern for justice in public speech. He deplores the current state of affairs in Athens, where the accused does not have 'an equal chance' of speaking. 'While we take our solemn oath at the beginning of each year that we will hear impartially both accusers and accused, we depart so far from this in practice, that when the accuser makes his charges we give ear to whatever he may say; but when the accused endeavours to refute them, we sometimes do not endure even to hear his voice.' Athenians complain about states where a 'citizen is put to death without a trial', yet 'we are blind to the fact that we are in the same case when we do not hear with equal good will both sides of the contest' (A 21–3)—Demosthenes made a fair complaint.

The appeal to fairness and justice for all is an impressive aspect of Isocrates' legacy, quite in the spirit of Protagoras and the elder Sophists. If the eirenic policies that he urges should prevail in Athens 'we shall have all mankind as our allies', Isocrates writes, reaffirming a fundamental distinction that Plato tried to erode—'who will not have been forced, but rather persuaded, to join with us' (*P* 21). Rhetoric is reclaimed from Plato's denigration, in a spirit of tolerance and enlightenment:

We ought, therefore, to think of the art of discourse just as we think of the other arts, and not to form opposite judgments about similar things, nor show ourselves intolerant toward that power which, of all the faculties which belong to the nature of man, is the source of most of our blessings. (*A* 253)

In other ways man is inferior to the animals, but, because 'there has been implanted in us the power to persuade each other and to make clear whatever we desire, not only have we escaped the life of wild beasts, but we have come together and founded cities and made laws and invented arts; and, generally speaking, there is no institution devised by man which the power of speech has not helped us to establish' (*A* 254).

Rehabilitating rhetoric from Plato's attack, and quoting something he had written to the young Nicocles, King of Cyprus, in the 360s (ii. 74–81), Isocrates gives one of the earliest extant accounts of the social and civilizing functions of eloquence:

For this it is which has laid down laws concerning things just and unjust, and things honourable and base; and if it were not for these ordinances we should not be able to live with one another. It is by this also that we confute the bad and extol the good. Through this we educate the ignorant and appraise the wise; for the power to speak well is taken as the surest index of a sound understanding, and discourse which is true and lawful and just is the outward image of a good and faithful soul. With this faculty we both contend against others on matters which are open to dispute and seek light for ourselves on things which are unknown; for the same arguments which we use in persuading others when we speak in public, we employ also when we deliberate in our own thoughts; and, while we call eloquent those who are able to speak before a crowd, we regard as sage those who most skilfully debate their problems in their own minds . . . [for] none of the things which are done with intelligence take place without the help of speech. (*A* 253–7)

That eloquent paragraph reaffirms the links between rhetoric and justice, stated by Gorgias in Plato's dialogue and parodied by Socrates. (Isocrates studied with Gorgias, and may be echoing his teachings.) It affirms the ethical function of the epideictic branch of rhetoric in confuting the bad and extolling the good, and underlines its role in education. It validates rhetoric both in the field of open dispute and in individual study, refusing any dichotomy between public and private discourse—which would privilege Plato's dialectic—seeing language as inescapably involved in all mental processes.

Disagreeing with Plato, Isocrates sets out to show the legitimate role of rhetoric, while avoiding bitter controversy. He refuses to descend to the level of his opponents, for although they call him contentious and are 'always saying disparaging things of me, I shall not answer them in kind' (A 259–60, 148). His dignity has been admired (ii. 270 n.), and marks him off from those Sophists who reviled and abused each other (A 147–8). His disagreements with Plato are by now clear, but both writers share a belief in the prime importance of education to society: 'as is the education of the youth so from generation to generation will be the fortune of the state' (A 174). Just as gymnastics develops the body, so does philosophy (in Isocrates' sense) strengthen the mind, its teachers imparting 'all the forms of discourse in which the mind expresses itself' (A 183). If Isocrates rejects here the malicious placing of rhetoric among the spurious arts in the Gorgias, he agrees with the Phaedrus (269 d–270 b) on the requisite qualities for one who wants to excel 'in oratory or in managing affairs or in any line of work', namely, 'a natural aptitude', which is 'paramount'; then training, learning to 'master the knowledge of their particular subject'; and lastly practice (A 186–7). He makes no exclusive claims for his teaching (A 193), and is more tolerant than others in seeing the value of subjects like astronomy and geometry, which may not be immediately applicable in life but do exercise and sharpen the mind (A 261–6).

Having earlier disclaimed the power to make men virtuous, Isocrates wins credibility by his more modest affirmation of the ethical effect of his teaching. In his earlier tract he announced that those who follow his system of teaching 'political discourse' may, 'if they will, be helped more speedily towards honesty of character than towards facility in oratory' (S 21; my italics): the pupil must want to be good. In the Antidosis, that 'true image of my thought and of my whole life' (A 7), he reports that the men who have been under his instruction 'have in no case been guilty of wrong-doing or of crime, while some of them have been crowned by the city in recognition of their worth' (A 144), and he lists those who received 'chaplets of gold' for their public services (A 93–4). (The same cannot be said for Socrates' pupils, as his critics have pointed out.) Other Sophists have produced pupils who were neither 'duped nor affected' by them, but 'turned out competent champions and . . . able teachers' (A 203–4), indeed the finest reward a Sophist can receive is 'when his pupils prove to be honourable and intelligent and highly esteemed by their fellow-citizens' (A 220). This dignified defence of his profession lends greater force to Isocrates' assertion— counter to Plato's allegations—that 'the principles which we instil into our students are such as we practise in our own lives' (A 239). Isocrates conceives of the orator as avoiding 'causes which are unjust or petty or devoted to private quarrels', preferring 'those which are great and honourable, devoted to the welfare of man and our common good . . .' (A 276). By selecting 'the most illustrious and the most edifying' examples of human action, and by 'habituating himself to contemplate' such deeds, the orator will 'feel their influence . . . in all the actions of his life', learning to love wisdom and honour (A 277). He will also realize that his own character must be above reproach, for 'words carry greater conviction when spoken by men of good repute than when spoken by men who live under a cloud', hence 'the argument which is made by a man's life is of more weight than that which is furnished by words' (A 278).

Isocrates here anticipates the doctrine of *ethos* set out in Aristotle's *Rhetoric*, but his, and the Sophists' conception of rhetoric generally, is much wider than Aristotle's. For by the *logos politikous* that he teaches Isocrates means a rhetoric worthy to be counted among 'the recognized arts' (A 202), but conceived on a broader plan. His system teaches 'those studies which will enable us to govern wisely both our own households and the commonwealth' (A 285), a broad practical concern which accounted for his great prestige with later exponents of the *vita activa*. To 'govern' has an ethical sense, too, not Plato's constant preoccupation with reason controlling the passions (although Isocrates shares that common Greek attitude setting virtue above pleasure: A 221, 289), but an awareness of the rights and entitlements of others. He believes that 'people can become better and worthier if they conceive an ambition to speak well', provided they 'set their hearts on seizing their advantage' in the true meaning of that term (*A* 275). He does not mean the 'advantage' gained by people who 'rob others or falsify accounts or do any evil thing' (*A* 281), indeed Isocrates is scathing in his attacks on people who 'overreach' in the way recommended by Plato's Callicles (*A* 284–5). Advantage in the good sense means following religion, justice, and all the virtues, neither working any disadvantage to others (ii. 77), nor becoming rich and powerful at another's expense. Those who advocate militarism and the profit motive for Athens have failed to grasp that

nothing in the world can contribute so powerfully to material gain, to good repute, to right action, in a word, to happiness, as virtue and [its parts, piety, justice, moderation]. For it is by the good qualities which we have in our souls that we acquire also the other advantages of which we stand in need. (*P* 28–35)

Like some other more famous moralists, Isocrates confuses two positions, 'virtue is its own reward' with 'virtue is beneficial', but at least he takes a consistent line against Athenian acquisitiveness and the social disorder that it produced. Perhaps the lasting contribution that Isocrates makes to rhetorical studies is ethical and political, the insight that where society is corrupt, language will be too. The Athens of his day had been 'plunged into such a state of topsy-turvy and confusion that some of our people no longer use words in their proper meaning but wrest them from the most honourable associations and apply them to the basest pursuits', as when Athenians 'think of men who indulge their depraved and criminal instincts and who for small gains acquire a base reputation as "getting the advantage", instead of applying this term to the most righteous and the most upright' (*A* 283–5). While nowhere near as incisive as Thucydides' famous account of the collapse of language in the civil wars on Corcyra,[5] Isocrates is at least aware of the many ways in which rhetoric reflects the health or sickness of a society.

One aspect of rhetoric strikingly absent in Isocrates concerns

---

[5] See Thucydides, *History of the Peloponnesian War*, 3. 82 ff., and Vickers 1973, pp. 599–602.

the °detailed techniques of language expounded by the
traditional textbooks. Apart from a general reference to the
processes of composition (S 16–17) he responds to Plato's
indictment of rhetoric by validating its social and educational
role, not by going back to first principles to ask what rhetoric is,
and how it functions. Luckily for posterity, Aristotle, who
regarded Isocrates with a contempt perhaps learned from Plato,[6]
took the second path. Having, in the *Poetics*, defended tragedy
from Plato's strictures, in the *Rhetoric* he answered part of his
master's indictment of the sister art, although agreeing with him
on some issues. The inferiority of judicial to political oratory, for
instance, was that the former is 'given to unscrupulous
practices', and is not just concerned with the facts at issue, for
'to conciliate the listener is what pays here' (1354^{b}29–34). This is
not as extreme as Plato's charge of flattery, but does similarly call
in question the integrity of the legal orator needing to please an
audience. Where Aristotle takes major issue with Plato is on the
status of rhetoric as a discipline, and its connection with other
branches of philosophy. While Plato had always seen rhetoric as
the inferior opponent of dialectic, Aristotle's text, as we have it,
begins baldly: 'Rhetoric is the counterpart of Dialectic. Both alike
are concerned with such things as come, more or less, within
the general ken of all men and belong to no definite science'
(1354^{a}1–3). He then passes to affirm its status as a *technē* (having,
therefore, *epistēmē*), again linking rhetoric and dialectic as arts
that are generally available, not the property of specialists.
Ordinary people use dialectic to 'discuss statements and
maintain them', and rhetoric 'to defend themselves and attack
others'. They use both arts, then,

either at random or through practice and from acquired habit. Both
ways being possible, the subject can plainly be handled systematically,
for it is possible to inquire the reason why some speakers succeed
through practice and others spontaneously; and every one will at once
agree that such an inquiry is the function of an art. (1354^{a}4–11)

---

[6] According to Cicero Aristotle once quoted a line from Euripides' *Philoctetes*
'with a slight modification: the hero in the tragedy said that it was a disgrace for
him to keep silent and suffer barbarians to speak, but Aristotle put it "suffer
Isocrates to speak"; and consequently he put the whole of his system of
philosophy in a polished and brilliant form, and linked the scientific study of
facts with practice in style' (*De Or.* 3. 35. 141).

Aristotle displaces dialectic from its privileged position in Plato, where it was virtually synonymous with philosophy, 'the whole process of rational analysis by which the soul was led into the knowledge of Ideas'.[7] Aristotle puts rhetoric and dialectic on the same level, both dealing with popular opinions, probable arguments, and a common subject-matter, while on a higher level he puts scientific reasoning, which 'starts with universal or necessary principles and proceeds to universal and necessary conclusions'.[8]

Having criticized extant rhetoric-books for their treatment of 'non-essentials', Aristotle takes up the charge made by Socrates several times in the *Gorgias*, that rhetoric was useless, or at any rate only useful for immoral ends, and simply asserts that 'Rhetoric is useful', giving four reasons (1355^{a}21 ff.). First, where Socrates had denied rhetoric and rhetoricians any knowledge of justice, Aristotle affirms rhetoric to be useful 'because things that are true and things that are just have a natural tendency to prevail over their opposites, so that if the decisions of judges are not what they ought to be, the defeat must be due to the speakers themselves, and they must be blamed accordingly'. That is, rhetoric *can* help justice to prevail, and it if fails neither the art nor the legal system is to blame, rather the speakers who have not exercised the art properly. Rightly used, then, rhetoric strengthens justice. Rhetoric is useful, too, not only for the specialist audience of the courtroom, but to persuade less well-educated audiences, using less technical means of argument.

The third use of rhetorical persuasion, similar to the 'strict reasoning' of dialectic, is when we argue 'on opposite sides of a question'. Far from being a sign of cynicism or amorality, we do so 'in order that we may see clearly what the facts are, and that, if another man argues unfairly, we on our part may be able to confute him'.

Finally, where Plato had laid great emphasis on Socrates' refusal to use rhetoric to defend himself, even if unjustly attacked (*Gorgias*, 521 d–e), Aristotle declares it

absurd to hold that a man ought to be ashamed of being unable to defend himself with his limbs, but not of being unable to defend

---

[7] Hunt 1961, p. 64.   [8] Ibid., p. 66.

himself with speech and reason, when the use of rational speech is more distinctive of a human being than the use of his limbs.

And since the charge in much of the *Gorgias* is that rhetoric lends itself to misuse, Aristotle adds this corollary:

And if it be objected that one who uses such power of speech unjustly might do great harm, *that* is a charge which may be made in common against all good things except virtue, and above all against the things that are most useful, as strength, health, wealth, generalship. A man can confer the greatest of benefits by a right use of these, and inflict the greatest of injuries by using them wrongly. (1355^{b}1–7)

To that list of good things that can be abused the modern student of Plato must add dialectic.

Aristotle's rehabilitation of rhetoric proceeds by defining it as 'the faculty of observing in any given case the available means of persuasion' (1355^{b}25). His target here is the passage where Socrates convinced Gorgias that rhetoric shared with other arts the role of persuasion through words. No, Aristotle replies, persuasion

is not a function of any other art. Every other art can instruct or persuade about its own particular subject-matter; for instance, medicine about what is healthy and unhealthy, geometry about the properties of magnitude, arithmetic about numbers. . . . But rhetoric we look upon as observing the means of persuasion on almost any subject presented to us. (1355^{b}25 ff.)

It is a general art, like dialectic, offering techniques useful to all the other arts. Aristotle sees rhetoric as a tool or instrument of human communication, with all the strengths and weaknesses that that implies. Far from opposing it to philosophy he connects it closely to dialectic, and is at some pains to integrate it into the whole circle of human sciences. Rhetoric is linked with logic, one of the three modes of persuasion being 'the proof, or apparent proof, provided by the words of the speech itself' (1356^{a}3). The two main modes of proof are the example, 'a rhetorical induction', and the enthymeme, 'a rhetorical syllogism' (1356^{b}1 ff.), both used less strictly than their counterparts in dialectic. The orator's other two resources, *ethos* and *pathos*, depend on his knowledge of 'human character and goodness in their various forms', and of the emotions. 'It thus appears that rhetoric is an offshoot of dialectic and also of ethical studies. Ethical studies may fairly be called political; and for this reason rhetoric masquerades as political science, and the professors of it as political experts', but without any right (1356^a1 ff., 21 ff.). Aristotle attacks the Sophists for their claim to teach politics, which he treated far more searchingly, but he underlines the importance of rhetoric as a political tool in deliberative oratory, a discussion which passes naturally into questions of ethics (1359^a30–1366^a22). Finally *pathos* demands understanding of the whole range of human emotions, leading to the treatise on psychology in Book Two (1378^a20 ff.).

Aristotle's *Rhetoric* (although lost for some time), together with the writings of Isocrates and later Greek rhetoricians, helped validate rhetoric in public life, and in the Hellenistic period it became firmly established in the educational system, alongside, and even at times above philosophy. The Romans took over Greek rhetoric and also inherited the dispute between rhetoric and philosophy. This flared up in the second century BC concerning their respective roles in education. In 155 BC three Greek philosophers went from Athens to Rome as ambassadors, Carneades, Critolaus, and the Stoic Diogenes. All three were hostile to rhetoric, and their criticism had a considerable impact.[9] Writing his *De Inventione* some seventy years later, Cicero described the schools of Aristotle and Isocrates as two 'opposing sects . . . one busy with philosophy, but devoting some attention to the art of rhetoric as well', the other entirely devoted to rhetoric (2. 2. 8 f.). In *De Oratore* Cicero lays the blame for this division at the feet of Socrates. Originally the liberal sciences were studied as a unity, entitled philosophy, but

Socrates robbed them of this general designation, and in his discussion separated the science of wise thinking from that of elegant speaking, though in reality they are closely linked together. . . . This is the source from which has sprung the undoubtedly absurd and unprofitable and reprehensible severance between the tongue [*lingua*] and the brain [*cor*], leading to our having one set of professors to teach us to think and another to speak. (3. 16. 59–60)

Where the Sophists had combined the study of rhetoric with

---

[9] See Kennedy 1972, pp. 53–4; Kennedy 1980, p. 72.

'the science of everything that concerns morals and conduct and ethics and politics', after Socrates' separation of the two domains 'the philosophers looked down on eloquence and the orators on wisdom' (3. 19. 71; also 3. 32. 126; *Orator*, 5.17).

Cicero's remedy for this separation is to urge rhetoric to take up philosophy, the discipline he reveres. At the outset of *De Oratore* he writes that 'most learned men hold what the Greeks call "philosophy" to be the creator and mother, as it were, of all the reputable arts' (1. 3. 9). Crassus is praised for being both orator and philosopher and for having thought 'matters relating to philosophy more important', since they are 'the source from which this oratorical fluency has been derived' (3. 22. 82)—that is, to give the words their fullest scope, a knowledge of *res* should precede competence in *verba*. In his later works Cicero becomes more insistent in urging that the orator must know the whole realm of *prudentia*, practical philosophy, dialectic, 'the mistress of all arts', and philosophy, 'the mother of excellence' (*Brutus* 6. 23, 41. 153, 93. 322). The orator is urged to study logic and moral science, especially as taught by the Middle Academy (*Part. Or.* 40. 139), to whom, rather than to 'the workshops of the rhetoricians', Cicero acknowledges that he owes 'whatever ability I possess as an orator ' (*Orator*, 3. 12; cf. *De Or.* 3. 20. 75). Philosophy is 'essential for the education of our ideal orator', for without it he cannot 'distinguish the genus and species of anything, nor define it, . . . nor separate truth from falsehood' (*Orator*, 4. 14. 16). Since 'the foundation of eloquence, as of everything else, is wisdom', then the orator must master logic, either the older science of Aristotle or the newer one of Chrysippus (ibid., 21, 70, 32. 113–16). 'He should not confine his study to logic, however, but have theoretical acquaintance with all the topics of philosophy', ethics, religion, politics, natural philosophy, civil law, history (ibid., 33. 118–34. 120).

Cicero's advocacy of a training in philosophy seems designed to answer Plato's objection that the rhetorician has no knowledge of such things. However, the desire to answer that attack leads to two counter-arguments that have less fortunate effects. First, the demands that Cicero makes on the ideal orator are widened until they take in virtually the whole field of human knowledge. As Crassus, Cicero's spokesman, puts it, 'in an orator we must demand the subtlety of the logician, the thoughts of a philosopher, a diction almost poetic, a lawyer's memory, a tragedian's voice, and the bearing almost of a consummate actor' (1. 28. 128). But these attributes only win approval in an orator when 'they are all assembled in perfection'. The 'genuine orator'—a more exclusive category than 'the perfect orator'?—'must have investigated and handled and debated the whole of the contents of the life of mankind', such being the field of his activity (3. 14. 54). He roams 'a vast immeasurable plain' (3. 19. 70), for

eloquence is so potent a force that it embraces the origin and operation and developments of all things, all the virtues and duties, all the natural principles governing the morals and minds and life of mankind, and also determines their custom and laws and rights, and controls the government of the state. . . . in short, the entire field of practical philosophy. (3. 20. 76, 3. 31. 122)

One of the interlocutors objects to the impracticability of this 'sublime and universal perfection' (1. 29. 131), but he is silenced by the flood of Crassus' oratory. The idols put up for imitation are all polymaths, such as the Sophist Hippias, who boasted 'that there was not a single fact included in any system of encyclopaedic knowledge with which he was not acquainted', and had not only mastered the liberal arts but when he appeared in public wore a ring, cloak, and boots that he had made himself (3. 32. 126). Gorgias was another such universal genius (3. 32. 120), as was the Roman Marcus Cato (3. 33. 135). Such claims may indeed answer Plato, but they leave rhetoric in the unfortunate position of having been propelled from nothing to too much. To demand such omni-competence is likely to deter students of rhetoric and alienate its critics.

Cicero's second response to Plato was also unfortunate. Although his injunctions to study philosophy seem both humble and sincere, expressing a non-aggressive desire for knowledge (as when he advises rhetoricians to 'put our pride in our pockets and borrow what we need' from the philosophers: 3. 27. 108), in a number of places Cicero visualizes this two-way traffic more in terms of an invasion. The philosophers are accused of having 'trespassed on our heritage':

For us to belong—assuming that we are really orators, that is, persons competent to be retained as leaders and principals in civil actions and criminal trials and public debates—to us, I say, belong the broad estates of wisdom and learning, which having been allowed to lapse and become derelict during our absorption in affairs, have been invaded by persons too generously supplied with leisure, persons who either banter and ridicule the orator after the manner of Socrates in Plato's *Gorgias*, or else write a few little manuals of instruction in the art of oratory and label them with the title of *Rhetoric*. (3. 31. 122)

To both groups having too much leisure and nothing better to do, philosophers and authors of rhetoric textbooks, Cicero replies that 'the province of the rhetoricians' is all-embracing, so that, since 'we can now no longer obtain these principles from elsewhere, we have to take them from the very persons who plundered us' (123). What was to Socrates the greatest blessing of the philosopher's life, its non-involvement in political affairs and public activity, becomes for Cicero and other exponents of the *vita activa* its very indictment. Philosophers may claim 'that all these matters are their exclusive province', Crassus says,

But when I have allowed that they may debate these subjects in their holes and corners, to pass an idle hour, it is to the orator none the less that I shall entrust and assign the task of developing with complete charm and cogency the same themes which they discuss in a sort of thin and bloodless style. (1. 13. 56)

In angulis: it is significant that Cicero should echo here the language of Callicles, who attacked the philosopher for shunning the arena of public affairs 'and living the rest of his life sunk in a corner and whispering with three or four boys' (*Gorgias*, 485 d). Plato was parodying the ordinary man's philistine attitude towards philosophy, but Cicero, despite his profession of admiration for philosophy, seems to endorse it. As Crassus continues this argument for the supremacy of rhetoric he adopts the claims of Gorgias, asserting that while all disciplines have their own subject-matter, only rhetoric can 'put these same arts in their full light' (1. 14. 61), and that whatever the subject on which the orator receives instruction, 'he will express himself far more gracefully than his master himself' (1. 14. 64–7).

Cicero's main and implicit response to Plato is to affirm that rhetoric takes all knowledge for its province, excelling philosophy or any other discipline in its ability to communicate whatever it chooses to discuss. One less serious, and more explicit response is to present Plato's attack on rhetoric as merely an example of rhetoric. So Cicero makes Crassus describe how he read *Gorgias* 'with close attention under Charmadas' at the Academy in Athens, and that 'what impressed me most deeply about Plato' there was 'that it was when making fun of orators that he himself seemed to me to be the consummate orator' (*De Or.* 1. 11. 47). The apparent victory of philosophy in the *Gorgias*, then, is actually a triumph for rhetoric. So another speaker in Cicero's dialogue, referring to Gorgias as 'advocate for the orator when he lost his case against the philosopher', describes him as 'an adversary who either in reality never was defeated by Socrates and [hence] Plato's famous dialogue is untrue, or if defeated he was, obviously Socrates was more eloquent and fluent and . . . a fuller and better orator' (3. 32. 129). Either way, it was rhetoric that triumphed. Quintilian follows this tactic of presenting the *Gorgias* as a victory for rhetoric, but with a more blatant misreading of it. Referring to Gorgias' definition of rhetoric as 'a creator of persuasion' (453 a) he can say, with correct critical judgement, that 'Plato intends it to be taken as the opinion of Gorgias, not as his own' (2. 15. 5). He also records, perceptively, that Gorgias is driven to give definitions 'under compulsion from the inexorable logic of Socrates' (2. 15. 10), and that Socrates allows Gorgias 'the power of persuading, but not of teaching', denying, as he does, rhetoric any authority in *docere* (2. 15. 18). Quintilian knows how to read Plato, then.

But Quintilian subsequently attacks 'the majority' of students who, 'content with reading a few passages' from the *Gorgias*, 'unskilfully excerpted by earlier writers, refrain from studying that dialogue and the remainder of Plato's writings, and thereby fall into serious error. For they believe that in Plato's view rhetoric was not an art, but a certain *adroitness in the production of delight and gratification* . . . ' (2. 15. 24). Summarizing the further charges, that rhetoric is 'the fourth department of flattery', a 'dishonest counterfeit' of justice, Quintilian comments:

All these statements occur in the *Gorgias* and are uttered by Socrates who appears to be the mouth-piece of the views held by Plato. But some of his dialogues were composed merely to refute his opponents and are styled *refutative* [*elenktikous*], while others are for the purpose of teaching and are called doctrinal [*dogmatikoi*]. (2. 15. 26)

Presumably Quintilian places this one in the former category:

Now it is only rhetoric as practised in their own day that is condemned by Plato or Socrates, for he speaks of it as 'the manner in which you engage in public affairs' [500 c]: rhetoric in itself he regards as a genuine and honourable thing, and consequently the controversy with Gorgias ends with the words, 'The rhetorician therefore must be just and the just man desirous to do what is just'. (27)

Reference to the text at that point (460 c) will show that the controversy with Gorgias by no means ends here, for this is just a stage in Socrates' development of the basic contradiction he finds between rhetoric notionally espousing justice but actually condoning injustice (460 e–461 b). Quintilian summarizes the rest of the dialogue in the same tendentious way. To Polus, 'a hot-headed and headstrong young fellow', Socrates

makes his remarks about 'shadows' and 'forms of flattery'. Then Callicles, who is even more hot-headed, intervenes, but is reduced to the conclusion that 'he who would truly be a rhetorician ought to be just and possess a knowledge of justice'. (2. 15. 28)

Reference to the text at that point (508 c) reveals that the 'conclusion' comes from Socrates, not Callicles, and is in no sense a conclusion, since the dialogue has some twenty pages to run.

If we are wondering why Quintilian should bother to misinterpret the *Gorgias*, the clue comes when we realize that he manages in this way to assimilate Plato to his own concept of the orator as a *vir bonus peritus dicendi* 'a good man skilled in speaking':

It is clear therefore that Plato does not regard rhetoric as an evil, but holds that true rhetoric is impossible for any save a just and good man. In the *Phaedrus* [261 a–273 e] he makes it even clearer that the complete attainment of this art is impossible without the knowledge of justice, an opinion in which I heartily concur. Had this not been his view, would he have ever written the *Apology* of Socrates or the Funeral Oration [*Menexenus*] in praise of those who had died in battle for their country, both of them works falling within the sphere of oratory? It was against the class of men who employed their glibness of speech for evil purposes that he directed his denunciations. (2. 15. 29–30)

It would be reassuring to think that Plato merely attacked the misuse of rhetoric, or the deficiencies of its teachers, who 'divorced rhetoric from justice and preferred plausibility to truth, as he states in the *Phaedrus*' (2. 15. 31). Yet Quintilian can reach this position only by knowingly distorting the sense of what Plato writes, at such length, and with such reiteration. Perhaps Quintilian thought that by claiming Plato as a friend of rhetoric he would enhance its stature and credibility. For generations of readers who had access to his account but not to the original he undoubtedly succeeded. One of them, the Neapolitan teacher Francesco Pucci, under his influence, 'transformed Plato's condemnation of rhetoric into a condemnation of the misuse of rhetoric'.[10]

For Quintilian this metamorphosis was perhaps a subtle way of responding to Plato, by misrepresenting and so denying his case. Elsewhere Quintilian preferred the direct approach, following Cicero by affirming the superiority of rhetoric to philosophy, but with a significant change of emphasis. He agrees with Cicero's diagnosis of the fatal split between rhetoric and philosophy brought about by Socrates (1. Pr. 13, 1. 10. 11), and holds that 'the material of rhetoric is composed of everything that may be placed before it as a subject for speech' (2. 21. 4). But whereas Cicero had urged the perfect orator to know all the arts, Quintilian regards it as 'sufficient that an orator should not be actually ignorant of the subject on which he has to speak' (2. 21. 14). More modest though this conception is, Quintilian, like Gorgias, believes that the orator will still be able to talk about these arts better than the experts (2. 4. 15–16). He recommends the budding orator to study geometry, music, and mathematics (1. 10. 3, 11, 34 ff.), and also dialectic, although that art is judged too cerebral for the needs of rhetoric addressing the general public (5. 11. 39, 10. 1. 36, 12. 2. 11–14). The most important subject for the orator is moral philosophy or ethics (12. 2. 15, 28), what Quintilian calls 'the better part of philosophy' (1. Pr. 14), and it is here that he goes beyond Cicero in the rhetorician's

---

[10] See Grafton 1985, p. 635, citing M. Fuiano, *Insegnamento e cultura a Napoli nel Rinascimento*, i (Naples, 1971), 88–9, 141.

proprietary attitude towards 'the principles of upright and honourable living'. Ethics has become the 'peculiar concern of philosophy', due to the 'indolence' of rhetoricians (1. Pr. 10, 13, 1. 10. 11, 2. 21. 13), but the time has come, Quintilian thinks, to attack 'those authors who have . . . presumptuously laid claim to the sole possession of the title of philosopher . . . [and] usurped the better part of oratory, and to demand back what is ours by right' (1. Pr. 14, 17). This department of knowledge 'was always the peculiar property of rhetoric, and the philosophers are really trespassers' (2. 21. 13), for when they discuss such virtues as 'equity, justice, truth, and the good' they 'are using the weapons of rhetoric, not their own' (12. 2. 5). The theft is more outrageous, Quintilian claims, since orators actually practise virtue while contemporary philosophers disguise their 'depravity of character' under 'a stern and austere mien' (1 Pr. 15), assuming a 'moral superiority while leading a life of debauchery at home' (12. 3. 12). So he looks forward to the day when

the perfect orator of our heart's desire shall claim for his own possession that science that has lost the affection of mankind through the arrogance of its claims and the vices of some that have brought disgrace upon its virtues, and shall restore it to its place in the domain of eloquence, as though he had been victorious in a title for the restoration of stolen goods! (12. 2. 9)

Quintilian can spin out such metaphors of reclaiming territory, and ousting the usurpers, but it is a lot easier to sustain a metaphor than to make a clear statement of intent. What would this mean in practical terms? Would the professors of rhetoric start teaching ethics again? Or would the philosophy teachers be bound in chains and sent as slaves to Africa? There is, the reader may feel, some discrepancy between the tone of Quintilian's remarks and their actual content. He seems to be advocating a reform of the curriculum, but does so in language redolent of the battlefield or a combat between two armed gladiators.

The fullest response to the *Gorgias* in antiquity was produced a hundred years after Quintilian, by the Sophist Aelius Aristides (AD 117–180). Famous for his precise Attic style, Aristides left over fifty orations, the most extensive being the three addressed

To Plato. In Defence of Oratory,[11] written between 145 and 147.
Aristides sets out to refute Plato's 'over-contentious remarks
about oratory, when he used the literary contrivance of a
meeting of Gorgias and Socrates at Athens' (§13), since in the
opinon of many 'silence confirms an accusation', and oratory
will otherwise seem 'incapable of protecting its own rights' (17).
Having invoked 'Hermes, God of Oratory' (19), Aristides quotes
that passage from the *Gorgias* (463 a–465 c) where rhetoric is
reduced to the level of cookery and accuses Plato—in terms
revived in our time by Terence Irwin—of *petitio principii*,
assuming what he has to prove:

Here there is no proof at all nor a chain of reasoning which had to be
arrived at. An assumption is simply made, as if he had the power to do
so, on a subject which formerly caused much difficulty. It is no different
than if he asked his hearers to make these concessions as a favour. Yet
if it is farcical to hypothesize the object of an investigation as a matter
agreed upon, how is it reasonable to hypothesize at the outset what it is
farcical even to investigate? For how is it not farcical to investigate
whether oratory and cookery are of the same nature? . . . The case
might be better understood, if the word 'oratory' were removed, and
'philosophy' were put in its place, and all the same arguments were
used in regard to this. (23–5)

Aristides sees the underlying quarrel between philosophy and
rhetoric, and laments that 'the defenders of one of two sciences
or faculties' should 'in any way slander the other side' (26). His
method will not involve slandering philosophy, but will show
Plato 'obviously refuted by his own statements' (50), starting
with those passages in the *Phaedrus* which seem to give a more
favourable account of rhetoric and poetry. This is part of a long
argument that rhetoric is an art, one of the main issues in the
controversies in this period, as H. M. Hubbell showed,[12] but
Aristides' account, unfortunately, is rather long-winded and
flabby.

[11] Quotations are from the Loeb Classical Library *Aristides*, vol. i, tr. C. A.
Behr (London, 1973); section numbers are given in the text following the
quotation. See also André Boulanger, *Aelius Aristide et la sophistique dans la
province d'Asie au IIᵉ siècle de notre ère* (Paris, 1923; 1968), especially pp. 210–70 (a
detailed but unsympathetic account); C. A. Behr, *Aelius Aristides and the Sacred
Tales* (Amsterdam, 1968); and G. W. Bowersock, *Greek Sophists in the Roman
Empire* (Oxford, 1969).
[12] Hubbell 1920, pp. 254–8, 365–82.

He is more convincing when he takes up Plato's 'sophism' that 'orators advise and only aim at what the multitudes approve' (178). If this were true, no 'herald or embassy would ask help from an orator', and no 'newly arrived ambassador would approach him to persuade the people' if they knew in advance that the orator would simply defer to the crowd rather than present their case (181). 'What defendant in a private or public suit would have sought for some orator to win him acquittal, if the orator intended to say what the jurors approved?' (182). In so doing, 'the defendant would have provided his own destruction', and might as well have brought with him 'the public executioner' as an orator (183). In fact, people accused of a serious offence, 'afraid of not receiving a fair hearing', beseech orators, and even 'grovel, believing that oratory is a curative for everything', for 'they know that orators do not practise to say what their seated audience'—the jury—approves, but rather 'all that is better to be said, so as to have the power of persuasion' (185–6). Orators, he claims, inverting Plato's terms, speak 'boldly', 'do not serve pleasures, but chastise desires, nor look to the multitude but the multitude looks to them'. For as even the pejorative term 'demagogue' shows, they lead the people, and thus the orator may be called 'ruler, patron, teacher' (189-91). Plato offers no proof for his charge that they merely 'gratify' the people (195), indeed the fact that he calls oratory 'the maker of persuasion' (*Gorgias*, 455 a) means that he grants it an independent status and a power of its own (199–201).

Turning to the lawcourts, Aristides argues that rhetoric is intimately related to justice. Since men are not born of equal strength, the stronger amongst us would get the bigger share by force if oratory did not restrain violence and ensure 'equality and justice for all' (206–7). Men originally lived in a state of violence, until

oratory was discovered and entered on the scene as an amulet for justice and as the bond of maintaining life for mankind, so that matters should not be decided for anyone by force, weapons, anticipation, numbers, size, or any other inequality; but that reason should calmly determine justice. This is the beginning and nature of oratory, the desire to save all men and to repel force through persuasion. (209–11)

Like Isocrates, Aristides restores force and persuasion to their rightful position as mutually exclusive opposites: as he says later, 'Where is persuasion, if force will prevail?' (228). He sees the 'two main points' of the laws as being 'to punish wrongdoers and to honour the decent' (213), to both of which oratory lends itself. Following Cicero, perhaps, Aristides argues that persuasion must have been used originally in order to get the laws accepted and force outlawed (215–16), and he praises the sensible division of powers in the lawcourt between advocate and judge, where 'oratory examines what takes place, and the art of justice renders a decision after the examination' (223). Rhetoric always 'desires the same ends as the art of justice' (224), justice being one of the four parts of virtue, and it partakes equally of the other three. 'Oratory was discovered by *intelligence* and for the sake of justice. The *moderation* and *courage* of those who have oratory preserve cities' (235; my italics). So Plato's distinction of genuine from spurious arts can be rejected:

Then of the four parts of 'flattery', oratory is not to justice, what cookery is to medicine. Rather of the four parts of virtue, every one is accomplished through oratory; and what gymnastics and medicine are in the body—I mean both of them together—, this oratory appears to be in the soul and in the conduct of city life. (235–6)

Wordy though he can be, Aristides does not lack penetrating arguments to defend rhetoric.

As for the tyrant Archelaus, held up as a model by Plato's Callicles, Aristides imagines oratory's response to the charge that she had created or endorsed his activities. She would say: 'I did not persuade those people to do these things. . . . far from having approved of [Archelaus'] actions, I should have immediately haled him into court, where he would have paid a proper penalty, . . . while he was still committing his first murders, if oratory had any place in Macedonia' (237–8). If oratory is 'solemnly expelled by Plato', Aristides warns, 'it will be driven out together with the laws, which are in sympathy with it' (271). The result would be a state of chaos or tyranny, ironically just what Plato accuses rhetoric of encouraging (*Gorgias*, 523 a ff.). Yet 'who is unaware that oratory and tyranny are as far separate as the use of persuasion and the use of force?' Therefore, 'if tyranny is an evil, on the same grounds oratory is a good' (307–8). Plato's animus to rhetoric is so great that it leads him to a logical absurdity, associating rhetoric with both *kolakeia* and *dunastaia*, classifying 'potentates and orators together, not only naming two qualities neither of which is appropriate to the faculty of oratory, . . . even totally foreign to it, but also combining two most contradictory accusations' (309). Orators cannot be at the same time potentates *and* flatterers, for flatterers are servants of tyrants, not themselves tyrants, and tyrants have no need of flattery, since they use force (ibid.). Plato is thus 'refuted by his own conflicting arguments' (310), the truth being that 'where oratory is preserved, a tyrant will clearly never arise . . .; nor again does oratory survive and rule where there is tyranny' (312).[13]

Aristides' attitude to democracy is far less jaundiced than Plato's, and in the second oration he answers Plato's attack on 'the Four Men', which he pronounces 'querulous in every way' (302). Where Isocrates had validated Miltiades, Themistocles, and Pericles by his own account of their public-spirited and courageous actions, Aristides writes a *prosopopoeia* in which they speak in their own defence. They apologize for not having been able to study Plato's philosophy—for the gods do not give everything to every man.

But what was ours, goodwill, eagerness, faith, and courage, these qualities we displayed, so that no one could surpass us, and in such times, Plato, when glory, safety, and the objects of our prayers lay in victory, and in defeat not even to exist at all. By our calculation and the kindly assistance of the Gods, your and our country is free, safe, untouched by the wanton and unlawful acts of the barbarians, . . . and there has been given to you and your comrades the power to be philosophers, and to sail in freedom wherever you wish, and to be able to remember us afterwards, though out of consideration, in a better way. (321)

That concise and effective defence of their achievements ends with a mild rebuke to Plato for his ingratitude, since he owes his freedom to pursue his profession to them. They repudiate the

---

[13] The modern reader following this argument may think of another state, neither democracy nor tyranny but the kind of totalitarian 'people's state' in the communist block, where leaders periodically make five- or seven-hour long speeches, a form of dead propaganda which only the very naïve take seriously. How would a Greek rhetorician classify this?

charge of fawning over the people of Athens, for even 'if we wished to fawn over them, we could not save them', and could never have been 'flatterers of the multitude' (322).

Speaking in his own person again, Aristides uses the *ad hominem* argument against Plato—'you were not even a leader at all'—and takes up his root accusation against 'the Four Men', that they failed to educate the citizens of Athens to virtue. Well, he asks,

is it possible to make a people good, blameless, and just, once and for all, or is this not even possible to affirm in the case of a single man? Indeed, if it is possible, why in the world have you not done it yourself . . .? If it cannot be done, why blame us if we have stumbled, those men would say again . . .? What if they did not make the Athenians best once and for all, but in some way improved them? (331–3)

Pursuing the *ad hominem* line, Aristides cites the awkward fact that the associates of the historic Socrates included Alcibiades, the 'wealthy, handsome, insolent, unscrupulous but able "democractic" politician', as an editor describes him,[14] and Critias, 'first among the Thirty Tyrants', as Aristides puts it, 'themselves the wickedest of the Greeks. These men they say must not be used as evidence that Socrates corrupted the young nor have their faults anything whatever to do with Socrates'. Therefore, if the pupils' faults are not to be 'accounted to the leaders themselves'—thus validating Gorgias' argument—then Themistocles and Pericles cannot be blamed if they 'did not once and for all educate the Athenians in political virtue' (335–6). This is a fair comment on the unreality of Plato's concept of education bringing a sudden and total conversion to good behaviour, and the nature of Socrates' associates may indeed have been a factor in the Athenians' enmity to him.[15]

[14] E. H. Warmington, in the Loeb edition, p. 478.

[15] Popper 1966, pp. 192–3, states that 'the main responsibility for the lost [Peloponnesian] war rests with the treacherous oligarchs who continuously conspired with Sparta. Prominent among these were three former disciples of Socrates, Alcibiades, Critias, and Charmides. After the fall of Athens in 404 BC, the two latter became the leaders of the Thirty Tyrants, who were no more than a puppet government under Spartan protection.' During the eight months of Critias' 'reign of terror', hundreds of Athenians were put to death, but he was defeated by the democrats, who brought peace and stability to Athens. 'As soon as the restored democracy had re-established normal legal conditions, a case was brought against Socrates. Its meaning was clear enough; he was accused of having had his hand in the education of the most pernicious enemies of the state, Alcibiades, Critias, and Charmides.'

Plato's demands on the Four Men were unreasonable. In fact, Aristides concludes, 'after all this time even now the Gods have never removed injustice from mankind, although they have governed from all eternity, and besides they see some men erring even against them' (338). Removing human defects is not as easy as Plato suggests.

Having switched from defence to attack, Aristides concludes with praise, affirming the power and value of rhetoric. Many of his arguments are familiar, by now, from the Sophist tradition as taken over by the Romans. God did not give reason to animals, only to men and gods (379); 'the product of oratory is the correct use of the mind, . . . a royal thing' (392). More original, surprisingly, is the literary evidence that he cites, for he brings out the fact that Plato is strangely silent on all the passages in Homer where oratory is praised as a powerful and beneficial gift. Homer describes how Phoenix was educated to be ' "a speaker of words and a doer of deeds" ', and presents human fame as deriving equally from the war and the council meetings (387–8: *Iliad*, 9. 440–3). In the *Odyssey* (8. 171–2) the orator is one who ' "speaks with assurance, with a gentle dignity, and is distinguished among those assembled" ', one of many places

where Homer clearly bears witness that the orator does not speak fawningly and abjectly, nor in awe, . . . nor pursuing the pleasure of the moment, changing himself for the occasion, as cooks do for the sake of another's pleasure, nor taking a posture like a slave of the powerful men of the moment. But he speaks with assurance, he says,

which means 'without stumbling', 'soundly', and with dignity and 'good order' (389–90). None of these passages would have endeared Homer to Plato, of course, but it is still good to be reminded by an ancient Greek of how much in Greek culture Plato ignored or misrepresented. An equally telling reference is to Hesiod's *Theogony* (80–7), which describes how 'kings participated in the power of argument by a divine portion and gift, saying that . . . "Whomever of the Zeus-cherished kings . . . the daughters of great Zeus will honour and look upon, upon his tongue they pour sweet song, and gentle words flow from his mouth" '. By persuasion, and 'upright justice'—not force—the king prevents strife (391). Protagoras, Gorgias, and Isocrates stand behind these words.

Having here associated rhetoric with Calliope, and previously with Hermes, Aristides now tells a myth, to match Plato's (equating Plato, in the course of it, with the boorish Zethus). In it Zeus tells Hermes 'to go to mankind with the art of oratory', not dividing it up into little parts but giving it whole to 'the best, the noblest and those with the strongest natures' (396–7). At the present time oratory 'still holds together and adorns cities', and in the future 'work remains for oratory so long as men have dealings with one another privately and publicly' (401–2). If some force removed diseases, Aristides argues, there would be no need for doctors. But if both legal disputes and wars 'should pass from mankind, oratory's power would not collapse', for it would still be needed by the national assemblies and the charms of peace, the honouring of gods, heroes, and good men (411). Warming to his panegyric, Aristides overreaches himself by claiming that 'one could rightly call oratory the bond of the Universe' (424)—love (with Boethius and Dante), yes: oratory, no! Luckily he does not end there, but goes on to prove his final point, 'that Plato himself enunciates the same views as I about oratory' (438), which he does to his own satisfaction, at least, by bringing together quotations from the *Statesman, Apology, Gorgias,* and *Timaeus* (438–9). Drawing on Quintilian, perhaps (if there was still a two-way traffic between Greece and Rome), Aristides suggests that Plato may have been attacking 'bad oratory' rather than oratory in general (446), just as one could attack bad dialectic, the type that 'will mislead, deceive, waste time, and use our tongues everywhere for no sound purpose' (449). So he reaches the comforting conclusion that 'in these arguments Plato has accused flattery and slander, not oratory' (454).

Aelius Aristides is no very distinguished writer, celebrated Atticist though he may have been. Yet his defence of oratory scores a number of valid points against Plato, especially his distorted view of politics and law. His reply, together with Isocrates', helps us to see the strengths of the Sophist tradition, especially its firm placing of rhetoric in the practical contexts of Greek society, its fair-mindedness, and balance. Neither writer has the penetration of Aristotle, obviously, and neither accepted the challenge to redefine or extend rhetoric. But they are mercifully free from aggressive attacks on philosophy. Apart from one scornful reference to the philosophers, who 'are proud and prance [I find it difficult to imagine a philosopher prancing!], and claim pre-eminence' (308), Aristides is content to let them do their job, if they will let him do his.

ii THE TRIUMPH OF RHETORIC

During the Middle Ages, as will be seen in Chapter 4, rhetoric was cast into a severely inferior position among the Liberal Arts, ousted first by grammar, then by logic. In the Renaissance, as Chapter 5 will show, it experienced a great revival in every way, enjoying privileged status as the humanist system spread from Italy into northern Europe. The second-generation humanists, successors to Petrarch and Salutati, evidently felt the need to exert their new powers, and soon revived the ancient quarrel with philosophy, ignoring the eirenic mode of Isocrates and Aristides. When Quintilian's work was recovered in the Renaissance his aggressive stance towards philosophy was taken over and extended, notably by Lorenzo Valla, who shocked his contemporaries by setting Quintilian above Cicero as a model for eloquence. In his dialogue *De Vero Falsoque Bono*, or *De Voluptate*[16] (1431–3), Stoic and Epicurean ideas of the good life are refuted in favour of Christianity, using the tactics of the church fathers, especially Lactantius, in setting the pagan philosophers in discord among themselves. In his preface Valla explains that, using the arguments of 'these same philosophers' against themselves, he will show 'that paganism has done nothing virtuously, nothing rightly'. Emulating biblical heroes, David and Jonathan, and using 'the sword that is the word of God', Valla expresses his hope that 'we shall destroy our enemies—that is, the philosophers—partly with their own swords, partly by inciting them to civil war and mutual destruction' (p. 51).

Valla's main goal in this dialogue is to defend the truly good life in heaven that is promised by the church to those who practise religion and virtue. In order to attack pagan philosophy effectively Valla draws on the language and attitudes of

---

[16] Quotations are from Valla, *On Pleasure. De Voluptate*, ed. and tr. Maristella Lorch and A. K. Hiëatt (New York, 1977). For an attempt to elucidate the complexities of this work see Vickers 1986.

classical rhetoric in its original dispute with philosophy. So his spokesman for the Epicurean cause, Matteo Vegio, explains that while defending Epicurus he has occasionally drawn on the writings of the rival camp, the Stoics, notably Seneca. He justifies this procedure on the grounds that he has been

initiated, not into the rites of philosophy, but into the more significant and lofty ones of oratory and poetry. Truly, philosophy is like a soldier or lower officer at the orders of Oratory, his commander and (as a great writer of tragedies [Euripides] calls her) his queen.

Vegio invokes the example of Cicero, who spoke 'freely in philosophy without being tied to any sect', yet criticizes him for not having been more aggressive towards that discipline:

Nevertheless, I would prefer that he had claimed to deal with those arguments not as a philosopher but as an orator, and that he had exercised the same license—or rather freedom—in firmly recovering from the philosophers all the oratorical trappings that he found among them (since everything that philosophy claims for itself is actually ours), and I would wish him to have raised against those sneak thieves of philosophers the sword he had received from Eloquence, queen of all, and to punish them as criminals. Truly how much more clearly, solemnly, and magnificently the same subjects are dealt with by the orators than by the obscure, squalid, and anaemic philosophers! (pp. 75–7)

That these views are meant seriously, not to be dismissed as a whim of this persona, is shown by Valla having another character, Bripio, praise Vegio for what he has said:

You do well when you try to return to oratory the very ample patrimony stolen from her by agents unknown to me. If indeed we diligently search through the different ages of history, we shall find that the orators spoke in the midst of cities about the best and most important subjects before the philosophers started to chatter in their nooks and crannies. And even in our own time, although the philosophers may call themselves leaders, it is the orators—as events show us—who must be designated leaders of others, and kings. I therefore approve of your design to speak as an orator instead of a philosopher, and I exhort you to follow it through. (p. 77)

Bripio echoes Cicero's contemptuous reference to philosophers chattering *in angulis*, and behind him we hear the voice of Callicles. It is as if Plato had defined the terms of the debate for all time.

Certainly Valla intends to emulate Cicero and Quintilian by returning Plato's charges with interest. In the final book his Christian spokesman rebukes Boethius for having been 'more friendly with the dialecticians than the rhetoricians':

How much better it would have been for him to speak oratorically rather than dialectically! What is more absurd than the procedure of the philosophers? If one word goes wrong, the whole argument is imperilled. The orator makes use of many different procedures: he brings in contrary points, seeks out examples, makes comparisons, and forces even the hidden truth to appear. . . . Boethius ought to have worked in this way; he, like many others, was deceived by excessive love of dialectics. But how much error has been in dialectics, and how no one has ever before written carefully about it, and how it is really a part of rhetoric—about all these things our Lorenzo here has begun to write, very much in accordance with the truth, in my opinion. (p. 273)

Valla's concluding self-praise describes one tactic in the Renaissance dispute, that of subsuming dialectic under rhetoric, as a more specialized and limited art.[17] The humanists generally dismissed scholastic logic as abstract and intellectual, with 'no true utility or direct relevance for human life'. Valla in particular attacked logic and scholastic philosophy with polemical violence, urging the 'revenge' on behalf of oratory that Cicero had not carried far enough, and claiming for rhetoric a total domination over the arts and sciences. Modern Valla scholars tacitly endorse these claims,[18] but to me they seem to revive the megalomania that Plato wickedly ascribed to Gorgias, when he

[17] On the rhetoricization of logic in the Renaissance see Cesare Vasoli, *La dialettica e la retorica dell'Umanesimo. 'Invenzione' e 'Metodo' nella cultura del XV e XVI secolo* (Milan, 1968).

[18] Seigel 1968 merely summarizes Valla's argument, referring to his 'total indictment' of Boethius for having preferred philosophy to both Christianity and rhetoric (pp. 157–8); or to Valla having declared 'all traditional philosophy to be outside the pale of true learning' (p. 168), without seeing the absurdity of that proposition; or to Valla's tactics for accomplishing 'that revenge on behalf of Oratory which [he] criticized Cicero for not having carried far enough' (p. 167). These seem to me places where an authorial disclaimer, rather than an endorsement, would be in order. Hanna-Barbara Gerl's study (Gerl 1974) is better balanced, but makes the same error of treating Valla's polemics with uncritical respect, accepting his claim that rhetoric is 'the true philosophy' (p. 74), and saying of his attack on Aristotle that 'Diesen Kampf bestreitet die Rhetorik . . . in einem unerhörten Totalitätsanspruch', to replace or transcend all other arts and sciences (p. 78). Valla seems to me, at any rate in his polemical works, to have been well-meaning but hysterical and unbalanced. Such claims achieve little, but can bring rhetoric into disrespect.

asserted that rhetoric 'includes practically all other faculties under her control' (456 b). What use is 'revenge' here? Renaissance apologists for humanism in effect fought out once again the 'Battles of the Liberal Arts' that had been so common in the medieval period. Professors starting their lectures each year made a practice of extolling their own subject at the expense of their colleagues', and this combination of vaunting and denigration continued for several centuries. Once rhetoric became thoroughly rehabilitated by the Florentine humanists it took up the campaign with great vigour. Rhetoric, and later poetry, were pronounced the supreme arts, often citing classical celebrations of eloquence, such as Tacitus: *omnium artium domina*, or Martianus Capella: *rerum omnium regina*.[19] Coluccio Salutati, Chancellor of Florence, in one place declared poetry to be 'the greatest of all arts and sciences', to which the others are merely preparatory, with Petrarch the greatest of all writers;[20] in another text he gave the palm to rhetoric.[21] Those who put rhetoric in the supreme position include George of Trebizond, Valla, Sperone Speroni ('signora della vita morale'), Guillaume Télin ('royne des hommes'), Vives, Guillaume Budé, and dozens more.[22] Those who elevated poetry include Giovanni Pontano, who deemed it 'mother of all knowledge', Benedetto Varchi, G. P. Pigna, and many Renaissance theorists of literature.[23]

As one reconstructs this debate even the most indulgent supporter of rhetoric begins to feel that it has pushed its case too far. In the mid-sixteenth century M. T. Nizolio, fanatical admirer of Cicero, took over the all-embracing claims of *De Oratore* in an un-Ciceronian spirit, rejecting the logical works of Aristotle as 'vicious', expelling dialectic and metaphysics, while making rhetoric the truly universal art, its subject-matter being all human knowledge.[24] Such claims, revealing as they do their

---

[19] Tacitus, *Dialogus de Oratoribus*, § 32; Martianus Capella, *De nuptiis Philologiae et Mercurii*, v. 427: tr. in Miller, Prosser, and Benson 1973, p. 3.

[20] See Ullman 1963, pp. 65, 95, 240.   [21] See Struever 1970, p. 53.

[22] See Monfasani 1976, p. 259; Garin 1973, p. 131 (Speroni); Gordon 1970, p. 30 (Télin); Bolgar 1970, pp. 199-215, at pp. 205 (Budé) and 207 (Vives).

[23] See Weinberg 1961, pp. 8-9, and *passim*.

[24] See R. P. McKeon, 'The Transformation of the Liberal Arts in the Renaissance', in B. S. Levy (ed.), *Developments in the Early Renaissance* (Albany NY, 1972), pp. 158–223, at pp. 217–19; and Nizolius, *De veris principiis et vera ratione philosophandi contra pseudo-philosophos*, ed. Q. Breen, 2 vols. (Rome, 1956).

own impracticability, do little harm beyond making rhetoric seem ridiculous. More damaging were the humanists' attacks on other sciences which did not threaten rhetoric's status as an art of language, such as medicine, or mathematics. The early humanists, led by Petrarch and Salutati, wrote formal invectives against medicine on the grounds that it was theoretical, concerned with nature rather than man, and incapable of generalization. Law, or humanism, by contrast, represented a fully human concern with language, God's gift to distinguish men from beasts, and with its essential role in the social and active life.[25] From the standpoint of the *vita activa* Aeneas Sylvius Piccolomini, in his *De Liberorum Educatione* (1450; printed *c.* 1475), made grammar and rhetoric central, recalling that Cicero had reproached Sextus Pompey for spending too much time on geometry, because 'the true praise of men lies in doing, and that consequently all ingenious trifling . . . which withdraws our energies from fruitful activity is unworthy of the true citizen'.[26] The humanists distrusted natural philosophy for its failure to help man face the supreme problem, as Petrarch put it, of how to live.[27] Juan Luis Vives, the Spanish humanist who had such a great influence on sixteenth-century Europe, warned against too much study of the *quadrivium* (arithmetic, geometry, astronomy, and music) because mathematical abstractions 'withdraw the mind from practical concerns of life, and render it less fit to face concrete and mundane realities'. Vives put grammar and rhetoric at the top of his educational priorities and virtually rejected science.[28] Roger Ascham, writing in the 1560s, warned his readers against 'all Mathematicall heades, which be onely and wholy bent to those sciences, how solitarie they be themselves, how unfit to live with others, and how unapte to serve in the world'.[29] One of the few changes made in the statutes of Cambridge University at the onset of Elizabeth's reign was to eliminate mathematics in favour of

[25] See Ullman 1963, p. 32; Garin 1965, p. 31; Gerl 1974, pp. 67 ff.
[26] See Woodward 1897, p. 155.
[27] Petrarch 1948, pp. 58–9: 'What is the use . . . of knowing the nature of quadrupeds, fowls, fishes, and serpents and not knowing or even neglecting man's nature, the purpose for which we are born, and whence and whereto we travel?'
[28] See Woodward 1906, pp. 202–3.
[29] Ascham, *English Works*, ed. W. A. Wright (Cambridge, 1904), p. 190; cit. Simon 1966, p. 119.

rhetoric. Fortunately for English science, perhaps, maths established itself all the same.[30]
The hostility of humanists and rhetoricians towards the sciences persisted as a form of jealousy and rivalry for a long time. One of the most bizarre instances was the attack by no less a rhetorician than Giambattista Vico on the work of no less a mathematician than Descartes. Vico, Professor of Rhetoric at the University of Naples for forty years, took issue with Cartesian geometry precisely on the grounds that recommended it to all students of mathematics, its 'defigurization of the geometrical, and . . . its conversion into algebraic values'.[31] Vico, arguing from the primacy of rhetoric and the *vita activa*, attacked Cartesian analysis for encouraging a solitary existence, rendering students incapable of civic life (this seems to have been a personal phobia against solitude rather than a justified complaint). To defend traditional values Vico rejected the new 'analytical geometry, by which the subject-matter of mathematics is, as far as possible, stripped of all concrete, figural elements, and reduced to pure rationality',[32] replacing them with the study of the Italian language and metaphor. Painting the picture in the blackest possible terms, Vico feared that a training in Cartesian geometry would blind the imagination, enfeeble the memory, slacken the understanding, and destroy perception. (This is rather like Victorian warnings of the dangers of masturbation.) The remedy was for students to return to 'plane' geometry, using figures instead of numbers, while cultivating their minds and tongues with rhetoric, especially the concrete teaching of the topics.[33] To modern commentators, once again, all this seems perfectly under-standable, for, as one Vico scholar puts it, Cartesian geometry 'worked contrary to the skills of effective public action and implied a spirit utterly repulsive to the mind of a jurist; for this reason, plainly and consistently, Vico rejected it'.[34] But also short-sightedly, one cannot help thinking. Like any other discipline, rhetoric should know its limitations.

[30] Simon 1966, p. 358. See now Mordechai Feingold, *The Mathematicians' Apprenticeship. Science, Universities and Society in England, 1540–1640* (Cambridge, 1984).
[31] Gianturco 1965, p. xxvi.
[32] Mooney 1985, p. 104. See my review of this book in *TLS*, 4 Apr. 1986, p. 365.
[33] Mooney 1985, pp. 127–9.   [34] Ibid., p. 103.

As we review these disputes between rhetoric and philosophy our reaction may be to say, 'Blessed are the peace-makers'. But few appeared in that role, each side in the quarrel rather exercising itself to become more provocative. One of the sad features of such disputes among the Liberal Arts is the lack of any longer view. The opponent of a discipline does his best to annihilate it as quickly and comprehensively as possible, not asking whether he or his mother-discipline might ever need it again. If some of the more extreme defenders of rhetoric had been presented with the assembled Liberal Arts together with a 'destruct button', I fear they might have wiped them out altogether. Of course, they claimed to have been provoked. Petrarch, as a modern scholar writes with studied neutrality, 'described the physicians' attempt to make rhetoric subservient to their own art of medicines as "an unheard-of sacrilege"'.[35] Vico, in the words of another commentator, was incensed by Descartes' 'professed antipathy, nay, utter contempt, for the *litterae humaniores* and pre-eminently for languages'.[36] Sometimes rhetoricians anticipated attack from philosophers and got in a 'pre-emptive strike'. Thus Ermolao Barbaro, writing from Venice to Giovanni Pico della Mirandola in April 1485, having heard about his studies from a mutual friend, praises him for having learned Greek, for 'during many centuries there has not stood out a memorable work in good Latin done by anyone who lacked Greek letters'.[37] Barbaro is asserting the sense of superiority that Renaissance humanists, especially those associated with the revival of Greek in the fifteenth century, felt over the medieval scholastic philosophers. The Venetian humanist describes them as 'dull, rude, uncultured, barbarians',

[35] Seigel 1968, p. 37.

[36] Gianturco 1965, p. xvi.

[37] The following discussion of the Barbaro–Pico–Melanchthon exchange is based on Breen 1968, which collects Breen's essays and translations of the correspondence between the three writers. All references will be included in the text, prefixed by the letter 'B': so here, B 13. (Two Latin texts by Pico and Barbaro are printed with Italian translations in E. Garin (ed.), *Prosatori Latini del Quattrocento* (Milan, 1952), pp. 804–22, 844–62.) Breen interprets Pico's part in this debate as a straightforward attack on rhetoric—rather than a mock-attack, parodying the extreme position of the logicians—but this is too simple, as any reader with a knowledge of Renaissance techniques in epideictic and mock-epideictic will recognize. A useful corrective by Letizia Panizza, 'Pico's 1485 Defence of Philosophy vs. Eloquence and Socratic Irony', was presented at the 1979 conference of the International Society for Neo-Latin Studies.

who may have 'said something of use', and were undoubtedly learned, but were wholly lacking in the 'shining and elegant style, at least pure and chaste' which brings 'an author immortal reputation' (B 13–14). True, they had *res*, 'material' or subject-matter, but that is not enough. A coppersmith or sculptor begins with material, but what shapes it is his art (B 14). Only those writers can excel who have a mastery of *verba* as well as *res*.

Pico replied from Florence in June 1485, and his opening paragraphs spell out the hidden target of Barbaro's letter. Ironically pretending to accept Ermolao's estimate of 'those barbaric philosophers, . . . dull, rude, uncultured', Pico apologizes for having spent six years studying Aquinas, Johñ Scotus, Albert, and Averroës, now realizing that he has lost 'the best years of his life' by studying philosophy instead of 'fine letters' (B 15–16). Pico was working at this time on his nine hundred *Conclusiones*, in the preface to which (1486) he formally abjured 'classical elegance' in favour of 'the manner and diction of the most celebrated Parisian disputants, the same being in most general use amongst the philosophers of our times' (B 4–5). The humanist attack on their medieval predecessors was of course a deliberate tactic in their own campaign of self-definition, and although some major changes of emphasis occurred in philosophical discourse, we now know that scholasticism, especially in its use of Aristotelian categories and methods of organizing knowledge, retained a strong influence on Renaissance philosophy.[38] It is with a conscious acceptance of this heritage that Pico now imagines how 'one of the slightly more eloquent' scholastics would defend his subject, and writes what we might call an 'Oration on behalf of scholastic philosophy' (B 16 ff.). The scholastics had slighted rhetoric—in Aquinas' hierarchy of the arts rhetoric and poetry had held the bottom position—but Pico's defence of them uses neither the form nor the content of scholastic arguments, but an essentially rhetorical mode, beloved of Renaissance humanists, the epideictic oration, alternating praise and blame. These procedures are interchangeable, of course, and I shall argue that

[38] See P. O. Kristeller, 'Humanism and Scholasticism in the Italian Renaissance', in Kristeller, *Studies in Renaissance Thought and Letters* (Rome, 1956; 1969), pp. 553–83; Kristeller 1979, pp. 85–105; C. B. Schmitt, *Aristotle and the Renaissance* (Cambridge, Mass., 1983); A. Grafton and L. Jardine, *From Humanism to the Humanities* (London, 1987): somewhat overstated.

in the course of the argument Pico indeed changes sides. What begins as an ostensible defence of scholasticism ends as an apologia for humanism and the study of eloquence and Greek. It is not easy to mark the point at which Pico switches direction, and it may be that he wished both sides to stand, not cancelling each other out.

Pico's persona starts by claiming that the scholastics have spent their lives enquiring into 'the reasons of things human and divine', not into the 'light nothings' of classical mythology. They have pursued truth with great care, but rather than being 'dull and heavy' they 'have had the god of eloquence not on the tongue but in the heart', for 'if eloquence they lacked they did not lack wisdom' (B 16). This argument might seem to be collapsing the distinction between the traditionally opposed terms, but if so it is just a stage in a campaign that now takes the offensive by pointedly rejecting Cicero's plea that *cor* and *lingua*, eloquence and wisdom, should be reunited. Pico's scholastic abjures any such compromise, flatly stating that 'eloquence should not be joined to wisdom', since to do so would be as wicked as if a reputable maiden or Vestal should use 'synthetic beauty, or rouge' (B 16). Rhetoric is still being judged with Plato's hostile metaphors and dismissive dichotomies, a debt that becomes clear in this uncompromising attack:

So great is the conflict between the office of the orator and the philosopher that there can be no conflicting greater than theirs. For what else is the task of the rhetor than to lie, to entrap, to circumvent, to practise sleight-of-hand? For, as you say, it is your business to be able at will to turn black into white, white into black; to be able to elevate, degrade, enlarge, and reduce, by speaking, whatsoever you will; at length you do this to the things themselves by magical arts, as it were, for by the powers of eloquence you build them up in such a way that they change to whatever face and costume you please. (B 16)

All that the rhetorician displays is 'sheer mendacity, sheer imposture, sheer trickery', being concerned 'either to enlarge by addition or to reduce by subtraction', whereas the 'entire endeavour' of the philosopher 'is concerned with knowing the truth and demonstrating it to others' (B 16–17).

Pico's scholastic shows a thorough knowledge of Plato's case against rhetoric, that paragraph reading like a swift review of the *Gorgias*, *Phaedrus*, and *Euthydemus*. As his argument develops it relies much on the major Platonic dichotomies, especially the opposition between thought and language. The philosophers' 'subject-matter' or *res* is solid, for 'in every subject concerned with true knowing nothing is more unseemly and detrimental than all that elaborated sort of discourse'. All such arts are like cosmetics, surface ornaments for a body whose inside is 'empty and hollow'. The philosophers 'search after the what of writing', others 'after the how' (B 18). Others write 'for the many', the philosophers for the few (B 19). The form of their discourse resembles 'the Sileni of our Alcibiades', with shaggy and loathsome faces, 'but within full of gems'. After Plato the scholastic invokes Cicero, saying that he did 'not desire eloquence in a philosopher, but that he be adequate in his subject-matter and teaching'. Cicero, he claims, knew that 'it is more important for us to set in order the mind than delivery; to be careful lest what strays be reason, not speech (*ratio non oratio*); that we attain to the word as thought, not to the word as expression' (B 20). But in fact Cicero would never separate *ratio* and *oratio*, for he regarded the one as the fulfilment of the other, and the union of both as the goal of his teaching (*De Inv.* 1.1, 1.4; *De Or.* 1. 13. 56, 1. 14. 51, 3. 16. 59 ff., 3. 19. 71, etc.). A touch of speciousness is evident here, perhaps to indicate the weakness of the case against rhetoric that it is forced to twist well-known texts to say the opposite of what they mean.

Pico's scholastic reverts to his dichotomies, claiming that wisdom 'and philosophers' teachings . . . are not brightened but obscured by word-painting' (B 21). It is 'the philosopher who alone contemplates and explores the nature of everything' (B 23), shunning 'the Muses' pleasant groves' for 'the horrendous cave in which Heracleitus said the truth lies hidden' (B 21). A long sequence of dichotomizing is employed to reject the atheism of the pagan poet Lucretius, although expressed 'in good Latin, elegantly', in favour of the truths of Christianity as set down by John Scotus, albeit 'without taste, crudely, in non-Latin words' (B 20–4). Pico, like Valla in his *De Voluptate* a half-century earlier, is declaring the inferiority of pagan to Christian culture. Yet, as a full reading of the text will show, Pico writes not like a scholastic, with a bare deductive logic, but like a humanist, with exuberance, grace, wit, and a wide range of allusions to poetry and mythology. Towards the end the argument visibly shifts ground, for the scholastic now concedes that 'eloquence and wisdom may be closely connected', but finds faults on both sides: 'It is the philosophers who have separated wisdom from eloquence [so conceding Cicero's case against Socrates]; and the historians, rhetoricians, and poets who have separated eloquence from wisdom.' It is the latter group, however, who must put their house in order, for although 'they are wrong who separate good sense (*cor*) from language (*lingua*)'—now admitting Cicero's complementary categories—language is less important than wisdom, the wisdom 'about things human and divine' that the philosopher is concerned with. And so we reach the most challenging dichotomy of all:

> We can live without a tongue, though not conveniently; but we cannot live at all without a heart. He is not cultured (*humanus*) who were alien to polite letters; he is not a man (*homo*) who were destitute of philosophy. The most inarticulate wisdom can be of use. [How?] Unwise eloquence, like a sword in a madman's hand, cannot be but most dangerous. (B 23–4)

Anyone familiar with Renaissance humanism will recognize that to call in question language is to challenge one of its deepest values, for the strength—and also the weakness—of that movement was its profound concern with the written and spoken word, from philology and textual criticism to rhetoric and hermeneutics. Our sense that the speech is in some way meant ironically begins to grow, although it still has no clear focus. There are instances of mock-attacks on rhetoric in the following century, as in H. C. Agrippas *De Incertitudine et Vanitate Scientiarum et Artium . . . Declamatio* (1530) and Bishop Jewel's *Oratio Contra Rhetoricam*[39] (c. 1548), but none that I know of before Pico. In his concluding comments *in propria persona* Pico informs us rather teasingly that 'I do not fully agree with' the arguments of the scholastic, and finally comes clean about his real purpose:

[39] See B. C. Bowen, 'Cornelius Agrippa's *De Vanitate*: Polemic or Paradox?', *Bibliothèque d'humanisme et Renaissance*, 34 (1972), 249–56; and (unaware of the preceding) E. Korkowski, 'Agrippa as Ironist', *Neophilologus*, 60 (1976), 594–607. For a translation of Jewel's mock attack see H. H. Hudson, 'Jewel's Oration Against Rhetoric: A Translation', *Quarterly Journal of Speech*, 14 (1928), 374–92.

I have given freely of myself in this matter, as in something of ill repute; so that, like those who praise the quartan fever, I might test my abilities. My special aim was like that of Plato's Glaucon, who praised injustice, not seriously, but to goad Socrates to the praise of justice. Likewise, so that I may hear you defend eloquence I have attacked it rather violently, for a little while even over the protest of my feelings and natural disposition. Had I thought the Barbarians right in their neglect of eloquence I should not almost wholly have left off studying them; I should not a short time ago have taken up Greek letters. (B 24–5)

So Pico has all along been playing the role of *advocatus scholastici* only in order to 'bring out' the rhetoricians to defend their subject. Like the mock-encomia, those praises of the fever, gout, or baldness, he has been testing—or rather, revealing his abilities in *inventio* and *elocutio*. It is a speech set up in order to be knocked down—yet obviously serious on some issues, notably Christianity. Pico records that he himself has moved away from scholastic philosophy to humanism, yet, he adds, 'certain grammaticasters turn my stomach, who when they have made a couple of etymological discoveries become such show-offs . . . that as compared with themselves they would have philosophers esteemed as nothing' (B 25). Humanist philology, as he rightly says, was not free from either pedantry or arrogance. The Barbarians, he concludes, have earned some praise for their knowledge of *res*: now the rhetoricians should show their ability in *verba*.

Pico's mocking, paradoxical attack on rhetoric succeeded in its goal of eliciting defences. Ermolao Barbaro wrote two letters in reply in 1485, one short and one long, and then a third participant entered the discussion—if one can still call it that when the first writers are dead—namely Philip Melanchthon, the German Reformation humanist, who in 1558 wrote his own *Reply to Pico*. Of the two, Barbaro, being closer in time, and a true correspondent, understands the immediate context, especially Pico's irony. He enjoys the piquant situation of Pico appearing as 'an enemy who champions the enemy', because 'under the guise of defending you utterly kill off those you defend' (B 27). As Cicero said of the *Gorgias* that Plato showed himself most a rhetorician when attacking rhetoric, so Barbaro sees that 'the foes of eloquence cannot maintain their cause save by eloquent men'. At the University of Padua, a centre of Aristotelian philosophy, he reports, Pico's defence has 'mightily annoyed the majority of those you defend', being described as a 'Laudation of Typhon and the Furies'—a mock-praise, that is, of things repugnant by nature. In humanist circles, though, 'with whom you quarrel in word but agree at heart, the thing you did is to everybody most gratifying, because we understand where you are leading and what you mean'. If Pico's mock-defence had represented his true sentiments, he would be 'a deserter' to the humanist cause.

Allow me this jest: if you are not a deserter, you are carrying water on both shoulders when by your method of defence you break down the case you have taken up. It does not matter by what method you betray the barbarians, your clients. But what more cunning scheme could you have hit upon than to try by the highest eloquence to defend the accused who confess themselves injurious to eloquence? (B 27)

Barbaro doubts whether any of the scholastics 'can understand the things you have said;—things endowed with so great splendour', so rich in rhetorical ornament of every kind (ibid.).

In order to show how little the scholastics understand, and how poorly they argue, Barbaro now attempts to emulate Pico by imagining a reply made by an arrogant Paduan philosopher (B 20–38). His Aristotelian persona records annoyance that in this dispute 'one who will give adverse sentence was elected to serve as judge and arbitrator', underlining the real thrust of Pico's argument. Resentful at this mock-defence, and at the humanist-rhetorical forms of argument it employed, Ermolao's scholastic now argues his case in search of *apodixis*, conclusive proof, and does so with a rash of technicalities, syllogisms, epicheiremes, dilemmas, and fallacies. In the Lucca codex these are illustrated in the margins by the symbols used to denote technical procedures in logic, double crescents, and isosceles triangles, upright and inverted (B 28 ff.). The style becomes a parody of the logician's mode of discourse:

Therefore their first rhetorical syllogism (*aggressio*) consists of both syllogism and prosyllogism, with true propositions and false assumptions, according to the first figure; or it consists of a single syllogism, using the second figure; as they desire to be taught by the rules of the *Analytics,* and they say this is altogether a paralogism of the kind called *per aliquid et simpliciter:* for example . . . (B 35)

Unfortunately, as readers of Nabokov or Sterne's *Tristram Shandy* know to their cost, parodies of pedantry end up as pedantry. The scholastics are mocked, but the modern reader experiences both tedium and puzzlement at the intricacies of their argument.

Barbaro complicates matters further by making his scholastic report at some length the arguments used by the *rhetorici* against him. Confronted with the humanists' claims that all philosophy is good, that the peripatetics held rhetoric to be part of philosophy, and that Aristotle assigned it to social knowledge, the scholastic can only mumble about the syllogistic categories involved and declare 'I do not know whether this or the contrary is true; nor can I find where Aristotle said it' (B 31). He would only have needed to consult the opening pages of his *Rhetoric,* but, as Barbaro makes the scholastic confess, 'inasmuch as almost all the books of this philosopher are obscure we neglect them', while the *rhetorici* study them constantly. In other words, the humanists have opened up the riches of the classical tradition, while the scholastics have given up reading texts, and remain trapped within their own logical system. Their spokesman reports how the humanists 'made sport of' him for attempting to divide philosophy strictly into theory and practice (including rhetoric): 'you want philosophers cut in two, half perfect, mutilated' (ibid.). The humanists' 'crowning argument' was that since Plato and Aristotle 'were men of such surpassing eloquence', then 'to say that philosophy conflicts with eloquence because the orator's business is but to deceive and lie, is clear calumny' (B 32). In reporting such arguments, and being unable to answer them, the scholastic is seen to be scoring a series of own goals. At times, however, the tissue of report and argument becomes so complex that it is hard to know who is arguing what, and we must conclude that Barbaro, like Valla, did not fully master the structure of an ironic treatise. The scholastic is certainly made to admit that their mode of speech is rude and clumsy (B 33); he is made to quote Cicero at great length, even though the passages turn out to be not 'a defence' but 'a betrayal' of his own position (B 33–5); he is forced to cite the humanists' case that a man lacking *prudentia*, practical knowledge, 'is not a philosopher, but a monster' (B 35). Unrealistic though it may be in terms of the persona's allegiance, he faithfully reports the rhetors' verdict on his 'crafty sort of argument', with 'its bad deductions from nonessentials and consequents', and its 'tissue of most impudent propositions' (B 36). Finally, although outwitted, he refuses to admit defeat, for 'it is our custom in debate always to stand firm, never to give an inch, never to yield, always to have some safe ground or hiding place'. This, too, the humanists attack, 'calling it boorishness and impudence born from our very contempt of polite letters' (B 37): the scholastics are ignorant of the debate form in rhetoric. As Ermolao says at the end, *in propria persona*, 'to defend a barbarous and stupid method of philosophizing' is like 'wanting to whiten an Ethopian' (B 38).

Now we can see that far from being opponents, Pico and Barbaro were actually collaborators. The one pretended to attack rhetoric yet actually mocked pagan philosophy and scholasticism; the other pretended to defend scholasticism yet actually attacked it. What neither had done, however, was to defend rhetoric, or at least do so openly and unequivocally. Melanchthon was a much more straightforward writer, with no taste for mock-encomium or irony, and in his *Reply to Pico* 'in behalf of Barbaro' (B 52–68) leaves us in no doubt as to his true opinion. He addresses Pico as if he were indeed an enemy of rhetoric. He has 'accused Eloquence', and Melanchthon intends to 'dissolve certain principal arguments of your letter', namely that the scholastics had 'complete knowledge of things', and 'were right in disdaining eloquence' (B 53). Farther from Pico in time, Melanchthon is even more removed in temperament, and fails to detect his ironic intent. The statement of Pico's scholastic that 'it is wrong to join eloquence to wisdom' is dismissed as 'a paradox which fights against nature itself', and 'tears apart . . . the virtues which nature has joined together' (B 54). Pico defends the scholastics 'in such a manner as to slash at Eloquence', and his 'entire discourse is not so much a defence of the barbarians as an arraignment of eloquence' (B 55). At every stage Pico is accused of misrepresenting the subject, of heaping up 'a mess of comparisons', one of which, Melanchthon says, 'turns my stomach' (B 61), and the sum of which are intended 'to confuse the reader so that he cannot have respect for the dignity of eloquence. I ask you, are these not the devices of a rhetorician or of a sophist?' (B 62). 'You vituperate poets, orators, historians—in short', Melanchthon complains, 'anything eloquent' (B 64).

We may complain, in turn, that Pico's irony has been missed, but we cannot doubt Melanchthon's sincerity. He sets about 'a defence of eloquence' that obeys the laws of epideictic rhetoric, alternating praise of eloquence with vituperation of scholasticism. Scholastic disputation, he claims, is incomprehensible even to initiates, 'for not only is it a new kind of words unknown to people generally, but everything is so confused that, as in a labyrinth, one can find neither beginning nor end for things'. The scholastics are constantly inventing 'monstrous expressions by which, since they have no basis in reality, nothing can be understood' (B 57). The schoolmen 'commit grammatical blunders' in Latin, do not finish their sentences, 'have no discretion or order in thoughts', and 'are guilty of solecisms . . . in their own schools' (B 58–9). Their parochialism has made them ignore the study of languages, 'which formerly was cultivated in the church', and thus they scorn God's gift of tongues (B 63). Where Jerome 'illuminated the Holy Scripture by his eloquence', Scotus 'brought into the church the most trifling disputations' (B 64). They have also 'corrupted philosophy', for not understanding 'good discourse' they have oppressed almost the whole of Aristotle with 'their fancies about common nature, hecceities, distinctions concerning first and second intentions, about instants, and similar ravings' (B 66). They have no knowledge of Greek mathematics, which Melanchthon—more enlightened than other humanists, due to his connections with Rheticus—sees as essential to recovering 'the true meaning of Ptolemy' (ibid.). And their application of dialectic to theology has been disastrous, since they cannot understand biblical discourse and 'build a new edifice' of their own, consisting of 'largely puerile disputations stitched together' (B 67). Finally, 'the most obstinate hatreds' they manifest against humanism 'prevent the possibility of a reflowering of the better studies' (B 68).

After this comprehensive attack on scholastic philosophy Melanchthon turns eagerly to the praise of his own discipline, 'for what subject can possibly be richer than that of the dignity

and utility of eloquence?' (B 53). Echoing Cicero, he affirms that
eloquence must be joined to wisdom, 'for clearly there is no use
for wisdom unless we can communicate to others the things we
have with wisdom deliberated and thought upon' (B54).
Eloquence is not 'adventitious ornament' but 'a peculiar power
and virtue given to men for a certain utility', namely 'for proper
and clear explication of mental sense and thought . . . in
appropriate and clear language' (B 54–6). Melanchthon,
somewhat opportunistically, invokes Plato's *Phaedrus* on
eloquence being 'necessary . . . for explication of things divine
and human', and Aristotle's *Rhetoric* for placing rhetoric among
the 'great and necessary things . . . concerning right and justice
and . . . every duty of virtue'. Then he turns to the Isocratean–
Ciceronian tradition of rhetoric as the instrument of civilization:

It has been said, with good reason, that when men were still dispersed
and nomadic they were gathered together by eloquence, and that by it
states were founded; by it rights, religions, legitimate marriage, and the
other bonds of human society were constituted. In fact, it is by
eloquence (*oratio*) that these things are maintained in commonwealths.
Should we agree with you and consider this divine power, so necessary
to mankind, as nothing but a game or pack of tricks? (B 56)

Whoever does not 'acknowledge the benefits of eloquence' is
guilty of 'ingratitude and impiety', to the Renaissance very
serious failings.

Melanchthon's defence of rhetoric moves along by now
familiar lines, basing itself on the superiority of the *vita activa*: 'I
call a philosopher one who when he has learned and knows
things good and useful for mankind, takes a theory (*doctrina*) out
of academic obscurity and makes it practically useful in public
affairs' (B 58). Like painting, he says, rhetoric strives to follow
nature by finding a style appropriate to the subject-matter. Its
'chief ornament is the thing's proper exposition itself, as in
painting it is the precise lineaments of bodies' (B 60). Philosophy
should indeed be communicated in the modest, not the grand
style, but other subjects 'require a certain splendour of
expression'. The fact that the Bible demonstrates various kinds
of style—the 'beautiful language' of the prophets, the 'Attic'
style of the Psalms, Paul's combination of disputation and
ornament—shows that eloquence is essential 'for expounding

sacred and great subjects', particularly for 'clarifying' them (B 63–4). Melanchthon values rhetoric as an aid to the exposition of difficult ideas, especially in theology, but also as a guide to living, for

> the orators bring into writing the best experience, which exercises and sharpens their thinking. That is why they transfer philosophy aptly to use and to common life. In their shadows your philosophers do not even understand the vigour of the precepts about which they quarrel. (B 65)

So Melanchthon can finally appeal to Pico with the appropriate rhetorical compliments ('you are gifted with many-sided learning . . . and I know you have the eloquence for elucidating such things') to take up the true business of the philosopher, that is 'to serve all mankind well by digging out and revealing truth', and then to 'do what pleases God, . . . again celebrate and praise Eloquence as given by heaven for the highest uses to men' (B 67–8).

Had Pico been alive when Melanchthon wrote this letter, he would have seen that his German fellow-humanist had missed the point of his ironic attack, but would have welcomed his defence of rhetoric, and his Christianity. Yet Pico, still in touch with scholasticism as a living influence, would not have approved of sixteenth-century Reformation attitudes, which could see no good in that school of philosophy, whether medieval or contemporary. Melanchthon expresses these attitudes vigorously, but nowhere argues them out. His attack is just as much the expression of prejudice against a type of philosophy as is Quintilian's, or Valla's. For him rhetoric is a social, communicative art, with great pedagogic or expository value. It is not an instrument of discovery, which is still the role of philosophy, to whose *res* rhetoric adds the *verba* which will make its meaning clear to audiences of mixed abilities, such as a typical congregation or even a school class. Melanchthon, the *'Præceptor Germaniae'*, writes always as a teacher or preacher. Quirinus Breen justly observes that Melanchthon's conception of philosophy is static, as if everything was already known and merely needed to be expounded, and that his 'subordination of philosophy to rhetoric leaves philosophy in a kind of beggarly position, for he does not leave it free to be itself' (B 46–7, 50). This is precisely the weakness of the humanist position in these debates, working from a single discipline that will not recognize the validity or equal status of others. Humanists spoke from a position of strength when they criticized the style or grammar of scholasticism, especially when judging medieval Latin by the criteria of their new-found classicism, and one can personally agree that philosophy ought not to be wholly detached from the concerns of human life. Yet the one-sided nature of their attack meant that the value of the *bios theoretikos*, the *vita contemplativa*, could never be recognized. Perhaps they felt that, being an alternative to their own way of life, it threatened or criticized them. But the aggression, one cannot help feeling, was their own.

iii THE REVENGE OF PHILOSOPHY

Rhetoric reached its highest degree of influence, in modern times, in the great expansion of European education between 1500 and 1750. At every level of society, for every literary genre, as for the arts of painting, architecture, and music, rhetoric was an indispensable accomplishment for the civilized man or woman.[40] But in the eighteenth century its hegemony came under attack. It still continued to be taught, schools and universities maintaining their usual conservatism over curricula, but in some important areas it lost its undivided supremacy. New and independent aesthetic systems emerged, as both the visual arts and music rejected the dominance of language and language-based criteria.[41]

The rhetorical tradition itself seems to lose vitality, and although we have as yet no reliable history or bibliography of the dissemination of rhetoric texts in this period, my impression is that the general attitudes of rhetoric had been absorbed by a literary culture some of whose members rejected its detail, and especially its technicalities. It is not the case of rhetoric being ousted at one go, for we know that the first generation Romantic

[40] See Struever 1970; Muntéano 1967; Jean Hagstrum, *The Sister Arts* (Chicago, 1958); Spencer 1957; Gombrich 1960; Roskill 1968; Le Coat 1975; Vickers 1984, and the literature cited there.

[41] See John Neubauer, *The Emancipation of Music from Language. Departure from Mimesis in Eighteenth-Century Aesthetics* (New Haven, Conn., 1986).

poets were still under its influence. Goethe made notes from
Quintilian, and in 1815 still held the view of Isocrates, Cicero, or
Vives that rhetoric is indispensable to humanity: as Curtius
says, 'in him the entire European tradition was alive'.[42]
Wordsworth quotes Quintilian with approval, as do Macaulay,
Disraeli, and John Stuart Mill.[43] Cicero continued to be a living
part of the educated Englishman or American's culture until
well into the nineteenth century.[44] De Quincey, writing in 1828,
declared that 'the age of Rhetoric, like that of Chivalry, has passed
among forgotten things'—even though his own prose style is as
full of antithesis, balance, and more exuberant figures of speech
as a Hellenistic romance.[45] But that year saw the publication in
London of Richard Whately's *Elements of Rhetoric* (seven editions
by 1846), while in Paris Pierre Fontanier published in 1818 a
Commentaire raisonné on the *Traité des tropes* (1730) by C. Chesnau
Du Marsais (1676–1730), from whom Diderot and D'Alembert
had commissioned the articles on grammar for the *Grande
Encyclopédie* (he died before he could write them). Fontanier
went on to produce his own *Manuel classique pour l'étude des
tropes* in 1821 (four editions by 1830), which was adopted as the
official manual by the University of Paris.[46] Among the French
romantics Lamartine, Vigny, and Victor Hugo had a thorough
grounding in rhetoric, while some 150 pages of notes taken by
Stendhal in the 1790s survive, based on the *Cours de rhétorique* of
Dubois. Flaubert, studying at the Rouen *lycée*, used a manual
containing 'les préceptes du genre et des modèles d'exercices'.
His extant juvenilia, written in 1835–6, when he was in the

---

[42] Curtius 1953, p. 63.
[43] See Dockhorn 1968, pp. 80–1, for Wordsworth quoting Quintilian and
Longinus; F. H. Colson (ed.), *M. Fabii Quintiliani Institutionis Oratoriae Liber I*
(Cambridge, 1924), pp. lxxxvi–lxxxviii and epigraph (title-page verso). Stone
1967 is an important study of the persistence of rhetorical doctrine in Romantic
literary theory.
[44] See Mary Rosner, 'Cicero in Nineteenth-Century England and America',
Rhetorica, 4 (1986), 153–82.
[45] De Quincey, *Collected Writings*, ed. David Masson (London, 1897), 81, 97;
on his prose style see Baldwin 1928, pp. 40, 44–7, 49.
[46] See Gérard Genette's editions of Fontanier, *Les Figures du discours* (Paris,
1968) and of Fontanier's re-edition of Du Marsais, *Le Traité des tropes* (Geneva,
1967). Du Marsais' treatise has also been reissued with a 'Postface' by Claude
Mouchard (Paris, 1981). On the continuing influence of rhetoric in the French
church see F. P. Bowman, *Le Discours sur l'éloquence sacrée à l'époque romantique.
Rhétorique, apologétique, herméneutique (1777–1851)* (Geneva, 1980).

fourth form, include six 'narrations' (five historical novellas and a portrait of Byron), which are extensions of his homework (the same holds for Georg Büchner at the Darmstadt Gymnasium in the 1820s). As Gérard Genette has said, 'pour un adolescent de cette époque, "se lancer dans la littérature" n'était donc pas, comme aujourd'hui, une aventure et une rupture: c'était le prolongement—on dirait volontiers l'aboutissement normal d'un cycle d'études bien conduites.'[47] Such manuals as Girardin's *De l'instruction publique* (1838) followed a tradition going back three centuries, laying down that pupils in the second form should learn the figures of rhetoric, and compose narrations in Latin and French, graduating in the following years to the more demanding texts of Fontanier. It was not until the reforms of 1885 and 1902 that 'rhétorique' was suppressed as a subject in the state *lycées*, and replaced by the history of literature.[48] Besides the flourishing of the classical tradition in the nineteenth century, one could show the emergence of new rhetorics in poetry and prose, so that De Quincey's obituary of 1828 can be seen to be premature.

The history of the continuity of the rhetorical tradition during this period is, however, less well known today than the attacks on it—an interesting phenomenon, reflecting the ultimate victory of the anti-rhetorical camp. The critics of rhetoric included a number of philosophers, influential in their own day and much studied in ours, whose diatribes have carried greater weight than the historical fact of continuity. The most widely read English philosopher to attack rhetoric was John Locke, in his *Essay Concerning Human Understanding*[49] (1690; continually revised to 1706, dozens of editions and translations by 1800). As he explains in Book 3, chapter 10, Locke sees the purpose of language as being 'First, To make known one Man's Thoughts or Ideas to another. Secondly, To do it with as much ease and

    [47] See Muntéano 1967, pp. 157–9, 176–9; Jean Bruneau, *Les Débuts littéraires de Flaubert* (Paris, 1962); Michel Crouzet, *Le Naturel, la grâce et le réel dans la poétique de Stendhal* (Paris, 1986); and Genette, 'Rhétorique et enseignement', in Genette, *Figures II* (Paris, 1969), pp. 23–42, at p. 26.

    [48] Genette, ibid. (n. 47 above), pp. 24–9; Fumaroli 1980, p. 5.

    [49] All references are to Locke, *An Essay Concerning Human Understanding*, ed. Peter Nidditch (Oxford, 1975), incorporated into the text. It was, of course, a traditional complaint by the philosophers that rhetoric moved the passions, even if they themselves did the same: see Aristotle's *Rhetoric* (cited above, pp. 68, 72–3), and Quintilian, 5 Pr. 1 f., 6. 1. 7 ff., 11. 1. 33, etc.

quickness, as is possible; and Thirdly, Thereby to convey the Knowledge of Things' (p. 504). 'Figurative speech', therefore, when we are seeking 'dry Truth and real Knowledge', is an 'Abuse of Language'. Rhetorical 'ornament', such as metaphor, is acceptable in discourses where we seek pleasure, but not if we wish to convey information. Plato's dichotomies are revived: *delectare* is the scope of rhetoric, but not *docere*. Worse still, 'truth' is set against 'deception', reason against the passions:

> But yet, if we would speak of Things as they are, we must allow that all the Art of Rhetorick, besides Order and Clearness, all the artificial and figurative application of Words Eloquence hath invented, are for nothing else but to insinuate wrong Ideas, move the Passions, and thereby mislead the Judgment; and so indeed are perfect cheat. (p. 508)

Locke refuses to be more specific, since 'the Books of Rhetorick which abound in the world will instruct those who want to be informed'. So he concludes by lamenting that 'the Arts of Fallacy' are promoted at the expense of truth and knowledge.

> 'Tis evident how much Men love to deceive, and be deceived, since Rhetorick, that powerful instrument of Error and Deceit, has its established Professors, is publickly taught, and has always been had in great Reputation: And, I doubt not but it will be thought great boldness, if not brutality in me, to have said thus much against it. *Eloquence*, like the fair Sex, has too prevailing Beauties in it, to suffer it self ever to be spoken against. (ibid.)

   Locke's concluding analogy reminds us that he was a contemporary of the Restoration dramatists; his artful structuring of that paragraph proves that his own time as a teacher of rhetoric at Oxford had taught him some skills; while throughout the *Essay* he makes fluent use of metaphor—for both clarificatory and derogatory, or epideictic purposes. For Locke, just as for Hobbes in *Leviathan* (1651) and Sprat in *The History of the Royal Society* (1667),[50] the general truth holds, that those who attack rhetoric, or metaphor, invariably have to use rhetoric, and metaphor. Sprat called for the banishment of eloquence from society, but retracted the call on Aristotle's grounds of its usefulness in defending goodness; Locke does not even attempt

---

[50] See Brian Vickers, 'The Royal Society and English Prose Style: A Reassessment', in Vickers and Struever, *Rhetoric and the Pursuit of Truth* (Los Angeles, Ca., 1985), pp. 3–76.

to banish it. Yet the desire to do so recurred in the following century. In the 'Discours préliminaire' (1751) to the *Encyclopédie* Jean d'Alembert reiterated the call:

A l'égard de ces puérilités pédantesques, qu'on a honorées du nom de Rhétorique, ou plutôt, qui n'ont servi qu'à rendre ce nom ridicule, & qui sont à l'art oratoire ce que la Scolastique est à la vraie Philosophie, elles ne sont propres qu'à donner de l'éloquence l'idée la plus fausse & la plus barbare. Cependant quoiqu'on commence assez universellement à en reconnaître l'abus, la possession où elles sont depuis long-temps de former une branche distinguée de la connaissance humaine, ne permet pas encore de les en bannir: pour l'honneur de notre discernement, le temps en viendra peut-être un jour.[51]

D'Alembert tries to drive a wedge between eloquence, which he sees as a natural gift, incapable of being learned by means of rules, and rhetoric as a science—a position reminiscent of Antonius at the beginning of *De Oratore*, or of Quintilian's many attacks on the 'puerilities' of the rhetoric-books compared to genuine oratorical skill. But D'Alembert, unlike Locke, accepts the legitimacy of communicating and thus concedes eloquence a role in life:

Les hommes en se communiquant leurs idées, cherchent aussi à se communiquer leurs passions. C'est par l'éloquence qu'ils y parviennent. Faite pour parler au sentiment . . . les prodiges qu'elle opère souvent entre les mains d'un seul sur toute une nation, sont peut-être le témoignage le plus éclatant de la supériorité d'un homme sur un autre.

The best reaction to this concession is Horace's wry remark, *Naturam expellas furca, tamen usque recurret* (adapted: 'You may drive rhetoric out with a pitchfork, but she will always come back in one form or another'). For that account of one man exceeding another due to the powers of his eloquence over the listener's feelings echoes the opening of *De Oratore* and *De Inventione*. D'Alembert then contradicts his denial that eloquence can be taught by recommending the would-be orator to study 'les hommes' and 'les grands modèles' of speech. Observing this, Marilyn Sides notes how his and other attacks

---

[51] *Encyclopédie ou Dictionnaire des Sciences, des Arts, et des métiers* (Geneva, 1777 edition), i, p. xix; cit. Sides 1983, pp. 111–14.

exist side-by-side with the persistence of rhetoric in 'good society, the theatre, the law-courts', and suggests that the call for 'a new scientific and logical' language remained 'the marginal discourse of an avant-garde élite until the nineteenth century, when it replaced rhetoric both in pedagogical and cultural institutions'.[52]

The danger is that historians take such calls for the banishment of rhetoric as proof that this duly took place ('peut-être un jour' is all that D'Alembert hazards). But, as Lessing says somewhere, 'all are not free who mock their chains'.[53] Those who attacked rhetoric continued to use it, and the pronouncements of 'an avant-garde élite' are as little use then, as now, for recording the whole picture. The attacks became sharper, however, nowhere more so than in Immanuel Kant's *Kritik der Urteilskraft* (1790) or 'Critique of Aesthetic Judgement'.[54] Like Plato, Kant combined formidable intellectual resources with great powers of expression. Also like Plato, he made much use of binary categories to privilege one discipline and dismiss another. Only here the favoured discipline is not philosophy, which Kant would probably have thought too valuable to put in the scales against rhetoric, but poetry. (He had declined a chair of poetry at the University of Königsberg before accepting one in philosophy.) While poetry, from the time of Aristotle to the seventeenth century, was regarded as essentially identical with rhetoric (having metrics as an additional resource), an autonomous poetic began to emerge in the eighteenth century. In Kant's work poetry is used as a stick with which to beat rhetoric. The arts of speech are said to consist of rhetoric and poetry, and are thus described:

Rhetoric is the art of transacting a serious business of the understanding as if it were a free play of the imagination; poetry that of conducting a free play of the imagination as if it were a serious business of the understanding.

The antithesis—in fact, *antimetabole*, interchanging 'serious business of the understanding' and 'free play of the imagination'—is clever, but of course question-begging, since

[52] Sides 1983.
[53] *Nathan der Weise*, iv. 4.
[54] Kant, *The Critique of Judgement*, tr. J. C. Meredith (Oxford, 1928, 1973); page-references incorporated into the text.

Kant offers no evidence to support either definition. Rhetoric is being used against itself, but in a mystifying way.

Kant extends his antithesis but without justifying his definitions. Poetry is said to be 'a free play of the imagination', which promises no intellectual or cognitive function, but in fact performs one. The orator, by contrast, 'announces a serious business, and for the purpose of entertaining his audience conducts it as if it were a mere *play* with ideas' (p. 185). The dichotomy is evidently intended to privilege the poet and disarm the orator, who is even denied the power of *movere*, a particularly arbitrary gesture given the growth in the seventeenth and eighteenth centuries—above all in Germany— of treatises analysing rhetoric's power over the feelings. Kant does not enquire how the orator works, simply denies him seriousness or understanding, making him an ineffectual entertainer. Continuing his demolition without examining rhetorical theory, and without analysing a single text, he declares that the orator totally 'fails to come up to his promise, and a thing, too, which is his avowed business, namely, the engagement of the understanding to some end'. One might have expected a philosopher to produce an argument, or at least some evidence, to support such a dismissive judgement.

When he comes to discuss rhetoric on its own, in section 53, Kant expresses his animus openly, but still without proper argument:

Rhetoric, so far as this is taken to mean the art of persuasion, i.e. the art of deluding by means of a fair semblance . . . is a dialectic, which borrows from poetry only so much as is necessary to win over men's minds to the side of the speaker before they have weighed the matter, and to rob their verdict of its freedom. Hence it can be recommended neither for the bar nor the pulpit.

For such serious activities it would be 'below the dignity' of their existence to know 'the art of talking men round and prejudicing them in favour of any one' (p. 192). Kant rejects 'the machinery of persuasion, which, being equally available for the purpose of putting a fine gloss or a cloak upon vice and error, fails to rid one completely of the lurking suspicion that one is being artfully hoodwinked' (p. 193). Almost as an afterthought, he reverts to his binary model, claiming that 'In poetry everything is straight and above board. It shows its hand . . . it does not seek to steal upon and ensnare the understanding with a sensuous presentation' (ibid.).

These are the prejudices of Plato, restated with more violence. Again the conception of rhetoric is totally negative; no contrary evidence is brought in. Persuasion is identified with violence, deception, imprisonment, exploitation. Since it suits his argument to do so, Kant concedes the orator total effectiveness, as if he succeeded automatically in his goal (a point derived perhaps from the *Phaedrus* above pp. 137–8). Yet Kant's reformulation of the power of rhetoric seems somewhat unreal in the late eighteenth century—a long time after the naïve propaganda of the Renaissance humanists—and would, if taken seriously, deprive men of the power to resist, deny them reason, or free will. His antipathy to rhetoric makes Kant create an unbelievable picture of man as an automaton driven by the orator. So, more explicitly, he adds a footnote to express his

disapproval of an insidious art that knows how, in matters of moment, to move men like machines to a judgment that must lose all its weight with them upon calm reflection. Force and elegance of speech (which together constitute rhetoric) belong to fine art; but oratory (*ars oratoria*), being the art of playing for one's own purpose upon the weaknesses of men (let this purpose be ever so good in intention or even in fact) merits no *respect* whatever [ist gar keiner Achtung würdig]. (ibid.)

Kant is pretending to believe all those claims of Cicero and Quintilian about rhetoric's 'irresistible power'! Bent on driving the last nails into its coffin, Kant even falsifies history, claiming that 'Besides, both at Athens and at Rome, it only attained its greatest height at a time when the state was hastening to its decay, and genuine patriotic sentiment was a thing of the past' (ibid.). The truth, of course, is quite the opposite.

Kant's desire to destroy rhetoric is notably short on argument, or logic. Like Plato, he uses binary categories to place rhetoric in the inferior position, before dismissing it altogether. He is more original in the strategies he invents to confuse and alarm the reader, who is to be stampeded into a judgement against rhetoric by being told that otherwise rhetoric will stampede him to judgement. Thus he will be manipulated like a machine over which some other person has total control—an early premonition of Frankenstein!—to a wrong or evil decision which he will certainly regret. The attack is inconsistent, however, like D'Alembert's. Kant rejects persuasion, yet is willing to accept 'Force and elegance of speech'. But you cannot drive a wedge into rhetoric like this, especially since persuasion (forbidden) derives from force (accepted). Samuel IJsseling has commented that Kant not only provides 'no critical justification for the use of such opinions but he even attempts quite inadvertently to force them on his readers'.[55] I am not sure about the 'inadvertently': Kant may have just been expressing a deep personal animus, but as a writer I think he knows what he is doing. However, if he can claim that the orator deprives man of freedom to think for himself, then he is now being guilty of attempting the same trick. Rhetoric did not attempt to deprive its listeners of free will, reason, and judgement, but to mobilize them on behalf of a specific issue, and it appealed to their strengths more than to their weaknesses. Kant was by any criterion a major philosopher, but it is hard to believe that he even attempted to do justice to rhetoric. His attempt to bully the reader lacks subtlety, coherence, and persuasiveness. Once again, like Plato, the opponent of rhetoric re-creates it in its worst possible form before attacking it: a double abuse.

A hundred years after Kant, and writing from a quite different standpoint, Benedetto Croce also eliminated rhetoric from an aesthetic system. Since Croce's whole *Aesthetic*[56] (1900) is committed to a holistic or monist concept of art, which refuses to make any distinction between style and content, idea and expression, it is not surprising that he should have rejected rhetoric. In an earlier theoretical chapter, with the title 'Indivisibility of expression into modes or degrees' (p. 67), he follows the Platonic and Kantian tactic, operating a whole series of excluding categories of the right/wrong model. Rhetoric's 'division of expression into various grades' is simply 'illegitimate'; the distinction of various types of trope and figure 'reveal their philosophic nullity when the attempt is made to develop them in precise definitions, because they either grasp

---

[55] IJsseling 1976, p. 86.
[56] Croce, *Aesthetic*, tr. D. Ainslie (London, 1906; 1959); page-references incorporated into the text.

the void or fall into the absurd' (pp. 68 f.). The emotive use of such words as 'nullity', 'void', 'absurd' should not obscure the point that, contrary to Croce's claims, rhetoric (alone!) is able to offer 'precise definitions' of all these devices. Croce takes as an example the 'very common' definition of metaphor as consisting *'of another word used in place of the proper word'*. Now Croce cuts off the definition at this point, omitting the crucial rider that this is done in order to extend its meaning or expressive power[57]—and then indulges in sarcasm: 'Now why give oneself this trouble? Why substitute the improper word for the proper word? Why take the worse and longer road when you know the shorter and better road?' A tyro in logic could see how Croce has loaded his argument by slipping in the terms 'improper', 'worse', and 'longer'. There would be many ways of discovering why we use metaphor, but not like this.

For Croce there is one terminology that is 'fixed as correct' for each writer or context, after which 'all other uses of it become improper or tropical' (p. 72). This yes/no, right/wrong model reappears in a later section of the *Aesthetic*, in an allegory (rhetoric lives!) of the birth of science and its struggle with 'forms of error', or 'negations of the concept of art itself', including—of course—rhetoric (pp. 420–1). Croce calls for 'scientific criticism' to be perpetually on the alert, not to rest content with mere statement of 'the truth', it being a sad fact that 'a simple affirmation of the truth has not always been accompanied by any considerable *recapture of enemy territory*' (p. 421; my italics). The aggression of Cicero, Quintilian, and Valla reappears, only now used against them. Croce sees the role of his new discipline, aesthetics, as being precisely to combat rhetoric. Earlier he had recommended that

the rhetorical categories should continue to appear in schools: to be criticized there. The errors of the past must not be forgotten and no more said, and truth cannot be kept alive save by making them combat errors. Unless an account of the rhetorical categories be given, accompanied by a criticism of them, there is a risk of their springing up again. (pp. 72–3)

[57] Quintilian writes that in metaphor 'a noun or verb is transferred from the place to which it properly belongs to another where there is either no literal term or the transferred one is better than the literal' (8. 6. 5). For his further account of the *functions* of metaphor see below, pp. 321–2.

Rhetoric is to be kept on as a tame Hydra for the budding aesthetician to decapitate from time to time.

Croce's prejudices colour every part of the supposedly historical survey that he now offers. Classical rhetoric is dismissed as 'a manual or *vademecum* for advocates and politicians', giving advice 'to those striving to produce certain effects by means of speech' (p. 422). Rhetoric's organic function in the state, its power to develop expressivity, its role in education and literature, are all ignored by this master of the rhetorical figure *meiosis*, or belittling. Croce next dwells on Plato's criticism of the Sophists, quotes Kant's 'gar keiner Achtung würdig'—if rhetoric is not worth any attention, one wonders, why do these philosophers devote so much space to it?—and travesties the Renaissance revival of rhetoric. Avoiding any comment on its new position in society and education, or its vast dissemination, he singles out three writers who supposedly criticized rhetoric for failing to be systematic, Vives, Ramus, and Patrizzi, casting them as reformers 'held up to odium by the traditionalists' and swept away by them (pp. 424–5). But while these writers fell into the stock routine of the prefaces to rhetoric-books—namely, criticizing the weaknesses of other rhetoric-books while recommending their own—Croce ignores the great contribution that they made to rhetoric. Vives' *De Ratione Dicendi* is the first modern treatise to be devoted to the anatomy and physiognomy of style, the first modern stylistics. His *De Tradendis Disciplinis* (nowhere mentioned by Croce) is one of the most thorough and intelligent accounts of the role of rhetoric in education. The reforms of Ramus and Talon may indeed have separated rhetoric from dialectic, but in their systematic development of *elocutio,* and their espousal of the vernaculars, the Ramists had a beneficial influence in applying rhetoric to literature. And far from being 'swept away', Vives' rhetorical works won much recognition and were widely used, while the Ramist reforms were absorbed by many writers, including some of a non-Ramist cast. The rhetorical tradition was more flexible than this historian could conceive. And despite the weaknesses that he diagnoses, rhetoric persisted, for Croce can list treatises appearing up to the 1880s. Yet he declares it dead.

Turning from history to analysis Croce levels the criticisms of the systematic philosopher that

Rhetoric can never be considered a regular science, being formed of a congeries of widely dissimilar cognitions. It included descriptions of passions and affections, comparisons of political and judicial institutions, theories of the abbreviated syllogism or enthymeme and of proof leading to a probable conclusion, pedagogic and popular exposition, literary elocution, declamation and mimicry, mnemonic, and so forth. (pp. 423 f.)

Once again, the critic is clever, but unscrupulous, producing an effect of confusion by lumping together the diverse social, political, and cultural roles of rhetoric with its teachings on psychology and with its internal processes (*inventio, dispositio, elocutio, pronuntiatio,* and *memoria*). These are all perfectly relevant in their contexts, but arranged higgledy-piggledy like this cannot seem but incoherent. The same trick could be played with the philosophy of Aristotle, or Descartes, or Hegel.

Croce sees rhetorical ornament as a mere 'addition or embroidery' (p. 427), although the texts presenting it as functional to expression were all available to him. Coming to the tropes and figures—the length of his treatment shows how much of a threat rhetoric seemed to him—Croce heaps up lists in a throw-away manner ('Figures of speech amounted to a score or so . . .', 'figures of thought to about the same number') before dismissing them all: 'considered rationally they are simply capricious'. There is more to be said about the functional nature of rhetorical figures, as I shall argue in Chapter 6. The gaps and contradictions in Croce's account become obvious when, after four more pages of mockery and abuse ('the fallacies of school doctrine', 'its inherent absurdity'), he comes to discuss those modern writers who followed traditional rhetorical theory about the figures' functional nature. When Vico stated that figures and tropes 'are not "caprices of pleasure" but "necessities of the human mind" ', Croce claims that he was 'framing his new concept of poetical imagination', necessitating a 'wholesale reconstruction of the theory of rhetoric' (p. 432): yet the idea is as old as Aristotle. Du Marsais is given credit for attacking 'the theory of rhetorical ornament' in 1730 when he wrote that the schemes or tropes derive from life, since 'nothing is more natural, ordinary and common than figures: more figures of speech are used in the town square on a market-day than in many days of academical discussion'. Yet this idea can be found in Aristotle, Quintilian, Longinus, Puttenham, Abraham Fraunce, Sidney, and many other writers. Croce imagines that by referring to Du Marsais giving 'instances of quite obvious and spontaneous expressions in which Rhetoric cannot refuse to recognize the figures of apostrophe, congeries, interrogation, ellipsis, prosopopeia' (p. 433), he is somehow disproving the theory of rhetorical ornament. But he is in fact proving another point, the organic relationship between the figures and the feelings, that unity formed by the 'natural language of the passions'.

At this point in his argument Croce seems to have got his historical perspective reversed. Whereas he has been arguing for the progressive decline of rhetoric from the time of Plato's criticism of the Sophists—a decline, if so, that had all the opposite features—he now begins to write in terms of an evolution or welcome advance. After Du Marsais, he says, 'the psychological interpretation of figures of speech, the first stage towards their aesthetic criticism, was not allowed to drop'. Although the psychological interpretation of the figures had been going on for two thousand years, to Croce it only gets under way with the *Elements of Criticism* (1762) of Henry Home, Lord Kames, who discovered that the rationale of the figures consists 'in the passional element', and analysed them 'in the light of the passional faculty'. This supposedly new movement is continued with Blair's *Lectures on Rhetoric and Belles Lettres* (1783), which defines the figures as 'language suggested by imagination or passion', and it finds analogous expressions in France (Marmontel) and Italy (Cesarotti), while in Germany 'an effort was made by Herder to interpret tropes and metaphors as Vico had done, that is to say as essential to primitive language and poetry'—an attempt of which Croce approves. With Herder we have reached Romanticism, which, Croce happily notes, 'was the ruin of the theory of ornament, and caused it practically to be thrown on the scrap-heap'. But accuracy makes him record that the Hydra has not yet been wiped out, for even Herder ('whose knowledge of art', Croce observes contemptuously, 'seems to have been confined to a little music and a great deal of rhetoric'), even Schelling, Solger, Hegel, and others, still retained discussions 'devoted to metaphor, trope and allegory' —yet 'for tradition's sake', he adds apologetically, 'without severe scrutiny'. Croce heaps odium on other writers who retain rhetoric, recommends De Sanctis and his 'anti-rhetoric', and closes with another invocation of what he claims to be 'the very nature of aesthetic activity, which does not lend itself to partition; there is no such thing as activity of type *a* or type *b*, nor can the same concept be expressed now in one way, now in another' (p. 436). It is important for Croce's whole system that he demolish rhetoric, and its distinction between *res* and *verba*, subject-matter as against linguistic expression. As two modern historians of literary criticism write, Croce's monistic system

denies the validity of all stylistic and rhetorical categories, the distinction between style and form, between form and content, and ultimately, between word and soul, expression and intuition. In Croce, this series of identifications leads to a theoretical paralysis: an initially genuine insight into the implications of the poetical process is pushed so far that no distinctions are possible.[58]

It would be easy to dismiss Croce as unrepresentative and idiosyncratic. But he has been, and continues to be influential, and not just in Italy, just as Kant's reputation has spread into every corner of the world. Croce could draw on a long tradition of philosophers attacking rhetoric, so that he in turn represents that deep split between *cor* and *lingua* which Socrates had brought about. But it is significant that Croce, like Kant and Plato before him, should have had to falsify history in order to present rhetoric at its worst. All three express a pre-existing prejudice which is not justified by rational argument. They use antithetical categories to privilege philosophy and dismiss rhetoric, turning a binary model into a monism. Intolerance, insinuation, abuse, the working up of emotions, especially fear and hatred—these are not tools that we associate with philosophy. They seem more like the resources of an unscrupulous and vindictive rhetorician. Philosophers attacking rhetoric first had to create a monstrous being before savaging it.

Rhetoricians attacking philosophy also travestied the rival discipline. To them it was impractical, cerebral, a tissue of abstractions with no relevance to life, expressed in barbarous Latin, clogged with technicalities, or revelling in the

[58] R. Wellek and A. Warren, *A Theory of Literature* (1949; Harmondsworth, 1963 edn.), p. 184.

proliferation of terminology and modes of argument for their own sake. Vico travestied Descartes just as Plato travestied the Sophists. Neither side would have recognized itself from the distorting mirror of its rival. Yet, of the two aggressors, I tend to blame rhetoric more. Rhetoric is, after all, committed to there being at least two sides to every question, and being able to speak for either. This can be presented as a trivial accomplishment, but it can also be seen as a more profound recognition that truth itself is not single and immutable, and that no one school of thought has a monopoly over it. A distinguished historian of Greek rhetoric has said that 'Gorgias' fondness for antithesis is a direct reflection of his belief that truth is relative and requires the clear expression of contrasts and alternatives as the basis of definition and choice'. In Sir Karl Popper's distinction between *'naïve monism'*, characteristic of a closed society or thought-system, and *'critical dualism'*, as characterizing and creating an open society,[59] rhetoric is by its very nature committed to freedom of thought and freedom of speech. It ought, then, to have recognized the liberty and independence of other disciplines, even if attacked by them.

Rhetoric continues to be attacked, or dismissed, in the name of philosophy. One of the leading modern Renaissance scholars, P. O. Kristeller, who has done so much to recover knowledge of the rhetoric and philosophy of the past, could still, in 1975, end a historical survey of rhetoric by professing himself 'at heart a Platonist' and stating his belief that 'Rhetoric in all its forms is based on mere opinion, and therefore . . . should be subordinated to philosophy, that is, to all forms of valid knowledge where such knowledge is available'.[60] Useful though it may be 'for expressing and conveying knowledge and insight', rhetoric should still 'be subordinated, not only to philosophy, but also to the sciences as well as to poetry and the other arts'. So we see that the Platonic dichotomy between 'real knowledge' (*epistēmē*) and 'opinion' (*doxa*) is still at work, still privileging philosophy and dismissing rhetoric to the most inferior position. Professor Kristeller aligns himself 'with many respectable philosophers' in holding that 'our true intellectual and moral freedom' consists in 'the submission to truth and to valid norms', another Platonic position, perhaps even more disturbing in its declaration of a single category, 'truth' or 'knowledge', as being the sole province of philosophy. Surely the history of philosophy, sociology, anthropology, and linguistics over the last hundred years has taught us how problematic such concepts as 'truth' or 'reality' really are, and how equally problematic is the language in which we formulate them. Given any such monistic conception of truth one is tempted to reply, in the words of the hero of a poem by Clough, a hero made sadder and wiser by experience—that in future

> I will look straight out, see things, not try to evade them;
> Fact shall be fact for me; and the Truth the Truth as ever,
> Flexible, changeable, vague, and multiform, and doubtful.[61]

By which I do not deny the concept of truth, but suggest that it is not an absolute, nor the prerogative of one group of scholars rather than another. Truth is relative, as all important concepts and values are relative, their exact nature being the individual's task to discover or ratify for himself. (As Socrates says in the *Phaedrus*, 'there are some words about which we all agree, and others about which we are at variance', such as 'just' and 'good'.) Our whole act of experiencing reality is subjective, our use of language inter-subjective, and any one in search of objective truths in a world after Nietzsche, Husserl, and Popper, say, is doomed to a dusty answer. Plato attacked the Sophists for their ethical relativism, and while scholars agree that the attack was unfair, we have now reached a stage in which relativism can be defended—not cynicism, not amorality, not indifference, but an honest admission that, in pheno-menological terms, the acts of perceiving the world, interpreting its signs, evaluating its actions, are all irremediably personal. They are not solipsistic, since individual interpretations can be shared, and in language as an exchange-system we can watch the process of individual experiences accumulating into group experiences, in a constant reciprocal movement between the person and larger social groups.

With the disappearance of a monist or categorical concept of truth the way is open, it seems to me, for rhetoric to achieve

---

[61] *Amours de Voyage* (1858), Canto V, ll. 100 ff.; in *Poems*, ed. F. L. Mulhauser (2nd edn., Oxford, 1974), p. 129.

respectability, at least, with philosophers, for its ability to present all that may be said on a topic, and for its encouragement to take part in dialogue. After all, the very acts of thinking, talking, and writing presuppose the existence of other people, the act of communication, and therefore the desire to persuade. As one writer has put it,

Speaking is always speaking *before another* and writing is always writing *for another*. . . . There must be some sort of invitation or challenge to speak and there is always the desire to find a hearing. . . . Each word is naturally an answer: an answer to a word which is older and more original than the word itself. This word is the word of another. Each word essentially demands an answer: a response in the sense of approval or disapproval. This word is also the word of another.[62]

Rhetoric, then, is indispensable, and its dispute with philosophy unreal, since thought cannot do without expression, any more than language can exist without ideas. At all events, it now seems pointless to dismiss rhetoric for not discovering 'the truth', as it is unhelpful to continue to rank the arts and sciences in some form of hierarchy. Each has its own role, and the totality of human knowledge requires co-operation rather than aggression—especially at a time when universities are being attacked from without.

Yet, before the reader says, with the dying Mercutio, 'A pox on both your houses!' (it took the further deaths of Romeo and Juliet to heal the strife between the families of Montagu and Capulet), we should record that this long-lived dispute at least helped each side to define its own goals and methods by opposition, as it were, and thus to clarify its own self-image. In the second century BC, when rhetoric regained something of its former vitality, the philosophical schools attacked it again by refurbishing the Platonic definitions denying rhetoric the status of an art, and so stimulated the rhetoricians to self-defence and self-analysis. As H. M. Hubbell records, 'it is hardly conceivable that any rhetorician was ever concerned to prove that he possessed an art until the philosophers began to question his position. Consequently all the pleas for rhetoric are coloured

[62] IJsseling 1976, p. 134.

more or less by the criticisms of it',[63] which become catalysts in the process of self-definition. Samuel IJsseling noted, similarly, that Plato's attack on rhetoric helped him to develop his own thinking, especially in establishing metaphysics as a philosophical discipline over and beyond words.[64] This controversy had at least beneficial effects for the combatants, whether Cicero or Quintilian, Valla or Locke. Otherwise it might seem a profound waste of time and energy, instructive though it is as to how divisions and classifications of knowledge seem to generate discord—as do languages, dialects, nationalities. But still, division is at least preferable to monism.

[63] Hubbell 1920, pp. 367, 381. For a stimulating review of Sextus Empiricus' answer to this question see Jonathan Barnes, 'Is Rhetoric an Art?' *darg Newsletter* (Discourse Analysis Research Group of the University of Calgary), 2 (1986), 2–22.

[64] IJsseling 1976, pp. 5, 14–15.

4

MEDIEVAL FRAGMENTATION

In following the fortunes of rhetoric, from the first-written records in the fourth century BC to its proliferation throughout the Roman empire, we have seen how rhetoric and society exist in a symbiotic relationship. In a democratic society, with free speech and due recognition of the individual's rights to being represented in legal and political activities, rhetoric has a real role to play. Either in the Greek version of personal involvement, or in the Roman, with representation through a professional orator, when the decisions of a court or assembly depend on a vote taken or decision passed after hearing speeches on both sides of the case, rhetoric can indeed claim to be a discipline essential to the life of a democracy. When emperors or dictators rule, however, and such issues are decided by edict or by appointed administrators, rhetoric's role in society inevitably declines. Yet even as a school subject it can still be a unifying force in education, affecting future lawyers, administrators, philosophers, writers of all kinds. And in this secondary role its models and ideals are still those of the orators in democracy, swaying the listener's emotions and will, enjoying that privilege of liberty, free speech.

If we turn to the medieval period the symbiosis between rhetoric and social conditions results in what I describe as a 'fragmentation' of rhetoric. I should say at once that I do not mean this as a negative judgement on medieval culture—how could one slight a culture that produced the cathedrals, a remarkable range of art, or the poetry of Dante and Chaucer? My aim is to show that rhetoric takes on very different forms according to the demands that society makes on it. It is a *technē* or *ars*, what we might call today a service rather than a manufacturing industry, and it performs the services required of it. In Shakespeare's powerful metaphor, its 'nature is subdu'd / To what it workes in, like the Dyers hand'.[1] As society and

---

[1] Shakespeare, *Sonnet* 111.

cultural ideals change, so does it. Even after its loss of a living role in Roman politics and law, rhetoric continued as a complete system of language and behaviour until late antiquity: its influence on early Christian writers has often been noted.[2] In the collapse of classical culture rhetoric suffered the general fate, and when it was revived it took on substantially different forms. My metaphor of 'fragmentation', then, is intended to describe, first, the situation of medieval rhetoric, *grosso modo*, compared with classical rhetoric. If I can risk a grand cultural generalization, I would define two great breakdowns in the rhetorical tradition: the first, in the Middle Ages, was followed by the long process of rebuilding and rediscovery in the Renaissance. The second, which started in the early nineteenth century, has persisted until our time, although we may now be seeing the beginnings of a second renaissance in rhetoric.

I

Medieval rhetoric is fragmented, first, in the obvious sense that many of the major rhetorical texts either disappeared or survived only in damaged form. Cicero's *Orator* and *Brutus* vanished altogether, and while *De Oratore* was known to a few scholars (Thierry of Chartres; Alanus, a twelfth-century commentator on the *Ad Herennium*), and was copied out by Lupus of Ferrières,[3] it was not part of a living educational tradition. Quintilian's *Institutes* came down to the Middle Ages in a badly mutilated version, with Books 5 to 8, 9, 10, and 12 missing completely or in part, and was otherwise known of through excerpts in florilegia.[4] To be fair, there is some evidence that these, the two most wide-ranging and demanding classical

---

[2] See Kennedy 1980; Kennedy 1983; C. N. Cochrane, *Christianity and Classical Culture: a Study of Thought and Action from Augustus to Augustine* (London, 1957); G. Kennedy, *New Testament Interpretation through Rhetorical Criticism* (Chapel Hill, NC., 1984); and James L. Kinneavy, *Greek Rhetorical Origins of Christian Faith: An Inquiry* (Oxford, 1986).

[3] Ward 1978, p. 54, and private communication.

[4] See P. Lehmann, 'Die Institutio Oratoria des Quintilianus im Mittelalter', *Philologus*, 89 (1934), 349–83, reprinted in Lehmann, *Erforschung des Mittelalters*, 5 vols., ii (Stuttgart, 1959), 1–28; P. Boskoff, 'Quintilian in the Late Middle Ages', *Speculum*, 27 (1952), 71–8; Curtius 1953, pp. 436–8; M. Winterbottom, 'Fifteenth-Century Manuscripts of Quintilian', *Classical Quarterly*, NS 17 (1967), 339–69; Winterbottom 1975, pp. 92–7; and Murphy 1974.

rhetoric texts, had already begun to lose readers in later antiquity. John Ward has pointed out that the *De Oratore* is used extensively by only one of the twenty-six treatises printed in Halm's *Rhetores Latini Minores*, while Quintilian seems to have undergone an eclipse in late antiquity, as Michael Winterbottom has suggested, perhaps because the *Institutio* 'was too long a book, and too technical, to win many readers'.[5] Be that as it may, had they been known these two works would have preserved a much wider conception of rhetoric's social and political role. In the event, the medieval rhetorician's knowledge of classical rhetoric texts was largely confined to those introductory and extremely practical school texts, Cicero's *De Inventione* and the anonymous *Ad Herennium*, often found combined in manuscripts, of which John Ward estimates that 'between 1,000 and 2,000 copies' survive, 'making them the major works of Latin antiquity for the Middle Ages', 'and arguably the most widely used classical Latin writings of all time'.[6] There were many commentaries on these works, some of them—such as Victorinus on the *De Inventione*—preserving other facets of the rhetorical tradition, but of course the circulation of manuscripts and commentaries was a haphazard affair, and many medieval writers had access to only a part of current knowledge. Classical rhetoric also survived in the encyclopedic tradition, but subject to the limitations of that genre. The encyclopedists, reducing knowledge to its most portable form, 'drew heavily upon abstracts of or commentaries on the earlier texts, not upon those texts themselves'. Thus the account of rhetoric in Isidore of Seville's *Etymologiae* (seventh century AD) derives from Cassiodorus Senator's *Institutiones* (sixth century), which in turn derives from the rhetoric of Fortunatianus (third century). These compilations abbreviate still further the digests on which they are based, and do not even convey their sources accurately. As Charles Faulhaber has shown, Isidore shortens Cassiodorus, leaves out passages where his author refers to rhetorical works that he does not know himself, and often reduces Cassiodorus' clarity to confusion. The result is a treatment of rhetoric so brief as to be almost useless: in Lindsay's edition it amounts to a mere twenty

[5] Ward, private communication; Winterbottom 1975, p. 93.
[6] Ward 1978, p. 54 n. 74; Ward 1983, p. 127.

pages, lacking even internal coherence.[7] Yet the *Etymologiae* is the only work containing information on rhetoric found in Spanish libraries in the tenth and eleventh centuries, and was a major channel of transmission. 'While not in itself sufficient for the adequate teaching of rhetoric, at least it kept some notion of the art alive.'[8]

The fragmentation of the texts was serious enough. Even more damaging was the fragmentation of their contexts. Readers of Alasdair Macintyre's *After Virtue* will recall the device he uses to describe the breakdown of the tradition of moral philosophy in our time. He invites us to 'imagine that the natural sciences were to suffer the effects of a catastrophe'. Science has been discredited, its teaching abolished, its books and instruments destroyed. Later, some

enlightened people seek to revive science, although they have largely forgotten what it was. But all that they possess are fragments: a knowledge of experiments detached from any knowledge of the theoretical context which gave them significance; parts of theories unrelated either to the other bits and pieces of theory which they possess or to experiment; instruments whose use has been forgotten; half-chapters from books, single pages from articles, not always legible because torn and charred. None the less all these fragments are reembodied in a set of practices which go under the revived names of physics, chemistry and biology.

These disciplines are carried out by people who do not realize that 'everything that they do and say conforms to certain canons of consistency and coherence, and those contexts which would be needed to make sense of what they are doing have been lost, perhaps irretrievably'.[9]

What may seem only 'A Disquieting Suggestion', as that chapter is called, an imaginative analogy with which to begin a discussion of the fragmentation of moral philosophy in the modern age, in fact describes what has happened many times in history. The Dutch historian of mathematics, B. L. van der Waerden, described a similar fragmentation in the sixth century BC: 'At the time of Thales, the Egyptian and the Babylonian mathematics had long been dead wisdom. The rules for

---

[7] Murphy 1974, pp. 43–76; Kendall 1978, pp. 147–8.
[8] Faulhaber 1972, pp. 53, 36, 54.
[9] Macintyre, *After Virtue* (London, 1981), pp. 1–2.

computing could be deciphered and shown to Thales, but the train of thought which underlay them was no longer known.'[10] This seems to have been a general phenomenon in the transmission of knowledge during the Middle Ages. In a recent survey of medieval science,[11] Michael Mahoney describes the rapid decline of mathematics in Rome and its virtual extinction after the fall of the empire, as the disappearance of an intellectual tradition. When the mathematical texts did become available, in the twelfth and thirteenth centuries, in translations from Greek and Arabic,

they posed fundamental problems of comprehension and assimilation. Unprepared to read them, medieval scholars had to learn almost from scratch and without teachers. In one sense, they learned quickly and well. In another sense, they never did quite learn. For they read the texts with their own intellectual concerns in mind: the union of faith and reason (a difficult problem exacerbated by the simultaneous introduction of Aristotelian philosophy), the education of the clergy, the effective governance of church and state. Hence, medieval mathematics assumed its own particular form in the period from the mid-eleventh to the mid-fifteenth century. Rarely pursued for its own sake, it served philosophical, pedagogical, and practical ends, and the internal technical development it underwent was largely dictated by those ends. (p. 146)

One example of this subordination of mathematics to some other end is geometry: 'the primary purpose for learning geometry in the Middle Ages was not to carry out further research in the area, but, rather, to understand the geometrical references of Aristotle and the Church Fathers', or to serve some specialist discipline, such as astronomy or optics (p. 153).

A similar pattern is found in the other sciences. In astronomy, as Olaf Pedersen shows, 'the works of Hipparchus, Ptolemy, and the other Greek astronomers disappeared or became useless when knowledge of Greek died out after the final collapse of the western half of the Roman Empire. Astronomical knowledge was limited to the fragments contained in Latin compilations, such as Book 2 of Pliny's *Natural History*,' Macrobius' commentary on the *Somnium Scipionis*, and Martianus Capella. From such works scholars of the early Middle Ages could, perhaps,

---

[10] B. L. van der Waerden, *Science Awakening* (Groningen, 1965), p. 89.
[11] In Lindberg 1978: page-references to this volume are included in the text.

get a vague inkling of the achievements of ancient astronomy. However, since the encyclopedic sources available to them completely ignored both the methods by which the results had been obtained and the mathematical form in which they had been expressed, there was no possibility of extending or even fully understanding the Greek achievement, either observationally or theoretically. (pp. 305–6)

In medicine, as Charles Talbot says, 'The Middle Ages did not create anything *ex nihilo sui et subjecti*, but took over the remnants and scraps that had survived destruction and neglect at the hands of successive hordes of barbarians' (p. 391). The basic textbooks were all classical, and the standard source of information was the commentary, but, paradoxically enough, the fragmentation of a subject was sometimes maintained by the very form which medieval scholarship took. Edward Grant's comment on natural philosophy makes this clear: 'the most common mode of expression was by means of a commentary on a traditionally recognized authoritative text', in the form of a series of *quaestiones* discussed pro and con in great detail, but in isolation from other related topics. So 'the virtues of such an approach, which emphasized thorough and systematic analysis of distinct problems in a prescribed order, were offset by the absence of any cohesive integration of the many derived conclusions as well as a failure to detect inconsistencies between questions treated within the same treatise'. The commentary, in focusing on particulars, probably discouraged the 'formulation of a coherent and consistent cosmology' (p. 267): attention to the parts was bought at the cost of the whole. (Perhaps the same judgement may be made of the rhetorical commentaries, once we know enough about them to gain an overview.)

The practicality that Mahoney noted in medieval mathematics—'rarely pursued for its own sake, it served philosophical, pedagogical, and practical ends'—seems to typify a general attitude to information in the Middle Ages. Where classical and—as I shall show—Renaissance readers and critics approached a literary work as a whole, medieval scholars tended to break it down into reusable parts. This tendency has been noted by a number of scholars. Hans Liebeschütz writes that medieval readers 'never considered the whole of classical antiquity', but 'looked upon it as a storehouse of ideas and forms, appropriating therefrom such items as seemed to fit in with the thought and actions of the immediate present'.[12] They valued the *auctores*, Curtius puts it, as providing 'a treasury of worldly wisdom and general philosophy', and a source for thousands of *sententiae*.[13] In Carolingian Italy ancient authors 'were read and interpreted for instruction in grammar and metrical rules'.[14] Similarly in rhetoric: Rabanus' *De Clericorum Institutione* (ninth century) 'foreshadowed the development of the central middle ages by the deliberate pragmatic selection of only the pertinent doctrines he wished to use', typifying what J. J. Murphy describes as 'the basic principle of medieval rhetoric . . . a frank pragmatism, making highly-selective use of ideas from the past for the needs of the present'.[15] This pragmatic or utilitarian attitude inevitably fragmented rhetoric texts, too. Seneca's collection of *Controversiae* was popular in the Middle Ages, but it 'was used as a collection of *exempla* rather than a preceptive guide to preparing future discourse'.[16]

The metaphor of fragmentation seems peculiarly appropriate to describe medieval rhetoric. Externally, the classical texts had survived in a damaged and haphazard state; internally, readers atomized what had been transmitted to fit their own needs. Further, rhetoric suffered a whole series of transformations, first as a university and school discipline, involving its status within the *trivium* (grammar, rhetoric, dialectic). These changes were sometimes the result of inter-faculty rivalry, the so-called 'Battle of the Liberal Arts', which generated much heat and little light.[17] But some important changes in the teaching of rhetoric derived from external influences, the needs of a new social group, both secular and ecclesiastical, involved in the growth of written communication—what might not unfairly be described as business correspondence. All these developments had the effect of making rhetoric more specialized, damaging its existence as a central and coherent educational system.

[12] Liebeschütz 1953, p. 271.
[13] Curtius 1953, pp. 57–8.
[14] Wieruszowski 1971, p. 419 n.
[15] Murphy 1971, p. xiv.
[16] Ibid., p. xii. John Monfasani has noted that the only Greek oration to be translated in the Middle Ages was the pseudo-Isocratean *Ad Demonicum*, which 'was viewed as a text in ethics rather than oratory' (Monfasani 1988).
[17] See Abelson 1906; Paetow 1910.

To begin with its place within the scheme of liberal arts, rhetoric's status was constantly being diminished. Part of its function had been usurped by grammar: 'in late Roman times, certainly by the fourth century, the teachers of language and poetry, called *grammatici*, had appropriated parts of the discipline of the *rhetores*',[18] including the lore of the schemes and tropes, and metrics. The final book of Donatus' influential grammar, the *Ars Major* (fourth century), deals with the schemes and tropes. This 'uncertain boundary dividing grammar and rhetoric' meant that the grammarian's explication of poets was limited to 'the parts of speech, correct syntax, the rhetorical figures', modes of argument, and metre, but never involved 'the structure or plan of the poem', which was left to the rhetor.[19] This was not simply a redisposition of a teaching-load: the figures of speech were handled in a far different way in the context of grammar. Divorced from a connection with the overall structure of a poem, unconnected with plot or character, and hence cut off from the passions, they became mere forms, patterns of word-formation or collocation without the literary function they had in antiquity and would have again in the Renaissance. Similarly with metrics, absorbed into grammar in the 'late and unproductive period' of the fourth century. As Curtius showed, the *ars* of the imperial age was taken over wholesale in the Middle Ages: 'the method of transfer was unintelligent, uninspired—and for that very reason it was durable.' Diomedes' 'purely formal' definition of poetry as a 'metrical structure' containing a narrative, for instance, persisted for many centuries.[20]

Grammatical studies were increasingly important after the seventh century, and with the Germanic migrations and the closing of the Romanized schools in southern Europe 'the burdens of culture fell on the shoulders of men to whom Latin was not a native language'. Grammar was a key subject up to the twelfth century, being called upon, as Marcia Colish puts it, 'to play a role which we might ordinarily expect to find assigned to rhetoric or dialectic'.[21] But it did not play it in the way that true rhetoric would have done.

[18] Campbell 1978, p. 174.   [19] Kelly 1966, pp. 274, 270.
[20] Curtius 1953, pp. 438–9.
[21] Colish 1968, pp. 92–7.

If rhetoric suffered from the rise of grammar, it suffered even more from the rise of logic and theology. In a now classic essay[22] Richard McKeon traced the fortunes of rhetoric over a thousand years, a period which he divided into four parts. The first, from about A D 400 to 1000, was dominated by the treatises of Martianus Capella, Isidore, Cassiodorus, and the pseudo-Augustine. The second, from 1000 to 1150, was the period of the Old Logic, the Cicero of *De Inventione* and the *Ad Herennium* (still ascribed to him), and Boethius. The third period, from 1150 to about 1300, was the age of the New Logic, while the fourth, from 1300 to the Renaissance, saw the rediscovery of Aristotle and other Greek rhetoricians, and the finding of the complete texts of Cicero and Quintilian (p. 273). During the first period rhetoric was concerned with 'civil philosophy', 'speaking well in civil questions' (p. 274). But this did not imply the full political and legal context of rhetoric in Greece and Rome. Rhetoricians of this period, such as Fortunatianus and Cassiodorus, defined civil questions as 'those which fall within the common conception of the mind', that is, involving common notions concerning the equitable and the good, which all men could discuss (p. 275). Whereas in Aristotle's *Rhetoric*, as in the classical tradition generally, the distinction of the three types of oratory—judicial, deliberative, demonstrative—depended on an external social context (the rhetoric of the lawcourts, political assemblies, and ceremonial speech-making), in Boethius 'the genus of rhetoric is no longer "civil science" (as it was for Cicero) but "faculty" ', a mere skill. The three kinds of oratory are now defined according to ethical criteria, independent of place and time: the just, the useful or honourable, and the good (p. 271). Rhetoric is taken out of a specific socio-political context. 'Civil' is to be distinguished from 'ecclesiastical', but it does not mean 'political': 'according to Aquinas, the matter with which rhetoric is concerned is civil, but rhetoric must not be confused with politics' (p. 285). This is one of many instances of a part of classical rhetoric surviving in medieval treatises in a wholly different context.[23]

[22] McKeon 1952: quotations will be incorporated into the text.
[23] For other instances of this asocial, apolitical concept of 'civil questions' see Leff 1978. Boethius' ethical distinction is also found in Gundissalinus' *De Divisione Philosophiae*: cf. Faulhaber 1972, p. 60.

McKeon's second period, from 1000 to 1150, saw the decisive subordination and breaking-up of rhetoric. 'Since its discipline was gradually limited by the transfer of the commonplaces, definitions, and, finally, proof . . . to the domain of dialectic, and since its subject matter was limited by the transfer of moral and political questions to theology, rhetoric developed . . . along three separate lines: as a part of logic, or as the art of stating truths certified by theology, or as a simple art of words' (p. 276). One cause of this shift of emphasis was the tendency to reclassify the sciences on a more systematic basis. Boethius taught that dialectic was concerned with theses or general questions, while rhetoric dealt merely with particular hypotheses or questions framed by circumstances. As McKeon says: 'the subordination of rhetoric to logic was based usually on the greater particularity of its subject matter, that is, its concern with hypotheses rather than with theses' (p. 276). Other historians have noted the redirection of energy by which logic became 'the vital study that taxes and develops men's minds', as C. S. Baldwin put it, while rhetoric came to lack 'educational vitality'.[24] Logic was the most important university subject, as the Paris curriculum of 1215 demonstrates,[25] where the set textbook for rhetoric was Book Four of Boethius' *De Differentiis Topicis*, a logic text with a 'narrow, limited, and technical focus' which paradoxically 'became one of the most popular medieval texts on rhetoric'. Michael Leff has shown how in Boethius 'rhetorical argumentation becomes a subordinate part of dialectical theory', in which 'rhetorical subjects are reducible to abstract propositional categories'.[26] The tendency to abstraction which becomes so strong in medieval rhetoric is anticipated in this work, written around AD 520, and is obviously connected with the vastly changed social conditions. As Leff puts it, in this

[24] Baldwin 1928, p. 151: see the whole of ch. vi, also Murphy 1974, *passim*, and Curtius 1953, pp. 480 ff., on how this move 'shattered the system of the *artes*', depressing rhetoric and poetics to the lowest rank.

[25] Curtius 1953, p. 483, observes that the rise of logic is connected with 'the fact that the flowering of Latin literature begins to fail from *c.* 1225'. Ward 1978, p. 45, places the 'apogee' of medieval rhetoric in the twelfth century: 'Its high points' include 'a much expanded interest in *elocutio*, the rhetorical *colores* of *Ad Herennium* IV . . .'. McKeon notes that 'if rhetoric is viewed as a form of literary criticism and associated with poetic, the decline of rhetoric is a symptom of the eclipse of the study of ancient literature' (McKeon 1952, p. 262 n.).

[26] Leff 1978, p. 24.

treatise (unlike, say, his *Consolation of Philosophy*), Boethius' 'concern for rhetoric is purely intellectual and schematic. He has no interest in practical application. Moreover, rhetoric-in-practice does not place an affective constraint on his theorizing, since the culture of Ostrogothic Italy renders oratory on public affairs trivial.'[27] As every historian of rhetoric must observe, the disappearance of legislative assemblies and lawcourts robbed rhetoric of its most important role in society. John Ward, commenting on the increasingly theoretical atmosphere of the schools, notes:

The fact . . . that the *De Inventione* could become the basic text-book of Latin rhetoric until *c.* 1150 AD, despite its failure to deal with *pronuntiatio, memoria,* and *elocutio,* illustrates in general the drift from practical to intellectual that characterises late antique and medieval rhetorical history.[28]

It is 'no accident', he writes, 'that all known ancient Latin rhetorical commentators chose the *De Inventione* to gloss', nor that Boethius should make it the basis of his system, one which became—with Victorinus' commentary on the *De Inventione*—the prime influence shaping medieval rhetorical theory.

The homogeneity of the textual tradition testifies to a homogeneity of approach. Cicero's early handbook, with its concentration on *inventio* and status-theory, was popular in the Middle Ages because it appealed to the general interest in logical methodology, the analysing of knowledge 'by means of definition, *differentia,* allocation of genus and species', dialectical topoi, and so forth. A system could be abstracted, detached from the context of social life, applied to issues still more remote from the reality of human affairs that classical rhetoric dealt with. So it was even adapted to Neoplatonist dialectic in Victorinus' commentary (fourth century), with its 'metaphysical concepts of time and substance', its theory of genus and species, syllogisms and categories. Where Cicero writes of society and civilization Victorinus transposes the discussion into the emancipation of the soul from the body, and Boethius applies to Cicero's text 'Neoplatonic and Aristotelian ideas of potentiality and actuality'. The scholastic emphasis is fixed by the time of the

[27] Leff 1978, p. 22.   [28] Ward 1978, pp. 42–3.

ninth-century commentaries on Book V of Martianus Capella, which 'see rhetoric as an intellectual discipline rather than a practical one', a form of dialectic, stripped of its teaching on delivery, arrangement, memory, and style.[29]

In other branches of rhetoric the break with the civic, political, and legal context of Greece and Rome is equally marked. As J. J. Murphy has said, 'the middle ages did not produce any major original works on secular speaking' because 'the political climate which had encouraged such writing in ancient Greece and Rome simply did not exist in medieval Europe'.[30] Even when classical texts were transmitted the editor or translator adapted them to current interests: reasonably enough, one might feel—except that the interests were narrower. Already Priscian, a teacher of Latin in fifth-century Byzantium, when translating Hermogenes' *Progymnasmata* (these *Praeexercitamina*, added to his grammar, became a standard text in the Middle Ages), transmitted Greek rhetoric theory but did so, as Curtius put it, 'with the omission of everything pertinent only to political and judicial oratory'.[31] Rhetoric's role in later antiquity as a purely written discipline was curiously prone to such surgery; perhaps because of the fundamental discrepancy between text and context. For the whole slant of *De Inventione*, as we have seen, is towards forensic rhetoric in the practice of the Roman lawcourts, especially the theory of *status*, determining which type of case the orator is pleading.

Given the disappearance of the Roman judicial system it was perhaps inevitable that medieval rhetoricians had to adapt Cicero to different purposes. However, the detachment of rhetoric from its social and political context had two damaging consequences. One was to encourage a split between theory and practice: some elements became excessively theoretical, others wholly practical. The theory was not tested by use, the practice lacked an adequate theoretical rationale for its existence. The other unfortunate consequence was that, being cut off from its

[29] Ibid., pp. 43–4.
[30] Murphy 1971, p. xxiii; similarly Curtius 1953, pp. 65–6, and Kennedy 1980, p. 24: 'The paradox of technical rhetoric is that throughout the Middle Ages . . . it remained theoretically concerned with addressing a jury in a court of law, even though such juries passed out of existence and judicial rhetoric had considerably reduced uses for around fifteen hundred years.'
[31] Curtius 1953, p. 442.

role as the art of communication between speaker and listener(s), rhetoric lost a concern with persuasion, psychology, and other factors involved in being addressed to an audience. Where Aristotle's *Rhetoric* makes rhetorical proof depend not only on logic but on the orator's knowledge of human character and emotions when appealing to the audience, Boethius ignores the 'ethical and emotional aspects of rhetorical persuasion'. Michael Leff points out that in Aristotle topics of argumentation 'refer both to the affective and cognitive states of an audience. No such conception is possible in Boethius.'[32] While we find survivals of the doctrine of the rhetor needing to arouse the feelings in order to achieve persuasion, this can be in a non-oratorical context, such as the *ars dictaminis*,[33] or in the twelfth-century written commentary tradition explicating the prologue to a speech, where *affectus* is supposed to be generated.[34] Lip-service is paid to the notion of eloquence or persuasion, but always divorced from its practical implications. For John of Salisbury 'eloquence had no special connection with rhetoric or oratory', nor was the orator a distinctive kind of thinker or speaker.[35] The tradition that did most to preserve the concept of *movere* is, of course, the art of preaching, from St Augustine onwards, where appeals to *affectus* occasionally occur.[36] But the organic link, in classical rhetoric, between the intention—to move and persuade—and the means, the rhetorical figures, becomes a rarity, when it does not disappear altogether. John Ward concludes that in 'the static, Christianised educational pattern' of the Middle Ages, which 'bore no specific relation to any particular sociological situation', rhetoric becomes 'a fossil', reduced to 'a source for largely extraneous disciplines', which did not—indeed could not—use the Ciceronian primacy of persuasive speech.[37] Curtius records the complaint of the

---

[32] Leff 1978, pp. 16–17.

[33] Alberic of Monte Cassino, *Flores Rhetorici* (c. 1087), in Miller, Prosser, and Benson 1973, pp. 143–9.

[34] Margareta Fredborg, personal communication.

[35] Seigel 1968, pp. 186–7. John Monfasani has pointed out that 'the leading medieval humanist, John of Salisbury, did not refer to a single Ciceronian oration in his famous defense of "eloquence", the *Metalogicon*, nor, I might add, in his other *chefs-d'oeuvre*, the *Policraticus* and *Letters*' (Monfasani 1988).

[36] See, e.g., Guibert de Nogent in Miller, Prosser, and Benson 1973, pp. 163, 174–5; Jennings 1978, pp. 114–15; McKeon 1952, pp. 282, 284, 286; Faulhaber 1972, pp. 18, 65.   [37] Ward 1978, p. 63.

celebrated statesman Wibald of Corvey (d. 1158) on the isolation
of rhetorical theory from practice. 'In the monasteries, he writes,
it was impossible to acquire a mastery of the art of speaking,
because there was no opportunity to use it for practical
purposes. Oratory was a lost art. There was no place for it in the
practice of either ecclesiastical or secular law.'[38] For this reason
Bede could ignore the relationship between rhetoric and oratory
entirely, and in the iconography of rhetoric there is a move from
voice and hand, the gestures of delivery, to stylus and wax
tablet, written compositions for a literary culture.[39]

The disappearance of the face-to-face, persuasive context of
rhetoric meant that rhetoric theorists lost sight of the audience.
Rhetoric was reduced from a two-way to a one-way system. The
energies that would otherwise go to elaborating a reciprocal
relationship turn inwards, away from a concern with a living
context, individuals or institutions susceptible to change, to an
intellectual structure. Rhetoric even loses its connotations of
creation and composition. As C. S. Baldwin has said of some
early medieval compilations: 'What rhetoric appears in these
surveys to lack most is distinct function. Writers as different
as John of Salisbury and Brunetto Latini seem to think of it as
polishing, decorating, especially dilating, what has been already
expressed. It comes in after the real job is done; it has lost its
ancient function of composing. The ancient lore of *inventio* kept
rhetoric in contact with subject matter and with actual
presentation. This had so much less scope in feudal society that
the lore easily lapsed, or was perverted.'[40] Since *inventio* was
developed as a logical or metaphysical classification-system it no

[38] Curtius 1953, p. 76.
[39] See Kendall 1978, p. 147; Curtius 1953, p. 39; and J. B. Trapp, 'Education in
the Renaissance', in Trapp (ed.), *Background to the English Renaissance* (London,
1974), pp. 67–89, at p. 78, who notes that in the twelfth-century *Hortus
Deliciarum* rhetoric carries 'stylus and tablets (instead of Martianus's jewels and
weapons)'. Rhetoric has been transformed from a spoken to a written art. For
the later iconography of rhetoric see P. d'Ancona, 'Le rappresentazioni
allegoriche delle arti liberali', *L'Arte*, 5 (1902), 137–55, 211–28, 269–89, 370–81;
Philippe Verdier, 'L'Iconographie des arts libéraux', in *Arts libéraux et philosophie
au moyen âge* (Montreal and Paris, 1969), pp. 305–55; and Marc Fumaroli,
'Réflexions sur quelques frontispices gravés d'ouvrages de rhétorique et
d'éloquence (1594–1641)', in *Bulletin de la société de l'histoire de l'art français*, 1975,
pp. 19–34.
[40] Baldwin 1928, pp. 181–2.

longer had a direct relationship with either composition or persuasion, outside the preaching manuals. The loss of a social role led to the atrophy, not only of the audience but of the speaker. R. O. Payne finds that in medieval English rhetoric and poetics 'the speaker seems indeed to have disappeared from the discussion altogether', and no 'psychology of audience response' exists.[41]

The inward-turning nature of medieval rhetoric had a curious effect on theory. There is a great deal of rhetorical theory in the Middle Ages, but it seems to exist as a self-contained system. On the other hand, there are many purely practical textbooks— lists of rhetorical figures, formulas for letter-beginnings, classifications of the types of *cursus* (patterns of prose-rhythm that marked the end of a sentence)—which seem to have no articulated *raison d'être*. Theory and practice, instead of leading into each other, strengthening, correcting, confirming, tend to go in separate directions. The commentators on *De Inventione*, having abandoned *elocutio, pronuntiatio,* and *memoria,* devoted their energies to a still greater elaboration of the system remaining. Classical rhetoric fascinated as an intellectual structure with a rich but disorganized terminology. As John Ward writes, 'The commentaries of the twelfth and thirteenth centuries turn upon the problem of smoothing away apparent terminological inconsistencies in Cicero: the "system", or codification of the *ars*,' had to be tidy, 'well sign-posted, neatly interlocking, and finite'.[42] The theoretical part busied itself with terminology, the practical part went on its way with increasingly elaborate devices. In Edmond Faral's pioneer study of the arts of poetry we find many instances of the development of a practical technique lacking a theoretical justification. *Interpretatio,* for instance, was a way of accumulating words and expressions around one thought, sometimes making use of etymology. Thus a manuscript gloss on Eberhard's *Laborintus* informs us how to deal with the phrase '*Mors* rapuit Heinricium': 'prolongamus *Meta omnium rerum sensibilium* rapuit Heinricium', in other words the term *mors* is 'expanded' or the thought 'prolonged' by each of its letters becoming the first letter of a new word.[43]

[41] Payne, in Murphy 1978, p. 272.
[42] Ward 1978, pp. 52, 56.
[43] Faral 1924, pp. 63, 65.

This is a testimony to the commentator's ingenuity, but it seems to belong to the world of crossword puzzles and acrostics rather than poetry. We detect a fracture between the goal or function of rhetoric and its processes or means. Often all that we have is a series of rules.

II

In McKeon's third period, from 1150 to about 1300, the influence of the New Logic 'led to separation of scientific or demonstrative proof from probable proof and to the location of rhetoric under the latter' (p. 277). Roger Bacon distinguished a theoretical rhetoric and poetic, which were parts of logic, from an applied rhetoric and poetic, which were parts of moral philosophy (p. 287). Once again, rhetoric was fragmented into theory and practice, and then assigned to separate disciplines. In theology rhetoric became an instrument to 'clarify the meanings and remove the ambiguities of scriptural statements' (p. 282), and to systematize collections of authorities, making discordant canons consonant. 'The "scholastic" method, as it came to be called, grew out of the assemblage of "sentences", which derived their name and their initial methods of treatment (p. 283). For Bonaventura rhetoric is treated 'by reduction to theology' (p. 286).

Rhetoric has always been a flexible tool, capable of being adapted to almost any context in human knowledge. It is not surprising, then, to find rhetorical texts being applied to other purposes. This practice goes back to the earliest encyclopedias. Isidore of Seville uses Quintilian on grammar and even on music, but 'looks elsewhere for information on rhetoric'.[44] Aristotle's *Rhetoric* survives, in Moerbeke's Latin translation, in more than a hundred manuscripts, and attracted distinguished commentators, yet most were interested in its connection with dialectic, and others used it as a textbook in ethics.[45] In these manuscripts the *Rhetoric* (along with the pseudo-Aristotelian *Rhetorica ad Alexandrum*) is often placed together with works on

[44] Winterbottom 1975, p. 93.
[45] Ward 1978, p. 55; Murphy 1966; Murphy 1969; and K. M. Fredborg, 'Buridan's *Quaestiones super Rhetoricam Aristotelis*', in J. Pinborg (ed.), *The Logic of John Buridan* (Copenhagen, 1976), pp. 47–59.

morals, politics, or economics, showing the subordination of
rhetoric to the moral and rational sciences (Aquinas drew on it
for his account of the passions: McKeon, p. 292), while
Aristotle's *Poetics* was 'taught and studied as a logical work
during the fourteenth century'.[46] Due to the mutilated version
of Quintilian that reached them 'most medieval scholars
considered the *Institutio* as a moral writing rather than a work on
education', for 'the strictly rhetorical portions were among those
missing' from one set of manuscripts.[47] In another set the
technographic sections survived, but could not be integrated to
the work's broader educational intent.[48] One Spanish *ars
praedicandi* discusses not preaching but 'The moral qualities
needed by the preacher', while another Spanish treatise
presents rhetoric as 'purely an instrumental science necessary
for work in the "sciences morales especulativas" '. As Charles
Faulhaber has noted, this work quotes Aristotle's *Rhetoric*, the
De Inventione, and the *Ad Herennium*, but also uses them 'merely
as sources of apophthegms, exempla or information about the
psychological characteristics of people of various ages and
conditions'.[49] This is a typical fragmentation and displacement
of the rhetoric text into some other discipline. Alcuin's dialogue
for Charlemagne 'is frankly moral not only in its traditional title,
On Rhetoric and the Virtues', but in its 'recognition that this
"sermonicandi ratio" must be supplemented by the other
virtues', so turning itself into a treatise on ethics (McKeon,
p. 274).

   Attacked and displaced from without, rhetoric also
fragmented itself from within. The third of McKeon's lines of
development for rhetoric during the Middle Ages was as 'a
simple art of words' (p. 276), a 'new art, which professed
an exclusive concern with practical issues and effective
applications, that is, with actions or with words', distancing
itself from both logic and theology. Attacked by those who had

---

[46] W. F. Boggess, 'Aristotle's *Poetics* in the Fourteenth Century', *Studies in
Philology*, 67 (1970), 278–94, at p. 284.
   [47] Faulhaber 1972, p. 14.
   [48] John Ward informs me that in one *Ad Herennium* commentary (MS Oxford
CCC 250), from *c.* 1200, 'the rhetorical portions of the mutilated Quintilian MS
tradition are used, but are excluded from the broad educational context that they
enjoyed in the classical text'.
   [49] Faulhaber 1972, pp. 71–2, 95.

assimilated rhetoric to dialectic, or to theology and edification (pp. 288–9), this tradition of rhetoric expressed itself in

a vast number of textbooks which grew in three distinct groups, differentiated according to the subject matters once treated by rhetoric but now concerned with verbal forms employed in those three fields in lieu of direct treatment of subject matter. First, rhetoric had contributed to the method of studying law, but the substantive consideration of law had moved into theology and had taken with it most of the appurtenances which might have made the law a learned profession, leaving only the verbal rhetoric of the *dictamen*. Second, the art of preaching, which had assumed in the Christian tradition an exhortative function approaching that of ancient deliberative oratory . . . gradually moved to a formalism in which doctrine was left to theology and attention was centered on three problems: propriety of division of the subject stated in the theme of the sermon, brevity of distinction, and utility of expansion. Finally, the art of poetry came to be considered, after the twelfth century . . . alternately a kind of argumentation or persuasion (and, as such, subordinate to logic or morals) and a form of composition (and, as such, to be treated in terms of style, organization, and figures borrowed from rhetoric).[50]

McKeon's analysis has been challenged on points of detail, but still seems the most perceptive general account of the reasons for rhetoric's vicissitudes in the Middle Ages. It alludes in passing to one of the most crucial changes in medieval rhetoric, to which we must return, the shift from 'subject matters' to 'verbal forms'.

In the development of separate *artes*, as John Monfasani puts it, 'the Middle Ages did not so much eradicate the art as dismember it to fit the needs and tastes of a different society'.[51] Or rather, societies, for the *artes poetriae, dictaminis, praedicandi*, and to a more limited extent, *arengandi*, each appealed to a different public, few of whom were likely to study or practise one of the others. The anonymous author of the *Rationes Dictandi*, produced in Bologna in about 1135, 'took it for granted that his readers were concerned only with letters and not with

---

[50] McKeon 1952, pp. 290–1, with full documentation.
[51] Monfasani 1976, pp. 245–6. For similar metaphors used by medievalists to describe the medieval 'destruction' or 'disintegration' of rhetoric see Faulhaber 1972, pp. 15, 19; Ward 1978, p. 51; Leff 1978, p. 23; Murphy 1974, pp. 87–8; and William D. Patt, 'The early "Ars Dictaminis" as response to a changing society', *Viator*, 9 (1978), 133–55.

any broader studies'.[52] The *artes poetriae* were composed by professional teachers of *ars grammatica*, but limit themselves to problems of teaching verse-writing, 'and display a constant disregard for the larger *ars grammatica* of which they form a part'.[53] This specialization is typical of the 'compartmentalization' in much medieval thought: 'the practice of distiguishing rigorously among the seven liberal arts dates from the twelfth and thirteenth centuries, when individual scholars began to specialize in one, and only one, art.'[54] This specialization reinforced both the insulation from the outside world and from other forms of rhetoric, that split already noted between theory and practice. The *artes praedicandi*, which emerge as 'a distinct rhetorical entity about 1200'—having separated themselves from the main body of rhetoric—concerned themselves with 'the *forma* rather than just the *materia* of sermon composition'. At first they posited a relationship between form and matter, but in the course of the fourteenth century 'theoretical explanations of the office and function of preaching tended to be lost as a great number of the preaching manuals concerned themselves almost exclusively with practical precepts'.[55] In the work of a leading medieval Spanish author, Alfonso the Learned, we see a clear gap between theory and practice. He 'draws almost no connection between the scanty fragments of rhetorical doctrine set forth' in one work and 'the much more detailed technical explanations' in another. 'In the former he is interested in rhetoric only as one of the liberal arts; in the latter he is interested only in its instrumental value, as a useful tool in problems of administration. In neither case is the king interested in the theoretical or esthetic aspects of rhetoric.'[56]

The most striking instance of the rise of a purely practical rhetoric is the *ars dictaminis*, developed in the Bolognese schools during the thirteenth century, which turned into 'an adjunct of the disciplines of law'. The art was initially conceived on two levels, one theoretical, giving general rules for the composition of all letters, the other more pragmatic, offering 'a series of form

---

[52] Murphy 1971, p. 4.
[53] Faulhaber 1972, p. 17, citing J. J. Murphy's 1951 dissertation.
[54] Colish 1968, p. 101.
[55] Jennings 1978, pp. 113, 116.
[56] Faulhaber 1972, pp. 96–7.

letters to be imitated by chancery notaries. Buoncompagno and Guido wrote both theoretical and practical works; by the beginning of the fourteenth century, however, theory was virtually eliminated while form books became more voluminous. *Dictamen* by that time was almost wholly oriented toward law', and treatises were produced which presented 'only those forms necessary for the drawing up of legal documents'.[57] The specialization of rhetoric led to the production of more specifically useful textbooks, but of use or interest to smaller groups. The more useful for the few, the less useful for the many: practicality had here lost sight of universality.

We are all committed to regarding practicality favourably—at any rate, the pejorative word is 'impractical'—but we must also register the disadvantages of a *praxis* cut off from *theoria*, or from wider cultural perspectives. The art of letter-writing is a typical product of medieval rhetoric's reshaping a tradition to meet new social needs, namely for communication models between clearly defined ranks and institutions within the hierarchy of medieval society. In discussing the *ars dictaminis* one can rightly praise the adaptability of rhetoric, and the textbooks' practicality—they are nothing if not practical—but one should note at the same time that specialization and practicality resulted in a further insulation from rhetoric as a unity and from other forms of culture. Many scholars today tend to be overly respectful towards the authors and topics they study, as if any criticism of them might reflect badly on themselves. Some recent work on medieval *dictamen* by very competent specialists has ignored the consequences of this new practicality, and to find an evaluation of the whole cultural context we must go back to Helen Wieruszowski, that pioneer in its study.[58]

The *ars dictaminis* was practical of necessity, Wieruszowski notes, for the teachers were unable 'to go beyond training their students for practical ends', having no further knowledge of

[57] Ibid., p. 16.
[58] Wieruszowski 1971, a collection of her essays of which the most important for rhetoric are: 'A Twelfth-Century *Ars Dictaminis* in the Barberini Collection of the Vatican Library' (pp. 331–45; from *Traditio*, 1962); '*Ars Dictaminis* in the Time of Dante' (pp. 359–77; from *Medievalia et Humanistica*, 1943); 'Arezzo as a Center of Learning and Letters in the Thirteenth Century' (pp. 387–474; from *Traditio*, 1953); and 'Rhetoric and the Classics in Italian Education of the Thirteenth Century' (pp. 589–627; from *Studia Gratiana*, 1967). Page-references will be incorporated into the text.

science or philosophy, and having learned what they knew of
ethics from collections of *sententiae* (p. 373). The thirteenth-
century *dictamen* was so absorbed in its political and practical
tasks that it could not share 'the general intellectual movements
of the age'. By contrast to 'rhetorical studies in the twelfth
century in Italy and France, this later teaching' did not
contribute to the revival of classical studies, for 'Mino and his
fellow schoolmasters remained unmoved by these currents'
(p. 375). The classics were not drawn on for quotations, they
were 'neglected also in the teaching of grammar and style, and
the letters exhibit not the slightest trace of classical influence'
(p. 376). This parochialism, which must surely cast doubt on any
claim that the medieval *dictator* is the father of the Renaissance
humanist, encouraged a new pragmatism, in which 'knowledge
and science replace wealth and noble birth' as the qualification
for worldly success (p. 377). The tendency in Italy towards
'practical and professional studies led to a subordination of the
liberal arts' to the 'higher' or more professional type of studies,
such as law and medicine (p. 424). Shortly after 1200 the liberal
arts course was remodelled to fit the needs of the faculty of law,
with rhetoric conceived as 'the study and practice of . . . *ars
dictaminis* in the stricter sense of the word', the use of
formularies, while grammar received 'still more drastic surgery':

Since all Latin instruction aimed at perfection in the technicalities
of letter-writing, grammar was in turn cut down to fit the needs of
rhetorical instruction, with the reading of Latin literature reduced to what
was absolutely indispensable. As a result of this process, both grammar
and rhetoric became detached from the sources that had once fed and
enlivened them and, for all practical purposes, became the lower and
higher stage respectively of what Paetow . . . called the 'business course',
which . . . 'usurped' almost the whole field of liberal arts. (p. 425)

The Bolognese schools must have resembled not so much a
university as a civil service training college.

Rhetoric here lost its connections with oratory and with
literary composition, both of which could help the production of
works meant for a reading public, and was reduced to the more
limited business of life, communication by writing between
separate parties for specific and therefore ephemeral purposes.
Typically the form-letter shows the correct way to address

someone superior or inferior to yourself (a lore that survives in modern protocol and etiquette books), and—often—how to ask a favour from them. Whether begging-letters from students asking their parents for more money, or attempts to secure secular or ecclesiastical office, the model letters in these collections are supplicatory, or utilitarian. They are not concerned with wider cultural issues, nor do they even encourage personal communication. The typical letter produced by this training has a single goal in mind, an item of business which will be mutually advantageous, or a request which, if granted, will benefit the writer, not the reader. The *dictamen* manual is written by one person to help another to write to a third to get what he or she wants. The leaders of this change were Buoncompagno della Signa and Guido Faba, whose manuals show some trace of rhetorical lore but effectively break with literature. Since their textbooks were central to success in the notarial profession (pp. 426–7), *dictamen* became still more class-coded and internal. Business turned its back on the wider spread of humanism (p. 462): in the specialization process disciplines became rivals, not partners.

The *artes dictaminis* show on every page this centripetal focus on the task in hand. As J. J. Murphy noted, they became an isolated and self-perpetuating genre:

> The first authors, like Alberic, were still close to their sources; once the genre was established, however, the *ars dictaminis* functioned independently and writers no longer bothered to justify their principles. Ultimately the genre fed upon itself, so that the 'authorities' became other dictaminal writers. . . . Moreover, the fully developed genre accumulated an auxiliary apparatus which included specialized treatments of small segments of the total art; in the case of the *ars dictaminis* it was separate treatises dealing only with salutations, or only with proverbs, or the like.[59]

Rhetoric-books naturally tend to proliferate detail, to cover all possible eventualities in the communication system, and rhetoric is in any case a tool rather than an end in itself. But even allowing for these traits, the 'practicality' of *dictamen* produced the most elaborate development of techniques for the manipulation of words in human history. Of Guido Faba's eight

[59] Murphy 1974, p. 329.

books four are simply collections of hundreds of *exordia*, one organized according to the virtues and vices, the remainder intended to be used by ambassadors, judges, members of various social classes.[60] Then there are three books of model letters, and one work of theory. All these works are practical, but the concentration on the individual components of letters leads to an odd imbalance. Where earlier authors had divided letters into five parts (the *salutatio* or greeting; the *captatio benevolentiae*, appealing for goodwill; the *narratio* or statement of the issue; the *petitio* or request; and the *conclusio*), Guido recognizes only three, eliminating *salutatio* as not being part of the letter. However, he then devotes nearly a third of his treatise to *salutatio*, giving to it 'eight times more space . . . than to the *exordium, narratio,* and *petitio* taken together'. Faulhaber records that such disproportion 'is not uncommon in the *artes dictandi*, possibly because the *salutatio* lent itself to that rational development of first principles so dear to the intellectual of the period'.[61] I would suggest that the very practicality of the *ars dictandi*, its ability to provide models to fit every possible combination of rank between sender and receiver, in a highly structured society, could only increase the gap between practice and theory.

This 'dismemberment' of rhetoric into three mutually exclusive *artes* gave the treatises in each *ars* a specialist, technical nature, where the part came to be regarded as more important than the whole. Their authors displayed what Robert Bolgar called 'the natural fanaticism of expertise'.[62] These books abound in concrete detail, itemizing specific devices, with little sense of meaning or function. In the *ars dictaminis* attention is given to form, shape, order, rhythm. The letter-writer, Guido says, has to cultivate 'devices of great elegance', such as varying the place of the verb, changing word-order, placing the 'more elegant words . . . at the beginning and end of the sentence', and even attending to 'word-stress'.[63] These are formal devices, easily systematized since they involve neither the expression of individual thoughts or feelings, nor the two-way process of communication. So the *dictatores* taught the use of the *cursus* as a fixed rule to be followed, without the rationale it originally had in spoken oratory as a mark to the audience of the completion of a period. Faulhaber concedes that the *cursus* is 'a mechanical procedure which lends itself easily to abuse in the hands of a mediocre writer', producing monotony and 'all sorts of unusual and ill-considered inversions',[64] but although Guido may have used it well himself we lack any justification for it other than its existence as a formal rule. Perhaps the medieval reverence for 'authorities' permitted this kind of' unthinking formalism. In grammar, likewise, Guido gives 'sets of causal and illative conjunctions to link *exordium* and *narratio*', and a whole sequence of rules for participial or noun-phrases, for verb-forms having a double subject. There are exercises for varying parts of speech, for learning to begin or end a sentence with a noun in any inflexional case, or a verb in any tense or mood.[65] The *ars dictaminis* started off by answering such real but limited queries as, 'can I begin a sentence with *docere* in the present perfect?', or 'how do I address a minor canon?', but it neither asked nor answered any more fundamental question. Guido's *Summa Dictaminis* is admitted to be heterogeneous, badly organized, its sole claim to originality consisting in 'putting the section on vices of style and composition at the beginning of his treatise' instead of at the back;[66] but its self-limitation to formalist concerns seems to typify the genre as a whole. Specialization and practicality were here inimical to imagination and to the sense that the whole should be more than the sum of its parts.

As for the parts, they are often transplanted from classical rhetorical models, not always appropriately. Isidore of Seville is still echoing the declamation-schools with such archaic illustrations as 'Shall we declare war upon Corinth or not?'[67] In

---

[64] Ibid., p. 103.
[65] Ibid., pp. 104–5.
[66] Ibid., pp. 107–8.
[67] Isidore, *Etymologies*, tr. D. V. Cerino in Miller, Prosser, and Benson 1973, p. 86. The source is either *De Inventione* (which Isidore knew only from Cassiodorus' summary: Faulhaber 1972, p. 52), 1. 12. 17, or *Ad Herennium* 3. 2. 2, on which Harry Caplan comments: 'Cato the Elder and Publius Scipio Nasica always ended their speeches, on no matter what question, the one with "In my opinion, Carthage must be destroyed", and the other with "In my opinion, Carthage must be spared" ' (p. 158 n.).

his *Flores Rhetorici*—a treatise that shows more grasp of the whole system of classical rhetoric than most—Alberic of Monte Cassino recommends both emphasis and its opposite, when we use words 'contemptuously so as to minimize, spurn, and crush an opponent's argument'.[68] This is good combative rhetoric, but seems a little out of place in a treatise on letter-writing! Alberic goes on to discuss types and categories of men, their age, nationality, much in the tradition of Horace, but although it would fit the requirements of fictional composition, this discussion of *ethopoeia* is not immediately relevant to the *ars dictaminis*.[69] It is difficult to see how Horace's teaching on *decorum* could help at the very elementary level of Latin verse composition dealt with in the *artes poetriae*.[70] Buoncompagno mentions *memoria*, but only in terms of content, not method.[71] Evidently these are all fragments of the genuine classical tradition whose true function was lost on medieval writers. It is as if they have an imperfect copy of the rules of a game such as cricket or bridge that they have never seen played, but are trying to reconstruct.

III

The disintegration of rhetoric into highly specialized disciplines brought about a major shift of focus within the art itself. Richard McKeon was the first to describe this shift, in his brief allusions to the reduction of *dictamen* to a purely 'verbal rhetoric', and the parallel move in preaching from a comprehensive 'exhortative function' to 'a formalism in which doctrine was left to theology' and textbook writers concentrated on techniques of division, 'brevity of distinction, and utility of expansion'. The arts of poetry derive both terms and organization from the *Ad Herennium* and the *De Inventione*, 'but the commonplaces which have been put to so many uses are no longer devices for discovering arguments of things and their traits but devices for remembering, for amplifying, for describing and for constructing figures' (pp. 291 f.). This diagnosis of a general

[68] Alberic, in Miller, Prosser, and Benson 1973, p. 149.
[69] Ibid., pp. 150–1.
[70] So Geoffrey of Vinsauf in Kelly 1966, p. 266 n., and in Parr 1968, p. 86.
[71] Wieruszowski 1971, p. 597.

movement away from subject-matter to a concern with verbal forms has been borne out by other students of the *artes poetriae*. The great pioneer, Edmond Faral, evaluated them in somewhat disappointed terms, finding them deficient in perception and scope. They lack a proper notion of the intellectual faculties, have only a vague idea of the function of art, 'a superficial ordering of their material, deprived of any deeper logic', and an erroneous classification of first principles.[72] We can understand the self-imposed limitations of the *artes* only when we realize that they are essentially exercise-books for schoolboys learning to write Latin verse. The four main treatises appeared in the fifty years around 1200, too close together, perhaps, for any innovation or development. The best known to students of English literature, thanks to Chaucer's praise, is Geoffrey of Vinsauf's *Nova Poetria*, 'a work', as C. S. Lewis said, 'whose value lies in its extreme naïvety'.[73] Matthew of Vendôme's *Ars Versificatoria* clearly belongs to an elementary grammar course, including specimen school exercises, designed for the younger pupils. As Douglas Kelly puts it, Matthew's main concern is 'verse composition in the narrower sense: the line of poetry, not the poem as a whole'. Although he briefly refers to the thought, Matthew is unconcerned with this 'non-formal aspect of poetry', concentrating on 'composition in the narrow sense of the word —the choice and arrangement of words in the sentence and rhetorical embellishment':[74] not composition as plot, structure, topics. *Inventio* in this context of literary creation has virtually disappeared: so has *dispositio*. But although historians classify the *artes'* discussion of the *colores rhetorici* as comprising *elocutio*, this label seems to me misleading. In classical and Renaissance rhetoric *elocutio* implies a whole context of persuasion, in which rhetorical figures are held to represent not just forms of language but states of feeling, and are used to arouse feeling in the audience, which implies in turn a coherent relationship between rhetoric and society. The *artes poetriae* list the figures much in the same way as they list adjectives ending in *-alis*, *-osus*, *-atus*, *-ivus*, *-aris*, as lexical items, unrelated to meaning or feeling.

[72] Faral 1924, p. xv.
[73] Lewis 1967, p. 191. See also Baldwin 1928, pp. 184–96 for a still useful discussion.
[74] Kelly 1966, pp. 263–4.

The reader who approaches these texts from a study of Renaissance poetics will be surprised to find how limited is their conception of poetry. It has nothing to do with *mimesis*, or the workings of the imagination, or the correction of a brazen world, or the construction of a golden one. Verse, Matthew tells us, 'is a metrical discourse proceeding succinctly member by member, decorated with the pleasing marriage of words and with the flowers of ideas, and containing neither too little nor too much'. What matters is 'the elegant joining of words, and the expression of the characteristics and the observed quality of a thing'.[75] This may be the way to instruct ten-year-old boys learning to read and write Latin poetry as a school-exercise, but is otherwise a severe impoverishment of literature. Rhetoric is reduced to beginner's Latin grammar, and derived from the bare digest of the encyclopedists.[76] Eberhard the German begins with even more basic topics in grammar, sees poetic instruction as dependant on grammar, and omits *dispositio* as being outside the grammarian's scope.[77] Geoffrey of Vinsauf has a wider range, as does John of Garland, who chides 'his predecessors for excessive specialization'.[78] But we still find an essentially fragmented view of both poetry and rhetoric. If the writers used the *Ad Herennium*, perhaps in a contemporary abridgement of Book 4, then either they or the abridgers deliberately omitted passages on the persuasive function of the figures, and rhetoric's role in society and education. The text that they used evidently contained elements which could not be assimilated to their conception of language, or rhetoric.

Denied a sense of the whole, the authors concentrated on the parts, with an atrophied sense of design or purpose. Matthew tells the budding student to begin his poem by using a *zeugma* ('*Zeugma* is making a single verb serve as the predicate of different clauses') or its opposite, *hypozeuxis* (where 'each clause has its own verb expressed').[79] John of Garland recommends beginning with a proverb, an exemplum, a simile, a metaphor, an 'if, while, or since' clause, or an ablative absolute.[80] Instead of

[75] Gallo 1974, p. 62.
[76] Kelly 1966, p. 266.
[77] Ibid., pp. 268–9.
[78] Ibid., p. 275.
[79] Galyon 1980, pp. 27, 29.
[80] Ibid., p. 119, n. 8.

a part of the oration, intended to establish the subject-matter or meaning of the composition, the prooemium, say, a *partitio* or a *propositio*, attention is displaced at the outset to a series of technical devices, irrelevant to the key position, and chosen apparently at random. Linguistic or purely formal grammatical elements are elevated to a position that elements of meaning ought to have. This is like telling the composer of a symphony always to begin with the chord of E flat, or with the cellos playing pizzicato. As with the *ars dictaminis* and its excessive attention to the *salutatio* and exordium, one feels that energies have got deflected through writers not knowing the why or wherefore.

This sense of deflection or dislocation applies to so many parts of the *artes poetriae*. Both Geoffrey of Vinsauf and John of Garland discuss whether to begin with the *ordo naturalis* or the *ordo artificialis*, a distinction which derives from Horace,[81] but which in these texts, as C. S. Baldwin said, 'provides a pattern, not to promote composition, but to obviate its necessity'.[82] For in Horace the doctrine applies to a whole sequence of events, as in the story of the Trojan War, a concept of plot quite lacking in these treatises. As for structure, the failure of the theorists to include any teaching on composition may account for the disorder of many medieval works. Both Curtius and Faral have commented on this feature of medieval narrative, where attention is given to episodes rather than to the unity of whole works. As Curtius puts it, 'the Middle Ages was far from demanding unity of subject and inner coherence of structure in a work of literature'. Indeed, he comments, in a remark that reveals the complete break-up of the system of interrelated compositional processes in classical rhetoric, 'only seldom is the disposition taken from the content presented'.[83] It is important not to confuse this issue with that of 'organic form', a much later aesthetic concept. The medieval writer could not have access to such writers as Coleridge or Schelling, but if the fragmentation of the rhetorical tradition had not taken the course it did he might have had access to useful classical ideas on the concept of

---

[81] See F. Quadlbauer, 'Zur Theorie der Komposition in der mittelalterlichen Rhetorik und Poetik', in Vickers 1982a, pp. 115–31.
[82] Baldwin 1928, p. 196.
[83] Curtius 1953, pp. 501–2; Faral 1924, pp. 59–60; Kelly 1966, p. 276 and n. 54.

unity. Ernest Gallo has dismissed the whole issue rather complacently: 'Medieval poets never heard of organic form, and they did quite well without it';[84] yet one could wish that better models had been available. Whatever Dante, or Chaucer, or the *Gawain* poet knew about form, they did not learn from the arts of poetry.

The point emphasized above, that medieval writers tended to interpret classical literature and philosophy to their own very different needs,[85] can be illustrated time and again from the *artes poetriae*, as in their discussions of *amplificatio*. In classical rhetoric (e.g. Quintilian, 8. 4. 1) *amplificatio* signified intensification, raising the emotional or ethical level of discourse. But in the medieval arts it meant extending a subject, spinning it out, and became 'la principale fonction de l'écrivain'.[86] It seems to have acted as a substitute for *inventio*, but once again we note a displacement or dislocation, in that instead of dealing with subject-matter it discussed a series of linguistic devices, such as *interpretatio*, periphrasis, comparison, apostrophe, or digression, which medieval theorists regarded as a special excellence.[87] 'On *Amplificatio* [Geoffrey] is almost embarrassing. He calls the various methods of "amplifying" your piece, quite frankly, *morae* (delays); as if the art of literature consisted in learning how to say much when you have little to say. . . . But this means not that the *morae* he recommends are all necessarily bad but that he misunderstands their real function.'[88] Other writers reassign devices with a similar lack of awareness. John of Garland 'cite les couleurs de rhétorique non comme les ornements, mais comme des variétés de l'apostrophe. Ce qui est à peu près absurde.'[89] Where classical rhetoric and poetics would give a complete account of the poet's activity, the medieval writers pick out one part: 'Matthieu considère la description comme l'objet suprême de la poésie.'[90] Here, at least, the survival of epideictic rhetoric meant that a poet was instructed to take up a definite attitude to his subject-matter,

[84] Gallo 1978, p. 84.
[85] See also Baldwin 1928, pp. 179–81, 191–6.
[86] Faral 1924, p. 61.
[87] Ibid., pp. 61–2; Curtius 1953, p. 501.
[88] Lewis 1967, p. 192.
[89] Faral 1924, p. 73.
[90] Ibid., p. 76.

either of praise or blame.[91] Elsewhere purely formal aspects ruled, such as the use of acrostic etymology for prolongation, or the enormous stress placed on word-play as a way of varying the shape of words, *annominatio*, or their combination, *determinatio*.[92] The rearrangement of letters or words became a substitute for any broader concept of meaning or feeling.

One of the most striking examples of the external, componential, formalist approach of the arts of poetry is the technique of *abbreviatio*, the obverse of *dilatio*. Faral listed the verbal devices itemized by Geoffrey and his fellow-writers, such things as *emphasis, articulus, ablativus absolute positus, verbum conversum in participium*.[93] He did not comment on the incongruity of an abstract category (*brevitas*) involving thought, or subject-matter, being dealt with in terms of separate linguistic manœuvres. As elsewhere in medieval rhetoric, matter appropriate to *res* is being dealt with as if it governed *verba*. The most penetrating analysis of this phenomenon was made by E. R. Curtius, who observed that whereas *auxesis* or *amplificatio* in classical rhetoric is the art 'of raising acts and personal traits above their real dimensions', to the thirteenth-century rhetoricians it indicates 'the purely linear extension, expansion, unrolling of a theme. *Amplificatio* as αὔξησις is elevation, and belongs to the vertical dimension, *amplificatio* as *dilatio* to the horizontal.'[94] As Curtius notes, 'Isocrates demanded brevity for the *narratio* in judicial oratory', and *brevitas* was counted among the *virtutes narrationis*, to be distinguished from the *virtutes dicendi*. In the Middle Ages the *brevitas*-formula received extensive but 'partially inappropriate use', for the original connotations of both *brevitas* and *narratio* disappeared early on, and brevity in the presentation of the facts at issue in a law case 'was absurdly enlarged into a *virtus dicendi* in general'.[95]

[91] For a rather bizarre instance of the influence of epideictic rhetoric see Faulhaber 1972, pp. 109–11.
[92] Faral 1924, pp. 65, 93–7, 97.
[93] Ibid., p. 85.
[94] Curtius 1953, Excursus XIII: 'Brevity as an ideal of style', pp. 487–94, at 492. It seems a serious misunderstanding for Ernest Gallo to claim that in the medieval arts of poetry 'amplification and diminution' give facts with more, or less, 'magnitude and emotional impact', retaining the classical concept of 'enhancing emotional impact' (Gallo 1974, pp. 54–5). He cites no evidence, however.
[95] Curtius 1953, pp. 487, 489.

The treatment of a *virtus narrationis* as if it were a *virtus dicendi*, or in my terms, the treatment of *res* in terms appropriate to *verba*, was cultivated by the authors of the arts of poetry, who seem to have thought it a new and modern device. But it led to the poet's subject-matter being conceived in purely quantitative terms. In Latin poetic theory, in about 1200, Curtius writes,

The art of the poet has first and foremost to prove itself in the rhetorical treatment of his material; for this he can choose between two procedures—either he ingeniously draws out his subject, or he dispatches it as briefly as possible. The absurdity of these excessively generalized precepts seems not to have entered the minds of the theoreticians. But, understandably enough, they devote more space to *amplificatio* than to *abbreviatio*; there was more to say about the former.[96]

Poetic skill, then, is displayed by being lengthy, or by being brief. Curtius, having analysed this doctrine in three of the *artes*, concludes that 'the examples show that the original meaning of *brevitas* as *virtus narrationis* had long since been obscured. The essence of brevity as of prolixity was seen in the use of particular artifices.'[97]

That comment sums up much medieval rhetoric. Deprived by the vicissitudes of history of the greater part of classical rhetoric, and denied a knowledge of the social and educational context within which these doctrines could make sense, medieval rhetoricians were faced with a tradition fragmented on two levels, text and context. Applying this basic fragmentation to a wholly different situation, with different needs and different habits of mind, they produced a rhetoric in which the original connections between the parts and the whole have been severed or replaced by a new set of links. The interrelationship between form and function has gone, form becoming an end in itself. Theory and practice resolve themselves into the abstract and the concrete, on levels that can never be brought together, except perhaps for the art of preaching. In the art of letter-writing, as in the art of poetry, the loss of the whole is accompanied by a flourishing but dislocated growth of the part.

[96] Curtius 1953, p. 490.   [97] Ibid., p. 491.

IV

Since rhetoric has varied in nature and fortune according to the state of human culture as a whole, it often reflects wider intellectual movements. My analysis, all too summary, of its dismemberment in the Middle Ages, and of the aesthetic consequences of that fragmentation, can be related to a general phenomenon long known to scholars studying the differences between medieval and Renaissance attitudes to antiquity. W. H. Woodward, that pioneer in the history of education, noted in 1897 that although the late medieval schools studied the classics, they did not do so in the spirit of a Renaissance humanist wishing to understand Roman literature, history, or civilization. 'The idea of Literature, or of an ancient author as a complete subject, was unknown outside Italy in the fourteenth century.'[98] Roberto Weiss, a pioneer of a later generation, making the by now familiar point that medieval scholars regarded the classics 'mainly as quarries of information . . . or as texts susceptible of an allegorical interpretation', emphasized that by contrast a Renaissance reader approached a classical text as a whole, 'a work of art from which inspiration of an aesthetic and stylistic nature could be derived'.[99] The art historian Jean Seznec, writing in 1940, dated the 'process of disintegration and dissociation' within the mythographic tradition to 'the last centuries of antiquity'—just when it took place in rhetoric. In the Middle Ages 'form and subject survived in isolation, so to speak, each distinct from the other'. The 'mythological heritage, like the classical patrimony as a whole', had disintegrated into 'a pictorial and a literary tradition which had become completely separate'.[100]

The most fruitful explanation of this tendency in medieval culture that I know of was provided by another art historian, Erwin Panofsky.[101] Setting out to define the difference between the classical revival of the twelfth century and the European Renaissance that started in fourteenth-century Italy, Panofsky

[98] Woodward 1897, p. 29.
[99] Weiss 1941, p. 3.
[100] Seznec 1953, pp. 211, 213.
[101] Panofsky 1960, p. 100. Further references incorporated into the text.

juxtaposed medieval and Renaissance sculpture. Romanesque artists could not perceive 'the essential principle of classical statuary: the interpretation of the human body as an autonomous, quite literally "self-centred" entity, distinguished from the inanimate world by a mobility controlled from within' (p. 60). Classical sculptors, we might say, had taken to heart the need for unity of form insisted on in the rhetorical tradition from Plato to Horace. The Romanesque sculptor, however, conceived his work as 'a piece of inorganic and homogeneous matter' rather than an organism with a 'differentiated structure', the result being that the parts compete against each other rather than interrelating (ibid.). When he imitates a classical model he often obscures it by an overdevelopment of the parts, or by attending too much to decorative detail (p. 95). If I could introduce a category from linguistics here, syntax (and larger syntactical structures, such as narrative) can be said to display either *parataxis*, where words or clauses are joined together by simple means, such as the copula 'and', or *hypotaxis*, where minor elements are subordinated to main ones. In these terms medieval art can be described as paratactic, part being added on to part, all existing at the same level of importance, while Renaissance art is hypotactic, where decisions about relative importance have been made and are expressed in terms of size and scale. It is the difference between two pulpit screens in the Siena Duomo—Nicola di Pisano's *Last Judgement* (Fig. 1) and Donatello's *Feast of Herod* (Fig. 2), two brilliant works of art organized on wholly different principles. In Panofsky's terms, Romanesque sculpture 'was conceived in terms of "mass" (inorganic and homogeneous matter) rather than "structure" (matter organized into different parts and parts of parts)' (p. 131). This paratactic, or aggregative approach is seen in Gothic art, where the parts are treated as being of equal value, not subordinate to a whole (pp. 132 f.).

   Other factors in medieval culture contributed to the distortion of the classical heritage. Panofsky notes that in art, too, the Middle Ages 'made classical antiquity assimilable by way of decomposition' (p. 100). Between 1050 and 1350 the whole corpus of classical mythology was passed down, 'absorbed, augmented, digested, and distorted' (p. 80), a process that Klaus Heitmann has described as the 'deformation' of ancient

Fig. 1. Pisano: *The Last Judgement: the Blessed*

Fig. 2. Donatello: *The Feast of Herod*

mythology.[102] Whereas Carolingian art never tried to 'infuse into a given classical image a meaning other than that with which it had been invested from the outset', in the proto-Renaissance of the eleventh to thirteenth centuries we find an essential change, as artists 'subjected classical originals to an *interpretatio Christiana*'. *Venus Pudica* could be changed into Eve, Dionysus into Simeon, Phaedra into the Virgin Mary (pp. 83–4). At the same time classical concepts, characters, and narratives were 'picturalized in a manner entirely independent from classical representational sources', either according to 'conventions familiar to the artist from the life and art of his day', or on the basis of verbal descriptions rather than actual images. These twin tendencies account for Panofsky's famous 'principle of disjunction', which states that

wherever in the high and later Middle Ages a work of art borrows its form from a classical model, this form is almost invariably invested with a non-classical, normally Christian, significance; wherever in the high and later Middle Ages a work of art borrows its theme from classical poetry, legend, history or mythology, this theme is quite invariably presented in a non-classical, normally contemporary, form. (p. 84)

In the classical revivals of the eleventh and twelfth centuries, 'in art as well as literature, classical form came to be divorced form classical content' (pp. 104, 107): similarly in medieval rhetoric, where questions involving content were treated in terms appropriate to form, so displacing *res* to the level of *verba*.

Another way in which the treatment of rhetoric reflects general habits of mind in the Middle Ages is in its tendency towards specialization. As Panofsky diagnosed it, the 'principle of disjunction' seems to express

a fundamental tendency or idiosyncrasy of the high-medieval mind . . .: an irresistible urge to 'compartmentalize' such psychological experiences as were to coalesce or merge in the Renaissance; and, conversely, a basic inability to make what we would call 'historical' distinctions. (ibid.)

Both symptoms are related, for the ability to perceive a unity depends on being able to see the past as a complete—and

[102] K. Heitmann, 'Typen der Deformierung antiker Mythen im Mittelalter' *Romanistisches Jahrbuch*, 16 (1963), 45–77.

therefore distant—unit. It is a case of 'where distance lends coherence to the view'. As Panofsky points out,

In the Middle Ages there existed—another instance of that 'compartmentalization' which, for example, prevented those who objected to Aristotle's theory of free-falling bodies on logical grounds from ever attempting to decide the question by experiment—a curious dichotomy between optic theory and artistic practice. (p. 138)

The Middle Ages had a theory of *perspectiva*, but it was connected with mathematics and astronomy, not with the problems of graphic representation. Romanesque and Gothic painters 'had learned to think of the painting surface as something impervious and opaque which . . . could not be connected with the theory of sight at all' (pp. 138 f.): the development of separate disciplines made it harder to see links or connections. We have seen the effects of such compartmentalization on the *artes*, developed by separate groups, intellectually as socially, unable to learn from each other or from rhetoric as a whole.

According to Panofsky, a crucial element in the formation of the Renaissance was the birth of the historical sciences, history, philology, and archaeology, all of which were 'foreign to the Middle Ages in spite of all the Carolingian and twelfth-century "humanists" '. This lack accounts for a fundamental difference between medieval and modern attitudes to classical antiquity:

In the Italian Renaissance the classical past began to be looked upon from a fixed distance, quite comparable to the 'distance between the eye and the object' in that most characteristic invention of this very Renaissance, focused perspective. As in focused perspective, this distance prohibited direct contact—owing to the interposition of an ideal 'projection plane'—but permitted a total and rationalized view. Such a distance is absent from both mediaeval renascences. (p. 108)

This admirable account can clarify what I mean, in discussing rhetoric, by context. The ability to conceive of a totality is not only a question of knowledge, of having access to the relevant documents, but also of being able to see a discipline, or a period, in its wholeness. The Middle Ages were certainly aware of the difference between a Christian present and a pagan past. However, they approached the classical world not historically but pragmatically, as a living continuum, albeit fragmented and distorted. As Panofsky suggests, the Middle Ages were too close to classical antiquity, stood in a direct, if dying-out line of descent from it:

For want of a 'perspective distance' classical civilization could not be viewed as a coherent cultural system within which all things belonged together. . . . Every phenomenon of the classical past, instead of being in context with other phenomena of the classical past, thus had to have one point of contact, and one of divergence, with the mediaeval present: it had to satisfy both the sense of continuity and the feeling of opposition . . . (pp. 110–11)

Given such a pragmatic attitude, with items from the past being applied out of context to fit the needs of the present, it is not surprising that the union of form and content in the visual arts should break apart, nor that, in rhetoric, classical devices and techniques should have been broken down into components which were then applied to often unsuitable ends.

One great achievement of the Renaissance, by creating a new awareness of its own identity, was to see classical antiquity as a whole. This process of self-definition can be seen very clearly in Renaissance philology. There, as Anthony Grafton has recently emphasized, we find

a form of historical awareness that seems to have few precedents. The humanists realized that any classical text was not just the product of a single intellect but a subordinate part of an organic cultural and historical whole. Accordingly, they set out to eliminate from the corpus of genuine antiques all works that used a vocabulary, employed concepts, or referred to events that their supposed authors could not have known.

Although they made mistakes, the humanists did demolish the claims to antiquity of a number of fakes, and in so doing 'framed the first clear general rules for testing the external form, internal consistency and vocabulary of documents'.[103] This conclusion links up with Panofsky's account of the self-conscious break with the immediate past that took place in the visual arts: 'the *intentio* of the Italian Quattrocento was to revert to the sources' (p. 166). In rhetoric, as we shall see, apart from letter-writing, which was a medieval genre without classical precedent, there

[103] Grafton 1985, pp. 624–5.

was an equally deliberate break with the immediate past, and a conscious revival of the systems of Greece and Rome.

One aesthetic consequence of this rediscovery of *antiquitas* as a whole was a new feeling for unity in works of art, and for the means by which unity could be achieved. In the fourteenth century 'the *disjecta membra* of classical perspective preserved or revived in Italian Dugento painting' were 'subjected to the unifying discipline' of the principles of 'mass consolidation' and 'surface consolidation' (p. 135), with the result that in Duccio and Giotto we already find a new 'impression of coherence and stability unmatched in all earlier painting'. Now 'incongruous and fragmentary material . . . has been reorganized and disciplined' (p. 136). Where, in the compartmentalization of the medieval sciences, perspective belonged to mathematics, and painters could not connect the impervious and opaque painted surface with a theory of sight, 'Brunelleschi and Alberti found the means of translating this idea into reality, thereby converting perspective as a mathematical theory of sight into a mathematical theory of design' (p. 139). Brunelleschian architecture is based on the classical system of proportion 'conceived in terms of focused rather than . . . diffused perspective' (p. 40).

When these developments in the theory of perspective were translated into general aesthetic terms, they were formulated, significantly enough, with the help of the newly revived classical rhetoric. Alberti's *De Pictura* (1435), the text in which fixed-point perspective was first described, applied rhetorical theory and terminology to painting, as a later chapter will show, and 're-introduced into the theory of the representational arts what was to become the central concept of Renaissance aesthetics', harmony (p. 26). Panofsky did not perceive the extent of Alberti's debt to rhetoric, but anyone who has recently read the classical texts will see how much he has been influenced by their concept of the unity of an oration. 'Composition', Alberti writes, 'is the procedure in painting whereby the parts are composed together in the picture', beginning with the principal part, surfaces, from the proper composition of which 'arises that elegant harmony and grace in bodies, which they call beauty'.[104] Next comes 'the composition

[104] Quotations are from Alberti 1972.

of members', where 'care should be taken above all that all the members accord well with one another', that is, 'when in size, function, kind, colour and other similar respects they correspond to grace and beauty' (p. 73). If the parts are disproportionate, he goes on, the result will be ugly. The painter must select one member, and 'the rest should be accommodated to it . . . in length and breadth', then ensuring 'that all the members fulfil their proper function according to the action being performed' (p. 75). Such terms as *accommodare* and *correspondere* derive from classical rhetoric's teachings on decorum, the adaptation of the parts to the whole.

This creative process, Alberti emphasizes, must come from a self-aware choice on the artist's part, for 'abundance' and 'variety' need to be controlled: 'I disapprove of those painters who, in their desire to appear rich or to leave no space empty, follow no system of composition, but scatter everything about in random confusion' (p. 79). The painter must make such fundamental decisions about major and minor elements well in advance, and 'will never apply his brush or style to his work before he has clearly decided in his own mind what he is going to do and how he will do it' (pp. 101–3). Rather like the orator using *dispositio* to set out his material, Alberti's painter will 'ponder at some length on the order and the means by which the composition might best be done', and have everything 'so well worked out beforehand that there will be nothing in the picture whose exact collocation he will not know perfectly' (p. 103). Panofsky calls this process 'aesthetic selection' and 'the rational organization of form' (p. 27), while I have compared it to *hypotaxis*, the subordination of the lesser clauses of a sentence to the main unit of sense. The linguistic analogy seems especially appropriate in the light of Michael Baxandall's demonstration that one of Alberti's main concepts, *compositio*, derives from classical and Renaissance grammar, where it refers to the organization of the constituent language-units into a whole.[105] The process of choice governs also the construction of sentences, especially the periodic sentence as described by Quintilian (9. 4. 124) and practised by Cicero, with its division into two or three main parts. Such a structure needs planning, and depends on a clear articulation of the constituent parts.

[105] Baxandall 1971, pp. 103 ff.

Medieval Latin, Baxandall points out, was not fitted for such a task: it had lost 'many of the sharper distinctions in the meaning of Latin conjunctions and connective adverbs', it used pronouns in 'a quite undifferentiated way', and it allowed the same 'blurring of distinctions' to affect word inflections. The general effect of these changes was to relax the system of classical Latin 'to a point where the delicate differentiation on which a periodic sentence depends became practically impossible. Medieval Latin writers often write long and complicated sentences but these are not often periodic' (p. 22). Renaissance humanists revived the periodic sentence with great fervour, indeed it became what Baxandall calls 'the basic art form' for them, a 'model of artistic composition in general' (p. 20).

From sentence-structure to the organization of whole works, then, a distinction can be drawn between the medieval tendency to treat individual units all at one level, and a Renaissance tendency to organize them into a whole which clearly differentiates structure and function. Rhetoric benefited from this new sense of unity, indeed helped to create it. To Quintilian the orator should only digress from his main argument if he could thereby increase emotional emphasis (4. 3. 4–15). In the Middle Ages, as we have seen, digression came to be treated as an end in itself, detached from the whole. In Renaissance rhetoric it was put back into place. Once launched on a digression, Vives advises, don't 'lose sight of the road that leads back home'. Although Giraldi Cinthio, writing in the 1550s, prefers multiple actions in romance, bringing 'the variety that is the spice of delight', he emphasizes that digressions should be made to depend on each other and be well linked to the main narrative. John Smith, or whoever published *The Mysterie of Eloquence* in 1657, laid down firmly that any digression ought to be 'pertinent to those matters which we have in hand'.[106] In this way, we might put it, Renaissance rhetoric got things back into the proper perspective.

---

[106] Vives 1966, p. 202; H. L. Snuggs, tr., *Giraldi Cinthio on Romances* (Lexington, Ky., 1968), pp. 23, 48 (attacking Trissino for an unrelated digression, making the fable faulty); Smith 1657, p. 241.

5

RENAISSANCE REINTEGRATION

If rhetoric in the Middle Ages was subject to larger cultural and historical changes, it was no less so in the Renaissance. The transformations of attitude that make the Renaissance a real event, not just a historian's fiction, can be seen in philology, philosophy, music, painting, and other arts and sciences.[1] To take up again two distinguished writers on art history, Jean Seznec commented that in the Middle Ages the mythological heritage had been split into two separate traditions, literary and pictorial, but that if properly interrelated 'these two traditions would have made it possible to rebuild the unity of ancient art'. The great achievement of the Renaissance, according to Seznec, was to bring about 'the reintegration of antique subject matter within the antique form'.[2] Erwin Panofsky similarly wrote that after the medieval decomposition of form and content, 'it was for the Italian Renaissance to reintegrate the separated elements', perform 'its task of reintegration'.[3]

'Reintegration' certainly seems the appropriate word to describe what happened to rhetoric in the Renaissance. In the first place, thanks to the humanists' search for ancient manuscripts—and they knew what they were looking for—the classical texts were rediscovered in a dramatic series of finds.[4] Poggio, hunting through the abbey of St. Gall in 1416, found a complete Quintilian 'safe and unharmed, though covered with

---

[1] For the decisive change of direction in Renaissance attitudes to the past see, e.g., W. J. Bouwsma, *The Interpretation of Renaissance Humanism* (Washington, DC, 1966), and *The Culture of Renaissance Humanism* (Washington, DC, 1970); D. R. Kelley, *Foundations of Modern Historical Scholarship: Language, Law, and History in the French Renaissance* (New York, 1970); G. M. Logan, 'Substance and Form in Renaissance Humanism', *Journal of Medieval and Renaissance Studies*, 7 (1977), 1–34; A. Grafton, *Joseph Scaliger: A Study in the History of Classical Scholarship*, Vol. 1 (London, 1983).

[2] Seznec 1953, p. 213.

[3] Panofsky, 1960, pp. 100, 106.

[4] See R. Sabbadini, *Storia e critica di testi latini* (Castania, 1914); and R. Pfeiffer, *History of Classical Scholarship* (Oxford, 1968).

mould and filthy with dust' in a cell at the foot of a tower, together with a manuscript of Asconius' commentaries on Cicero's speeches. Poggio had already discovered eight speeches of Cicero, including *Pro Roscio*, *Pro Murena*, and *Pro Cluentio*, and in 1421 Gerardo Landriani, bishop of Lodi, found a complete manuscript of Cicero's *De Oratore*, *Orator*, and *Brutus*, the last totally unknown, the other two known only from mutilated versions. These discoveries were rapidly disseminated: transcripts of Quintilian went to Barzizza in Padua, Bruni and Niccoli in Florence, and Guarino in Venice.[5] All the major treatises were given great diffusion through the invention of printing, and many minor but still important works soon appeared in print. In 1508–9 Aldus Manutius published at Venice a popular collection of *Rhetores Graeci*, containing Aristotle's *Rhetoric* and *Poetics*, Dionysius of Halicarnassus' *On Composition*, Hermogenes' *On Ideas*, and Demetrius' *On Style*.[6]

I

The history of Renaissance rhetoric is in part the story of the assimilation and synthesis of a great number of classical treatises, together with the many handbooks in the European vernaculars that they inspired. Lest this seems an obvious and unnoteworthy process we should realize that a receptive climate must first exist before assimilation can take place. Richard McKeon noted the increasingly 'perfunctory' treatment of rhetoric in the Middle Ages, despite the increased knowledge available:

The translation of the *Rhetoric* of Aristotle, of the pseudo-Aristotelian *Rhetorica ad Alexandrum*, and of the *De elocutione* of Demetrius in the thirteenth century would seem to have had . . . no effect comparable to that of the other translations of the century in stimulating interest in its subject; and the return of rhetoric to prominence during the Renaissance is explained only on the supposition that men's minds were turned once more, after a long interval, to literature and life.[7]

The discovery of lost texts, or the granting them true status— Aristotle's *Rhetoric* now enters the rhetorical tradition in its own

---

[5] Kennedy 1980, p. 199.
[6] Woodward 1897, p. 26.
[7] McKeon 1952, pp. 260–1.

right, not as a work on ethics or psychology—could only increase the autonomy of rhetoric, its recognition as an independent subject. The truly staggering number of editions, commentaries, and new works listed in J. J. Murphy's pioneering bibliography,[8] involving some six hundred Renaissance authors, testifies to the great eagerness with which rhetoric was cultivated. If there were perhaps two thousand rhetoric books published between 1400 and 1700, each in an edition of between two hundred and fifty and a thousand copies, and if each copy was read by anything from one reader to the dozens using a school text, then there must have been several million Europeans with a working knowledge of rhetoric. These included many of the kings, princes, and their counsellors; popes, bishops, ordinary clergymen (whether Catholic, Jesuit, Protestant, Calvinist), all the professors, schoolteachers, lawyers, historians; all the poets and dramatists, including the women, who were otherwise not granted much education.

If these figures seem at first sight exaggerated, we should realize that rhetoric occupied a privileged position in the school curriculum, being reserved to the higher classes, forming the climax of a pupil's education. At the Collège de Guyenne in Bordeaux (founded by the great educational reformer Andrea de Gouvéa: the teachers included Mathurin Cordier, George Buchanan, and Muretus) the top class was called 'Classe de Rhétorique', while in the fifth and final class of the Jesuit schools 'la rhétorique couronnait la formation littéraire'.[9] The most detailed studies of Renaissance education made so far, for sixteenth-century England (chronicled in T. W. Baldwin's[10] analysis of all extant grammar-school curricula), show how Renaissance humanism gave rhetoric a greater status than ever before. In 1510 and 1511 John Colet and Erasmus, apparently independently, outlined a scheme for a humanist reform of

[8] Murphy 1981. For critical evaluations of this pioneering reference work, with corrections, see my review in *Quarterly Journal of Speech,* 69 (1983), 441–4, and 70 (1984), 335–8; and Heinrich Plett in *Wolfenbütteler Renaissance Mitteilungen,* 8 (1984), 142–5.

[9] See Vickers 1981; Dainville 1968, p. 20; and L. W. B. Brockliss, *French Education in the Seventeenth and Eighteenth Centuries. A Cultural History* (Oxford, 1987), pp. 121–33: 'The Study of Grammar and Rhetoric'.

[10] Baldwin 1944. Further references to this massive work (over 1,500 large pages) will be included in the text in the form Vol. i. p. 118: i.118.

secondary education, set out most clearly in Erasmus' *De Ratione Studii*. By 1512 Colet had invited Erasmus to put it into practice at St Paul's (i. 78). Colet's instructions of 1518 emphasize that the best authors must be chosen for study, such as have 'the veray Romane eloquence joynyd with wisdome' (i. 128). Although the early curriculum of St Paul's is not known in detail, enough survives to prove that Wolsey's curriculum for Ipswich in 1528 derived from it (i. 118), a pattern repeated many times. A school was founded at Saffron Walden in 1525, and in 1530 its timetable was based on those of Winchester and Eton (i. 134). Founders of schools naturally looked to the authorities for models, and so the ideas of a few great educators (Erasmus, Vives, Sturm) and the curricula of the pioneer schools (St Paul's, Eton, Winchester, Westminster) were copied all over the country, with slight variations and compromises. The rate of expansion was high, and by 1575 there were about 360 grammar-schools. In this standardized education-system the major aim was to achieve fluency in spoken and written Latin. Grammar was studied first, from the parts of speech onwards, using such techniques as parsing, translation from Latin into English and back again. Gradually pupils ascended to the writing of themes on a set subject and impromptu disputations in Latin, while working through Latin literature in stages of increasing linguistic difficulty.

The curriculum was not large, but the teaching was incredibly thorough. New facts were released sparely (new words at the rate of three a day), and after the master's explanation the pupil would repeat it, memorize it, be asked to recite it; be tested again, repeat it, and be made to use it over and over until there was no chance of forgetting it. The amount of repetition required is frightening. School hours were from 6 a.m. till 9, then breakfast; 9.15 till 11, then lunch; 1 till 5, then supper; 6 till 7, for pure repetition; for thirty-six weeks a year, and for four to six years. First thing in the morning pupils were tested on the facts they had been given to learn the previous day. Then some new work was introduced, to be studied until lunchtime; that afternoon it would be repeated, and a little bit more added. All would be rehearsed in the evening, tested next day, and so on. Fridays and Saturdays the whole week's work was reviewed and repeated. 'A sixteenth-century schoolmaster estimated that one hour of instruction would require at least six hours of exercise to apply the principles to writing and speaking.'[11] One is glad not to have been a boy at such a school—or, perhaps more, not to have been a master.

This remorseless process of repetition amd memorization testifies to the determination of the Renaissance educator to leave nothing to chance. But it has important consequences for literature, since writers' thought-processes and reading habits were conditioned by having to absorb countless *sententiae* or memorize quantities of Ovid's *Metamorphoses*. Since eloquence was the greatest human acquirement, and rhetoric the key to all literature, schoolboys were thoroughly drilled in every stage of the art. In their reading as in their own writing they were taught to observe the larger process of rhetoric (the five parts of an oration, the three styles, how to write using a 'formulary' system) and—most important in some educationalists' eyes—to know the name, definition, and use of a large number of figures of speech. In the fourth form (at the age of about ten) they would use that seminal work Erasmus' *De Copia*, 'On the copy [i.e. *copia*, amplification] of Words and Things', and in the fifth form they would graduate to the list of figures in Susenbrotus' popular collection *Epitome Troporum ac Schematum* (1541; 24 + printings in less than a hundred years), or in *Ad Herennium*, Book 4. What pupils actually did when confronted with these compilations may be expressed very simply: 'learn the figures; identify them in whatever you read; use them yourself' (although the processes could be followed in a different order, or simultaneously). For the first stage Erasmus is the guide, advising the pupil simply to 'have on the tip of your tongue a *summa* of rhetoric' (i. 81), advice which Vives addresses more to the master, who is as it were to pick a posy from a huge field of rhetoricians.[12] The principle of memorizing the figures is solemnly recorded in a host of school statutes—St Paul's, Ipswich, Eton, Canterbury (Marlowe's school), Bury St Edmunds, Aldenham, and many more. So those for Rivington in 1576 specify that the master should introduce his pupil into the *Ad Herennium* in order 'to let him understand the divers kinds, and parts of an Oration, giving him examples out of other

[11] Joseph 1947, p. 11.   [12] Vives 1913, p. 183.

authors, and how to furnish his sentences with figures of all sorts, as they be plainly set forth in the fourth book, which will be more easy to follow *by daily practice*' (i. 349; my italics).

Rotherham in the early seventeenth century used Butler's Ramist rhetoric, and with equal diligence: 'Their fore-noone Lessons were in Butler's *Rhetorick*, which they said *memoriter*, and then construed, and applyed the example to the definition' (i. 427). An account by Archbishop Laud of Westminster School in the early 1630s (Dryden was there in the 1640s) notes casually that 'Betwixt 4 and 5 they repeated a leafe or two out of some book of Rhetoricall figures' (i. 360). It was simply accepted as routine, and given the crushing degree of memorization one can assume that anyone who had attended grammar school in Renaissance England (or Europe) would know a good proportion of the 132 figures and tropes in Susenbrotus.

Secondly, after memorization and repetition, the pupil noted the figures in everything that he read, and transferred many examples to his own notebook—Every Man his Own Orator. Susenbrotus himself had urged the teacher to 'fully point out' the grammatical and rhetorical figures in both sacred and profane authors so that the pupil can more easily 'understand the mind of the author who is being read', stressing that 'tropes and schemes . . . must especially be pointed out while expounding', as if with the finger (ii. 139). If we looked into the classroom of any school in England in the sixteenth or seventeenth centuries we would find confirmed the process that Richard Sherry[13] recorded as early as 1550: 'The common schole-masters be wont in readynge, to saye unto their scholers: *Hic est figura:* and sometimes to ask them, *Per quam figuram?*' But, he says, 'what profit is herein if they go no further?' One must have a complete working knowledge of the figures in order to understand any literature, 'For thys darre I saye, no eloquente wryter maye be perceived as he shulde be, wythout the knowledge of them' (ii. 36). The schools recommended constant

[13] Sherry published *A treatise of the Schemes and Tropes gathered out of the best grammarians and oratours* in 1550, reissuing it five years later as *A Treatise of the figures of Grammar and Rhetorike*, with a subtitle revealing the shift from primary rhetoric to secondary, from speech to reading: *profitable for all that be studious of Eloquence, and in especiall for such as in Grammar Scholes doe reede most eloquent Poets and Orators . . .* (Sherry 1550).

observation of the figures. At Westminster, between 1 and 3 in the afternoon the master expounded the day's lesson 'out of Cicero, Virgil, Homer, Euripides, Isocrates, Livy, Sallust', a lesson which 'was to be exactlie gone through by construing and other grammatical waies, examining all the rhetorical figures' (i. 359–60). At Hertford the practice of aiding teaching and furthering memorization by having a higher form examine a lower one on its lesson was followed, but with the proviso that the synonyms, phrases, 'with the Figures and Order of composicion of the sentence shalbe added of the master, observed by the schollers and inserted by them into their paper books' (i. 373).

What was good for the schoolboy's notebook in the sixteenth century was often good for a printed book. So in 1540 John Palsgrave published a translation of the Latin comedy *Acolastus* in which he added in the margin notes pointing out the metaphors, *sententiae*, and the 'schemes or exornations rhetoricall', drawing attention to such figures as *aposiopesis*, *auxesis, epiphonema*,[14] and Angel Day in his manual of epistolary rhetoric *The English Secretorie* (1596) indicated in the margin the figures used in his model letters.[15] Elizabethan rhetoricians even went to the surely unnecessary lengths of advising readers to mark the figures in books themselves. John Hoskins informs the person for whom he wrote his *Directions for Speech and Style* that in the copy of Sidney's *Arcadia* presented with the treatise he has written 'M' against the metaphors, and 'des' against 'evident and lively descriptions'.[16] Similarly the schoolmaster John Brinsley, author of *Ludus Literarius or The Grammar Schoole* (1612), recommended that in the left-hand margin it was good to list the various parts of the oration, 'and in the latter side of the page towards the right hand to set the several tropes and figures, but in two or three letters. As for metonymia, efficientia, no more but met, effic, or the like, marking some time under the word in which they are.'[17] Milton's copy of Harington's translation of *Orlando Furioso* still exists, and we can see how Milton the model

[14] John Palsgrave, *Acolastus*, ed. P. L. Carver (London, 1937), pp. 145–6.
[15] Further examples of writers and printed books listing rhetorical figures in the margin can be found in Joseph 1947, and Herrick 1950, pp. 189–214.
[16] Hoskins 1935, pp. 9, 42.
[17] Cit. K. Charlton, *Education in Renaissance England* (London, 1965), p. 114.

pupil dutifully marked the metaphors and rhetorical figures.[18] One teaching aid that Vives described in 1531 was prepared by Peter Mosellanus, namely 'a table of figures of speech, which can be hung up on the wall so that it will catch the attention of the pupil as he walks past it, and force itself upon his eyes'.[19] No opportunity must be lost to impress this art on their tender minds.

The last stage, the pupil using the figures himself, is the one for which abundant written evidence exists and which need not be elaborated on here. One of the earliest English theoretical works, *The Education of Children* (1588) by William Kempe, advises that once the pupil has learned 'the tropes and figures' and observed 'every trope, every figure' in the work he reads, he should then 'take in hand the exercise of all these 3 Artes at once in making somewhat of his owne', keeping decorum or 'the fineness of speech in the Rhetoricall ornaments, as comely tropes, pleasant figures' (i. 446). A fuller account is provided by the influential seventeenth-century educationalist Charles Hoole, in his *New Discovery of the Old Art of Teaching Schoole* (c. 1637; published 1660). Given the topic for his theme, the pupil should first take his notebook, look up everything that might be useful, sketch the argument, and then put it into the five-part oration, endeavouring to use the formulae 'proper to each part, so as to bring their matter into handsome and plain order; and to flourish and adorn it neatly with Rhetorical Tropes and Figures, always regarding the composure of words'.[20] Thus by the triple process, endlessly repeated, the average Renaissance schoolboy knew as much about the rhetorical figures as his Hellenistic or Roman counterpart.

As a final insight into the English educational institution of rhetoric we can look briefly at surviving school exercises. Virtually all of these have disappeared, of course, but the teaching of royalty was of sufficient importance for the notebooks of King Edward VI to have been preserved. The king had the best humanist teacher in England, Sir John Cheke (who

[18] D. L. Clark, *John Milton at St. Paul's School: A Study of Ancient Rhetoric in English Renaissance Education* (New York, 1948), pp. 176–7.

[19] Vives 1913, p. 134.

[20] Hoole 1660, p. 183.

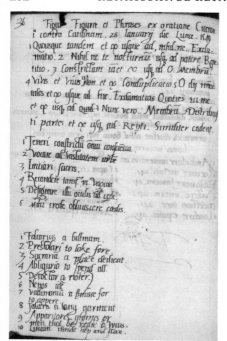

FIG. 3. King Edward VI: School notes on rhetoric

was to have such an enormous influence on Cambridge), and one can trace the progress of instruction in his pupil's exercise-book. In 1547–8 he was taught the figures and the parts of an oration from the *Ad Herennium* (Edward's own copy of this has survived and is well thumbed, especially in the relevant parts here, Books 4 and 1: Baldwin 1944, i. 231–4), and he simply memorized them like everyone else. We can also trace the next stage, rhetorical analysis of the works studied. In 1548 he was reading the most popular book of moral philosophy in the Renaissance, Cicero's *Offices*, extracting *sententiae* and phrases from it, then making an analysis of its structure. On 28 January 1549 he made a rhetorical analysis of Cicero's famous first speech against Catiline, noting the 'figures and phrases' used in it. Against the celebrated direct opening ('Quousque tamen abutere, Catilina, patientia nostra?'—'In heaven's name, Catiline, how long will you abuse our patience?') he wrote *Exclamatio*; of another passage repeating 'nihil' at the beginning of six succeeding clauses he wrote *conduplicatio* (or 'anaphora'—

he uses the *Ad Herennium* terminology). Another ('vivis, et vivis'—'you are living, and you are living') he correctly described as *membrum*, the figure which ends the construction suddenly, but not the sense; and of the sequence of clauses beginning with verbs similarly inflected ('Fuisti . . . distribuisti . . . statuisti . . . delegisti . . . discripsisti . . . confirmasti . . . dixisti') he wrote *similiter cadens*, that is, *homoioteleuton* or prose-rhyme (i. 227–8). It is a formal enough exercise, but at least as good as that performed by a modern historian of rhetoric.[21] The first stage of the schoolboy's absorption of rhetoric can also be seen here, for in 1549 the young king wrote a Latin composition on the theme 'love is a greater cause of obedience than fear', an especially interesting topic for a ruler. First he collected all his main arguments (*inventio*), also listing similes and examples which he intended to use; then he divided the material up in the form of the five parts of speech (*dispositio*); lastly he wrote the whole thing out, neatly using up all his quotations (i. 250–1).

King Edward VI may have had more individual supervision than other Renaissance schoolboys, but the teaching system and its dominance by rhetoric was the same for him or for Queen Elizabeth (Ascham taught her and records how she too learned her figures of speech[22]), as for thousands of other pupils, including all the great writers of this period. As C. S. Lewis rather charmingly puts it, we must picture medieval and Elizabethan poets

growing up from boyhood in a world of 'prettie *epanorthosis'*, *paronomasia, isocolon,* and *similiter cadentia.* Nor were these, like many subjects in a modern school, things dear to the masters but mocked or languidly regarded by the parents. Your father, your grown-up brother, your admired elder schoolfellow all loved rhetoric. Therefore you loved it too. You adored sweet Tully and were as concerned about *asyndeton* and *chiasmus* as a modern schoolboy is about cricketers or types of aeroplane.[23]

If that last sentence might seem to confuse the enthusiasm of hobbies with the discipline of work, Lewis's statement of the familiarity and respect with which a boy regarded rhetoric can

[21] Clarke 1953, p. 72.   [22] Joseph 1947, p. 29.
[23] C. S. Lewis, *English Literature in the Sixteenth Century* (Oxford, 1954), p. 61.

be vigorously endorsed. And the Elizabethans' familiarity with the figures is demonstrated by their many references to them, usually by the appropriate name, a practice that continues well into the eighteenth century. We must postulate, therefore, their keen appreciation of other people's skilful use of the figures, whether as readers or as members of an audience. (The way that characters in *Love's Labour's Lost* or *Romeo and Juliet* demonstrate their wit through sleight-of-hand with the figures has to be appreciated instantaneously in live performance or else the whole point is lost. The many Elizabethan parodies of bad rhetoric demand the same keenness.) A characteristically witty account of their awareness of rhetoric is provided by Nashe, as his *Unfortunate Traveller*, Jack Wilton, describes an orator in full possession of his rhetoric and his audience: 'And ever when he thought he had cast a figure so curiously as he dived over head and eares into his auditors admiration, hee would take occasion to stroke up his haire, and twine up his mustachios twice or thrice over while they might have leisure to applaud him.'[24] This account makes oratory resemble again the improvisatory, performing art it used to be.

Credit for the ability of so many Renaissance writers to use the full expressive resources of language must be given to the humanist school-system and to the masters who so energetically enforced it. As we can see from their later compositions, the schools exerted a lasting impression on the writers who attended them—Marlowe at Canterbury, Spenser at Merchant Taylor's (under Mulcaster), Sidney and Fulke Greville at Shrewsbury, Shakespeare almost certainly at Stratford Grammar School, at Westminster Ben Jonson (under the revered Camden) and later George Herbert, Hooker at Exeter Grammar School. Here they all achieved a 'solid grounding' in the most ancient and powerful literary discipline, and within the framework of rhetoric they were free to develop. In fifteenth-century Italy the initiative in reforming the educational curriculum was taken by a few enterprising individuals, such as Vittorino da Feltre, who challenged the moribund universities by introducing the new humanist education. Vittorino's school at Mantua was ahead of any Italian university of its day in the study of letters, and an equally important role was played by

[24] Cit. Joseph 1947, p. 49.

Guarino da Verona at Ferrara, the schools of the Brethren of the Common Life at Deventer (imitated at Liège and Strasburg), André Gouvéa at Bordeaux, Erasmus and others with the Collegium Trilingue at Louvain, Melanchthon at Wittenberg.[25] It was easier for a gifted individual to found a new institution than to change an old one: as Roberto Weiss once said, 'all intellectual movements are started by amateurs, and their professional adherents only appear once the movement has established itself securely'.[26] The innovations of Erasmus and Colet at St Paul's had been followed out in so many towns by the 1560s that the generation born then, which includes many of the greatest writers of the English Renaissance, were able to benefit from a remarkably intense education in the arts of language.

Those who went on to university acquired still more rhetoric. The universities were older than the grammar-schools, and they experienced first the humanist reforms in teaching which were to have so vital an influence on the schools. Oxford and Cambridge, like all European universities in the Middle Ages, had been dominated by scholasticism, the study of Aristotle's logic being the single most important element. The early sixteenth-century English humanists began to put into practice the ideals of studying classical literature which had been developed in fifteenth-century Florence under the inspiration of the Byzantine educationalist Chrysoloras,[27] and they made far-reaching changes in the university curricula. Where logic had held the main place, rhetoric and grammar (including study of the classics) now shared it with logic, and Greek was added. In the words of a recent historian of Oxford and Cambridge in this period, an important readjustment of emphasis took place:

By reforming the study of grammar, by increasing the time spent in the study of rhetoric, by transferring rhetoric from the more advanced part of the arts course to preparation for the B.A., and by enlarging work in both fields through the introduction of some readings from the *litterae humaniores*, they reduced the overriding emphasis formerly put upon logic and allowed, if they did not invite, a new spirit to guide a student's work.[28]

[25] Woodward 1906, pp. 14, 22, 32–3, 82, 86–7, 140, 181, 218, 229, 232.
[26] Weiss 1941, p. 4. See ibid., pp. 8, 179 ff. on the diffuse and uncoordinated nature of English humanism during the fifteenth century.
[27] Bolgar 1954, pp. 87–8, 268–9.
[28] Curtis 1959, p. 94.

The new spirit was soon there, not least because in addition to university lectures the colleges took more and more responsibility for organizing teaching, and in the establishment of colleges we have further evidence of the advance of rhetoric. When Bishop Foxe founded Corpus Christi College, Oxford, in 1517, he specified that lectures should be given on Cicero's *Orator*, his *Parts of Rhetoric*, Quintilian's *Institutes*, and the *Declamations* attributed to Quintilian. Trinity, Oxford, adopted the same texts in 1555 and added what has been called 'the Bible of the later Humanists',[29] the *Elegantiae* of Laurentio Valla. In the same year St John's, Oxford, accepted this list and added to it further works by Cicero, Hermogenes, Isocrates, and Demosthenes, and the two Renaissance collections by Trapezuntius and Cassander (Baldwin 1944, i. 103–4). At Cambridge Henry VIII passed on an injunction in 1535 that 'students should be instructed in the liberal arts', and after the 1549 visitation with its new statutes rhetoric was given more room in the second year of the arts course. Rhetoric gained, indeed, at the expense of other subjects: 'one of the few changes made in the Edwardian statutes at the outset of Elizabethan's reign was to eliminate mathematics in favour of rhetoric.'[30]

In the colleges, as in the university lecture-halls, the new humanist attitudes to the culture of the past took firm hold. Just as Renaissance sculptors, painters, and architects made a conscious break with medieval tradition in returning to the classics, so the rhetoric of the period expressed the same wish for a new beginning. Where the Middle Ages had downgraded rhetoric with the trivium, subordinating it to dialectic or theology, the Renaissance reversed the trend, with interest. Leonardo Bruni set grammar and rhetoric against 'that vulgar, threadbare jargon' of theology,[31] while Colet dismissed the Latin of the scholastics punningly: 'it rather may be called blotterature than literature.'[32] To Vittorino da Feltre grammar and rhetoric, combined, implied the critical scholarship of Greek and Latin literature, history, and thought. 'Dialectic, instead of dominating all other subjects', dropped in importance: 'degustasse sat erit', Aeneas Sylvius said of it.[33] Rudolph

---

[29] Bolgar 1954, p. 270.   [30] Simon 1966, pp. 199, 252–3, 358 n.
[31] Woodward 1897, p. 123: translating Bruni, *De Studiis et Litteris*.
[32] Simon 1966, p. 79.
[33] Woodward 1897, p. 38.

Agricola, whose rhetoricization of logic was to become so important in the sixteenth century, started his treatise *De Formando Studio* in 1484 by rejecting the entire discipline of the medievalists.[34] Erasmus likewise attacked medieval scholasticism, especially in logic and theology, and in his own educational treatises went back to Quintilian, as did Budé in his praise of eloquence as the faculty without which knowledge is useless.[35] Specific medieval arts or systems were attacked: in the 1530s Melanchthon rejected fourfold allegory, while in the same period Sir Thomas Elyot gave little špace to the *ars dictaminis*.[36] One need only recall the attacks on Aristotelian philosophy from Ramus and Galileo to Bacon, Hobbes, and Boyle, to realize how totally the balance of the *trivium* had changed. The early English humanist poet John Skelton, in his *Speke Parrot* (*c*. 1521), described how the grammarians and logicians were being expelled:

> *Albertus de modo significandi*
> And *Donatus* be dryven out of scole;
> Priscians hed broken now handy dandy,
> And *inter didascolos* is rekened for a fole;
> Alexander, a gander of Menanders pole,
> With *Da Causales*, is cast out of the gate,
> And *Da Racionales* dare not show his pate.

> *Plauti* is his comedies a chyld shall now reherse,
> And medyll with Quintylyan in his *Declamacyons* . . . [37]

That gleeful inconoclasm could be followed through in the changes that took place in the school and university curricula.

Renaissance grammarians were scathing about their predecessors' weaknesses. Many medieval grammars, such as the *Doctrinale* of Alexandre de Villedieu and the *Graecismus* of Evrard de Béthune, were written in verse as a help to memorization, but at the cost of clear exposition. Verse grammars were dismissed by the humanists for their 'pedagogical ineffectiveness', and 'the grandiose attempt of the scholastic grammarians to transform grammar into a demonstrative science, an attempt that had culminated around 1300 in the treatises on the modes of meaning, was

---

[34] Woodward 1906, p. 99. [35] Ibid., pp. 101, 123, 134.
[36] Melanchthon 1968, pp. 342–6; Woodward 1906, p. 284.
[37] Cit. Sweeting 1940, p. 64.

abandoned'.[38] Rejection of modistic grammar accompanied a drastic reduction of the grammatical curriculum. Where the Middle Ages had developed grammar as an end in itself, the Renaissance subordinated it to the total scheme of learning. Although some medieval manuals continued to be used, they were gradually replaced by texts with radically changed emphases. The first humanist manual, the *Regulae Grammaticales* (*c.* 1418) of Guarino Veronese, 'completely lacks the logical and metaphysical underpinnings' characteristic of scholastic grammars, defining its humanistic approach by 'what it excludes'.[39] Later humanist grammars, such as the *Rudimenta Grammaticales* (1468) of Niccolò Perotti, and a composite treatise by Giulio Sulpizio Verulano, expanded their scope by including a manual on epistolary style, while Despauterius' vast *Commentarii Grammatici* (1537) include treatises on poetic genres, letter-writing, and an extensive *Ars Versificatoria*.[40] Conversely, the new manuals on epistolography, such as the *Novum Epistolarium* (1484) of Giammario Filelfo, added unexpected sections on the divisions of the oration, the figures of speech, the orator's three *genera*, and even one on *pronuntiatio*, admittedly irrelevant to letter-writing, while Sulpizio actually included *memoria*.[41] The prestige of classical rhetoric was so great that the new language arts took over its doctrines wholesale, whether strictly relevant or not.

The rhetoric manuals themselves vary in size and scope, as ever, according to the educational needs they aimed to fulfil. But a steady trend can be seen towards ever-more inclusive treatises, absorbing classical traditions wholesale, with somewhat daunting results. The *Rhetorica* of Bartolomeo Cavalcanti, begun in 1541 and published in 1559, is a huge digest of classical rhetoric in seven books, based on Aristotle, Cicero, Quintilian, Hermogenes, Trapezuntius, and two contemporaries, Pier Vettori and Vincenzo Maggi.[42] Other substantial tomes from this period include the *De Oratione Libri VII* (1558) of A. Lullius; the

[38] Percival 1983, pp. 305, 310.   [39] Ibid., p. 315.   [40] Ibid., pp. 319, 321–2.
[41] Henderson 1983, p. 337. See ibid., pp. 340–2, 346–7, 354 on Renaissance rejection of the medieval *artes dictaminis*.
[42] Roaf 1959 is a useful study of its genesis and sources, but shows little sympathy for it as a rhetoric-book, finding it 'excessively tedious to modern readers' (p. 310), dull, diffuse, wearisome, repetitive, and so on (pp. 312, 321. 338, 398 ff.).

De Universa Ratione Elecutionis Rhetoricae (1576) of Johannes Sturm, which runs to more than 800 pages, with 226 pages on rhetorical ornament alone (Sturm produced no less than sixteen books on rhetoric); and the *Thesaurus Rhetoricae* (1559) of Giovanni Baptista Bernardi, an encyclopedia defining some five thousand rhetorical terms.[43] The seventeenth century continued this trend towards the all-inclusive work, especially the Jesuits, such as Louis de Cressolles, whose *Vacationes Autunnales sive de perfecta oratoris actione et pronunciatioŋe libri III* (1620) contain over 700 pages on delivery and pronunciation, and Nicholas Caussin, who addresses a wider area in the 1,010 pages of his *Eloquentiae Sacrae et Humanae Parallela Libri XVI* (1619).[44] All Renaissance rhetoric-books were of course eclectic, derivative, which did not deter some authors from claiming that their method was 'entirely new', as Vives did, or asserting that 'after centuries of disuse I shall try to bring rhetoric again into the light'[45]—another humanist not lacking in self-confidence. Some performed their task of digesting and reorganizing the classical tradition efficiently—Melanchthon, Susenbrotus, Soarez, Peacham, for instance; others, such as Thomas Wilson, were less successful.[46] The author of a rhetoric textbook is a kind of *bricoleur*, taking his overall plan from one source, his definitions from two or three other authorities, his examples from further afield—or he might show his originality by inventing his own, or quoting from some contemporary work.

While the Renaissance rhetoric-text has neither a definite form nor an agreed-on scope, and can be expanded or contracted as the energy of the author and the demands of the publisher determine, the majority of these texts attempt to treat rhetoric as a unity. In this sense, rhetoric was reclaiming its own domain. As J. J. Murphy noted, 'Medieval rhetoric, with its fragmentation into specialized genres, did not provide the humanists with the kind of synthesizing approach for which they yearned'.[47] John Monfasani's study of that pioneer humanist

---

[43] See Ward 1983, p. 157; Murphy 1983, pp. 26–7.
[44] Soarez 1955, p. 48; Fumaroli 1980, pp. 279–326, 362–71.
[45] Vives 1966, pp. 26, 28.
[46] See, e.g., Melanchthon 1968, Susenbrotus 1953, Soarez 1955; for Wilson see R. H. Wagner, 'Thomas Wilson's *Arte of Rhetorique*', *Speech Monographs*, 27 (1969), 1–32, at p. 27: Wilson's treatment of *elocutio* 'is unusual, and confusing . . . not convincing'.   [47] Murphy 1974, pp. 359–60.

Trapezuntius (George of Trebizond) has shown that 'In being the first humanist to write a synthetic exposition of rhetorical invention, George literally took back the topics from the logicians'. When he decided to treat all five of the orator's duties he 'reunited the parts of classical rhetoric which the various medieval *Artes* had separated or suppressed'.[48] Another Renaissance rhetoric-book that reintegrated the tradition, independently of Trapezuntius, was the Hebrew rhetoric of Judah Messer Leon, *Sēpher Nōpheth Sūphīm*, or *The Book of the Honeycomb's Flow*, which appeared at Mantua in about 1475.[49] Here the unifying source was the *Rhetorica ad Herennium*. Other Renaissance writers rejected specific medieval deformations of the rhetorical tradition. In the enormously popular *De Arte Rhetorica* of Cyprian Soarez, the chapter on the emotions states that 'An orator is most effective in arousing the minds of men, and he does this by amplification'. In making *amplificatio* the chief means of arousing the emotions, Soarez ignored the medieval tradition which made it a question of *verba* not *res*, of the mere quantity of words involved, and has gone back to classical sources, notably Cicero's *De Partitione Oratoria*.[50] Richard McKeon, having been the first to notice that trend in the medieval specialization of the *artes* towards a purely 'verbal rhetoric', a 'formalism' concerned with words separated from 'arguments of things', recorded the contrary trend in the Renaissance. The purely linguistic analysis of figures made in the grammatical and *ars poetria* traditions was now turned into a more complete theory of poetry, 'which dealt with imagination, passion, truth, and virtue'. Rhetoric was returned not only to literature but to life, indeed 'political philosophy has never entirely lost the rhetorical turn from which its theories derived their modern concreteness and practicality'.[51]

II

The stress on practicality is perhaps the most distinctive feature

[48] Monfasani 1976, pp. 277, 269.

[49] Isaac Rabinowitz, *The Book of the Honeycomb's Flow*, a translation of Judah Messer Leon, *Sēpher Nōpheth Sūphīm* (Ithaca, NY, 1983).

[50] Soarez 1955, p. 169. Similarly Melanchthon 1968, p. 202: 'from all logical places we shall provide amplifications in order to arouse people's minds, by exaggerating either the dignity or the meanness of the object.'

[51] McKeon 1952, pp. 290–2, 294–5.

of the Renaissance rediscovery of classical rhetoric. When George of Trebizond cites the traditional definition of rhetoric as 'the civil science by which we speak in civil questions with the assent, as much as possible, of the listeners'—a mosaic of passages from *Ad Herennium, De Inventione,* and later texts—the concept of civil questions, which survives in medieval rhetoric without any real understanding of its meaning, is now interpreted as referring to rhetoric's role in society and especially the *vita activa*.[52] According to this way of life, often opposed to the *vita contemplativa,* and sometimes to the *vita voluptuosa,*[53] the individual's duties should go first to the country that has given him citizenship and a language, then to his fellow-citizens, his family, and friends, and lastly to himself. He must put others before him, as Cicero—echoing Plato and Aristotle—said so many times,[54] most memorably in *De Officiis*:

Since . . . we are not born for ourselves alone, but our country claims a share of our being, and our friends a share, and since . . . everything that the earth produces is created for man's use; and as men, too, are born for the sake of men, that they may be able mutually to help one another; in this direction we ought to follow Nature as our guide, to contribute to the general good by an interchange of acts of kindness, by giving and receiving, and thus by our skill, our industry, and our talents to cement human society more closely together, man to man. (1. 7. 22)

As in those passages from the rhetorical works quoted above (pp. 10–11), Cicero again sees *ratio* and *oratio*, reason and speech, as constituting a 'bond of connection between all the members of the human race . . . which by the processes of teaching and learning, or communicating, discussing, and reasoning associate men together and unite them in a sort of natural fraternity' (1. 16. 50–1). The knowledge so produced should be 'made available for the use of as many as possible' (1. 26. 92). Although 'the whole glory of virtue is in activity' (1. 6. 19), scholars who devote their lives to 'the pursuit of knowledge' still

[52] Monfasani 1976, p. 267. On the medieval 'survival' of this concept see, e.g., Baldwin 1928, pp. 142, 178; Leff 1978, p. 22; Ward 1978, p. 49 n.
[53] See Garin 1965; Rice 1958; Vickers 1985; and Seigel 1968.
[54] See Plato, *Rep.* 520 a–b; Aristotle, *Nic. Eth.* 1169ᵃ 18 ff.; Cicero, *De Rep.* 1. 1. 1; 3. 4; 4. 8; fr. 2; 6. 13. 13, 16, 25–6, 29; *De Fin.* 3. 19. 62; 4. 7. 17; 5. 23. 65. Salutati virtually reproduces Cicero verbatim: see Witt 1983, p. 73.

contribute to 'the advantages and blessings of mankind', either as teachers training many 'to be better citizens', or by writing books for the improvement of posterity. All such actions are valuable because men of 'learning and science' thus

apply their own practical wisdom and insight to the service of humanity. And for that reason also much speaking (if only it contain wisdom) is better than speculation never so profound without speech; for mere speculation is self-centred, while speech extends its benefits to those with whom we are united by the bonds of society. (1. 44. 156)

The impact on the Renaissance of these pages from *De Officiis* (an inescapable textbook at school and university), together with related passages in Cicero's rhetorical works, was immense. So many utterances of Renaissance humanists between Petrarch and Milton are reminiscences, or deliberate quotations of Cicero. To the humanists *ratio* and *oratio* were the defining attributes of human nature, yet, as George of Trebizond put it, 'reason does not do any good unless bodied forth in speech'.[55] Coluccio Salutati, writing in the 1370s, saw these gifts as linking men with angels:

For if intelligence and reason, by which the human race has some common property with superior beings, are a source of beauty; if men are clearly distinguished from other living creatures because they can use words; how much more excellent than other men is he who, relying on his reason, stands forth with brilliant eloquence?[56]

This turning the orator into a culture-hero also derives from Cicero,[57] and was echoed by Poggio Bracciolini and Georg Harsdörffer, Fracastaro, Soarez, and Sir Philip Sidney, to name but a few.[58]

If speech is the precondition of social exchange then silence and solitude, the *bêtes noires* of Ciceronian humanism, are its denial. In one of his early 'Familiar Letters' Petrarch describes the reciprocal relationship between mind and speech: 'each

---

[55] Monfasani 1976, p. 259. For other Renaissance writers praising speech as the gift separating men from beasts see Castor 1964, p. 135, citing Erasmus and Louis le Roy; Bolgar 1970, p. 205, citing Budé.

[56] Witt 1983, p. 67; also Ullman 1963, p. 113; Struever 1970, p. 53.

[57] See *De Or.* 1. 8. 30 ff., 2. 9. 35 ff., 3. 5. 19–20; *De Inv.* 1. 1–5; and K. Barwick, *Das rednerische Bildungsideal Ciceros* (Berlin, 1963).

[58] See, e.g., Dyck 1966, pp. 25–6; Fracastaro 1924, p. 67; Soarez 1955, pp. 110–1; Melanchthon 1968, p. 221; Sidney 1965, pp. 121–2.

depends upon the other, but while one remains in one's breast, the other emerges into the open'. Speech can then be 'of great assistance' to others, so the study of eloquence should be cultivated out of both 'charity toward our fellow men' and for the cure and solace of ourselves.[59] In the Renaissance all forms of speech, including poetry, were valued as modes of communication,[60] so that to write or think purely for oneself would have been regarded as perverse. Aeneas Sylvius Piccolomini, giving advice to rulers, stressed the futility of silence: 'As Homer says, silence is becoming in a woman, but in a man, and that man a king standing before his people, it is rather a shame and a disgrace.'[61] Solitude was also viewed with disapproval, as a denial of our basic humanity. Cicero had said that a man placed in a wholly solitary existence would soon die (*De Off.* 1. 43. 153), and his humanist followers denounced monasticism or the contemplative life as betraying the Christian ideal of *caritas*. Solitude is variously described as barbarous isolation, illiterate, inferior, fruitless, infertile, treasonous, inhuman, rotting in laziness, sterile, unjust, vain.[62] Where the earlier humanists could see the gift of speech as bringing man nearer the status of angels, later writers denounced the contemplative life for presumptuously aspiring to the prerogative of angels to be not doers but lookers on.[63]

The humanists' justification for making rhetoric central to their work was that eloquence was both natural and social. As Stefano Guazzo wrote in 1574,

Nature herself has given man the power of speech. But certainly not in order that he converse with himself . . . rather as a means of communication with others . . . a means by which men can come together and love one another.

To Guazzo, then, the solitary man is 'not far from an animal' and 'deserves the Helleborre as much as the madman'. For the philosopher and rhetorician Alessandro Piccolomini man is 'a

---

[59] *Rerum Familiarum*, i. 9 (Petrarch 1975–85, i. 47–9).
[60] Muntéano 1967, p. 225; Dyck 1966, p. 30.
[61] Cit. Woodward 1897, p. 143.
[62] Garin 1965: pp. 21 (Petrarch); 39–42 (Leonardo Bruni); 45 (Poggio Bracciolini); 61 (L. B. Alberti); 67 (Palmieri); 151 (Speroni); 152 (Guazzo and Galileo); 157 (Nizolio).
[63] Ibid., pp. 172 (Figliucci); 174 (Piccolomini); 176 (Segni).

social and communicative being' intended to exchange 'useful and virtuous behaviour'. The man who places himself outside human relationships, fleeing to the forests and mountains, will not only have to stoop to 'conversing with thorny shrubs and stones' but will soon be 'taken for a wild beast rather than a man'.[64] To Vergerius, writing a treatise on education, idleness leads to self-indulgence and to an 'unsociable, solitary temper', while the man who surrenders himself entirely to speculative thought follows 'a self-regarding end and is useless as a citizen or as a prince'.[65] Humanist disapproval of solitude sometimes invokes one of its other bugbears, *philautia* or self-love. Erasmus proclaimed, echoing Cicero, that 'no man is born to himself, no man is born to idleness', but to serve their country and God.[66] In his *Praise of Folly* Erasmus expressed the general Renaissance hostility to *philautia* as the denial of *caritas*, a position echoed in Shakespeare and embodied so memorably in the figure of Panurge in Rabelais' *Le Tiers Livre*.[67]

While attacking all the enemies of eloquence Renaissance humanism held out to its followers the promise of success to those who mastered rhetoric. In his *De Ratione Dicendi* Vives, drawing on Isocrates and Cicero, argued that since 'the bonds of human society are justice and speech' nothing is 'more advantageous to human society than well-formed and well-developed language'. The prudent man knows what is useful to human society and 'holds sway over the minds of men by speech alone'.[68] In his more inclusive work *De Tradendis Disciplinis* Vives describes rhetoric as having 'the greatest influence and weight. It is necessary for all positions in life', since 'no human activity can continue without speech'. Lacking

[64] Garin 1965, pp. 159 (Guazzo); 173 (Piccolomini).
[65] Woodward 1897, pp. 100, 110.
[66] Woodward 1906, p. 187.
[67] Erasmus, *Praise of Folly*, tr. B. Radice (Harmondsworth, 1971), pp. 59, 94–5, 131–5, 153. See also Shakespeare, *All's Well that Ends Well*, 1. 1. 157, where Parolles describes virginity as 'peevish, proud, idle, made of self-love, which is the most inhibited [prohibited] sin in the canon'; also *Twelfth Night*, 1. 5. 97: 'O, you are sick of self-love, Malvolio'; and *Coriolanus*, 4. 6. 32: 'Ambitious past all thinking, / Self-loving!' For Rabelais see *Le Tiers Livre*, ed. M. A. Screech (Geneva, 1974), pp. xiv–xvi, 30–3, 46–8, 54–7, 180, 204–5, 246–7; Screech, 'Rabelais. Le Tiers Livre de Pantagruel', in P. H. Nurse (ed.), *The Art of Criticism* (Edinburgh, 1969), pp. 27–39; and Screech, *Rabelais* (London, 1979), pp. 235–8, 258–9, 261–2, 280–1, 307–9, 343, 431–2, 460–1.
[68] Vives 1966, pp. 22–4.

the complacency of some Renaissance commentators Vives sees speech as 'the cause of the greatest of the goods and ills of life', hence

the more corrupt men generally are, so much the more ought the good and intelligent men to cultivate carefully the art of Rhetoric, which holds such sway over the mind, so that they may lead others from misdeeds and errings to, at least, some care for virtue.[69]

If Renaissance theorists tended to justify aesthetic activities on moral grounds, with how much more right did they claim an ethical intent for rhetoric. Poliziano wrote that oratory or eloquence 'is the only means of penetrating men's minds and, without violence, making them follow goals useful for all'.[70] For Jacopo Zabarella rhetoric and poetics were instrumental faculties which the citizen employed 'to make his fellow citizens good', a belief shared by Salutati.[71]

The success of rhetoric in the *vita activa* was visible to all. As Chancellor of Florence Coluccio Salutati's letters were crucial to its fight against the papacy. A modern commentator has said that 'Salutati's missives were among Florence's most important weapons', while Giangaleazzo Visconti remarked that 'Salutati's letters were worth more to Florence than a thousand horsemen'.[72] Subsequent chancellors of Florence saw the importance of rhetoric, and both by their theoretical writings and their own praxis demonstrated the power of eloquence.[73] In his *Life of Cicero* Leonardo Bruni presented the orator as 'a hero of civic humanism combining eloquence and learning with political leadership', and George of Trebizond modelled himself on both Bruni and Cicero.[74] For this reason it seems wrong to suggest that 'Trebizond's starkly utilitarian explanation of rhetoric' in his *Rhetoricorum Libri V* (1433–5) was 'conditioned by the need to "sell" the usefulness of his instruction to the

[69] Vives 1913, pp. 180–1.
[70] Cit. Garin 1973, p. 121.
[71] Weinberg 1961, p. 22; Witt 1983, pp. 69–70.
[72] Witt 1983, p. 125; Ullman 1963, p. 14; V. Kahn, 'Coluccio Salutati on the Active and Contemplative Lives', in Vickers 1985, pp. 153–79, at p. 153.
[73] Garin 1965; Garin 1972; P. Herde, 'Politik und Rhetorik in Florenz am Vorabend der Renaissance', *Archiv für Kulturgeschichte*, 47 (1965), 141–220; D. Cantimori, 'Rhetoric and Politics in Italian Humanism', *Journal of the Warburg and Courtauld Institutes*, 1 (1937), 83–162.
[74] Monfasani 1976, p. 42.

pragmatic merchants of the Venetian Republic'.[75] All writers on rhetoric emphasized its *utilitas*, but we must beware of giving that word Benthamite connotations: in the Renaissance it was interchangeable with such words as *caritas* and *philanthropia*.[76] As Vives, that far-sighted educationalist, wrote, 'this then is the fruit of all studies; this is the goal. Having acquired our knowledge, we must turn it to usefulness, and employ it for the common good. Whence follows immortal reward. . . .'[77] The practicality of rhetoric in civic business was emphasized by many writers. To Aeneas Sylvius Piccolomini 'eloquence is a prime accomplishment in one immersed in affairs'; George of Trebizond advised that if a man 'hungers for the glory of ruling the republic, let him devote himself to rhetoric'; and Francis Bacon observed that, although 'profoundness of wisdom will help a man to name or admiration, . . . it is eloquence that prevaileth in an active life'.[78]

III

The effectiveness of rhetoric derived, as everyone who had read the classical texts knew only too well, from its power over the emotions. Renaissance rhetoricians gave enormous attention to this topic, and related it to the new emphasis in psychology on the will as the source of freedom and responsibility. Rhetorical *movere* was increasingly conceived of as mobilizing the will to good ends. As Eugenio Garin has shown, in attacking medieval abstraction and quietism, Salutati defended 'the primacy of the will', insisting that 'man is made free through a free act of the will', and that human nature is only realized in action and communication.[79] In Petrarch's formulation, 'the object of the

[75] Monfasani 1976, p. 298.

[76] Brian Vickers, 'Bacon's so-called "utilitarianism": sources and influence', in M. Fattori (ed.), *Francis Bacon. Terminologia e fortuna nel XVII secolo* (Rome, 1984) pp. 281–313.

[77] Vives 1913, p. 283. See also J. C. Scaliger's rejection of the sharp theoretical distinction between the virtues, where justice is connected with judicial rhetoric, utility with deliberative, and honesty with eulogies: 'utility is the end of all the virtues, wherefore also of justice' (Scaliger 1905, p. 50).

[78] Woodward 1897, p. 143; Monfasani 1976, p. 295; Bacon 1857–74, iii, 409.

[79] Garin 1965, pp. 29–33; Charles Trinkaus, *In Our Image and Likeness: Humanity and Divinity in Italian Humanist Thought*, 2 vols. (London, 1970), i. 51–102.

will, as it pleases the wise, is to be good; that of the intellect is truth. It is better to will the good than to know the truth.'[80] In Salutati, too, 'the pre-eminence of the will over the intellect is fundamental', expressing a new voluntarist psychology which Nancy Struever sees as deriving from the Sophists.[81] Alberti, like so many Renaissance figures, 'possessed great strength of will', his favourite motto being 'gli uomini possono tutto quando lo vogliono', and he stressed the role of education in fashioning the personality and its powers of self-determination.[82] The route to the will, as Renaissance psychology understood it, lay partly through the reason, and it would be wrong to describe the working of rhetoric as irrational. We must beware of using the clear-cut modern distinction between 'feelings and thoughts'. As a great pioneer in rhetorical criticism, Rosemond Tuve, wrote in 1947, 'several of the faculties are concerned, in both parties to the communication'. Rhetorical devices 'move a reader's affections', but also 'affect his judgments; they move him to feel intensely, to will, to act, to understand, to believe, to change his mind'.[83]

The hinge, though, the channel through which persuasion worked, was the *affectus*, the source of affection (passion), that power to feel which the orator, poet, painter, or musician aroused in himself before transmitting to this audience. As Juan Luis Vives, who made an important contribution to Renaissance psychology, put it in 1531,

in man the highest law and government are at the disposal of will. To the will, reason and judgment are assigned as counsellors, and the emotions are its torches. Moreover, the emotions of the mind are enflamed by the sparks of speech. So, too, the reason is impelled and moved by speech. Hence it comes to pass that, in the whole kingdom of the activities of man, speech holds in its possession a mighty strength which it continually manifests.[84]

Or, in Francis Bacon's pithier formulation, 'the duty and office of Rhetoric is to apply Reason to Imagination for the better moving of the will'.[85] The passions had received separate

[80] Petrarch, 1948, p. 105.
[81] Struever 1970, pp. 58–9; also pp. 13–14, 18, 74, 79–80.
[82] Woodward 1906, pp. 49, 52; for similar emphases in other humanists see ibid., pp. 169, 201.
[83] Tuve 1947, p. 183.   [84] Vives 1913, p. 180.
[85] *The Advancement of Learning* (1605), in Bacon 1857–74, iii. 409.

treatment in several of the classic rhetoric-texts: in Book Two of
Aristotle's *Rhetoric*, in *De Oratore* (2. 44. 188–91), and in
Quintilian (6. 2. 20–36). In Renaissance rhetorics they receive
more and more emphasis. When Daniel d'Auge published his
Deux dialogues de l'invention poétique in 1560 he gave five pages to
the analysis of the passions; when the Jesuit Caussinus
published his *De Eloquentia Sacra et Humana* in 1619 he devoted
nearly a hundred pages to the topic.[86] Vossius, the Dutch
humanist whose treatise on rhetoric (1606) was widely read
throughout Europe, devotes the second of his six books
ostensibly to *inventio*, but it is in fact 'largely a treatise on the
passions'.[87] The increasingly systematic treatment of the
emotions in the seventeenth century (well studied recently by
German scholars[88]) resulted in a new sub-discipline of rhetorical
psychology, *pathologia*. While not without its eccentricities, such
as the 'weird imaginings'[89] of Cureau de la Chambre in *Les
Caractères des passions* (1640) and *Le Système de l'âme* (1664), the
revival of interest in the passions could only intensify awareness
of the functionality of rhetoric. Even new concepts in literary
theory, such as the marvellous, and purgation, were referred to
the passions.[90]

Several of the treatises just cited deal with poetics, and we
might note here that the subsuming of poetry with prose or
oratory under rhetoric, endorsed by Cicero, Ovid, and
Quintilian (above, p. 60), continued through the Middle Ages,
so that to speak of a 'confusion of rhetoric and poetic' in the
Renaissance is anachronistic.[91] Both drew on common
resources, with the poet given extra licence in vocabulary but
being more restricted in his choice of rhythm. Bernard
Weinberg's massive history of Italian Renaissance criticism
(which unaccountably omits rhetorical treatises, although it
concedes that every part of poetic theory was shot through with
rhetoric), has shown that in the rhetoricization of poetry almost

[86] Gordon 1970, p. 37; Sieveke 1974, p. 55.
[87] Bayley 1980, pp. 31–2.
[88] See Dyck 1966, Plett 1975, Rotermund 1969, Sieveke 1974, and Stolt 1974.
[89] France 1965, p. 164.
[90] See Weinberg 1961, pp. 137, 172, 283, 545, etc.; and Index s.v. 'Passions'
and 'Moving of passions (movere)'.
[91] C. S. Baldwin made such anachronistic statements in the 1920s (Baldwin
1928, pp. 39, 194; Baldwin 1939, pp. 15, 57, 59, 166), but it is disappointing to
find Weinberg doing so a generation later: Weinberg 1961, pp. viii–ix, 72.

all 'poetic concerns' were reduced to 'the three styles' and the language appropriate to each, so that the main stress in these treatises is 'on diction, on figures and styles, and on the "topics" which are curiously transformed into stylistic procedures'.[92] Critics read and analysed poetry according to the rhetorical processes of *inventio, dispositio,* and *elocutio,*[93] and saw as the special glory of the poet his ability to arouse the passions. Antonio Posio wrote in 1562 that 'the poet must arouse anger, fear, hope, and the other passions'; for Viperano in 1569 it was clear that 'history guides the mind, poetry arouses and calms the passions'; Giovanni Pontano, in the 1470s, saw the poet's aim as being 'to move and carry away the listener', impressing 'admiration' in his soul and thus acquiring 'fame and reverence'; Giason Denores, interpreting Horace in 1553, stated that 'if the poet wishes to arouse the passions, he must attend to "ornaments" and "figures"'; Antonio Minturno in 1559 updated Cicero, telling the poet that the *vis* of his art enables him to lead the people 'where you will, or from whatever place it may please you'; and Bartolomeo Maranta praised Virgil in 1564 for his excellence in *movere*: 'how variedly—and always wherever he wishes—he draws away the souls of men, inflames, calms, teaches, impels, excites, diverts, discourages them.' As Weinberg comments, this claim that poetry 'exercises upon the reader or hearer a kind of irresistible power, a superior rhetorical force which sways his passions and imposes upon him the teachings of the poem' played into the hands of the opponents of poetry, since just this moving power made it dangerous.[94] However, every treatise attacking poetry merely

[92] Weinberg 1961, pp. 108–10, 151–2, 196–9, 804. For examples of critics who identify poetic and rhetoric see ibid., pp. 4, 5, 10, 56, 66, 71, 87, 100, 108, 112, 137, 150, 181, 191, 205, 213–14, 244, 267, 370, 398, 462–3, 594, 642, 644, 748, 825, etc. One advantage of Weinberg's vast scope is that his 1200-page book, with its generous quotations, amounts to an anthology of critical ideas in Renaissance Italy. For his later collection of complete texts see Weinberg 1970–4.

[93] For critics finding the triad of *inventio, dispositio,* and *elocutio* in poetry (often via a commentary on Horace's *Ars poetica*) see Weinberg 1961, pp. 55, 56, 80–1, 86, 89, 95, 101, 102–3, 114, 123, 125, 128–9, 134, 137, 144, 150, 153, 157–8, 168, 184, 195, 208, 216, 222, 227, 232, 240, 383, 432, 434, 439, 500, 645, 646, 650, 724, 733, 741, 754, 757, 795, 848, 880, 905, 921, 984, 1017, 1084: a total of over forty critics, within an admittedly incomplete survey.

[94] Ibid., pp. 17, 43, 87–8, 129, 171–2, 237, 294. For other critics linking poetics and rhetoric in these terms see ibid., pp. 42, 213, 231, 284, 290, 701–2, 703, 884, 908, 929.

produced others defending it and reiterating its rhetorical power.

In Renaissance France a great revival of poetry led to treatises on poetics outnumbering formal rhetoric-books, yet adopting all their teaching.[95] Robert Griffin, in an enlightening study of the links between poetic and rhetoric, has shown that French Renaissance poetic was 'inclusive, not exclusive, in the sense that thought and intention, eloquence and imagery, feeling and meaning, mental concept and spatial construct are all creatively linked'.[96] The sixteenth century saw a decisive 'shift of interest', from the *Instructif de la seconde rhétorique* (1501), a typical late medieval manual emphasizing purely formal properties, such as rhyme systems and rhythm, to Guillaume des Autelz's *Réplique aux furieuses défenses de Louis Meigret* (1550), where emphasis shifts to 'the rhetorical persuasion that comes from a knowledge and application of functional rhetorical figures', and the poet is instructed to do 'tout à mouvoir les affections' (p. 22). Where the medieval treatises of the 'seconde Rhétorique' (devoted to versification, the 'première' to prose) had stressed pattern and decoration as the skills of the poet (a significant parallel with Panofsky's description of medieval art quoted above, p. 246), the new poetics insisted on 'functional expression' and the adoption of rhetorical *movere*. So in Fabri's *L'Art de rithmer* rhetoric is seen as 'la royne de la pensee des hommes, qui tourne les couraiges, suadant et dissuadant en tel fin qu'il plait, and Du Bellay insists, in his *Deffense et illustration de la langue Francoyse* (1549), that 'the poets be steeped in examples of rhetorical persuasion, "quand aux figures des sentences & des motz, & toutes les autres parties de l'eloquution, les lieux de commiseration, de joye, de tristesse, d'ire, d'admiration, & toutes autres commotions de l'ame . . ."' (p. 31).

Poets took to heart his advice 'qu'il entreprenne quelque hault & excellent ouvraige', with the result that in this and the

---

[95] See Gordon 1970, pp. 28–45: 'L'Alliance de la Poésie et de la Rhétorique'; France 1965; France 1972.

[96] Griffin 1969, p. 23. Later quotations in this paragraph are from Griffin. On the late medieval 'seconde Rhétorique' see also Castor 1964, who describes its concern with the surface of poetry rather than its substance (p. 7), its obsession with the 'technological aspects of poetry' producing endless discussions of shape and style (pp. 14 ff.), resulting in a 'formalisation and bare prescription' (p. 18) rather than a theory of function and expression.

following century the poet's power to influence the passions
was reiterated untiringly. As Basil Muntéano put it, rhetoric,
based on observations drawn from the depths of the human
consciousness, produced 'une véritable *esthétique de la persuasion
passionnelle*'.[97] Thus Du Bellay made the homage to Cicero that
writers on rhetoric in every generation must pay, describing the
ideal poet as one 'qui me fera indigner, apaiser, éjouir, douloir,
aimer, haïr, admirer, étonner, bref, qui tiendra la bride de mes
affections, me tournant çà et là à son plaisir'.[98] Whereas critics
earlier in this century, still working with a Romantic aesthetic,
saw Ronsard and his contemporaries as introspectives, A. L,
Gordon rightly presents the sixteenth-century French poet as
being concerned to win power over his readers' souls and hearts
to effect persuasion, and drawing on the rhetoric handbooks for
lists of the passions and the specific devices that would arouse
them: 'Les rhéteurs savent que les mots enflamment l'imagination des hommes et qu'une similitude ou une amplification peut
déclencher les passions et pousser à l'action.' Thus Daniel
d'Auge, having spent his five pages analysing the affections,
briefly lists the figures that can be used to arouse them: 'Toutes
ces affections se meuvent ou par extenuation, ou par amplification, ou par similitude, ou par comparaison & exemple, . . . ou
par exclamation' and so on,[99] a list that also derives from *De
Oratore* (quoted below, pp. 311–12). Later theorists added to
Aristotle's classification of the passions the newer system of
Descartes.[100]

In Germany, where, due to a combination of cultural and
historical factors, the Renaissance made its effect felt later, the
passions became even more the concern of rhetoric and poetics.
The great pioneer of German rhetoric, Philip Melanchthon,
made the distinction that 'the end or purpose of dialectics is to
teach, but the function of rhetoric is to move and stimulate
minds and thus to affect a person'.[101] It is doubtless no accident

[97] Muntéano 1967, p. 164.
[98] Cit. France 1972, p. 29; Gordon 1970, p. 35; Griffin 1969, p. 320.
[99] Gordon 1970, pp. 36–7.
[100] Muntéano 1967, p. 145; France 1965, p. 17; and R. Behrens, *Problematische
Rhetorik. Studien zur französischen Theoriebildung der Affektrhetorik zwischen
Cartesianismus und Frühaufklärung* (Munich, 1982).
[101] Melanchthon 1968, p. 85.

that in his Protestant rhetoric-book *docere* and *movere* rule, and *delectare* is dropped. Melanchthon never lost sight of the orator's need to make emotional appeals, especially in the peroration of a speech, and in his chapter *de affectibus* urged that emotion be added to ethical evaluations, so that the congregation will be turned to the good.[102] The work of Klaus Dockhorn and Joachim Dyck has established that in seventeenth-century Germany 'rhetorische Stillehre' was no 'trockener Schematismus', but had its function 'als Mittel der psychologischen Wirkung'.[103] Poetry using the rhetorical figures was seen throughout this period as guaranteed to arouse the emotions, with the obligatory references to Cicero and Quintilian.

The increasing stress on the role of the passions in persuasion led, between 1540 and 1640, to an important readjustment of emphasis within rhetoric. Of the three goals of rhetoric, *movere*, *docere*, and *delectare*, *movere* became the most sought-after; of the five parts of the compositional process, *elocutio* received the greatest attention. The two changes were connected, of course, since the resources of language were developed by *elocutio* in the service of persuasive ends. Some historians lament this disturbance of the 'ideal balance' between the constituent parts of rhetoric, but it should be seen, rather, as another instance of the discipline adapting itself to new needs and demands. The dominance of *movere* within the 'Affekt-Trias' has been shown by several scholars independently,[104] and involved sacred as well as secular oratory. Quintilian's description of *elocutio* as the hardest to master, yet most important skill, without which oratory would be like a sword in its sheath (quoted above, p. 43), was echoed by Melanchthon, Richard Sherry, Webbe, Du Bellay, Peletier, Speroni, Vida, Tasso, Puttenham, and no doubt many more—some rhetoricians actually found *elocutio* more important than *inventio*.[105] W. S. Howell once distinguished four types of rhetoric-book in the sixteenth century: Ciceronian,

---

[102] Melancthon 1968, pp. 176, 200–3.

[103] Dyck 1966, pp. 16, 22 (acknowledging a debt to Klaus Dockhorn, whose essays, written between 1944 and 1966, are collected in Dockhorn 1968).

[104] Dockhorn 1968, Muntéano 1967, Plett 1975, Weinberg 1961.

[105] For a small sample of Renaissance rhetoricians giving *elocutio* the place of honour see the authors cited in Gordon 1970, pp. 42 ff. Monfasani 1976, pp. 282, 332 n.; Dyck 1966, pp. 66, 162, etc.; France 1965, pp. 32 ff.; Plett 1975, pp. 18, 28, 77–8, 79, 105, etc.; Weinberg 1961, Index s.v. 'Elocution' and 'Invention—disposition—elocution'.

teaching all five processes; Ramist, teaching at least three (having assigned *inventio* and *dispositio* to logic); elocutionary, teaching *elocutio* alone; formulary, teaching the *progymnasmata* methods.[106] I note that *elocutio* figures in three out of the four types, and plays a dominant role in those. Credit for the supremacy of *elocutio* used to be given to the Ramists, who in the mid-sixteenth century split off the first two processes for logic, but Vives' *De Ratione Dicendi* (1533) is devoted wholly to *elocutio*, while Cavalcanti's *Retorica* (1559) 'deals in considerable detail with *elocutio*', and 'dismisses with unwonted brevity' *dispositio* and *pronuntiatio*.[107] The fact is that the textbooks give more space to *elocutio* than to the other processes, and while, as A. Kibédi-Varga has reminded us,[108] this may partly be because it takes more room to set out all the definitions and examples, it is clear that the Renaissance pursued *elocutio* with enormous zest. Susenbrotus listed 140 rhetorical figures; Shakespeare has been shown to know nearly 200; while Bernardi's *Thesaurus* (1559), as we have seen, lists approximately 5,000 rhetorical devices. Modern distaste for stylistic rhetoric, then, is wholly unhistorical. If you cannot pick up a list of the figures and read it through avidly, thinking of all the instances of their application and re-creation in Petrarch or Racine, Shakespeare or Milton, then you have not yet thought yourself back into a Renaissance frame of mind.

If we were to regard *elocutio* as mere ornament then its rise to dominance in the sixteenth century would be inexplicable, unforgivable almost. But for those who strove to teach, or acquire it, eloquence was neither trivial nor decorative. As Edward Surtz defines it, *elocutio* was 'a complex term in the Renaissance', which basically described 'the *perfect expression* of one's ideas' but also implied the possession of 'prudence and knowledge', and thus connoted 'fine address and practical *savoir-faire* in all pursuits of public and private life'.[109] As we shall

---

[106] Howell 1956, ch. 3.

[107] Vives 1966, p. 8; Roaf 1959, p. 334. Dr. Roaf finds Cavalcanti's discussion of *elocutio* 'surprisingly detailed' (p. 336).

[108] Kibédi-Varga 1970, p. 17. See the whole discussion, pp. 16–36, especially the conclusion that in French rhetoric of the seventeenth and eighteenth centuries 'les *passions* sont considérées comme un chapitre très important, sinon le chapitre principal, de la rhétorique' (p. 35).

[109] Edward Surtz, SJ, *The Praise of Pleasure. Philosophy, Education, and Communism in More's Utopia* (Cambridge, Mass., 1957), p. 81.

see, *ornamentum* signified in Latin 'equipment or accoutrements', a soldier's 'gear' or weapons (below, p. 314). Joachim Dyck has independently emphasized that 'the *ornatus*, the body of rules covering the use of tropes and figures of speech, is also part of the emotional effect to be achieved by words; it is not an adornment to delight the intellect but a means of producing and reducing emotion'.[110] This is the explanation of J. C. Scaliger's use, in his *Poetices Libri Septem* (1561) of the chapter-heading *Efficacia* to describe 'the controlled use of figures of diction for persuasion to certain emotions'.[111] Figures were efficacious: they achieved their effect.

To bring out the nature of this new emphasis in the Renaissance we might remind ourselves of the basic categories in classical rhetoric. The figures were traditionally divided into three groups, which were then classified according to their emotive power (as were the individual figures). Similarly the three styles were ranked in terms of emotional intensity. The Grand Style was allowed to use all the figures, to achieve maximum effect: it was like a gale force 9; the Middle Style was force 5, the *genus humile* force 3, with a correspondingly smaller power to affect the listener or reader. The first and most effective category consisted of the *figurae sententiae*, 'les grandes figures' as the French called them, which comprised such figures as *exclamatio, apostrophe, imprecatio, aposiopesis, prosopopoeia*, and all types of visual representation. In a few weeks' reading I once counted, for the period between 1545 and 1657, no less that twenty-three rhetoricians who describe the *figurae sententiae* as being an automatic way of arousing the feelings. They include Ramists, such as Talaeus, Fenner, Fraunce, and Butler; non-Ramists, such as Susenbrotus, Sherry, Puttenham; the Italian poetic theorists, Lionardi and Minturno; French theorists, such as d'Auge, d'Aubignac, La Mesnardière; the Jesuit Caussinus, and the encyclopedist Alstedt. The types of rhetoric-book which make this identification include the standard Ciceronian and Ramist texts, works of epistolary rhetoric, preaching, poetics, and dramatic criticism.[112] We are

---

[110] Dyck 1983, p. 236; Dyck 1966, p. 88.
[111] Griffin 1969, p. 74 n.
[112] It would take too much space to document these findings fully; but see the works listed in nn. 81, 96, and 97 for a beginning.

dealing with a central rhetorical tradition, found throughout Europe, in all types of school, that, if the appropriate devices are used, appeal to the feelings is guaranteed to be effective. Certainly the humanists had 'an almost incredible faith in the power of the word',[113] and one may feel that both the rhetoricians' promise of automatic success and their inability to conceive that speech could be put to evil ends show a fundamental lack of realism.[114] But these interlinked beliefs in the social nature of man, the centrality of language to human exchange, the rhetorician's ability to influence people, his dedication to truth and virtue—this whole system made it inevitable that attention should be focused on *elocutio* as eloquence in the service of the noblest human ideals, and the figures of rhetoric as the best means of realizing them.

This new, vastly expanded emphasis on *movere* and *elocutio*, then, is another sign of the practicality that distinguishes Renaisssance rhetoric from the medieval, or even classical version of the art. The decline of forensic and deliberative eloquence, the continuing shift from primary rhetoric (spoken, often in face-to-face confrontation) to secondary (written, at a distance), left more space for epideictic, now the dominant mode, and underlined the need to make persuasion effective. J. C. Scaliger summed up the beliefs of many Renaissance rhetoricians when he asked,

is there not one end, and one only, in philosophical exposition, in oratory, and in the drama? Assuredly such is the case. All have one and the same end—persuasion . . . The soul of persuasion is truth, truth either fixed and absolute, or susceptible of question. Its end is to convince, or secure the doing of something.

The goal of oratory is persuasion, in all three genera: the orator 'speaks in the forum that good may be meted to good men, and punishment to evil men; in assemblies and councils that public affairs may be well administered; and in eulogies that we may be won from evil by good example, and may pursue and practice that which is set forth as honest.'[115] Scaliger can still conceive of the orator in his full social context, but to most Renaissance theorists rhetoric was a written art addressed to the individual

---

[113] Gray 1968, p. 205.
[114] Vickers 1983a.
[115] Scaliger 1905, pp. 3, 5.

reader. Yet while the emphasis on persuasion was translated from the spoken to the written medium it inherited the whole force and energy that classical rhetoric had given to it as a public and performing art. All the power and skill of the ancient orators was claimed by Renaissance writers, so that the ability to move the affections through language—now written—became a fundamental property of literature.

IV

Having firmly anchored itself into the structure and function of Renaissance society, and reasserted its persuasive powers, rhetoric simultaneously extended its scope. It developed genres neglected or too partially developed during the Middle Ages, and it was itself made use of by the other arts, and even by the sciences.

Within its own system, besides the vast profusion of textbooks setting out the traditional prescriptive system, we find new developments in two areas, the oration and the letter. The Middle Ages had shown virtually no interest in ancient oratory, even though some of Cicero's speeches, and collections of declamations were still extant. The pioneer in reclaiming classical oratory was Petrarch, who discovered Cicero's *Pro Archia* at Liège in 1333, being followed by other humanists, including Leonardo Bruni, who found six more orations of Cicero, and Poggio Bracciolini, who found another ten. By the time Giovanni Bussi published the first edition of Cicero's orations in 1471, he was able to bring together all but one of the fifty-eight known to us.[116] It took longer for the Greek orators to be rediscovered and translated into Latin, which is hardly surprising when one considers how foreign their culture must have seemed in Quattrocento Italy. Roman history and customs had become much familiarized by the work of humanists from Petrarch to Valla and Poliziano, but Greek legal oratory must have seemed very strange. When the extant Greek orations began to be translated, those with a moralizing or political relevance were much more popular than the forensic speeches.

---

[116] Monfasani 1988, citing Remigio Sabbadini, *Le scoperte dei codici latini e greci ne' secoli XIV e XV*, 2 vols. (Florence, 1905–14; repr. Florence, 1967).

Isocrates' corpus did not get into Latin until 1528, Demosthenes' not till 1549.[117] The next step in disseminating knowledge of the classical orations was to produce commentaries. This was done for Cicero by Antonio Loschi as early as 1392–6, in his *Inquisitio Super XI Orationes Ciceronis*, a work which inaugurated the truly rhetorical (as opposed to merely grammatical) analysis of classical oratory, using the appropriate categories of argument, structure, and style. As John Monfasani points out, Loschi's analysis 'was not an exercise in antiquarianism, but an eminently practical way of grasping and teaching classical eloquence'.[118] In the following century, other humanist commentators added their notes, the typically cumulative nature of such scholarship culminating in a collective volume published in 1477. Northern European humanists such as Melanchthon, Latomus, Ramus, and Sturm were even more diligent, and the sixteenth century saw the publication of several massive volumes.[119] Cicero's speeches re-entered the rhetorical tradition, becoming—as they had been for Quintilian —the touchstone of practical eloquence. Yet the study of classical oratory remained a school and university subject, a stage in one's education rather than an end in itself. No humanist earned his living solely as an orator, and few of them emulated Cicero in publishing their own orations—no doubt due to the greatly changed conditions in politics and law.[120] By the sixteenth century, as Christine Roaf has said, 'the oration itself had already become a literary genre rather than a means of political persuasion', and many of those published were epideictic, intended for the reader, not for a live audience.[121]

[117] Monfasani 1987.
[118] Ibid.; Monfasani 1976, p. 265; G. W. Pigman III, 'Barzizza's Studies of Cicero', *Rinascimento*, 21 (1981), 121–63.
[119] Ward 1983, pp. 146–57, surveying commentaries on Cicero between the invention of printing and the end of the sixteenth century, finds at least 479 printed commentaries on individual speeches (excluding editions of collected speeches), that is almost four editions a year, twice the number of commentaries on *De Inventione* and *Ad Herennium* (pp. 152–3).
[120] For representative anthologies see Karl Müllner's pioneering collection, *Reden und Briefe Italienischer Humanisten* (Vienna, 1899), reissued with new introduction and useful bibliographies ed. H.-B. Gerl (Munich, 1970); G. Lisio (ed.), *Orazioni scelte del secolo xvi* (Florence, 1957). For the many declamations that Salutati wrote (one of them, *Lucretia*, exists in over 50 manuscripts, the most popular of all his works), see Ullman 1963, p. 34.   [121] Roaf 1959, p. 272.

In the other genre given great prominence in the Renaissance, however, letter-writing, the humanists challenged comparison. Petrarch was again the pioneer, discovering in 1345 three collections of Cicero's letters in the chapter library of Verona: *Ad Atticum, Ad Brutum,* and *Ad Quinctum Fratrem.* In the 1390s the other extant collection, the *Ad Familiares,* was copied for Coluccio Salutati, while the letters of Pliny, father and son, resurfaced in the next century.[122] The Greek letter collections were available to the Quattrocento humanists following the Byzantine influx after the fall of Constantinople in 1453, and the main authors were all translated into Latin and gathered into Musurus' corpus of Greek epistolography in 1499. Here, for once, the Greek tradition was more useful than the Latin since it actually included a number of manuals on letter-writing, which were translated in the sixteenth century and helped stimulate the humanist vogue for writing new treatises.

Letters were soon added to the grammar-school curriculum. In 1430 Guarino made an anthology of fifty of Cicero's *Epistolae ad Familiares,* their easy but idiomatic Latin becoming one of the formative stylistic influences in humanistic schools. At about the same time Gasparino Barzizza compiled *Epistolae ad Exercitationem Accommodatae* in which 'fictive letters supposedly exchanged by classical figures' served as a teaching-text. Subsequent Italian treatises contained sections on letter-writing, notably Agostino Dati's *Elegantiolae,* with some 56 printings between 1470 and 1500 alone, and Francesco Nigri's *Modus Epistolandi,* 26 editions between 1488 and 1500.[123] But the real boom in epistolary manuals comes later, in Northern Europe, especially in Germany, with such works as Conrad Celtis's *Modus Epistolandi* (1492), Christopher Hegendorff's *Methodus Conscribendarium Epistolarum* (1526), Heinrich Bebel's *Commentaria Epistolarum Conficiendarum* (1500), and the anonymous *Epistolae Obscurorum Virorum* (1515: the authors were probably Orotus Rubianus and Ulrich von Hutten). The Netherlands alone produced some 13 *artes epistolandi* in the Renaissance, the most famous being Erasmus' *Opus de Conscribendis Epistolis,* published in 1522 and 1534, with 55

---

[122] Monfasani 1987, also Monfasani 1976.
[123] Monfasani 1987, and Clough 1976, pp. 47, 58–61.

editions by 1540.[124] Other important works included the Spaniard Vives' *De Epistolis Conscribendis* (1533), and the *Epistolica Institutio* (1587) of the Flemish classical scholar Justus Lipsius. While distancing themselves from the medieval *ars dictaminis*, with its barbarous Latin and stereotyped formulae, the humanists were well aware that no real classical models existed for their treatises, and attempted to create their own by adapting the full rhetorical model to a new context. *Memoria* and *pronuntiatio* obviously fell away, and *dispositio* was treated less in terms of the five-part oration (as it had been in medieval treatises) than according to the letter's topics. Erasmus stated that letters could be written in any of the traditional three types of rhetoric (deliberative, forensic, epideictic), and added a fourth, the familiar—no doubt inspired by the letters of Cicero and Petrarch. Another move towards informality was his placing of epistolary style within the category of *sermo*, daily speech. After the elaborations of the medieval arts, Renaissance rhetoric returned to the domain of normal life.

The fruit of the humanists' interest in letter-writing came in the letters they themselves wrote, and often self-consciously collected. Petrarch was the pioneer once more, emulating Cicero by collecting his own 'Familiar Letters'. Written between 1325 and 1366, he edited them for publication between 1345 and 1366, revising, inventing, rewriting as if they were just another literary work, not a unique person-to-person communication, and dividing them into the same number of books as the *Iliad* and *Odyssey*. The *Rerum Familiarum Libri XXIV*,[125] together with his two other collections, constitute an invaluable document, bringing Petrarch nearer to us than any other Renaissance man except Montaigne; but they pose certain critical problems, lying as they do somewhere between the informal, personal missive and the formal essay. The fact that Petrarch seems to contradict himself in a number of places, both here and in his treatises, is another sign of the influence of rhetoric, for from Aristotle on writers knew that compositions were to be created with a view

---

[124] See Henderson 1983; Monfasani 1987.

[125] See Petrarch, *Le familiari*, ed. V. Rossi and U. Bosco, 4 vols. (Florence, 1933–42); G. Billanovich, *Lo scrittoio del Petrarca* (Rome, 1947); and E. H. Wilkins, *Petrarch's Correspondence* (Padua, 1960). An English translation has been made by Aldo S. Bernardo: Petrarch 1975–85.

to the audience or recipient. Despite Erasmus' definition of the letter (borrowed from Libanius, incidentally) as *absentis ad absentem colloquium*, 'the familiar and mutuall talke of one absent friend to another', as Angel Day translates it,[126] the chief problem with Renaissance letters is to know whether they are straightforward communications, formal treatises, cultivations of a self-image through exemplary models of behaviour, or (at times!) specimens of correct Latin style. Certainly the genre of collected letters had an enormous success, as represented in Italy by the epistles of Traversari, Poggio, Filelfo, Poliziano, Bruni, Piccolomini, Ficino, and Bembo—by 1580 Montaigne could claim that he owned more than a hundred volumes of printed Italian letter collections. Northern Europe emulated Italy, led by Erasmus (who said that he 'devoted half his day to the reading and writing of letters': some 3,165 of his own survive[127]), Melanchthon, Wimpfeling, Lipsius (some 4,300 letters, 1,500 still unpublished), Pirckheimer, Celtis, as well as the great family collections, such as that of the Amerbachs in Basle, which extends from 1481 to 1591, with more than 6,000 letters extant.[128]

The letter was simultaneously an art-form and a practical communication. The same holds true of the sermon, the other genre for which the Renaissance humanists had no classical precedent. There were medieval models aplenty, of course, but both preaching-theorists and preachers in the Renaissance broke with the immediate past. The medieval sermon-manuals, which began to appear around 1200, and of which over three hundred are extant, show 'a remarkable homogeneity'.[129] Typically, they are based on a theme taken from Scripture, which must be sufficiently long to accommodate divisions into several parts, each of which is then 'proved' by citing authorities and by logical argument, above all syllogistic. The emphasis is on *docere*, and there is little concern with the shape of the whole.[130] By the late fourteenth century, as John O'Malley has

[126] Henderson 1983, p. 345; Angel Day, *The English Secretorie* (London, 1586; facs. edn. Menston, 1967), p. 18. Cf. Also Donne: 'More than kisses, letters mingle souls; / For, thus friends absent speak.'
[127] Clough 1976, pp. 34 (Montaigne), 33 (Erasmus).
[128] Much information can be gathered from the studies assembled by Franz Josef Worstbrock, *Der Brief im Zeitalter der Renaissance* (Weinheim, 1983).
[129] Murphy 1974, p. 332.   [130] See ibid., pp. 269–355, and Jennings 1978.

shown, sacred orations had begun to break with medieval traditions of preaching and apply the methods of classical rhetoric, especially the epideictic genus. Preachers saw the sermon as embodying the twin techniques of praise and blame, used various types of structure (including at least an exordium and peroration), and laid a new emphasis on *movere*.[131] This development brought preaching into line with the general trend in Renaissance rhetoric towards epideictic, the specific goal being to direct the audience to ethical conduct. Where the medieval sermon had discussed abstract doctrine, preachers now 'focused more clearly on God's deeds and actions—his *beneficia*', in order to arouse a desire for imitation, the possibility of which was premissed on the widely shared belief in the 'dignity of man'.[132] The style of these sermons is more lyrical, uninhibitedly emotional, and makes frequent use of *ekphrasis*, that visual element so strong in epideictic, with its belief that sight was the most powerful of the senses.[133] The appeal to the emotions, the celebration of the mercy and generosity of God and Christ, the emphasis on the congregation's potential for good—these are common elements in the theory and practice of many Renaissance and Reformation preachers and theologians, from Martin Luther to Lancelot Andrewes and John Donne.[134] Luther laid down the duties of the preacher as including the practice of rhetoric, especially in warning the congregation, and blaming the evil, obstinate, and lazy—the epideictic category of *vituperatio*.[135] As Joachim Dyck has noted, in sixteenth-century Germany, after the reforms of Luther and Melanchthon, 'training in rhetoric became for the very first time in history a basic requirement in the training for the priesthood'.[136] The first reformer to deal with the duties of the ministry in German was

[131] See O'Malley 1979, and O'Malley 1983, pp. 238–52.
[132] O'Malley 1983, p. 240. On the secular theory of epideictic as promoting emulation, especially in the theory of the epic, see Vickers 1982b.
[133] O'Malley 1979, pp. 51–3, 62–4, 79; Fumaroli 1980, pp. 258–61, 281 ff., 371–7.
[134] On Luther see Dockhorn 1974 and Stolt 1974. On the English Renaissance sermon see W. Fraser Mitchell, *English Pulpit Oratory from Andrewes to Tillotson* (London, 1932) and J. W. Blench, *Preaching in England in the late Fifteenth and Sixteenth Centuries* (Oxford, 1964). Bayley 1980 contains a useful discussion of the place of rhetoric in secondary education (pp. 17–37) and in the Church (pp. 38–71), including preaching manuals from Germany, Spain, and France.
[135] Stolt 1974, p. 52.
[136] Dyck 1983, p. 224.

Erasmus Sarcer, and in his *Pastorale oder Hirtenbuch* (1559), like Luther and Melanchthon, he drew much from Quintilian, refurbishing the traditional rhetorical teaching that to produce an emotional response the preacher must 'have been moved in his heart likewise'. All three German Protestant theologians 'derived their concept of faith from Quintilian's rhetorical theory of emotions, in so far as faith for them means the capacity to visualize that which is absent and to conjure it up emotionally', what Sarcer, following Quintilian (6. 2. 32–6) calls *illustrior*.[137] In this rather surprising context we see again the remarkable range of Quintilian's 'after-life'.[138]

The influence of classical rhetoric extended to the form as to the content of many Renaissance works. When Sir Philip Sidney came to write *An Apology for Poetry* in the early 1580s, he cast it into the seven-part form of a classical oration, *exordium, narratio, propositio, divisio, confirmatio, refutatio*, and *peroratio*.[139] This, too, is a work of epideictic rhetoric, praising poetry and downgrading other verbal arts (especially philosophy), another form of the *paragone*. We are not surprised that Sidney, poet and prose-writer, should have used the structure of a classical oration, but we may be to find that Johannes Kepler used exactly the same form for his *Apologia Pro Tychone Contra Ursum* (c. 1601). As Nicholas Jardine has shown, this work is 'cast as a judicial oration, composed strictly in accordance with the strategies for conduct of a legal defence' laid down by Roman rhetoric.[140] Kepler had been commissioned by Tycho Brahe to defend him from the attacks of Ursus, and he did so by following the form and methods of legal oratory, down to convicting his opponent of a whole series of logical fallacies, and making devastating use of the rhetorical figure *concessio*, where the orator argues from his opponent's premises to show that 'no matter how charitably' one considers his case, 'it still fails'.[141] The modern

---

[137] Dyck 1983, pp. 234–5.

[138] On Quintilian's influence see above, Ch. 1, n. 42, also Ch. 3, n. 42.

[139] See K. O. Myrick, *Sir Philip Sidney as a Literary Craftsman* (Cambridge, Mass., 1935), pp. 46–83, and Sidney 1965, pp. 12–16.

[140] *The Birth of History and Philosophy of Science. Kepler's 'A Defence of Tycho against Ursus' with Essays on its Provenance and Significance* (Cambridge, 1984), pp. 72–9.

[141] Ibid., pp. 77–8.

reader's surprise at this application of rhetoric to astronomy may be qualified when he realizes that Kepler had been educated at Tübingen University, where Melanchthon's rhetoric-books were set texts in the first-year course, and that he actually had taught rhetoric at Graz. Galileo, too, used epideictic rhetoric to promote his own world-system and rout the Aristotelians.[142] The fact that two of the greatest scientists of the age could use such models proves that classical rhetoric was able to validate its claim to be of use to contemporary life by adapting itself to new subjects, and new forms.

[142] See Vickers 1983b.

6

THE EXPRESSIVE FUNCTION OF
RHETORICAL FIGURES

—But away with these figures of speech: they are
troublesome to manage, and have been worn to rags.
Unhappily, there is no such thing as speaking—nor even as
thinking—without such figures.

Jeremy Bentham[1]

The movement in music and painting, during the sixteenth and
seventeenth centuries, towards greater expressiveness and a
more powerful hold over the audience's feelings reflected the
changes that were taking place within rhetoric itself. As many
passages quoted in the last chapter will have shown, the
ultimate power of rhetoric in written communication was
thought to reside in the figures and tropes, the last stage in the
elaboration of persuasive composition. If we are prepared to
accept this theory, stated so often and with such conviction, we
must take with it the rhetoricians' insistence on the minutiae to
which they devoted so much time. Yet, of all the aspects of
rhetoric this remains the least appreciated, the most
misunderstood. That people who have never studied rhetoric
should dismiss them is only to be expected. Yet historians of
rhetoric, who have devoted much of their professional lives to
the art, can still be found complaining that the figures were
'impractical', and caused the 'decay' of rhetoric;[2] that 'the dreary
and trivial instruction of the rhetoricians' produced 'almost
interminable lists';[3] that in discussing the figures they 'shed little
light' and 'wasted much effort on introducing confusing

---

[1] 'Jeremy Bentham to his Fellow-Citizens of France, on Houses of Peers and
Senates' (1830), in *The Works of Jeremy Bentham*, ed. John Bowring, 11 vols.
(London, 1843), iv. 422.

[2] Clark 1922, p. 29.

[3] Kennedy 1963, pp. 277, 321–2. Kennedy 1972, p. 376, is glad that Longinus
avoids 'the interminable lists of figures'.

innovations of terminology' in a 'tedious and unprofitable' system—which, nevertheless, ought to be studied, 'however repellent or frivolous it may seem'[4]—one could hardly think of a more inappropriate word for the doctrine of the figures than 'frivolous'; that human energy was wasted on 'this interminable enumeration of stylistic devices', an interest 'more concerned with the husks than the kernels of style';[5] that writers of rhetoric-books produced 'mechanistic theories of style' with a disturbing 'proliferation of *figurae*' in a 'highly schematized treatise' or a 'markedly schematic handbook'.[6] If all these diatribes were true, then the study of the rhetorical figures would have been one of the most colossal instances of time-wasting in the history of human culture. Happily, they are not true, for however much modern historians would like to fragment rhetoric and relegate the figures to the dustbin, classical and Renaissance writers knew that they functioned as the last and crucial link in the whole process of persuasion.

I

All rhetoric-books offer a classification of verbal devices. Particular structures are identified, named, their function discussed, and rules given concerning their use and abuse. Breaking off a phrase or sentence in mid-flow, for instance, was recognized as a specific linguistic act, and was called *aposiopesis* in Greek, *reticentia* in Latin. Then various types of interruption were distinguished, according to the speaker's own emotional state, and—by extension, assuming that his hearers will vibrate in sympathy with him—according to his intention towards the audience. Mixing up the right order of thoughts, and thus of

[4] Clarke 1953, pp. 34, 23. Ward 1978 describes the technical terms of rhetoric in late antiquity as constituting 'terminological jungles' that brought on the 'dinosauric extinction' of rhetoric, and dismisses the 'details of the classical rhetorical system' as 'dessicated and arid'. Yet he still concedes that they could 'form the sensibilities of each new generation' (p. 31), and finds 'surprising . . . the adaptability of the classical academic rhetorical tradition' (p. 41). That self-contradiction might have provoked a rethinking of the initial rejection of the details.

[5] Howell 1956, pp. 33–4.

[6] Murphy 1974, pp. 8–9, 109, 185, 230, 360. Murphy 1978, discussing *The Owl and the Nightingale*, reassures us that he won't 'drag the reader through a catalogue' of figures (p. 199), a dismissive attitude shared by another contributor to that symposium, R. O. Payne: pp. 270, 272.

words, out of haste, or confusion, or an inadequate education, is another easily observed verbal act in everyday life, and was given various names by the rhetoricians—*hysteron proteron, hyperbaton,* or *cacosyntheton.* In anger human beings will cry out, appeal to some stander-by, to God, or to part of the scenery to bear witness to their sufferings: this gesture came to be known as *apostrophe* or *exclamatio.* Thus the lore of rhetorical figures could be seen as deriving originally from life. It was mimetic, an attempt to classify emotional states and the resulting speech forms, both being regarded as deviations from normal behaviour, signalling a loss of balance. In this respect the figures were treated as the final, stylistic manifestation of the point from which we began, that the eloquence of rhetoric is merely a systematization of natural eloquence.

In his *Rhetoric,* giving advice on the need to make language 'appropriate', that is, correctly expressing 'emotion and character' (quoted above, p. 80), Aristotle noted that 'aptness of language is one thing that makes people believe in the truth of your story. . . . Besides, an emotional speaker always makes his audience feel with him . . .' (1408ᵃ10–19). 'Truth' and conviction in rhetoric, then, partly depend on the propriety of expression in relation to feeling. Propriety itself is a difficult concept, needing more discussion, but what seems to be implied here is that the listener will judge the speaker's accuracy in expressing emotion by reference to what he has himself felt on similar occasions. Gerald Else explains that in Aristotle's system the spectator or listener will share and sympathize with the feelings of a character if he uses 'the "forms" of speech which we know from experience to be in fact the true signs of that feeling'.⁷ Aristotle subsequently classifies the audience's reaction as varying according to age, nationality, sex, and the 'dispositions . . . which determine the character of a man's life. . . . If, then, a speaker uses the very words which are in keeping with a particular disposition, he will reproduce the corresponding character' (1408ᵃ27–32). Although he makes disparaging remarks about prescriptive rhetorics, Aristotle goes on to correlate specific figures with particular 'dispositions'. Thus, to him *hyperboles* 'are for young men to use; they show vehemence of character; and this is why angry people use them

⁷ Else 1957, p. 493.

more than other people' (1413ᵃ28 ff.). He quotes Achilles
rejecting Agamemnon's placatory offer of his daughter's hand:
'I will not marry [her] . . . even if she rivalled golden Aphrodite
in beauty and Athena in her handiwork' (Iliad, 9. 388–91). As
Else has noted, the juxtaposition of analysis and quotation
implies that 'Homer, having observed how men speak in anger,
has correctly (plausibly) put a hyperbole in Achilles' mouth', so
that the audience will gauge, and respond to Achilles' anger.
Else also drew attention to the technical terminology of this
passage, which alludes to 'the actual turns or "figures" of
speech that characterize various feeling-states', and he
perceptively linked it with the requirement in the Poetics (ch. 17)
that the tragedian must render the conflict in the play's action in
its 'patterns [of speech]' also. In Aristotle's words, 'those who
are in the grip of the emotions are most persuasive because they
speak to the same natural tendencies in us, and it is the
character who rages or expresses dejection in the most natural
way who stirs us to anger or dejection' (1455ᵃ29–33). The word
here translated as 'patterns of speech' is related to *schemata* (the
normal term for rhetorical figures), and in glossing it Else makes
an observation which is peculiarly relevant to our enquiry:

The forms or figures which the poet is to incorporate in the speech of
his characters are 'figures of speech' not so much in the technical sense,
i.e. manipulations of language *per se*, as in the broader sense of *modes of
the expression of feeling* in language. Their appropriateness is not to be
tested so much, therefore, by formal stylistic criteria as by the ear of the
spectator or reader, who says to himself, 'Yes, this is the way men do
talk when they are angry or downcast or full of admiration; I have
heard things said just that way many times'.[8]

The best comment here is La Rochefoucauld's maxim: 'les
passions sont les seuls orateurs qui persuadent toujours.'[9] The
orator must re-create those passions.
    Although Aristotle's *Rhetoric* virtually disappeared until the
Renaissance, a tradition persisted in Greek rhetoric linking

[8] Ibid., pp. 486, 494–5; my italics. In her version of the *Poetics* in Russell and
Winterbottom 1972, M. E. Hubbard translates: 'So far as possible one should also
work it out with the appropriate figures', and glosses 'i.e. of speech and
thought'.
[9] France 1965, p. 164.

specific figures with specific states of mind. Given the highly formalized nature of Greek prose, with its strict conventions of grammar and syntax, one group of figures frequently commented on involved the dislocation of normal or expected word-order. The psychological basis for this effect was the belief that, since language is the expression of thought and emotion, a disturbance in personality will be represented in a dislocation of the normal modes of syntax. Hence, whenever orators or writers use fragmented expression it will signal an emotional disturbance, and the audience will respond accordingly (with fear, anxiety, or sympathy). The author of the remarkable treatise *On Sublimity* (late first century A D, ascribed to one 'Longinus'), is acutely aware of how the *schemata* of rhetoric imitate life. So he writes of the figure *hyperbaton*, which represents a violent disruption of the natural order of words and ideas:

It is a very real mark of urgent emotion. People who in real life feel anger, fear, or indignation, or are distracted by jealousy or some other emotion (it is impossible to say how many emotions there are; they are without number), often put one thing forward and then rush off to another, irrationally inserting some remark, and then hark back again to their first point. They seem to be blown this way and that by their excitement, as if by a veering wind. They inflict innumerable variations on the expression, the thought, and the natural sequence. Thus *hyperbaton* is a means by which, in the best authors, imitation approaches the effect of nature. Art is perfect when it looks like nature, nature is felicitous when it embraces concealed art. (22. 1)

Here the rhetorical figure is seen as a direct *mimesis* of a human psychological state, and described with considerable insight into both psychology and style. The author makes some acute analyses of how Herodotus and Thucydides used this figure (22. 2–3), and illustrates Demosthenes' 'lavish' use of it by the very form of his own sentence:

His transpositions produce not only a great sense of urgency but the appearance of extemporization, as he drags his hearers with him into the hazards of his long *hyperbata*. He often holds in suspense the meaning which he sets out to convey and, introducing one extraneous item after another in an alien and unusual place before getting to the main point, throws the hearer into a panic lest the sentence collapse altogether, and forces him in his excitement to share the speaker's peril, before, at long last and beyond all expectation, appositely paying off at the end the long due conclusion; the very audacity and hazardousness of the *hyperbata* add to the astounding effect. (22. 3–4)

Longinus declines to give any examples, there being 'so many' such in Demosthenes,[10] but in his own analysis he has re-created the excitement of a real speech incomparably. And if we recall that he is writing in the first century A D, some five hundred years after Demosthenes, then we must celebrate the power of rhetorical criticism, in the hands of a sensitive writer, to emulate the object that it describes.

The Latin rhetorical tradition was always aware of the expressive function of the tropes and figures, and also shared the belief that rhetoric had essentially codified real life. Cicero advises the orator using the plain style to be sparing with ornament, apart from metaphor, which he may 'employ more frequently because it is of the commonest occurrence in the language of townsman and rustic alike. The rustics, for example, say that the vines are "bejewelled" [with buds], the fields "thirsty", the crops "happy", the grain "luxuriant" ' (*Orator*, 24. 81). Aristotle had said that everyone uses metaphor in conversation (1404^{b}32 ff.), while the anonymous Latin rhetoric made the same comment about *metonymy* (*Ad Her.* 4. 32. 43). Quintilian similarly described metaphor as 'so natural a turn of speech that it is often employed unconsciously or by uneducated persons' (8. 6. 4), and noted that 'allegory is often used by men of little ability and in the conversation of everyday life' (8. 6. 51), as are *emphasis* (8. 3. 86), and even *synecdoche* (8. 6. 21). The motives behind such uses are revealed in his comment on *hyperbole*, that it 'is employed even by peasants and uneducated persons, for the good reason that everybody has an innate passion for exaggeration or attenuation of actual facts, and no one is ever contented with the simple truth' (8. 6. 75). As M. L. Clarke (who dismisses the figures as 'tedious and unprofitable') rightly commented, 'everyday speech does not consist in the main of plain, straightforward, unimpassioned speech', and Roman orators were aware that the expressive

---

[10] In his outstanding edition D. A. Russell unfortunately does not supply any examples either: Longinus 1964, p. 139.

devices they used 'had their roots in popular speech'.[11] When Quintilian completes his discussion of that type of *enargeia* which concerns itself with 'vivid illustration', where facts are 'displayed in their living truth to the eyes of the mind', he pauses to reassure his readers that in this branch of the art of rhetoric, as in others, it is nature that gives the rules: 'the mind is always readiest to accept what it recognises to be true to nature' (8. 3. 71).

The rationale of rhetorical figures as the crystallization of real-life emotional states was rediscovered in the Renaissance. One of the best statements of it is given by George Puttenham towards the end of his *Arte of English Poesie:*

And with these examples I thinke sufficient to leave, giving you information of this one point, that all your figures Poeticall or Rhetoricall, are but observations of strange speeches [i.e. outside the norm of human communication: Aristotle's 'foreign'], and such as without any arte at all we should use, and commonly do, even by very nature without discipline [instruction]. But more or less aptly and decently, or scarcely, or aboundantly, or of this kind or that kind of figure, and one of us more than another, according to the disposition of our nature, constitution of the heart, and facilitie of each mans utterance: so as we may conclude, that nature herselfe suggesteth the figure in this or that forme, but arte aydeth the judgement of his use and application . . .[12]

Both Aristotle and Longinus seem to lie behind that passage. As for the objection that the terminology of rhetoric is artificial, proving that it has nothing to do with life, Abraham Fraunce had the appropriate answer ready in 1588, while defending logic:

Neyther let any man thinke, that because in common meetings and assemblies the wordes and tearmes of Logike bee not named, therefore the force and operation of Logike is not therefore used & apparant. For, as in Grammar wee name neyther Noune, Pronoune, Verbe, nor any other parte of speech: and as in Rhetorike, wee make mention neyther of Metonymia, Synecdoche, Exclamatio, nor any other Rhetorical figure or trope: yet use in our speech the helpe of the one in speaking grammatically, and the direction of the other in talking eloquently,

---

[11] Clarke 1953, pp. 39–40.
[12] Puttenham 1936, p. 298.

so in logic too the names stand for real linguistic acts.[13] We all use the figures in our everyday speech and writing, whether we know their names or not. When Tristram Shandy's father went to enter his son's name 'at Jesus College in ****' the scholars were amazed at his natural abilities as a rhetorician, especially 'that a man who knew not so much as the names of his tools, should be able to work after that fashion with them'.[14] He did not need to read rhetoric-books to become eloquent.

That quotation from Sterne is no isolated fluke, for the rhetorical tradition flourished vigorously right through the eighteenth century. Dryden, the leading critic and theorist of neo-classicism, in his *Apology for Heroic Poetry and Poetic License* (1677), developed the hint of Longinus that rhetoric originally drew from life. The first poets showed how to raise the passions by drawing directly from life, before the conventions were formalized: 'from hence have sprung the tropes and figures for which they wanted a name who first practised them, and succeeded in them.' Hence 'those things which delight all ages must have been an imitation of nature', and 'therefore is rhetoric made an art; therefore the names of so many tropes and figures were invented: because it was observed they had such an effect upon the audience'.[15] Drawing nearer Longinus, Dryden outlines the occasions on which the 'bolder' or more forceful figures may be used—but not flaunted—in order to

work their effect upon the mind without discovering [revealing] the art which caused it. And therefore they are principally to be used in passion; when we speak more warmly, and with more precipitation, than at other times: for then, *si vis me flere, dolendum est primum ipsi tibi*; the poet must put on the passion he endeavours to represent: a man in such an occasion is not cool enough, either to reason rightly, or to talk calmly. Aggravations are then in their proper places; interrogations, exclamations, hyperbata, or a disordered connection of discourse, are graceful there because they are natural.[16]

Dryden here joins the tradition extending from Puttenham back to Aristotle two thousand years before him: language reveals the inner man, especially when in the grip of emotions.

[13] Fraunce 1588, fo. 120ʳ.
[14] *Tristram Shandy*, Book I, ch. 19.
[15] Dryden 1962, i. 200–1.
[16] Ibid., p. 203.

The link between rhetoric and real life remained unquestioned until the 1800s at least. Writing in 1730, Du Marsais began his treatise *Des Tropes* by disagreeing with the traditional definition of rhetorical figures as forms of speech deviating from the norm: 'D'ailleurs, bien loin que les Figures soient des manières de parler éloignées de celles qui sont naturèles et ordinaires, il n'y a rien de si naturel, de si ordinaire, et de comun que les Figures dans le langage des homes.' He quotes Abbé de Bretteville's *Eloquence de la chaire et du barreau* (1689), which states that the figures are both easy and natural: '"J'ai pris souvent plaisir", dit-il, "à entendre des paysans s'entretenir avec des figures de discours si variées, si vives, si éloignées du vulgaire, que j'avois honte d'avoir si long-tems étudié l'éloquence, voyant en eux une certaine Rhétorique de nature beaucoup plus persuasive, et plus éloquente que toutes nos Rhétoriques artificèles".'[17] Du Marsais' comment is an elaboration of this:

En éfet, je suis persuadé qu'il se fait plus de Figures un jour de marché à la Halle, qu'il ne s'en fait en plusieurs jours d'assemblées académiques. Ainsi, bien loin que les Figures s'éloignent du langage ordinaire des homes, ce seroient au contraire les façons de parler sans Figures qui s'en éloigneroient, s'il étoit possible de faire un discours où il n'y eût que des expressions non figurées.[18]

Thus Du Marsais turns the old theory round: it would be more unnatural to do without figures.

Du Marsais' book was republished in 1818 'avec un commentaire raisonné' by Pierre Fontanier, one of the last great French rhetoricians in the classical tradition, who could still express agreement on this point:

Sans doute que les figures sont naturelles, et que nous n'avons besoin ni d'étude ni d'art pour les employer; sans doute qu'elles entrent dans

[17] Du Marsais 1984, pp. 2–3. As Roland Barthes put it, the art of rhetoric '*choisit* les figures . . ., il ne les crée pas; en somme le figuré est une combinaison artificielle d'éléments naturels' (Barthes 1970, p. 221).

[18] Du Marsais 1984, p. 3. Barthes 1970, p. 221, cites Racine: 'Il ne faut qu'écouter une dispute entre les femmes de la plus vile condition: quelle abondance dans les figures! Elles prodiguent la métonymie, la catachrèse, l'hyperbole, etc.'; and the verses of F. de Neufchateau: 'A la ville, à la cour, dans les champs, à la Halle, / L'éloquence du coeur par les tropes s'exhale.' Samuel Butler's jibe, in *Hudibras*, against a sectarian who no sooner opened his mouth 'than out there flew a trope' needs to be put back into this context.

le langage le plus commun et le plus ordinaire . . . c'est une vérité qu'on a reconnue de tout temps, et Boileau, je crois, avait dit avant Dumarsais, qu'il se fait plus de métaphores en un jour de marché aux halles, qu'il n'y en a dans toute l'Enéide.

However, he goes on, that does not mean that the figures do not differ from plain, un-figured language, in the sense that they present 'quelque chose de plus relevé . . . de plus fort, de plus énergique, ou de plus gracieux, de plus aimable'. What happens to figures once they become widely used, Fontanier acutely notes, is that they end up by not seeming like figures but part of 'ordinary language'.[19] In that sense, then, speech has reclaimed her own, for the devices identified and enumerated by the rhetoricians have been returned to their matrix.

English eighteenth-century theories of poetry, as P. W. K. Stone showed so well,[20] are still fundamentally rhetorical, and continue to posit a reciprocal relationship between rhetoric and natural feeling. In his *Lectures on Rhetoric and Belles Lettres* (1783) Hugh Blair could simply remark: 'Let nature and passion always speak their own language, and they will suggest figures in abundance.'[21] In his essay 'On Poetry' (1776) James Beattie explained how, conversely, 'Natural Language is improved in Poetry by means of Tropes and Figures', affirming that 'there are hundreds of tropical expressions in common use, incomparably more energetic than any proper words of equal brevity that could be put in their place'.[22] Robert Lowth accounts for the 'great force and efficacy' of rhetorical figures on the grounds that 'they in some degree imitate or represent the present habit and state of the soul'.[23] In the second half of the eighteenth century it is still 'widely held that figurative language occurs spontaneously to the mind in a state of emotion',[24] a condition that applies both to the person of the

---

[19] Du Marsais 1984 part 2 (Fontanier), pp. 3–7. Cf. a modern scholar on how Boileau's *L'Art poétique* passed on many rhetorical precepts unnoticed: 'Si parfaite est cette assimilation, que l'on ne l'aperçoit plus guère' (Muntéano 1967, p. 152).

[20] Stone 1967, especially pp. 58–76. See also Dockhorn 1968, pp. 22–3, on the rhetorical tradition extending to Wordsworth; and Ian Thomson, 'Rhetoric and the Passions, 1760–1800', in Vickers 1982a, pp. 143–8.

[21] Cit. Stone 1967, p. 167 n. 22.

[22] Beattie, *Essays* (1776), p. 264.

[23] Cit. Stone 1967, p. 66.

[24] Ibid., p. 62.

orator (stated by Dryden in the tag from Horace's *Art of Poetry*: 'If you wish me to grieve you must first grieve yourself') and to the audience. As Stone puts it, 'Figures are obviously useful only as they *demonstrate* feeling: they are signs of a state of mind in the speaker which his audience will readily interpret, and instinctively react to', by the workings of sympathy.[25] So Joseph Priestley writes in 1777:

Figurative speech . . . is indicative of a person's real feelings and state of mind, not by means of the words it consists of, considered as *signs of separate ideas* . . . but as circumstances naturally attending those feelings which compose any state of mind. Those figurative expressions, therefore, are scarcely considered and attended to as *words*, but are viewed in the same light as attitudes, *gestures*, and *looks*, which are infinitely more expressive of sentiments and feelings than words can possibly be.[26]

Interestingly enough, to these theorists of language the greatest feelings are expressed without language, or through its breakdown. The figure *asyndeton*, which creates an effect of 'dissolution', as Quintilian describes it, by 'the absence of connecting particles' (9. 3. 50), still continues to be associated with emotional disturbance. Thus an anonymous writer in 1762 says that 'Joy, grief, and anger are most naturally expressed by exclamations, sudden starts and broken sentences'; James Beattie in 1783 states that 'The Language of enthusiasm, and of all those passions that strongly agitate the soul, is naturally incoherent'; Robert Lowth, lecturing *On The Sacred Poetry of the Hebrews* in 1753, observes that the more violent affections of the heart 'break and interrupt the enunciation by their impetuosity; they burst forth in sentences pointed, earnest, rapid, and tremulous'; while in 1774 Alexander Gerard provides an elaborate psychological explanation of the phenomenon.[27] This chronological sequence, incidentally, shows again how Croce tried to distort history.

Thus from Aristotle to the end of the eighteenth century the

[25] Stone 1967, p. 64.
[26] Ibid., p. 66.
[27] Ibid., pp. 68–70. See also France 1965, p. 34, citing d'Aubignac in 1657: 'Ainsi . . . par la variété sensible des Figures, on garde une resemblance du desordre de la Nature'; and Diderot in 1757: 'Ce qui émeut toujours, ce sont des cris, des mots inarticulés, des voix rompues, quelques monosyllabes qui s'échappent par intervalles, je ne sais quel murmure dans la gorge, entre les dents.'

figures and tropes were regarded mimetically, as capturing specific and clearly defined emotional states.

II

If we turn from these descriptive accounts of rhetoric to the prescriptive tradition, which teaches the writer how to use individual figures, and what effects they can produce, we find a surprising amount of detail (surprising, that is, after modern historians' denials that the ancients had a rationale for the figures). Rhetoricians, always aware of decorum, the need to integrate the part to the whole, frequently relate the figures to style and function. In his manual *On Style (c.* 270 BC) Demetrius[28] distinguishes four styles (the plain, the grand, the elegant, and the forceful), and says that we 'must assign to each style the figures that are appropriate to it' (p. 76). Repetition is one of the most useful devices, as in a speech by Ctesisas, where it gives both vividness and a 'passionate tone' (pp. 109–10), and he distinguishes a whole category of 'forceful figures'. These include *anadiplosis* (repeating a word from the end of one clause to the beginning of the next), *anaphora* (repeating a word at the beginning of subsequent clauses), and *gradatio* or *climax* (Greek for 'ladder') which he illustrates with a famous example from Demosthenes' speech *On the Crown*:

'I did not say these things and then refuse to move a proposal; I did not move a proposal and fail to go as an envoy; I did not go as an envoy and fail to persuade the Thebans.' This passage is like a man climbing higher and higher. If you were to put it like this: 'After my speech, after moving a proposal I went as an envoy, and persuaded the Thebans', he would be narrating facts, but saying nothing forceful. (p. 121)

The comment is acute, as is the rewriting of the idea to destroy the figure, and with it the effect—a device frequently used in the tradition of stylistic rhetoric. Demetrius notes quite subtle rhetorical effects. Within the forceful style, for example, repetition is not the only method: 'Brevity is so useful in this style that it is even more forceful *not* to say something, as when Demosthenes says: "Now I might remark—but I myself certainly do not wish to say anything offensive, and my accuser

---

[28] Quotations are from Demetrius 1961, and will be incorporated into the text.

has the advantage in slandering me" ' (p. 117)—this is the *aposiopesis*, the sudden breaking-off of speech. Related to it is *paralipsis*, pretending to pass over topics while actually hinting at them, as in this example from Demosthenes: ' "I make no mention of Olynthus, Methone, Apollonia, and the thirty-two cities in Thrace." With these words the orator has said all he wanted to say, and he says he will not mention them in order to give the impression that he has even more dreadful things to say' (p. 120).

This is the beginning of rhetorical criticism, the analysis of texts in terms of specific rhetorical devices. Demetrius is sensitive to the effects possible in Greek prose by the dislocation of conventional grammar or word-order. The forceful style, he writes, expresses 'a vehement brevity, like men aiming blows in a close fight' (p. 122), and in syntactical terms a 'lack of connectives, more than anything else, produces forcefulness' (p. 122)—this is, once again, *asyndeton*. The principle of dislocation also applies on a larger scale, for

> Just as we mentioned that the figure of omitted connectives contributes to forcefulness, so does an altogether loose word-arrangement. A proof of this is found in Hipponax. When he wants to attack his enemies he breaks his rhythm, makes it halting instead of straightforward, less rhythmical, and this suits the forcefulness of his attack. (p. 128)

Demetrius is not categorical in defining the states of emotion that can be produced through syntax and word-repetition, for he knows that a variety of effects is possible from one figure. His modern editor has noted with some puzzlement that Demetrius gives three separate examples of the figure *anaphora* (or initial repetition) and attributes three quite different results to them. The first (borrowed in fact from Aristotle's *Rhetoric*, 1413^{b}33–1414^{a}7) is from the *Iliad*'s catalogue of ships (2. 671–4), where by repeating the name Nireus at the beginning of three consecutive lines Homer makes the act of leading only three ships to Troy (Nireus is never heard of again) seem impressive, more so perhaps than it was (p. 76). Secondly, a poem by Sappho to the evening star opens with a list of its influences: 'all things you bring; you bring the sheep, you bring the goat, you bring the child to its mother', the repetition being said to produce an effect of charm (p. 95). The charm lies in the meaning, of course, but the echoing structure certainly underlines it. The last example is from the speech of Aeschines against Demosthenes, an impassioned accusatory repetition (p. 121) which communicates great intensity. G. M. A. Grube suggests that 'the fact that these effects are so different may raise doubts as to the soundness of Demetrius' basic categories',[29] but it is a sign, rather, of Demetrius' recognition of what I would call the polysemous nature of rhetorical figures. That is, in considering the figures we must attend to a three-way relationship:

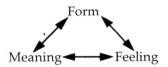

The form is fixed, in the rhetorician's classification of verbal devices—the breaking-off of a sentence is always the same thing formally—but both meaning and feeling are infinitely flexible, as resourceful in expressive potential as language itself. As we will see, the poly-functional nature of the figures is attested to by many rhetoricians.

The same Greek tradition of stylistic rhetoric also produced Longinus' treatise *On Sublimity*, which, fragmentary though it is, and not rediscovered until 1554, remains the outstanding union of rhetoric and literary criticism. For this author rhetorical figures constitute the third source of 'sublimity' (I follow Donald Russell in preferring this term to 'the sublime', which has come to have very different connotations). Sublimity implies not so much 'grandiose diction' as 'high thinking and strong passion':[30] more than half the extant text is devoted to this theme (chs. 16–29). His general thesis is that the figures 'are natural allies of sublimity' and that to use them in conjunction with strong emotions disarms suspicion of the 'artifice' involved in rhetoric (17. 1–2). Longinus' excellence as a rhetorician consists, first, in his eye for specific verbal effects in the great works of Greek literature. So he notes how Demosthenes, in one of his

[29] Demetrius 1961, p. 27.
[30] Longinus 1964, pp. xxx–xlii.

speeches, in place of a straightforward argument, suddenly invokes the oath made by the heroes of Greece:

'By those who risked their lives at Marathon, you have not done wrong!' Observe what he effects by this single figure of conjuration, or *apostrophe* as I call it here. He deifies his audience's ancestors. . . . He inspires the judges with the temper of those who risked their lives. He transforms his demonstration into an extraordinary piece of sublimity and passion. . . . At the same time he injects into his hearer's minds a healing specific. . . . In short, the figure enables him to run away with his audience. (16. 1–2)

This single figure has a multiple effect: it is 'an illustrative example, a confirmation, an encomium, and an exhortation' (16. 3).

Longinus shares Aristotle's belief that the 'truth' of a rhetorical figure is attested by the reactions of the listener or reader, who compares its verbal form to his own utterances when under the influence of a similar emotion. Like other theorists of rhetoric he links the mimetic state to its communicative or self-reproductive power. So he discusses rhetorical questions and answers (the figure *anthypophora*), once again casting his own observations into the form of the figure he is treating: 'Should we not say that they increase the realism and vigour of the writing by the actual form of the figure?' (18. 1). His example is again from Demosthenes: 'Let us sail to Macedonia. "Where shall we anchor?" says someone. The war itself will find out Philip's weak spots.' Longinus' comment moves from the figure to the speaker, from him to the audience, and back:

Put in straightforward form, this would have been quite insignificant; as it is, the impassioned rapidity of question and answer and the device of self-objection have made the remark, in virtue of its figurative form, not only more sublime but more credible. For emotion carries us away more easily when it seems to be generated by the occasion rather than deliberately assumed by the speaker, and the self-directed question and its answer represent precisely this momentary quality of emotion. Just as people who are unexpectedly plied with questions become annoyed and reply to the point with vigour and exact truth, so the figure of question and answer arrests the hearer and cheats him into believing that all the points made were raised and are being put into words on the spur of the moment. (18. 1–2)

The credibility of rhetorical effect is once again seen as depending on truth to life in the emotion presented. An Aristotelian would have applauded that analysis; a Platonist would have been shocked at the degree of manipulation implied by the words 'seems' and 'cheats'. All rhetoricians are at bottom actors, who adopt personae and act out the roles prescribed: but then one could argue that poets, novelists, and the rest of us involved in 'the presentation of the self in everyday life' do the same.

Longinus is outstanding in his ability to connect particular figures of rhetoric with specific states of feeling, either in the persona presented in the literary work, or in the audience's reaction to it. So he writes of *asyndeton*, the absence of connectives, that in it 'the words tumble out without connection, in a kind of stream, almost getting ahead of the speaker'. He cites two examples, the first from Xenophon: 'Engaging their shields, they pushed, fought, slew, died.' The second is from the *Odyssey* (10. 251–2), on which he makes this acute comment on the effect the figure has on our experience and rhythm of reading:

Disconnected and yet hurried phrases convey the impression of an agitation which both obstructs the reader and drives him on. Such is the effect of Homer's *asyndeta*. (19. 1–2)

Longinus also discusses the 'conjunction of several figures in one phrase', which produces 'a very stirring effect', as in a speech by Demosthenes, where, combining *anaphora* and *asyndeton*, the orator breaks up the settled rhythm of a sentence —which risks 'inertia' and 'monotony'—with some deliberately choppy phrases. Longinus applauds this decision, for 'disorder goes with emotion, which is a disturbance and movement of the mind'. Then he shows how Demosthenes' syntax uses the rhetorical figures to mimic the action described. In the end 'his order becomes disorderly, his disorder in turn acquires a certain order' (20. 1–3).

That kind of sensitivity to the playing off of irregularity against a norm of regularity is seen again in his analysis of the 'opposite' figure, *polysyndeton*, where you 'add the conjunctions'. He quotes a rather dull passage from one of 'Isocrates' school' and comments:

As you proceed with these insertions, it will become clear that the urgent and harsh character of the emotion loses its sting and becomes a spent fire as soon as you level it down to smoothness by the conjunctions. If you tie a runner's arm to his side you take away his speed; likewise, emotion frets at being impeded by conjunctions and other additions, because it loses the free abandon of its movement and the sense of being, as it were, catapulted out. (21. 1–2)

Whatever the identity of Longinus, he was the most sensitive reader and style critic of antiquity. His analysis of the shift from singular to plural for Oedipus' speech of horrified recognition of his deeds done in ignorance (23. 2–3), or the shift from past to present tense in Xenophon (25. 1), or from reported to direct speech in the *Iliad* (27. 1–2—'the use of this figure is appropriate when the urgency of the moment gives the writer no chance to delay, but forces on him an immediate change from one person to another'), or on Plato's overfondness for *periphrasis* (24. 1), are all perceptive observations that any critic would have been proud to have made. But what sets him apart is his recognition of the functional relationship between figures and feeling: 'they all make style more emotional and excited', and emotion (*pathos*) is an 'essential part of sublimity' (29. 2). But at all times with decorum: the use of the plural, he writes, 'is only to be followed when the subject admits amplification, abundance, hyperbole, or emotion—one or more of these. Only a sophist has bells on his harness wherever he goes' (23. 4). It is not until the sixteenth century—in my reading experience, at least—that we find again such a sensitivity to the effect of rhetoric on style.

The Roman rhetorical tradition offers nothing comparable to this treatise. There are some extended passages on style in Cicero's *Orator* and *Brutus*, of course, but they are largely concerned with prose rhythm and vocabulary, and are, furthermore, exercises in self-validation, designed to show that he had always used an effective style, whatever the new Atticists were saying about him. Cicero is, in general, rather disappointing on the details of how an orator should control his final stage of composition. *De Inventione* was meant to be a treatise on the whole of rhetoric, but he abandoned it before reaching *elocutio*, and in his later work he evidently felt it below his dignity to write a rhetoric handbook. Although adept at using the figures himself in a great range of emotional and forensic contexts, he was seldom inclined to enlarge on their function. Perhaps the great practitioner does not need to explain the theoretical basis of his art: in Pascal's famous aphorism, 'La vraie éloquence se moque de l'éloquence'. Cicero 'is generally satisfied with an enumeration of the Figures',[31] and when he does so it is in an off-hand, almost apologetic way. In the *Orator* he simply lists the patterns which characterize figures without deigning to name them or discuss their function (39. 135–9), and confines his comments to saying that the figures of thought are more important, and are frequently used by Demosthenes (136). In the more wide-ranging discussion in *De Oratore*, although we are told that the orator must intimately understand 'all the mental emotions with which nature has endowed the human race . . . because it is in calming or kindling the feelings of the audience that the full power' of oratory is shown (1. 5. 17); and that 'the orator's virtue is pre-eminently manifested either in rousing men's hearts to anger, hatred, or indignation, or in recalling them from these same passions to mildness and mercy' (1. 12. 53; also 1. 14. 60, 1. 51. 219), Cicero seems to take for granted our knowledge of the verbal means by which these effects would be brought about. In Book II Antonius discusses the technique of exciting and urging 'the feelings of the tribunal towards hatred or love, ill-will or well-wishing, fear or hope, desire or aversion, joy or sorrow, compassion or the wish to punish', and other associated emotions (2. 44. 185). The power of eloquence over even those who resist is celebrated (187); the complete orator's union of voice, gesture, and passion is described (45. 188); and we are reminded that the listener will not feel any emotions unless the advocate is himself stirred by them (189). Indeed this topic of the orator's emotional state receives greatest attention (45. 190–55. 216), with the new idea, as we have seen, that the orator's power to move himself as well as others lies in the language he has himself composed: 'the very quality of the diction, employed to stir the feelings of others, stirs the speaker himself even more deeply than any of his

---

[31] D'Alton 1931, p. 112; Clarke 1953, p. 51.

hearers' (46. 191). This auto-arousal, or self-persuasion is one of the most striking instances of rhetoric's belief in the power of *elocutio,* yet still Cicero disdains to give further details. When Crassus has finished his all too brief account of the figures of thought (3. 52. 200–54. 208)—'for these more or less are the figures'—Cotta is made to draw attention to this peculiarity in his exposition: 'I notice that you have poured them out without giving definitions or examples, in the belief that we are familiar with them' (55. 208). Yes, Crassus says, I am sure you know all this already, and in any case it is getting dark. (Quintilian's reverence for the great practitioner is so great that he reproduces both lists verbatim, despite their laconic and confusing nature: 9. 1. 25–45.)

Cicero ignores the minutiae, but he obviously knows which devices are appropriate. In the technique of *amplificatio* 'a great impression is made by dwelling on a single point', as well as by the opposite method of *praecisio,* the 'suggestion that causes more to be understood than one actually says' (*De Or.* 3. 52. 202). He describes 'imitation of manners and behaviour' as 'a considerable ornament of style, and extremely effective in calming down an audience and often also in exciting it' (204); other resources include 'putting [them] on the wrong scent', 'raising a laugh', 'relapse into silence, compliment', 'free use of the voice and even uncontrolled vociferation to amplify the effect', 'anger, invective, promise of proof, deprecation, entreaty, . . . self-justification, ingratiation, hard-hitting, appeals to the powers above and imprecation' (205). This throwaway list shows that Cicero knew his trade, and his speeches reveal a brilliant and ruthless ability to advance his own case and damage the opposition's.[32] All these have been figures of thought, and Cicero reminds us of their superiority over figures of words, namely 'that the figure suggested by the words disappears if one alters the words, but that of the thoughts remains whatever words one chooses to employ' (200). Cicero then dismisses the subject by making Crassus rattle off the names of thirty-eight figures of words in one paragraph, in the barest possible manner. But he at least bears witness to what I have called the polysemous nature of the figures, describing diction as 'a weapon either employed for use, to threaten and to

[32] Classen 1982.

attack, or simply brandished for show. For there is sometimes force and in other cases charm in iteration of words . . .' (206).

The author of the *Rhetorica ad Herennium* did get as far as *elocutio*, in his much-imitated fourth book, and although not as perceptive as the Greek rhetoricians, he shows some awareness of the specific effects of figures. He sums up the difference between *colon*, the brief clause which needs another to complete the sense, and *articulus* (or *brachylogia*), where the discourse is cut up by the force of expression (in his example: 'You have destroyed your enemies by jealousy, injuries, influence, perfidy'):

the former moves upon its object more slowly and less often, the latter strikes more quickly and frequently. Accordingly in the first figure it seems that the arm draws back and the hand whirls about to bring the sword to the adversary's body, while in the second his body is as it were pierced with quick and repeated thrusts. (4. 19. 26)

The image is repeated with variation in describing *conduplicatio* (or *ploche*), 'the repetition of one or more words for the purpose of Amplification or Appeal to Pity': 'The reiteration of the same word makes a deep impression upon the hearer and inflicts a major wound upon the opposition—as if a weapon should repeatedly pierce the same part of the body' (4. 28. 38). Though a simple explanation, it does bring out the combative effect of the figure.

The distinctively Roman emphasis on forensic rhetoric can be seen in his location of rhetorical figures in specific courtroom situations. So he explains the function of 'Reasoning by Contraries' (*contrarium*—denying the contrary of an idea before affirming it) that

by means of the contrary statement it . . . forcibly proves what the speaker needs to prove; and from a statement which is not open to question it draws a thought which is in question, in such a way that the inference cannot be refuted, or can be refuted only with much the greatest difficulty. (4. 18. 26)

He gives the same forensic power to other large-scale figures of argument: *hypophora*, *similitudo*, *permissio*, which provokes pity, *aposiopesis* ('Here a suspicion, unexpressed, becomes more telling than a detailed explanation would have been'). He makes an acute comment on a figure later to be very popular with

Renaissance writers, *correctio* (*epanorthosis*), which 'retracts what
has been said and replaces it with what seems more suitable' (as
in the famous instance from Thomas Kyd, *The Spanish Tragedy*:
'O eyes—no eyes, but fountains fraught with tears'), writing
that 'This figure makes an impression upon the hearer, for the
idea when expressed by an ordinary word seems rather feebly
stated, but after the speaker's own amendment it is made more
striking by means of the more appropriate expression' (4. 26 36).
As well as other comments on the argumentative force of figures
the author of the *Ad Herennium* stresses that rhetorical art should
not draw attention to itself. Some elaborate figures 'are to be
used very sparingly when we speak in an actual cause, because
their invention seems impossible without labour and pains' (4.
22. 32). Most rhetoricians from Aristotle on (*Rhetoric*, 1404^{b}18)
urge that art must be concealed by nature.

The fullest treatment of the figures in Roman rhetoric comes
in Quintilian, as we might expect, and includes an explicit
rationale for their use. In Book 8, having praised the power
of *elocutio* in that celebrated passage (quoted above, p. 43),
Quintilian next considers *ornatus*. This word is inevitably
rendered in English as 'ornament', with the unfortunate
connotation of 'adornment', the use of unnecessary trappings or
incidental decoration. But as George Kennedy pointed out, 'to
the Roman ear the word "ornament" suggests distinction and
excellence, the possession of resources ready for any challenge;
it is a vital and useful quality', which 'aids the orator's practical
purpose, for by it he compels attention and bends the audience
to his will'. Walter Ong noted independently that in Latin
ornamentum signified 'equipment or accoutrements', a soldier's
'gear' or weapons, and has nothing to do with purely
ornamental devices.[33] It is with this military metaphor in mind
that Quintilian says of *ornatus* that where the orator's other
accomplishments appeal to the learned 'this gift appeals to the
enthusiastic approval of the world at large, and the speaker who
possesses it fights not merely with effective, but with flashing

[33] Kennedy 1969, p. 81; Ong 1958, p. 277; cf. Griffin 1969, p. 49. Dyck 1966,
p. 88, writes that in seventeenth-century German rhetoric *ornatus* was connected
with 'Wirkung', moving the hearers' emotions. Curtius 1953, p. 71, traces this
functional concept of *ornatus* from Quintilian to Dante and into the eighteenth
century.

weapons' (8. 3. 2)—so echoing the sword-fighting metaphor used in the *Ad Herennium* to describe the force of figures of repetition. If properly used, as by Cicero in defence of Cornelius, 'the brilliance and the weight' of eloquence can rouse an audience to 'a kind of frenzy',

> filled with delight, and sometimes even transported by admiration. The flash of the sword in itself strikes something of terror to the eye, and we should be less alarmed by the thunderbolt if we feared its violence alone, and not its flash as well. Cicero was right when, in one of his letters to Brutus, he wrote 'Eloquence which evokes no admiration is, in my opinion, unworthy of the name'. (8. 3. 4–6)

(We should remember that *admiratio* was a strong emotion, aroused by such powerful genres as tragedy.) The most elegant restatement of the metaphor of rhetorical armaments is in Alexander Pope's *Essay on Criticism* (1711):

> In grave Quintilian's copious work we find
> The justest Rules, and clearest *Method* join'd;
> Thus *useful Arms* in Magazines we place,
> All rang'd with *Order*, and dispos'd with *Grace*,
> But less to please the *Eye*, than arm the Hand,
> Still fit for Use, and ready at Command. (ll. 669–74)

The eighteenth century still knew what the figures were for.

In all systematic treatments of these resources a distinction is made between tropes and figures (or schemes). A trope (or 'turn') involves a change or transference of meaning, and works on the conceptual level: the recognition, and appreciation, of a metaphor is a mental event. A figure involves the placing or disposition of words into a structure which is natural yet goes beyond the normal or minimum needs of communication. Cicero alludes to the Greeks' name for figures of thought and language, *schemata*, 'postures' or 'attitudes' (*Brutus*, 17. 69, 79. 275)—another term taken over directly by Renaissance art-theorists, as we shall see. Quintilian also uses the term *schemata* as a synonym for *figurae* (2. 13. 19), and explains that the word 'figure' can be taken in two senses, both as 'form' or 'shape' in general, and more specifically as a *schema* or 'rational change in meaning or language from the ordinary and simple form, that is to say, a change analogous to that involved by sitting, lying down on something for looking back' (9. 1. 10–11). This corporeal metaphor is developed further, to describe the deviation from normal posture in these 'attitudes, or I might say gestures of language' (9. 1. 13). Again the physiological analogy opens the path from rhetoric to the visual arts. Quintilian goes on to group the figures into the traditional categories of 'figures of thought' (9. 1. 17)—general tactical processes such as rhetorical question, apostrophe, dissimulation, insinuation; and 'figures of speech', which he divides into four types:

   (*a*) variations of syntax, such as *hyperbaton*;
   (*b*) modes of iteration: *anaphora, ploche, polyptoton*;
   (*c*) word-play: *paronomasia, antanaclasis, syllepsis*;
   (*d*) balance and antithesis: *parison, isocolon*, . . . (9. 3. 1–102)

Although the latter group is numerically the larger, it is the former, the 'figures of thought, that is of the mind, feeling or conceptions', to which the greatest power is ascribed. Quintilian first emphasizes their 'great and manifold' utility in every branch of oratory, their ability to 'steal their way secretly into the minds of the judges'. 'For', he goes on, reviving the metaphor of sword-play, just as 'the task of the skilful swordsman is to give the impression that his design is quite other than it actually is, even so the oratory in which there is no guile fights by sheer weight and impetus alone' (9. 1. 19–20). The emotional power of figural language is its great glory:

Further, there is no more effective method of exciting the emotions than an apt use of figures. For if the expression of brow, eyes and hands has a powerful effect in stirring the passions, how much more effective must be the aspect of our style itself when composed to produce the result at which we aim? (9. 1. 21)

Repetition, in general, is to be used 'to fix one point in the minds of the audience' (9. 2. 4). *Apostrophe* 'is wonderfully stirring' (9. 2. 38); the orator must cultivate variety so as to 'rivet the attention of the mind' (63). He should cultivate those types of figure which 'serve to attract the attention of the audience and do not allow it to flag, rousing it (*excitatum*) from time to time by some specially striking figure' (9. 3. 27), in order to excite their ears and minds (*aures et animos excitat*: 9. 3. 66). *Asyndeton* 'is useful when we are speaking with special vigour: for it at once impresses the details on the mind and makes them more numerous than they really are' (9. 3. 50), while *anaphora* can be used to produce 'force and emphasis' (9. 3. 30). 'The origin' of these figures of repetition, he writes, 'is one and the same, namely that they make our utterances more vigorous and emphatic and produce an impression of vehemence such as might spring from repeated outbursts of emotion' (9. 3. 50, 54). In the rhetorical tradition to seem is to be.

Quintilian, like the Greek rhetoricians, is aware that figures are polysemous, or polypathous, ascribing a whole range of emotional emphases. For the figure *aposiopesis*, which breaks off a sentence leaving the sense 'uncertain [how] to be understood' (9. 3. 60), Quintilian gives three different applications. First, it can 'indicate passion or anger, as in the line

> *Quos ego—sed motos praestat componere fluctus.'*

In this famous verse from the *Aeneid* (1. 35), the *locus classicus* for most later definitions of the figure (and immortalized in an oil-sketch by Rubens—Fig. 4), Neptune rebukes the winds for raising a storm, but breaks off without actually saying what he

FIG. 4. Rubens: '*Quos Ego*' (*Neptune Calming the Tempest*)

will do to them ('Whom I— / But better first these billows to assuage'). The same figure, Quintilian goes on, 'may serve to give an impression of anxiety or scruple', as in a speech of Cicero about some lawless politician: 'For as regards all of us—I do not dare to complete the sentence.' It can also be used 'as a means of transition', although Quintilian doubts whether it is then really a figure (54–5). His awareness of the polysemous or many-functional nature of rhetorical devices applies equally to the class of figures which involve repetition, such as the doubling of words, either 'with a view to amplification, as in "I have slain, I have slain, not Spurius Maelius" (where the first *I have slain* states what has been done, while the second emphasizes it), or to excite pity, as in "Ah! Corydon, Corydon"' (Virgil, *Eclogues*, 2. 69). Yet, Quintilian notes, 'the same figure may also sometimes be employed ironically, with a view to disparagement' (9. 3. 28–9).

The forensic emphasis in Roman rhetoric comes out again as Quintilian, too, places specific rhetorical devices in the context of a courtroom, with an advocate preparing his case. So he advises that 'the figures best adapted for intensifying emotion consist chiefly in simulation. For we may feign that we are angry, glad, afraid, filled with wonder, grief or indignation' (9. 2. 26). The legal context necessarily involves an awareness of the reactions of judge and jury, as in the device whereby

we excite some suspicion to indicate that our meaning is other than our words would seem to imply; but our meaning is not in this case contrary to that which we express, as is the case in *irony*, but rather a hidden meaning which is left to the hearer to discover. (9. 2. 26)

In this manœuvre the facts must be so presented as to 'excite the suspicions of the judge', suppressing all details save those that will 'suggest the truth' which the advocate wishes to argue. Here Quintilian delivers a truly perceptive comment on the effect produced by this sort of withholding of information:

For thus the judge will be led to seek out the secret which he would not perhaps believe if he heard it openly stated, and to believe in that which he thinks he has found out for himself. (71)

Again he finds several reasons for not speaking openly: if it is unsafe to do so; or unseemly; or just to give variety (66).

(Shakespeare, as we will see, knows of another and more sinister reason!) But always, Quintilian writes, the orator must convince his audience of the genuineness of his feeling by suiting style to subject and to the appropriate emotions, for anger cannot be credibly expressed in neat antitheses (9. 3. 102). It is a passage which provides an illuminating gloss on the failure of Brutus' rhetoric in *Julius Caesar*.[34]

That injunction is one of several where Quintilian applies the theory of decorum to the details of style, insisting on an organic relation between form and content. Our pleasure should be derived 'both from the figurative form and the excellence of the sense' (9. 3. 71), for 'it is as ridiculous to hunt for figures without reference to the matter as it is to discuss dress and gesture without reference to the body' (9. 3. 100): *res* and *verba* must cohere. Again we have the stress on the need to avoid display, lest it damage the effect constantly sought for, of language naturally expressing feeling: '*Gradatio*, which the Greeks call *climax*, necessitates a more obvious and less natural application of art and should therefore be more sparingly employed' (9. 3. 54). Feeling must be expressed in language, as all rhetoricians know, and the figures are the natural means of doing so. But art is still a selection from nature, and Quintilian warns against treating the relationship 'emotions : : figures' on a one-to-one basis:

I must repudiate the view of those who hold that there are as many types of figures as there are kinds of emotion, on the ground, not that emotions are not qualities of the mind, but that a figure, in its strict, not its general sense, is not simply the expression of anything you choose to select.

The mere expression of emotion does not create a figure, even though 'superficial observers are deceived by the fact that they find figures in all passages dealing with such themes', that is, expressions of 'anger, grief, pity, fear, confidence or contempt' (9. 1. 23–6). It is art, not nature, that describes or codifies a figure. The emotions are extremely varied, but the verbal forms that they take, although authentic repositories of feeling, are not infinite, but represent a deliberate process of choice and

---

[34] Vickers 1968, pp. 241–5.

systematization. As Vives put it, perhaps thinking of this passage, 'words are limited; realities infinite'.[35]

As for the tropes, although by and large less emotional power was attributed to them, metaphor, at least, was seen as able to generate emotional intensity. In Book Three of his *Rhetoric* Aristotle advises the writer to select his words carefully, since 'one term may set [a thing] more intimately before our eyes' (1405^b12). Metaphor is valuable because it gives us 'something fresh', 'a new idea, a new fact' (1410^b12 ff.), and a good metaphor 'sets the scene before our eyes; for events ought to be seen in progress rather than in prospect' (1410^b33). The writer must aim at 'actuality' and 'liveliness', qualities that are attained by 'being graphic (i.e. making your hearers *see* things)'—that is, by 'using expressions that represent things in activity' (1411^a21 ff.). From his examples and comments it seems that Aristotle means 'activity' both literally, where events are described as in a state of motion, and also figuratively, as when inanimate things are personified. Metaphor conveys liveliness, and also surprise: 'because the hearer expected something different, his acquisition of the new idea impresses him all the more. His mind seems to say, "Yes, to be sure; I never thought of that" ' (1412^a17 ff.). A further criterion is that metaphors must be 'related to the original thing, and yet not obviously so related—just as in philosophy also an acute mind will perceive resemblances even in things far apart' (1412^a9 ff.). The ability to create, or perceive metaphor, is a mark of intellectual penetration, and originality. As the complementary discussion of metaphor in the *Poetics* puts it, 'by far the most important' gift of a writer 'is to be good at metaphor. For this is the only one that cannot be learnt from anyone else, and it is a sign of natural genius, as to be good at metaphor is to perceive resemblances' (1459^a5 ff.). Nothing in Latin rhetoric matches Aristotle's discussion of metaphor, either in range or in perception.

The *Ad Herennium*, that useful witness to the Romans' adoption of the systematized rhetoric of the Hellenistic period, merely says that metaphor is used 'for the sake of creating a vivid mental picture': *rei ante oculos ponendae causa* (4. 34. 45). The same criterion of vividness is attributed to several other

[35] Vives 1966, p. 266.

figures, *descriptio* (4. 39. 51), *similitudo* (4. 47. 61), 'character delineations', such as *effictio*, the portrayal of bodily form, and *notatio*, the portrayal of a person's character (4. 48. 61 ff.), also *demonstratio* (4. 55. 68–9). In all these instances we should remember the prime concern of Roman forensic rhetoric, the advocate speaking in court and attempting to persuade the judge and jury. Bringing the scene *ante oculos* is obviously crucial, a passage to the eyes of the mind via the ears (compare Aristotle: 'making your *hearers see* things'). Our anonymous author did not go on to make the connection with *movere* and *persuasio*, but his two great successors did. In his early treatise Cicero advises the advocate to use *indignatio* in his peroration so as to 'bring the action as vividly as possible before the eyes of the judge . . . so that a shameful act may seem as shameful as if he had himself been present and seen it in person' (*De Inv.* 1. 54. 104). The defence counsel can also 'lay the blame on someone else . . . by placing the scene vividly before the eyes of the jury' (2. 28. 83). In *De Oratore* Antonius gives, exceptionally, a theoretical rationale for the effectiveness of this device:

the most complete pictures are formed in our minds of the things that have been conveyed to them and imprinted on them by the senses, but . . . the keenest of all our senses is the sense of sight, and . . . consequently perceptions received by the ears or by reflexion can be most easily retained in the mind if [conveyed] by the mediation of the eyes. (2. 87. 357; also *Part. Or.* 6. 20)

For this reason every good metaphor 'has direct appeal to the senses, especially the sense of sight' (3. 40. 160), the highest praise of a metaphor being that it 'directly hits our senses' (3. 41. 163).

Quintilian similarly recommends the orator to develop the 'power of vivid imagination, whereby things, words and actions are presented in the most realistic manner', such as an imagined murder scene. 'It is the man who is really sensitive to such impressions who will have the greatest power over the emotions' of the judge (6. 2. 29–30). Referring to Cicero's terms for this activity, *illustratio* and *evidentia* (*Part. Or.* 6. 20), Quintilian adds the Greek term for it, *enargeia*, 'which makes us seem not so much to narrate as to exhibit the actual scene' (6. 2. 32). When he comes to discuss *ornatum*, in which brilliance and forcefulness are added to clear expression, Quintilian repeats the term *enargeia* to describe *evidentia* or *repraesentatio*, the 'vivid illustration' which 'thrusts itself upon our notice', praising it as 'the highest of all oratorical gifts', for it can make the judge feel that 'the facts on which he has to give his decision are . . . displayed in their living truth to the eyes of his mind' (8. 3. 61–2, 71). Various forms of producing this effect are discussed, among them an actual word-picture of the scene (63), simile (72), and 'reciprocal representation', which 'places both subjects of comparison before our very eyes, displaying them side by side' (77—'Look here, upon this picture, and on this'). Quintilian's chapter on the tropes has been criticized as unsatisfactory, ill-arranged, and poorly illustrated,[36] but it does at least contain an awareness of the persuasive function of metaphor, as being 'designed to move the feelings, give special distinction to things, and place them vividly before the eye . . .' (8. 6. 19). All these tropes have to proceed via the ear to the mind's eye in vivid language, *sub oculos subiectio* (9. 2. 40). In accord with the coherence between orator and audience fundamental to classical rhetoric, the intensity of his perceptions cannot but move our feelings.

III

No attentive reader could come away from the classical texts thinking that the tropes and figures were 'dry formulae'. It is only the persistence of a post-Romantic animus against rhetoric that has prevented us from grasping this fact earlier. Certainly Renaissance readers knew what classical rhetoric meant by the expressive functionality of the figures, and we can find those precepts echoed, often in the same terms and with the same examples, in all the European vernaculars. (A comparative study of the reception and application of rhetoric in Renaissance Europe would be of immense value.) Most of my examples will come from the English Renaissance, which I know best, but I note in passing how writers in continental Europe reflected the classical emphasis on the *figurae sententiarum* as being most able to mobilize feeling. Heinrich Plett's study of the development of

---

[36] Kennedy 1969, pp. 83–5.

affective rhetoric in the sixteenth century brings out very clearly how a group of *schemata sententiae*—*ecphonesis, aposiopesis, prosopopoeia, apostrophe, dubitatio, interrogatio, hypotyposis*—recurs time and again in the rhetoric-books as guaranteeing effective persuasion, whether by the Englishmen Farnaby, John Clarke, and Richard Sherry, the Dutchman Vossius, the Spaniard Luis de Granada, the Germans Macropedius and Susenbrotus (to preserve their Latinized names), or the Frenchmen Nicholas Caussin and Omer Talon.[37] The Abbé d'Aubignac, in his *Pratique du théâtre* (1657), as Peter France notes, stated that 'the tragic poet's business being to express and excite passions he will make copious use of "les grandes Figures qui sont aux choses et aux sentiments" '—such figures as apostrophe, exclamation, hyperbole, interrogation, imprecation—and avoid figures based on purely verbal distinctions, such as antitheses and puns. In *La Poétique* (1639) La Mesnardière also recommended the dramatist to use in general the *figurae sententiarum*. Other writers were more explicit, seeing the repetition of words as being the best means of expressing passion: in his *Art de parler* (1675) Bernard Lamy described repetition as 'une figure fort ordinaire dans le discours de ceux qui parlent avec chaleur'.[38] Omer Talon said that the figures of repetition affect the soul, while Sainct-Fleur, writing in 1569, recommended that *epizeuxis* (repeating a word with no other words intervening: 'Howl, howl, howl, howl, howl') should be used 'pour produire un effet de véhémence'.[39] Here, too, the emotions expressed by the poet, such as the use of rhetorical questions to arouse pathos, were seen as producing an answering response in the hearer. In Malebranche's laconic —and rhetorical—formulation, 'les personnes passionnées nous passionnent'.[40]

In Germany a whole group of writers vied with each other in producing ever larger and more systematic treatises, in which specific figures were correlated with specific 'affects'. Thus Johann Heinrich Alstedt, the Ramist synthesizer, wrote in his *Encyclopaedia* (1630) that 'Figurae rhetoricae inprimis sententiae, sunt validissimae machinae, quibus arx affectuum expugnari

---

[37] Plett 1975, pp. 26, 32, 44, 47, 70, 77–8, 84, 89, 93–4.
[38] France 1965, pp. 27, 33, 166–7, 117–18.
[39] Gordon 1970, pp. 109, 110.
[40] Ibid., p. 133; France 1972, pp. 29–30.

potest'. Some of his claims seem rather dubious (the tropes *metonymy* and *synecdoche* as producing emphasis, or showing vehement commotions in the soul), but one can agree that a figure of repetition should be used 'in affectu vehementioris amoris, admirationis, odii, irae, doloris'.[41] Meyfart's *Teutsche Rhetorica* (1634) describes *epizeuxis* as 'eine heffige und gewaltige Figur'; likens *anadiplosis* to a sword striking twice on the same place; and rediscovers the polysemous quality of the figures, writing that *synecdoche* can be used when the orator wants to flatter the listener, 'oder ihm den Zorn / Neyd, Hass und Furcht einjagen will'.[42] For the Jesuit Caussinus, in his vast tome, as for his contemporaries in France, 'zur Gemüts- und Affekterregung . . . spielen bei weitem die heftigeren *Figurae sententiae* eine dominante Rolle, wie z.B. die Figuren der exclamatio, der aversio, der deprecatio, der sermonicatio usw.'[43]

In the dozen or so English rhetoric-books published between 1550 and 1620 we find the same pattern as in the classical rhetorics and—unless I am much mistaken—the contemporary continental treatises, whereby tropes are granted less power to move the feelings. Alex Gordon, in his very helpful study of rhetoric in sixteenth-century France, says that in this period tropes were respected, 'mais on ne leur donne pas la place privilégiée qu'ils occupent dans la poésie moderne'.[44] In general tropes seem to be assigned a cognitive or explanatory function, clarifying the sense or making clear internal relationships. Melanchthon, much used by English rhetoricians, finds metaphor useful for increasing clarity and perception.[45] The Ramist Dudley Fenner, in his *Artes of Logike and Rhetorike* (1584) gives the standard account of the formation of tropes ('first found out by necessitie, for the want of words, afterwards confirmed by delight, because such wordes are pleasaunt and gracious to the eare'), but has no awareness of their emotional function.[46] Abraham Fraunce, another Ramist, draws on the

[41] Dyck 1966, pp. 81–4.
[42] Ibid., pp. 85–6.
[43] Sieveke 1974, pp. 55, 60–2, 66–7.
[44] Gordon 1970, p. 196. He notes the relatively low prestige of metaphor in French Renaissance poetics (p. 196), and records finding only one important example of irony in Ronsard (p. 219).
[45] Melanchthon 1968, p. 265.
[46] Fenner 1584, Sig. D₁ᵛ.

standard classical texts to describe metaphor as a 'flourishing' trope, 'especially fit to be applied to the senses'.[47] More perceptive is Henry Peacham, in the most complete of the English manuals, *The Garden of Eloquence* (1577, 1593), which is based partly on Susenbrotus' *Epitome Troporum ac Schematum* (1541), but much amplified.[48] Peacham defines five uses for metaphors:

First, they give pleasant light to darke things, thereby removing unprofitable and odious obscuritie. Secondly, by the aptnesse of their proportion, and nearnesse of affinitie, they worke in their hearer many effects, they obtaine allowance of his judgement, they move his affections, and minister a pleasure to his wit. Thirdly, they are forcible to perswade. Fourthly to commend or dispraise. Fiftly, they leave such a firme impression in the memory, as is not lightly forgotten. (p. 13)

That is perhaps too generalized and schematic, but it is one of the few accounts of the tropes in English rhetoric that grants them any emotive power.

Peacham gives much more emphasis to the figures, and shows that he has noted the passages in the classical texts describing their expressive functions. Indeed, when producing a much enlarged version, in 1593, he added a section on each figure giving 'The Use' and 'The Caution', stressing the need for the rhetorical device to be related to the sense and not to be used excessively. In 1577 he had described the effect of *anaphora* in the rather vague terms used in the *Ad Herennium*: 'when with much comelynesse one word is repeated in diuers clauses . . .' (Sig. Hiiii^v). But in 1593 he brings out its function: 'The use hereof is chiefly to repeate a word of importance and effectual significication', adding the cautions that the figure must not be used too often, nor tautologically, and that 'heede ought to be taken that the word which is least worthie or most weake be not taken to make the repetition, for that were very absurd' (pp. 41–2). As an example of the correct use of *anaphora* he quotes Psalm 29: 'The Lord sitteth above the water floods. The Lord remaineth a King

---

[47] Fraunce 1588, p. 15.

[48] Quoted from Peacham 1593, incorporated into the text. As an instance of the amount that Peacham adds to his sources, Susenbrotus treats metaphor in about 150 words, running together passages from Cicero and Quintilian. Peacham devotes eight pages to the trope, integrating passages from Aristotle's *Poetics,* and developing his own ideas (pp. 6–14).

for ever. The Lord shall give strength unto his people. The Lord shall give his people the blessing of Peace.'

In many of these figures of repetition Peacham insists that the writer fit sound and structure to sense, with the figure being based on 'a word of importance' in the text. For the figure *epistrophe*, 'which endeth diverse members or clauses still with one and the same word', he adds an awareness of the audience and the persuasive intent of rhetoric reminiscent of Quintilian: 'The use of this figure . . . it serveth to leave a word of importance in the end of a sentence, that it may the longer hold the sound in the mind of the hearer' (p. 43). Again, for *diaphora* or *ploche*, the repetition of a word, Peacham urges that it should serve 'both to the pleasure of the eare and sense of the mind', and that the word repeated be the most meaningful one (p. 45). *Epanalepsis*, he maintains, should place 'a word of importance in the beginning of a sentence to be considered, and in the end to be remembered' (p. 46). *Paragmenon*—his name for *polyptoton*—('a figure which of the word going before deriveth the word following') is used 'to delight the eare by the derived sound, and to move the mind with a consideration of the nigh affinitie and concord of the matter', for example, on the relationship between Adam and Christ (1 Cor 15:45): 'The first man was of the earth earthly, the second man was the Lord from Heaven heavenly' (p. 55). He recalls the classical rhetoricians, such as Quintilian on *gradatio*, in urging the avoidance of artifice. The figure *paronomasia* 'ought to be sparingly used, and especially in grave and weightie cases, both in respect of the light and illuding forme, and also forasmuch as it seemeth not to be found without meditation and affected labour' (p. 56). He joins Longinus in describing *articulus* (or *asyndeton*) as a figure 'very convenient to expresse any vehement affections: in peacable and quiet causes it may be compared to a semi-breefe in Musicke, but in causes of perturbation and haste it may be likened to thicke and violent strokes in fight, or to a thick and thundring peale of ordinance' (p. 57). His analogies update Quintilian's metaphor of sword-fighting, and look ahead to Monteverdi's description of the *stile concitato*.

Like other Renaissance writers, Peacham is so convinced of the potential of the figures to express feeling that he groups them according to their degree of emotional power. Figures of 'the second order' (*figurae sententiarum*) 'are such as do make the oration not onely pleasant and plausible but also verie sharpe and vehement, by which the sundrie affections and passions of the minde are properly and elegantly uttered (by a forme of outcrie) and that either by the figures of Exclamation, Moderation, Consultation, or Permission' (pp. 61–2). These figures 'do attend upon affections as ready handmaids at commaundement to express most aptly whatsoever the heart doth affect or suffer' (p. 120). And within this group he distinguishes between the more violent forms of exclamation and the 'lesse vehement than those', which 'pertaine to more milde affections, and do require a more moderate forme of pronuntiation' (p. 84). The criteria for classifying the figures are emotional and psychological, and Peacham responds both to their emotional function and their intellectual or argumentative force. Thus he says of the figure *apodixis* (*evidens probatio*) that 'Of all the formes of speech there is not one more apt, or more mighty to confirme or confute than this, which is grounded upon the strong foundation of experience confirmed by all times . . .' (p. 87). He credits similar power to *antimetabole*, quoting the example used in the *Ad Herennium*, but giving a more intelligent account of it than that work's mere epithet 'neat': '*Antimetabole* is a forme of speech which inverteth a sentence by the contrary, thus: "It behoveth thee to eate that thou maist live, and not live that thou maist eate". . . . The use hereof serveth properlie to praise, dispraise, to distinguish, but most commonly to confute by the inversion of the sentence' (p. 164). No reader of Peacham could come away without seeing that the figures of rhetoric have a great persuasive power, appealing both to the emotions and to the intellect.

Of the many other Elizabethan rhetoricians, the least interested in stressing the imaginative potential of rhetoric are the Ramists, surprisingly so in view of the fact that they illustrated their textbooks with examples taken from contemporary poetry. One looks in vain for any advance on the generalized concept of rhetoric as being ornament or 'garnishing' in Dudley Fenner's *Artes of Logike and Retorike*, or Charles Butler's *Rhetoricae Libri Duo* (1597). In a more adventurous Ramist work, Abraham Fraunce's *Arcadian Rhetoric*,[49] there are a few signs of a more intelligent awareness. In one of these places, discussing the power of 'figures in Sentences, which in the whole sentence express some notion of the minde', he seems to be merely echoing Peacham: 'These are more forcible & apt to perswade than those of words, which be rather pleasant and fit to delight' (p. 63). But in discussing such figures as *epanorthosis* or *aposiopesis* he makes a more original psychological point: 'The calling backe of a mans selfe followeth when any thing is revoked, and it is as it were, a cooling of that heate of exclamation . . .' (p. 78). This stress on 'cooling', however, is opposed to the traditional interpretation of the figure's pathetic or passionate effect, such as Peacham's enlargement of Quintilian: '*Aposiopesis*: by which the Orator through some affection, as either of feare, anger, sorrow, bashfulness or such like, breaketh off his speech before it be all ended. *Virgil*: "How doth the childe Ascanius, whom tymely *Troy* to thee—" breaking off by the interruption of sorrow' (Peacham 1593, p. 118; *Aen.*, 3.33 f: a unique instance in virgil of an *aposiopesis* coinciding with an incomplete verse line).

Weak though the Ramists are on this point, further evidence of the literary-psychological relations of rhetoric is found in a writer formerly, and dubiously, associated with the Ramists, Sir Philip Sidney. In his *Apology for Poetry* (c. 1582)[50] he attacks the misuse of imitation, often done mechanically and without regard to context. Sidney illustrates his point by reference to the famous opening of the first *In Catilinam*, which both Quintilian and the young King Edward VI had analysed:

Tully, when he was to drive out Catiline, as it were with a thunderbolt of eloquence, often used that figure of repetition, *Vivit. Vivit? Imo vero etiam in senatum venit*, &c. Indeed, inflamed with a well-grounded rage, he would have his words (as it were) double out of his mouth, and so do that artificially which we see men do in choler naturally. And we, having noted the grace of those words, hale them in sometime to a familiar epistle, when it were too much collar to be choleric. (p. 138)

By his scornful concluding *paronomasia* ('collar . . . choleric') as by his allusion to the figure *conduplicatio* in 'double out of his mouth' (*ploche* is called by Puttenham 'the doubler') Sidney

---

revives the technique used by Longinus of describing a rhetorical figure by imitating its effect. And, like his predecessors in classical antiquity, he connects rhetoric to its natural sources in human emotion: 'so do that artificially, which we see men do in choler naturally'. In an earlier passage in the *Apology*, arguing that every art 'delivered to mankind . . . hath the works of Nature for his principal object', Sidney (perhaps echoing Aristotle) concisely indicated the proper relationship between nature and art: 'the rhetorician and logician, considering what in Nature will soonest prove and persuade, thereon give artificial rules', that is—in no pejorative sense— rules made by art (pp. 99–100).

Sidney, as poet and writer of a major prose romance, is taken as the acknowledged model of expressive language in a work marked by great psychological penetration, *Directions for Speech and Style*[51] (*c.* 1599) by John Hoskins, who in this might be called the English Longinus. Here too is evidence of a considerable literary intelligence (the illustrations are well chosen from Sidney's *Arcadia*), a rare sensitivity to the style of individual writers, and this work, also, is tantalizingly brief. Hoskins in the main follows Susenbrotus (or Peacham), but adds several explanations of his own. So in discussing figures of repetition he makes the perceptive suggestion that 'as no man is sick in thought upon one thing but for some vehemency or distress, so in speech there is no repetition without importance' (p. 12). This psychological justification for a figure, relating it to an obsessive emotional state, is quite in the tradition of Demetrius and Longinus. Elsewhere he combines artistic and more utilitarian ends, as did Quintilian and Peacham (p. 105) before him: the figure *anaphora* 'beats upon one thing to cause the quicker feeling in the audience, and to awake a sleepy or dull person' (p. 13).

Hoskins has the ability to take a familiar figure and interpret it afresh. Of all the accounts of *antimetabole* (e.g. from Sidney: 'they misliked what themselves did, and yet did still what themselves misliked'), none is more acute: 'this is a sharp and witty figure and shows out of the same words a pithy distinction of meaning . . .' (p. 15). Hoskins, like Quintilian, insists on figures being tied to sense and structure: 'let discretion [i.e.

---

[51] Quoted from Hoskins 1935, incorporated into the text.

decorum] be the greatest and general figure of figures' (p. 15); and again, the use of a figure should 'come from some choice and not from barrenness' (p. 17). He underlines the needs of the artistic moment: 'In these two sorts of amplifying you may insert all figures *as the passion of the matter shall serve*' (p. 21; my italics), and has a good sense of the varying effects possible from any one device. So *polyptoton* 'is a good figure, and may be used *with or without passion*' (p. 17). Some figures, he warns, such as exclamation, are so emotionally intense that they are 'not lawful but in extremity of motion [emotion], as Pirocles, seeing the mild Philoclea innocently beheaded, cried out: "O tyrant heaven, traitor earth, blind providence, no justice! How is this done! How is this suffered? Has this world a government?"' (p. 33). His sympathy with one of Sidney's favourite tropes, *synoeciosis* (or *oxymoron*, 'a composition of contraries'—such as 'witty ignorance') again takes a psychological turn: 'This is a fine course to stir admiration in the hearer and make them think it a strange harmony which must be expressed in such discords' (p. 36). In trying to re-create the 'body of rhetoric' as the Renaissance knew it, John Hoskins is the most intelligent and helpful guide, and one wishes his book were longer.

Hoskins was one of the sources—together with Blount and Farnaby—of *The Mysterie of Rhetorique Unvail'd*[52] (1657), by John Smith, which had ten editions by 1721. Smith makes the standard distinction between a *figura dictionis*, which expresses the matter or 'body' of speech, and a *figura sententiae*, which expresses its 'soul' (p. 5). The latter is superior for 'the forcible moving of affections', carrying 'with it a certain manly majesty, which far surpasses the soft delicacy of the former Figures', and may justly be called 'pathetical' (pp. 7–8). In *ploche*, for instance, 'a word is by way of Emphasis so repeated that it denotes not only the thing signified, but the quality of the thing' (p. 109), the emotions associated with it. *Ecphonesis* (or *exclamatio*) 'is a pathetical figure, whereby as the Orator or speaker expresses the vehement affection and passion of his own mind, so he also excites and stirs up the minds and affections of those to whom he speaks' (p. 140). *Aposiopesis* may arise through 'some affection, as either of sorrow, bashfulnesse, fear, anger, or

---

[52] Quoted from Smith 1657, incorporated into the text. Some authorities ascribe this book to the Catholic controversialist John Sargeaunt (1622–1707).

vehemency', and has a direct emotional design on the audience: 'a figure, when speaking of a thing we yet seem to conceal it, though indeed by this means we aggravate it' (p. 148). Even *pleonasmus*, which other writers or periods would see as a vice of style, is described in the affect-oriented seventeenth century as 'a figure whereby some superfluous word is added in a sentence to signifie emphatically the vehemency and earnestnesse of the speaker, and the certainty of the matter spoken'. Having quoted several biblical instances of this figure, Smith insists that 'these Pleonastical inculcations are not vain, but serve to work things the better upon our hard hearts' (pp. 186–7).

All these figures come under the general category of *pathopoeia*, 'a form of speech whereby the Speaker moves the minds of his hearers to some vehemency of affection, as of love, hatred, gladnesse, sorrow, &c. It is when the speaker himself (being inwardly moved with any of those deep and vehement affections), doth by evident demonstration, passionate pronunciation and suitable gestures make a lively expression thereof' (p. 266). Cicero, Quintilian, and Horace continue to be newly discovered by each generation. In keeping with the general tendency I have noted, Smith gives the tropes a cognitive or didactic, not an emotional function. *Synecdoche* 'gives a grace unto speech, . . . enforcing the understanding of the hearers to a deeper consideration of the sense and meaning' (pp. 32–3). *Metalepsis*, 'a kinde of Metonymie, signifying by the effect a Cause far off by an effect nigh at hand, . . . teaches the understanding to dive down to the bottom of the sense, and instructs the eye of the wit to discern a meaning afar off' (p. 52). Smith even goes out of his way to deny *similitudo* an affective function: 'Note that similitudes are rather to make dark things plain, than to prove any doubtful thing; similitudes are not argumentative, as appears by the parable of the unjust Steward, in Luk. 16. 6. 7, &c' (pp. 211–12).

Like so many rhetoricians, Smith is a synthesizer rather than an originator: as Susenbrotus modestly—and accurately—wrote of his work, '*Collector, non auctor, ego sum*'. Rather more original was George Puttenham, for the author of *The Arte of English Poesie*[53] (written *c.* 1569–85; printed 1589) moves with equal ease

[53] Quoted from Puttenham 1936, incorporated into the text.

332 THE EXPRESSIVE FUNCTION OF RHETORICAL FIGURES

from philosophical and historical aspects to both technicalities and *jeux d'esprit*. Here rhetoric is held to be essential to poetry, as he explains in the first chapter of the third book, 'Of Ornament': 'the chief prayse and cunning of our Poet is in the discreet using of his figures . . . with a delectable varietie, by all measure and just proportion, and in places most aptly to be bestowed' (p. 138): decorum must rule. The next chapter argues that although we should not 'use figurative speeches foolishly', it would be a grave error not to use them at all, by which our writing or speeches would be 'but as ordinary talk, than which nothing can be more unsavourie and farre from all civilitie'. If the highest persons in the land were to speak, they 'ought to doe it cunningly and eloquently, which can not be without the use of figures' (pp. 138–9). Here is the basic principle of Renaissance literary language: figures are the *sine qua non* of excellence, and 'plain speeche' is simply crude. Puttenham also provides the best statement of the need for an organic relation between the figure and the sense, commenting on such a clumsy repetition as

'To love him and love him, as sinners should doo.' These repetitions be not figurative but phantastical, *for a figure is ever used to a purpose, either of beautie or of efficacie*: and these last recited be to no purpose, for neither can ye say that it urges affection [passion], nor that it beautifieth or enforceth the sence, nor hath any other subtilitie in it, and therefore is a very foolish impertinency of speech, and not a figure. (p. 202; my italics)

The harshness of tone here, from this generally urbane writer, is an additional sign of the seriousness with which the Renaissance took its notion of decorum.

The writer must use the figures, then, in an organic relationship to his subject-matter, either for emotional or intellectual conviction, or just for beauty. So the poet is urged to make use of the sententious figures, which are not only pregnant with meaning, but also have a melodious, 'auricular' effect, 'because the eare is no lesse ravished with their currant tune than the mind is with their sententiousness. For the eare is properly but an instrument of conveyance for the minde, to apprehend the sence by the sound' (p. 196). This is surely for its date a remarkable awareness of the relationship between sound and sense. In his comments on particular figures Puttenham can be very perceptive. To *aposiopesis* (pp. 166–7), which he describes as 'the figure of silence, or of interruption', he gives several possible psychological motives: 'if we doo interrupt our speech for feare' it is suitable; or 'for shame'; or 'for anger or by way of menace'. The figure is equally apt 'to show a moderation of wrath as the grave and discreeter sort of men do', or just 'upon some sodaine occasion', and he adds a further hint as to the sort of character who might be shown using it: 'This figure is fit for phantasticall heads and such as be sodaine or lacke memorie.' Here are five possible states of mind which the figure *aposiopesis* can re-create: the polysemous quality of the figures is recognized once more. Again, like contemporary and classical rhetoricians, Puttenham sees the specific power of *asyndeton*: 'we utter it in that fashion, when either we be earnest, or would seeme to make hast' (p. 213). Like Hoskins, he has a good sense of the particular figures which characterize a writer's style, noting Ralegh's frequent use of figures of repetition (*anaphora*, p. 198; *epizeuxis* and *ploche*, p. 201), and Sidney's involuted wit (p. 202).

Puttenham, as we have seen, made one of the most perceptive statements of the relationship between rhetoric and life (quoted above, p. 300). His conception of the rhetorical figures as imaging human thought and emotion had been stated before, but Puttenham goes beyond other theorists by invoking the perennial dispute between nature and art, and resolving it into a philosophical view of the artistic process which suggests at once Plato and Coleridge. Of the three liberal arts which make up the traditional trivium, he writes,

I call those artes of Grammer, *Logicke*, and *Rhetorick* not bare imitations, as the painters or kervers craft and worke in a forraine subject viz. a lively purtraite in his table or wood, but by long and studious observation rather a repetition or reminiscens naturall, reduced into perfection, and made prompt by use and exercise. (p. 306)

The ancient triad 'Art, Imitation, Exercise' is thus given a philosophical extension, the artist using language not just to observe nature but to re-create it. It follows that the poet, having mastered the art of expressing himself in the most effective 'maner of language and stile . . . whereof the many moodes and strange phrases are called figures', must transcend this art and return to nature, where he began. His work, 'even as nature herselfe working by her owne peculiar vertue and proper instinct and not by example or meditation or exercise as all other artificers do, is then most admired when he is most naturall and least artificial' (p. 301). The sanity and perceptiveness of Puttenham's book is such that we might well accept his linking of the growth of rhetoric and the development of poetry in the way that Sir John Harington did in 1591. Appending 'A Brief Apology for Poetry' to his translation of Orlando Furioso, Harington earnestly recommended his readers to study the Arte of English Poesie 'where, as it were, a whole receit of Poetrie is described, with so manie new named figures as would put me in great hope in this age to come would breed manie excellent Poets'.[54] The living proof that in this period theory was put into practice can be found in the supremely fluid 'reminiscens naturall' of rhetoric in the works of Sidney, Shakespeare, Donne, George Herbert, Milton. Art and nature were one.

Sir Ernest Gombrich once said that 'in classical writings on rhetoric we have perhaps the most careful analysis of any expressive medium ever undertaken'.[55] Renaissance treatments of rhetoric, I would argue, are even more sensitive to its literary value, and to its importance for the practising poet. The flourishing of rhetoric attended the emergence of Greek literature: evidently rhetoric played a key role in the rise of a language as well as of its greatest literature. The decline of rhetoric in the wake of logic's rise to power in the Middle Ages was followed by a decline in poetry. Certainly the rediscovery of rhetoric in the Renaissance coincided with a great spurt of literary creativity in all the vernaculars. The intense verbal discipline of rhetoric, its emphasis on invention, composition, and an expressivity suited to context and feeling, can now be seen not as the perverse development of 'arid' devices lacking any rationale, but as a training offering both stimulus and guidance. While we concede that the rhetoricians occasionally overstated the automatic nature of persuasion, and may have ascribed to some tropes affective qualities that we cannot

[54] Smith 1904, ii. 196.
[55] Gombrich 1960, p. 317.

conceive of, this wide agreement over a long period of time—from Aristotle to the seventeenth century and beyond—that 'a figure is ever used to a purpose, either of beautie or of efficacie', justifies the claims of rhetoric to be a coherent and functional system, from the first conception of a literary work to the finest details of its language.

IV

Rhetoric-books commonly use examples to illustrate their argument. To complete my case that the descriptions given to specific figures and their effects were not exaggerated, I should like to illustrate them from some familiar passages in Shakespeare.[56] The figure *aposiopesis*, to start with, breaking off a sentence uncompleted, had a wide range of effects ascribed to it, the least dignified being Puttenham's 'fit for phantasticall heads and such as . . . lacke memorie'. We think of Polonius, perhaps:

POLONIUS. And then, sir, does 'a this—'a does—
   what was I about to say?
   By the mass, I was about to say something.
   Where did I leave?
REYNALDO. At 'closes in the consequence'.
POLONIUS. At 'closes in the consequence', ay, marry.
   He closes thus: 'I know the gentleman . . .'
(*Hamlet*, 2. 1. 49 ff.)

Or we recall Justice Shallow losing the thread of his discourse:

SHALLOW. Death, as the Psalmist saith, is certain to all, all
      shall die. How a good yoke of bullocks at Stamford fair?
SILENCE. By my troth, I was not there.
SHALLOW. Death is certain. Is old Double of your town living yet?
SILENCE. Dead, sir.
SHALLOW. Jesu, Jesu, dead! . . . How a score of ewes now?
(2 *Henry IV*, 3. 2. 36 ff.)

---

[56] The text quoted is the Riverside Shakespeare, ed. G. B. Evans (Boston, 1974). See also Joseph 1947; Vickers 1968, and Vickers, 'Shakespeare's Use of Rhetoric', in *A New Companion to Shakespeare Studies*, ed. K. Muir and S. Schoenbaum (Cambridge, 1971), pp. 83–98

For another old man Shakespeare applied *aposiopesis* to evoke a state that no rhetorician thought of, impotent anger:

> No, you unnatural hags,
> I will have such revenges on you both
> That all the world shall—I will do such things—
> What they are yet I know not, but they shall be
> The terrors of the earth!
>
> (*King Lear*, 2. 4. 278 ff.)

The broken-off sentence, Shakespeare observed, is also a peculiarly appropriate way of symbolizing death, as with Hamlet's uncompleted message to Fortinbras:

So tell him, with th'occurrents more and less
Which have solicited—the rest is silence. [*Dies*
(*Hamlet*, 5. 2. 357 f.)

It is typical of Shakespeare's conception of Hamlet that he should himself comment on his expiring life. In other plays it is left to a bystander to complete the sentence:

HOTSPUR.   O, I could prophesy,
   But that the earthy and cold hand of death
   Lies on my tongue. No, Percy, thou art dust,
   And food for— [*Dies*
PRINCE HAL. For worms, brave Percy. Fare thee well, great heart!
(1 *Henry IV* 5. 4. 83 ff.)

More invention—the privileged knowledge of the dramatist, in fact—is needed to complete this last utterance:

CLEOPATRA. As sweet as balm, as soft as air, as gentle—
   O Antony!—Nay, I will take thee too:
·   What should I stay— [*Dies*
CHARMIAN. In this vile world? So fare thee well!
(*Antony and Cleopatra*, 5. 2. 311 ff.)

A different kind of incompleteness is created when *aposiopesis* is used in dialogue. The author of *Ad Herennium* said that 'here a suspicion, unexpressed, becomes more telling than a detailed explanation would have been'. Quintilian, we recall, took the psychology of this process a stage further in describing how the speaker can inject 'some suspicion to indicate that our meaning is other than our words seem to imply', leaving the hearer to discover the hidden meaning. As the hearer does so, the judge —or dupe, we must add—is 'led to seek out the secret which he would not perhaps believe if he heard it openly stated, and to believe in that which he thinks he has found out for himself' (9. 2. 65, 71). The Spaniard Vives, discussing *aposiopesis* and the difference between life and art, writes that 'if someone were to express his true feeling of anger or fear by a moment of silence, this would be natural, for excitement does impede the power of reason. . . . But if the excitement is simulated, we consider it a figure of speech, and call it reticence.' He gives two functions for *reticentia*, one passionate, when 'we try to make our audience believe that we stop speaking for a moment and suppress an outburst of words by doing violence to ourselves'. The other is less passionate, more calculated, for reticence is very suspect 'among men of suspicious natures, who go to great lengths to see sinister conjectures everywhere'.[57] We recall Edmund's manipulation of Gloucester (*King Lear*, 1. 2. 27 ff.), which fits that pattern perfectly, or this more painful sequence:

OTHELLO.   What hath he said?
IAGO. Faith, that he did—I know not what he did.
OTHELLO. What? what?
IAGO. Lie—
OTHELLO. With her?
IAGO. With her? On her; what you will.
OTHELLO. Lie with her? lie on her? We say lie on her, when they belie her. Lie with her! 'Zounds, that's fulsome! Handkerchief—confessions—handkerchief! To confess, and be hang'd for his labour. . . . It is not words that shakes me thus.

(Othello, 4. 1. 31 ff.)

But it is only words, appealing to his fears, and sharpened by the ambiguity (or *syllepsis*) that Iago exploits on 'lie'. Othello's final collapse into unreason is expressed through the figure *hyperbaton*, dislocated word-order mirroring the confusion in his thoughts. A similar figure is used to capture a less tragic

---

[57] Vives 1966, p. 74.

experience, Sylock's double loss and double lament, first in a report of his raving exclamations:

> My daughter! O my ducats! O my daughter!
> Fled with a Christian! O my Christian ducats!
> Justice! the law! my ducats, and my daughter!
>
> (*Merchant of Venice*, 2. 8. 12 ff.)

The Jew's 'confus'd' passion is seen directly later on, when he simultaneously laments Jessica's loss and gloats over Antonio's misfortune (3. 1. 85 ff.).

Shylock's lamentations naturally express themselves in *exclamatio*, a figure Shakespeare uses both in tragic and in mock-tragic situations, such as the parody of Pyramus and Thisbe—'O dainty duck! O dear!' (*Midsummer Night's Dream*, 5. 1. 276 ff.), or the Nurse's erroneously premature lament for the death of Juliet:

> O woe! O woeful, woeful, woeful day!
> Most lamentable day, most woeful day
> That ever, ever, I did yet behold!
> O day, O day, O day, O hateful day!
>
> (*Romeo and Juliet*, 4. 3. 49 ff.)

Since the grief is unfounded, those lines are obviously meant to be ridiculous. Yet in the later tragedies impassioned repetition is expressed through the same figures *ploche* and *epizeuxis* to a devastating effect:

> OTHELLO. If she come in, she'll sure speak to my wife.
>   My wife, my wife! what wife? I have no wife.
>   O insupportable! O heavy hour! (5. 2. 96 ff.)

There the recoil against the word just spoken—'what wife?'—is the figure *epanorthosis*. It is striking to note that Shakespeare only ever uses *epizeuxis* (repeating a word with no other word intervening) for the extremes of tragic feeling, whether madness:

> I'll put't in proof,
> And when I have stol'n upon these son-in-laws,
> Then kill, kill, kill, kill, kill, kill!
>
> (*King Lear*, 4. 6. 185 ff.)

—or anguish:

Howl, howl, howl!   (5. 3. 257)

—or despair:

> Thoul't come no more,
> Never, never, never, never, never.   (309 f.)

—or meaninglessness:

> To-morrow, and to-morrow, and to-morrow,
> Creeps in this petty pace from day to day,
> To the last syllable of recorded time.
>
> *(Macbeth,* 5. 5. 19 ff.)

As one classical rhetorician put it, 'the reiteration of the same word makes a deep impression on the hearer', since, as a Renaissance counterpart saw, 'no man is sick in thought upon one thing but for some vehemency or distress'.

May those few examples, and the coherence of rhetorical theory behind them, make anyone tempted to dismiss the minutiae of rhetoric accept the figures and tropes as expressive devices in their own right, linguistic forms that contain, and arouse, many possible relationships between meaning and feeling.

7

RHETORIC AND THE SISTER ARTS

One distinctively new application of rhetoric in the Renaissance was to the fine arts, sculpture, architecture and, above all, painting. Classical rhetoric and art criticism had made some general claims for the relationship between poetry, rhetoric, and the visual arts, claims which crop up time and again in the Renaissance. The most often quoted parallels come from Horace's *Ars Poetica*,[1] the famous tags *ut pictura poesis* (361 ff.) and *pictoribus atque poetis* (9 ff.). The latter derives from the work's opening injunction not to mingle violently differing styles or subject-matter, to which Horace imagines an objection:

'Painters and poets', you say, 'have always had an equal right in hazarding anything'. We know it: this licence we poets claim and in our turn we grant the like; but not so far that savage should mate with tame, or serpents couple with birds, lambs with tigers. (9–13)

Even more influential was Horace's later comparison of the two arts in terms of their scale and intended effect:

A poem is like a picture: one strikes your fancy more, the nearer you stand; another, the farther away. This courts the shade, that will wish to be seen in the light. (361–3)

Usually taken to mean 'as is poetry so is painting', and frequently misunderstood,[2] this tag was ubiquitous in art as in literary criticism between the fifteenth and the eighteenth centuries. Almost as popular was the idea which Plutarch ascribed to Simonides, that 'painting is mute poetry, poetry a speaking picture'.[3] Less influential, but certainly known to

---

[1] The translation used is by H. R. Fairclough, Loeb Classical Library (London, rev. edn., 1929).

[2] Lee 1967, p. 3; Trimpi 1973 and 1983 are the best studies of the deformation of Horace by the critical tradition. For his role in literary—and hence rhetorical—criticism see Weinberg 1961.

[3] Plutarch, *De Gloria Atheniensium, Moralia* 346f–347c. Partially cit. Baxandall 1971, pp. 100–1.

humanists, were those passages in Quintilian comparing the
development of oratory with that of painting and sculpture
(12. 10. 2), or references to specific ancient works of art.[4]

I

While absorbing these classical ideas Renaissance humanists
went far beyond them, systematizing the discussion of the
visual arts by superimposing on them the categories and
processes of rhetoric. In a sense, it was inevitable that they
should do so, since rhetoric offered the only complete and
integrated communication system. What had been done for
language—on the grounds of its usefulness to life and business
—had not been done for painting, architecture, or music. Given
the revival, in the fourteenth and fifteenth centuries, of an
educational system based on the language-arts, it was also
inevitable that theorists should have applied concepts derived
from grammar, logic, and rhetoric to arts which did not use
language, sometimes resulting in a certain deformation of
the sister arts. As Michael Baxandall has shown so clearly, the
learned treatises of the early humanists carried over into the
visual arts both the strengths and weaknesses of the Latin
language: clarity and control at the level of syntax, but a certain
stiffness and abstraction in vocabulary.[5] If the habits of Latin
were deeply ingrained in the writings of the pioneers in the
Quattrocento, they also revealed a debt to rhetoric which was to
become still more evident in those writing later in Italian and the
other vernaculars. The 'fundamental critical attitudes of
Renaissance writers', as David Summers has written, derived
from rhetoric; but this is not to say that the 'end or means of
painting or poetry were in all respects rhetorical. Rather, the
essential elements of these arts . . . were formed along lines
prepared for them by assumptions almost universally held
throughout the long and continuous history' of rhetoric.

---

[4] See R. G. Austin's edition of Quintilian, Book 12 (Oxford, 1948, 1965); his
article, 'Quintilian on Painting and Statuary', *Classical Quarterly*, 38 (1944), 17–20;
and Baxandall 1971, pp. 117–18.
[5] Baxandall 1971, pp. 8–50. For further comment on the aesthetic concepts and
categories in Quattrocento art theory see Baxandall, *Painting and Experience in
Fifteenth Century Italy* (Oxford, 1972).

Questions of subject-matter, style and audience could be discussed only in the terminology of rhetoric.[6]

Although not necessarily affecting the end or means of painting, in fact rhetoric was often called on to do both. The pioneer treatise, Alberti's *De Pictura* (1435) applies a generally Ciceronian attitude to painting, urging the painter—as Cicero and Quintilian had urged the orator—to master the liberal arts, and associate with learned men.[7] Alberti was himself a humanist, and followed the standard career as a secretary to humanist prelates, joining the hundred or so scholars employed in the papal chancery. His writings include a brief Latin treatise on the rules of rhetoric (written for Lorenzo de' Medici), a small work on moral philosophy, a mock-epideictic poem, and a number of important dialogues on central humanist topics.[8] The very form of *De Pictura* derives from classical rhetoric, in general from the isagogic or elementary treatises which discuss (1) the elements; (2) the art; and (3) the artist.[9] So Alberti devotes his first book to the elements of optics; the second to the branches of painting; and the third to the painter and his moral and professional conduct. More particularly, as D. R. E. Wright has recently shown, Alberti's overall plan corresponds to the structure of Quintilian's *Institutes of Oratory*, in its *elementa / ars / artifex* division.[10] However, comparison of the individual parts will show considerable differences in scale: the second section, on *ars*, occupies nine books, and several hundred pages in Quintilian, only two dozen in Alberti. The classical treatises provided an organizing frame for Alberti, visible to readers versed in classical rhetoric, but the contents and scope of his book were original. Its importance remains, for us as for the Renaissance, of being the first treatise to attempt the union of mathematical theory with painting technique, using geometrical optics to create a coherent system of perspective—although not without difficulties, as commentators have shown.

[6] Summers 1981, pp. 88–9.

[7] Alberti 1972, pp. 95–7; Lee 1967, pp. 17–18.

[8] J. Gadol, *Leon Battista Alberti, Universal Man of the Early Renaissance* (Chicago, 1969), pp. 5, 10, 220, and *passim*.

[9] Gilbert 1943–5, pp. 91 ff., endorsed by Baxandall 1971, p. 126 n. Spencer 1957 suggested, somewhat improbably, that Alberti had based his work on the five-part form of a Ciceronian oration.

[10] Wright 1984. Quintilian at one point states that rhetoric is 'best treated under the three following heads, the art, the artist, and the work', *ars*, *artifex*, and *opus* (2. 14. 5), but he does not follow the scheme through.

Rhetoric is secondary, then, but still accounts for some characteristic emphases that were to be taken further in the more literary, less practical treatises that followed. Alberti knows enough about rhetoric to include a disclaimer of eloquence, although he draws on Cicero and Quintilian frequently.[11] His praise of painting (pp. 60–6) echoes the techniques of epideictic rhetoric, including the *paragone* or formal claim for the superiority of one art to its rivals, in which the twin modes of *laus* and *vituperatio* are used to elevate painting and depress sculpture, architecture, or whatever else. He uses *partitio* to outline his treatment of painting in Book II (p. 66), and ends it with the matching summing-up (p. 92). Alberti defines the aim of painting as being 'to represent things seen', proceeding in three stages: *circumscriptio*, where the painter draws the outline of the things to be represented; *compositio*, which unifies the 'several surfaces of the object seen'; and *luminum receptio*, the reception of light as it defines 'the colours of surfaces' (p. 67). Two of his three categories have certain analogues in the language-arts. *Circumscriptio* is a term in rhetoric, 'an encircling', referred to briefly by Cicero (*De Or.* 3. 54. 207), and apparently means 'definition'.[12] *Compositio*, as Michael Baxandall has shown, is a term in grammar and rhetoric, 'the putting together of the single evolved sentence or period', in which words make up phrases, phrases make up clauses, and clauses make up sentences.[13] In just the same way

[11] Alberti 1972, p. 59. For sources in classical rhetoric see ibid., pp. 60 ff., nn. 6, 9, 12, 38, 47, 49, 50, 51, 53, 53a, 60, 61, 63, 64, 79; Spencer 1957, pp. 32–4. Future quotations are from this translation, by Cecil Grayson. John Spencer's version, Alberti 1966, translates the later Italian text, and while less reliable than Grayson's is considerably more helpful on Alberti's use of rhetoric. For the rhetorical elements in Alberti's *De Re Aedificatoria* see, e.g., H. Mühlmann, *Ästhetische Theorie der Renaissance. Leon Battista Alberti* (Bonn, 1981). Alberti designed temples in accordance with the rhetorical concept of the *'genus grande'*; memorials in terms of epideictic rhetoric; and domestic buildings as instances of the *'genus humile'*.

[12] Sonnino 1968, p. 67, says that *circumscriptio* is a synonym for *definitio*: but as often without giving any authority for her statement. The Loeb translator of Cicero renders *circumscriptio* as *periphrasis*, but in Thomas Wilson's *The Arte of Rhetorique* (1533; rev. 1560) it is defined as 'a briefe descrybing or declaryng of a thyng': Wilson 1982, p. 413.

[13] Baxandall 1971, p. 130. Wright 1984, pp. 63–4, however, insists on the derivation of *compositio* from Pliny's history of painting, *Naturalis Historia*, 35. 5. 16, 35. 11. 29; but also acknowledges the elaboration of the idea through the component parts in rhetoric (*Inst. Or.* 8. 5. 26–9). On *compositio* in classical rhetoric see Cicero, *Brutus*, 8. 34; *De Or.* 3. 48. 171–98; *Orator*, 61. 204–67. 226; Quintilian, 8. 2. 22, 6. 62–7, 9. 4. 1–147. One of the pioneers of the rhetorical

Alberti defines composition as

> that procedure in painting whereby the parts are composed together in a picture. The great work of the painter is the 'historia'; parts of the 'historia' are the bodies, part of the body is the member, and part of the member is a surface. (p. 71; repeated, evidently for didactic reasons, on p. 73)

He then goes on to describe the practical applications of optics to perspective in the drawing of planes (pp. 70 ff.).

Alberti's term for the subject of a painting derives ultimately from the Greek word *historia*, which originally had no connotations of diachronic, or chronologically ordered narrative. As in Aristotle's *Historia Animalium* it merely meant a synchronic treatment of a subject, as systematic as the limits of knowledge and the scale of the treatise would allow. Alberti never defines what he means by *historia*, but his discussion of its component parts and effect on the viewer reveals that he is still thinking in literary, and specifically in rhetorical terms. In rendering surfaces, he writes, the painter must seek for 'grace and beauty', observing and imitating nature. When he reaches the more detailed stages of members he must first take care 'that all the members accord well with one another', which will happen 'when in size, function, kind, colour and other similar respects they correspond to grace and beauty' (p. 73). This is the rhetorical concept of *decorum*, an idea which runs throughout the whole of Book II, carrying with it the notion of internal coherence, a functionality in which 'all the members fulfil their proper function according as to the action being performed' (p. 75). This injunction to 'see to it that all the members perform their appropriate movements' (p. 77) has obvious parallels in the

revival in Italy, Gasparino Barzizza, in his treatise *De Compositione* (1420), defined three essential qualities of rhetorical composition, *compositio* (divided into *iunctura* or *nexus; ordo; numerus* or *rhythmus), elegantia,* and *dignitas* (Woodward 1897, p. 55): his source is *Ad Herennium*, 4. 12. 17 ff. An important modern study is Aldo Scaglione, *The Classical Theory of Composition from its Origins to the Present. A Historical Survey* (Chapel Hill, NC, 1972), who lists some twenty-three ancient sources for *compositio* (pp. 25–6), before analysing the classical theories (pp. 8–96), their development in the Renaissance (pp. 126–58), and the period 1600–1800 (pp. 159–336). This book seems to be unknown to art-historians. For further comment on *compositio*, narrative, and other verbal concepts, see Georg Kauffmann, 'Sprache und bildende Kunst in der Renaissance', in A. Buck (ed.), *Die Rezeption der Antike* (Hamburg, 1981), pp. 237–79.

rhetoricians' emphasis that all the parts of a speech should cohere, like the limbs of a body.[14] Quintilian's long discussion of order and unity in a speech, replete with metaphors from the human body, warns the orator that 'it is not enough merely to arrange the various parts: each several part has its own internal economy . . .'. We must attempt 'not merely to place [our] thoughts in their proper order, but to link them together and give them such cohesion that there will be no trace of any suture: they must form a body, not a congeries of limbs' (7. 10. 16). Alberti's recommendation of *decorum* includes appropriateness of dress, movement, and personality (p. 75), all topics discussed at length in the classical rhetoric books.

The rhetorical influence on Alberti comes out most strongly in his discussion of the effect of the *historia*. A painting, he believes, consists of an imitation of nature made with an eye to its impact on the spectator. That *historia* will be praised which will 'be so charming and attractive as to hold the eye of the learned and unlearned spectator'—it is for the world at large, not for an élite—with a 'sense of pleasure and emotion' (*animi motu*: p. 79). Alberti is now applying to painting the three *officia oratoris: docere, delectare, movere*. He says least about the first, although some would ascribe a didactic purpose to *historia*,[15] and Alberti certainly uses the word *docere*. He also describes the painter as a man of good morals, which presumably means that he will produce 'good' works. As for *delectare*, 'the first thing that gives pleasure in a *historia* is a plentiful variety . . . variety and abundance' (p. 79). These are the rhetorical concepts of *copia* and *varietas*,[16] to which Alberti correctly adds the caution to apply decorum and control, in order to produce unity, not 'random confusion' (p. 79). His greatest emphasis, appropriately in tune with the whole direction of Renaissance rhetoric, is on *movere*:

A 'historia' will move [*movebit*] spectators when the men painted in the

[14] On organic unity in the rhetoric-books see also *De Inv.* 1. 18. 26; *De Or.* 2. 80. 325, 2. 88. 359, 3. 45. 179–3. 46. 180; *Brutus*, 17. 68; Quintilian, 7. Pr. 2, *et seq.; Ad Her.* 4. 45. 58, with Caplan's note giving other examples.

[15] Wright 1984, p. 52 n. 3.

[16] For *copia* see Quintilian, 10. 1. 5 (the phrase *copia rerum ac verborum* which also occurs in Book III of *De Oratore*), 8. Pr. 13 ff., and much of Book 8. For *varietas* see *De Inv.* 1. 41. 76; Quintilian, 2. 13. 8 ff.; Shearman 1967, pp. 139, 141; and H. L. F. Drijepondt, *Die antike Theorie der 'varietas'* (Hildesheim, 1979).

picture outwardly demonstrate their own feelings [*animi motum*] as clearly as possible. Nature provides—and there is nothing to be found more rapacious of her like than she,—that we mourn with the mourners, laugh with those who laugh, and grieve with the grief-stricken. Yet these feelings are known from movements of the body. We see how the melancholy, preoccupied with cares and beset by grief, lack all vitality of feeling and action, and remain sluggish, their limbs unsteady and drained of colour. In those who mourn, the brow is weighed down, the neck bent, and every part of their body droops as though weary and past care. (p. 81)

Alberti adds similarly graphic accounts of anger and happiness, before urging the painter to use 'the necessary study and care' to learn about 'the movements of the body, which I believe he must take from Nature with great skill. It is extremely difficult to vary the movements of the body in accordance with the almost infinite movements of the heart' (ibid.). Here is where skill in imitation must also draw on suggestion, leaving 'more for the mind to imagine than is seen by the eye'.

Alberti is here drawing on the major principles of classical rhetoric concerning *movere*, the natural response of the listener or spectator to the orator's or poet's grief or happiness. A well-known passage in Horace (quoted above, p. 50) describes the poet's affective power in identical terms, and as we have seen, both Cicero and Quintilian emphasize the need for the orator to feel the emotions he wishes to present (above, pp. 79–80). The painter must similarly depict the emotional and psychological states of the people he represents, through their bodily movements and gestures. Here Alberti opens up a link between painting theory and the doctrine of rhetorical gesture which was to prove enormously fruitful for painting theory in the next three centuries. To enhance the emotional impact, he suggests, the artist should include a commentator within the painting, to guide the viewer's eye and feelings:

I like there to be someone in the 'historia' who tells the spectators what is going on, and either beckons them with his hand to look, or with ferocious expression and forbidding glance challenges them not to come near, . . . or points to some danger or remarkable thing in the picture, or by his gestures invites you to laugh or weep with them. Everything the people in the painting do among themselves, or

Fig. 5. Masaccio:
The Trinity

perform in relation to the spectators, must fit together to represent and explain [*ad agendam et docendam*] the 'historia'. (p. 83)

At the end of that passage Alberti explicitly invokes the rhetorical concept of *docere*, while his account of the commentator's range of, and power over whatever emotions he chooses to summon up ('to laugh or weep') is a stock ingredient of the rhetoric-texts discussing *movere*. In effect Alberti's commentator within the painting fulfils the same role as the Greek or Roman orator in a lawcourt, describing the events which have led up to the law case, and the emotions of his clients or himself, in terms of outrage, anger, or pity. A number of passages in Cicero and Quintilian come to mind describing the deportment of an advocate in court in rather similar terms.[17]

At this point the urge to cite actual examples of the representation of emotions becomes very great. (My own

[17] See, e.g., *De Or.* 2. 44. 188, 2. 47. 197; *Brutus*, 84. 290 and 49. 187: the 'listening throng is delighted, is carried along by' the orator's words, and 'feel now joy now sorrow, are moved now to laughter, now to tears; . . . are stirred to anger, wonder, hope, fear'.

candidate, if I may briefly impose, would be Masaccio's Trinity, in Santa Maria Novella, where the figure of Mary standing before the crucified body of Christ looks out at us while her left hand points limply backwards towards the dead body in a gesture of flaccid grief, as if her feelings were numbed, deprived of energy.) Alberti cites one classical example, the immolation of Iphigenia (which he had learned about from Cicero and Quintilian, especially the latter's Book 2, chapter 13, much studied by Renaissance art-theorists[18]), and one modern, the mosaic of the 'Navicella' (Christ walking on the water) which Giotto made for Old St Peter's:

They also praise in Rome the boat in which our Tuscan painter Giotto represented the eleven disciples struck with fear and wonder at the sight of their colleague walking on the water, each showing such clear signs of his agitation in his face and entire body that their individual emotions are discernible in every one of them. (p. 83)

In connection with such passages we might recall *De Oratore*, where Cicero declares *actio*, the union of voice and gesture, to be 'the dominant factor in oratory' (3. 56. 213) because it presents every emotion forcefully (above, p. 66). Gesture 'is wholly the concern of the feelings' (3. 59. 221), and in gesture

the body talks, so it is all the more necessary to make it agree with the thought; and nature has given us eyes . . . to indicate the feelings of the mind . . . . And all the factors of delivery contain a certain force bestowed by nature.

Rhetorical gesture 'gives the emotion of the mind expression', which accounts for its great effectiveness, even on the unlearned (223). This graphic account of gesture as expressing inner feeling-states had a considerable influence on Alberti, and beyond him on many other art theorists.

Following the tradition of Aristotle, Cicero, Quintilian, and others, Alberti now briefly itemizes the 'movements of the mind, which the learned call dispositions [*affectiones*], such as anger, grief, joy, fear, desire' (p. 83). Then he considers movements of the body, always in connection with rhetoric's emphasis on the need to exteriorize feeling:

We painters . . . who wish to represent emotions through the

<hr>

[18] Quintilian, 2. 13. 13; Cicero, *Orator*, 22. 74; Pliny, *Nat. Hist.* 35. 36. 73–4.

movements of limbs, may leave other arguments aside and speak only of the movements that occur when there is a change of position. Everything which changes position has seven directions of movement, either up or down or right or left, or going away in the distance or coming towards us; and the seventh is going around in a circle. I want all these seven movements to be in a painting. (p. 83)

Apparently original here, in fact, as John Spencer first showed,[19] Alberti is very close to Quintilian (11. 3. 105). Spencer expresses surprise that, 'instead of turning to the observation of nature as one would expect a Renaissance man to do, he turns to Roman oratorical practice',[20] but this is not as odd as it seems once we recall the degree to which Roman writers insisted that rhetoric drew from life. Alberti's subsequent account of the *varietas* in the postures of the human body also derives from a much-quoted passage in Quintilian (2. 13. 8–10).

Alberti did claim to have 'gathered from nature' the following observations 'about the attitude and movements of the limbs'. Noting that 'in every attitude a man positions his whole body beneath his head, which is the heaviest member of all', he observed that

the movements of the head in any direction are hardly ever such that he does not always have some other parts of the body positioned beneath to sustain the enormous weight, or at least he extends some limb in the opposite direction like the other arm of a balance, to correspond to that weight. When someone holds a weight on his outstretched hand, we see how, with one foot fixed like the axis of a balance, the rest of the body is counterpoised to balance the weight. (p. 85)

At one level this is sensitive empirical observation; at another, it both draws on rhetoric and opens the way for others to extend its borrowing. David Summers has stated that theories of human movement in the Renaissance were based on the idea of contraposition, which derives from an Aristotelian definition of movement as 'a condition of axial disequilibrium of parts of the body'. But, more specifically, the word

contrapposto, now exclusively used for a figural posture in which the weight of the body is shifted to one leg with a consequent adjustment of the other parts of the body, is taken from the Latin *contrapositum*, in

---

[19] Alberti 1966, p. 127 n. 65; Alberti 1972, p. 82 n. 49.
[20] Spencer 1957, p. 33.

turn translated from the Greek *antithesis*, a rhetorical figure in which opposites were set directly against one another. In the Renaissance, *contrapposto* had a wider meaning than it has now, and could refer to any opposition—*chiaroscuro*, for example, or the juxtapositions of old and young, male or female.[21]

One further type of *contrapposto*, I would add, can be found in epideictic rhetoric, with its juxtaposition in the same descriptive sequence of a beautiful and a 'loathly' lady, as recommended by medieval arts of poetry and practised by Boccaccio, among others.[22] This may account for the frequent occurrence, in Leonardo's notes and drawings, of the head of a young boy and an old man, side by side. Leonardo certainly supplies one of the best instances of *contrapposto* in his Leda and the Swan, a chiastic interplay of forms which was to have great influence on Raphael, Michelangelo, and later artists.[23]

From the same chapter in Quintilian which Alberti had drawn on, almost verbatim, for the account of Timanthes' painting of the sacrifice of Iphigenia (2. 13. 13), and for its description of the *varietas* in bodily postures (2. 13. 8–10), Renaissance art-theorists read with great interest this comparison between sculpture and rhetoric:

Dress, expression and attitude are frequently varied. The body when held bolt upright has but little grace, for the face looks straight forward, the arms hang by the side, the feet are joined and the whole figure is stiff from top to toe. But that curve, I might almost call it motion, with which we are so familiar, gives an impression of action and animation. . . . Where can we find a more violent [*distortum*] and elaborated attitude than that of the Discobolus of Myron? Yet the critic who disapproved of the figure because it was not upright, would merely show his utter failure to understand the sculptor's art, in which the very novelty and difficulty of execution is what most deserves our praise. A similar impression of grace and charm is produced by rhetorical figures. . . . For they involve a certain departure from the straight line and have the merit of variation from the ordinary usage. (2. 13. 8–12)

    [21] Summers 1981, p. 76. On *contrapositum* see Quintilian, 9. 3. 81, 83; *contraposita*: 9. 3. 32.
    [22] Faral 1924, pp. 76–7; Boccaccio, *Filocolo*; *Sir Gawain and the Green Knight*, ll. 942–69; E. Gallo, *The Poetria Nova and Its Sources in Early Rhetorical Doctrine* (The Hague, 1971), pp. 181 ff.; Gordon 1970, p. 39.
    [23] Summers 1981, pp. 80–5.

This passage, in which Quintilian lays down one of the fundamental justifications for *elocutio* and the doctrine of the figures, was echoed by numerous Renaissance art-theorists.[24] It also provided part of the theoretical justification, as Summers has shown, for the evolution of the 'serpentine figure', so important in the art of the high Renaissance, and discussed at length by Lomazzo (drawing on both Alberti and Quintilian), in his *Trattato dell'arte de la pittura* (Milan, 1584).[25]

Other elements of rhetoric appear in Alberti's third book. The 'aim of the painter' is said to be 'to obtain praise, favour and good-will for his work much more than riches' (p. 95). In addition to *delectare*, this passage contains a number of elements drawn from rhetoric. According to the somewhat optimistic scheme of classical and Renaissance ethics, fame was the public response to an individual's virtue, as if excellence were automatically awarded. Epideictic rhetoric existed in order to praise virtue and dispraise vice, and it was encouraged to use the classical philosophical–rhetorical distinction which set intrinsic values (virtue, goodness) over extrinsic ones (fortune, riches).[26] Hence Alberti's repeated stress on fame as the painter's goal. The notion of good will, secondly, derives from the rhetorical category of *ethos*, as Alberti shows more clearly in urging the painter to be, or become 'a good man, well versed in the liberal arts. Everyone knows how much more effective uprightness of character is in securing people's favour than any amount of admiration for someone's industry and art.' (p. 95). Their good will is moved 'by kindness more than by expert knowledge of art', so the painter is urged to be of sound morals, and display 'good manners and amiability' (ibid.). As we have seen (above, pp. 19–20, 35) Aristotle first formulated this concept of the orator's character as a major ingredient of his success, and the Roman developments of the *captatio benevolentiae* were

[24] Baxandall 1971, pp. 18–19; Summers 1981, pp. 91–2.
[25] Summers 1981, Index s.v. *'figura serpentina'*; Shearman 1967, p. 84.
[26] See, e.g., Cicero, *De Inv.* 2. 53. 159, 2. 59. 178; *De Or.* 2. 84. 342 f.; *Part. Or.* 24. 86–7; Quintilian, 3. 7. 10–14, 26. It is one of the disappointments of his valuable study that David Summers should have grasped only the superficial, trivialized concept of epideictic rhetoric as display for a learned audience, rather than its serious ethical function, which I have outlined in Chapter 1 (pp. 54–62). See Summers 1981, pp. 18, 42–3, 165–7, and 483 n. 54.

designed to evince aspects of character very close to those described by Alberti.[27] Thirdly, his call for the orator to be a *vir bonus*, placed in his final book in a position parallel to Quintilian's twelfth book, makes his debt to that work explicit. Alberti recommends that the painter master all the liberal arts, especially geometry (p. 95), a subject which Quintilian had praised highly (1. 10. 34–49). Artists, he recommends, should 'take pleasure in poets and orators, for those have many ornaments [i.e. expressive resources] in common with the painter'. Further, 'literary men' could be very useful to a painter 'preparing the composition of a 'historia', [for] the great virtue of this consists primarily in its invention. Indeed, invention is such that even by itself and without pictorial representation it can give pleasure' (p. 95). Alberti's two instances of fruitful inventions both became popular in Renaissance painting, the Calumny of Apelles and the Three Graces.[28] Poets and rhetoricians, he stresses again, can assist the painter 'in those very inventions which . . . may gain him the greatest praise' (p. 97).

To invention Alberti joins the matching concept from rhetoric, imitation, the complementary processes that formed the main sources of literary creativity for classical and Renaissance writers. The version of imitation that he recommends is where the artist assembles an ideal form by selecting the most beautiful individuals, illustrated by the famous story of Zeuxis, who chose the best features from 'five outstandingly beautiful girls, so that he might represent in his painting whatever feature of feminine beauty' he chose (p. 99). Alberti's version closely resembles that found in Cicero's *De Inventione*, and his concept of the 'idea of beauty' probably owes more to Cicero than to Plato.[29] Almost any of the classical rhetorics, from Aristotle to

[27] See, e.g., Aristotle, *Rhet.* 1415ª 34 ff.; *Ad Her.* 1. 4. 6–1. 7. 11; *De Inv.* 1. 15. 20–1. 18. 26; *De Or.* 2. 42. 182 f., 2. 43. 184, 2. 46. 192; *Part. Or.* 9. 32; Quintilian, 2. 15. 2–33, 12. 1. 1 f.

[28] See Jean-Michel Massing, *Du texte à l'image. La Calomnie d'Apelle et son iconographie* (Strasbourg, 1988); and Edgar Wind, 'Seneca's Graces', *Pagan Mysteries in the Renaissance* (rev. edn., Harmondsworth, 1967), pp. 26–35.

[29] Alberti 1966, pp. 93, 133. On imitation see Lee 1967, pp. 7–8, 10, 25; Baxandall 1971, pp. 40, 43, 103; Summers 1981, Index s.v. 'Imitation'; although I do not see how Summers can describe the traditional metaphor of the poet gathering his material like a bee going from flower to flower as another version of 'poetic furor' (p. 192): these are surely very different.

the *Ad Herennium*, could lie behind Alberti's insistence that the artist's 'fundamental principle' is to learn from Nature, but that 'the means of perfecting our art will be found in diligence, study and application' (p. 97).[30] Quintilian (1. 1. 24–35) seems to be the inspiration for his recommendation that 'those who begin to learn the art of painting do what I see practised by teachers of writing. They first teach all the signs of the alphabet separately, and then how to put syllables together, and then whole words' (p. 97). The literary analogy recurs when he recommends painters to use their notebook drawings for the finished painting, transferring 'our sketch models . . . from our private papers' (pp. 103–5). The notebook technique, so vital to Renaissance humanist culture,[31] finds its rightful place in the arts. In the closing pages two injunctions recur over and over: that 'the gifts of Nature should be cultivated and increased by industry, study and practice' (p. 103), and that painters 'should first think well about what they are going to do, and then carry it out with great diligence. Indeed diligence is no less welcome than native ability in many things' (p. 105). Parallels in the rhetorical tradition, particularly Quintilian, may by now seem superfluous.[32]

For all the comparative brevity of his work, especially considering the space he devotes to purely technical considerations of drawing and painting, Alberti succeeded in anticipating almost all the applications of rhetorical theory to the visual arts during the Renaissance. The range of later treatises applying rhetorical criteria is striking: from Filarete on architecture in the 1430s to Pomponius Gauricus on sculpture in 1504, from the *Dialogo di pittura* (1548) of Paolo Pino, and the *Dialogo della pittura intitolato l'Aretino* (1557) of Lodovico Dolce to the later work of Danti, Comanini, and Lomazzo.[33] Predictably

[30] For the triad 'Nature, Theory, Practice' see *Ad. Her.* 1. 2. 3; *De Inv.* 1. 1. 2; *De Or.* 1. 4. 14; and Quintilian, 7. 10. 14, 11. 3. 11.

[31] See Bolgar 1954. Spencer 1957, p. 37, cites *De Oratore*, 2. 28. 117–51.

[32] See, e.g., *De Or.* 2. 35. 147; *Brutus*, 93. 321 (Cicero's account of how he perfected himself as an orator: 'I . . . did not cease from my efforts to increase such gifts as I had by every type of exercise . . . '); and Quintilian, 2. 13. 15, 2. 17. 42, 7. 10. 14, 10. 7. 24.

[33] The best collections of this material are those edited by Paola Barocchi, *Trattati d'arte del Cinquecento*, 3 vols. (Bari, 1960–2), which reprints whole treatises (with an excellent index); and *Scritti d'arte del Cinquecento*, 3 vols. (Milan–Naples, 1971–6), which groups them usefully according to topic. See also

enough, we find these theorists continuing to systematize painting in rhetorical terms. Where Alberti had used only *inventio*, in his *De Viris Illustribus* (1456) Bartolomeo Fazio writes that 'both painting and poetry . . . involve *inventio* and *dispositio'*, balking, as Baxandall has noted, at adding *elocutio*, falling back on the more general term *exprimere*.[34] Leonardo's notes relate *'invenzione* to *disegno*, *moto*, and *varietà',*[35] where the painting terminology may still dominate the rhetorical, and it was left to Paolo Pino to make the decisive step of applying the whole triad: 'L'arte della pittura . . . dividerò in tre parti a modo mio: la prima parte sarà disegno, la seconda invenzione, la terza et ultima il colorire.'[36] Lodovico Dolce, writing a few years after Pino, made a more sustained attempt to apply the rhetorical system to painting. His knowledge of rhetoric was considerable, having produced Italian translations of both the *Ars Poetica* (1535; revised 1559) and the *De Oratore* (1547), and in addition to their influence his contemporary Italian sources—Alberti, Castiglione, Vasari—all drew on the same rhetorical tradition.[37] His treatise is cast into the form of a dialogue between Pietro Aretino, distinguished man of letters and Venetian, who has the main expository role, and Giovan Francesco Fabrini, a Florentine, who asks questions at the right time. The expository section is set within the context of a dispute between the two men as to who are the greatest Italian painters, and in what area

A. Filarete, *Treatise on Architecture*, tr. J. R. Spencer, 2 vols. (New Haven, Conn., 1965); G. P. Lomazzo, *Scritti sulle arti*, ed. R. Ciardi, 2 vols. (Florence, 1973–4); and Roskill 1968, which gives the text of Dolce's *Aretino*, a translation, and extensive commentary. Lee 1967 also considers seventeenth-century theorists, notably Pietro Bellori and Roger de Piles, while Jensen 1976 extends the survey of painting, music, and rhetoric into the eighteenth century. V. M. Bevilacqua, 'Ut Rhetorica Pictura: Sir Joshua Reynolds' Rhetorical Conception of Art', *Huntington Library Quarterly*, 34 (1970), 59–78, shows the tradition still functioning in the 1760s.

[34] Baxandall 1971, pp. 100–1.

[35] Summers 1981, pp. 74–5.

[36] Barocchi 1960–2, i. 113, 116 ff., and 408 n. Cf. also Gilbert 1943–5, pp. 93–8 for comments on Pino's rather untidy linking of painting and rhetoric. Gilbert also notes (p. 105) that 'the obscure Florentine writer Francesco Lancilotti used a fourfold division of *Disegno, Colorito, Compositione*, and *Inventione* in his poetic *Tractato di Pictura* (Rome, 1509)', but denies him any place in the tradition and concedes credit for the systematic application of rhetorical concepts to Pino, who may have drawn on Bernardino Daniello's *La poetica*, published at Venice in 1536 (p. 106).

[37] See Roskill 1968 for details of biography and sources. Page-references to this edition will be incorporated into the text.

they excel. Evidently responding to Vasari's *Vite de' più eccellenti pittori scultori ed archittetori* (1550), which had pronounced Michelangelo to represent the perfection of Italian painting, Dolce's Aretino recognizes his excellence in *disegno* (draughtsmanship) but pronounces Raphael superior in every other department, and judges Titian the master of both, especially in *colorito*. (In the *Proemio* to the second edition of his *Vite* in 1568 Vasari responded by declaring 'disegno padre delle arti'.) In arguing his case Dolce's Aretino divides painting into three parts, 'Inventione, Disegno, e Colorito'. The invention is the 'favola, o historia' that the painter either chooses for himself or receives from some literary collaborator (p. 116). Invention must attend to 'l'ordine e la convenevolezza', ('order and propriety'), the latter involving decorum of costume, setting, and bearing (p. 118). As for 'l'ordine' (which Roskill rather confusingly translates as 'disposition'), Dolce lays down that the artist must 'move from section to section following the course of time in the narrative he has undertaken to paint', not placing 'later in time what ought to come earlier', or vice versa (p. 120). We might recall Horace's distinction between beginning *ab ovo* or *in medias res* (*Ars Poet.*, 147–9), a distinction later codified into *ordo naturalis / ordo artificialis*, but Dolce himself cites Aristotle's *Poetics* (1450^{b}22 ff.), which was variously interpreted in the sixteenth century.[38] He is evidently referring to the chronological sequence of events, either in a fresco-cycle or in a composite narrative painting, rather than to the disposition of characters and events, or visual forms, within a painting.

Dolce has more to say on invention, emphasizing the need for decorum with the anecdote of Timanthes' painting of the veiled Agamemnon (p. 122: from Quintilian, via Alberti), the need for unity (p. 124), appropriateness of gesture and posture (p. 128: from Quintilian, via Alberti), the need to be versed in history and poetry (Alberti alone), and to make preliminary sketches (Alberti again). Invention, he goes on, derives from two sources, the 'historia' itself and the painter's 'ingegno' or intellect, manifested in 'l'ordine e la convenevolezza' and resulting in 'l'attitudini, la varietà, e la (per cosi dire) energia delle figure'—and we recognize further rhetorical categories. 'Disegno', which corresponds to *dispositio*, is defined as 'the

[38] Roskill 1968, pp. 276–8; Weinberg 1961, Index s.v. 'Order'.

form imparted by the painter to the things which he sets about imitating; and it is really a winding movement of lines, which travel along various paths to give shape to the figures' (p. 130), another echo of Quintilian as a source for the 'serpentine figure'. Dolce has earlier defined painting as 'nothing other than the imitation of nature' (p. 96), a principle which, as Roskill rightly says, 'stands at the heart of Renaissance art theory' (p. 239), and he now adds the corollary, that 'the painter should try not only to imitate nature but to surpass it' (p. 130), a fundamental principle in rhetoric. Correct design also depends on knowledge of the proportions of the human body (pp. 136 ff.), and, like every other branch of art, involves applying the rhetorical categories of decorum (pp. 140 f.), and variety (p. 144).

Dolce's third element, 'colorito', corresponds to *elocutio*, notionally at least, and this is where the parallel with rhetoric becomes problematic. His criteria for colour, naturally enough, are mimetic, verisimilar—the painter must produce 'a good imitation of the tones and softness of flesh and the rightful characteristics of any object there may be' (p. 152)—and also technical, involving 'contrast, perspective, tone and texture, modulation and unity', as Roskill summarizes them (p. 297). The student of rhetoric instantly notes that Dolce does not invoke the main quality of *elocutio* as understood in the Renaissance, its power to move the feelings by employing a range of expressive and affective devices. But after a very brief account of *colorito*, Dolce comes to a topic not announced in his original division:

Lastly the painter should have at his command one other element, of such a kind that the painting which does not possess it remains cold, as the saying is, and like a dead body that is totally inactive. What is needed is that the figures should stir the spectators' souls—disturbing them in some cases, cheering them in others, in others again inciting them to either compassion or disdain, depending on the character of the subject matter [*historia*]. Failing this, the painter should not claim to have accomplished anything. For this is what gives the flavour to all his virtues.

As with the poet, historian, or orator, if their works 'lack this power to move, they lack also spirit and life' (p. 156).

His modern editor has criticized Dolce for destroying the

'structural cohesion and symmetry of presentation' by adding this 'subjective' criterion, which is 'quite arbitrarily introduced'.[39] But, as we have seen, by the mid-sixteenth century the symbiosis between *elocutio* and *movere* was firmly established. Recognizing that *colorito* could not do justice to the need for emotional expressivity, Dolce has made a quick transition from the processes of composition (*inventio* . . .) to the *officia oratoris* (*movere—docere—delectare*), which describe the effect that the artwork should have on its audience. Dolce had earlier invoked *delectare* as the goal of painting (which, having been invented 'principalmente per dilettare, se'l Pittor non diletta, se ne sta oscuro e senza nome': p. 148), but he does not explicitly specify *docere*, although he describes the 'usefulness' of painting in inflaming men to emulate heroism, in the traditional linking of epideictic and ethics ('images of the upright and the virtuous excite mankind to virtue and good deeds': p. 112). Roskill interestingly suggests that Dolce's espousal of *delectare* but not *docere* derives from Horace's reworking of the triad—inseparable in rhetorical theory—into 'mutually exclusive alternatives' (*aut prodesse, aut delectare*), which was understood literally in sixteenth-century Venice (p. 13). This may well be the case, since Dolce's further remarks on *movere* make the by now obligatory quotation from the *Ars Poetica*:

Nor can the painter stir emotion unless he already experiences in his own being, while executing the figures, those passions—or shall we say 'states of mind' [*affetti*]—which he wishes to imprint on the mind of another. And this is why Horace, who has been quoted so many times, observes *si vis me flere dolendum est primum ipsi tibi*. (p. 156)

Rather than seeing Dolce's advocacy of *movere* as destroying the coherence of his compositional scheme, we should see it as complementary, indeed an essential attribute of the Renaissance art-work. The other interlocutor in the dialogue picks out this point, 'that paintings need to move the spectator', as having given him 'the highest pleasure' (p. 158), and singles out Titian as the great instance of this power (p. 160), only for his partner to describe Raphael as 'supremely moving' (p. 174), unequalled

---

[39] Roskill 1968, pp. 23, 301; see also pp. 267, 271–2 for further criticisms of Dolce's inconsistencies. Roskill does not always perceive the connections within rhetoric.

in 'stirring the emotions' (p. 176). *Movere* remains the criterion of artistic excellence (as it still does: we talk of being 'moved' by this work of art, 'left cold' by that).

Other aspects of rhetoric could be followed out in the sixteenth-century theorists *ad libitum*, such as the growth of individual aesthetic concepts: *terribilità*, so common in evaluating Michelangelo's art, which came from the concept of *deinotes* referred to by Quintilian (6. 2. 24; cit. above p. 78), and much developed in later Greek rhetoric; *difficultà*, already glimpsed in Quintilian; and concepts of visual vividness, present in Roman rhetoric in such phrases as *ante oculos ponere*, strengthened by the ekphrastic tradition derived from Hermogenes.[40]

When art theory developed in seventeenth-century France *movere* figured in a major controversy, well studied by Jacqueline Lichtenstein, between the older guard of the French Academy and some more adventurous theorists, led by Roger de Piles. The more conservative group urged that 'dessin', *disegno*, was the vital quality for a painter to possess, embracing as it did the twin rhetorical processes of *inventio* and *dispositio*. The revisionists responded that *colore* was the single crucial aptitude needed, corresponding as it did to *elocutio*.[41] This may seem a fruitless dispute, since rhetoric needs all its parts, and cannot set one against the other; but the shift of emphasis is further evidence of the tendency in this period towards more expressive art forms. The implicit equation of *elocutio* with *movere* was still active for Roger de Piles, writing between 1688 and 1699, who drew on this alliance to urge that 'un tableau doit "saisir" le spectateur comme par surprise, le frapper du premier coup d'oeil, l'attirer violemment et "le forcer pour ainsi dire à le regarder"'. Painting, he wrote, should be '"une espèce de création qui nous divertit et met nos passions en

---

[40] On *terribilità* see Summers 1981, pp. 234–6; on *difficultà*, *idem*, pp. 177 ff., and 507 n. 17 (although he does not pick up some of the forerunners in classical rhetoric, e.g. *De Or.* 3. 22. 84); on *ekphrasis* see, e.g., Baxandall 1971, pp. 85–7; Svetlana Alpers, '*Ekphrasis* and Aesthetic Attitudes in Vasari's *Lives*', *Journal of the Warburg and Courtauld Institutes*, 23 (1960), 190–215; and S. C. Hulse, '"A Piece of Skilful Painting" in Shakespeare's "Lucrece"', *Shakespeare Survey*, 31 (1978), 13–22.

[41] Lichtenstein 1982, p. 171–3. On this opposition in sixteenth-century Venice see Roskill 1968, pp. 25, 65, etc., and Bernard Teyssèdre, *Roger de Piles et les débats sur le coloris au siècle de Louis XIV* (Paris, 1957).

mouvement" '.[42] The affective tradition of Cicero and Quintilian is revived for yet another generation by the most up-to-date theorist. Although sometimes described as an opponent of rules and systems,[43] the fact that, in his later work, de Piles could draw on the newly translated treatise of Longinus, shows that the rhetorical tradition still had important ideas to offer theorists of painting.

Valuable though rhetoric was to art criticism, its legacy was not altogether beneficent, involving as it did the application of a language-based system to a purely visual medium. Rensselaer Lee believed that some sixteenth-century critics applied to art 'in a more or less Procrustean manner' that fusion of Aristotle with Horace that characterizes so much of Renaissance theory in poetics and rhetoric, thus 'imposing on painting what was merely a reconditioned theory of poetry', without asking 'whether an art with a different medium could reasonably submit to a borrowed aesthetic'.[44] Michael Baxandall's analysis of Alberti's use of *compositio* would partly support this judgement, for he showed that Alberti transferred to painting the grammatical concept of '*structura aspera* . . . the disagreeable conjunction of two "rough" consonants between the end of one word and the beginning of the next', a discord frowned on by the rhetoricians. But in displacing '*verbum* by its equivalent *superficies* or plane' Alberti produced an 'ambiguous' statement, 'not easy to reconcile with experience', and quickly passed on to another topic, as if sensing the danger.[45] David Summers has noted, similarly, that Dolce 'equivocates' when he comes to work in more detail, ending up with a group of concepts— *l'attitudine, la verità,* and *l'energia*—occupying 'an ambiguous

---

[42] Cit. Lichtenstein 1982, pp. 178–9.

[43] Lee 1967, pp. 26–7. For other reservations about transplanting analytical categories from one art to another see Jensen 1976, pp. xiv–xv, 169; and James Merriman, 'The Parallel of the Arts: Some Misgivings and a Faint Affirmation', *Journal of Aesthetics and Art Criticism,* 31 (1972), 153–64, 310–21.

[44] Lee 1967, p. 7. Just though this verdict is in some cases, Lee's subsequent remark, that Lomazzo and other critics who applied Horace's *si vis me flere* in detail lose 'all semblance of that essential detachment which in aesthetic experience mysteriously accompanies and qualifies emotional participation' (p. 24), seems anachronistic. Detachment may be a quality celebrated by Diderot or Joyce, but it was not one valued by Alberti, Leonardo, or Michelangelo.

[45] Baxandall 1971, pp. 131–3.

position . . . since they stand at the very fount of pictorial invention' but are also parts of *elocutio*. A fusion of categories results, for 'what is being put forward as the model for painting is not rhetoric but poetry'.[46]

Difficulties evidently arise over correlating the separate categories of the two arts, and no doubt more examples could be found of conflation, confusion, or silent omission. But the link between rhetoric and painting was made a great deal easier by the fact that classical rhetoricians had drawn so many illustrations from sculpture and painting. In an influential passage Quintilian had invoked painting to explain the power of oratorical gesture:

> Nor is it wonderful that gesture which depends on various forms of movement should have such power, when pictures, which are silent and motionless, penetrate into our innermost feelings with such power that at times they seem more eloquent than language itself. (11. 3. 67)

Literary language was also full of metaphors taken from painting. Many of the critical terms that Leonardo Bruni applied to literature—*figura, status, ingressus, color, lineamenta, forma*—were, as Baxandall points out, 'by origin visual metaphors and so applicable to painting too', so that Alberti could draw on the humanists' imagery and simply reverse 'the analogy from painting to writing into an analogy from writing to painting'.[47] If a two-way traffic already exists then some of the deformations caused by trying to read one art in terms of another can be avoided.

II

In Renaissance music we find a similar process of rhetoricization of a distinct art-form, carried to even greater lengths. The influence of rhetoric came later than on painting, not till the early 1500s,[48] but it soon established its hold. Quintilian's parallel between the history of rhetoric and the history of

---

[46] Summers 1981, pp. 73–4; similarly Roskill 1968, pp. 267, 271–2.

[47] Baxandall 1971, pp. 26, 135.

[48] R. M. Ellefsen, 'Music and Humanism in the early Renaissance: their Relationship and its Roots in the Rhetorical and Philosophical Traditions', Ph.D. Diss. Florida State University, 1981; University Microfilms order no. 8125766. A useful recent symposium is *Musik in Humanismus und Renaissance*, ed. W. Rüegg and A. Schmitt (Weinheim, 1983).

painting provided a historical scheme which the Swiss humanist Glareanus could apply to Renaissance music in his *Dodekachordon* (1547), just before Vasari used it for his *Lives of the Painters* in 1550.[49] Quintilian provided the model for the title of Gioseffe Zarlino's *Istitutione armoniche* (1558), which invokes the work of many rhetoricians, while other treatises modelled themselves on *De Oratore*.[50] Given the logocentric world of the humanists, it is no surprise that a whole series of terms for grammar and rhetoric should have been taken over for music: 'theme, motive, phrase, metrics, rhythm, period, exposition, episode, accent, articulation, figure, style, composition'—these are still with us, while we have discarded earlier borrowings, such as trope, prose, *clausula, punctum, color*, and others.[51] Since both oratory (or poetry) and music are performing arts, events in time, then other analogies can be drawn from punctuation—pause, question-mark, exclamation.

The prime reason for the humanists' rhetoricization of music was their basic concept of art as a mimesis. Music, too, was an 'imitation of nature',[52] an innocent-looking concept which in fact implied a literary model, namely the fable, with all the connotations of form and function that went with it. Just as for Alberti the painter's aim was to construct a good *historia*, so these later theorists described the composer's art as being based on the *favola* (which usually meant 'plot' or 'structure'), to which he added appropriate music. The 'imitative arts remained . . . techniques of story-telling centering on man's activities',[53] sacred and secular, with a consequent down-valuing of purely instrumental music. The first thing to be sought for in every composition, Zarlino wrote in 1558, was 'the subject, . . . without which one can do nothing'; the composer must make or choose some 'history or fable' on which he 'founds his

---

[49] Shearman 1967, p. 34.

[50] See Strunk 1950 for Zarlino. The *Proportionales musicales* of Johannes Tinctoris (1473) modelled its prœmium on *De Oratore*, substituting contemporary England for Rome in Cicero's account of the revival of rhetoric. I owe this information to an unpublished paper by Dr Ronald Woodley (Newcastle), 'Music, Theory and Humanism in the Early Renaissance'.

[51] Gurlitt 1966, p. 65; also H. H. Eggebrecht, *Handwörterbuch der musikalischen Terminologie* (Freiburg, 1979–).

[52] See A. Carapetyan, 'The Concept of *Imitazione della Natura* in the Sixteenth Century', *Journal of Renaissance and Baroque Music*, 1 (1946–7), 47–67, and Le Coat 1975, ch. 1: 'Mimesis: a humanistic discipline'.

[53] Le Coat 1975, p. 30.

composition'. It follows that the construction of a *favola* in music will be approached in just the same way as with literature, using rhetorical *inventio*. So, Zarlino continues, 'in every musical composition, what we call the subject is that part from which the composer derives invention to make the other parts of the work'.[54] As Gerard Le Coat has pointed out, Zarlino's *Istitutione armoniche*, published one year after Dolce's *Aretino* (1557), 'gave the same definition of *invention*, i.e. the choice of a subject by the artist "in accordance with the loftiness of his imagination" '.[55] Zarlino takes over the next two stages of the rhetorical process, with some variation, renaming *dispositione* as *compositione*, and turning *elocutio* into the general category of ornament. Monteverdi's *Orfeo* (1607) was described on its title-page as a '*FAVOLA in musica*', and one of its first reviewers praised it under the appropriate rhetorical categories: 'Poet and composer have presented the affections in such an extraordinary manner that nothing remains to be criticized. The poetry is beautiful in the *invention* of the material, still more beautiful in its *disposition*, and most beautiful in its *expression*', while the music—in the subordinate place, as so often at this time—was 'in this case not inferior'.[56]

The application of rhetorical terms to the processes of composition continued through the Italian sixteenth century into Germany in the next two centuries, the country and period in which *musica rhetorica* was developed to an astonishing degree. The 'fable' or 'poem' continues to be the starting-point, music following literature, and the processes of *inventio* and so on are still applied to music.[57] While these are harmless analogies we also find the appearance of much more thorough-going identifications of the two arts, which begin to strain the

---

[54] Strunk 1950, pp. 229–31.   [55] Le Coat 1975, p. 31.

[56] Ibid., citing Leo Schrade, *Monteverdi* (New York, 1950), p. 226.

[57] See e.g., Strunk 1950, p. 319 (Galilei, 1581); Unger 1941, pp. 35 (Athanasius Kircher, 1650), 39 ff. (Mauritius Vogt, 1719: surely a parody of mechanical processes in *inventio*, recommending bending four 'Hufnägel' into shapes, and setting them to music, or rolling a dice, or drinking wine), 41 (Heinichen, 1728: a fifty-page demonstration of using the *loci topici* as aids to musical *inventio*: see G. J. Buelow, 'The *Loci Topici* and Affect in late baroque Music. Heinichen's practical Demonstration', *The Music Review*, 27 (1966), 161–76), and 42–4, 50 (Mattheson, 1739). For a bibliography of later works on music and rhetoric see G. J. Buelow's entry for 'Rhetoric and Music', in *The New Grove Dictionary of Music and Musicians*, xv. 793–803, subject to the caveats about the confusion of terminology expressed in Vickers 1984, pp. 39–40.

parallel. Gallus Dressler, writing in Magdeburg in 1563, applies the term *exordium* to music, and says that as the sentence has eight constituent parts (period, comma, clause, etc.) so does music.[58] Sethus Calvisius, in 1592, says that a composition, like an oration, can have three parts, '*Exordium, medium et finis*',[59] while Joachim Burmeister develops this point out of classical rhetoric, adding that the musical *exordium* also affects a *captatio benevolentiae* of the listener.[60] This is still a suggestive idea, not putting the analogy between music and rhetoric under any great strain (it cannot be taken much further, of course, as we realize when we recall what qualities of character the orator is meant to display at this point: see above, pp. 20, 68). But Burmeister, the pioneer in this respect, and another dozen theorists (mostly German) over the next century and a half, went on to claim a specific identity between the two arts at the level of the rhetorical figures. While some modern scholars have accepted these claims more or less uncritically, it seems to me that a degree of scepticism is in order.[61] The prime difference between

[58] Unger 1941, pp. 30–1.

[59] Ruhnke 1955, pp. 137–8.

[60] Burmeister, *Musica poetica* (Rostock, 1606), facs. edn. M. Ruhnke (Kassel and Basle, 1955), p. 72.

[61] The leading exponents of *musica rhetorica* that I refer to are Brandes 1935; Unger 1941; Ruhnke 1955; Palisca 1959; Palisca 1972; Butler 1977; and Butler 1980. The German writers occasionally express caution about the identification of the two arts (e.g. Brandes 1935, pp. 25–7; Unger 1941, p. 80), but they (and Butler) are all too prone to accept the theorists' claims. See Vickers 1984 for a detailed analysis. It seems important to express some caution in the application of rhetorical criticism to the others arts, since scholars can get carried away by their enthusiasm. Thus Ursula Kirkendale ('The Source for Bach's *Musical Offering*: The *Institutio oratoria* of Quintilian', *Journal of the American Musicological Society*, 33 (1980), 88–141), makes large claims for Bach's direct modelling on Quintilian on what seems to me a slender base. So, in the opening Ricercar Quintilian's requirements for the *exordium*, that it contain 'simple speech' and 'common usage', is said to be seen in the fact that 'Simple eighth notes, mostly in conjunct motion, pervade the entire piece, passing smoothly from one voice to another' (p. 97), while the 'happy mean' that Quintilian calls for between *docere* and *delectare* is said to be shown 'as always in Bach's vocal music, [where] the interpolation of triplet passages, usually rising, in a context of binary eighth notes, expresses joy and produces pleasure' (ibid.). The 'alternating *alla zoppa* and Pyrrhicius rhythm' shows that 'Bach is listening to Quintilian's words on the exordium' on the ways in which the mind of the judge can be stirred up (p. 98), while the 'chromatic descent in parallel minor sixths' supposedly echoes Quintilian's discussion of arousing pity in the judge (p. 99). Bach's 'Canon Perpetuus' is linked with Quintilian's account of *narratio* (4. 2. 40 ff.) in this way: 'Characteristic of the *narratio* is *oratio perpetua*, which, like Bach's infinite canon proceeds straight ahead, without an end in sight' (p. 101). The crab canon is

language and music is that language has a constant semantic dimension, uses words with definite meanings—subject, of course, to personal and regional differences: but these too can be registered—while music has no such fixed system of denotation. Certain modes, or in modern terms keys and tonalities, have traditionally been associated with certain feeling-states, but the association is not only arbitrary (in a much profounder sense than the 'arbitrary' association, in language, of signified with signifier, which is at least widely shared within a country, dialect, or social group), but has suffered some drastic changes[62]—before disappearing altogether in recent music.

If we examine in detail the music theorists' account of the rhetorical figures we see that in all cases the literary effect has to be narrowed down, or fundamentally transposed.[63] Where *anaphora* in rhetoric describes the repetition of a word at the beginning of clauses or sentences, in Burmeister it involves 'the imitation of a musical subject in only some of the voice parts'. In rhetoric *gradatio* is a specific term for the repeating of a word at the end of one clause and the beginning of the next: in musical rhetoric it implies a generalized notion of enlargement. *Aposiopesis* in rhetoric describes a speaker's breaking off a sentence with the sense incomplete: in Burmeister it means only a general pause (since music cannot use the idea of a sense unit). In these cases the figure is applied to music in a more generalized way, but in others a whole-scale transposition is involved, shifting from content to form. In rhetoric *hyperbole* means going beyond normal criteria of truth or proportion, a figure obviously based on linguistic decorum and usage: Burmeister used it to refer to a note written above the stave. *Hypallage* in rhetoric is the misplacing of words ('see the

related to Quintilian's advice, on *narratio longa*, that 'we say nothing contrary to nature', with this justification: 'Bach fulfills this brilliantly, for the crab is one of the very few *natural* phenomena which has a terminological and technical equivalent in music' (p. 104). With such naïve and fanciful analogies the application of rhetoric to music cannot have much validity.

[62] See D. P. Walker, *Studies in Musical Science in the Late Renaissance* (London, 1978), ch. 5, 'The Expressive Value of Intervals', at pp. 71–2, where he shows that the emotions attributed to the major and minor modes have undergone a complete reversal between the sixteenth and seventeenth centuries and the eighteenth and twentieth; also Winn 1981, pp. 143–4.

[63] For the details of these comparisons see Vickers 1984, pp. 28–34.

Epilogue'): to Burmeister it is 'a fugue by contrary motion; when the subject rises, the answer descends, and vice versa'.[64] As in so much medieval rhetoric (where Burmeister's fundamental affinities lay) the semantic element has been transposed into a formal one, involving the visual or figural disposition of music on the page.[65] *Metalepsis* in rhetoric is a figure where a statement must be understood either from what precedes or from what follows: Burmeister uses it for music in which some voices enter with the first words of a text, while others begin with a later section. Further analysis could show that whenever writers attempt precise identification of rhetorical figures with musical form the whole level of denotation has to be drastically adapted, or turned into a more general notion of form. Although such terms as 'the language of music' and 'musical metaphors' are common, and easy, a more searching analysis will conclude that they soon lose their applicability.[66] Language and music derive from fundamentally different resources.

The humanists' application of rhetoric was more valid when it described goals which music could reach by using its own

[64] Claude V. Palisca has kindly supplied this definition, correcting the erroneous one given in Butler 1977, p. 58, and cited in Vickers 1984, p. 30.

[65] Winn 1981 comments, aptly enough, that although Burmeister's 'opening pages talk about using music to make arguments, to move the affections, and to influence the heart', in his actual examples he 'patiently equates each rhetorical figure with its musical equivalent as if both were geometric designs' (p. 191), thus revealing his affinities with medieval 'constructive' rather than Renaissance 'expressive' forms (p. 129). Compare Panofsky's account of medieval sculpture, and Griffin's description of the medieval 'seconde Rhétorique' in terms of patterns and design, above, pp. 246, 280.

[66] Metaphor is, of course, the mental translation of a concept from one realm into another, an essentially linguistic phenomenon. Dene Barnett (personal communication) doubts whether metaphor can exist in music, 'except by analogy. [Its proponents'] favourite example is a short descending scale passage which they say is a metaphor for death or descent from the Cross, etc. But a descending scale passage does not have a fixed primary meaning.' It can 'suggest death (but even then, only in certain contexts) but it suggests death not by metaphor, but by a certain resemblance between the sign and what it refers to; i.e., the acoustic descent of the passage has something in common with the physical descent of the body of Christ. But this only means that the musical sign is an icon . . . ', otherwise 'the lack of a genuine semantical meaning to any passage in music means that the resemblance is pretty remote'. The independence of music from denotation, he adds, is shown by the fact that 'one melody was often used in the 18th century to accompany (and to "express") two different sets of words. Bach, for example, used one melody for the quite licentious words of "Wollust" in his cantata *The Choice of Hercules* and later chose the same melody for an aria by the virgin Mary in the Christmas Oratorio.'

resources. Given the presence of a literary text (psalm, motet, madrigal, opera, monodic song) as the 'subject', it followed that the musical composition as a whole must fulfil the criteria otherwise expected of the fable: it must be complete, unified but showing variety, must maintain decorum in adapting style to subject-matter, and fulfil the duties of the orator: *docere, delectare, movere*. Of these three claims the first, that of teaching or being morally improving, sends us back to the text, and strengthens still further what one cannot help seeing as the unhealthy predominance of words over music.[67] Zarlino, in his major work (1558), could invoke Horace's injunction, *aut prodesse volunt, aut delectare poetae*, and maintain a healthy balance by seeing the composer working 'to improve or delight the minds of his listeners with harmonious accents', a balance found in other early humanists, such as Calvin in 1545 and Glareanus in 1547.[68] But in the last quarter of the sixteenth century a movement arose in Florence which consciously set *prodesse* in opposition to *delectare*, by placing words above music. Count Giovanni de' Bardi, inspired by the theories of Girolamo Mei, who in his unpublished treatise 'De modis musicis veterum libri quator' attempted to revive the ancient Greeks' ideas about music, founded a 'Camerata' or music academy in the 1580s. As his son Pietro explained some fifty years later, the academy was an association of virtuous men studying the arts and sciences, and trying to 'extract the essence of the Greek' and Latin theorists.[69] They seem to us like orthodox Renaissance humanists doing what they were supposed to do, recovering ancient learning in order to stimulate modern creativity.

But as always, the recovery of the past is not a simple act, for it depends on which sources are revived, and for which

[67] Walker 1941–2, a fundamental study, has expressed this view most forcefully; see also Winn 1981, pp. 177 ff. Walker's long essay was translated into German as *Der musikalische Humanismus im 16. und frühen 17. Jahrhundert* (Kassel and Basle, 1949), with some additional comments and bibliography in his 'Vorwort' (pp. 3–4), which were unfortunately not included in the recent collection of his essays, *Music, Spirit and Language in the Renaissance*, ed. P. Gouk (London, 1985).

[68] Horace, *Ars Poetica* 333–4: 'Poets aim either to benefit, or to amuse, or to utter words at once both pleasing and helpful to life.' For this idea in Zarlino, see Strunk 1950, p. 229; Glareanus: ibid., p. 221; Calvin: ibid., p. 347, also Charles Garside, 'Calvin's Preface to the Psalter. A Re-Appraisal', *Musical Quarterly*, 37 (1951), 566–77.

[69] Strunk 1950, pp. 363–4.

purposes. Starting from Plato and Aristotle—rather than from Quintilian—they derived a body of knowledge which, as the late D. P. Walker showed so well, they applied at one point in good faith and at another by ignoring what they found in their sources,[70] adding to it some Christian attitudes, notably those of Paul and St Augustine. Starting from Plato's attack on pleasure, here equated, unfortunately, with harmony and melody and thus with the senses, and taking over the Platonic exclusion of everything but morally improving literature, the Camerata theorists once again made music the servant of the words. From Galilei in 1581 to the Monteverdis in the 1600s—since, as Caccini put it, according to Plato 'music is nothing other than the fable' —*harmonia* waited dutifully on *parole*.[71] This complex of ideas led, in musical terms, to a strange series of positions. Their ideal was of a single voice declaiming a text over a tactfully restrained accompaniment, so that the words could be understood, and thus their 'conceit' penetrate the mind (not the senses, somehow), but still fulfil the rhetorical goal of moving the auditory's feelings. This theory gave rise to monodic song, and the birth of opera from the union of fable and recitative, in the works of Peri, Caccini, and Monteverdi, an important development in music by any standards. But in order to validate their own position they had to calumniate the rival, namely polyphony, producing a whole campaign of mockery and abuse. Where many voices sang at once, they claimed, the sense was obscured, as it was where parts entered in delayed sequence or 'answered' each other. Polyphony and counterpoint, according to the monodists, confused the text, and hence the mind, showing that these techniques ignored the intellect and appealed to the passions through the senses, thus encouraging all forms of bad behaviour. The polemics of de' Bardi, Galilei, and G. C. Monteverdi,[72] add up to a damning but biased and somewhat pointless indictment of the music of Josquin, Di Lasso, and their predecessors. Platonist though he is, Vincenzo Galilei cites Quintilian's concept of the *vir bonus* to describe the new composer of monody, obviously dismissing the polyphonists to an inferno.[73]

[70] Walker 1941–2, pp. 64–6.
[71] Strunk 1950, pp. 312, 319, 364–5, 371–2, 374–5, 378, 380–1.
[72] See ibid., pp. 293–4, 307–21, 374, 378–80, 405–7.   [73] Ibid., p. 321.

To us the whole dispute must seem like that in the French Academy between *dessin* and *couleur*, two complementary expressive resources unnecessarily fighting each other. And, just as in that controversy, the new men claimed to have rhetoric on their side. According to these neoterics, the monodic style had rediscovered the power to move the feelings, but this time indirectly, via the mind not the feelings (we may think this an unreal and unworkable distinction). De' Bardi senior states that the composer using their reformed style has 'the power to dispose the mind with his harmony to any moral quality'. Galilei takes the completely rhetorical position that since music arose 'primarily to express the passions with greater effectiveness', and to 'communicate these with equal force to the minds of mortals', then monody alone can express the 'conceptions' of the text clearly, in order 'to impress the passions of the listener'. Jacopo Peri (composer of *Euridice*, one of the first operas) describes how he has attempted in his music to imitate 'the inflections and accents that serve us in our grief, in our joy, and in similar states'; and Giulio Caccini asserts that in his 'late compositions' he has used 'a certain noble neglect of the song' (*sprezzatura!*) and highlighted the words, since 'songs for a single voice . . . accompanied by a single stringed instrument', have greater power to 'penetrate the perception of others and to produce those marvellous effects' ascribed to music.[74] Some modern scholars have taken the monodists' propaganda at face value,[75] but a broader perspective will show that they were merely claiming for their style powers which had long been ascribed to music in general. Descriptions of the power of music over the emotions, and hence over the moral faculties, begin with Plato and Aristotle, and reappear over the succeeding millennia in many guises. One *locus classicus*, imitated constantly, as James Hutton showed in a seminal essay,[76] was Quintilian, himself drawing on a long tradition when he appealed, 'Give me the knowledge of the principles of music, which have power to excite or assuage the emotions of mankind', a power which he illustrated with anecdotes from life (1. 10. 32–3). Plutarch and other ancient sources made such

[74] Strunk 1950, pp. 294, 307, 314, 374, 378–9.
[75] Shearman 1967, p. 101.
[76] Hutton 1951.

stories as how Timotheus, with his playing of the lyre, raised and quelled the emperor's passions at 'Alexander's Feast' a commonplace until the time of Dryden; and once Handel set that poem to music it became an eternal touchstone of the expressive resources of harmony and rhythm. Music's power to move the passions is celebrated by such very different writers as Glareanus, Zarlino, Calvin, Thomas Morley, and Claudio Monteverdi;[77] by the encyclopedic Marin Mersenne in his *Harmonie universelle* (1636);[78] and by the exponents of the 'Prose mesurée', a French invention in which declamation, with musical rhythms exactly duplicating those of the verse, was supposed to move the audience to whatever emotions composers would wish.[79]

All schools of music in the Renaissance, then, claimed to be able to harness *movere* in a way that equalled or excelled rhetoric. The humanists of the first half of the sixteenth century had proudly rejected medieval composers as *mathematici*, mere counters of notes, makers of abstract patterns which had no organic connection with the text. The newer *musici poetici*, as defined by Adriano Coclico in his *Compendium musices* (1552), and as led supremely by Josquin des Prez, applied 'any note to the due syllable' of the text, and were 'diligent and careful', as Hermann Finck put it in his *Practica Musica* (1555) 'in fitting the text so that it agrees with the notes placed above it, and so that these notes express in the best possible way the meaning of the discourse and the various affections'.[80] Anyone familiar with rhetoric will recognize at once the source of such terms as 'applying', 'agreeing', 'fitting', 'adapting', and 'accommodating' music to words in the concept of decorum, where style is accommodated to subject-matter. This becomes, throughout the Renaissance, one of the major criteria to be applied to vocal compositions. As early as More's *Utopia* (1518), the inhabitants of that imaginary isle are said to excel the rest of the world, for their music 'so renders and expresses the natural feelings, so suits the sound to the matter [*ita sonus accommodatur ad rem*],

---

[77] For these five musicians see Strunk 1950, pp. 227, 250, 275, 346–7, 413–4.

[78] On Mersenne see Le Coat 1975, pp. 23, 52–7; Winn 1981, p. 194; and D. T. Mace, 'Marin Mersenne on Language and Music', *Journal of Music Theory*, 14 (1970), 2–34.

[79] Walker 1941–2, p. 308.

[80] Coclico and Finck are quoted from Le Coat 1975, p. 19.

whether the words be supplicatory or joyful or propitiatory or untroubled or mournful or angry, and so represents the meaning by the form of the melody that it wonderfully affects, penetrates, and influences the souls of the hearers'.[81] That classic account of music conceived of in terms of rhetorical *movere* refers, of course, to polyphony.

Other early humanists praise polyphonic composers by applying the rhetorical ideal of vividness, in the phrase *ante oculos ponere*, originally applied to metaphor but extended to such figures as *hypotyposis* and *ekphrasis*. So Glareanus, friend of Erasmus, praised Josquin for expressing 'the passions of the soul' [*affectus animi*] with a power matching Virgil's:

For just as Maro . . . was accustomed to adapt his poem to the subject so as to set weighty matters before the eyes of his readers [*ante oculos ponere*] with close-packed spondees, fleeting ones with unmixed dactyls, to use words suited to his every subject, . . . so our Josquin, where his matter requires it [*ubi res postulat*] now advances with impetuous and precipitate notes, now . . . in longdrawn tones.[82]

Glareanus is sensitive to the imaginative qualities implied in a setting, such as Lassus' putting to music the 'Genealogy of Christ our Saviour according to the Evangelists Matthew and Luke'. 'The motet has great majesty, and it is wonderful that from material so sterile, namely, from a bare catalogue of men, he has been able to fashion as many delights as though it had been some fertile narrative.' Lassus excelled here in *inventio*, we might say; Josquin in *elocutio*, as in expressing the greatest passion at a specific word, or sustaining throughout a whole motet ('*Planxit autem David*') the emotions befitting a mourner, 'who is wont to cry out at first frequently, then to murmur to himself, turning little by little to sorrowful complaints, thereupon to subside or sometimes, when passion breaks out anew, to raise his voice again, shouting a cry'. All these fluctuations of feeling are recorded in Josquin's music, which 'everywhere expressed the passion in a wonderful way'.[83]

In these and other accounts of the expressive power of

[81] More, *Utopia*, ed. and tr. E. Surtz, SJ and J. H. Hexter (New Haven, Conn., 1956) pp. 236–7.
[82] Glareanus, *Dodekachordon* (Basle, 1547), Book 3, ch. 24, pp. 326–3; tr. Strunk 1950, pp. 220–1.
[83] Tr. Strunk 1950, pp. 224–5.

polyphony,[84] the early humanists are deriving from their rhetorical education concepts and categories which are then used for practical criticism, which judges music as a mimetic art representing human feelings. Instead of granting the later monody a monopoly over rhetorical *movere*, we should see music theory in the whole period as sharing a common debt to rhetoric and its concern with expressivity. Claudio Monteverdi embraced the new style, of course, but forsook neither the madrigal nor choral music, while his operatic recitatives can be seen to derive some of their affective quality from 'rhetorical madrigalising', polyphony, and even from popular Italian genres such as the *vilanella* and *canzonetta*.[85] This composite tradition lies behind Monteverdi's *Madrigali Guerrieri ed amorosi* (1638), in the Foreword to which he states:

I have reflected that the principal passions or affections of the mind are three, namely, anger, moderation, and humility or supplication. . . . The art of music also points clearly to these three in its terms 'agitated', 'soft', and 'moderate'.[86]

—that is, *concitato*, *molle*, and *temperato*. Monteverdi writes that he has been unable to find in music any examples of the genre *concitato* (corresponding to *vehemens* in rhetorical terminology), which Plato describes as the kind of 'harmony that would fittingly imitate the utterances and the accents of a brave man' engaged in warfare, and so he began to experiment with the musical rhythms that would correspond to the more forceful classical metres. He found that 'sixteen semiquavers, struck one after the other, and combined with words expressing anger and disdain', would give 'a resemblance to the passion which I sought, although the words did not follow metrically the rapidity of the instrument'. Then he took his *favola* from Tasso's

---

[84] Similarly the Dutch humanist Samuel Quickelberg praised Orlando di Lasso in 1560 for expressing the content of the Penitential Psalms 'so aptly with lamenting and plaintive melody, adapting where it was necessary [the music] to the subject and the words, expressing the power of the different emotions, presenting the subject as if acted before the eyes [*rem quasi actam ante oculos ponendo*], that one cannot know whether the sweetness of the emotions more adorns the plaintive melodies', or vice versa: tr. Gustav Reese in Reese, *Music in the Renaissance*, (rev. edn., London, 1954), p. 513.

[85] Winn 1981, pp. 176, 189.

[86] Tr. Strunk 1950, p. 413, who notes the classical sources: Plato, Aristotle, Aristoxenus, and Boethius.

Gerusalemme Liberata, setting to music the episode of Tancred and Clorinda as a way of 'describing in music contrary passions, namely warfare and entreaty and death'.[87] As anyone who listens to the work will confirm, Monteverdi certainly succeeded in his 'attempt to depict anger', and his control of rhythm to suggest horses galloping is as expressive as the melody and harmony used in the lament of the dying Clorinda.

While this document certainly shows the influence of the Florentine Camerata in its experiment with rhythms to make a 'resemblance to agitated speech', it also belongs in the main line of musical rhetoric going back to antiquity. It was, after all, Quintilian who had first linked the two arts, urging the orator to learn from musicians flexibility in voice-inflexion, above all 'the variation of arrangement and sound [*compositio et sonus*] to suit the demands of the case'. Both arts, he stated, know how to adapt form to feeling, find the appropriate expression for emotions. Rhetoric, like music, can vary

> both tone and rhythm, expressing sublime thoughts with elevation, pleasing thoughts with sweetness, and ordinary with gentle utterance, and in every expression of its art is in sympathy with the emotions of which it is the mouth-piece. It is by the raising, lowering or inflexion of the voice that the orator stirs the emotions of his hearers, and the measure . . . of voice and phrase differs according as we wish to rouse the indignation or the pity of the judge. For, as we know, different emotions are roused even by the various musical instruments, which are incapable of reproducing speech. (1. 10. 22–7)

As with Alberti reversing the direction of Quintilian's analogies between painting or sculpture and rhetoric, so with music: for some humanists it was enough to use these words to describe music.[88] The common element was the striving for expressivity, which should reach a high degree of emotional intensity while remaining natural. In the music of Monteverdi, or Purcell, rhetoric united natural feeling and expressive form.

Music, painting, sculpture, all arts concerned with the representation of human thoughts and feelings, the 'move-

---

[87] Strunk 1950, pp. 413–15.
[88] Hutton 1951, p. 19. For Quintilian's influence on Renaissance musical rhetoric see Unger 1941, pp. 11–15, and Ruhnke 1955, pp. 94–7, 99–100.

ments of the mind' as expressed in their own media, drew on the whole tradition of Greek and Roman rhetoric. As new rhetoric texts became available, so they were adapted to each art. Gerard Le Coat has shown that Hermogenes' *Peri Ideōn*, which came into vogue at the end of the sixteenth century, was taken over by theorists of both music and painting. Hermogenes identified seven main qualities of style: clarity, grandeur (with six sub-divisions), beauty, speed, ethos (four sub-divisions), verity, and gravity. This scheme reappears in substantially the same form in much literary criticism, appropriately enough, but in musical writings we find it in Mei and Mersenne, while in art it is adapted by Lomazzo and Poussin.[89] Poussin, as well as applying the rhetorical concept of *actio* to gesture in painting, took from Zarlino's *Istitutione armoniche* the account of how Greek music used Modes to produce 'marvellous effects', grave and severe in the Dorian Mode, 'intense, vehement, violent' in the Phrygian. Excited by his reading, Poussin announces in 1647 that 'I hope, before another year is out, to paint a subject in this Phrygian Mode. The subject of frightful wars lends itself to this manner.'[90]

It follows that a truly historical method can use rhetoric as the basis for interpreting art and music side by side, as has already been attempted for the somewhat vexing problem of 'Mannerism'.[91] Le Coat devotes the second part of his book to a comparative analysis, using rhetoric as the common medium, of three seventeenth-century representations of anger, in poetry (Marino's *Strage degl' Innocenti*), painting (Poussin's *Massacre des Innocents)*, and music (Monteverdi's *Combattimento di Tancredi e Clorinda).*[92] H. W. Jensen has analysed Poussin's *Judgment of Solomon* in terms of the oratorical practice of *actio*, while he too has worked laterally, across the arts, comparing Dryden's *Song for St Cecilia's Day* (1687) with paintings by Rubens and Michelangelo, showing how many artists of this period deploy 'rhetorically oriented conventions and devices', intended to arouse in an audience 'the strong passions of admiration and

[89] Le Coat 1975, pp. 35–9 and *passim.*
[90] Ibid., pp. 73–190.
[91] See Shearman 1967, pp. 35, 38, 97–104, 135–51, 163–6; and M. R. Maniates, *Mannerism in Italian Music and Culture, 1530–1630* (Chapel Hill, NC, 1979).
[92] Le Coat 1975, pp. 73–190. This enterprising study deserves to be better known.

astonishment'.[93] In an age which has come to value interdisciplinary study we can see that rhetoric remains the most natural, perhaps the fundamental tool, for understanding the expression of feeling in artistic form.

[93] Jensen 1976, pp. 60–2, 179–86, and *passim*. See also D. T. Mace, 'Musical Humanism, the Doctrine of Rhythms, and the St. Cecilia Odes of Dryden', *Journal of the Warburg and Courtauld Institutes*, 27 (1964), 251–92.

8

RHETORIC IN THE MODERN NOVEL

> Pour nous, aujourd'hui, l'œuvre de la rhétorique n'a plus,
> dans son contenu, qu'un intérêt historique (d'ailleurs sous-
> estimé). L'idée de ressusciter son code pour l'appliquer à
> notre littérature serait un anachronisme stérile. Non qu'on
> ne puisse retrouver dans des textes modernes toutes les
> figures de l'ancienne rhétorique: mais c'est le système qui
> s'est désaccordé, et la fonction signifiante des figures a
> disparu avec le réseau de relations qui les articulait dans ce
> système.
>
> Gérard Genette[1]

Like all other forms of writing, in prose or verse, the novel has
drawn on rhetoric's transmitted skills in the organization of
language. The influence of rhetoric here is seen less at the level
of composition—there could be nothing comparable to Kepler or
Sidney using the seven-part oration for their treatises—than in
individual stylistic contexts: tropes and figures used for
description, characterization, emotional intensification. It
follows that analysis of the rhetorical element in fiction must
concern itself with the the details of style, and I have chosen
three well-known novels for close reading. But as an
introduction to those longer readings I should like to consider
some smaller pieces of evidence for the survival or revival of
rhetoric in the modern novel, evidence that has cropped up in
my general reading rather than by systematic study.

I

The teaching tradition of rhetoric survived, as we have seen,
into the nineteenth century. In some isolated outposts it
survived even longer. The novelist V. S. Naipaul, whose family
emigrated from India to the West Indies, is a witness to the

---

[1] *Figures I* (Paris, 1966), p. 221.

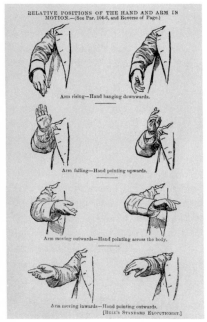

FIG. 6. *Bell's Standard Elocutionist:* Frontispiece

unlikely survival of 'elocutionary rhetoric' in such far-flung areas just before the Second World War. (This teaching method, developed in eighteenth-century England, used lessons in reading aloud and the study of spoken oratory and gesture as the basis for a literary education.[2]) In his partly autobiographical novel, *A House for Mr Biswas* (1961), set in Port of Spain, Trinidad, elementary education is still based on such outmoded anthologies of poetry or oratory as 'The *Royal Reader*', or '*Nelson's West Indian Readers*, by Captain Cutteridge, Director of Education'. Trinidadian children learn by heart and recite, with their hands behind their back, such poems as 'The Three Little Piggies. By Sir Alfred Scott-Gatty', or ' "Bingen on the Rhine" from *Bell's Standard Elocutionist*'[3]—a compilation first published in 1860. Mr Biswas, the book's hero (in real life the

[2] The fullest study of the elocutionary tradition is Howell 1971, but from an unsympathetic viewpoint, since the author makes it the scapegoat for the general decline of rhetoric. See Vickers 1981, pp. 114–16.

[3] Quotations are from the Penguin edition (Harmondsworth, 1969). For reflections of the educational system and its out-moded textbooks see pp. 46, 50, 111, 129, 137, 233–4, 238, 315, 339–40, 356–7, 382, 463, 479, 483, 490, 531. The

novelist's father), who gradually overcomes his deprived childhood and becomes a newspaper reporter, inadvertently takes his school copy of this work with him when he moves house. His son Anand subsequently studies the same text, being made to 'sit down there and call out this speech'—some Macaulay—so that his father, a newly-fledged journalist, can practise his shorthand (p. 337). The text becomes a source of family entertainment, too, for Mr Biswas reads from it at Christmas (p. 393), and the son once uses it to try and cheer up some relatives, a couple that looked sad, for reasons as yet beyond him.

    Anand, wishing to animate them and to show off a new accomplishment, offered to recite a poem to them. He had just mastered all the gestures illustrated on the frontispiece of *Bell's Standard Elocutionist*. Hari and his wife looked moved; they smiled and asked Anand to recite.

    Anand drew his feet together, bowed, and said, 'Bingen on the Rhine.' He joined his palms, rested his head on them, and recited:

    '*A soldier of the legion lay dying in Algiers.*'

He was pleased to see that the smiles of Hari and his wife had been replaced by looks of the utmost solemnity.

    '*There was lack of woman's nursing, there was dearth of woman's tears.*'

    '*But a comrade stood beside him while his life blood ebbed away.*'

Anand's voice quavered with emotion. Hari stared at the floor. His wife fixed her large eyes on a spot somewhere above Anand's shoulder. Anand had not expected such a full and immediate response. He increased the pathos in his voice, spoke more slowly and exaggerated his gestures. With both hands on his left breast he acted out the last words of the dying legionnaire.

    '*Tell her the last night of my life, for ere this moon be risen,*

    '*My body will be out of pain, my soul be out of prison.*'

Hari's wife burst out crying. Hari put his hand on hers. In this way they listened to the end; and Anand, after being given a six-cents piece, left them shaken.

most influential of these texts is by Alexander Melville Bell (1819–1905), author of numerous works on oratory: *Bell's Standard Elocutionist. The principles of elocution and relative exercises; followed by an extensive collection of classified extracts in prose and poetry adapted for reading and recitation* (Edinburgh, 1860); it was still being reprinted in America fifty years later. On the autobiographical nature of this novel see Naipaul's touching memoir in the *New York Review of Books* for 24 Nov. 1983 (vol. 30 no. 18), pp. 22–3. Mr Naipaul has kindly confirmed that the illustration from Bell reproduced here (Fig. 6) is indeed the one he remembers as a boy.

Less than a week later Hari died. It was only then that Anand learned that Hari had known for some time that he was going to die soon. (pp. 414–15)

Despite his mastery of pathos and rhetorical gesture Anand was wholly lacking in decorum, unwittingly choosing the most unsuitable piece possible for this audience. But the novelist remembered his rhetoric-book.

To Gerald Brenan, autobiographer and historian of Spain, at a prep school in Winchester before the First World War, the pedantry of a classics master made the whole of rhetoric unpalatable. The headmaster, Mr Johns, took the senior boys (aged 12 or thereabouts) in Greek, and would make them

construe Homer or Xenophon. If he was in a good mood puns would fly about and sweets be distributed, but if he frowned one had to be careful. Yet he was not a good teacher. He made no attempt whatever to arouse our interest in what we were reading. Either he made jokes about Homeric epithets or else he set us searching for odd figures of speech, as though they were the principal objects of interest in literature. What I remember from these hours is chiefly therefore a rag-bag of onomatopoeias, oxymorons, hypallages, anacoluthons, hysteron-proterons and so forth—all of course quite pointless. Like James Joyce, he seemed to love words in order to make fun of them.[4]

But rhetoric becomes 'quite pointless' only when taught so perfunctorily, and Joyce's interest in words—and rhetoric— went rather deeper than mockery. Unfamiliarity, and the waning of rhetoric in education, has made these terms sound strange to modern ears. Yet some of the names of these figures, and many of the verbal effects they describe, recur in contemporary fiction. *Hysteron proteron*, for instance, the 'preposterous' misplacing of words, is the figure at work in this comic anecdote from a recent novel set in Northern Ireland, where the horn summoning the workers to the factory blows 'very loud' in the mornings:

At one time they used to blow it at quarter to eight, to give people time to rush to work. Da always told us about the old fellow who worked with him and he was always late and when he got into work he talked fast, like talking faster was getting him there earlier, but he was always

---

[4] *A Life of One's Own. Childhood and Youth* (London, 1962) pp. 58–9.

late Da says and he always got his words arse about face. He said to Da one morning: 'I put my foot in the horn as the trousers blew eight and left the door in bed and Maggie lying wide open.'[5]

A figure is used, and named, in Flann O'Brien's comic novel *At Swim-Two-Birds* (1939), where the narrator recalls how his uncle prepared to play some records on an old wind-up gramophone:

My uncle was occupied with inserting a cranking device into an aperture in the machine's side and winding it with the meticulous and steady motion that is known to prolong the life and resiliency of springs. Fearing that his careful conduct of the task was not observed, he remarked that fast winding will lead to jerks, jerks will lead to strain and strain to breakage, thus utilizing a figure of speech to convey the importance of taking pains.

Name of figure of speech: Anadiplosis (or Epanastrophe).

Moderation in all things, he said, that is the trick that won the war.[6]

A more sustained use of rhetoric illuminates the pages of Raymond Queneau's brilliant *Exercices de Style*.[7] In this work (which the British Library, at least, catalogues as 'fiction') Queneau, a novelist best known for *Zazie dans le métro*, takes a banal incident on a Paris bus and retells it in ninety-nine different ways (a procedure that a Renaissance writer would have instantly recognized as a form of 'varying', practised to increase facility in expression, as in Erasmus' *De Copia*, where a single sentence is varied more than two hundred ways; Beckett performed a similar operation in *Watt*). The basic incident, told as '*Récit*', begins: 'Un jour vers midi du côté du parc Monceau, sur la plate-forme arrière d'un autobus à peu près complet de la ligne S . . .'. This is then subjected to various rhetorical procedures, such as '*Polyptotes*' (varying forms from the same root): 'Je montai dans un autobus plein de contribuables qui donnaient des sous à un contribuable qui avait sur son ventre de contribuable une petite boîte qui contribuait à permettre aux autres contribuables de continuer leur trajet de contribuables'; or '*Homeoptotes*' (like endings): 'Un jour de canicule sur un

---

[5] Ian Cochrane, *A Streak of Madness* (London, 1973); quoted from the Penguin edition (Harmondsworth, 1977), p. 49.

[6] Quotations from the Penguin edition (Harmondsworth, 1971), p. 94. Unfortunately the effect is rather spoiled by the misprint 'anadipolsis'.

[7] Quotations are from the typographically elaborate edition (Paris, 1956). Barbara Bray has bravely attempted an English translation (London, 1980).

véhicule où je circule, gesticule un funambule au bulbe minuscule . . .'; or *'Onomatopées'*: 'Sur la plate-forme, pla pla pla, d'un autobus, teuff, teuff, teuff.'

Queneau's invention does much more than merely display the figures and tropes: he adds definition to the scene cumulatively (rather like composing a colour photograph in a series of separate printing stages of the component colours), and he reveals most economically the variations in style and attitude caused by the choice of a figure. Thus for *'Exclamations'*: 'Tiens! Midi! temps de prendre l'autobus! que de monde!'; or *'Apartés'* (asides): 'L'autobus arriva tout gonflé de voyageurs. *Pourvu que je ne le rate pas, veine il y a encore une place pour moi'*; or *'Apostrophe'*: 'O stylographe à la plume de platine, que ta course rapide et sans heurt trace sur le papier . . .'. Some sections exploit those rhetorical figures describing the possible compressions or deformations of language, whether spoken forms such as *'Aphérèses'*: 'Tai tobus yageurs', or *'Apocopes'*: 'Je mon dans un auto plein de voya', or written such as *'Syncopes'*: 'Je mtai ds aubus plein dvyageurs', or *'Métathèses'*: 'Un juor vres miid, sru la plate-forme aièrrre d'un autobus . . .'. Queneau's examples are so clearly differentiated that—an exemplary feature of a rhetoric-book—definitions are hardly needed. Finally, two figures to rejoice English-speakers, *'Anglicismes'*: 'Un day vers midday, je tèque le beusse et je sie un jeugne manne avec un grète nèque et un hatte avec une quainnde de lèsse tressée', and the matching *'Poor lay Zanglay'*: 'Ung joor vare meedee ger preelotobüs poor la port Changparay. Eel aytay congplay, praysk.'

Raymond Queneau's exuberant invention created a work that is strictly speaking inimitable. Michel Tournier's *Friday or the other island*[8] is an imitation, so to speak, of *Robinson Crusoe*, retaining the eighteenth-century setting with Crusoe a castaway into solitude, but differing radically with Defoe's reconstruction of his life on the island. Tournier re-creates much more profoundly the effects of solitude, which threaten to break down his protagonist's personality altogether, making him withdraw for long periods to a protozoic existence in a primeval slime, or a

---

[8] *Vendredi, ou les limbes du Pacifique* (Paris, 1967); I quote from the English version by Norman Denny (London, 1969; Harmondsworth, 1974).

foetal posture in the depths of a cave. One striking sequence explores the consequences of being cut off from society and denied the use of language, a topic central to the rhetorical tradition. (Tournier knows, perhaps, Cicero's *De Officiis*, where the corollary of language as the tool of social exchange is the vision of solitude and the deprival of speech leading to madness and death.) The novel alternates a third-person narrative with excerpts from Robinson's journal, whose passages of sustained reflection counterpoint the narrator's smoother flow of events (an effect unfortunately ruined when one quotes the journal alone, which thus seems too pat). As Robinson comes to realize that he is 'in a land bereft of human kind', the dialogue that he has been continuing in his mind with 'the vanished crew and the people of the island' turns into a 'soliloquy', of which he soon wearies, noting the 'corrosive influence' of solitude, 'the dehumanizing process which I feel to be inexorably at work within me' (pp. 47–8). His solitude, he finds,

does not destroy the meaning of things. It undermines them at the very root of their being. More and more do I come to doubt the evidence of my senses. I know now that the very earth beneath my feet needs to be trodden by feet other than mine if I am to be sure of its substance.

The 'surest guard' against hallucination and delirium is 'our brother, our neighbour, our friend or our enemy—anyway, God save us, *someone*!' (p. 49).

Solitude not only undermines his belief in his own perception, the 'process of erosion' also leads to a 'disintegration of language'. Although he constantly talks aloud, communicating every idea or observation he has 'to the trees or clouds', he notes a daily

collapse of whole sectors of that citadel of words within which our thought dwells and moves, like a mole in its network of tunnels. Those fixed points which thought uses for its progression, like crossing a river on stepping stones, are crumbling and vanishing beneath the surface. I am losing my sense of the meaning of words which do not represent concrete objects. I can only talk literally. Metaphor, litotes and hyperbole call for a considered effort which has the effect of emphasizing everything that is unreal and conventional in those figures of speech. (p. 58)

That is, denied contact with other people, and with the 'natural language of the passions', as an eighteenth-century rhetorician would describe them, with thought reduced to a literalness that cannot make more abstract transitions, to use such figures demands a conscious exercise of the will. (A perspective that would have pleased those theorists, such as Vico and Rousseau, who held that the first forms of language were the tropes, invented to express human feelings.) Robinson goes on to question the evaluations implicit in some of the tropes we use in everyday speech:

For example, the notion of *depth*, which I never troubled to scrutinize when using it in such expressions as 'a deep thinker' or 'a deep love'. It is a strange prejudice which sets a higher value on depth than on breadth, and which accepts 'superficial' as meaning, not 'of wide extent' but 'of little depth', whereas 'deep', on the other hand, signifies 'of great depth' and not 'of small surface'. (ibid.)

Similarly with that process of thought that 'prefers the inward to the outward being', as if men are 'to be regarded as riches enclosed in a worthless shell, and the more deeply we penetrate within them, the greater is the treasure we discover. But what if there were no treasure? What if that outer shell were solid, filled with sameness like a doll stuffed with bran?' (p. 59). To question that metaphor would be to challenge an evaluation of outer and inner that goes back beyond Plato, but this sensitivity to language and the implications of rhetoric is just one aspect of Michel Tournier's profound rethinking of this received narrative.

Rhetoric plays a smaller part in a modern English novel, also set in the eighteenth century, William Golding's *Rites of Passage*.[9] Its meticulous narrator, one Edmund Talbot, keeps a journal, for his patron to read, of his voyage on a British ship to take up a post in one of 'His Majesty's colonies'. Mr Talbot is young and eloquent, too much so for the ship's officers, to whom he expresses surprise that there is no chaplain on board:

'How is order to be maintained? You take away the keystone and the whole arch falls!'

[9] Quotations from *Rites of Passage* (London, 1980), with page-references incorporated into the text.

Mr. Cumbershum did not appear to take my point. I saw that my language must not be figurative with such a man and rephrased it. (pp. 21–2)

This mannered story-teller, self-conscious about his stylistic economy ('I will get myself up, relieved, shaved, breakfasted in a single sentence': p. 28—where 'relieved', however, sounds anachronistic), and clever with his use of parenthesis ('throughout the day I have walked, talked, eaten, drunk, explored—and here I am again, kept out of my bunk by the—I must confess it—agreeable invitation of the page!': p. 29), appropriately enough draws attention to his own rhetoric when reflecting on

the *strangeness* of this life in this strange part of the world among strange people and in this strange construction of English oak which both transports and imprisons me! (I am aware of course, of the amusing 'paranomasia' in the word 'transport' and hope the perusal of it will afford you some entertainment!) (pp. 228–9)

Actually the figure is not *paronomasia* (variously defined as 'repeating the same word in different cases', or using two or more words resembling each other in sound but differing in sense), but *syllepsis*, another form of pun which alludes to a second meaning without repeating the word; and had Mr Talbot known a bit more about rhetoric he could have commented on his use of *ploche* and *polyptoton* in the repetition of 'strangeness . . . strange' earlier on. Yet he is clearly proud to know the name of one figure and uses it again (just as inappropriately) to describe the death of James Colley, from the thought of whose position 'many miles down' under the sea it seems 'a different sort of *bathos* (your lordship, as Colley might say, will note the amusing "paranomasia") to return to the small change of day . . .' (p. 264).

Golding's narrator writes his journal down, but the novelist captures a remarkably direct, almost spoken tone of voice. Another narrator who speaks his story, a vastly more complex narrative sequence, rich in flash-back, flash-forward, and intercalated episode, figures in Graham Swift's novel *Waterland*.[10] The narrator is Tom Crick, history master at an East

---

[10] Quotations from *Waterland* (London, 1983), with page-references in the text.

Anglian grammar school for thirty-two years, who has just been told that he is to be 'retired early'. He stands mentally, as it were, before his 'children'—'I addressed you, silently, as "children"'—and asks them to 'listen, one last time, to your history teacher' (p. 4). The story he tells them has interludes and reflections dealing with history, but essentially concerns his own family history, a not untypical Fenland tale involving incest, murder, an abortion, and the resulting barrenness and schizophrenia. The narrative is not spoken out loud but internally, a form of monologue that seems to rely, none the less, on specifically oral devices, especially repetition. The most common figure of repetition, as usual, is *anaphora* (the same word beginning a sequence of clauses or sentences), as in the teacher's exposition of a 'theory of reality': 'Reality's not strange, not unexpected. Reality doesn't reside in the sudden hallucination of events. Reality is uneventfulness, vacancy, flatness. Reality is that nothing happens' (p. 34). But that example already shows one peculiar feature of this narrative style, that the repetition is not emphatic-persuasive, generating a strong emotional response, but rather meditative or reflective, allowing the mind to brood over a point, make a list, accumulate details. Such are the sentences beginning with the name of a character, 'Freddie Parr' (p. 42), or an abstract noun like 'curiosity' (p. 44), or 'rumour' (p. 88). Worse still, *anaphora* is used for such relatively unimportant words and phrases as 'not to the men' (p. 8), 'perhaps' (p. 10), 'he was hoping' (p. 24), 'that' (pp. 26–7), 'because' (p. 29; and p. 94), 'who' (p. 101; also p. 129), 'whether' (p. 102), 'why was it that' (p. 123), 'they've got . . .' (p. 135), 'how' (p. 190), and so on. Reading these inert sequences of repetition inevitably makes one recall the advice of Renaissance rhetoricians that the word chosen for emphasis should be one important to the sense, which in a novel would mean not just the sentence but the larger narrative design.

The narrator of this novel uses rhetoric unconsciously, or better still unknowingly—he doesn't know how it should be made effective. *Anadiplosis*, the linking repetition of the word ending one period and beginning the next, is used without wit or energy here, for instance: 'the land in that part of the world is flat. Flat, with an unrelieved and monotonous flatness . . .' (p. 2); Fen families 'adapt themselves, as we might say, to technology. To technology, and to ambition' (p. 13); 'That I realised. I realised I was looking at a dead body' (p. 25); ' . . . of her grandmother? Her grandmother who . . .' (p. 88). These repetitions may mark the slowness of the narrator's brain, or his pause to take stock, but they have little energizing function in the narrative. Longer passages of repetition end up being, simply, repetitive, a speech or thought mannerism that seems just to recapitulate itself (e.g. pp. 139, 'Added to' beginning three sentences; p. 149, listing thirteen 'stages of intoxication'; p. 157, four clauses ending 'has drunk'; p. 202, 'He drank' beginning three sentences). The narrator's use of *epistrophe* (the same word ending a sequence of clauses or sentences) fails to exploit the possibilities of wit and surprise that the figure can create. So he speculates parenthetically on ('. . . History: a lucky dip of meanings. Events elude meaning, but we look for meanings. Another definition of Man: the animal who craves meanings—but knows—)' (p. 122). There is little here of the unexpected return of a word that *epistrophe* can create. (See also p. 15: three sentences ending 'reality'; p. 32, ending 'machine'; p. 141, ending 'drunkenness', p. 276, ending 'stuff'.) *Correctio* (or *epanorthosis*), recalling a word to replace it with one more suitable, is used rather woodenly to tell us that the teacher's drawer contains 'one—no, two—bottles of J & B' (p. 132); or to describe how a character 'opens his eyes, and his eyes, or rather his limbs— . . . tell him' where he is (p. 292: three successive paragraphs begin 'He opens his eyes'). *Anadiplosis* is used to describe the 'stages' of love: 'It begins with adoration. Then adoration turns to desire, and desire to cleaving, and cleaving to union' (p. 196). This is tidy enough, but one has to ask, what has been gained by putting this commonplace idea into the form of a rhetorical figure? In a functional use of rhetoric figure and expression are linked by necessity. *Epizeuxis*, repeating a word for passionate emphasis, becomes an empty repetition as the narrator explains 'why so many historical movements fail, fail at heart, is because they fail to take account of the complex and unpredictable forms of our curiosity' (p. 168). Such writing is neither complex nor unpredictable.

The most frequent of these figures of repetition is actually one that was never meant to be used in repetition, namely the rhetorical question. The narrator is inordinately given to bombarding his class of children—imagined class, imagined discourse—with sequences of questions, fifteen in a row on page 80, for instance ('Children, why this seeking for omens? Why this superstition? Why must the zenith never be fixed? . . .'), and eleven on the opposite page ('How do the Atkinsons mark, in 1874, the ninety-second birthday of Sarah? With beer and merriment? With raised tankards and toasts?') A hectoring note sometimes enters these questions: 'But what is the greater cause for astonishment . . .? What is the greater cause for alarm . . .?' (p. 87), and they are not, in any case, 'rhetorical' questions in the root sense of the term—a question whose answer is self-evident. We readers cannot answer these questions since we don't have the information, which is in the hands of the man telling the story. The doctor visits Cable House early one morning: 'What has brought him in such haste? Has something terrible taken place within? No—or, that is, no and perhaps yes too' (p. 91; part of fifteen questions in three pages). Instead of piling up the questions, we sometimes feel, the narrator could simply tell us the answers. Rather than a verbal device to be used in specific situations, the rhetorical question becomes a monotonous way of conveying information, heaping up detail, or provoking speculation (see, e.g., further sequences on pp. 111, 114, 152–3 (two paragraphs!), 165, 176, 185, 220, 221, etc.). No other modern text I know of uses so many rhetorical questions. A rhetoric teacher examining the narrator's composition would have told him to cultivate variety, avoid wearying the reader.

The formation of the narrator in Graham Swift's novel is no less an act of deliberate artistic choice than it was in William Golding's. Golding's story-teller, though, witty, dapper, eager to tease and please, is more stimulating. But Swift's narrator is perhaps intended as a study of the *déformation professionnelle* resulting from a lifetime teaching school. The author occasionally makes his rhetorical inheritance explicit:

Children, something of my father's fulminating and faltering rhetoric infects my teacherly oratory. Something of his predicament, before that Town Hall assembly, those heckles, those jeers, revives itself in my classroom confrontations, when I face resentment and hostility over the desk-tops. (p. 141)

It is unclear to what extent this is meant as a justification for the narrator's style. Had his rhetoric been either 'fulminating' or 'faltering' it might have been more interesting. The term 'rhetorical' recurs in this episode, where Mr Crick is confronted by an awkward pupil (who turns out to be surprisingly loyal) and sees himself as 'Blathering again. Talking too much. Rhetorical hand-sweeps over empty desks' (p. 143), but changing from this defensive posture to a feeling of liking for the boy: 'A hand raised—but not in rhetorical gesture. A hand raised, almost unconsciously, to touch Price's shoulder' (p. 144). There 'rhetorical' seems to be opposed to 'sincere', but although the narrator drops his gesture on this occasion his style remains to the end repetitive, pleonastic, verbose. The narrator is so fully rendered in his linguistic over-plus that he comes between us and the events he describes. His self-justifying retrospections clog the movement of thought and action, his voice absorbs and obliterates all other voices. It is no doubt appropriate for a schoolmaster to be condescending to his pupils (e.g. p. 55), but to use a pedant as a narrator is to run into certain risks caused by verisimilitude—pompous and boring story-tellers can just deter readers. *Waterland* survives being told by Mr Crick, and does so because of the author's grasp of a complex narrative, and his evocation of the Fen milieu and its social history. But although rhetoric is frequently used, it is within a narrow spectrum, repetitively, and to little creative purpose.

II

The modern novel that best demonstrates the continuing power of rhetoric is James Joyce's *Ulysses* (1922). Joyce's fascination with language almost as an end in itself is well known, and his education, at the Jesuit Belvedere College and University College, Dublin, may have introduced him to the basic rhetorical processes. As Matthew Hodgart reminds us, oratory played a large role in Irish society then, especially in politics, and Joyce reused several speeches delivered in the Ireland of his youth. The 'hell-fire' sermon in *Portrait* derives from one Joyce heard delivered by Father James Cullen at a retreat in November 1896, while in *Ulysses* he records, and reworks, examples of famous Irish orators: Seymour Bushe, whom he had heard

speak in 1899 (he included one passage from that speech in a
1904 notebook), and John F. Taylor, who addressed the UCD
Law Students Debating Society on 24 October 1901.[11] When
Joyce began to take further notes for the revision of *Ulysses* in
1918 (the first version had begun to appear in the *Little Review*
in March of that year), working in the Zentralbibliothek, Zurich,
he did some special research on rhetoric for the 'Aeolus'
episode.[12] Thanks to the detective work of Philip Herring, we
know two of his sources: a translation of Aristotle's *Rhetoric* into
French by François Cassandre (Paris, 1654; Joyce used the 1733
Amsterdam reprint), and the *Oxford English Dictionary* (from
which he copied out the examples given for three rhetorical
figures).[13] Joyce also used some manual of rhetoric, probably
nineteenth-century, which he may have shown to Stuart Gilbert
when the latter was preparing his authorized explication of
Ulysses in the late 1920s. As Gilbert records, Joyce approved of
the whole work and suggested 'several passages' directly: 'thus
the long list of examples of rhetorical forms which concludes my
commentary on the "Aeolus" episode was compiled at his
suggestion, and we spent several industrious afternoons
collaborating on it.'[14] Gilbert includes a list of ninety-five
rhetorical devices used in the 'Aeolus' episode, some of which
are erroneously defined or illustrated,[15] but if these errors are

[11] Hodgart 1974, pp. 120–2. Groden 1977, pp. 96–7 and 82 n. (with details of a
modern reprinting of Taylor's original peroration).

[12] I also live in Zurich (for some years in the street next to where Joyce was
living at this time), and discovered about his use of rhetoric from a book that I
myself borrowed from the Zentralbibliothek. The *genius loci* has evidently been
at work.

[13] Herring 1977, pp. x, 9–10, 25–6. Boileau, the great French critic, wrote in
1674 of Cassandre's translation of Aristotle's *Rhetoric*, 'j'avoue franchement que
sa lecture m'a plus profité que tout ce que j'ai jamais lu en ma vie' (Muntéano
1967, p. 175). It was also used by Racine (France 1965, p. 39).

[14] Gilbert 1952, p. viii; the commentary is on pp. 177–98.

[15] Since Matthew Hodgart has put me on record as stating that Gilbert's list
includes a number of errors (Hodgart 1974, p. 122 n.), I ought to specify them,
although they might better be called 'non-standard' definitions. Epideictic
rhetoric is not well defined as 'expository' (p. 188), and the compilers of classical
rhetoric-texts were hardly 'the Schoolmen' (p. 190). I doubt whether Joyce
deals with 'nearly all the important, misleading enthymemes elenchated by
Quintilian and his successors' (ibid.), and the example Gilbert gives of an
enthymeme (p. 194) is incorrect, as Hodgart has noted (Hodgart 1974, p. 124),
being only an elliptical sentence. Some of Gilbert's spellings are unusual, if they
be not printer's errors (*metonomy* instead of *metonymy*; similarly *synonomy*,
exergasia, antinomasia, paranomasia, incremetum). *Ploche* is said to be 'the using of a

not Gilbert's own they might help us to identify the books that Joyce used. The only writer referred to by Gilbert is 'Professor Bain' (p. 189) that is, Alexander Bain (1818–1903), author of *English Composition and Rhetoric* (1866; 2 vols., 1887–8), and other similar studies.

Although rhetorical devices figure in every episode of *Ulysses*, at times on every page, they are used most intensively, and appropriately, in the 'Aeolus' episode. Following out his parallel with Homer (Odysseus, Penelope, Telemachus: Leopold and Molly Bloom, Stephen Dedalus), Joyce here treats the experiences of Odysseus, as described in Book X of the *Odyssey*, on the floating island of Aeolia (Stromboli), where Aeolus lives, god of the winds. When Odysseus leaves, Aeolus gives him a bag containing all the dangerous winds, thanks to which he almost reaches Ithaca, but his companions open the bag by mistake and drive the ship back to Aeolia. At this point Aeolus loses his temper with Odysseus and drives him away with a curse. Joyce's equivalent for the floating and erupting island is the office of two Dublin newspapers, the *Freeman's Journal* and *National Press*, which Bloom visits in order to have an advertisement placed on behalf of his client Alexander Keyes.

name, in the same phrase, both as a name and to signify the qualities of the person to whom it is applied' (p. 194–cf. p. 330 above): it usually denotes mere repetition. *Epanalepsis* is said to be 'beginning a clause with a word that is made to end the next clause' (pp. 195–6), a figure which is more often known as *anadiplosis*. The words "Twas rank and fame that tempted thee' are said to form a *synoeciosis* (p. 196), but that term refers to a 'union of contraries', otherwise known as *oxymoron*. Lenehan's pun in 'I caught a cold in the park. The gate was open' is not an *auxesis* (p. 196), which means arranging terms in ascending order of importance, an effect which Gilbert subsequently names *anabasis* (p. 198). It is wrong to describe *anaphora* as a 'redundant repetition of same words at the beginning of clauses' (p. 196): there is nothing redundant about emphasis. Sometimes Gilbert's definition describes the verbal effect correctly, but attaches the wrong name to it (as with *epanodos*, p. 198); at other times the definition is right, but the example quoted does not match it (as with *epitrope*, p. 197). In *Notes for Joyce. An Annotation of James Joyce's 'Ulysses'* (New York, 1979), Don Gifford reprints some eighty of Gilbert's identifications of the figures and adds a further forty suggestions of his own (pp. 519–25): both lists still contain errors, and they remain lists. Fifty years on, critical analysis of Joyce's *use* of rhetoric seems overdue. R. Saldívar, *Figural Language in the Novel. The Flowers of Speech from Cervantes to Joyce* (Princeton, NJ, 1984) devotes a chapter to Joyce, discussing *Stephen Hero* and *Ulysses*—but not, surprisingly, the 'Aeolus' episode. The critical method derives much from Derrida, taking over his punning discussion of metaphor as 'héliotrope' (in his essay 'La Mythologie blanche', *Poétique*, 5 (1971), 1–52), and developing the notion of 'flowers of speech' in Joyce's text in an ingeniously literal-minded fashion.

The same building includes the premises of an evening paper, whose editor, Myles Crawford, plays the role of Aeolus. Bloom is hoping to persuade Crawford to give his client a 'puff' in the Saturday issue, and when Bloom leaves the office to contact his client, Crawford dismisses him with a joking reference to the ending of *Paradise Lost*: 'Begone! he said. The world is before you.'[16]

But when Bloom telephones back, '—Tell him to go to hell, the editor said promptly' (p. 285)—and when Bloom returns in person with his client's offer to run the advertisement for two months only, not three, as the journal wants, Crawford says of Keyes that he can 'kiss my royal Irish arse' (p. 307). There are many precise parallels with Homer, including even an imitation of Odysseus' north-east-to-south-west movement around Italy in the toings and froings of Bloom and Stephen across Dublin.[17]

Joyce not only constructed elaborate echoes between his eighteen episodes and Homer's text, but gave each of his episodes a series of correspondences, physical, temporal, symbolic, which were intended to unify the whole work and give it some kind of encyclopaedic status. For the 'Aeolus' episode the first schema that he produced was sent to Carlo Linati in September 1920 and has eight main headings:

> Time—12–1
> Colour—Red
> Persons—Aeolus, Sons, Telemachus, Mentor, Ulysses (2)
> Technic—Simbouleutike, Dikanike, Epideictic, Tropes
> Science, Art—Rhetoric
> Sense (Meaning)—the Mockery of Victory
> Organ—Lungs
> Symbol—Machines: Wind: Hunger: Kite: Failed Destinies:
>   Press: Mutability[18]

[16] *Ulysses* is cited from the new critical text, ed. H. W. Gabler *et al.*, 3 vols. (New York, 1984). All my quotations are from Vol. I; here, p. 285. Compare here the closing lines of *Paradise Lost*:

The world was all before them, where to choose
Their place of rest, and providence their guide:
They hand in hand with wandering steps and slow,
Through Eden took their solitary way. (xii. 646 ff.)

[17] See Groden 1977, pp. 76–91, and literature cited there.

[18] Ibid., pp. 100–1. When he sent another scheme to his friend Valery Larbaud in the following year, Joyce simplified it, omitting his hints about its meaning and symbolism, and replacing the itemization of 'Technic' with one laconic word, 'enthymemic' (ibid., pp. 112–13). As Matthew Hodgart has shown, the revised formula is rather unhelpful: Hodgart 1974, pp. 123–5.

The events take place between 12 noon and 1; the colour-symbolism (not the most convincing part of Joyce's scheme) associates the newspaper world with red; the characters include many of those from the comparable section in the *Odyssey*; while both the thematic and symbolic references include the idea of failure, or a hollow victory (Odysseus driven back by the winds over which he had had power; Bloom seeming to have had his client's deal accepted, then spurned). The reference to 'technic' has Joyce using the correct Greek terms, as found in Aristotle, for the three kinds of rhetoric, deliberative, forensic, and panegyric. Furthermore, within the action of this episode, the conversation among the hangers-on in the newspaper office, Joyce included examples of each of the three kinds of oratory.

The epideictic oration is that delivered by Dan Dawson, reported in the day's newspaper, and read aloud by Ned Lambert, one of the editor's cronies. (Epideictic speeches, Joyce doubtless knew, were usually written down and read out or published, not delivered in an actual forum.) It is a speech in praise of 'ERIN, GREEN GEM OF THE SILVER SEA' (p. 255), as one of the head-titles that Joyce subsequently inserted into the text informs us, and is a mass of clichés and poetic diction ('*purling rill*', '*gentlest zephyrs*', '*mossy banks*'): in the *Rhetoric* (1406ª11–35) Aristotle had advised the orator to avoid poeticisms. 'How's that for high?' (p. 255), Ned Lambert asks, alluding to the three styles of traditional rhetoric, and adding his own coarse *paronomasia* for '*overarching leafage*': '*overarsing leafage*' (p. 257). In the peroration the panegyrist celebrates Erin's

Peaks, . . . *towering high on high, to bathe our souls, as it were* . . .— Bathe his lips, Mr Dedalus said . . . —As *'twere, in the peerless panorama of Ireland's portfolio, unmatched, despite their wellpraised prototypes in other vaunted prize regions, for very beauty* . . . *steeped in the transcendent translucent glow of our mild mysterious twilight* . . . —The moon, professor MacHugh said. He forgot Hamlet. (p. 261)

But sure enough, that '*glowing orb*' soon enters and '*shines forth to irradiate her silver effulgence*', only to be dismissed by Mr Dedalus's coarse *meiosis*, 'O! . . . Shite and onions!' (p. 261).

This spineless collection of poeticisms is justly mocked, we may feel, if the parody is not indeed overdone. Epideictic comes off worst, 'forensic eloquence' (p. 289), as represented by the celebrated advocate Seymour Bushe, does rather better.

Contrasting 'Roman justice . . . with the earlier Mosaic code, the *lex talionis* . . . he cited the Moses of Michelangelo in the Vatican' (p. 291). As one of the characters recalls,

—He said of it: *that stony effigy in frozen music, horned and terrible, of the human form divine, that eternal symbol of wisdom and prophecy which, if aught that the imagination or the hand of sculptor has wrought in marble of soultransfigured and of soultransfiguring deserves to live, deserves to live.* His slim hand with a wave graced echo and fall. (p. 293)

To the modern reader that passage, with its shameless borrowing from Blake ('the human form divine'), its calculated rhyme ('aught . . . wrought'), elaborate *polyptoton* ('soul-transfigured . . . soultransfiguring'), and above all the carefully stage-managed repetition of the last clause, may seem self-regarding, narcissistic, not much better than Dawson's poeticisms. Yet the character who quotes it describes it as 'one of the most polished periods I think I ever listened to in my life' (p. 291), while the others hail it as 'the divine afflatus' (p. 293). And the workings of rhetorical *movere* and the orator's delivery are summed up in its effect on young Dedalus: 'Stephen, his blood moved by grace of language and gesture, blushed' (ibid.).

The third and last speech, which receives most space and most adoration, is, appropriately, in the deliberative genre, which Aristotle pronounced the noblest. The character nicknamed 'professor' MacHugh reports that 'the finest display of oratory I ever heard was a speech made by John F. Taylor at the college historical society', debating 'the revival of the Irish tongue' (p. 293). In contrast to the abrupt treatment of the two previous specimens, Joyce now gives us an oration within an oration, for the professor himself is a would-be orator, with his modern version of *actio*. He 'raised an outspanned hand to his spectacles and, with trembling thumb and ringfinger touching lightly the black rims, steadied them to a new focus' (p. 295). Recalling Quintilian's pronouncement that the eye is the most expressive organ, 'his gaze turned at once but slowly from J. J. O'Molloy's towards Stephen's face and then bent at once to the ground, seeking' (ibid.). Having caught their attention he delivers the longest and most elaborate of the three specimens of Irish oratory. As the professor reports, Taylor had arisen 'from a sickbed', and appeared unshaven, wearing 'a loose white silk neckcloth and altogether he looked (though he was not) a dying man' (p. 295). Perhaps this was a deliberate choice of costume, that method of appealing to an audience's sympathies recommended by Quintilian (quoted above, pp. 78–9). As he begins speaking, Taylor claims to feel *'transported into a country far away from this country, into an age remote from this age'*— a double *epanalepsis*—and imagines himself in ancient Egypt, *'listening to the speech of some highpriest of that land addressed to the youthful Moses'* (p. 297).

There follows a *prosopopoeia*, a device much recommended by rhetoricians for its emotional force, which is built up around a sustained antithesis between the Egyptians and the Jews: *'—Why will you jews not accept our culture, our religion and our language? You are a tribe of nomad herdsman; we are a mighty people . . .'* (p. 297). The antithesis is pursued through six more sentences, all artfully varied to avoid monotony, ending *'Vagrants and daylabourers are you called: the world trembles at our name'* (ibid.). At this point Joyce punctuates the professor's recital (among the symbols present in this episode, as he told Linati, are 'wind' and 'hunger') with a reminder of the modern orator's body: 'A dumb belch of hunger cleft his speech.' Undeterred, the professor sweeps on to Taylor's conclusion: *'had the youthful Moses listened to and accepted that view of life, had he bowed his head and bowed his will and bowed his spirit before that arrogant admonition'*—piling up the figures of emphasis, *anaphora* and *ploche*, with *auxesis*, the terms arranged in ascending order of importance (—*head*—*will*—*spirit*), all made more clear-cut with the symmetries of *isocolon* and *parison*—had Moses been influenced by such a speech (if ever, the sceptical reader thinks by now, such a speech was delivered) then

he would never have brought the chosen people out of their house of bondage . . . He would never have spoken with the Eternal amid lightnings on Sinai's mountaintop nor ever have come down with the light of inspiration shining in his countenance and bearing in his arms the tables of the law, graven in the language of the outlaw.

He ceased and looked at them, enjoying a silence . . . —That is oratory, the professor said uncontradicted. (p. 299)

This speech within a speech ended, after more instances of the figures of symmetry traditionally associated with Gorgias (*isocolon, parison, anaphora*), with a most artful *paromoion* (where every word in a two- or more part structure corresponds to its neighbour: 'the tables of the . . . / the language of the'), capped by an *antithesis* or *polyptoton* on 'law/outlaw'. It is significant that in the notes that Joyce took from Cassandre's version of Aristotle's *Rhetoric* (Book Three, section ix), he picked out the component parts of a compound period, noting the distinction between *parisose* (in Cassandre's French), where the period is 'composée de membres égaux', and *paromoeose*, where 'les extrémités de châque membre se ressemblent pour la terminaison', in the latter case it being acceptable that 'la ressemblance se trouve dans les dernières syllabes'. In Joyce's brief notes this appears as:

antithesis in clauses to sustain length of equal limbs = parisose
   equal ends = Paromoeose
   equal starts?
         (isocolic isocolon)

Then he turned to the *OED* and copied out their examples for *parison* ('the good is geason and short is his abode / the bad bides long and easy to be found') and *paromoion* ('O Tite, tute, Tati, tibi tanta Tyranne tulisti', that celebrated example of alliteration from Ennius' *Annals*, recorded for posterity by Priscian).[19] Careful as he was, like all good rhetoric students, to reuse the contents of his notebook, when he came to revise this speech in late 1918, Joyce inserted into Taylor's speech an additional *parison*: '*Israel is weak and few are her children: Egypt is an host and terrible are her arms*' (p. 297).[20]

Further, and fascinating evidence of the care Joyce took over his use of rhetoric in the 'Aeolus' episode is provided by modern retrieval of the corrections he made during the first printing. His Parisian printers provided no less than six sets of proofs between early August and October 1921, three of the *placards* or galley-proofs and three sets of page-proof, all happily extant. The analyses made by A. Walton Litz and Michael Groden[21] show a process of accretion that may remind us of

[19] Herring 1977, pp. 25–6; Groden 1977, pp. 80–1, 93–4.
[20] Groden 1977, p. 94. Joyce also 'polished' these speeches in both the intermediate revisions (ibid., p. 96) and the final ones (pp. 104–5).
[21] Litz, cit. Groden 1977, p. 93; Groden's own admirable account of the final stages of revision can be found on pp. 64–9, 101–14.

'*amplificatio*' as practised in medieval rhetoric, or 'augmentation' as Groden calls it. Joyce piled up the rhetorical devices in the latest stage of revision out of a 'desire for all-inclusiveness', to produce what Stuart Gilbert described as 'a veritable thesaurus of rhetorical devices'.[22] So dense are these figures in some places as to raise the critical problem of whether they are integrally related to character and setting, or whether they represent that later change in Joyce's style, away from individual voices towards more abstract schemes and correspondences.[23] It seems to me that the evidence points both ways. Given that the setting is a newspaper office, some of the devices are completely functional in rendering the noise and bustle that runs through the episode. This is sometimes done by *onomatopoeia*, as with an office door that 'whispered: ee: cree. They always build one door opposite another for the wind to. Way in. Way out' (p. 243), or with the brilliant description of the presses at work:

Sllt. The nethermost deck of the first machine jogged forward its flyboard with sllt the first batch of quirefolded papers. Sllt. Almost human the way it sllt to call attention. Doing its level best to speak. That door too sllt creaking, asking to be shut. Everything speaks in its own way. Sllt. (p. 254)

The noise breaks into the sentence-structure of Bloom's thoughts, the sound even becoming a verb at one point ('the way it sllt to call attention'). When Bloom wants to speak he adapts to the machines, 'slipping his words deftly into the pauses of the clanking' (p. 299). Figures of repetition also represent these noises, 'Thumping thump' (p. 245); 'The machines clanked in threefour time. Thump, thump, thump' (p. 247); 'Clank it. Clank it' (p. 249).

Joyce adapts rhetoric to the situation of a printing-press in more subtle ways. Typesetters have to be able to spell correctly, and one of them sets the others a 'spellingbee conundrum'. The practice sentence, as successfully negotiated, would read: 'It is amusing to view the unparalleled embarrassment of a harassed pedlar while gauging the symmetry of a peeled pear under a cemetery wall.' (Long-sufferers will regret the absence of

---

[22] Ibid., p. 93; Gilbert 1952, p. 189.
[23] See the sensitive discussion of this change in Groden 1977, pp. 13–43, and especially pp. 17, 37, 114.

'accommodation'.) But as set out by Joyce, using the rhetorical technique of dividing up words (*tmesis*) as a *mimesis* of the typesetter's mental act, it reads:

> It is amusing to view the unpar one ar alleled embarra two ars is it? double ess ment of a harassed pedlar while gauging au the symmetry with a y of a peeled pear under a cemetery wall. Silly, isn't it? Cemetery put in of course on account of the symmetry. (p. 251)

The last sentence, with the *paronomasia* at the beginning and end, sounds like *epanalepsis*, too. Another specific printing-house figure comes as Bloom watches 'a typesetter neatly distributing type. Reads it backwards first. Quickly he does it. Must require some practice that. mangi D. Kcirta P.' (p. 253). Bloom mentally inverts the name of the man whose funeral he has just attended. Another form of printing-house inversion concerns word-order, as in one of the headlines that punctuate the text of this episode: 'WITH UNFEIGNED REGRET IT IS WE ANNOUNCE THE DISSOLUTION . . .' (p. 245). This heading represents the announcement of Mr Dignam's death, which is just being set in type, with a characteristic printer's error in word-order, no doubt to be corrected during proofing.

The headlines, most of which Joyce added in the latest stages of correction in August 1921,[24] are at one level an affectionate parody of the zippy style of modern newspapers: 'DAMES DONATE DUBLIN'S CITS SPEEDPILLS VELOCITOUS AEROLITHS, BELIEF' (p. 309). But many of them, as Matthew Hodgart observed, read more like 'captions under imaginary illustrations, probably photographs, added by an anonymous sub-editor'.[25] It is clear that a title like 'WE SEE THE CANVASSER AT WORK' (p. 247) or 'IN THE HEART OF THE HIBERNIAN METROPOLIS' (p. 239) could refer to illustrated articles rather than summaries of the contents of a news item. The identity of their author is a critical problem, for they exist at a level somewhere between the reader and the text, anticipating and guiding our responses to it in much the same way as the marginal notes or 'postils' added to Galileo's *Dialogue of the Two*

---

[24] Groden 1977, pp. 105–10, with facsimile on p. 106.
[25] Hodgart 1974, p. 129.

Chief World Systems tell you what is coming next and what you should think of it.[26] Towards the end of the episode there is an increasing interplay between the titles and the text (e.g. p. 309).

By making the rhetorical forms appropriate to the newspaper office Joyce maintains the decorum of place. The decorum of character is observed by allocating a specific device to one speaker. Thus the idler and parasite Lenehan, a survivor from *Dubliners* (the story 'Two Gallants'), is given to confusing languages, saying '*Thanky vous*' (p. 271) and '*Muchibus thankibus*' (p. 293). He also indulges in 'Spoonerisms', the rhetorical figure *metathesis*, as in 'I hear feetstoops' (p. 265), and 'Clamn dever' (p. 287). He also sports with *hysteron proteron*: 'O, for a fresh of breath air!' (p. 281), and palindromes: 'Madam, I'm Adam. And Able was I ere I saw Elba' (p. 285). He puns, too, especially with figures of sound, referring to 'our old ancient ancestors' (a parodic tautology) 'as we read in the first chapter of Guinness's' (p. 273). Worse still, when Bloom collides with him he claims to be hurt in the '—Knee . . . —The accumulation of the *anno Domini*' (p. 267). He riddles, too: 'What opera resembles a railwayline?' (p. 275). *Answer: 'The Rose of Castile*. See the wheeze? Rows of cast steel' (p. 279). [Groan!] Lenehan, complete with limerick (p. 279), is a kind of semi-professional joker, with a repertoire of ready-mades. Professor MacHugh, as we have seen, is an orator manqué, given to unrelated oratorical gestures, as when he 'extended elocutionary arms from frayed stained shirtcuffs' (p. 273).[27] Like a typically garrulous pedagogue he is always supplying gratuitous information, quite unable to follow his own rhetorician's injunction that 'We mustn't be led away by words, by sounds of words' (p. 271). This failing he shows when he describes John F. Taylor's speech as

the speech . . . of a finished orator [Quintilian's *orator perfectus*], full of courteous haughtiness [*paronomasia*] and pouring in chastened diction I will not say the vials of his wrath [a *paralipsis* or *occupatio*, declining to say what you nevertheless do say] but pouring the proud man's contumely [quotation] upon the new movement. It was then a new

[26] Vickers 1983b, pp. 83–4.
[27] Hodgart 1974, pp. 126–9, has a brilliant analysis of the use of gesture in this episode.

movement [*epistrophe*].   We   were   weak,   therefore   worthless
[alliteration]. (p. 295)

As guardian of ancient culture, with more than a passing
resemblance to Shakespeare's pedant Holofernes, MacHugh can
pounce on a banal remark by the editor 'Ohio! . . . My Ohio!'
and pronounce it a rare metrical unit: '—A perfect cretic! the
professor said. Long, short and long.' (p. 263—itself an example
of *epanalepsis*).

Rhetoric can be seen as functional to 'Aeolus' on a thematic
level if we recall Joyce's original description of its 'Sense
(Meaning)—the Mockery of Victory', and 'Symbol . . . Failed
Destinies'. The appropriate figure here is of incomplete
utterance, *aposiopesis*. As Stuart Gilbert noted, 'the theme of
undeserved frustration, of a goal nearly, but not quite attained,
recurs under several aspects in this episode', exemplified by
Moses, Mr Bloom, J. J. O'Molloy, and even Seymour Bushe, of
whom MacHugh remarks: '—"He would have been on the
bench long ago, the professor said, only for. . . . But no
matter"' (p. 291). As Gilbert says, 'the professor's aposiopesis
guards its secret; in the cause of Bushe's frustration we have one
of the few instances in *Ulysses* of a mystery unsolved'.[28] (It has
been since, needless to say: Bushe was caught in bed with the
wife of an Irish nobleman.) However, in this novel, uniquely,
aposiopesis must be distinguished into the unspoken and the
spoken: that is, in the interior monologues the sense is
sometimes left incomplete as a realistic *mimesis* of how, in our
thoughts, we do not follow through to the end a familiar or
predictable development. So Bloom's monologues include such
incomplete sentences as 'Published by authority in the year one
thousand and.' (p. 245), or 'Maybe he understands what I.'
(p. 247). Another type of *aposiopesis* used here is where one
speaker relies on another to complete the sense: '—Did you?
Hynes asked' (p. 247), referring to drawing money from the
cashier, or '—I beg yours', Bloom says (p. 259). O'Molloy
interrupts the professor once (p. 287) as Lenehan interrupts him
(p. 273). The thematic articulation of frustration is thus carried
out through rhetorical resources.

The narrator also uses rhetoric functionally, to describe and

[28] Gilbert 1952, pp. 186–7.

evaluate character and event. In his reading of Aristotle's *Rhetoric* Joyce studied the section on metaphor carefully, noting that the 'object' of this trope was 'to make folk learn easy .˙. foreign words', and summarizing the main heads of Aristotle's argument:

Metaphor prefer to comparison
Comparison makes folk wait and tells you only what
    smthg is like.
Good diction tria metaphor, antithesis, energy.[29]

As the virtual narrator of this episode, Joyce makes little use of simile, but applies metaphor thematically, with over forty instances of his basic trope of words as 'wind', ranging from the mystical-magical to the coarsely fundamental.[30] He also uses metaphor to describe his characters, and certainly meets Aristotle's requirement that metaphors should be vivid, and show things in motion. Our first view of the editor, Myles Crawford, comes when 'the inner door was opened violently and a scarlet beaked face, crested by a comb of feathery hair, thrust itself in' (p. 263). This visual, almost caricatural effect is repeated later, when they are leaving to go to the pub: Crawford 'appeared on the steps, his hat aureoling his scarlet face' (p. 305). If Crawford looks like a cockerel, Lenehan has the hands of a dog or bear (he 'began to paw the tissues up from the floor': p. 267), while the professor resembles a bird ('raising two quiet claws': p. 271). The most brilliant of these unflattering animal metaphors is for professor MacHugh at the centre of attention, about to deliver John F. Taylor's speech: 'He raised his head firmly. His eyes bethought themselves once more. Witless shellfish swam in the gross lenses to and fro, seeking outlet' (p. 295). Skill in metaphor is a sign of genius, Aristotle wrote, an ability to show resemblances that no one has seen before. Joyce shows it again in his description of the professor's audience: 'His listeners held their cigarettes poised to hear, their smokes ascending in frail stalks that flowered with his speech. *And let our crooked smokes*' (p. 297). The quotation from *Cymbeline* (5. 5. 476 ff.) translates the metaphor a stage further, since the 'crooked smokes' are those of sacrificial altars, for which the

[29] Herring 1977, p. 26.
[30] Hodgart 1974, p. 117.

cigarette is a bathetic modern equivalent, complementing the equivalence set up earlier between the Romans' love for water-closets and the Irish for Guinness.

Joyce as narrator gives his characters a sensitivity to rhetoric almost as great as his own. Towards the end of 'Aeolus' Stephen is telling his story of the two Dublin vestals (whose view of Dublin from the top of Nelson's column is likened to Moses' glimpse of the promised land from Pisgah) to a largely uncomprehending professor MacHugh. But when Stephen includes the detail that one of them rubs on Lourdes water for her lumbago while the other drinks 'a bottle of double x for supper every Saturday'—double x being the normal strength for Guinness, triple x the export brew—'Antithesis, the professor said, nodding twice' (p. 305). Trust a rhetorician to recognize his own categories! When Bloom is trying to explain the advertisement that his client wants to place, a pair of crossed keys, he says 'House of Keys, don't you see? His name is Keyes. It's a play on the name' (p. 305). Rhetoricians distinguished various types of pun: this is an example of *syllepsis*, where two meanings of the same word are invoked without repeating it. The narrator also uses it to describe Ned Lambert asking a question 'with a reflective glance at his toecaps' (p. 263), and J. J. O'Molloy uses it to rebuke Crawford: 'Your Cork legs are running away with you' (p. 289). *Antanaclasis* involves repeating a word and shifting meanings, as when O'Molloy says of Gerald Fitzgibbon that 'He is sitting with Tim Healy . . . rumour has it, on the Trinity college estates commission', and Crawford coarsely corrects him: 'He is sitting with a sweet thing . . . in a child's frock' (p. 295). *Paronomasia* echoes words resembling each other in sound, as done frequently by Lenehan, or by the narrator, describing someone discarding the flimsy *'sports* tissues': 'He tossed the tissues on the table' (p. 265).

Much as one may strive against it, any account of the use of rhetoric in 'Aeolus' ultimately declines to a list. Joyce uses so many different figures, many of them once or twice only, that it becomes difficult to synthesize them into any coherent sequence. One gets the impression, if not of a thesaurus then of a display-piece or demonstration of verbal skills. Joyce's sensitivity to the physical shape or texture of language was immense, and he never tires of repeating, transforming, or rearranging words. The first section gives us a list of place-names and verbs to describe the tram-routes across Dublin, followed by mimetic syntax and sound-effects:

Right and left parallel clanging ring a doubledecker and a singledeck moved from their railheads, swerved to the down line, glided parallel. (p. 239)

(Parallel lines meet at infinity: the trams are also a metaphor for Bloom and Stephen, who come close in this episode, but do not meet.) The second section, headlined 'THE WEARER OF THE CROWN', begins with this highly polished sentence, a copybook specimen of prose-rhythm, dactyls yielding to trochees:

Under the porch of the general post office shoeblacks called and polished. (p. 239)

Joyce's notes from Aristotle's *Rhetoric* included definitions and illustrations of 'dactyl, spondee, iamb, trochee, pean', with hints as to the subject-matter for which they should be used: for spondee 'narrative solemn', for iamb 'conversat', and for trochee 'dance'.[31] From the shoeblacks we move to the post-office, with its 'sacks of letters, postcards, lettercards, parcels, insured and paid, for local, provincial, British and overseas delivery' (p. 239), that sense of untrammelled movement across great distances giving way to the slow and heavy and serious activity of delivering Guinness:

Grossbooted draymen rolled barrels dullthudding out of Prince's stores and bumped them up on the brewery float. On the brewery float bumped dullthudding barrels rolled by grossbooted draymen out of Prince's stores. (p. 241)

The figure *antimetabole* repeats and inverts words, usually to make a semantic distinction. Here the inversion is not quite exact (if one assigns a letter to each word the sequence is *ab cd e fg : gf dc ba e*), and it functions rather to make us live through the activity twice, so conveying the weight and bulk involved. When 'Aeolus' was first published in the *Little Review* for October 1918, this sentence was printed twice, in the same word-order, perhaps as a printer's error; Joyce only reversed the order in a hand-written addition sent to the printer in 1921.[32]

---

[31] Herring 1977, p. 25.
[32] Groden 1977, p. 70.

Joyce may have capitalized on an error, or he may have changed his mind: either way, his mastery of the mimetic resources of prose-rhythm and prose-rhetoric is already apparent.

Joyce, and his characters, use verbal repetitions for many purposes. Mr Bloom has the proprietor of the newspaper pointed out to him as he arrives at the office:

> The broadcloth back ascended each step: back. All his brains are in the nape of his neck, Simon Dedalus says. Welts of flesh behind on him. Fat folds of neck, fat, neck, fat, neck. (p. 241)

There the repetiton, whether *ploche* (repeating one word) or *epanodos* (repeating two or more in sequence), serves both to describe Brayden's appearance and to render his movement up the steps. Bloom sees, or thinks those words, in an interior monologue. Similarly Stephen, told by J. J. O'Molloy that '—Professor Magennis was speaking to me about you', thinks to himself 'Speaking about me. What did he say? What did he say? What did he say about me? Don't ask' (p. 293)—so he doesn't. Repetition of word with no words intervening is *epizeuxis*, a figure to be used for passionate outbursts, appropriately for Lenehan's mocking conclusion to the professor's account of Pyrrhus, who failed 'to retrieve the fortunes of Greece' (another instance of unfulfilment)—'Owing to a brick received in the latter half of the matinée. Poor, poor, poor, poor, Pyrrhus!' (p. 279). If the words repeated are conjunctions, that is known as *polysyndeton*, as when Bloom thinks of his father reading the 'hagadah book' backwards (like the typesetter), with the story of the 'twelve brothers, Jacob's sons. And then the lamb and the cat and the dog and the stick and the water and the butcher' and so on (p. 253). Repeating words but removing the conjunctions is *asyndeton*, apt to describe an aged printer, 'bowed, spectacled, aproned' (p. 253), or Lenehan's peremptory demand for an answer to his riddle: 'Reflect, ponder, excogitate, reply' (p. 275). The most frequently used form of repetition in this episode, significantly enough for the future of *Finnegans Wake*, is *polyptoton*, where the stem of a word is repeated and transformed. Bloom 'passed in through the . . . passage' (p. 243); the professor shows himself, despite his warnings, constantly 'led away by words, by sounds of words. We think of Rome, imperial, imperious, imperative' (p. 271). *Polyptoton* is the wordsmith's standby, and just before the professor launches a disquisition on 'Kyrios! Shining word! . . . Kyrie! . . . Kyrie eleison!' we can see the glow of anticipated transformations spreading polyptotically over his face: 'A smile of light brightened his darkrimmed eyes, lengthened his long lips' (p. 277). Stephen, too, uses the figure as he thinks of Seymour Bushe's allusion to Michelangelo's Moses, 'that stone effigy': 'stonehorned, stonebearded, heart of stone' (p. 297). Later he recalls an occult belief in the permanence, despite its apparent transitoriness, of the spoken word: 'Akasic records of all that ever anywhere wherever was' (p. 299).

Repetition and transformation affect not just individual words but longer sequences, as Joyce displays his skills in using *anaphora, epistrophe, symploce, parison, isocolon, anadiplosis, epanalepsis, parenthesis,* and other figures involving the disposition of whole sentences (the studious reader will soon discover examples of each). Most of the time these figures are appropriate to the general context, but in one respect Joyce strains our belief in the naturalness of his art. Word-order in prose can be varied from the normal grammatic conventions for specific effects, such as those dislocations of the norm to represent mental disorder, favoured by the Greeks, while word-order in verse may be varied according to metrical constraints. But Joyce sometimes disturbs the natural order without either justification, creating a somewhat mannered effect. As the newsboys scamper through the hall the draught disturbs the '*Sports* tissues' just 'tossed on to the table': 'The tissues rustled up in the draught, floated softly in the air blue scrawls and under the table came to earth' (p. 265).—An oddly beautiful sentence, none the less, slowing the reader down as he has to work out the right order the words should take, the tissues dropping softly meanwhile. Myles Crawford inverts: 'A Hungarian it was one day . . .' (p. 277), as does Lenehan: '— Clever, Lenehan said, Very.', being pre-echoed, as it were, by the writer of the headline 'CLEVER, VERY' (p. 285). So does the professor, describing John F. Taylor's appearance at the debate: 'That he had prepared his speech I do not believe . . . ' (p. 295), and again: 'The masters of the Mediterranean are fellaheen today' (p. 301). If such utterances seem mannered, other instances of inversion can be defended as representing the movement of the mind, which does not always find the standard word-order. So Bloom thinks of the great age of 'old Chatterton, the vicechancellor . . . Close on ninety they say. Subleader for his death written this long time perhaps' (p. 257), or considers the unfulfilled promise of J. J. O'Molloy: 'Cleverest fellow at the junior bar he used to be' (p. 259). If at times the characters in 'Aeolus' seem to become vehicles for a rhetorical *tour de force* (as someone says of the characters in that word-sick play *Love's Labour's Lost*, 'they have been at a great feast of language and stolen the scraps'), then at other times we have to concede that Joyce has been true to the principles of rhetoric, using art to illuminate nature.

III

After the verbal exuberance of *Ulysses*, the eight years Joyce spent in collecting words, phrases, ideas, allusions, years of patient sifting and assembling, where no detail was too small for his—and his printers'—attention, a process brought to a premature halt, thankfully, by his decision to publish it on his fortieth birthday, 8 February 1922[33]—after this richness of reference, making his novel seemingly inexhaustible to exegesis, it may come as a shock to turn to George Orwell's *Nineteen Eighty-Four*. Shorter, narrower in scope, with a much smaller vocabulary, produced with great pain and in improvised surroundings over the last eighteen months of a short life,[34] Orwell's novel has a proportionally smaller use of rhetoric. Some readers, indeed, aware of Orwell's concern for clarity and simplicity in language as an index of individual and social health, might wonder whether it has any rhetoric at all. It does, but within a narrower spectrum than *Ulysses*, and totally lacking the charm and beguiling quality of Irish oratory, with its tendency towards narcissism and display. In this fable of how

[33] Groden 1977, p. 13 and note, records that Joyce not only used in *Ulysses* passages rejected for *A Portrait of the Artist* but carried over some of his *Ulysses* notes into *Finnegans Wake*.

[34] For the circumstances of composition see *The Collected Essays, Journalism and Letters of George Orwell*, ed. S. Orwell and I. Angus, 4 vols. (London, 1968), and Bernard Crick, *George Orwell. A Life* (London, 1980). Orwell's first draft of the novel, dating from 1943, is reprinted in an appendix to Crick's book, pp. 407–9. For its later progress see ibid., pp. 309, 360–1, 376–7, 380–5, 391–9; and the *Collected Essays*, iv. 544 (Index).

the future might be, if totalitarianism were allowed to flourish, rhetoric is given a large-scale political function, to control not just individuals but a whole society. The goal of learning to love Big Brother is achieved by an unrelenting manipulation of mind and feelings, from the visual image to sound, music, gesture, and physical contact in the mass rallies, and—as Winston Smith discovers in Room 101—torture and betrayal. Plato reserved for the state the use of force and lies to serve its own interests: it is hard to see how his beliefs could prevent a world such as this coming to be.

This state systematically destroys memory, denies or rewrites the past, aiming to deprive its citizens of any firm hold on reality. Another way of achieving this goal is to use language to deny itself. The union of contraries in rhetoric is called *synoeciosis* or *oxymoron*, as in Joyce's Mr O'Madden Burke, having been poked 'mildly in the spleen': 'Help! he sighed. I feel a strong weakness' (p. 279). It is a figure traditionally associated with the Petrarchan lover and his 'freezing fires' or 'fair cruelty'. Juan Vives said of antitheses that they 'wage a kind of war between themselves', and John Smith wrote that '*Contraries* are qualities which mutually destroy one another'; but no traditional rhetorician could have foreseen the application of this figure to political purposes, in the three slogans of the party:

WAR IS PEACE
FREEDOM IS SLAVERY
IGNORANCE IS STRENGTH[35]

The first two slogans, especially, are simultaneous assertions and denials, extreme forms of paradox that cannot be resolved, and so create a confusion of values. In our logic p cannot be at the same time $-p$. The Party's aim is not the transvaluation of values but their perversion, transformation into their opposites by the power of propaganda and the systematic rewriting of the past. If everyone 'accepted the lie which the Party imposed—if all records told the same tale—then the lie passed into history and became truth' (p. 31). ' "Reality control", they called it: in Newspeak, "double-think".' As Winston Smith contemplates 'the labyrinthine world of double-think', the union of opposites,

[35] Vives 1966, p. 83; Smith 1657, p. 40. *Nineteen Eighty-Four* is cited from the Penguin edition (Harmondsworth, 1954); here pp. 7, 16, 25, 86.

synoeciosis, is seen as fundamental to the 'denial of reality' on which the system is based.

To know and not to know, to be conscious of complete truthfulness while telling carefully constructed lies, to hold simultaneously two opinions which cancelled out, knowing them to be contradictory and believing in both of them; to use logic against logic, to repudiate morality while laying claim to it, to believe that democracy was impossible and that the Party was the guardian of democracy; to forget whatever it was necessary to forget, then to draw it back into memory again at the moment when it was needed, and then promptly to forget it again: and above all, to apply the same process to the process itself. That was the ultimate subtlety: consciously to induce unconsciousness, and then, once again, to become unconscious of the act of hypnosis you had just performed. Even to understand the word 'doublethink' involved the use of doublethink. (pp. 31–2)

There *synoeciosis*, coupled with *ploche* and *polyptoton*, are no longer just figures of rhetoric but a way of life, as we see from the long excerpt from Goldstein's textbook on 'Oligarchic Collectivism' which substantially repeats and extends this analysis (pp. 169–72).

In the novel, Winston Smith's awareness of this process is juxtaposed with that of other characters, who are unconcerned by it. Syme, the enthusiastic exponent of Newspeak, predicts a time when the literature, and even the slogans of the Party will have to change. 'How could you have a concept like "freedom is slavery" when the concept of freedom has been abolished? The whole climate of thought will be different. In fact there will be no thought, as we understand it now. Orthodoxy means not thinking—not needing to think. Orthodoxy is unconsciousness' (p. 46). This is a true 'mise en abîme'. Winston's lover Julia, however, denied any political awareness by Orwell, is not horrified by the 'impudent forgeries' that Winston commits in the Records Department: 'She did not feel the abyss opening beneath her feet at the thought of lies becoming truths' (p. 126). Yet the process is so thoroughgoing, Winston reflects, that perhaps every word in the history books 'was pure fantasy. . . . The past was erased, the erasure was forgotten, the lie became truth' (p. 63). Newspeak includes a number of words that have 'Two mutually contradictory meanings', such as *duckspeak*, a term of abuse to an opponent, praise to someone you agree with (p.147) or *blackwhite*: 'Applied to an opponent, it means the habit of impudently claiming that black is white, in contradiction of the plain facts. Applied to a Party member, it means a loyal willingness to say that black is white when Party discipline demands this' (pp. 169–70)—but also 'to *know* that black is white, and to forget that one has ever believed the contrary. This demands a continual alteration of the past', a falsification designed to unhinge memory and 'dislocate the sense of reality' (pp. 170–1). The denial of logic, the simultaneous accepting of two contradictory beliefs, 'this peculiar linking-together of opposites—knowledge with ignorance, cynicism with fanaticism', preserves the hierarchy of the ruling powers by creating a 'prevailing neutral condition' of 'controlled insanity' (p. 172). When Winston is tortured in the Ministry of Love (by a cynical antithesis the titles of the four ministries—of Peace, Truth, Love, Plenty—refer to their precise opposites), he is at first beaten up, just to 'destroy his power of arguing and reasoning', then browbeaten by hours of verbal violence: 'in the end the nagging voices broke him down more completely' than physical violence (p. 194). Accused of being 'mentally deranged', and having 'a defective memory' (p. 197), O'Brien's torture machines then destroy his sense of logic and reality. If he learns to see five fingers when four are shown him then he will 'become sane', accept the reality that exists only in the mind of the Party (pp. 200–1, 212, 222).

The union of opposites, a real denial of perception and reality, is one of the organizing schemes of *Nineteen Eighty-Four*. Another major trope, already glimpsed, is *euphemismos*, originally a way of preserving decency while referring to something unpleasant—a virtue of style, in classical rhetoric. In Orwell's world—as already in Thucydides' account of the effects of political upheaval on language during the civil war on Corcyra—euphemism is a sign of the calculated destruction of human feelings. If found guilty of Thoughtcrime, 'you were abolished, annihilated: *vaporized* was the usual word' (p. 7). Winston's job in the Ministry of Truth consists in altering or 'rectifying' the record of the past to show that whatever Big Brother predicted had happened, that production forecasts had been met, or exceeded, generally falsifying history. The instructions he receives 'never stated or implied that an act of forgery was to be committed: always the reference was to slips, errors, misprints, or misquotations' needing correction (p. 36). Where other power-states have tried to control the way people think, this one aims to destroy words, to make language smaller in order 'to narrow the range of thought'. In the end Thoughtcrime will be 'literally impossible, because there will be no words in which to express it' (p. 45). Ambiguity and shades of meaning will be rigidly eliminated, words will stand in a one-to-one relationship with things, ideas and other free thought-processes stamped out. But the 'revision' of the past is made more difficult 'because the processes that it involved could not be called by their true names' (p. 148). Euphemism defeats all clarity of purpose. It is not enough to lie, the lies have to be made to look like truths, or deeds of charity. O'Brien tells Winston that he has been brought to the Ministry of Love 'to cure you! To make you sane!' (p. 203).

These are corrective measures, after the event, or for troublesome individuals. For the masses, and for day-by-day control, the Party uses what we might describe as rhetorical *movere* on a massive scale. Teachers of forensic eloquence in ancient Greece and Rome advised their students, innocently enough, of the need to arouse the resentment and hatred of judge and jury against the opposition. They might have revised their opinions had they seen the Two Minutes Hate period, where the face of Emmanuel Goldstein, the Enemy of the People, is flashed on the telescreen, and collective feelings aroused by flicking a switch. Within thirty seconds 'uncontrollable exclamations of rage were breaking out from half the people in the room', for 'the sight or even the thought of Goldstein produced fear and anger automatically' (p. 14). The feelings aroused are so intense 'that it was impossible to avoid joining in. . . . A hideous ecstasy of fear and vindictiveness' possessed them, yet the rage they felt was 'an abstract, undirected emotion which could be switched from one object to another like the flame of a blowlamp' (p. 15). This is uncomfortably close to the celebrations that we have read in Cicero and Quintilian of the orator's power to move people now to joy, now to fear, just as he wishes. From *vituperatio* the Party switches to *laus*, reversing the poles of epideictic rhetoric, by showing the face of Big Brother filling the screen, 'full of power and mysterious calm', arousing 'an overwhelming emotion' in people, which they express in a 'sub-human chanting' of his name (pp. 16–17). The Party exploits the rhetoric of the image just as ruthlessly, following Goldstein's appearance with that of a 'huge and terrible Eurasian soldier' (pp. 14–16), and covering London with posters of a 'monstrous figure of a Eurasian soldier . . . striding forward with expressionless Mongolian face and enormous boots, a sub-machine gun' pointing straight at you (p. 122). Fear has a rhetorical force, too. The portrait of Big Brother has been given a hypnotic effect by emphasis and repetition:

It was as though some huge force were pressing down upon you— something that penetrated inside your skull, battering against your brain, frightening you out of your beliefs, persuading you, almost, to deny the evidence of your senses. (p. 67)

This is again rhetorical persuasion, taken to a totalitarian extreme.

The Party mobilizes every possible source of feeling, including sexuality. They enforce a 'sexual puritanism' not merely because 'the sex instinct created a world of its own which was outside the Party's control and which therefore had to be destroyed if possible'. More important to them is the knowledge that 'sexual privation induced hysteria', which is easily 'transformed into war-fever and leader-worship' (p. 109). Frustrated energies can be redirected; fulfilled energies not. General humanitarian feelings, too, are numbed or replaced by political loyalties. At mass rallies and demonstrations the Party's orators, 'contorted with hatred, catalogue the enemy's 'atrocities, massacres, deportations, lootings, rapings, torture of prisoners', producing the desired effect of such oratory on the listeners, who are 'first convinced and then maddened' (p. 147). The way in which the Party's rhetoric bypasses reason and appeals to the basest emotions is demonstrated in a scene of high comedy when a party orator receives news that the official enemy has been changed from Eurasia to Eastasia. Having quickly read the message,

nothing altered in his voice or manner, or in the content of what he was saying, but suddenly the names were different. . . . The Hate continued exactly as before, except that the target had been changed.—

The thing that impressed Winston in looking back was that the speaker had switched from one line to the other actually in mid-sentence, not only without a pause, but without even breaking the syntax. (pp. 47–8)

Had the young Plato been able to read that passage it might have confirmed his worst suspicions about rhetoric. Another reader would say, that confirms all we have known about totalitarianism. Rhetoric, after all, is only a tool.

The Party's control of personal life, thought, and feelings is so great that they might seem to be in less need of verbal rhetoric; or one might suspect that details of style are not a real centre of interest for Orwell. Certainly *Nineteen Eighty-Four* does not match *Ulysses* in either the range or intensity of its rhetoric. But Orwell does use specific devices, and effectively. Mrs Parsons, terrorized by her children's loyalty to the Party (they subsequently denounce their own father), apologizes to Winston for the mess they have made in the flat: ' "They haven't been out to-day. And of course—" She had a habit of breaking off her sentences in the middle' (p. 21). One cause of *aposiopesis*, we recall from the rhetoric-books, is fear. After Winston has been broken by being exposed to his greatest terror, of being eaten alive by rats, he, too, takes refuge in this device of not completing his sentences. In his drunken and apathetic state the worst thing

was that the smell of gin, which dwelt with him night and day, was inextricably mixed up in his mind with the smell of those—
He never named them, even in his thoughts, and so far as it was possible he never visualized them. They were something that he was half-aware of . . . (p. 231)

On the dust on the table in the café he traces '2+2= ' (p. 233); and when he picks up a chessman to make 'a tentative move . . . it was evidently not the right move, because—' (p. 237). Here a memory intervenes, of his mother giving him a game of Snakes and Ladders, but 'he pushed the picture out of his mind. It was a false memory. He was troubled by false memories occasionally. They did not matter so long as one knew them for what they were. Some things had happened, others had not happened' (p. 238). He is sane now.

The Party also uses rhetoric in public address, but less inventively than their other resources. Goldstein's speech on the telescreen is delivered in a 'rapid polysyllabic speech which was a sort of parody of the habitual style of the orators of the Party' (p. 14), hardly an impressive characteristic. Winston, having to compose a completely fictitious panegyric to a new hero of the Party,

pulled the speakwrite towards him and began dictating in Big Brother's familiar style: a style at once military and pedantic, and, because of a trick of asking questions and then promptly answering them ('What lessons do we learn from this fact, comrades? The lesson—which is also one of the fundamental principles of Ingsoc—that,' etc., etc.), easy to imitate. (pp. 40–1)

This rather laboured use of *anthypophora* makes Big Brother a less formidable figure: Orwell was perhaps undecided whether to make his enemies look dangerous, or ridiculous.

The most sustained use of Party rhetoric is by O'Brien in his cross-examination and 'brain-washing' of Winston. Because this is face-to-face address—one can hardly call it persuasion, since O'Brien also uses torture—we find greater verbal patterning. *Polyptoton*, the figure of transformation, is peculiarly appropriate for the double-think involved in O'Brien's denial that a photograph of three men executed for treason exists which proves that they were innocent: 'It does not exist. It never existed.' To Winston's agonized appeal—'But it did exist! It does exist! It exists in memory. I remember it. You remember it'— O'Brien, who has just destroyed it (or a copy of it), replies 'I do not remember it'. This creates in Winston the confusion of values, that 'deadly helplessness' produced by mutually contradictory statements:

If he could have been certain that O'Brien was lying, it would not have seemed to matter. But it was perfectly possible that O'Brien had really forgotten the photograph. And if so, then already he would have forgotten his denial of remembering it, and forgotten the act of forgetting. (pp. 198–9)

Such contortions of thought can only be communicated through contorted language. After his mind has been shattered by the torture Winston 'accepted everything. The past was alterable. The past never had been altered . . . He remembered remembering contrary things, but those were false memories

. . .' (p. 223). Words can be easily transformed, people too with such methods.

As the torture grows in intensity O'Brien's language takes on a more repetitive, incantatory nature. The Inquisition, he says, was at error, for it 'killed its enemies in the open, and killed them while they were still unrepentant: in fact, it killed them because they were unrepentant' (p. 203), thus turning its victims into martyrs. That sentence used *anaphora* and *epistrophe* to emphasize their mistake, and this latter figure recurs as O'Brien points to another instance of the Inquisition's failure to make proper use of its victims: 'the confessions that they had made were obviously extorted and untrue. We do not make mistakes of that kind. All the confessions that are uttered here are true. We make them true' (p. 204: by rewriting the past). *Antimetabole, anaphora,* and *epistrophe* are used to characterize the Party's superior methods:

We do not destroy the heretic because he resists us: so long as he resists us we never destroy him. We convert him, we capture his inner mind, we reshape him. We burn all evil and illusion out of him. . . . We make him one of ourselves before we kill him. (p. 205)

(Which by now must seem a rather pointless procedure.) The increasingly rigid patterns of the syntax convey their ruthless elimination of humanity:

Never again will you be capable of ordinary human feeling. Everything will be dead inside you. Never again will you be capable of love, or friendship, or joy of living, or laughter, or curiosity, or courage, or integrity. You will be hollow. We shall squeeze you empty, and then we shall fill you with ourselves. (p. 206)

Those antitheses give us our last glimpse of normal humanity— Orwell's original title for the novel was 'The Last Man in Europe'.

O'Brien's rhetoric is obviously constructed so as to convey the effect of inescapability, of closed options. That Winston is hearing it while strapped to a table and having great currents of pain shot through him makes the rhetoric in one sense redundant, since there is truly no need for persuasion. But the scene allows Orwell to bring out the nature of totalitarian politics, given a coherent exposition by O'Brien to an intelligent listener. Unlike other oligarchies of the past, who pretended that they had seized power only for a limited time, 'the Party seeks power entirely for its own sake. We are not interested in the good of others; we are interested solely in power. Not wealth or luxury or long life or happiness: only power, pure power': *ploche* and *epistrophe* are used to stress the key word, 'power'. Orwell's disillusioned insight into totalitarianism's real goal matches the bitter lecture 'Politik als Beruf' that Max Weber gave in 1918, both recording how politics, especially the struggle for power, destroys all ideals about human nature. In O'Brien's rhetoric the antitheses are like fixed poles within which human life.will be broken. Using such figures as *ploche* (repetition), *antimetabole* (inversion), and *epanalepsis* (the same term at the beginning and end of a sentence), the key words are reiterated, drilled into our consciousness:

> Power is not a means, it is an end. One does not establish a dictatorship in order to safeguard a revolution; one makes the revolution in order to establish the dictatorship. The object of persecution is persecution. The object of torture is torture. The object of power is power. . . .
>
> The first thing you must realize is that power is collective. The individual only has power in so far as he ceases to be an individual. You know the Party slogan: 'Freedom is Slavery'. Has it ever occurred to you that it is reversible? Slavery is freedom. (pp. 211–12)

Either way it is a grotesque lie.

The range of rhetorical figures in *Nineteen Eighty-Four* is smaller than in *Ulysses,* and although this reflects a great difference in their authors' attitudes to language, Orwell has clearly made a deliberate selection to characterize one form of political rhetoric. Like many orators, O'Brien uses the basic figures of emphasis, *anaphora, epistrophe, ploche,* and *antithesis* to ram home the Party's beliefs, such as their denial of religion, science, and history: 'Before man there was nothing. After man, if he could come to an end, there would be nothing. Outside man there is nothing' (p. 213). To prove their assertion of power the Party will make men suffer constantly:

> Power is in inflicting pain and humiliation. Power is in tearing human minds to pieces. . . . Progress in our world will be progress towards more pain. . . . In our world there will be no emotions except fear, rage, triumph, and self-abasement. Everything else we shall destroy—

everything. . . . The more the Party is powerful, the less it will
be tolerant: the weaker the opposition, the tighter the despotism.
(pp. 214–15)

The Party will keep puppet enemies, such as Goldstein, so as to
maintain a constant hatred, in which 'they will be defeated,
discredited, ridiculed, spat upon'—but preserved, in order to
foster collective identity. The pressure that the Party exerts is
seen almost in terms of a giant body, a macrocosmic power
principle. The world they are preparing is 'A world of victory
after victory, triumph after triumph after triumph: an endless
pressing, pressing, pressing upon the nerve of power' (p. 215).
The insistence, the hammering home of this viewpoint through
such figures of repetition has the effect traditionally ascribed to
this form of rhetoric: 'As usual, the voice had battered Winston
into helplessness' (p. 216). Having brought him to his lowest
point his persecutors fatten him up again, and his ideological
cure seems complete. But O'Brien knows his real thoughts,
knows that he still hates Big Brother (p. 227), and the final
horror with the rats and his betrayal of Julia are needed to bring
about his definitive conversion. In the book's last paragraph
Orwell shifts from the figures to a trope, using *exclamatio* most
effectively to convey Winston's new feelings for the enormous
face on the telescreen:

Forty years it had taken him to learn what kind of smile was hidden
beneath the dark moustache. O cruel, needless misunderstanding! O
stubborn, self-willed exile from the loving breast! Two gin-scented tears
trickled down the sides of his nose. But it was all right, everything was
all right, the struggle was finished. He had won the victory over
himself. He loved Big Brother. (p. 239)

Rhetoric, a tool with many uses, is seen in its most negative light
in this novel, as the agent of oppression, intimidation, and
betrayal. But then language itself is used for the same ends,
and anyone who shares Orwell's concern with language in
politics and public life will recognize his greatest fear.

IV

The 'flahool', or a gift of the gab, characterizes rhetoric in *Ulysses*
as a vocal art, oratory used to persuade an audience to noble

ends, such as Irish independence, or to delight them with the speaker's artistry. Of the three goals of the orator, Joyce's speakers favour *docere* and *delectare*. In Orwell's utopia *delectare* has long been abandoned, while *movere* and *docere* are put to the most ruthless political ends. In the third and last contemporary novel that I want to consider, *Pictures from an Institution*[36] (1954), by Randall Jarrell, rhetoric is essentially a written, not a spoken art, and belongs less to the utterances of the characters in the novel than to the narrator's analysis, and judgement of them. Randall Jarrell (1914–65) was a gifted poet and an influential judge of modern poetry, author of several critical works and this one novel, set in a small women's liberal arts college, and covering one academic year. From Jarrell's letters[37] and comments on the novel we know that Benton College is based on Sarah Lawrence College, New York, where he taught in the late 1940s and 50s. The President of Benton, Dwight Robbins, 'shared certain traits' with Harold Taylor, President of Sarah Lawrence from 1945 to 1959 (*Letters*, p. 288), indeed Jarrell had to defend himself from possible legal action when an excerpt from *Pictures* was to appear in *Kenyon Review*. He wrote to the editor, John Crowe Ransom, that while the two presidents shared 'a few particulars like curly hair, ingenuous sincerity . . . perpetual youngness, perfect adjustment to [their] surroundings', his president was 'a Molière-esque type, . . . a sort of *idiot savant* of Success', who 'talks ordinary President-banalities'. Taylor, by contrast, was 'much shrewder, more pretentious and hypocritical, more intellectual, etc.', altogether less likeable. Jarrell concludes: 'as you'll see later in the book, I rather like Robbins, and think about him, "Poor creature, if he could only become human!" ' (*Letters*, pp. 366–7).

The main character in the book is Gertrude Johnson, a novelist who comes at short notice to teach the creative writing course, and who decides to write a novel about Benton (*Pictures*,

[36] All quotations are from *Pictures From an Institution. A Comedy* (New York, 1954), incorporated in the text. A reprint (Chicago and London, 1987) is welcome.
[37] Quotations from *Randall Jarrell's Letters. An Autobiographical and Literary Selection*, ed. Mary Jarrell (Boston, 1985), incorporated into the text as *Letters*. For the genesis of the novel, which took place in two stages—in the second half of 1951, and from the spring of 1952 to the summer of 1953—see the *Letters*, pp. 250–1, 256, 264–5, 279, 285, 291, 302, 313, 334, 337, 360–3, 366–7, 373, 375, 377–8, 381–3, 392. See also the memorial volume, *Randall Jarrell, 1914–1965*, ed. Robert Lowell, Peter Taylor, and Robert Penn Warren (New York, 1967).

p. 8). She then treats everyone in this academic community as material for her novel, with a ruthless disregard for their feelings. As Jarrell told Ransom, of those who had read the manuscript Gertrude reminded them 'violently of five or six lady writers, whichever one they happen to know, but there are many deplorable writers of the sort' (*Letters*, p. 367). But one writer in particular seemed to be alluded to, Mary McCarthy, as Philip Rahv objected when considering publishing an excerpt in *Partisan Review*. Jarrell replied that

> Gertrude is so large and real to me (I can make up in my sleep a sentence for her to say about anything) that it seems funny to have her confused with Mary McCarthy, whom I know slightly and don't know too much about: but she *is* the same general type as Mary McCarthy, her books are like, and I got five or six happenings or pictures from M. M. But the readers who know Jean Stafford best think *she's* Gertrude, and the ones who know—but I won't go on with this list of Lady Writers. I hope (this is said in a grandiloquent tone) that Gertrude will survive when all of them are forgotten. One of the other characters says about her, 'She is one of the principles of things—a naked one,' and I hope this is right too. (*Letters*, p. 383)

Two other characters in the novel, Irene and Gottfried Rosenbaum, are modelled on Jarrell's friends Hannah Arendt and her husband Heinrich Blüchner:[38] all four are German *émigrés* working in America, representing an older and, Jarrell thought, more impressive culture. Yet, in taking models from life, Jarrell added to them, telling Hannah Arendt in 1954 that she is more like Irene than her husband is like Gottfried, because 'I used a lot of things from myself for him, just as I did for Gertrude' (*Letters*, p. 392). This is borne out by what Irene, in the novel, says about Gertrude the woman novelist as a specifically American phenomenon: ' "She does not exist in Europe, not in quite this state. She is hidden, or distributed among several, or a man, there" ' (*Pictures*, p. 154).

One part of himself which Jarrell did put into Gertrude was his combination of wit and cruelty. As we can tell from the *Letters*, and from tributes by fellow-poets and critics, Jarrell could be a wounding reviewer and a devastating critic from the floor of a lecture. One of his reviews, of Conrad Aiken's poetry,

---

[38] See *Letters*, pp. 180–1, 256, 279, 367, 392, and Arendt's memoir of Jarrell in the memorial volume and in her *Men In Dark Times* (London, 1970).

was so savage that it produced a very understandable protest from Aiken, and an aggrieved self-defence from Jarrell, who always seemed unaware of how much he could hurt people (*Letters*, pp. 192–5). He once overheard a man in his audience, as he reported in a letter, 'say, about my lecture, "whatever he says has an edge to it," '—and, Jarrell commented, 'it's kind of true, but it's also a kind of Midas-blessing. It's *so* hard for me to write prose sentences so that they don't, even if I'm trying to be mild. I suppose that wit is a good slave and a bad master' (*Letters*, p. 210). While teaching at Princeton in 1951–2, he saw a lot of R. P. Blackmur, who was both hospitable and quarrelsome, tension between the two colleagues reaching the point where Jarrell responded in public, as he wrote to his future wife:

> My lecture last night was a *great* success, and this time I wasn't long-suffering but just demolished old Blackmur (quite politely, most of the time); he was incredibly rude both to me and two members of the audience. I felt *so* good when it was all over; the audience was excited . . . (ibid., pp. 346–7)

Public quarrels between academics are a sure guarantee of success with the audiences who come to hear them. John Crowe Ransom recorded that he had 'more than once' seen Jarrell 'rising in the academic forum when the official speaker had finished, and . . . ruining him with three or four perfect satirical sentences uttered in that high and piercing voice' (ibid., p. 397). So, in the novel, Gertrude ruins other people, and Jarrell ruins Gertrude.

The novel's title alludes to Mussorgsky's musical account of an art-gallery, *Pictures from an Exhibition*: by calling his *Pictures from an Institution* Jarrell puts his work outside the traditional connected narrative of a novel. The events it chronicles are the typical ones in any academic community: the cocktail party at the beginning of the year, lunch on Founder's Day, a memorable faculty dinner-party, grades and exams, the annual display of work in the creative and performing arts, the end of the year and everyone's departure. But it could equally have been called *Characters from an Institution*, since most of the seven chapters are named after the actors ('1. The President, Mrs., and Derek Robbins; 2. The Whittakers and Gertrude; 3. Miss Batterson and Benton; 4. Constance and the Rosenbaums; 5. Gertrude and

Sidney; 6. Art Night; 7. They All Go'). The book consists in effect
of a series of descriptions—*Imagines* we might call them—of
individual characters, relationships, and social events. There is
no ongoing narrative, and, against the normal expectation of
novel readers nothing 'happens'. At the end of the year its
characters are older, some are wiser, and all are glad that the
year is up. President Robbins, in particular, is delighted that
Gertrude's temporary position is nearly over: 'But then he said—
—and he smiled like the newly created angels who can't yet
believe their bliss—"Only twenty-three more days!"' (p. 236).

Despite the absence of a conventional plot, reading *Pictures
from an Institution* is a continual delight, as the tributes paid by a
very distinguished group of readers when it first came out
testify.[39] Jarrell's wit and intelligence are shown in a prose-style
which is highly structured, with an unending flow of verbal
invention. As an example of his style at its most carefully
organized we could take the encounter between President
Robbins and Gertrude at the welcoming party, where the
friendship previously set up at their first meeting came to an
end,

after eleven days. Without the party, they both felt bitterly, it might
have lasted for weeks. One could not help blaming Gertrude a little
more than one blamed the President; the President, like most people,
behaved in a different way after he had had a great deal to drink, but
Gertrude, knowing no other, behaved as she always behaved. But the
drinks at the party, the almost unavoidable intimacies at the party,
what they had said and what Mrs. Robbins had said and what people
had said they all of them had said at the party—these, the memory of
these, made Gertrude and the President look narrowly at each other,
and their eyes widened at what they saw. George looked at the dragon
and thought, *Why, that woman's a dragon*, and the dragon looked at
George and thought, *That's no man, that's an institution.* (p. 7).

Jarrell's best jokes often depend on careful rhetorical patterning.
Running through that passage is a series of antitheses (days/
weeks; behaved in a different way/behaved as she always
behaved; narrowly/widened; woman—dragon/man—institution,

[39] The dust-jacket quotes approving comments from Wallace Stevens, Jean
Stafford, Marianne Moore, Eric Bentley, James Agee, Orvielle Prescott, and
others, while the *Letters* record further admirers, Robert Lowell, Hannah Arendt,
Louis Untermeyer, and J. C. Ransom.

which make the basic character discriminations while avoiding monotony. Then Jarrell uses *epistrophe*, the repeated words 'at the party' closing three of the clauses, with the unexpected heaping up (*ploche*) in 'what they had said . . . had said . . . had said they all of them had said', both figures re-creating the clash of voices and conflicting accounts that belong to these occasions. After the event their differing reactions are also expressed in rhetorical forms: *paronomasia* for the President, whose 'ordinary disorderly executive existence had not prepared him for life', and *antimetabole* for Gertrude, to whom the party was 'one more pearl on the string of her existence, and she had come here to string pearls' (p. 8). The rhetorical figure *epanorthosis*, or *correctio*, where a phrase or word is recalled and replaced with one more suitable, catches the very moment when Gertrude conceives of writing a novel about Benton: 'But Dwight Robbins; President Robbins, that is; the President, that is—the President *interested* Gertrude. She realized, suddenly, that she was no longer between novels' (ibid.). The repetitions there (using *epistrophe, anaphora*) capture the mind's hesitation, then decision.

These few quotations from the opening sequence highlight the practical difficulty facing a rhetorical analysis of Jarrell's novel, which is ten times longer than the 'Aeolus' episode, longer than *Nineteen Eighty-Four* and far more densely packed with rhetoric: how to do justice to its range and scale? Jarrell may use fewer individual figures than Joyce, since he is not trying to construct a thesaurus or display-piece, but he uses them more frequently. There are perhaps twenty rhetorical figures that recur most often, but some of them do so fifty or sixty times. Their use is more obviously functional than in *Ulysses*, however, since they largely serve to convey the narrator's description and evaluation of his characters. People do use rhetoric in the spoken dialogue, but less frequently. Given this density of usage, selection is essential, and I find it truer to the experience of the novel to arrange the discussion in terms of the characters involved, rather than make a lexicon of the figures. This will also bring out the range of Jarrell's writing, the many ways in which his prose-style enacts moral and social judgements.

The President is described with a mixture of contempt and affection. His faults are so transparent, the result of vanity and complacency rather than malice, that he is a figure of fun, not danger. In a sentence that Hannah Arendt admired, *antimetabole* finds a perfect balance for his lack of individuality: 'President Robbins was so well adjusted to his environment that sometimes you could not tell which was the environment and which was President Robbins' (p. 11). The President has curly hair, is handsome and youthful-looking—an ex-Olympic diver, he still does his routine of somersaults in the college pool—but it is youth bought at a price, for, in Jarrell's distinctive metaphor, 'he possessed, and would possess until he died, youth's one elixir, Ignorance; he drank each day from the only magic horn, Belief' (p. 16). Or, to vary the metaphor for his simple-mindedness, 'He was a labyrinth in which no one could manage to remain for even a minute, because there were in it no wrong turnings' (ibid.). His utterances are of a striking banality, with portentous pauses:

He would say to you in private in his office, about the teachers of Benton: 'We like to feel that we educate [there was a slow, chaste separation between the next two words: they seemed youths and maidens who have become strong and sublimated through remaining apart] each . . . other.' (p. 25)

The narrator's parenthesis imitates the speaker's, stops the flow, holds up for more intense inspection the words that finally complete the sense, with a much greater effect of anti-climax. Interruptions characterize other people's treatment of the President. Asked a question in midflow of some totally unmemorable remarks on the novel, 'the President replied stiffly—he hated to be interrupted, and it seemed to him that he was always being interrupted— . . .' (p. 46). Sure enough, two sentences later he starts off '"I was reading just the other day—where was it I was reading—"

"In the *Swiss Family Robinson*, I'll bet", Gertrude broke in' (p. 47), with a typically malicious *insinuatio* as to his reading habits.

The narrator also breaks up the President's flow, less by interrupting than by not marking: 'He went on to say that something—I missed the word—was a commitment, and it was a commitment we must implement' (p. 61). One can, cruelly, leave out the key word that contains the sense of his remarks, yet it makes no great difference, they are all clichés. If *aposiopesis* characterizes the President in conversation, *antithesis* is used for him in action, to evoke the gap between what he is and what he thinks he is. He often goes on fund-raising tours to Hollywood, appealing to former alumnae while sitting 'at the grassy verge of swimming-pools: as he looked thoughtfully into the thoughtless water he seemed to [them] some boyish star who, playing Tom Sawyer, fancies for the moment that he is Narcissus' (p. 27). From Tom Sawyer to Narcissus: which role suits him best? Neither is actually flattering. But the President is popular, in a way: he 'had so many friends that, as Gertrude said'—exploiting to the full the ambiguity—' "they fell over each other going out the door" ' (p. 21). 'Of course', the narrator goes on, 'the President's friends didn't like him as well as many of our enemies like *us*, but they took pleasure in his misfortunes . . .' (ibid.). This double antithesis sets up a gradation of relative friendship and enmity which leaves the President in a somewhat forlorn position. Antithesis shows the gap between his surface and his real feelings, as in his reaction to the news that Miss Batterson is going to leave Benton: 'But he hid the joy he felt, and expressed, a little shortly, the sorrow he did not feel' (p. 107). The syntactical balance and delay catches his assumption of hypocrisy. When the news of Miss Batterson's death comes, shortly afterwards, Gertrude 'behaved badly in her own way, and the President behaved well in his: he expressed grief in its Instant or powdered form' (p. 115). Antithesis is usually a very definite figure, setting up clear-cut oppositions, but in Jarrell's hands it opens up larger possibilities: if this is to behave well, perhaps Gertrude's way is preferable—at least she was sincere. As the narrator says of President Robbins, 'he wasn't the hypocrite that Gertrude said he was. He had not evolved to the stage of moral development at which hypocrisy is possible' (p. 72). That is a memorably dismissive phrase.

The teaching faculty at Benton do not claim as much attention as the President, but their foibles, amusing or more serious, are also transfixed by the figures of rhetoric. To begin with the appropriate figure confessing inexpressibility (*adynaton*), the narrator records that the people of Benton 'were so liberal and selfless, politically that—but what words of men, or tongue of man or angel, can I find adequate to this great theme?' (p. 104). Yet, as he finds words, the ironies become more withering: 'You felt about the people of Benton: *If only they weren't so complacent! If only they weren't so*—then you stopped yourself, unwilling to waste an afternoon on *if only's*, and mumbled a summary *If only we were all dead or better!*' (ibid.). *Correctio* or *epanorthosis* stops a phrase in order to substitute one more fitting: in Jarrell's book the revision is always more damaging. Yet there are more ways to kill a cat. Antithesis, for instance, can convey one curiously pointless academic pattern, conveyed in an explanatory—or is it apologetic?—parenthesis: '(Dr. Whittaker spent his life either explaining things or having them explained to him.)' (p. 48). Antithesis can start off by registering the difference between the students and staff: 'And, soon, the girls would change before your eyes: they got older and sadder and wiser, and [*not 'but' but 'and'*] the professors never got any younger or gayer or stupider . . .' (p. 219). As you finish that sentence you realize that the apparent opposition turned into an identity, since all are moving on the same life continuum. Jarrell's antitheses are unpredictable, their outcome unexpected:

The people of Benton, like the rest of us, were born, fell in love, married and died, lay sleepless all night, saw the first star of evening and wished upon it, won lotteries and wept for joy. But not at Benton. (p. 222)

There the antithesis leaves open the question, how many of the preceding statements are negated? But since the chapter ends with those words, we cannot tell.

Some of the antitheses are self-contained, as in the *chiasmus* used to describe visitors' reactions to the art professor's varied products: 'Miss Rasmussen also designed furniture; but people persisted in sitting down in her sculpture, and in asking "What is that named?" of her chairs' (p. 228). Many of these effects depend upon a reversal of expectations: as in other universities, professors at Benton did fall in love with the students, 'but this happened distressingly seldom' (p. 63). (What a bloodless lot they are!) The students are controlled by an admissions policy in which 'girls who had read Wittgenstein as high school baby-sitters were rejected because the school's quota of abnormally intelligent students had already been filled for that year. (The normality of the intellectual environment of Benton was rigorously maintained.)' (p. 80). That delicious parenthesis opens up the word 'normality' to inspection. Repetition of words is usually an emphatic figure, but in Jarrell's hands it acquires subtlety and suggestiveness, as with the faculty's attitude to publication: 'One teacher had last had something printed in a 1928 *Dial*; they respected him for that article, but they respected him much more for having put away such things, and gone on to where they were' (p. 87)—namely, not publishing. But figures of repetition (*ploche, parison*) can also convey a child's view of academics, as the son of one of the faculty says to the narrator: '"Haven't you noticed how they all talk just the same, and dress just alike, and read the same books, and—and leave the same day and come back the same day? . . . They're androids"'—that is, as the narrator kindly spares us a trip to the dictionary, 'synthetic human beings, robots who look just like you and me' (p. 271). A hit, a palpable hit.

Every page of *Pictures from an Institution* carries some new invention, some lovingly executed sentence—if I am allowed a pun—or new turn of phrase or figure. Not all the characters are treated with this genial, tolerant amusement. The President's wife, ex-colonial English—with 'her Achilles leg, that unlucky South Africa' (p. 51), haughty and overbearing, is put down comprehensively. *Anaphora, correctio, antithesis,* and metaphor combine to describe Mrs Robbins's self-absorption: 'Her every sentence sang itself to a melody so thin-lipped, so emptily affected, so bloodless, so heartless, so senselessly and conclusively complacent, that it was not merely inhuman but inanimate, not merely lifeless but the negation of life' (p. 14). *Antimetabole* says all that is needed about her relations with the rest of the world: 'People did not like Mrs. Robbins, Mrs. Robbins did not like people; and neither was sorry' (p. 11). Even her own dogs dislike her:

To understand what Pamela Robbins was, one didn't need to listen to what she said, to understand English, to understand human speech; the Afghans . . . —they knew what Mrs. Robbins was, and as she fed them they wagged their tails distrustingly. (p. 14)

Correctio, looking for a more suitable term, diminishes her further: 'Mrs. Robbins fought to acquire as much—not merit; what did she know about merit?—as much prestige or position or face as possible' (p. 13). In Jarrell's hands this figure exploits to the full its power to fracture a statement, arrest the reader while searching for a more suitable formulation, and finally send us away satisfied that justice has been done. Yet Jarrell is seldom witty about Mrs Robbins: whatever she represents was not something he could occasionally forgive. Almost the only tender—no, potentially tender—description of her comes towards the end of a long and in every sense exhausting dinner-party given by Gertrude, as the guests, one by one, pass out.

In a corner of the sofa Mrs. Robbins slept. Sleep, settling on her hard face, had begun to soften it; begun, and got nowhere, and dropped off to sleep. (p. 60)

In that marvellous sentence, an *epanalepsis* beginning and ending with the word 'sleep', the repetition of 'begun' in the second half leads to an unexpected reversal, as the attempt of sleep to humanise Mrs Robbins's face is defeated, and sleep becomes itself, restoring the face to its *status quo ante*: hard. A modern American writer perfectly fulfils the mimetic claims made for the figures of rhetoric by the critics of Greece and Rome.

Jarrell's greatest care, his most searching and varied use of rhetoric, is devoted to his main character, the novelist Gertrude Johnson, an egotist who takes on mythic, almost archetypal dimensions. *Correctio*, the figure of qualification, creating a gap between perception and evaluation, sums up the narrator's relationship to her: 'My wife and I . . . were very old acquaintances—I could say *friends*, but Gertrude had no very old friends—of Gertrude's' (p. 35). The same figure describes Gertrude's major, and most damning fault as a writer: 'she did not know—or rather, did not believe—what it was like to be a human being' (p. 189). This ignorance of humanity means that 'even the best of Gertrude's books were habitat groups in a Museum of Natural History: topography, correct; meteorological information, correct; condition of skins, good; mounting of horns, correct . . .'—the repetition of these terms at the end of the clauses (*epistrophe*) makes us alert for the qualification—'Inside there were old newspapers, papier-mâché, clockwork' (p. 190). Our experience of reading, especially of Jarrell's use of balance and opposition, made us expect some kind of devastating contrast, although not perhaps such a coherent extension of the metaphor of lifeless models. The amazing, the perverse thing about Gertrude as a novelist is that she distrusts invention: 'the novelist's greatest temptation, Gertrude felt, is to create' (p. 47). She relies on direct transcription from life, reducing her relationships with people to the level of material for a novel. To put it in antimetabolic terms, for Gertrude 'there were two species: writers and people; and the writers were really people, and the people weren't' (p. 22). Jarrell's ability to deploy rhetoric inventively comes out strikingly here, for the form of the figure makes us expect a sentence ending, 'the people weren't writers'. To cut it off here, leaving the possible construction, 'and the people weren't people', conveys how Gertrude denies ordinary people any value, collapses the distinction to privilege one side of it, deny the other. An even wittier use of *antimetabole* rewrites one of Dwight Robbins's banalities:

The President went on to say, with a smile at his homely metaphor, that Gertrude's bark was worse than her bite. This was foolish— Gertrude's bark *was* her bite; and many a bite has lain awake all night longing to be Gertrude's bark. (p. 51)

Here it is the narrator who collapses the terms into one subsuming what would be the stronger in most beings (the bite) into the weaker (the bark), thus showing how ferocious Gertrude must be. We appreciate the imaginative flight, too, by which Jarrell gives the bite a life of its own, insomniac with envy at her superior force.

As a novelist Gertrude manifests a form of misanthropy, seeing the worst in everyone—'it was, indeed, her only principle of explanation'—and by doing so gains a dubious popularity with her readers. 'They wanted her to tell them the worst about themselves, and [*not 'but' but 'and'*] after they had met her they whispered to one another the worst about *her*' (p. 189). In that sentence the pronouns revolve about the central term, 'worst' (they—her—them—themselves; they—her —they—her), to show how her negative view of life rebounds on her. Jarrell's revenge on Gertrude is to effect for her the same erosion that she makes of the distinction between life and art:

> this American novelist wanted life to be Art, not seeing that many of the values . . . of life and art are irreconcilable; so that her life looked coldly into the mirror that it held up to itself, and saw that it was full of quotations, of data and analysis and epigrams, of naked and shameful truths, of *facts*: it saw that it was a novel by Gertrude Johnson. (p. 214)

The detonation in that sentence, the unpatterned final clause, gains more force in its free statement from the symmetries and repetitions (*anaphora* and *ploche* in the 'ofs' and 'ands') that precede it. Other sentences achieve a similar effect with different means, as in the description of her amazing knowingness, equal to that of *Time* magazine: 'all clichés, slogans, fashions, turns of speech, details of dress' and much else 'lived in Gertrude as though in nutrient broth; and Gertrude nourished them unharmed, knowing all, believing none' (p. 133). That single antithesis (with its biblical echoes), postponed to the latest point, demolished all that has gone before. Why does she treasure them then, we ask, knowing the answer, that she paid no attention to the society she lived in 'except as a giant nursery of facts' (p. 215).

The rhetorical figure with which Jarrell consistently characterizes Gertrude is antithesis, which expresses the way she stands outside normal human life: 'If she was superior to most people in her courage and independence, in her intelligence, in her reckless wit, in her extraordinary powers of observation, in her almost eidetic memory'—a great build-up, keeping us waiting for the detonation—'she was inferior to them in most human qualities' (p. 190). Jarrell uses this device in many and varied forms, giving with one hand and taking away —but more, much more—with the other. In that sentence the seven positive terms, which begin to seem like an admiring portrait, are more than wiped out by the single point opposed to them, for what would such gifts be in an inhuman being? As if anticipating such a question, the narrator goes on:

> Most of the time Gertrude was not an ordinary human being but an extraordinary human animal. Her hand was against every man's and every man's was against hers. She had not signed the human contract when the rest of us signed it. (p. 190)

Antithesis, antimetabole, ploche—all define her misanthropy.[40] Her anti-social feelings are given a remarkable and disturbing dimension by being shown as a projection on to society of her feelings about herself. Gertrude 'knew that people must be, at bottom, like herself, and this was enough to justify—to make imperative—any measures she could take against them. And if everybody had been, at bottom, what Gertrude thought she was, she would have been right to behave as she behaved, though it would have been better simply to curse God and die' (p. 191). Self-hatred can go no further.

'Tragic' would be the wrong word to apply to Gertrude, since she shows almost no redeeming features. Yet Jarrell's sustained analysis of her—using the barest minimum of 'plot' in the conventional sense of conflicting goals, narratives of success, failure, transformation—reaches a degree of understanding which becomes almost compassionate. It may be a case of *tout comprendre, c'est tout pardonner*. Even the evasions, the mental dishonesties she uses to sustain her misanthropy, are registered. Her books condemn mankind for being 'stupid and bad': what then, the narrator wonders, would become of Gertrude if people were 'clever and good'? For this reason,

when she met someone who was either good or clever, she looked at him in uneasy antagonism. Yet she need not have been afraid. Clever people always came to seem to her, after a time, bad; good people always came to seem to her, after a time, stupid. She was always able to fail the clever for being bad, the good for being stupid; and if somebody was both clever and good, Gertrude stopped grading. (p. 134)

In that sequence Jarrell subtly repeats the terms 'clever' and 'good' (the figure *epanodos*), which would call in question Gertrude's judgement on life, re-creating the process by which she then juggles them around to form the equations she wants, clever = bad, good = stupid. When this manœuvre fails she just ducks out of the game; and the antithesis collapses, accordingly. Elsewhere Jarrell sustains an antithesis to show her odd vision of life, at once penetrating and facile: 'She showed that anything, anything at all, is not what it seems; and if

[40] Compare Jarrell's remark in a letter, dated September 1951, about a friend who was incapable of love: 'Really complete egotism is so hard on you because you feel that everyone else is, *essentially* is or should be, like you—so you're alone, really alone. It's Gertrude's war of all against all' (*Letters* p. 269).

anything is not anything, it is nothing' (p. 187). She is a
deconstructionist before her time.

This portrait gains conviction, due to the authority with which
Jarrell knows and describes her—as one of his reviewers said,
'the reader continually feels that no one person should be given
so deep an understanding of another human being as Jarrell
manifests' here.[41] It convinces also because so many of these
traits cohere. But egotism of this order can bring only
unhappiness, even to someone as apparently self-sufficient as
Gertrude. In her social relations Gertrude loved to shock people,
and to make them laugh: 'Both gave her a sense of animation
and assurance: she was sure, then, that—What was it she was
sure of then? Of something; she was not sure what. But her
sense of assurance was real' (p. 69). That sentence first ascribes
certainty to her, then uses *aposiopesis*, the figure of incompletion,
to deny or undermine it. The insecurities become transparent in
the descriptions of Gertrude's insomnia, where *epistrophe*, a
word repeated at the end of sentences, is especially effective.
Jarrell uses *epistrophe* more often than *anaphora*, which is
unusual. *Anaphora* comes easily, even to ordinary people
(compare Graham Swift's narrator), but *epistrophe* demands
planning and control, if the word chosen is to achieve the
proper effect of unexpected recurrence and meaningful
emphasis. (But Jarrell has any amount of control.) As Gertrude
lies awake, tossing and turning, she remembers what

someone once cried out upon the scaffold: *O God, if there is a God, save
my soul, if I have a soul!* Instead of these two things there were herself
and the people in the world; she thought of herself, of them, of what
they had done to her, of what she had done to them, of what they say
and feel and *are*—and it was unbearable beyond belief, worse, surely,
than any nightmare. She had never had a nightmare; this was her
nightmare. (p. 197)

Many of the figures associated with Gertrude combine there—
correctio (if . . . if . . .), *antithesis* (herself . . . people), *antimetabole*
(they had done to her . . . she had done to them)—but the
clinching *epistrophe* on 'nightmare', appropriately enough,
crowns this picture of unhappy misanthropy. Again, lying there
she sometimes gets lost in her own thoughts: 'then for an

---

[41] Paul Engle, quoted on the dust-jacket.

instant even habit was no help, as she identified her anger—or was it anguish?—was, for the instant, her anguish' (p. 197). There *paronomasia* (anger/anguish) builds up to the echoing key word, 'anguish'. This devastating section ends with another *epistrophe* also correctly based, as a Renaissance rhetorician would say, 'on a word of some significance':

But sometimes in bed beside her sleeping, her perpetually sleeping husband, she felt herself shaking so that, faintly, with a little steely sound, the springs of the bed shook: she said to herself, in wondering agony, *Why am I so angry?* She was *right* to be so angry; and yet, why was she so angry? (p. 198)

There Jarrell registers, simultaneously, her insecurity about her own feelings and her sense of them being right. The anger, however, remains unexplained.

Yet Gertrude has a husband, Sidney, her one weakness, and her one redeeming feature. He is in fact an extremely indeterminate person, easily absorbed into her world. The narrator appreciates Gertrude's 'gift for decoration': 'she and Sidney had gone into a bare apartment and after a few days had got it looking barer' (p. 38). Amusing though these unexpected inversions are, they all associate Gertrude with notions of bareness or emptiness. 'Gertrude didn't eat much, and Sidney had accustomed himself to not eating much.' She could get along 'on crackers, a sucked lemon, and the last lettuce-leaf in the back of the vegetable-drawer of the refrigerator. *What women eat when they live alone!* a doctor has said—and that is what Sidney ate' (p. 195). The surprise comes from the absorption of Sidney into the categories 'women: Gertrude'—he offers no resistance. He is devoted to her, but quite passive: 'Sidney went behind her like a shadow, useless and waiting to be used' (p. 74), an antithesis (with *polyptoton*) made more effective by the device Jarrell uses a number of times, putting the copula 'and' where we might expect the disjunctive 'but'. *Polyptoton* is used again, with antithesis or *chiasmus*, to explain why Gertrude finds 'something soothing about Sidney . . . it was absurd of her to feel that way. . . . She had made her living, her life, out of the rejection of the absurdities of existence; Sidney was an absurdity she had grown accustomed to—accepted willingly, almost' (p. 75). The last word, though, has that familiar Jarrell effect of giving with one hand and promptly withdrawing. Vives noted that the figure *epanorthosis* (*correctio*) was used often by St Paul, and commented: 'an adjustment between word and reality takes place whenever we wish to be understood or believed more or less differently from what we wish or the listeners think we wish.'[42] The narrator uses the figure brilliantly to define the sense that Sidney is totally subordinate to Gertrude, when he is

reminded of a sentence of Freud's, about love-affairs, that I could apply to Gertrude and Sidney—they were *a group of two*. Yet this didn't sound right, somehow. I compromised with: they were a group of one and a half. (p. 105)

Jarrell fully realizes the ability of this device to open up a gap between perception and evaluation, where the second look is always for the worse. Sidney's share in the relationship declines further in the metaphor used to describe Gertrude and himself: 'she lay there beside that homely negligible extension of herself, that fifth limb, Sidney' (p. 213). Or, as another character describes Sidney: 'He is—he is St. Jerome's lion's lion' (p. 153).

The value of Sidney to Gertrude is that he is the only human being with whom she can have something resembling, at least, a normal sharing or exchange relationship. Gertrude 'betrayed toward Sidney, alone among mortals, a rudimentary and anomalous good-nature' (p. 75). Her denial of reciprocity to everyone save him is rendered in another antithesis having an unexpected outcome:

In the world there were people who were bad to her and people who were good to her, people she was bad to and people she—and Sidney. Sidney was what Gertrude could be good to. (p. 206)

In such sequences Jarrell's prose has the characteristic that Jonas Barish, writing of the prose of Lyly and Shakespeare, has described as 'logicality', that is, 'the habit of proceeding disjunctively, of splitting every idea into its component elements and then symmetrizing the elements so as to sharpen the sense of division between them'.[43] Such disjunctions have a predictive

---

[42] Vives 1966, p. 76.

[43] *Ben Jonson and the Language of Prose Comedy* (Cambridge, Mass., 1960), p. 23: see the first two chapters for a penetrating juxtaposition of Shakespeare's preference for symmetry and prediction, with the highlighting of surprise, as against Jonson's liking for asymmetry and formlessness.

effect, for when we hear a sentence referring to 'the one' we await the completing member giving 'the other'. Jarrell sets up such frameworks but sometimes collapses them unexpectedly, as in this example, where the *aposiopesis* denies the antithesis we had been led to expect, so that instead of 'people she was good to', which the sentence predicts, we have 'Sidney'. Her life with him—'absurd' though it was, she felt, 'to waste herself' on him—was premissed on the principle, ' "Sidney needs me" ' (p. 75). She likes to think that in this relationship she retains her independence none the less, since to her, being 'free' means recognizing neither commitments nor loyalties to other human beings. 'She was free to destroy Sidney too, if she wanted to; she just, just—just didn't want to . . .' (p. 190). There *epizeuxis* and *aposiopesis* combine to suggest a note of impotence undermining the assertion, as if her mind were unwilling to recognize a deeper truth. In the great crisis that Jarrell subjects Gertrude to, with her anguished insomnia, the situation is definitely reversed, as she moves through *paromoion* and *parison*, matching structures, into *antimetabole*, their inversion:

> She had trusted Sidney entirely because Sidney needed her entirely: how could Sidney possibly get along without *her*? But now that she saw that she could not possibly get along without Sidney, her trust was shaken. When Sidney found out that she was in his power—if he found out, her heart substituted hastily—what would he do? How could you trust *anyone* with such power? (p. 206)

In the third sentence we have a rare use of *correctio* being ascribed to one of the characters, as Gertrude makes that 'adjustment between word and reality' that Vives described, recalls the word she most fears and substitutes a less damaging one, 'if' for 'when'. But 'she knew about Sidney and herself, now', and the 'newness of her knowledge' (*paronomasia* on knew/now/newness; *polyptoton* on knew/knowledge) gives Gertrude anxieties:

> She felt that she must not at any price let Sidney see what she had seen—just mustn't give him a *chance* of seeing; how glad she was that Sidney wasn't smarter! (p. 209)

There the multiple forms of 'see—seen—seeing' catch Gertrude's wish to preserve Sidney from knowing a truth which the narrator, and his readers, share with her. Gertrude lives on, but rhetorical figures have recorded the growing insecurity over the basis of her existence.

At the end of the novel 'they all go', as the chapter title has it, echoing a Shakespearian stage-direction. Gertrude is going off to Peru to write a travel book, and Sidney will accompany her. He has always had some quite nondescript employment in whatever place she happens to be. His insignificance, wherever he works, is beautifully rendered by the fact that his resignation can be given and accepted all in one parenthesis. As the narrator explains 'she and Sidney (he had said to his employers, *I have to go, Gertrude is leaving*; they had said, *All right*) were going to Peru or Chile or Ecuador . . .' (p. 254). (Hamlet said he could be 'bounded in a nutshell', Sidney is contained in a parenthesis.) But there is little possibility of him getting a job in Peru:

Sidney said, 'It'll be a vacation for *me*—Gertrude will be working harder than ever.' As he said this he looked at her. For that look you forgave him everything—and after all, what was there to forgive?—you even forgave Gertrude everything; or, at least, were willing to consider the possibility of making the attempt, foredoomed to failure as it was. (p. 266)

That final pivoting, at the word 'or', with the following five successive stages of qualification diminishing the possibility of forgiving Gertrude, can stand as an appropriate summation of Randall Jarrell's use of rhetoric to describe and evaluate his characters. As so many examples have shown, his trick of giving but withdrawing approval makes the reading experience echo, sequentially, the process of judgement. We go through the same second thoughts with the narrator, which in the case of President Robbins and Gertrude are always revisions for the worse. Yet there are exceptions to this rule, indeed some of the other characters—especially Gottfried Rosenbaum, the lovable German music professor and his wife Irene—are lacking in any malice and are celebrated accordingly.

Gottfried knew more than you did, and could do more with what he knew; and when you looked for a clause, beginning with *but*, that would end the sentence in your favour, you could not find one. (p. 172)

It is reassuring to know that to some characters *correctio* does not apply.

Yet it is the gallery of satirical sketches that makes this novel memorable, above all Gertrude, whom Jarrell himself came to love (*Letters*, p. 401). In these satiric 'characters' Jarrell's prose is a model of variety, invention, and elegance. The grace with which he despatches his targets reminds me of Dryden's exclamation, in his *Discourse Concerning the Original and Progress of Satire* (1693), 'how easy is it to call rogue and villain', but 'how hard to make a man appear a fool, a blockhead, or a knave, without using any of these opprobrious terms'. This 'fineness of raillery', Dryden says, resembles 'the mystery of that noble trade', the public executioner's, where

there is still a vast difference betwixt the slovenly butchering of a man, and the fineness of a stroke that separates the head from the body, and leaves it standing in its place.[44]

Jarrell's prose has that precision, that cutting edge. In his novel, as in the very different ones by Orwell and Joyce, rhetoric shows that it lives on, available in many forms to writers creating imagined worlds.

In this sense I must disagree with Gérard Genette, whose judgement (in the words that form the epigraph to this chapter[45]) that rhetoric is not relevant to modern literature seems to me refuted by the novelists considered here (including those two brilliant French writers). It is true that rhetoric as a whole network of relationships and procedures is now available only to those who reconstruct it by study, but the expressive function of the figures remains, whether or not as part of a larger system. For their forms, and the range of expression possible within them, are indigenous to many languages in many historical periods. Genette himself has emphasized the value of studying the evolution of rhetoric as a system, 'car elle nous apprendrait beaucoup sur l'histoire des représentations du monde et de l'esprit pendant toute l'époque classique, d'Aristote à La Harpe' (p. 216)—only, I would add, in much later periods, too. For although representations of the world and of the human intellect have varied greatly in this period, one constant has been the forms of tropes and figures. An *antimetabole* or a *synecdoche* is the same figure, whether used by Aeschylus or

[44] Dryden 1962, ii. 136–7.
[45] *Figures I* (Paris, 1966), p. 221. Further references included in the text.

Joyce. And Genette also saw, at one point, that the semiology of rhetoric 'consiste à distinguer les figures les unes des autres, en fixant à chacune d'elles une valeur psychologique précise, selon le caractère du détour imposé à l'expression. Cette valeur est donnée (pour anticiper sur le vocabulaire de la stylistique moderne) soit comme *impressive* (telle figure est destinée à provoquer tel sentiment), soit comme *expressive* (telle figure est dictée par tel sentiment),' or both at once. As he goes on to show, it was precisely the Cartesian Bernard Lamy who, among French rhetoricians, 'a poussé le plus loin l'interprétation psychologique (affective) des figures, jusqu'à chercher dans chacune d'elles le "caractère", c'est-à-dire la marque d'une passion particulière: autant de figures, autant de symptômes' (pp. 217–18). Lamy's examples, and definitions, can be fitted into our literary tradition anywhere between Longinus and Raymond Queneau. If we attend to what I have called the polysemous nature of rhetorical figures, their ability to use the same form for an almost infinite range of functions and feelings, then we might conclude that rhetoric has always been an integral resource of linguistic expression, and always will be.

9

EPILOGUE: THE FUTURE OF RHETORIC

On nous reprochera peut-être de voir la Rhétorique
partout. Et si, par hasard, elle y était vraiment?

Basil Muntéano[1]

Having carried the story of rhetoric from the past to the present,
from Homer to the works of living novelists, I now link the
present to the future, and suggest what might be hoped for in
rhetoric studies, and what not.

To start with the negative side, we might by now expect that
the significance of rhetoric in the classical world would be
clearly recognized, given its importance in politics, law,
philosophy, poetry, history, and literary criticism, and indeed
as one of the main preservers of classical culture. Yet in two
recent compilations from our ancient universities rhetoric is
nowhere given adequate treatment, either as a cultural
phenomenon or as a discipline affecting all forms of literary
composition. In *The Cambridge History of Classical Literature*,[2]
neither the Greek nor Latin volume treats rhetoric as a subject in
its own right, with a continuous history. There are references to
it, unavoidably so, as concerns Cicero (ten pages out of over
nine hundred in the Latin volume), Quintilian (three pages, his
'grave deficiencies' apparently including a sketchy knowledge
of Greek literature, his 'narrow vision' and 'scant historical
sense' having created canons 'which have constricted the study
of Latin literature over the last five hundred years'—with the
grudging admission that his influence 'has been beneficent as
well as stultifying'), and oratory under the later principate
(seven pages). In the Greek volume Aristotle's *Rhetoric* receives
one page, where it is virtually dismissed as being 'now of largely

---

[1] Muntéano 1967, p. 171.
[2] *The Cambridge History of Classical Literature*. Vol. I, *Greek Literature*, ed.
P. E. Easterling and B. M. W. Knox (Cambridge, 1985); Vol II, *Latin Literature*,
ed. E. J. Kenney and W. V. Clausen (Cambridge, 1982).

historical interest' (a dangerous formulation for a classicist to use), Dionysius, Longinus, and Demetrius together receive six, but oratory nearly thirty pages (by George Kennedy): what emphasis there is is on end-products rather than shaping forces. It is evident that for many practitioners of traditional classical philology literary criticism has begun to exist as a respectable category, but not rhetoric. The rival production from Oxford,[3] of smaller scope but with equally distinguished authors, gives no separate attention to rhetoric, although it has sections on 'Life and Society' and 'The Arts of Living'. *Quis custodiet?*—It might be said in defence that these books are addressed to the general reader, or under-graduate—but then all the more need to get some fundamental elements of classical culture into the right perspective from the first.

Where proper scholarly histories of rhetoric do exist, these can have serious defects. The two volumes on British logic and rhetoric by W. S. Howell,[4] although pioneering in their day, and giving the first full account of many texts, are examples of internalist and parochial history. They are limited to English rhetoric-books, ignore the school and university background, and consider neither the international neo-Latin texts used in England nor the continuing tradition of editing, commenting, and teaching the major classical texts. A proper history of rhetoric, or any other discipline, however, will consider not just new titles but the totality of teaching-material, ancient or modern, in Greek, Latin, and the vernaculars, since the presence of Cicero or Quintilian is often more important than the latest modern digest. It will also consider the parallel presence of rhetoric in major literary forms, such as poetry, history, the sermon, the letter, the novel, and the other arts, for these are all ways in which rhetoric has influenced the thought-habits and modes of expression in a society. A properly-balanced history will also be responsive to the actual emphases in rhetoric at each point in time or within a culture: Howell, for instance, was notoriously dismissive of *elocutio* and the figures and tropes in any form, whether in education or in real life. A true history of rhetoric will need to consider the role

---

[3] *The Oxford History of the Classical World*, ed. J. Boardman, J. Griffin, O. Murray (Oxford, 1986).

[4] See Vickers 1981, commenting on Howell 1956 and Howell 1971.

of eloquence in institutions, such as parliaments, lawcourts, universities, academies.

A model history in this respect, which far outdistances anything done for any other country, is Marc Fumaroli's survey of 'the Age of Eloquence' in France from 1580 to the 1660s.[5] This begins with the classical heritage as it was being refashioned at the turning-point between the inherited values of the European Renaissance and the newer spirit of French classicism. The dispute over Cicero, especially the concept of *imitatio* as applied to models of style, which begins in Italy in the late fifteenth century,[6] was fought out in France just as bitterly, the old cat-calls of 'Asianism' and 'Atticism' taking on a new lease of life. Professor Fumaroli devotes the second part of his history to the Jesuits, whose growth, flourishing, and final extinction between 1551 and 1763 is treated in its full context, social and intellectual. The Jesuits are shown as embracing simultaneously both the scholarly history of rhetoric, sifting the printed records of the past to form an ever-more complete picture, and newer interests in the visual effects possible with such figures as *hypotyposis* and *ekphrasis*, resulting in a vogue for emblems and hieroglyphs as a sacred language. The Jesuits were under constant attack from the University of Paris: another institution conscious of its image as an academy of eloquence was Parliament, which used the formal addresses delivered at its opening to enhance its legitimacy and antiquity, and to mark its independence from Rome. The 'Remonstrances' or harangues delivered by the royal advocates twice a year represented an important fusion of legal and political eloquence, a new genre which had its parallel in England, in the 'Charges' delivered by Sir Francis Bacon in his capacity as Attorney-General and Solicitor-General.[7] The outstanding figure in France at this time was Richelieu, the politician who legitimized rhetoric by taking his own orators with him when he came to power, and helped institutionalize rhetoric more firmly by founding the Académie française. All

---

[5] See Fumaroli 1980 and Brian Vickers, 'The Age of Eloquence', review essay of Fumaroli in *History of European Ideas*, 5 (1984), 427–37.

[6] See H. Gmelin, 'Das Prinzip der Imitatio in den Romanischen Literaturen der Renaissance', *Romanische Forschungen*, 32 (1932) 83–360; F. Ulivi, *L'imitazione nella poetica dal Rinascimento* (Milan, 1959); G. Santangelo (ed.), *Le epistole 'De Imitatione' di G. F. Pico della Mirandola e di P. Bembo* (Florence, 1954).

[7] See Bacon 1857–74, xi. 265–75, 399–416; xii. 136–46; xiii. 182–93, 211–14.

these developments are linked by Fumaroli in their consequences for literature, from Muret and Montaigne to Guez de Balzac, a unification of history which should provoke students of other literatures to emulation.

If this study is exemplary in its grasp of rhetoric as a cultural phenomenon, other recent books arouse expectations which they do not fulfil. A book with the ambitious title *Rhetorical Norms in Renaissance Literature*,[8] by W. J. Kennedy, offers an investigation of the literary conventions in Renaissance lyric poetry, ironic prose, and the epic, all in under two hundred pages. Rhetoric is treated not only skimpily but with a disabling lack of historical understanding. In the seven pages given to classical rhetoric Kennedy states that the influence of Aristotle's *Rhetoric* was 'decisive', or 'tremendous', and that Cicero and Quintilian reproduce Aristotle wholesale. In addition to these obvious errors, the author ignores major forces in the tradition such as Isocrates, the *Rhetorica ad Herennium*, and the Hellenistic texts, while dismissing the three centuries from Petrarch to Milton in three pages. Any subject may be treated concisely, of course, but the haste and superficiality of this survey is accompanied by a fundamental misconception of Renaissance rhetoric. Kennedy states that the Middle Ages regarded rhetoric 'almost exclusively as an art of ornamentation', yet sees no difference between this period and the Renaissance, when a concept of *elocutio* as supposedly 'ornate speech' is said to have gradually 'reduced rhetoric to nothing more than a mere classification of figures and tropes'. This is such a travesty of the multiform nature of Renaissance rhetoric—the author was, at the time of writing, a professor at Cornell, and chairman of the Department of Comparative Literature—that one wonders how it can have been acquired. Far from being 'superficial elocutionary devices', used for 'embellishment or ornamentation', the figures carried out the expressive and persuasive function ascribed to *ornatus* as a whole. The author goes on to discuss lyric poetry in terms of 'speech and address', but fails to see the relevance of epistolary rhetoric; he discusses appeals to other persons or places within Petrarch's poems but never investigates the figure *apostrophe*; and he is quite unable to read the conventions of the proœmium in the invocation to

[8] New Haven, 1978: see my fuller account in *Rhetorik*, 2 (1981), 106–12.

Paradise Lost, saying that its 'questions have no answer and the dilemmas no resolution'. All this might not matter, had he not claimed in his title and chapter headings to be talking about rhetoric. As so often today, the word 'rhetoric' is used as a legitimizing counter in a book's title, but is in fact exploited, the reader likewise.[9]

I

The deficiencies of William Kennedy's book—by no means the only one of its kind—derive from a half-hearted or inadequate attempt to reconstruct rhetoric as a historical reality. But we also find, in contemporary work on rhetoric, evidence of a progressive atrophy of the discipline, not just from a primary to secondary role—from oral to written communication—but to *elocutio* alone, now detached from its expressive and persuasive functions, and brought down finally to a handful of tropes. It is not easy to reconstruct the process by which this atrophying has come about, but one name sometimes evoked as exemplar is that of Vico. In his *New Science,*[10] discussing 'Poetic logic', which 'considers things in all the forms by which they may be signified' (p. 127, §400), Vico argues that the first form taken by language was anthropomorphic metaphor, for 'the first poets attributed to bodies the being of animate substances, with capacities measured by their own, namely sense and passion, and in this way made fables of them. Thus every metaphor so formed is a fable in brief', and metaphor remains 'the most luminous and therefore the most necessary and frequent' of all the tropes (p. 129, §404). After the invention of metaphor, Vico believes, followed metonymy, the substitution of agent for act resulting from 'the fact that names for agents were commoner than names for acts', and that of subject for form and accident

[9] A recently announced series by the University of Wisconsin Press is called 'Rhetoric of the Human Sciences', which will analyse 'various disciplines, not as the "sciences" they sometimes claim to be, but as "rhetorics"—that is, as systems of belief and practice, each of which has its own characteristic form and structure': announcement in *The New York Review of Books,* 30 Jan. 1986, p. 17. This is to widen the meaning of rhetoric to the point of no return.

[10] Quotations are from Vico 1968, with references incorporated into the text. Earlier rhetoricians who designated the four 'basic' tropes include Talaeus (1547), Ramus (1549), Vossius (1605), Keckermann (1606), Farnaby (1625), and Smith (1657). Who originated the practice?

being due to the early poets' 'inability to abstract forms and qualities from subjects' (p. 130, §406). The third trope Vico considers is synecdoche, which, he claims, 'developed into metaphor as particulars were elevated into universals or parts united with the other parts together with which they make up their wholes' (p. 130, §407). Vico's speculative history of the genesis of tropes ends with irony, which, he thinks, 'could not have begun until the period of reflection, because it is fashioned of falsehood by dint of a reflection which wears the mask of truth' (p. 131, §408).

That really marks the extent of Vico's interest in the tropes, which are brought in not as rhetorical devices in their own right but as stages in a hypothetical scheme of the evolution of language and poetry. But before leaving the topic he makes a further reductive gesture:

From all this it follows that all the tropes (and *they are all reducible to the four types above discussed*), which have hitherto been considered ingenious inventions of writers, were necessarily modes of expression of all the first poetic nations, and had originally their full native propriety. But these expressions of the first nations later became figurative when, with the further development of the human mind, words were invented which signified abstract forms or genera comprising their species or relating parts with their wholes. (p. 131, §409; my italics)

Behind Vico's theory of the genesis of tropes one can just see the traditional argument of rhetoricians that eloquence was natural before it became systematized into an art. Like other rhetoricians, Vico uses this argument as a tool to attack a neighbouring discipline, wishing to 'overthrow . . . two common errors of grammarians'. But his reduction of the tropes to four is unfortunate, and in fact unworkable, as anyone will see who tries to reduce *prosopopoeia, antiphrasis, onomatopoeia, antonomasia,* or *hyperbole* to one of the privileged four. Each of these tropes has a specific nature, and a specific role to play in the elaboration of discourse, so that to claim that all the others may be ignored can only impoverish rhetoric. Vico seems to be the source—typically, unacknowledged—behind Kenneth Burke's adding to one of his books an appendix discussing 'Four Master Tropes', namely the same four, metaphor, metonymy, synecdoche, and irony.[11] Burke also subordinates them to his own concerns, free-wheeling, allusive, unhistorical philosophizing, a system that rearranges the components of classical rhetoric so idiosyncratically as to be virtually unusable.

Vico is the acknowledged inspiration for the 'four trope' theory of the contemporary American historian Hayden White,[12] who has revived the ancient (if somewhat confusing) term 'tropics' to describe 'the tropical element in all discourse' (p. 1). White believes that this element is 'inexpungeable from discourse in the human sciences, however realistic they may aspire to be', for 'tropics is the process by which all discourse *constitutes* the objects' which it then describes and analyses (p. 2). The 'turning' of words and thoughts effected by tropes allows us to move from 'one notion of the way things are related' to another, and to see that the connection between things 'can be expressed in a language that takes account of the possibility of their being otherwise' (ibid.). So White indirectly refutes Croce's monism, and justifies the adaptive power of language. No text, he goes on, 'can represent "things as they are" without rhetorical adornment or poetic imagery', and even the syllogism works by using synecdoche and metonymy as it moves 'from the plane of universal propositions to singular existential statements' (p. 3). I agree with some of White's principles, and I endorse his comment that those thinkers (he cites Vico, Rousseau, Hegel, and Nietzsche) who held that the first languages derived from tropes and figures did not oppose these 'prefigurative modes of cognition' to 'rational modes', and were interested in integration rather than opposition (p. 7). But I cannot do much with his claim to have discovered an 'archetypal plot of discursive formations' which moves, in Vico's sequence but for a different purpose, from metaphor to

---

[11] *A Grammar of Motives* (New York, 1945), pp. 503–17. Burke's debt to Vico is clear in such passages as these: 'If you trail language back far enough, of course, you will find that all our terms for "spiritual" states were metonymic in origin. . . . Language develops by metaphorical extension, in borrowing words from the realm of the corporeal, visible, tangible and applying them by analogy to the realm of the incorporeal, invisible, intangible, then in the course of time, the corporeal reference is forgotten . . .' (p. 506).

[12] *Tropics of Discourse. Essays in Cultural Criticism* (Baltimore, Md., 1978); references in the text.

metonymy to synecdoche to irony. White claims to find this pattern in Piaget's division of children's cognitive development into four phases ('sensorimotor, representational, operational, and logical'); in Freud's interpretation of dreaming (condensation, displacement, representation, secondary revision), in Marx, and in Hegel (pp. 6–20). In another essay he finds the same 'quaternary pattern' in the levels of interpretation in historical narrative, which are 'structurally homologous with one another' (p. 70). So to the four 'basic' tropes, metaphor, synecdoche, metonymy, irony, correspond four 'modes of emplotment' (romance, comedy, tragedy, satire), four 'modes of explanation' (idiographic, organistic, mechanistic, contextualist), four 'modes of ideological implication' (anarchist, conservative, radical, liberal), and four nineteenth-century historians (Michelet, Tocqueville, Ranke, Burckhardt: pp. 70–4). This is an unusual recurrence of a technique that I have called 'category-fit', common in the occult sciences,[13] and a venerable way of making sense of the world. But as far as rhetoric is concerned, White's practice is doubly unfortunate, being not only reductive in its concern with four tropes only, but also subordinating them to a different and, let it be said, alien interest.

The other tradition behind the atrophying of rhetoric in modern theory reduces the tropes to two only, metaphor and metonymy. The instigator of this reduction was of course Roman Jakobson, who wanted to apply 'purely *linguistic* criteria to the interpretation and classification' of aphasia.[14] I have italicized the term that shows how rhetoric has once again been subordinated to another discipline, here linguistics, especially the kind practised by Jakobson, which never shook off the influence of structuralist phonology and its concern with binary oppositions. Any linguistic sign, according to Jakobson, 'involves two modes of arrangement' of its constituent parts, combination and substitution or selection, these two ways of treating constituent signs yielding the 'context' of a linguistic unit and the 'code' (pp. 60–1). So the 'constituents of a context',

[13] See Brian Vickers, 'On the Function of Analogy in the Occult', in A. Debus and I. Merkel (eds.), *Hermeticism and the Renaissance* (Cranbury, NJ, 1988), pp. 265–92.
[14] 'Two Aspects of Language and Two Types of Aphasic Disturbances', in R. Jakobson and M. Halle, *Fundamentals of Language* (The Hague, 1956), pp. 53–82; references in the text.

he argues, can be thought to be 'in a state of *contiguity*, while in a
substitution set signs are linked by various degrees of *similarity*,
fluctuating between synonyms and antonyms (ibid.). These two
operations, contiguity and similarity, 'provide each linguistic
sign with two sets of *interpretants*', to use the terminology of
C. S. Peirce, two references 'which serve to interpret the sign—
one to the code, and the other to the context' (pp. 61–2).
Jakobson's binary system, finally, allows him to distinguish two
types of aphasics, those with 'Similarity Disorder' and those
with 'Contiguity Disorder', and it is at this point that he invokes
rhetoric, claiming that the two types correspond to the tropes
metaphor and metonymy.

Before examining Jakobson's argument it may be worth
recalling the meaning of these terms in rhetoric. 'By a trope',
Quintilian writes, 'is meant the artistic alteration of a word or
phrase from its proper meaning to another.' The alteration
involves not just words but 'our thoughts and the structure of
our sentences', so that those writers are 'mistaken who have
held that tropes necessarily involved the substitution of one
name for another', such as indicating an invention by
substituting the name of the inventor (Vulcan for fire, Ceres for
bread), or substituting 'that which contains for that which is
contained' ('a cup was drunk to the lees', implying a cup of
wine), or cause for effect ('slothful ease'), or vice versa (8. 6. 23).
Synecdoche gives 'variety to our language by making us realise
many things from one, the whole from a part, the *genus* from a
species, things which follow from things which have preceded'
(8. 6. 19). Other rhetoricians agree substantially, or are more
explicit, such as the *Ad Herennium*, describing metonymy as 'the
figure which draws from an object closely akin or associated [*ab
rebus propinquis et finitimis*] an expression suggesting the object
meant, but not called by its own name', substituting greater for
lesser, instrument for possessor, and so on (4. 32. 43). *Metaphor*,
as everyone knows, involves describing one thing or concept in
terms of another, so as to relate or combine attributes not
commonly associated. *Antonomasia* is 'the substitution of an
epithet as equivalent to the name which it replaces', or
'indicating the most striking characteristics of an individual, as
in the phrase "Father of gods and king of men"'. Periphrasis
and allegory are large-scale ways of using one verbal sequence

to describe another; irony and related tropes substitute a form of discourse that means the opposite of what it seems to say.

All the tropes, then, work by a form of substitution based on resemblance and difference, with the listener or reader being expected to make the mental operations necessary to relate one term to another within the same class. In one context 'Mars' will be a metonymy for 'war', 'gold' for 'wealth', 'Venus' for 'love'. The movement can be within a logical class (part for whole, container for contained), and demands a certain power of abstraction in both writer and reader, that 'ability to see resemblances' that Aristotle praised so highly where metaphor is involved. The tropes form a rather miscellaneous group, notoriously so, standard lists ranging from eight to thirty or more. Some rhetoricians attempted to classify them by their general operations, a typical example, found as late as Alexander Bain in the 1880s,[15] being the grouping into 'Figures Founded on Similarity' (similitude, metaphor), 'Figures Founded on Contiguity' (metonymy, synecdoche, transferred epithet), and 'Figures Founded on Contrast' (irony, interrogation). It is important to realize that all such groupings place the tropes in various classes but without implying fundamental differences between them: 'contiguity', as in the *Ad Herennium*'s description of metonymy, is a variant form of 'similarity', not a polar opposite to it. What Jakobson does is to take the binary oppositions that he has established for linguistics—combination/substitution, code/context, paradigmatic/syntagmatic—and then forcibly impose these on to the two tropes that he has picked out. Even within his own terms, 'combination' is hardly a polar opposite to 'selection', just a different process, and to see 'syntagm' and 'paradigm' as opposites involves taking a metaphor very literally, spatializing it ('pole' or 'axis') and then subordinating it to a dichotomy.

In the first kind of aphasia, he argues, with 'impaired substitution and intact contexture', operations of contiguity are said to replace those based on similarity:

From the two polar figures of speech, metaphor and metonymy, the

[15] *English Composition and Rhetoric*, enlarged edition, 2 vols. (London, 1886–7), i. 135–232.

latter, based on contiguity, is widely employed by aphasics whose selective capacities have been affected. *Fork* is substituted for *knife*, *table* for *lamp, smoke* for *pipe, eat* for *toaster*. . . . Such metonymies may be characterized as projections from the line of a habitual context into the line of substitution and selection. (p. 69)

I shall return to this metaphor of 'polar figures of speech', but must say first that Jakobson is using the term 'contiguity' in a loose, indeed metaphorical way, to describe how aphasics, unable to recall the proper word, substitute the *next* best, or the *nearest* word they can think of. But in rhetoric, as we have seen, metonymy involves the substitution of a 'related' term (where *propinquis* does not mean literally 'next to') according to fixed transitions or tropings within a category on different levels, such as putting the container for the thing contained, or the sign for the thing signified. In Jakobson's examples there is no such movement across the levels within a category, only the attempt to find a substitute corresponding to the unrecallable word, some of which are very approximate indeed. 'Table' and 'lamp' are two domestic objects sometimes found in physical contiguity but which do not imply each other, neither do 'eat' and 'toaster'. It takes a reader with a special knowledge of the clinical context to recognize what the aphasic means by these terms. One may doubt whether they are figures of speech in the sense that we normally give that phrase. In fact, when he describes the other type of patient, one 'confined to the substitution set (once contexture is deficient')', Jakobson himself substantially qualifies his claim that these are rhetorical processes. Such an aphasic

deals with similarities, and his approximate identifications are of a metaphoric nature, contrary to the metonymic ones familiar to the opposite [*sic*] type of aphasics. *Spyglass* for *microscope*, or *fire* for *gaslight* are typical examples of such *quasi-metaphoric expressions*, . . . since, in contradistinction to rhetoric or poetic metaphors, they present no deliberate transfer of meaning. (p. 72)

In that case, they are not really metaphors, and since the items in the first class are not really metonymies Jakobson's use of rhetorical terms can be seen to be both opportunistic and vague. Just as with the attempt to apply rhetorical terms to music or painting, the *translatio* of rhetoric to linguistics, and thence to psychology and neurology, involves both a simplification and a distortion of rhetoric.

Yet Jakobson was unconcerned by such reflections, returning to his earlier metaphor in a chapter entitled 'The metaphoric and metonymic poles'. Here he asserts that either of those two relations, similarity and contiguity, can appear 'on any verbal level—morphemic, lexical, syntactic, and phraseological' (p. 77). That may well be, especially given the rather vague terms in which they are defined, but where his argument becomes really damaging is when he asserts that 'either of the two gravitational poles [gravity provides a further reinforcing metaphor] may prevail', that is, what he calls 'metaphor' *will dominate over* 'metonymy', or vice versa, not just in the disordered mental world of aphasics but in literary genres or large-scale artistic movements. Jakobson actually proposes (pp. 77–8, 81–2) the following dichotomy, based on the 'dominance' of either 'pole':

Metaphor	*Metonymy*
Russian lyrical songs	Russian Heroic epics
Romanticism and symbolism	Realism
Surrealism	Cubism
Poetry	Prose

He argues that 'the predominance of metonymy' underlies realism, which belongs to 'an intermediary stage between the decline of romanticism'—he must mean in the mid-nineteenth century—'and is opposed to them both'. This case is argued in two sentences, in terms of 'the realistic author metonymically' digressing from the plot to atmosphere, or from characters to action, and illustrated with two quotations from Tolstoy (p. 78). One hardly knows which to admire most, the vastness of the thesis or the paucity of argument. Perhaps further analysis would only have complicated the issue. The same mixture of grandiose assertion and non-existent argument characterizes his dichotomizing of poetry and prose: 'Since poetry is focused upon sign, and pragmatical prose primarily upon referent'—let us not stop to discuss that proposition—'tropes and figures were studied primarily as poetical devices. The principle of similarity underlies poetry. . . . Prose, on the contrary, is forwarded essentially by contiguity' (pp. 81–2).

This reveals too clearly Jakobson's ignorance of rhetoric, in which tropes and figures were studied primarily as expressive devices, first in prose and only later in poetry. But the distinction is so vast as to be meaningless.

In Jakobson's work, as in Vico and White, rhetoric is fragmented and then subordinated to an alien enterprise. This is a pattern we have met before, in medieval rhetoric, with its disintegration of a unified tradition into components that were reused for different and usually more restricted ends. In Jakobson the guiding spirit is the binary opposition basic to structuralist phonology after Trubetzkoy, which here not only divides rhetoric into two terms, and two only, but then conceives of them in fundamental opposition. Invoking what he claims to be '*the bipolar structure of language (or other semiotic systems)*, and in aphasia, the *fixation* on one of these poles to the *exclusion* of the other' (pp. 78–9; my italics), Jakobson states as a general law that 'A competition between both devices, metonymic and metaphoric, is manifest in any symbolic process, either intrapersonal or social' (p. 80). The reader may well feel at this point that such an opposition, and the further desire to exclude one half of the field, is manifest most of all in Jakobson's thought-processes. In other words, aphasia provides the norm for wide-scale social and intellectual movements. His supporting evidence is what he calls the 'decisive question' in analysing the structure of dreams, namely whether the symbols and narratives that occur there 'are based on contiguity (Freud's metonymic "displacement" and synecdochic "condensation") or on similarity (Freud's "identification and symbolism")' (p. 81). Freud provided Hayden White's quaternary scheme with four terms: the same text accommodates Jakobson's binary theory with two. These categories are malleable, evidently, and once again too vast to be usable. Jakobson's other evidence is the wholly outmoded anthropology of J. G. Frazer, who, as Jakobson innocently puts it, 'resolved' the principles underlying magic rites into similarity and contiguity—'this bipartition is indeed illuminating', he says (p. 81).

Jakobson was a great linguist, whose contribution will stand when most of us writing in this century will have long been forgotten. But on this issue he is merely expressing a general

attitude to rhetoric in modern times, which first reduces its
scope, and then applies it to purposes that it never dreamt of.
No rhetorician before Vico could have thought of describing the
evolution of human consciousness in terms of the interaction of
four tropes, or summing up the complex nature of poetry and
prose in two.

The effects of Jakobson's dichotomizing reduction of rhetoric
have, I believe, been disastrous, as a whole critical school has
attempted to read literature solely in terms of metaphor versus
metonymy, ignoring all other verbal devices. The kind of
undisciplined and unhistorical criticism that may use this
method as a form of self-legitimization is illustrated from an
unexpected side in a recent work by Gordon Williams which
appears to be about rhetoric in Latin poetry.[16] In fact the author
claims that between the major compositions of Catullus and the
death of Horace (60–8 BC) poets used a technique of composition that 'ran counter to rhetorical theory as it has come
down to us (mostly from later periods)', in particular by denying
'the fundamental distinction between form and content' basic to
rhetoric with its categories of *inventio* and *elocutio* (p. ix). But
unfortunately rhetorical theory was already fully formed in this
period, as an examination of the *Rhetorica ad Herennium, De
Inventione*, and what we know of their Hellenistic sources, will
soon show; indeed rhetoric was already a part of Roman
education then, and its impact is clearly visible in the poetry of
Catullus, and Horace; while the distinction between *res* and
verba is inherent in the Latin language and in general thought
categories.[17] 'Once that comfortable distinction between form
and content was disregarded', Williams goes on (so it must
already have existed, then!), 'conventional rhetorical analysis
was impotent'. But this is to confuse creation with criticism,
since it does not consider how poets constructed their poems,
and to substitute an animus against rhetoric for an informed and
responsible attitude to history. Williams claims that the poetry
of this period is 'a poetry of meditation', not 'a rhetorical
poetry' which would try to 'manipulate an audience by making

[16] *Figures of Thought in Roman Poetry* (New Haven, Conn., 1980).
[17] See, e.g., Clarke 1953; Bonner 1977; D'Alton 1931, ch. 8, 'The supremacy of
rhetoric', pp. 438–524; and Kennedy 1972, pp. 384–419 on 'Rhetoric and Poetry'
in the Augustan period.

immediate impact', a process that, according to him, only arose later, during the age of Augustus, when 'rhetorical theory' succeeded in forcing its 'impertinent impositions' on to poetry, assimilating it 'to the condition of prose (with the addition of metre). . . . It is only fairly recently that the imposture has been seriously questioned' (pp. x–xi)—namely by Professor Williams himself, in two previous books.

Whether 'a poetry of meditation' is the right description for the poetry of Catullus, or Horace, is a question that can be left to other readers, but what this dichotomy—privileging one side and dismissing the other—reveals is just another instance of classicists' continuing hostility to rhetoric. Williams's case is interesting in that he admits to having been 'faced with difficult problems of terminology', since he scorns to use that of the 'ancient rhetorical theorists'. Apparently they 'confined their analysis to simple structures for the most part, like rhetorical questions or aposiopesis, and devoted their attention otherwise to figures of speech': since these are all figures of speech, that is a meaningless statement. Worse still, the 'close distinctions' they made between terms (unlike Williams) can easily get the modern user into 'a scholastic nightmare of labelling in which the important issues simply disappear from view' (pp. xi–xii)— another travesty of classical rhetoric. Therefore he decided to use Jakobson's simpler binary opposition, even though he knows that

ancient theorists used the words 'metaphor' and 'metonymy' to describe modifications of meaning that are produced by the fact that a sign or group of signs is connected to an unexpected or unusual referent. The resulting modification is intelligible to the reader because a relationship of similarity or of contiguity links the normal or expected referent with the new referent,

which presupposes in the reader the capacity to recognize the relationship (p. xi). This is, despite the general dismissal of rhetoric, an acute observation on the actual functioning of these tropes as conceived of in the classical treatises, well supported by his later survey of the relevant texts (pp. 23 ff.). Yet although the author knows how unhistorical and non-rhetorical Jakobson's terminology is, he finds it convenient for the real aim of his book, which is equally non-rhetorical. By 'figures of thought' in his title he refers not to the *figurae mentis* of the handbooks (which in any case meant figures expressing 'the mind, feeling or conceptions': Quintilian, 9. 1. 17), but to a special technique which he claims operated in Roman poetry of this period. For these poets, it seems 'an idea . . . could be regarded as a semantic unit, analogous to a word, and could be subject to configurations with other ideas just as had been done previously with words [thus sabotaging his chronology again!]. Consequently . . . new techniques could be devised for managing transitions of thought, and the poet could say one thing while expecting his reader to understand that he meant something else . . . ' (pp. ix–x). That seems to me, I confess, a wholly unfounded idea, and one that opens the door to any interpretation of a text, whatever its overt meaning, putting the critic in a state of privileged communication with the *manes* of his poets, since he alone, after nearly two thousand years, knows what their poems are really about. The prospect is alarming, but in the event this turns out to be a largely conventional piece of criticism, using such concepts as 'thematic anticipation' and 'objective correlative'. Yet it dismissed rhetoric; and sought legitimization by using Jakobson's two 'polar' tropes.

Some dangers of this reductive attitude to rhetoric have been brought out by Gérard Genette, a critic who has devoted much thought to rhetoric and its history and who has edited two classic French rhetoric texts.[18] Commenting on the appearance in 1970 of the *Rhétorique générale* of the 'Groupe μ de Liège' (a team of Belgian critics who adopted the first letter of 'metaphor' for their name), and of two articles discussing 'la figure généralisée' and 'la métaphore généralisée', Genette observed

---

[18] Genette's three volumes entitled *Figures* include a number of essays on rhetoric. *Figures I* (Paris, 1966) has an interesting study of Etienne Binet's 1621 rhetoric-book (pp. 170–83), and an essay called 'Figures' (pp. 205–21) that unfortunately regards figures solely as 'deviations' from normal speech rather than expressive devices in their own right. *Figures II* (Paris, 1969) has an excellent essay on 'Rhétorique et enseignement' (p. 23–42), while *Figures III* (Paris, 1972) includes the text I shall discuss, 'La Rhétorique restreinte' (pp. 21–40), also available in English as 'Rhetoric Restrained' in Genette, *Figures of Literary Discourse*, tr. A. Sheridan (Oxford, 1982), pp. 103–26. (Instead of 'restrained' I would translate 'reduced' or 'restricted'.) My quotations are from the last-named essay, in the original. For Genette's editions of Du Marsais and Fontanier see p. 197 n. 46.

that in all these cases rhetoric was being neither generalized nor enlarged, but reduced, restricted. Aristotle's *Rhetoric* was a truly general treatise, including some remarks on metaphor, but now the term 'generalized' is applied to what is in effect a handbook of figures (pp. 21–2). Rhetoric has always had a smaller role in modern times, of course, compared to its status in Greece and Rome, but Genette thinks that the final process of reducing it to a study of tropes took place with the publication in 1730 of the treatise *Des Tropes* by Du Marsais, the grammar expert for the *Encyclopédie*, whose interest in rhetoric was that of 'a linguist, and more precisely a semantician' (p. 23). Du Marsais was concerned with the process by which tropes offered a substitution of a 'figurative' sense for 'the proper' sense, a concern that was taken further by Fontanier when he re-edited Du Marsais' treatise in 1818, and made the trope the model for all other figures, as if by right. Although including eighteen tropes, in a somewhat chaotic order, Du Marsais had proposed that they should be arranged hierarchically, a suggestion, Genette points out, already made by Vossius in the seventeenth century (perhaps Vico's unacknowledged source), who defined four main genera, metaphor, metonymy, synecdoche, and irony (pp. 23–4). Du Marsais proposed an alignment based on the three main associative principles of similitude, contiguity, and opposition (Genette does not note that these principles are already clearly defined in the classical rhetoric texts). Fontanier rejected irony, and stated that the only tropes worthy of the name were metonymy, synecdoche, and metaphor. As Genette puts it, one has only to combine the two approaches to obtain 'le couple figural exemplaire, chiens de faïence irremplaçables de notre propre rhétorique moderne: Métaphore et Métonymie' (p. 25): china dogs, or 'bookends' as the English version has it.

The final reduction of all tropes to these two was carried out, as we have seen, by Jakobson (anticipated, apparently, by Eikhenbaum in 1923, who also made the correlation metonymy = prose, metaphor = poetry), but Jakobson's borrowing from rhetoric involved, as Genette shows, a drastic reduction of the scope of these figures. In classical rhetoric the categories of analogy and contiguity refer to signifiers placed in a substitutional relation within metaphor and metonymy, such as 'gold' and 'corn' (having in common the colour yellow), 'steel' and 'sword' (exchanging substance for artefact). Jakobson assimilated that opposition to one derived from linguistics, between paradigm and syntagm, equivalence and succession, but these oppositions refer to what is signified, not to the signifiers. As well as creating an opposition where none exists in the original, and then displacing it within the linguistic sign (from signifier to signified), Jakobson's 'drastic reduction' of scope continues what Genette sees as a general trend in modern rhetoric, one that prefers tropes of a more semantically concrete, 'spatio-temporal' nature, excluding those that rely on intellectual operation. This 'displacement of the object . . . privileges the two relations of contiguity (and/or inclusion) and resemblance, while weakening those of association' (pp. 25–6). The trope *synecdoche* depends on similarities being grasped by the intellect, and cannot be subsumed under physical contiguity: 'sail' for 'ship', as Genette points out, is a substitution not by contiguity—which would demand 'mast', say—but within a class defined logically (p. 27). Perhaps for this reason it was of no use to Jakobson in his attempt to define aphasia in 'purely linguistic terms'. The 'pseudo-spatial' concept of contiguity, as Genette calls it, may privilege metonymy but it also creates a further reduction within the figure itself, for many of the relations described by classical rhetoric—effect for cause, sign for the thing signified—'cannot be easily reduced to an effect of contact or spatial proximity, unless by using metaphor' (pp. 27–8). Contiguity in this physical sense cannot relate 'heart' and 'courage', 'bowels' and 'pity', so that 'to reduce all metonymy to a purely spatial relationship is to restrict the mode of action of this figure to a single physical' or material aspect (p. 28). As with my earlier analysis of the attempt to apply figures of rhetoric to music, the field of application of the rhetorical device taken over into another discipline is immediately limited.

The same reductive process has operated with the figures of resemblance, benefiting metaphor at the expense of others, especially comparison or similitude. Genette's detailed and original analysis of the functioning of analogy—which reveals, too, the inadequacy of a Jakobsonian binary model (pp. 29–31)— shows that metaphor is only one of several figures of analogy, and that to reduce all such tropes to 'the metaphoric pole' is to do violence to language and to thought. The opposition metonymy–metaphor, he concludes somewhat mockingly, could be assimilated to other grand binary schemes, such as the correspondence between heaven and earth, or between the sisters in the Gospel: metonymy is Martha, the active one, busy about the house, passing from one object to another, duster in hand, while metaphor is Mary, who having chosen 'the better part', namely contemplation, will go straight to heaven. Or they could be seen as horizontal versus vertical, or materialists (prosaic people privileging 'contact') versus spiritualists (poetic souls preferring 'similitude'), or—but 'nous ne pousserons pas plus loin', he comments with a rare sarcasm, 'ce jeu d'extrapolations manichéistes, dont les stations terminales ne réservent aucune surprise' (pp. 37–8). Genette's target in these closing pages is the elevation, more marked in French literary theory than elsewhere, of metaphor to 'the trope of tropes', the figure of figures, the only part of rhetoric worth saving (p. 28–40). I agree with him that this is the ultimate reduction of rhetoric, the penultimate stage being Jakobson's binary opposition, its apotheosis a monism that, from the vast corpus of the art, privileges one single trope, a rare survivor from 'the great shipwreck of rhetoric' in the nineteenth century (p. 32).

My last example of the reduction, fragmentation, and misapplication of rhetoric in modern literary discourse is the work of the late Paul de Man, in three collections of essays. *Blindness and Insight. Essays in the Rhetoric of Contemporary Criticism* (New York, 1971) contained work produced between 1966 and 1969. *Allegories of Reading. Figural Language in Rousseau, Nietzsche, Rilke, and Proust* (New Haven, 1979) brought together essays from 1972 to 1976, while *The Rhetoric of Romanticism* (New York, 1984) assembled essays written between 1956 and 1983. This last volume discusses Wordworth's *Essays upon Epitaphs* in terms of the figure *prosopopoeia*, here claimed to be 'the trope of autobiography', since it 'deals with the giving and taking away of faces, with face and deface, *figure*, figuration, and disfiguration' (pp. 75–6)—a self-centred playing with the word (here the figure *polyptoton*) that de Man sometimes indulged in. Another essay, 'Anthropomorphism and Trope in the Lyric', claims that in Baudelaire's 'Correspondances' the 'anthropomorphic' symbolism of seeing nature as a 'temple' of trees with living 'pillars'—surely referring to architecture and therefore not primarily *anthropo*morphic—means that 'anthropomorphism' can be elevated to the ranks of rhetoric as a 'figure of amplification' (pp. 246–7). Both essays are typical of de Man in limiting their interest in rhetoric to one stage, *elocutio*, then to one category within it, namely a specific trope (sometimes misnamed figure), which then becomes the fragile basis for a vastly elaborated theory. But at least this rather miscellaneous volume does not attempt to turn rhetoric against itself, as the two other collections do.

Blindness and Insight uses 'rhetoric' in the subtitle, but the term only appears in an essay called 'The Rhetoric of Blindness', which finds Jacques Derrida guilty of 'blindness' in his reading of Rousseau. The rhetoric text in dispute is Rousseau's *Essai sur l'origine des langues*[19] (c. 1756), especially the discussion of how imitation works differently in the various arts. Readers of my account of the translation of rhetorical categories to the visual arts will recognize the tradition behind Rousseau's giving the priority to drawing—'le dessin'—over colour. Much of Rousseau's thinking on language derives from familiar emphases in the rhetorical tradition: language distinguishes men from beasts (p. 27); gestures express emotion vividly, and history has many examples of 'ces maniéres d'argumenter aux yeux' which prove that 'on parle aux yeux bien mieux qu'aux oreilles: il n'y a personne qui ne sente la vérité du jugement d'Horace à cet égard' (pp. 31–3). The passage in Horace that Rousseau alludes to is *ut pictura poesis* once again, and his account of the emotional impact of metaphor—'les discours les plus éloquens sont ceux où l'on enchâsse le plus d'images' (p. 35)— derives from a long and well-known tradition of the power of visual appeal, recently flourishing in France (Rousseau cites Lamy's *L'Art de parler*). The origin of language, Rousseau reasons, was due not to the satisfaction of human needs— gestures are more appropriate for that—but to the expression of feeling. The original languages resembled poetry, not geometry, man's first words being formed to express immediate emotional needs: 'pour émouvoir un jeune coeur, pour repousser un

[19] Quotations are from J.-J. Rousseau, *Essai sur l'origine des langues, où il est parlé de la mélodie et de l'imitation musicale*, ed. C. Porset (Paris, 1970), incorporated into the text. The editor reproduces Rousseau's manuscript orthography.

aggresseur injuste la nature dicte des accens, des cris, des plaintes: voilà les plus anciens mots inventés' (pp. 41–3).

Within the argument I have been developing in this book it will come as no surprise that Rousseau should connect language with human feelings, nor that he conceives rhetoric as being the natural language for feeling. Chapter III of his treatise is entitled 'Que le premier langage dut être figuré', and at once links rhetoric and feeling:

Comme les prémiers motifs qui firent parler l'homme furent des passions, ses prémiéres expressions furent des Tropes. Le langage figuré fut la première à naître, le sens propre fut trouvé le dernier. . . . D'abord on ne parla qu'en pöesie; on ne s'avisa de raisonner que longtemps après. (p. 45)

Anticipating the reader's objection that an expression cannot become figurative before its literal sense has been established—a serious objection, still—Rousseau replies that

pour m'entendre il faut substituer l'idée que la passion nous présente, au mot que nous transposons; car on ne transpose les mots que parce qu'on transpose aussi les idées, autrement le langage figuré ne signifieroit rien.

In a trope *res* and *verba* must cohere in the process of *translatio* (the Latin term for metaphor) from one level of discourse to another. The motive force in Rousseau's theory of the trope's *translatio* is 'passion', strong feelings such as fear. His example is of a savage who encounters other men for the first time and in his fear sees them as bigger and stronger than himself, and so calls them 'giants'; later, as he gets used to them, he substitutes the term 'men'. The example may not be well chosen, as de Man complains, but my point is that Rousseau uses it to connect tropes with feeling: 'Voilà comment le mot figuré nait avant le mot propre, lorsque la passion nous fascine les yeux. . . . L'image illusoire offerte par la passion se montrant la première, le langage qui lui répondoit fut aussi le premier inventé' (p. 47).

Of Rousseau's theory as such I have little to say beyond noting the organic connection it preserves between rhetoric and feeling. But I find it strange that de Man's discussion of Rousseau, and Derrida, should totally ignore the affective significance of tropes. In his view, the title of Rousseau's Chapter III 'must be understood' as saying, 'the only literal statement that says what it means to say is the assertion that there can be no literal statements' (*Blindness*, p. 33). Rousseau's chronology—first trope, then literal meaning—is collapsed into a simultaneity that produces an impasse of contradiction. De Man wishes to argue that all literary language, and so literature itself, is figurative, and therefore ambivalent, but he foists this theory into Rousseau's text, which is given the additional hazard of undermining itself: 'Accounting for the "rhetoricity" of its own mode, the text also postulates the necessity of its own misreading.' That is, it writes in 'an indirect, figural way that knows it will be misunderstood by being taken literally' (p. 136). But if this reader, any reader, can distinguish literal and figurative, why is misreading a necessity? Because, de Man might reply, reading is impossible. Rousseau supposedly makes metaphor 'the cornerstone of a theory of rhetoric'—I cannot discover that Rousseau had a 'theory of rhetoric': this text merely argues that communication of feeling results in the invention of figurative language—but 'a rhetoric that can assert itself only in a manner that leaves open the possibility of misunderstanding'. It not only 'leaves open' that possibility, but 'opens up', much more excitingly, 'the possibility of the archetypal error: the recurrent confusion of sign and substance' (ibid.). So, de Man concludes, any text can be called 'literary' that 'implicitly or explicitly signifies its own rhetorical mode and prefigures its own misunderstanding as the correlative of its rhetorical nature; that is, of its "rhetoricity"' (ibid.). Derrida accused Rousseau of blindness, but, de Man says, he either read Rousseau in terms of Rousseau's critics or else he deliberately misread him (p. 139). Either way, he is himself blind—or rather, he shows 'blindness to be the necessary correlative of the rhetorical structure of literary language' (p. 141).

Paul de Man's discussion of Rousseau's rhetoric is typical of his whole critical method, being based on a very small amount of text, which is here interpreted in a way quite different to that meant, indeed insisted on by the author. Rousseau's emphasis on tropes as representing passion, feelings, poetry as against rational discourse—a web of ideas derived from the rhetorical tradition, most immediately from Vico[20]—is ignored in favour of a modern intellectualist discussion of metaphor in terms of literal and figurative levels. This line of discussion is then subjected to a mode of simultaneous assertion and negation which results in a logical impasse: 'rhetoricity' is found to be the state of making assertions that are fated to be misunderstood. In *Allegories of Reading* this process is repeated on a larger scale, both as a general theoretical statement and as a reading of Nietzsche. In the opening chapter, 'Semiology and Rhetoric', de Man explains that he uses the word rhetoric to signify 'the study of tropes and of figures', and 'not in the *derived* sense of comment or of eloquence or persuasion' (p. 6; my italics). But this is a *hypallage*, that gets things back to front: tropes and figures are the verbal means by which persuasion is carried out, not an alternative to it, to be detached for separate discussion. And persuasion is not a 'derived' but a primary conception of rhetoric. In the hands of de Man rhetoric no longer means oratory, civic eloquence, moving the feelings, or constructing the whole of an artistic discourse; it refers to a few well-known tropes, not even figures. The modern fragmentation of rhetoric is carried further, reducing it from persuasion or 'actual action upon others' to the workings of a self-contained 'intralinguistic figure or trope' (p. 8). It has been made introverted, solipsistic.

Whether de Man ever read Aristotle, Quintilian, or any other rhetorician remains unclear. (Derrida by contrast, cites Aristotle in Greek.) His actual knowledge of rhetoric as revealed in these essays is limited to a fundamentally misguided conception of the art, and to a few tropes, not always correctly understood. But this did not prevent him from making grand generalizations. The continuity between grammar and rhetoric, a constant in the language arts for over two thousand years, is swept away in three pages (9–11). On the basis of one invented

[20] See Vico 1968, passages quoted in the text above, also Bk. 2, §2, ch. 4, 'Corollaries concerning the origins of languages and letters', para. 431, which argues that 'the first men of the gentile world . . . expressed themselves by means of gestures or physical objects which had natural relations with the ideas' (p. 139), and ch. 5, para. 456, 'Corollaries concerning the origins of poetic style', which argues that 'poetic language' was 'born entirely of poverty of language and need of expression. This is proved by the first lights of poetic style, which are vivid representations, images, similes, comparisons, metaphors . . .' (p. 153).

anecdote, in which a husband responds to his wife's solicitous question with the irritable reply 'What's the difference?', de Man builds up a whole theory of a 'tension between grammar and rhetoric'. Since the question is capable of being misunderstood (either asking 'what is the difference between x and y?', or implying 'it makes no difference to me'—one would have thought that the speech-context, especially the tone of the speaker's voice, would have made it quite clear to the wife what her husband meant), de Man concludes that 'the same grammatical pattern engenders two meanings that are mutually exclusive: the literal meaning asks for the concept (difference) whose existence is denied by the figurative meaning' (p. 9). This trivial incident, describing a banal misunderstanding (if it ever took place) actually gives de Man the cue to define the 'difference between grammar and rhetoric', namely that 'grammar allows us to ask the question, but the sentence by means of which we ask it may deny the very possibility of asking'. Unfortunately, de Man has misunderstood the term 'rhetorical question', which means a question posed without the expectation of a reply, the speaker implying the answer to be self-evident. De Man, however, says that a question 'becomes rhetorical . . . when it is impossible to decide by grammatical or other linguistic devices which of the two meanings [literal or figurative] prevails.' (This would simply be a muddled or ambivalent question.) But, insisting on his idiosyncratic and anachronistic late twentieth-century conception, de Man takes it to a melodramatic and paranoiac conclusion, with the rhetorical question now seen as a 'semiological enigma', recording the despair that a speaker feels 'when confronted with a structure of linguistic meaning that he cannot control', a state that can only lead to 'an infinity of similar future confusions' (p. 10). So de Man reaches the amazing conclusion that in the rhetorical question, as such, 'Rhetoric radically suspends logic and opens up vertiginous possibilities of referential aberration'. And he promptly equates this 'rhetorical, figural potentiality of language' with literature, similarly bound to an autotelic absorption with itself, not with the world or experience it purports to describe, and equally liable to self-undermining. After a brief analysis of a passage in Proust, made to deny 'the intrinsic metaphysical superiority of metaphor over metonymy'—a pointless enough exercise in the Jakobsonian mode of setting one trope off against another—de Man concludes by reaffirming that 'a literary text simultaneously asserts and denies the authority of its own rhetorical mode'. (p. 17).

In deconstructionist theory, we may say, the binary oppositions of structuralism, originally conceived in spatial or skeletal terms, are confronted in a linear equation, and made to negate each other. An older modern critical school, the so-called 'New Criticism', with its concepts of 'tension' and 'irony', has also contributed to this critical mode.[21] But the oppositions, polarities, deconstructions, vertigo, are in the minds and method of the critics, not in the material itself. They may be expressing modern anxieties about language, with the curiously self-satisfying claim that language is an unreliable tool, but they ought not to foist these anxieties on to rhetoric.

De Man's essays on Nietzsche, especially 'Rhetoric of Tropes' (pp. 103–18), and 'Rhetoric of Persuasion' (pp. 119–31), further extend the deconstructionist deformation of rhetoric. As with the Rousseau essay, some references to rhetoric by Nietzsche (mainly the notes he took for the course on rhetoric given to an audience of two students at Basle University during the winter semester 1872–3), form the starting-point of de Man's enquiry, an enquiry that will end, like the Rousseau piece, in an impasse. Nietzsche made excerpts from several recent German books on rhetoric, Richard Volkmann's still unequalled survey, *Die Rhetorik der Griechen und Römer in systematischer Uebersicht* (1872), Gustav Gerber's *Die Sprache als Kunst* (1872), and the twin studies by Friedrich Blass, *Die griechische Beredsamkeit* (1865) and *Die attische Beredsamkeit* (1868). As a classical philologist anxious to establish his career, Nietzsche was diligent in taking notes, but added his own comments and interpretations, still not published in their totality.[22] He had excellent authorities, and

---

[21] See my review of Stanley Fish's *Self-Consuming Artifacts*, in *Renaissance Quarterly*, 27 (1974), 117–22.

[22] The most coherent presentation of this material to date is in the French translation by P. Lacoue-Labarthe and J.-L. Nancy, 'Friedrich Nietzsche, *Rhétorique et langage*', *Poétique*, 5 (1970), 99–142, from which I quote in summary or paraphrase, with references in the text. They reprint, with useful annotation, texts available in Nietzsche's *Gesammelte Werke* in the following editions: Leipzig (Kröner), vols. 17–19 (1912–13), and Munich (Musarion), Vol. 5 (1922), pp. 287–319; this volume also includes Nietzsche's early 'Geschichte der griechischen

produced a well-balanced account of the art. The course as a whole discussed: 1. the concept of rhetoric; 2. the main divisions; 3. the relationship between rhetoric and language; 4. *elocutio*: linguistic purity, clarity, decorum; 5. decorum of character and ornament; 6. neologism; 7. tropes; 8. figures; 9. prose rhythm; 10. the doctrine of *stasis*; 11. *genera et figurae causarum*; 12. judicial rhetoric and its types; 13. deliberative rhetoric; 14. epideictic rhetoric; 15. *dispositio*; 16. *memoria* and *actio*; Appendix: a brief history of eloquence.

Only the first seven chapters have been published (modern editors' interest expired, significantly enough, when they reached the rhetorical figures), but we can see that Nietzsche covered the whole subject, with perhaps insufficient attention to *inventio*. To pick out some of the main emphases, Nietzsche begins with the prestige of rhetoric in the ancient world, as the final stage in the formation of culture and intellect. He shows his awareness of the recent history of rhetoric, noting its decline in the nineteenth century, and quoting the attacks by Locke and Kant (p. 104). To illustrate the great status of the orator in Rome he cites Schopenhauer's account of the power of eloquence to penetrate the listener's mind and feelings, leading them wherever he will, even against their desires (p. 105)—Cicero and Quintilian made new, once again. In the present time, he writes, 'rhetorical' has come to mean 'artificial' in a pejorative sense, but of course, he asserts, 'natural' is itself a relative concept, and in fact rhetoric is only a development of artifices already present in language. Invoking Aristotle's description of rhetoric as a force (*dynamis*), Nietzsche argues (like Rousseau) that the purpose of language is not to pass on abstract truths or instruction, but to communicate an individual's emotions and judgements (p. 111). Drawing very closely on Gerber's work, Nietzsche equates rhetoric and language, since all words originated as tropes, and continue to be fundamentally trope-like (pp. 112–13; p. 128 n. 38). This idea also resembles Rousseau, but we note that Rousseau's linking of tropes and the feelings has disappeared from the nineteenth-century rhetorical

Beredsamkeit', pp. 1–42. The admirable *Nietzsche, Werke. Kritische Gesamtausgabe*, ed. G. Colli and M. Montinari (Berlin, 1967–ー), will contain a full transcript of these notes, probably in Abteilung II, Band 2, but the recent death of the surviving editor will undoubtedly delay things.

tradition. Returning to the relation between art and nature, Nietzsche makes the traditional points that the orator must avoid any impression of artifice, must imitate nature, and win the audience's belief in his sincerity (pp. 117–18). The 'agonistic', competitive nature of rhetoric in the ancient world, he writes (perhaps echoing his friend Jacob Burckhardt), meant that the weapons with which orators fought had to be not only powerful but beautiful, so that eloquence was meant to be both ethically moving and aesthetically pleasing, arousing the audience's *admiratio*, which Cicero and Quintilian—both quoted by Nietzsche—held to be an essential result of oratory (see above, p. 315).

Whether Nietzsche got his knowledge of rhetoric direct from the classical sources or from modern surveys (the latter seems the case for his somewhat confusing account of the tropes: p. 129 n. 67) is irrelevant. Once the full texts become available (including his lecture notes on Aristotle's *Rhetoric*) we should be able to confirm an interim judgement that Nietzsche was fully aware of the whole social and political function of classical rhetoric, its powers of persuasion, its use of *movere*, its various genres and categories, and its detailed teaching on the tropes and figures. Yet in Paul de Man's account Nietzsche's interest in rhetoric seems oddly one-sided. De Man makes two major claims. First, that 'Nietzsche moves the study of rhetoric away from techniques of eloquence and persuasion (*Beredsamkeit*) by making these dependent on a previous theory of *figures of speech or* [sic!] *tropes*' (*Allegories of Reading*, p. 105; my italics). Secondly, that for Nietzsche 'the figurative structure is not one linguistic mode among others but it characterizes language as such' (ibid.). The passages cited to substantiate both points derive from the same section in Nietzsche's notes, §7, on tropes, itself largely derivative from Gerber. De Man claims that the second point 'marks a full reversal' of established priorities, from a conception of language 'in its adequation to an extralinguistic referent or meaning' to one directed to 'the intralinguistic resources of figures' (p. 106).

Even from the very brief account I have given of Nietzsche's notes on rhetoric it is clear that the first point is quite without substance. Nietzsche has no programme to move the study of rhetoric away from eloquence and persuasion. Nor does he make persuasion 'dependent on a previous theory' of the tropes: this is de Man's own formulation, stated earlier in his book (p. 6), and in fact Nietzsche fails to make an explicit connection between the tropes and persuasion. As for the second point, de Man represents Nietzsche's opinions more accurately, but the deduction that a belief in the figurality of language means a shift from an extralinguistic to an intralinguistic concept of rhetoric is not Nietzsche's but de Man's, already made in his opening essay, *in propria persona* (p. 8). It should by now be evident that de Man is ascribing to Nietzsche attitudes towards rhetoric that he himself holds. De Man's account is highly selective, once more, again using small points from his author to support his own much larger claims. A fragment in *The Will to Power* (1888) on chronological reversal, the fluctuating priorities of cause and effect, inside and outside, is set beside the account of metonymy or metalepsis in the rhetoric notes (1872) to claim that both texts give language 'the possibility of substituting binary polarities such as before for after, . . . cause for effect, without regard for the truth-value of these structures' (p. 107–9). By running together two texts working at radically different levels and in quite different contexts de Man is able to diagnose what he calls 'the general drift of Nietzsche's thought', no less, namely 'the possibility of escaping from the pitfalls of rhetoric by becoming aware of the rhetoricity of language' (p. 110). That seems, however, his problem, not Nietzsche's. The underlying deconstructionist's preoccupation appears unmistakably in de Man's judgement of Nietzsche's essay 'On Truth and Lie in an Extra-Moral Sense', that 'although it presents itself legitimately as a demystification of literary rhetoric' it 'remains entirely literary, rhetorical, and deceptive itself' (p. 113). Once again, the desired impasse is achieved, with an air of satisfaction at having reached the *quod erat demonstrandum*.

In de Man's mental universe rhetoric is fated to a condition of deceit and mystification from which it is ceaselessly but fruitlessly trying to escape. Literature, and indeed language, suffer similar fates, so that, rather like Plato's arraignment of rhetoric with tragedy and music, the defender of rhetoric once again finds himself in congenial company. Yet why should rhetoric be ascribed this self-disruptive, fruitlessly un-self-healing fate? That is a hard question to answer, but the other essay on Nietzsche, 'Rhetoric of Persuasion' (given de Man's rejection of persuasion this is perhaps meant as a deliberate *oxymoron* or self-contradiction), pushes this diagnosis to its extreme point. De Man starts with a long passage from the posthumous fragments known as *The Will to Power* which challenges that basic tenet of philosophy since Aristotle, the principle of non-contradiction, the impossibility of affirming and denying the same thing (pp. 119–21). Readers must judge for themselves the cogency of Nietzsche's argument on this head, and de Man's account of it (as he says, 'the text does not simultaneously affirm and deny identity but it denies affirmation': p. 124). I want to pick up the discussion later, where de Man surprisingly bends his account of *The Will to Power*, sections 477 to 479, which is said to effect the deconstruction of consciousness and of thought as act (p. 129), back to his earlier discussion of Nietzsche's rhetoric.

De Man now claims that the Course on Rhetoric 'starts out from a pragmatic distinction between rhetoric as a system of tropes and rhetoric as having to do with the skills of persuasion' (p. 136). Anyone who takes the trouble to consult the text will see that it does nothing of the kind, as my summary above has shown. To understand de Man's reading of Nietzsche we must read him as he said we should read Derrida or Rousseau, namely substituting the critic's name for the author's. So, he goes on,

Nietzsche [de Man] contemptuously dismisses the popular meaning of rhetoric as eloquence and concentrates instead on the complex and philosophically challenging epistemology of the tropes . . . Privileging figure over persuasion is a typically post-Romantic [de Man] gesture. (p. 130)

The references to history and specific texts begin to take on a hallucinatory or purely imaginary quality, as in the comments that in Plato 'rhetoric becomes the ground for the furthest-reaching dialectical speculations conceivable to the mind' (a grandiose affirmation with little content or meaning), whereas in the 'text books that have undergone little change [*sic!*] from Quintillian [*sic!*] to the present', rhetoric 'is the humble and not-quite-respectable handmaiden of the fraudulent grammar used in oratory; Nietzsche himself begins his course by pointing out this discrepancy and documenting it with examples taken from Plato and elsewhere' (ibid.). Nietzsche did not in fact begin his course like that, but that is how de Man began his book—or at least placed first an essay which called grammar in question.

The degree of assimilation of Nietzsche to his own views on rhetoric, language, and literature, reaches its height in the last page of de Man's essay, where he ascribes to Nietzsche the 'final insight' that 'what is called "rhetoric" is precisely the gap' that de Man has just posited between the 'philosophical' and 'pedagogical' traditions, represented by Plato (!) and Quintilian:

> Considered as persuasion, rhetoric is performative but when considered as a system of tropes, it deconstructs its own performance. Rhetoric is a *text* in that it allows for two incompatible, mutually self-destructive points of view, and therefore puts an insurmountable obstacle in the way of any reading or understanding. The aporia between performance and constative language is merely a version of the aporia betweeen trope and persuasion that both generates and paralyzes rhetoric and thus gives it the appearance of a history. (p. 131)

That is perhaps the most extraordinary statement about rhetoric made in its long history. Yet it is entirely typical of de Man's deconstructionist methods in the way it fractures rhetoric into persuasion on the one hand, tropes on the other, dismisses the first without discussion, finds an inherent flaw in the second, and then juxtaposes them as 'incompatible, mutually self-destructive'—one of those activities being superfluous (a deliberate *pleonasmus*?). This is as if to say that verbs and nouns were always fighting against each other, or themselves, thus making communication impossible. In Paul de Man's theory of literature rhetoric becomes grist to the deconstructionist mill, which 'both generates and paralyzes' not just rhetoric but literary criticism, discourse itself.

De Man's influence on contemporary criticism, especially in America, has been great, and it may well be beneficial. But as regards rhetoric, his effect can only be harmful, for the totally unhistorical and self-confusing nature of his raids on rhetoric could paralyse and stultify any further thought.[23] The concern

[23] It is a sign of the times that the Folger Shakespeare Library should currently justify a course on rhetoric by reference to 'the recent revival of interest in rhetoric following the work of Paul de Man'. The nature and effect of his

that any responsible student of rhetoric must feel over this idiosyncratic distortion has been expressed by at least one reviewer of *Allegories of Reading*, Jeffrey Barnouw.[24] Analysing de Man's account of Proust, which claims to find an opposition between metaphor and metonymy (de Man's definition of which, Barnouw says, is 'scandalously loose and slippery': p. 460), and hence a disjunction between 'the aesthetically responsive and the rhetorically aware reading', Barnouw comments that

the wide gap between his 'reading' and the textual basis in the passage from Proust suggests that the model, far from being derived from the experience of reading, is *a priori* and arbitrary. Its affinities with the

influence can be seen from an issue of *New Literary History* (vol. 9, no. 3, Spring 1978) devoted to 'Rhetorical Analyses' (a more than usually abused term here), which includes an essay by Jonathan Culler, 'On Trope and Persuasion' (pp. 607–18). Culler parrots de Man (unacknowledged) in claiming that 'the relationship between trope and persuasion is always problematic and discontinuous', and that 'rhetoric is fated' to an 'incalculable textuality' (p. 608), a hesitation or 'aporia' between 'structure and event' (p. 609) that makes rhetoric itself an 'irony' (p. 611), the 'aporia of trope and persuasion' leading Culler to a further vision of 'rhetoric as language cut loose from a ground' (p. 615). This tradition has already reached a cul-de-sac: what next? In a matching essay, with the ambitious title 'Rhetorical Analysis: Towards a Tropology of Reading' (pp. 619–25), Marie-Rose Logan acknowledges her debt to de Man, which is so total and uncritical that she hasn't even bothered to read Nietzsche for herself, repeating as gospel truth de Man's claim that 'At the beginning of his course on rhetoric Nietzsche' makes a 'pragmatic distinction between rhetoric as a system of tropes' and rhetoric as eloquence, dismissing 'the latter in favour of the former . . . because he intends to concentrate on the philosophic epistemology of tropes' (p. 620). But as I have shown, this is de Man's rejection, not Nietzsche's. The reverence for *auctoritas*, which is another parallel between the medieval and modern fragmentations of knowledge, a talismanic worship of 'modern masters', is seen in the way Logan links Nietzsche with Derrida and de Man, and then claims that their 'deconstruction' of rhetoric—'(understood as the study of tropes and figures)' she adds parenthetically—has been carried further by linguistics and formalism: 'for, indeed, such critics as Jakobson, Todorov, Barthes, Genette, Greimas, and Riffaterre have all contributed . . . to the elaboration of a *refined* theory of rhetoric which could be termed a *sophisticated epistemology of rhetoric*' (ibid.). I have italicized the terms meant to valorize the 'enterprise' supposedly carried out by this heterogeneous group of critics, since the root metaphors connote on the one hand the purifying processes of alchemy and on the other the degeneration of a substance from its original and integral state: a suitably muddled metaphor for this topsy-turvy argument.

[24] In *Comparative Literature Studies*, 19 (1982), 459–63, page-references incorporated into the text. See also Barnouw's essay on Fish, 'The Experience of Bacon's *Essays*: Reading the Text *vs.* "Affective Stylistics" ', *Proceedings of the 9th Congress of the International Comparative Literature Association*, Vol. 2 (Innsbruck, 1979), pp. 351–7.

'self-consuming artifact' of Stanley Fish include the capacity to create difficulties in and for a text. The difficulties in either case are not real, however, but simply needed for the therapeutic effects of reading. (p. 461)

'Therapeutic' for the deconstructionist implies reading a text so as to reach what de Man calls a 'state of suspended ignorance' (*Allegories*, p. 19), the sceptic's *aporia* or doubt, what I have called the impasse.

Quoting de Man's conclusions to his Nietzsche chapters, with its discovery (or creation) of what we might call structural *aporiai* within rhetoric, Barnouw comments that de Man's claim to reach this conclusion 'by means of reading and presumably understanding what Nietzsche wrote is just the sort of "paradox" that de Man would see as in some way confirming his approach' (p. 462). But Barnouw re-examines the long excerpt from *The Will to Power* which de Man quotes and shows that his account of it is seriously misleading. In it Nietzsche argues that the principle of identity 'reflects not an objective impossibility and necessity but a subjective inability', the subject's 'need to reduce things to a manageable order', to 'posit and arrange a world that should be true for us'. He is referring to logic, not language, arguing that 'our sense of reality, our awareness of entities, precedes and underlies logic', so that it is a basic error to ' "make of logic a criterion of true being" ' (p. 462). De Man, however, applies Nietzsche's point to a much larger and tendentious argument about 'types of utterance' and the fundamental schism that he finds within rhetoric, as within language itself. The way de Man applies to language what in fact refers to logic is an example of what I mean by saying that he 'bends' Nietzsche's thought to his own concerns. As Barnouw shows, having followed out de Man's development of his reading, 'the paradoxical deconstructive discourse is not Nietzsche's, it is read in by de Man against the intrinsic direction of the text' (p. 463). In the end we are left with a critical methodology 'in which a theory of reading effectively undermines the capacity to read' (ibid.). In such a method, we can now see, it was inevitable that rhetoric should have to be split in two and made to attack itself. De Man may have thought of himself as a friend to rhetoric, but his use of it for his own purposes is more destructive than many of its enemies' explicit attacks.

It is worth refuting this deconstruction of rhetoric, even at the risk of being called antipathetic to 'modern literary theory', since a rather important issue is at stake, namely the nature of human communication. De Man aims to deny language any power to refer to events or objects or experience outside itself. All tropes, then, can be faulted in so far as they claim to refer to an outside world that exists independent of language. So, he baldly asserts,

> metaphor is error because it believes or feigns to believe in its own referential meaning. . . . Metaphor overlooks the fictional, textual element in the nature of the entity it connotes. It assumes a world in which intra- and extra-textual events . . . can be distinguished. . . . This is an error, although it can be said that no language would be possible without this error. . . . To the extent that all language is conceptual, it always already speaks about language and not about things. (*Allegories*, pp. 151–2)

In his final sentence de Man disintegrates the linguistic sign, which Saussure formulated (in terms that actually go back to classical linguistics) as 'signified over signifier', that is, drawing a clear distinction between the word (signifier) and the thing or concept (signified) that it denotes. In Saussure's terminology the two parts of the sign are divided by a line (as used in the representation of fractions) in order to emphasize that they exist on different planes, but nevertheless form a unity. Whereas linguistic materialists collapse the distinction, turning words into things, deconstructionists throw away half of it, creating a mental world in which signifiers 'float freely', or are 'liberated' from the burden of meaning.

We can understand deconstruction historically, as a phase in twentieth-century thought reflecting a loss of confidence by some highly intelligent, highly educated people about the nature of language, or as another reaction against positivism, a further calling in question of received certainties. Such questioning can be exhilarating, and salutary, but in this case I feel it to be an inward-turning, self-disruptive process, which denies literature a 'mimetic' relationship with the world just as it denies language a referential aspect. Of course, many literary texts contain an element of commentary on, or at least awareness of their own status as works fashioned by one human being according to certain artistic conventions for other humans to read and, presumably, enjoy—that is, to have their lives enriched by a greater awareness of the possibilities of literature, and language. But to declare such an element of self-awareness or self-commentary to be the primary function of literature, and to deny it any ability to represent human behaviour, is to start from a dualism (represent the world/represent itself) and turn it into a monism that is peculiarly debilitating, since it condemns literature to a self-reflexive concern with its own inability to represent, or with the incapacity of language to do so. As Jeffrey Barnouw has said,

> If a 'text' can only qualify itself as 'literature' by deconstructively turning on itself, the eventual result will be an impoverishment of what literature can say to us, because we no longer bring to it questions about our world. Awareness of the metaphorical and reflexive character of language in use, and particularly in literature, should rather lead us to recognize and explore the way language gives us access to the world at the same time that it informs the world.[25]

Deconstruction is a challenge to modern critical theory in that it calls in question the whole of our thinking about language, and literature, since the earliest records of the Greeks. The challenge has come from a highly ingenious and articulate sector of modern philosophy, which seems to have lost touch with ordinary reality. We need to remind ourselves, perhaps, of some emphases in modern linguistics that offer an alternative view of language. R. H. Robins, in his brief but penetrating history of grammatical theory,[26] objected to the Stoics' distinction between signified and signifier because, if taken literally, 'it leads to the unhelpful conception of "the meaning" as something actually existing' as an isolatable entity which can be evaluated in purely logical terms (p. 26). But the 'completeness' or otherwise of an utterance, he asserts, 'depends on its fulfilling the purpose intended by speaker or

---

[25] Barnouw, reviewing the Rousseau chapters in de Man's *Allegories of Reading*, in *The Eighteenth Century: A Current Bibliography*, ns. 6 (1980), 338–9.

[26] R. H. Robins, *Ancient and Medieval Grammatical Theory in Europe with Particular Reference to Modern Linguistic Doctrine* (London, 1951); page-references included in the text.

writer in its context of situation and can only be tested in relation to that context' (pp. 28–9). One weakness of Greek and Roman grammar was that 'language was considered too much as the expression of thought complete in itself, and its dependence on context, the world around, for its functioning was largely ignored' (p. 44). Later, medieval speculative grammarians made grammar the handmaid of philosophy. 'Language was for them'—as it is, I interject, for the deconstructionists, albeit with different implications—'the verbal expression of the thought of the intellect. This extraordinarily narrow and distorted conception of language', Robins writes, has persisted into our time, hindering the development of linguistics. To understand language fully, we must see it 'in its proper light as part of human co-operation, part of social action, in all the everyday situations in which men and women find themselves' (p. 89). We must situate language in the world, in concrete human situations, for 'it is contextual function alone that constitutes and guarantees linguistic meaning' (p. 92). Deconstructionists, living in social contexts, using language according to social codes, interacting with the world around them, nevertheless deny language any reliable function in reporting or creating that world, and grant literature even less relation to reality. This does seem a major paradox, especially since deconstructionist theory flourishes on its own gestures of denial and restriction. Some sense must be getting through.

My concern is to defend rhetoric, and a proper defence of language in its referential mode and its social context can be left to linguistics, phenomenology, and some of the social sciences. I would doubt whether the isolation and introversion of language created by deconstructionism would survive an honest confrontation with their work, but that is a task that must be left to other hands.[27]

[27] For a defence of the referential nature of language see, to begin with, R. H. Robins, *General Linguistics: an Introductory Survey* (London, 1971); R. Brown, *Words and Things. An Introduction to Language* (New York, 1968); R. Wells, 'Meaning and Use', in S. Saporta (ed.), *Psycholinguistics* (New York, 1961), pp. 269–83; H. S. Sørensen, 'Meaning and Reference', in A. J. Greimas, R. Jakobson, *et al.* (eds.), *Sign, Language, Culture* (The Hague, 1970), pp. 67–80; and the challenging discussion by Raymond Tallis, *Not Saussure. A Critique of Post-Saussurean Literary Theory* (London, 1988).

II

That brief survey of the fate of rhetoric in the work of some influential modern critics is not encouraging. It would, I think, be catastrophic if the image of rhetoric given by Jakobson or de Man were to prevail, or become universal. It would be regrettable, also, if my critique of their use of the art were taken to mean that historians of rhetoric were antipathetic to modern criticism. Such is not the case, and anyone who reflects for a moment on the equally disastrous alternatives of uncritical history or unhistorical criticism—by which I mean criticism unaware that it is itself the product of a specific historical context—will surely agree that a union of the historical and the critical faculties is not just desirable but necessary. As a general rule, too, if we want to do interdisciplinary work we should try as hard as possible to understand the subject area into which we move, hoping to illuminate our own interest. My complaint is that some moderns have not tried to understand rhetoric, either as a historical reality or as a complex but coherent system of communication. I would welcome literary theory and practical criticism that tries to be truly responsive, and responsible, to rhetoric.

If we now turn to work that at least approaches rhetoric in the appropriate cultural and historical terms—not that it always manifests acute critical intelligence—we will be almost overwhelmed by its range and diversity. As every year's work confirms, rhetoric was a world-wide historical phenomenon, with a remarkable ability to adapt to new social contexts, speech situations, aesthetic and cultural demands. Given its protean form, its ability to pop up in the most unlikely places and times, it is not surprising that so far no survey or bibliography exists that covers more than a fraction of its extent. The classical period is the best served,[28] but even here, as every scholar knows, titles

---

[28] The coverage of *L'Année philologique* is exemplary, albeit the indexing could be more helpful. The *Bulletin signalétique* of the Centre National de Recherches Scientifiques includes rhetoric, as does the Modern Language Association annual bibliography (recently). The documentation in George Kennedy's ongoing history of rhetoric (Kennedy 1963 etc.) is admirable, but would have been much more useful if collected as a separate bibliography. Six authors contribute sections of uneven value to W. B. Horner (ed.), *The Present State of Scholarship in Historical and Contemporary Rhetoric* (Columbia, Mo., 1983). Some idea of its general level can be gleaned from this comment on the *Rhetorica ad Herennium*:

alone are not reliable accounts of the contents of books and articles, which must be read to discover their real scope. Scholars who know the literature ought to take more initiative than they have so far in publishing or collaborating on bibliographies. For the medieval and Renaissance periods some helpful guides exist,[29] but with many gaps and inconsistencies. Given the virtual identification of poetics and rhetoric in the Renaissance, for instance, it is frustrating to discover that Bernard Weinberg's pioneering history of literary criticism excluded rhetoric, although he was tempted to include 'rhetorical theory' with literary criticism, 'for the problems are the same or nearly so, and the documents themselves readily lead from one discipline to another'. But he did not. When J. J. Murphy produced his bibliography of Renaissance rhetoric, he conversely (similarly?) excluded 'treatises on the composition of poetry'.[30] Historians should treat a discipline in its totality, as it was actually practised in whatever period they are studying. We have a long way to go before we overcome the post-Romantic hostility to rhetoric, and it is no doubt this hostility that explains why there are so few guides to rhetorical studies since 1750, say. Given the belief that rhetoric no longer existed after this date, its actual presence was seldom noted, and many students of nineteenth- and twentieth-century literature still feel that they can safely ignore it. I hope that this book does something to change that frame of mind.

The fact is that historians—if that is not yet a pejorative word —of the most diverse cultures and literatures have found rhetoric relevant. It is a valuable aid to understanding the work of dramatists from Menander and Aristophanes to Georg

'Reading of the text could be tedious, except that the store-house of rhetorical figures . . . provide[s] invaluable evidence for historians of rhetoric' (pp. 13–14); or the description of de Man's book as 'possibly the most influential book in English in the Nietzsche-Derrida tradition [sic!]. . . . De Man does consider "persuasion" as an alternative to a figural notion of rhetoric, but he questions whether they may not be the same in the long run' (p. 193)—a sublime missing of the point.

[29] See Murphy 1971, 1974, 1978, 1981, and 1983, and Brian Vickers, 'A Bibliography of Rhetoric Studies, 1970–1980' in *Comparative Criticism*, 3 (1981), 316–22.

[30] Weinberg 1961, pp. viii–ix, 72; Murphy 1981, p. xi. On the fusion of the two disciplines see also Brian Vickers, 'Rhetoric and Poetics', in the *Cambridge History of Renaissance Philosophy*, (Cambridge, 1987), pp. 715–45.

Büchner,[31] and philosophers from Pascal to Freud.[32] It can be observed flourishing in Hellenistic Greece and Egypt, or medieval Byzantium.[33] Its importance in England,[34] France,[35] Germany,[36] Italy,[37] and Spain[38] has been documented, but also in America,[39] Russia, and elsewhere in Eastern Europe.[40] Nor was its domain limited to Europe: we have studies, some going back a century or more, of its influence in China,[41] India,[42] and Persia,[43] and in Arabic,[44] African, and Oceanic cultures.[45] So far

---

[31] For Aristophanes see C. T. Murphy, 'Aristophanes and the Art of Rhetoric', *Harvard Studies in Classical Philology*, 49 (1938), 69–113; for Menander, see J. W. Cohoon, 'Rhetorical Studies in the Arbitration Scene of Menander's *Epitrepontes*', *Transactions of the American Philosophical Association*, 45 (1914), 141–230; Büchner see Gerhard Schaub, *Georg Büchner und die Schulrhetorik* (Berne and Frankfurt, 1975). Büchner attended the Gymnasium at Darmstadt from 1825 to 1831 (Lichtenberg had been there in the 1750s) and some of his school exercises are happily extant, published by W. Lehmann in the Hamburg edition, *Sämtliche Werke und Briefe*, vol. 2 (1971). His 'Abiturientenrede', Menenius Agrippa addressing the Roman people, is lost, but from his 'Rede zur Vertheidigung des Cato von Utika' (1830) it is but a short step to *Dantons Tod* (1835).

[32] See Patricia Topliss, *The Rhetoric of Pascal* (Leicester 1966); T. Todorov, *Théories du symbole* (Paris, 1977), 'La rhétorique de Freud', pp. 285–321; E. Benveniste, 'Remarks on the Function of Language in Freudian Theory', in Benveniste, *Problems in General Linguistics*, tr. M. E. Meek (Coral Gables, Fla., 1971), pp. 65–75; and S. Jaffe, 'Freud as a Rhetorician: *Elocutio* and the Dream-Work', *Rhetorik*, 1 (1980), 42–69. The relevant text is Freud's *The Interpretation of Dreams*, tr. J. Strachey (New York, 1965), pp. 378–84, 526–44.

[33] See B. P. Reardon, *Courants littéraires grecs des IIᵉ et IIIᵉ siècles après J-C* (Paris, 1971), which devotes five chapters to rhetoric; R. W. Smith, *The Art of Rhetoric in Alexandria* (The Hague, 1974); G. L. Kustas, *Studies in Byzantine Rhetoric* (Thessaloniki, 1973) and 'The Function and Evolution of Byzantine Rhetoric', *Viator*, 1 (1970), 55–73.

[34] For England see R. C. Alston, *A Bibliography of the English Language from the Invention of Printing to the Year 1800*, 20 vols., vol. 6, *Rhetoric, Style, Elocution, Prosody, Rhyme, Pronunciation, Spelling Reform* (Bradford, 1969), pp. 1–53, and *Additions and Corrections, Volumes I–X* (Leeds, 1973), pp. 46–55; and H. F. Plett, *Englische Rhetorik und Poetik 1479–1660. Eine systematische Bibliographie* (Wiesbaden, 1985). Partial bibliographies in Howell 1956, 1971, and G. P. Mohrmann in Murphy 1983, pp. 68–83.

[35] For France see Gordon 1970, Griffin 1969, Fumaroli 1980, and P. L. Kuentz's bibliography of seventeenth-century works—alas, only those in French, an especially short-sighted decision for this period, where neo-Latin was the more important language for international scholarship—in *XVIIᵉ Siècle*, no. 80–81 (1968), 133–42.

[36] For Germany see R. Schmidt, *Deutsche Ars Poetica. Zur Konstituierung einer deutschen Poetik aus humanistischem Geist im 17. Jahrhundert* (Meisenheim am Glan, 1980); C. Winkler, *Elemente der Rede. Die Geschichte ihrer Theorie in Deutschland von 1750 bis 1850* (Halle, 1931); U. Stötzer, *Deutsche Redekunst im 17. und 18. Jhdt.* (Halle, 1962); E. Haas, *Rhetorik und Hochsprache. Ueber die Wirksamkeit der Rhetorik bei der Entstehung der deutschen Hochsprache im 17. und 18. Jahrhundert* (Frankfurt,

1980); M.-L. Linn, *Studien zur deutschen Rhetorik und Stilistik im 19. Jahrhundert* (Marburg, 1963); Barner 1970, pp. 456–87; D. Breuer and G. Kopsch, 'Rhetorik-Lehrbücher des 16. bis 20. Jahrhunderts', in Schanze 1974, pp. 217–355; R. Jamison and J. Dyck, *Rhetorik–Topik–Argumentation. Bibliographie zur Redelehre und Rhetorikforschung im deutschsprachigen Raum 1945 bis 1979/80* (Stuttgart, 1983). Joachim Dyck is currently preparing a bibliography of eighteenth-century German rhetoric which will include some eight hundred titles.

[37] It is especially frustrating that for Italy, birthplace of the revival of rhetoric in modern times, no adequate bibliography, and no reliable history, exist. See at best the literature cited by La Russo in Murphy 1983, pp. 37–55.

[38] For Spain see M. Menendez y Pelayo, *Historia de las ideas estéticas en España* in his *Obras completas*, ii. (Madrid, 1947), 145–203; A. Marti, *La preceptiva retórica española en el Siglo de Oro* (Madrid, 1972); J. R. Verdu, *La retórica española de los siglos XVI y XVII* (Madrid, 1973); and A. García Berrio, *Formación de la teoría literaria moderna*, 2 vols. (Madrid, 1977, 1980).

[39] For America see W. Guthrie, 'The Development of Rhetorical Theory in America, 1635–1850', a series of articles in *Speech Monographs*, 13 (1946)–18 (1951), inclusive; K. R. Wallace (ed.), *A History of Speech Education in America* (New York, 1954).

[40] For Russia see R. Lachmann (ed.), *Die Makarij-Rhetorik* (Cologne-Vienna, 1980); id. (ed.), Feofan Prokopovic, *De Arte Rhetorica Libri X* (Cologne-Vienna, 1982), both in the 'Rhetorica Slavica' series. For a Polish Renaissance rhetoric see F. Kumaniecki (ed.), *Rhetorica* of Callimachus Experiens (Warsaw, 1950); on rhetoric in the seventeenth century see M. K. Sarbiewski, *Wykłady Poetyki (Praecepta Poetica)*, ed. S. Skimina (Wrocław-Krakow, 1958), Polish and Latin; for the eighteenth century see Z. Rynduch, *Nauka o stylu w retorykach polskich XVII wieku* (Gdańsk, 1967), with English summary; and for a collection of modern studies see B. Otwinoska (ed.), *Retoryka a Litteratura* (Wrocław, 1984). The Rumanian historian Vasile Florescu has had one book translated into French (by M. Munteanu): *La rhétorique et la néorhétorique. Genèse, Evolution, Perspectives* (Paris, 1982). For Hungary see A. Kibédi-Varga, 'Rhétoriques et Poétiques de Hongrie—Etat présent de la question', *Rhetorik*, 3 (1983), 145–9.

[41] For China see R. T. Oliver, *Communication and Culture in Ancient India and China* (Syracuse, NY, 1971); *The Complete Works of Han Fei Tzu*, tr. W. Liao (London, 1959), for the treatise *Difficulties in the Way of Persuasion*, 3rd cent. BC; also Kennedy 1980, p. 7.

[42] For India see Oliver (last note); S. K. De, *History of Sanskrit Poetics* (Calcutta, 1960); P. Regnaud, *La Rhétorique sanskrite* (Paris, 1884); P. Narayan, *Indian Rhetoric* (Allahabad, 1894); G. Jenner, *Die poetischen Figuren der Inder von Bhamaha bis Mammata. Ihre Eigenart im Verhältnis zu den Figuren repräsentativer antiker Rhetoriker* (Hamburg, 1968); E. Gerow, *A Glossary of Indian Figures of Speech* (The Hague, 1971); and M.-C. Porcher, *Figures de Style en Sanskrit. Théorie des Alamkāraśāstra* (Paris, 1978).

[43] For Persia see F. Rückert, *Grammatik, Poetik und Rhetorik der Perser* (Gotha, 1874).

[44] On Arabic rhetoric see A. F. Mehren, *Die Rhetorik der Araber* (Copenhagen and Vienna, 1853); Hildesheim, 1970); G. E. von Grunebaum, *A Tenth-Century Document of Arab Literary Theory and Criticism* (Chicago, 1950); S. A. Bonebakker, 'Aspects of the History of Literary Rhetoric and Poetics in Arabic Literature', *Viator*, 1 (1970), 75–95, and *Materials for the History of Arabic Rhetoric* (Naples, 1975); H. Ritter (ed.), *The Mysteries of Eloquence of 'Abdalqāhir al-Jirjānī* (Istanbul, 1954), and (tr.), *Die Geheimnisse der Wortkunst (Asrār al-Balāġa) des Abdalqāhir Al-Curćānī* (Wiesbaden, 1959); G. J. H. Van Gelder, *Beyond the Line. Classical*

all these studies exist in isolation, and at very varied levels of scholarly accuracy or historical insight. Some international study-centre, or recurring conference should be set up to encourage comparative study. It would be fascinating to identify similarities, whether caused by comparable speech-situations or debt to a common tradition, and then go on to trace the differences caused by national cultures.

The range of vitality of modern interest in rhetoric can be seen from the number of journals published recently. Previously the only long-lived journals had been the organs of the departments of speech (and drama, and education, and composition or writing) in American universities, some of which did include valuable historical or cross-cultural essays, but which tended to reflect the emphases within those departments, a parochial concern with rhetoric in modern English or in translation, adapted to the needs of a contemporary American under-graduate who had been granted little or no access to the classical or European traditions, and wished to apply rhetorical skills to modern commercial or professional life. Despite some hon-ourable exceptions, this has been a restricting tradition, and new journals have been set up in opposition to it: *Philosophy and Rhetoric* (1968–   ), *Rhetorik. Ein internationales Handbuch* (1980–   ), and the most varied and interesting, *Rhetorica* (1983–   ).[46] The range of topics recently dealt with includes ancient Egyptian and early Jewish rhetoric, medieval German drama, the painting theory of Constable, and the influence of rhetoric on double-entry book-keeping.[47] Elsewhere detailed studies have been

Arabic Literary Critics on the Coherence and Unity of the Poem (Leiden, 1982); K. Abu-Deeb, *Al-Jurjani's Theory of Poetic Imagery* (Warminster, 1979).

[45] See M. Bloch (ed.), *Political Language and Oratory in Traditional Society* (London, 1975) for studies of oratory in the Maoris, Tikopia, and Bali; R. Finnegan, *Oral Literature in Africa* (Oxford, 1976); A. C. Hozda and G. Fortune (eds.), *Shona Praise Poetry* (Oxford, 1979); S. D. Ngcongwane, *The Influence of the Traditional Praise-Poem on modern Bantu Poetry* (Kwa-Dlangezwa, 1974).

[46] *Philosophy and Rhetoric* is published by Pennsylvania State Univ. Press, University Park, Pa.; *Rhetorik* by Frommann-Holzboog, Stuttgart; *Rhetorica* by the International Society for the History of Rhetoric and the University of California Press. Other journals available to members of the societies are *Rhetoric Newsletter* (also the ISHR), and *Rhetoric Society Quarterly* (Rhetoric Society of America).

[47] See, e.g., *Rhetorica*, 1 (1983): M. Fox, 'Ancient Egyptian Rhetoric' (pp. 9–22); 2 (1984): K. M. Wilson, 'Antonomasia as a Means of Character-Recognition in the Works of Hrotsvit of Gandersheim' (pp. 45–54); V. M. Bevilacqua, 'The

made of specific rhetorical figures, such as *aposiopesis, chiasmus, hendiadys, systrophe,* and *hyperbole.*[48] This is a legitimate area of rhetorical research, if pursued with sensitivity, a real interest in literature, and without erecting grandiose interpretative schemes on evidence which is bound to be partial and local.

Modern rediscovery of the rhetorical tradition has been, inevitably enough, patchy, subject to the usual conditions of accidental and unsystematic research that govern most activities in the arts. Some surprising imbalances exist—the German sixteenth century, and the French, have been better studied, so far, than the truly innovative Italian fifteenth or sixteenth centuries, an imbalance that needs to be urgently redressed. But in other areas advances have taken place that have brought with them reactions and corrections. The first detailed modern study of a Renaissance rhetorician was that made by Walter Ong, SJ, in 1958, of Ramus, accompanied by a bibliographical inventory of the editions of Ramus and his collaborator Talaeus.[49] Ong brought an admirable historical and scholarly concern to Ramus's life and works, and genuinely illuminated much of this *œuvre,* the cause of many controversies in the late sixteenth and early seventeenth centuries. But as our grasp of the subject has improved we have been able to see some wrong emphases. One of Ong's main interpretative claims was that Ramus' preference for bracketed tables of contents, where a topic was divided into two headings, most often, each of those into a further two, until he had dealt with the whole subject he was treating—that this

Rhetorical Theory of John Constable's *Reflections upon the Accuracy of Style'* (pp. 75–92); 3 (1985): J. A. Aho, 'Rhetoric and the Invention of Double Entry Bookkeeping' (pp. 21–44); I. Rabinowitz, 'Pre-Modern Jewish Study of Rhetoric' (pp. 137–44).

[48] See L. Ricottilli, *La scelta del silenzio. Menandro e l'aposiopesi* (Bologna, 1984); J. W. Welch (ed.), *Chiasmus in Antiquity. Structures, Analyses, Exegesis* (Hildesheim, 1981); H. Horvei, *'The Chev'ril Glove': A Study in Shakespearean Rhetoric* (Bergen, 1984): on the figure *antimetabole*; G. J. Wright, 'Hendiadys and *Hamlet'*, *PMLA* 96 (1981), 168–93; S. Hegnauer, *Systrophe: The Background of Herbert's Sonnet 'Prayer'* (Berne and Frankfurt, 1981); B. Vickers, 'The "Songs and Sonnets" and the Rhetoric of Hyperbole', in A. J. Smith (ed.), *John Donne. Essays in Celebration* (London, 1972), pp. 132–74; N. B. Smith, *Figures of Repetition in the Old Provençal Lyric: a Study in the Style of the Troubadours* (Chapel Hill, NC, 1976).

[49] Ong 1958, and W. Ong, *Ramus and Talon Inventory* (Cambridge, Mass., 1958).

lay-out in printed books led to a 'spatializing of consciousness' in the Renaissance mind, and was somehow bound up with the influence of print. (One detects the influence of Marshall McLuhan on this theory: Ong has always claimed that the debt was the other way round.) Several scholars have voiced doubts about this thesis, and anyone familiar with the textbook tradition knows that bracketed tables exist aplenty in manuscripts long before printing, and in printed books before, or independently of Ramus.

Ong, and other scholars after him, made much of Ramus's claim to be innovating in using the concept of 'method'. Yet John Monfasani has shown that the word *'methodus'*, which George of Trebizond took over from Hermogenes, and which was adopted in turn by French writers before Ramus, signified a specific topic, namely the treatment of the figures of speech, and 'reflected no methodological concern and had no influence on the development of humanist method'. Furthermore, a term to describe a 'well ordered and commodious way of proceeding or explaining', it was well known in scholastic circles.[50] Ramus is traditionally said to have 'reformed' rhetoric by transferring *inventio* and *dispositio* to logic, leaving it the three remaining processes, a shift which supposedly led to the greater Renaissance emphasis on *elocutio*. But H.-J. Lange has pointed out that *inventio* had been 'neglected' for *elocutio* long before Ramus.[51] Marc Fumaroli has criticized the McLuhanite emphasis on print, which downplays Ramus' interest in spoken oratory: 'contrairement à ce que prétend . . . le P. Ong, Ramus veut former un orateur. Il ne sacrifie nullement la parole agissant directement sur un public, dans le vif social, au profit de l'écriture et de la lecture silencieuses.'[52] One of the strengths of a scholarly tradition is its power of self-correction, and I give this small example of historical evaluation to show that rhetoric studies are neither uncritical nor static. Indeed, the recent publication of two book-length studies on Ramus, together with

[50] Monfasani 1976, pp. 325–6, 322 n. Monfasani also notes that both Ong and Vasoli were mistaken in taking the term *synthesis* in sixteenth-century rhetoric as a description of method. In fact, it was simply 'one of the eight elements of every form', as defined by Hermogenes, and 'concerned the sound and rhythm of a group of words; it had nothing to do with argumentation, and certainly not with methodology' (ibid., p. 327 and n.).

[51] See Schanze in Murphy 1983, p. 117.

[52] Fumaroli 1980, p. 434.

THE FUTURE OF RHETORIC

a translation of his attack on Quintilian, show a healthy development.[53] Yet, although we can now correct false emphases in Ong's work, it is thanks to him that Ramus remains the best-studied rhetorician of the Renaissance. We could wish that the same attention were devoted to Sturm, or Scaliger,[54] Cavalcanti or Soarez, and dozens of other writers.

There are a number of admirable modern studies of the rhetorical tradition, and France in particular has been well served, from the books by Robert Griffin and Alex Gordon on the sixteenth century to those by Peter France on the seventeenth, and the magisterial work of Marc Fumaroli spanning the whole period from the Renaissance to classicism.[55] Yet, if I had to select one book that shows modern re-creation of rhetoric at its best, it would be John Monfasani's study of George of Trebizond (1395–1472/3), or Trapezuntius to the Latin world.[56] Historically, George was an extremely important figure in the introduction of Greek and Byzantine rhetoric into the Italian Renaissance, fusing that tradition with the Latin works of Cicero and Quintilian to produce the first reintegrated work of modern times, the *Rhetoricum Libri V* (1433–5). This book circulated widely in manuscript, and had ten printed editions by 1547 (p. 322), becoming a valued source and model for many compilers of rhetoric-books over the next two centuries. George also wrote the first humanist textbook in logic, the *Isagoge dialectica*, which had fifty-three editions between 1508 and 1567 (p. 329). In his long career, starting as Greek scribe for the young Venetian humanist Francesco Barbaro, rising to apostolic secretary to the Popes Eugenius IV and Nicholas V, and becoming professor of rhetoric and humanities to the Venetian

[53] See N. Bruyère, *Méthode et dialectique dans l'œuvre de La Ramée. Renaissance et âge classique* (Paris, 1984); K. Meerhoff, *Rhétorique et poétique au XVIe siècle en France. Du Bellay, Ramus, et les autres* (Leiden, 1986): on rhythm in verse and prose, and such related concepts as *figura, numerus,* and *concinnitas*; P. Ramus, *Arguments in Rhetoric against Quintilian. Translation and Text of Peter Ramus's 'Rhetoricae Distinctiones in Quintilianum'*, tr. C. Newlands (De Kalb, Ill., 1986).
[54] See, however, a valuable recent symposium ed. C. Balavoine and P. Laurens, *La Statue et l'empreinte. La Poétique de Scaliger* (Paris, 1986), harbinger of a forthcoming annotated French translation of the *Poetices libri septem*, ed. Pierre Laurens. Another welcome recent publication is R. L. Freeman, *Leonard Cox's 'The Arte or Crafte of Rhetoryke': a Critical Edition* (Lanham, Md., 1986).
[55] See Griffin 1969, Gordon 1970, France 1965 and 1972, Fumaroli 1980.
[56] See Monfasani 1976 (and my review: *The Quarterly Journal of Speech*, 63 (1977), 443–8). Quotations are from this source.

republic, George was in much demand as a translator. He put most of Aristotle's works into Latin, becoming the leading humanist Aristotelian of his generation, and also rendered major works by Demosthenes and Plato.

Professor Monfasani follows his author through every phase of this long and productive career, not just describing but evaluating George's performance in every department. In so doing he also brings out the realities of being a humanist: the need to find patrons, to whom one had to dedicate a major book, or celebrate in encomium (George compared one Pope to Moses, John the Baptist, and St Paul!); the competition for patronage and status which, together with a certain innate quarrelsomeness, produced many disagreements between humanists. George was expelled from several cities, came to blows with the notorious Poggio Bracciolini (pp. 109–10), and spent three periods in gaol. In order to reconstruct both life and works Professor Monfasani has scoured the archives of the Vatican and some forty other libraries all round the world, bringing to light hitherto unknown letters, treatises, and manuscript notes by his author, meticulously recording every detail, even retrieving one colophon which was partly erased by water used to extinguish a fire in the University of Basle in 1904 (p. 346). He has reprinted much of this new material, in fifteen appendices to his monograph and in a later collection of texts.[57] Re-creating his author's world, he has become a philologist, editor, and translator himself. As well as mastering the history of rhetoric and logic, with special attention to the Byzantine tradition (not an easy subject), he exemplifies the role of the historian in thinking himself back into a distant cultural context, re-creating a writer's intellectual and social milieu, reconstituting not only what he read but how he read it. His comment on this dual process is a classic statement of the historical approach: 'much of Trebizond's work is understandable only in terms of the doctrines he appropriated from his predecessors and of the problems he inherited with the doctrines' (p. 241). Monfasani's account of the doctrines, and

---

[57] See J. Monfasani (ed.), *Collectanea Trapezuntiana. Texts, Bibliographies, and Documents of George of Trebizond* (Binghamton, NY, 1984). All that we now need is an edition and translation of the *Rhetoricum Libri V*, which would crown his labours.

what George made of them, is the most detailed analysis we have of any post-classical rhetorician, and a work of great historical penetration. It has a sense of the whole (as in some perceptive comments on the differing attitudes to rhetoric north and south of the Alps: pp. 330–3), and a complete grasp of the details. It shows how much of a past cultural context can still be recovered, given the historian's skill , and energy. Monfasani's book establishes a basis on which others can build with confidence.

Although the greater part of the history of rhetoric remains to be written, there are grounds for optimism about the current state of the art, and its future prospects. We need wide-ranging historical and critical studies, biographies, editions of texts, analyses of specific issues within rhetoric and in its relationship to the other arts, to politics, and to society.[58] If scholars can expand our historical knowledge, while sharpening their critical and analytical powers, we can advance one major goal of history, the progressive recovery of the past. After all, as Melanchthon put it, 'what subject can possibly be richer than that of the dignity and utility of eloquence?'

[58] Some recent publications may be grouped here: J.-M. Valentin, *Le Théâtre des Jésuites dans les pays de langue allemande (1554–1680)*, 3 vols. (Berne and Frankfurt, 1978), on the use of rhetoric in Jesuit education and drama, complemented by B. Bauer, *Jesuitische 'ars rhetorica' im Zeitalter der Glaubenskämpfe* (Berne and New York, 1986). *The Collected Works of Erasmus*, Vol. 28 (Toronto, 1987), contains the *Ciceronianus*, tr. B. Knott. M. G. Van der Poel, *De 'Declamatio' bij de Humanisten. Bijdrage tot de Studie van de Functies van de Rhetorica in de Renaissance* (Nieuwkoop, 1987), English summary pp. 343–51, is an important study of declamation in schools and universities from ancient Rome to the seventeenth century, with much new material, concluding that Renaissance writers in the genre, such as Erasmus and H. C. Agrippa, meant their works seriously, not ironically. R. Norrman has expounded *Samuel Butler and the Meaning of Chiasmus* (London, 1986), and L. D. Green has edited *John Rainold's Oxford Lectures on Aristotle's 'Rhetoric'* (Cranbury NJ, 1985). Karin M. Fredborg has produced a long-needed edition of *The Latin Rhetorical Commentaries by Thierry of Chartres* (Toronto, 1988), while Antonio García Berrio has produced a commented edition of the *Tablas Poéticas* (1579) of Francisco Cascales (a dialogue showing the fusion of Aristotelian, Horatian and rhetorical literary theory) to provide an *Introducción a la Poética Clasicista* (Madrid, 1988). Recent monographs include Moshe Barasch, *Giotto and the Language of Gesture* (Cambridge, 1987); Sarah Spence, *Rhetorics of Reason and Desire, Vergil, Augustine and the Troubadors* (Ithaca, NY, 1988); Deborah K. Shuger, *Sacred Rhetoric, The Christian Grand Style in the Renaissance* (Princeton, NJ, 1988).

BIBLIOGRAPHY

ABELSON, P. (1906), *The Seven Liberal Arts: A Study in Mediaeval Culture*, New York.

ALBERTI, LEON BATTISTA (1956; rev. 1966), *On Painting*, ed. and tr. J. R. Spencer, New Haven, Conn.

—— (1972), *On Painting and on Sculpture*, ed. and tr. C. Grayson, London.

BACON, FRANCIS (1857–74), *Works*, ed. J. Spedding, R. L. Ellis, and D. D. Heath, 14 vols., London.

BALDWIN, C. S. (1928), *Medieval Rhetoric and Poetic (to 1400)*, New York.

—— (1939), *Renaissance Literary Theory and Practice: Classicism in the Rhetoric and Poetic of Italy, France, and England 1400–1600*, ed. D. L. Clark, New York.

BALDWIN, T. W. (1944), *William Shakspere's Small Latine & Lesse Greeke*, 2 vols., Urbana, Ill.

BARNER, W. (1970), *Barock-Rhetorik*, Tübingen.

BAROCCHI, P. (1960–2), *Trattati d'arte del Cinquecento*, 3 vols., Bari.

BARTHES, R. (1970), 'L'Ancienne Rhétorique: Aide-mémoire', *Communications*, 16, pp. 172–229.

BAXANDALL, M. (1971), *Giotto and the Orators: Humanist Observers of Painting in Italy and the Discovery of Pictorial Composition 1350–1450*, Oxford; repr. 1986.

BAYLEY, P. (1980), *French Pulpit Oratory 1598–1650*, Cambridge.

BOLGAR, R. R. (1954), *The Classical Heritage and its Beneficiaries*, Cambridge.

—— (1970), 'Humanism as a Value System with Reference to Budé and Vives', in A. H. T. Levi (ed.), *Humanism in France at the end of the Middle Ages and in the early Renaissance*, Manchester, pp. 199–215.

BONNER, S. F. (1977), *Education in Ancient Rome. From the elder Cato to the younger Pliny*, London.

BRANDES, H. (1935), *Studien zur musikalischen Figurenlehre im 16. Jahrhundert*, Berlin.

BREEN, Q. (1968), *Christianity and Humanism. Studies in the History of Ideas*, ed. N. P. Ross, Grand Rapids, Mich.; originally in *Journal of the History of Ideas*, 13 (1952), pp. 384–426.

BUCHHEIT, V. (1960), *Untersuchungen zur Theorie des Genos epideiktikon von Gorgias bis Aristoteles*, Munich.

BURGESS, T. C. (1902), *Epideictic Literature*, University of Chicago Studies in Classical Philology 3, Chicago, pp. 89–261.

BUTLER, G. G. (1977), 'Fugue and Rhetoric', *Journal of Music Theory*, 21, pp. 49–109.

—— (1980), 'Music and Rhetoric in Early Seventeenth-Century English Sources', *The Musical Quarterly*, 66, pp. 53–64.

CAMPBELL, J. J. (1978), 'Adaptation of Classical Rhetoric in Old English Literature', in Murphy 1978, pp. 173–97.

CASTOR, G. (1964), *Pléiade Poetics*, Cambridge.

CLARK, D. L. (1922), *Rhetoric and Poetry in the Renaissance. A Study of Rhetorical Terms in English Renaissance Literary Criticism*, New York.

CLARKE, M. L. (1953), *Rhetoric at Rome. A Historical Survey*, London.

CLASSEN, C. J. (1982), 'Ciceros Kunst der Ueberredung', in *Eloquence et rhétorique chez Cicéron*, ed. W. Ludwig, Geneva, pp. 149–84.

CLOUGH, C. H., ed. (1976), *Cultural Aspects of the Italian Renaissance. Essays in Honour of Paul Oskar Kristeller*, New York.

COLISH, M. (1968), *The Mirror of Language: A Study in the Medieval Theory of Knowledge*, New Haven, Conn.

CURTIS, M. H. (1959), *Oxford and Cambridge in Transition, 1558–1642*, ·Oxford.

CURTIUS, E. R. (1953), *European Literature and the Latin Middle Ages*, tr. W. R. Trask, New York.

DAINVILLE, F. de, SJ (1968), 'L'Évolution de l'enseignement de la rhétorique au XVIIᵉ siècle', *XVIIᵉ Siècle*, 80–81, pp. 19–43.

D'ALTON, J. F. (1931), *Roman Literary Theory and Criticism*, London; repr. New York, 1962.

DEMETRIUS (1961), *A Greek Critic: Demetrius on Style*, ed. G. M. Grube, Toronto.

DOCKHORN, K. (1968), *Macht und Wirkung der Rhetorik*, Bad Homburg.

—— (1974), 'Rhetorica movet. Protestantischer Humanismus und Karolingische Renaissance', in Schanze 1974, pp. 17–42.

DRYDEN, JOHN (1962), *Of Dramatic Poesy and other Critical Essays*, ed. George Watson, 2 vols., London.

DU MARSAIS, C. C. and FONTANIER, P. (1984): Du Marsais, *Les Tropes* (1729) and Fontanier, *Commentaire raisonné sur les tropes* (1818), ed. G. Genette, Geneva.

DYCK, J. (1966), *Ticht-Kunst. Deutsche Barockrhetorik und rhetorische Tradition*, Bad Homburg.

—— (1983), 'The First German Treatise on Homiletics: Erasmus Sarcer's *Pastorale* and Classical Rhetoric', in Murphy 1983, pp. 221–37.

ELSE, G. (1957), *Aristotle's Poetics: the Argument*, Cambridge, Mass.

ERASMUS, DESIDERIUS (1904), *Desiderius Erasmus concerning the Aim and Method of Education*, tr. W. H. Woodward: containing *De Ratione Studii* (1511) and *De Pueris* (1529), Cambridge.

—— (1978), *Collected Works of Erasmus*, Vol. 24: *Literary and Educational*

Writings 2, including *De Copia* (tr. B. I. Knott) and *De Ratione Studii* (tr. B. McGregor), Toronto.

FARAL, E. (1924), *Les Arts poétiques du XIIᵉ et du XIIIᵉ siècle*, Paris; repr. 1971.

FAULHABER, C. B. (1972), *Latin Rhetorical Theory in Thirteenth and Fourteenth Century Castile*, Berkeley and Los Angeles.

—— (1978), 'The *Summa dictaminis* of Guido Faba', in Murphy 1978, pp. 85–111.

FENNER, DUDLEY (1584), *The Artes of Logike and Rhetorike*, facs. edn. in *Four Tudor Books on Education*, ed. R. D. Pepper, Gainesville, Fla., 1960.

FRACASTORO, GIROLAMO (1924), *Naugerius sive de poetica dialogus* (Venice, 1555); Eng. tr. R. Kelso, introduction by M. W. Bundy, Urbana, Ill.

FRANCE, P. (1965), *Racine's Rhetoric*, Oxford.

—— (1972), *Rhetoric and Truth in France. Descartes to Diderot*, Oxford.

FRAUNCE, ABRAHAM (1588), *The Arcadian Rhetorike*, London; facs. edn. Menston, 1969.

FUHRMANN, M. (1984), *Die antike Rhetorik. Eine Einführung*, Munich and Zurich.

FUMAROLI, M. (1980), *L'Âge de l'éloquence. Rhétorique et 'res literaria' de la Renaissance au seuil de l'époque classique*, Paris.

GALLO, E. (1974), 'Matthew of Vendôme: Introductory Treatise on the Art of Poetry', *Proceedings of the American Philosophical Society*, 118, pp. 51–92.

—— (1978), 'The *Poetria nova* of Geoffrey of Vinsauf', in Murphy 1978, pp. 68–84.

GALYON, A. E., tr. (1980), Matthew of Vendôme, *The Art of Versification*, Ames, Iowa.

GARIN, E. (1965), *Italian Humanism: Philosophy and Civic Life in the Renaissance*, tr. P. Munz, Oxford, from *L'Umanesimo italiano: filosofia e vita civile nel Rinascimento*, rev. edn., Bari.

—— (1972), *Portraits from the Quattrocento*, tr. V. and E. Velen, New York.

—— (1973), 'Discussioni sulla retorica', in Garin, *Medioevo e Rinascimento*, Bari, pp. 117–39; 1st edn. 1954.

GERL, H.-B. (1974), *Rhetorik als Philosophie: Lorenzo Valla*, Munich.

GIANTURCO, E., tr. (1965), Giambattisto Vico, *On the Study Methods of our Time*, Indianapolis, Ind.

GILBERT, C. (1943–5), 'Antique Frameworks for Renaissance Art Theory: Alberti and Pino', *Marsyas*, 3, pp. 87–106.

GILBERT, S. (1952), *James Joyce's 'Ulysses': A Study*, New York; 1st edn. 1930.

GOMBRICH, E. H. (1960), *Art and Illusion: A Study in the Psychology of Pictorial Representation*, London.

GORDON, A. L. (1970), *Ronsard et la rhétorique*, Geneva.

GRAFTON, A. (1985), 'Renaissance Readers and Ancient Texts: Comments on Some Commentaries', *Renaissance Quarterly*, 38, pp. 156–49.

GRAY, H. H. (1968), 'Renaissance Humanism: The Pursuit of Eloquence', in *Renaissance Essays*, ed. P. O. Kristeller and P. P. Wiener, New York; from *Journal of the History of Ideas*, 24 (1963).

GRIFFIN, R. (1969), *Coronation of the Poet. Joachim du Bellay's Debt to the Trivium*, Berkeley and Los Angeles.

GRODEN, M. (1977), *'Ulysses' in Progress*, Princeton, NJ.

GURLITT, W. (1966), 'Musik und Rhetorik. Hinweise auf ihre geschichtliche Grundlageneinheit', in Gurlitt, *Musikgeschichte und Gegenwart*, ed. H. H. Eggebrecht, 2 vols., Wiesbaden, vol. I, pp. 62–81; originally in *Helicon*, 5 (1944).

HARDISON, O. B., Jr. (1962), *The Enduring Monument. A Study of the Idea of Praise in Renaissance Literary Theory and Practice*, Chapel Hill, NC.

HAVELOCK, E. A. (1957), *The Liberal Temper in Greek Politics*, London.

HENDERSON, J. R. (1983), 'Erasmus on the Art of Letter-Writing', in Murphy 1983, pp. 331–55.

HERRICK, M. T. (1950), *Comic Theory in the Sixteenth Century*, Urbana, Ill.

HERRING, P. F. (1977), *Joyce's Notes and Early Drafts for 'Ulysses'*, Charlottesville, Va.

HODGART, M. J. C. (1974), 'Aeolus', in C. Hart and D. Hayman (eds.), *James Joyce's 'Ulysses'. Critical Essays*, Berkeley and Los Angeles, pp. 115–30.

HOOLE, CHARLES (1660), *A New Discovery of the Old Art of Teaching Schoole*, facs. edn. Menston, 1969.

HOSKINS, JOHN (1935), *Directions for Speech and Style (c. 1599)*, ed. H. H. Hudson, Princeton, NJ.

HOWELL, W. S. (1956), *Logic and Rhetoric in England, 1500–1700*, Princeton, NJ.

—— (1971), *Eighteenth-Century British Logic and Rhetoric*, Princeton, NJ.

HUBBELL, H. M., tr. (1920), *The Rhetorica of Philodemus*, New Haven, Conn. = *Transactions of the Connecticut Academy of Arts and Science*, 23, pp. 243–382.

HUNT, E. L. (1961), 'Plato and Aristotle on Rhetoric and Rhetoricians', in R. F. Howes (ed.), *Historical Studies of Rhetoric and Rhetoricians*, Ithaca, NY, pp. 19–70; originally in *Studies in Rhetoric and Speaking in Honor of James Albert Winans* (New York, 1925).

HUTTON, J. (1951), 'Some English Poems in Praise of Music', *English Miscellany*, 2, pp. 1–63.

IJSSELING, S. (1976), *Rhetoric and Philosophy in Conflict. An Historical Survey*, The Hague.

JENNINGS, M., CSJ (1978), 'The *Ars componendi sermones* of Ranulph Higden', in Murphy 1978, pp. 112–26.

JENSEN, H. J. (1976), *The Muses' Concord. Literature, Music and the Visual Arts in the Baroque Age*, Bloomington, Ind.

JOSEPH, SISTER M. (1947), *Shakespeare's Use of the Arts of Language*, New York.

KELLY, D. (1966), 'The Scope of the Treatment of Composition in the Twelfth-Century Arts of Poetry', *Speculum*, 41, pp. 261–78.

—— (1978), 'Topical Invention in Medieval French Literature', in Murphy 1978, pp. 231–51.

KENDALL, C. B. (1978), 'Bede's *Historia ecclesiastica*: The Rhetoric of Faith', in Murphy 1978, pp. 145–72.

KENNEDY, G. (1963), *The Art of Persuasion in Greece*, London.

—— (1969), *Quintilian*, New York.

—— (1972), *The Art of Persuasion in the Roman World (300BC – AD300)*, Princeton, NJ.

—— (1980), *Classical Rhetoric and Its Christian and Secular Tradition from Ancient to Modern Times*, Chapel Hill, NC.

—— (1983), *Greek Rhetoric Under Christian Emperors*, Princeton, NJ.

KIBÉDI-VARGA, A. (1970), *Rhétorique et littérature. Études de structures classiques*, Paris.

KRISTELLER, P. O. (1979), 'Philosophy and Rhetoric from Antiquity to the Renaissance', in P. O. Kristeller, *Renaissance Thought and its Sources*, ed. M. Mooney, New York, pp. 213–59.

LE COAT, G. (1975), *The Rhetoric of the Arts*, Berne and Frankfurt.

LEE, R. W. (1967), *Ut pictura poesis: The Humanistic Theory of Painting*, New York (originally in *Art Bulletin*, 22, 1940).

LEFF, M. C. (1978), 'Boethius' *De differentiis topicis*, Book IV', in Murphy 1978, pp. 3–24.

LEWIS, C. S. (1967), *The Discarded Image. An Introduction to Medieval and Renaissance Literature*, Cambridge.

LICHTENSTEIN, J. (1982), 'Eloquence du coloris: rhétorique et mimésis dans les conceptions coloristes au 16ᵉ siècle en Italie et au 17ᵉ siècle en France', in *Symboles de la Renaissance*, Vol. 2, ed. D. Arasse, Paris, pp. 171–84.

LIEBESCHÜTZ, H. (1953), 'Das zwölfte Jahrhundert und die Antike', *Archiv für Kulturgeschichte*, 35, pp. 247–71.

LINDBERG, D. C., ed. (1978), *Science in the Middle Ages*, Chicago.

LONGINUS (1964), *On the Sublime*, tr. D. A. Russell, Oxford; repr. 1970.

McKEON, R. P. (1952), 'Rhetoric in the Middle Ages', rev. repr. in R. S. Crane (ed.), *Critics and Criticism*, Chicago, pp. 260–96; from *Speculum*, 17 (1942).

MARROU, H. I. (1964), *A History of Education in Antiquity*, tr. G. Lamb (1956) from *Histoire de l'éducation dans l'antiquité* (Paris, 1948); cit. from Mentor edition, New York.

MELANCHTHON, PHILIP (1968), *Elementorum Rhetorices libri duo* (Wittenberg, 1531), ed. and tr. Sister J. M. La Fontaine, Ph. D. Diss., U. Michigan.

MILLER, J. M., PROSSER, M. H., and BENSON, T. W., eds. (1973), *Readings in Medieval Rhetoric*, Bloomington, Ind.

MONFASANI, J. (1976), *George of Trebizond. A Biography and a Study of his Rhetoric and Logic*, Leiden.

—— (1983), 'The Byzantine Rhetorical Tradition and the Renaissance', in Murphy 1983, pp. 174–87.

—— (1988), 'Humanism and Rhetoric', in A. Rabil, Jr. (ed.), *Renaissance Humanism: Foundations, Form and Legacy*, Philadelphia, Pa.

MOONEY, M. (1985), *Vico in the Tradition of Rhetoric*, Princeton, NJ.

MUNTÉANO, B. (1967), *Constantes dialectiques en littérature et en histoire*, Paris.

MURPHY, J. J. (1966), 'Aristotle's Rhetoric in the Middle Ages', *Quarterly Journal of Speech*, 52, pp. 109–15.

—— (1969), 'The Scholastic Condemnation of Rhetoric in the Commentary of Giles of Rome on the *Rhetoric* of Aristotle', *Arts libéraux et philosophie au Moyen Age*, Montreal and Paris, pp. 833–41.

—— ed. (1971), *Three Medieval Rhetorical Arts*, Berkeley and Los Angeles.

—— (1974), *Rhetoric in the Middle Ages. A History of Rhetorical Theory from St. Augustine to the Renaissance*, Berkeley and Los Angeles.

—— ed. (1978), *Medieval Eloquence. Studies in the Theory and Practice of Medieval Rhetoric*, Berkeley and Los Angeles.

—— (1981), *Renaissance Rhetoric. A Short-Title Catalogue of Works on Rhetorical Theory from the Beginning of Printing to A.D. 1700*, New York.

—— ed. (1983), *Renaissance Eloquence. Studies in the Theory and Practice of Renaissance Rhetoric*, Berkeley and Los Angeles.

O'MALLEY, J. W. (1979), *Praise and Blame in Renaissance Rome: Rhetoric, Doctrine, and Reform in the Sacred Orators of the Papal Court, c. 1450–1521*, Durham, NC.

—— (1983), 'Content and Rhetorical Form in Sixteenth-Century Treatises on Preaching', in Murphy 1983, pp. 238–52.

ONG, W. J. (1958), *Ramus Method and the Decay of Dialogue*, Cambridge, Mass.

PAETOW, L. J. (1910), *The Arts Course at Medieval Universities with Special*

Reference to Grammar and Rhetoric, Champaigne, Ill.

PALISCA, C. V. (1959), 'A Clarification of "Musica Reservata" in Jean Taisnier's *Astrologiae*, 1599', *Acta Musicologica*, 31, pp. 133–61.

—— (1972), '*Ut Oratoria Musica*: the Rhetorical Basis of Musical Mannerism', in *The Meaning of Mannerism*, ed. F. W. Robinson and S. G. Nichols, Jr., Hanover, NH, pp. 37–65.

PANOFSKY, E. (1960), *Renaissance and Renaissances in Western Art*, Stockholm; repr. London, 1970.

PARR, R. P., tr. (1968), *Geoffrey of Vinsauf: Documentum de modo et arte dictandi et versificandi (Instruction in the Method and Art of Speaking and Versifying)*, Milwaukee, Wis.

PEACHAM, HENRY (1577), *The Garden of Eloquence*, facs. edn. Menston, 1971.

—— (1593), *The Garden of Eloquence*, 2nd edn.; facs. edn. W. G. Crane (New York, 1977).

PERCIVAL, W. K. (1983), 'Grammar and Rhetoric in the Renaissance', in Murphy 1983, pp. 303–30.

PETRARCH (1948), 'On His Own Ignorance and That of Many Others', tr. H. Nachod, in E. Cassirer, P. O. Kristeller, and J. H. Randall, Jr. (eds.), *The Renaissance Philosophy of Man*, Chicago, pp. 47–133.

—— (1975–85), *Rerum familiarum*, tr. A. S. Bernardo, 3 vols., Albany, NY (vol. I) and Baltimore, Md. (vols II–III).

PLATO (1963), *The Collected Dialogues*, ed. E. Hamilton and H. Cairns (by fourteen translators), New York.

PLETT, H. F. (1975), *Rhetorik der Affekte. Englische Wirkungsästhetik im Zeitalter der Renaissance*, Tübingen.

POPPER, K. (1966), *The Open Society and Its Enemies*. Vol. 1: *The Spell of Plato*, 5th rev. edn., London.

PUTTENHAM, GEORGE (1936), *The Arte of English Poesie* (London, 1589), ed. G. Willcock and A. Walker, Cambridge; repr. 1970.

RICE, E. F. (1958), *The Renaissance Idea of Wisdom*, Cambridge, Mass.

ROAF, E. C. (1959), 'Bartolomeo Cavalcanti, 1503–62: A Critical and Biographical Study', D.Phil. Diss., Oxford.

ROSKILL, M. W. (1968), *Dolce's 'Aretino' and Venetian Art Theory of the Cinquecento*, New York.

ROTERMUND, E. (1969), 'Der Affekt als literarischer Gegenstand: Zu Theorie und Darstellung der Passiones im 17. Jahrhundert', in H. R. Jauss (ed.), *Die nicht mehr schönen Künste*, Munich, pp. 239–69.

RUBEL, V. L. (1941), *Poetic Diction in the English Renaissance. From Skelton through Spenser*, New York.

RUHNKE, M. (1955), *Joachim Burmeister. Ein Beitrag zur Musiklehre um 1600*, Kassell and Basle.

RUSSELL, D. A. and WINTERBOTTOM, M., eds. (1972), *Ancient*

Literary Criticism. The Principal Texts in New Translations, Oxford.

SCALIGER, J. C. (1905), *Select Translations from Scaliger's Poetics*, ed. and tr. F. M. Padelford, New York.

SCHANZE, H., ed. (1974), *Rhetorik. Beiträge zu ihrer Geschichte in Deutschland vom 16.–20. Jahrhundert*, Frankfurt.

SEIGEL, J. E. (1968), *Rhetoric and Philosophy in Renaissance Humanism: the Union of Eloquence and Wisdom, Petrarch to Valla*, Princeton, NJ.

SEZNEC, J. (1953), *The Survival of the Pagan Gods. The Mythological Tradition and Its Place in Renaissance Humanism and Art*, New York; tr. B. F. Sessions from *La Survivance des dieux antiques* (London, 1940).

SHEARMAN, J. (1967), *Mannerism, Style and Civilization*, Harmondsworth.

SHERRY, RICHARD (1550), *A Treatise of Schemes and Tropes*, facs. edn. H. W. Hildebrandt, Gainesville, Fla., 1961; repr. New York, 1977.

SIDES, M. (1983), 'Rhetoric on the Brink of Banishment: d'Alembert on Rhetoric in the Encyclopédie', *Rhetorik*, 3, pp. 111–24.

SIDNEY, SIR PHILIP (1965), *Apology for Poetry* (1595), ed. G. K. Shepherd, London.

SIEVEKE, F. G. (1974), 'Eloquentia sacra. Zur Predigttheorie des Nicolaus Caussinus S. J.', in Schanze 1974, pp. 43–68.

SIMON, J. (1966), *Education and Society in Tudor England*, Cambridge.

SMITH, G. G. (1904), *Elizabethan Critical Essays*, 2 vols., Oxford.

SMITH, JOHN (1657), *The Mysterie of Rhetorique Unvail'd, wherein above 130 the Tropes and Figures are severally derived from the Greek into English, together with lively Definitions and Variety of Latin, English, Scriptural Examples . . .*, London; facs. edn. Menston, 1969; Hildesheim, 1973.

SOAREZ, CYPRIAN (1955), *De Arte Rhetorica Libri Tres* (Cologne, 1557), ed. and tr. L. Flynn. S. J., Ph.D. Diss., U. Florida.

SONNINO, L. A. (1968), *A Handbook to Sixteenth Century Rhetoric*, London.

SPENCER, J. R. (1957), 'Ut Rhetorica Pictura. A Study in Quattrocento Theory of Painting', *Journal of the Warburg and Courtauld Institutes*, 20, pp. 26–44.

STOLT, B. (1974), *Wortkampf: Frühneuhochdeutsche Beispiele zur rhetorischen Praxis*, Frankfurt.

STONE, P. W. K. (1967), *The Art of Poetry 1750–1820. Theories of Poetic Composition and Style in the late Neo-Classic and early Romantic Periods*, London.

STRUEVER, N. S. (1970), *The Language of History in the Renaissance. Rhetoric and Historical Consciousness in Florentine Humanism*, Princeton, NJ.

STRUNK, O., ed. (1950), *Source Readings in Music History*, New York.

SUMMERS, D. (1981), *Michelangelo and the Language of Art*, Princeton, NJ.

SUSENBROTUS, JOANNES (1953), *The 'Epitome Troporum ac Schematum'
of Joannes Susenbrotus: Text, Translation and Commentary*, by J. X.
Brennan, Ph.D. Diss., U. Illinois.

SWEETING, E. J. (1940), *Early Tudor Criticism, Linguistic and Literary*,
Oxford; repr. New York, 1964.

TAYLOR, W. (1937), *Tudor Figures of Rhetoric*, Ph.D. Diss., U. Chicago;
repr. Whitewater, Wis., 1972.

TRIMPI, W. (1973), 'The Meaning of Horace's "Ut pictura poesis" ',
Journal of the Warburg and Courtauld Institutes, 36, pp. 1–34.

—— (1983), *Muses of One Mind. The Literary Analysis of Experience and Its
Continuity*, Princeton, NJ.

TUVE, R. (1947), *Elizabethan and Metaphysical Imagery. Renaissance Poetic
and Twentieth-Century Critics*, Chicago, Ill.

ULLMAN, B. L. (1963), *The Humanism of Coluccio Salutati*, Padua.

UNGER, H.-H. (1941), *Die Beziehungen zwischen Musik und Rhetorik im
16.–18. Jahrhundert*, Würzburg; repr. Hildesheim, 1969.

VICKERS, B. (1968), *The Artistry of Shakespeare's Prose*, London.

—— (1973), *Towards Greek Tragedy*, London.

—— (1981), 'Rhetorical and anti-rhetorical Tropes: On writing the
History of *elocutio*', *Comparative Criticism*, 3, pp. 105–32.

—— ed. (1982a), *Rhetoric Revalued. Papers from the International Society for
the History of Rhetoric*, Binghamton, NY.

—— (1982b), 'Epideictic and Epic in the Renaissance', *New Literary
History*, 14, pp. 497–537.

—— (1983a), ' "The Power of Persuasion": Images of the Orator, Elyot
to Shakespeare', in Murphy 1983, pp. 411–35.

—— (1983b), 'Epideictic Rhetoric in Galileo's *Dialogo*', *Annali
dell'Istituto e Museo di Storia della Scienza di Firenze*, 8, pp. 69–102.

—— (1984) 'Figures of Rhetoric/Figures of Music?', *Rhetorica*, 2,
pp. 1–44.

—— ed. (1985), *Arbeit, Musse, Meditation. Betrachtungen zur Vita activa
und Vita contemplativa*, Zurich.

—— (1986), 'Valla's ambivalent Praise of Pleasure: Rhetoric in the
Service of Christianity', *Viator*, 17, pp. 271–319.

VICO, GIAMBATTISTA (1968), *The New Science of Giambattista Vico*,
rev. tr. of 3rd edn. (1744), by T. G. Bergin and M. H. Fisch, Ithaca,
NY.

VIVES, JUAN LUIS (1913), *On Education*, tr. from *De tradendis disciplinis*
by F. Watson, Cambridge; repr. Toronto, 1971.

—— (1966), *De Ratione Dicendi* (1533), tr. J. F. Cooney, Ph.D. Diss., Ohio
State U.

WALKER, D. P. (1941–2), 'Musical Humanism in the Sixteenth and
early Seventeenth Centuries', *The Music Review*, 2, pp. 1–13, 111–21,
220–7, 288–308; and 3, pp. 55–71; repr. in Walker, *Music, Spirit and*

Language in the Renaissance, ed. P. Gouk (London, 1985).

WARD, J. O. (1978), 'From Antiquity to the Renaissance: Glosses and Commentaries on Cicero's *Rhetorica*', in Murphy 1978, pp. 25–67.

—— (1983), 'Renaissance Commentators on Ciceronian Rhetoric', in Murphy 1983, pp. 126–73.

WEINBERG, B. (1961), *A History of Literary Criticism in the Italian Renaissance*, 2 vols., Chicago.

—— ed. (1970–4), *Trattati de poetica e retorica del '500*, 4 vols., Bari.

WEISS, R. (1941), *Humanism in England During the Fifteenth Century*, Oxford; repr. 1957.

WIERUSZOWSKI, H. (1971), *Politics and Culture in Medieval Spain and Italy*, Rome.

WILSON, THOMAS (1982), *Arte of Rhetorique* (1553, 1560), ed. T. J. Derrick, New York.

WINN, J. A. (1981), *Unsuspected Eloquence. A History of the Relations between Poetry and Music*, New Haven and London.

WINTERBOTTOM, M. (1975), 'Quintilian on Rhetoric', in T. A. Dorey (ed.), *Empire and Aftermath. Silver Latin II*, London, pp. 79–97.

WITT, R. G. (1982), 'Medieval "Ars Dictaminis" and the Beginnings of Humanism: a New Construction of the Problem', *Renaissance Quarterly*, 35, pp. 1–35.

—— (1983), *Hercules at the Crossroads. The Life, Works, and Thought of Coluccio Salutati*, Durham, NC.

WOODWARD, W. H. (1897), *Vittorino da Feltre and other Humanist Educators*, Cambridge; repr. 1912.

—— (1906), *Studies in Education during the Age of the Renaissance 1400–1600*, Cambridge.

WOOTEN, C. W., tr. (1987), *Hermogenes' On Types of Style*, Durham, NC.

WRIGHT, D. R. E. (1984), 'Alberti's *De Pictura*: Its Literary Structure and Purpose', *Journal of the Warburg and Courtauld Institutes*, 47, pp. 52–71.

APPENDIX

Definitions of Rhetorical Figures and Tropes

Note: further illustrations and discussions of the figures and tropes may be found in Taylor (1937); Rubel (1941); Joseph (1947); Heinrich Lausberg, *Handbuch der literarischen Rhetorik*, 2 vols. (Munich, 1960) and *Elemente der literarischen Rhetorik* (Munich, 1963); L. A. Sonnino, *A Handbook to Sixteenth-Century Rhetoric* (London, 1968); Richard A. Lanham, *A Handlist of Rhetorical Terms: A Guide for Students of English Literature* (Berkeley and Los Angeles, 1968); Arthur Quinn, *Figures of Speech: 60 Ways to Turn a Phrase* (Salt Lake City, Utah, 1982); Bernard Dupriez, *Gradus: Les procédés littéraires (Dictionnaire)* (Paris, 1984). All the illustrations are from Shakespeare's works.

Adynaton, the impossibility of expressing oneself adequately to the topic:

> *3 Gent.* Did you see the meeting of the two kings?
> *2 Gent.* No.
> *3 Gent.* Then have you lost a sight which was to be seen, cannot be spoken of.
>
> *Winter's Tale*, 5. 2. 39

Anadiplosis (or *reduplicatio*), where the last word(s) of one clause or sentence become(s) the first of the one following:

> Wishing me like to one more rich in hope,
> Featur'd like him, like him with friends possess'd.
>
> Sonnet 29

Anaphora (or *repetitio*), where the same word is repeated at the beginning of a sequence of clauses or sentences:

> Some glory in their birth, some in their skill,
> Some in their wealth, some in their body's force . . .
>
> Sonnet 91

Antanaclasis, where a word is used twice (or more) in two (or more) of its senses:

> Put out the light, and then put out the light.
>
> *Othello*, 5. 2. 7

Anthypophora (or *rogatio*), to ask a question and to answer it oneself:

> What is in that word honour? What is that honour? Air. A trim reckoning!
> Who hath it? He that died a' Wednesday. Doth he feel it? No. Doth he hear it?
> No.

1 Henry IV, 5. 1. 131

Antimetabole (or *commutatio*), where two or more words are repeated in inverse order:

> Music to hear, why hear'st thou music sadly?

Sonnet 8

Antithesis (or *comparatio*), where contraries are opposed and distinguished:

> A bliss in proof; and prov'd, a very woe;
> Before, a joy propos'd; behind, a dream.

Sonnet 129

Antonomasia (or *pronominatio*), substitution of name, either (1) of a descriptive phrase for a proper name; or (2) of a proper name for a quality associated with it:

> (1) Cupid is 'that same wicked bastard of Venus. . . . that blind rascally boy.'

As You Like It, 4. 1. 211

> (2) I am no great Nebuchadnezzar, sir;
>   I have not much skill in grass.

All's Well, 4. 5. 21

Aposiopesis (or *praecisio*), breaking off a sentence with the sense incomplete.

> I will have such revenges on you both,
> That all the world shall — I will do such things —
> What they are yet I know not, but they shall be
> The terrors of the earth!

King Lear, 2. 4. 281

Apostrophe (or *aversio*), a turning of speech from one topic or person to another, often for emotional emphasis:

> Within a month . . .
> She married—O most wicked speed: to post
> With such dexterity to incestuous sheets . . .

Hamlet, 1. 2. 153

Asyndeton (or *dissolutio*), the absence of connecting particles between clauses:

Gor'd mine own thoughts, sold cheap what is most dear,
Made old offences of affections new.

Sonnet 110

Auxesis (or *incrementum*), where words are arranged in ascending order of importance:

Since brass, nor stone, nor earth, nor boundless sea,
But sad mortality o'er-sways their power . . .

Sonnet 65

Brachylogia (or *articulus*), the absence of connecting particles between single words, which are thus separated only by commas:

. . . till action, lust
Is perjur'd, murd'rous, bloody, full of blame,
Savage, extreme, rude, cruel, not to trust . . .

Sonnet 129

Chiasmus, repeating ideas (not necessarily in the same words, contrast *antimetabole*) in inverted order:

But O, what damned minutes tells he o'er
Who dotes, yet doubts; suspects, yet strongly loves.

Othello, 3. 3. 169

Climax (or *gradatio*), where the last word of one clause or sentence becomes the first of the one following, as in *anadiplosis*, but continued through three or more stages—like the rungs of a ladder:

My conscience hath a thousand several tongues,
And every tongue brings in a several tale,
And every tale condemns me for a villain. . . .

Richard III, 5. 3. 193

Ecphonesis (or *exclamatio*), the exclamation of extreme emotion such as anger, grief, admiration:

O sides, you are too tough!
Will you yet hold?

King Lear, 2. 4. 197

Epanalepsis (or *resumptio*), where the same word is repeated at the beginning and end of clause, a line, or sentence:

> Kind is my love today, tomorrow kind . . .
>
> Sonnet 105

Epanodos (or *regressio*), where the main terms in an argument are repeated in the course of it:

> Mine eye and heart are at a mortal war
> How to divide the conquest of thy sight:
> Mine eye my heart thy picture's sight would bar,
> My heart mine eye the freedom of that right.
>
> Sonnet 46

Epanorthosis (or *correctio*), where a word or idea is corrected and replaced by one more suitable:

> A good heart, Kate, is the sun and the moon, or rather the sun and not the moon; for it shines bright and never changes, but keeps his course truly.
>
> *Henry V*, 5. 2. 162

Epiphonema (or *acclamatio*), a pithy summing-up of an argument, often in the form of an epigram or *sententia:*

> This I do vow and this shall ever be:
> I will be true despite thy scythe and thee.
>
> Sonnet 123

Epistrophe (or *conversio*), where the same word is repeated at the end of a sequence of clauses or sentences:

> Is this nothing?
> Why then the world and all that's in't is nothing,
> My wife is nothing, nor nothing have these nothings,
> If this be nothing.
>
> *Winter's Tale*, 1. 2. 292

Epizeuxis (or *subjunctio*), where a word is repeated two or more times with no other word intervening:

> Howl, howl, howl!
>
> *King Lear*, 5. 3. 257

Euphemismos, substituting a more favourable for a pejorative term:

> *Falstaff* . . . when thou art king, let not us that are squires of the night's body ['we that take purses'] be call'd thieves of the day's beauty. Let us be Diana's foresters, gentlemen of the shade, minions of the moon . . .
>
> *1 Henry IV*, 1. 2. 13 ff.

Homoioptoton (or *similiter cadens*), where corresponding words (often at the end of a sequence of clauses or sentences) have similar case endings (not possible in uninflected languages):

Veni, vidi, vici.

Homoioteleuton (or *similiter desinens*), where corresponding words (often at the end of a sequence of clauses or sentences) have similar endings:

My mother weeping, my father wailing, my sister crying, our maid howling, our cat wringing her hands . . .

Two Gentlemen of Verona, 2. 3. 6

Hypallage (or *submutatio*), 'changing the true construction and application of the words whereby the sense is perverted and made very absurd' (Puttenham):

The eye of man hath not heard, the ear of man hath not seen, man's hand is not able to taste, his tongue to conceive, nor his heart to report, what my dream was.

Midsummer Night's Dream, 4. 1. 211

Hyperbaton (or *transgressio*), the alteration of word order for purposes of emphasis:

Yet I'll not shed her blood,
Nor scar that whiter skin of hers than snow . . .

Othello, 5. 2. 3

Hyperbole (or *superlatio*), exaggeration of scale in order to describe outstanding qualities:

His legs bestrid the ocean, his rear'd arm
Crested the world, his voice was propertied
As all the tuned spheres, and that to friends . . .

Antony and Cleopatra, 5. 2. 82

Hypotyposis (or *demonstratio, evidentia*), vivid description appealing to the sense of sight:

Think, when we talk of horses, that you see them
Printing their proud hoofs i'th' receiving earth . . .

Henry V, 1. Pro. 26

Hysteron proteron (or *praeposteratio*), the placing first in a sentence or clause of words which, in terms of sense, ought to come later:

Th'*Antoniad*, the Egyptian admiral,
With all their sixty, fly and turn the rudder.

Antony and Cleopatra, 3. 10. 2

Isocolon (or *compar*), where a sequence of clauses or sentences is of an identical length (and often of an identical structure: see *parison*):

> Was ever woman in this humour woo'd?
> Was ever woman in this humour won?

Richard III, 1. 2. 227

Meiosis (or *extenuatio*), a form of 'diminishing' a topic by belittling it:

> But when my glass shows me myself indeed,
> Beated and chopp'd with tann'd antiquity . . .

Sonnet 62

Metalepsis, attributing a present effect to a remote cause:

> There spake my brother! There my father's grave
> Did utter forth a voice.

Measure for Measure, 3. 1. 86

Metaphor (or *translatio*), when a word is transferred from one thing to another, for illumination and for emotional emphasis:

> That time of year thou mayst in me behold
> When yellow leaves, or none, or few, do hang
> Upon those boughs which shake against the cold,
> Bare ruin'd choirs, where late the sweet birds sang.

Sonnet 73

Metonymy (or *transmutatio*), the substitution of one name for another, as of an author for his work, the sign for the signified:

> O thou, my lovely boy, who in thy power
> Dost hold Time's fickle glass, his sickle, hour . . .

Sonnet 126

Onomatopoeia (or *nominatio*), where language is used to imitate the sound of the animal ('Tu-whit tu-whoo') or thing described:

> Blow, winds, and crack your cheeks! rage, blow!
> You cataracts and hurricanoes, spout . . .

King Lear, 3. 2. 1

Paralipsis (or *occupatio*), when one pretends to pass over a matter and so draws attention to it:

> Let but the commons hear this testament [Caesar's will] —
> Which, pardon me, I do not mean to read —

And they would go and kiss dead Caesar's wounds . . .
Have patience, gentle friends; I must not read it.
It is not meet you know how Caesar loved you . . .

Julius Caesar, 3. 2. 130

Parison (or *compar*), corresponding or symmetrical structure of a sequence of clauses or sentences:

As Caesar lov'd me, I weep for him; as he was fortunate, I rejoice at it; as he was valiant, I honour him; but as he was ambitious, I slew him.

Julius Caesar, 3. 2. 24

Paronomasia (*agnominatio* or *allusio*), where two or more words are used in proximity which are similar in sound but different in sense:

Mad in pursuit and in possession so.

Sonnet 129

Periphrasis (or *circumlocutio*), the use of a number of words to describe at greater length and with fuller emphasis something which could be stated much more briefly:

   . . . when that fell arrest
Without all bail shall carry me away . . .

Sonnet 74

Ploche (or *conduplicatio, diaphora*), the repetition of the same word or words:

Music to hear, why hear'st thou music sadly?
Sweets with sweets war not, joy delights in joy.

Sonnet 8

Polyptoton (*paragmenon, traductio,* or *adnominatio*), repeating a word in a different form:

And death once dead, there's no more dying then.

Sonnet 146

Polysyndeton (or *acervatio*), the profusion of connecting particles between clauses:

Then, in the blazon of sweet beauty's best,
Of hand, of foot, of lip, of eye, of brow,
I see their antique pen would have express'd
Even such a beauty as you master now.

Sonnet 106

Prosopopoeia (or *confirmatio*), representing an imaginary or absent person as speaking or acting; attributing life, speech or human qualities to dumb or inanimate objects:

> Methinks I hear
> Antony call; I see him rouse himself
> To praise my noble act. I hear him mock
> The luck of Caesar . . . Husband, I come!

Antony and Cleopatra, 5. 2. 283

Syllepsis (or *conceptio*), where a word is used once only but where by the context and tone two different meanings are suggested:

> Therefore I lie with her, and she with me . . .

Sonnet 138

Synecdoche (or *subintellectio*), where one thing is substituted for another, part for whole, genus for species, and vice-versa:

> These are the ushers of Martius: before him he carries noise, and behind him he leaves tears . . .

Coriolanus, 2. 1. 158

Synoeciosis (*oxymoron* or *contrapositum*), uniting (not opposing, as in *antithesis*) contrary and incompatible-seeming terms or states:

> Have we, as 'twere with a defeated joy,
> With an auspicious and a dropping eye,
> With mirth in funeral, and with dirge in marriage,
> In equal scale weighing delight and dole,
> Taken to wife.

Hamlet, 1. 2. 10

Zeugma (or *adjunctio*), where one verb serves two or more clauses:

> Since saucy jacks so happy are in this,
> Give them thy fingers, me thy lips to kiss.

Sonnet 128

INDEX: RHETORICAL TERMS

INDEX: NAMES